A Copious Fountain

A History of Union Presbyterian Seminary, 1812–2012

William B. Sweetser Jr.

WESTMINSTER
JOHN KNOX PRESS
LOUISVILLE • KENTUCKY

© 2016 Union Presbyterian Seminary

First edition
Published by Westminster John Knox Press
Louisville, Kentucky

16 17 18 19 20 21 22 23 24 25—10 9 8 7 6 5 4 3 2 1

Scripture quotations from the New Revised Standard Version of the Bible are copyright © 1989 by the Division of Christian Education of the National Council of the Churches of Christ in the U.S.A. and are used by permission.

Material published herein from interviews is used with permission of the interviewees. The map of Virginia (illustration 1) is published herein courtesy of Lou McKinney, Union Presbyterian Seminary Media Services Department. The photograph of Samuel Goven Stevens (illustration 33) is published herein with the permission of Lincoln University. The photograph of Union students on the picket line at Thalhimers (illustration 35) is published herein with permission of the *Richmond Times-Dispatch*. All other photographs and illustrations are published herein with permission from Union Presbyterian Seminary.

Book design by Drew Stevens
Cover design by Allison Taylor
Cover photography by Duane Berger

Library of Congress Cataloging-in-Publication Data

Names: Sweetser, William B., Jr., author.
Title: A copious fountain : a history of Union Presbyterian Seminary,
    1812–2012 / William B. Sweetser Jr.
Description: Louisville, KY : Westminster John Knox Press, 2016. | Includes
    bibliographical references and index.
Identifiers: LCCN 2015034517 | ISBN 9780664238346 (hardback)
Subjects: LCSH: Union Presbyterian Seminary—History. | BISAC: RELIGION /
    History. | RELIGION / Christian Theology / History. | RELIGION / Christian
    Church / History.
Classification: LCC BV4070.R66 S94 2016 | DDC 230.07/351755451—dc23 LC record
available at http://lccn.loc.gov/2015034517

Most Westminster John Knox Press books are available at special quantity discounts when purchased in bulk by corporations, organizations, and special-interest groups. For more information, please e-mail SpecialSales@wjkbooks.com.

To Sheila and Amanda

We were always in this together

Contents

List of Illustrations

List of Abbreviations

Institutions, Organizations, and Programs

AATS	American Association of Theological Schools (from 1978, the Association of Theological Schools: ATS)
ABCFM	American Board of Commissioners for Foreign Missions
ACS	American Colonization Society (full name: The Society for the Colonization of Free People of Color of America)
ATS	Assembly's Training School (full name: General Assembly's Training School for Lay Workers; from 1959, PSCE)
ATS	Association of Theological Schools (successor to AATS)
BTSR	Baptist Theological School in Richmond
CPE	clinical pastoral education
ECP	Extended Campus Program
GI	government issue
HSC	Hampden-Sydney College
NPC	National Presbyterian Church (a separation from PCUS in 1973)
OFINE	Office of Institutional Effectiveness
PCA	Presbyterian Church in America (= NPC, renamed in 1974)
PC(CSA)	Presbyterian Church in the Confederate States of America (1861–65)
PCUS	Presbyterian Church in the United States (1861–1983)
PC(USA)	Presbyterian Church in the United States of America (1789–1837, 1869–1958, 1983–)
PSCE	Presbyterian School of Christian Education
RTC	Richmond Theological Center (1968–80s), then Consortium
SACS	Southern Association of Colleges and Schools
SCLC	Southern Christian Leadership Conference
SIM	Student in Ministry
SMI	Society of Missionary Inquiry
STVU	School of Theology of Virginia Union University
SVM	Student Volunteer Movement
UPC	United Presbyterian Church in the United States of America (1958–83)
UPS	Union Presbyterian Seminary (2009–)
UTS	Union Theological Seminary in Virginia (1824–1997)
UTS (NY)	Union Theological Seminary in New York

| UTS-PSCE | Union Theological Seminary and Presbyterian School of Christian Education (1997–2009) |
| WRFK | Call letters of the UTS radio station |

Degrees

AB	bachelor of arts
BA	bachelor of arts
BD	bachelor of divinity
DD	doctor of divinity
DDS	doctor of dental surgery
DMin	doctor of ministry
DPhil	doctor of philosophy
Dr. theol.	*doctor theologiae*
EdD	doctor of education
LLD/LL.D.	doctor of laws
MA	master of arts
MACE	master of arts in Christian education
MATS	master of arts in theological studies
MD	doctor of medicine
MDiv	master of divinity
MDS	master of dental surgery
MSW	master of social work
MTS	master of sacred theology
PhD	doctor of philosophy
STB	bachelor of sacred theology
STM	master of sacred theology
ThD	doctor of theology
ThM	master of theology

Timeline

For presidents of UTS and their years in office, see the list of illustrations.

	Union Seminary	Denomination	National
1705		First presbytery meeting	
1741–58		Old Side/New Side split	
1743			Presbyterians tolerated
1747		Samuel Davies begins preaching in VA	
1749	Augusta Academy founded; renamed Liberty Hall in 1776		
1755		Hanover Presbytery formed	
1776	Hampden-Sydney College founded		
1789		First General Assembly	Constitution
1800			Second Great Awakening
1801		Plan of Union	
1806	Hanover Presbytery establishes Theological Library at HSC		
1807	Moses Hodge elected HSC president		
1808	Moses Hodge serves as Professor of Theology (1808–20)	General Assembly proposes plan for establishing seminary	
1810		Cumberland Presbyterian Church formed	

	Union Seminary	Denomination	National
1812	Synod of Virginia votes to establish seminary		
1824	John Holt Rice serves as Theology Professor (1824–31)		
1826	The Theological Seminary of the Presbyterian Church, under the care of the Presbytery of Hanover, becomes Union Theological Seminary in Virginia		
1831	George A. Baxter serves as Professor of Theology (1831–41)		
1837		Old School/New School split	
1841	Samuel B. Wilson serves as Professor of Theology (1841–69)		
1861–65			Civil War
1869	Robert L. Dabney serves as Chairman of the Faculty (1869–83)		
1861		PC(CSA) formed	
1865		PCUS formed	
1883	Thomas E. Peck serves as Chairman of the Faculty (1883–93)		
1890s			Progressive era begins (1890s–1920s)
1893	Clement R. Vaughan serves as Chairman of the Faculty (1893–96)		
1896	Givens B. Strickler serves as Chairman of the Faculty (1896–1904)		
1898	Classes begin in Richmond		Spanish-American War
1904	Walter W. Moore serves as first president (1904–26)		
1911	First time over 100 enrolled; First million-dollar budget		
1917–18			World War I
1926	Benjamin Rice Lacy Jr. serves as second president (1926–56)		

	Union Seminary	Denomination	National
1929	Walter W. Moore Fund		Great Depression begins
1941–45			World War II
1949	Mid-Century Campaign		
1950–53			Korean War
1956	James Archibald Jones serves as third president (1956–66)		
1960			Woolworths sit-in
1964–75			Vietnam War
1965	Advance Campaign		
1966	Balmer Hancock Kelly serves as interim president (1966–67)		
1967	Frederick Rogers Stair Jr. serves as fourth president (1967–81)		
1968			Poor People's Campaign
1981	T. Hartley Hall IV serves as fifth president (1981–94)		
1983		Reunion	
1994	Louis B. Weeks serves as sixth president (1994–2007)		
1997	Union Theological Seminary becomes Union Theological Seminary–Presbyterian School of Christian Education		
2002	Charlotte Campus begins		
2007	Brian K. Blount inaugurated as seventh president		
2009	Union Theological Seminary–Presbyterian School of Christian Education becomes Union Presbyterian Seminary		

Preface

When President Brian Blount called me at noon on April 16, 2008, I was making grilled-cheese sandwiches for my church's weekly Bible study luncheon. I had not expected a phone call from the seminary president and was even more surprised when he asked me if I would write the bicentennial history of Union Presbyterian Seminary. I was both honored and disappointed; this should have been Jim Smylie's book to write. The shadows of age would prevent Jim from working on the book, and I eagerly jumped at the chance to tell Union's story. About a month later three huge archive boxes were sitting in my den and reams of jottings on Jim Smylie's yellow legal-pad paper started my research. His voluminous notes served as signposts in writing this history, and I am grateful for him as a teacher and for the foundation he laid in this history.

I was surprised to find that a systematic history of Union, founded in 1812, has never been written. Although Moses Hoge helped write an article for the *Virginia Argus* in 1810 as a retrospective justifying the need for a theological school and library, the first "official" history was a short paper written by Samuel B. Wilson, Secretary to the Board of Trustees, in 1867. As Union was trying to find its way after the Civil War, Wilson wrote his account to be included in the board's minutes, to give context to the school's struggle for survival. Seminary histories appear as adjuncts to commemorative events thereafter. Thus we find a brief history written for the 70th anniversary celebration in 1894; article-length histories in the 1884, 1907, and 1976 *General Catalogue*; biographies and historical notes in the 1899 *Appreciations* by Walter W. Moore (published to celebrate the "Removal" of the campus from Hampden-Sydney to Richmond); a book of biographies for the 1912 centennial celebration; and scattered historical notes in both the *Union Seminary Magazine* and the *Union Seminary Review*. The first modern history is *The Days of Our Years*, written by several professors as part of Union's 150th anniversary celebration in 1962. There are also unpublished speeches from the 175th anniversary celebrations in 1987 along with an entire issue of *Focus* magazine devoted to Union's history (written by Jim Smylie). The traumatic "Removal" was analyzed and commemorated on the 25th (1923), 50th (1948), and 100th (1998) anniversaries of the move to Richmond from Hampden-Sydney. These histories, except for the *Days of Our Years* and the materials for the 175th anniversary celebration, focus on the administration of the seminary and do not put the school into context with its times or trends in theological education.

There is one constant in the 200-year history of Union Presbyterian Seminary: the five-course curriculum inherited from the Church of Scotland. This traditional core curriculum consists of Old and New Testament exegesis (including a proficient knowledge of the original languages), theology, church history, and polity. Early in its history, Union developed a unique outlook; while it retained the traditional curriculum as its foundation, it was also introducing innovative subjects into the curriculum and employing pioneering ways to teach. Yet five themes have been in constant tension within Union's history. How these five themes ebbed and flowed in relation to each other through the first 200 years helps explain why John Holt Rice's school is unique and can be fruitful in putting Union's history into a wider context. The first theme is how the definition of an educated ministry has changed in 200 years. Second, how Union has functioned as both a "Southern" and a "national" institution. Third, how Union engaged the world even as it served a small denomination. Fourth, how Union students and graduates resolved the tension between conserving the cultural status quo and advocating for reform. Finally, how Union Seminary influenced the denomination and theological education.

My intent is for this book to be both a celebration of what makes Union unique and an examination of the forces that made Rice's "school of the prophets" what it is today. I have followed the work of Glenn T. Miller in his analysis of Protestant theological education, especially *Piety and Profession* (2007). His thesis on the specialization of theological education is particularly helpful in understanding the Removal and subsequent curricular developments.

I have tried to let the student voices predominate. To do this, I have used letters and diaries, student publications and monographs, and conducted over a hundred interviews in an effort to let generations of students speak for themselves. To give a sense of the culture in which those students lived, I have kept the archaic language, grammar, spelling, and capitalization in the letters, minutes, articles, and titles for courses and personnel (yet adding a few commas for clarity). Since the spelling of Hampden-Sydney College was not standardized until the twentieth century, I have used the archaic "Sidney" where it appears in older documents. From these documents we can see how Union students have been shaped by their culture, and yet they also remade the world in which we live. May we do as well in our time.

Where a specific word or reference is unfamiliar, such as the term "black flag" in chapter 5, I have included a short definition in the text or in a note. There can also be some confusion with regard to the nationality of some students. Throughout the nineteenth century several students are described as coming from a European county, usually Scotland, England, or Germany. These students were considered "foreign" but were probably immigrants since they went on to serve churches in the United States. The first student who would meet our definition of a foreign student, meaning one who attended Union with the intention of returning to his country, was Isaac Yohannan (1901) from Persia.

I am grateful to Jack Kingsbury, Dean McBride, and Doug Ottati, who helped me understand the currents of theology and biblical studies over the last two centuries and how they have impacted Union. I confess that I have used their insights perhaps too sparingly. Very quickly I discovered that a critical discussion of theological trends, currents in biblical studies, and issues in denominational politics would take my focus away from student life. Ken McFayden introduced me to the works of Glenn T. Miller and clarified recent developments in the Doctor of Ministry (DMin) program. My conversations with Bob Bryant helped me to focus and shape my approach to the later chapters.

Many people have asked me if I am including PSCE in this history. Although the stories of UTS and PSCE do intersect at many points (and finally converge), PSCE was a separate institution, with its own life and traditions. Consequently, I only mention PSCE when its history overlaps with Union. PSCE was a unique school in American Christianity and valuable to the PC(US). It deserves its own history. The best current resource is *The First 70 Years: A History of the Presbyterian School of Christian Education*, by Louise McComb.

Whenever I quote a graduate (or attendee), I have placed the date of graduation (or attendance) in parentheses after the name. Prior to 1900, degrees were not awarded, so only the last year of attendance is noted. After 1900 I record the degree received and the date. After the 1980s there are UTS graduates who participated in the dual-degree program with PSCE. I only note their degree from UTS out of respect for the integrity of the history of PSCE. Although names can change due to marriage, when quoting from student publications I have used the name of the person writing the article at the time. All information as to graduates prior to 1976 came from the 1907 and 1976 *General Catalogue*.

Gregory of Nazianzus (329–90) is reputed to have said that "we are but dwarfs standing on the shoulders of giants." What is true for fourth-century theological controversies is also true for seminary education—and for researching this book. I would have foundered without the help of many people. I cannot thank my wife, Sheila, enough. I started out in our downstairs den, invaded the living room with stacks of papers arranged "just so," and ended up in the bedroom upstairs. Through the deaths of her mother and my father, she was gracious as I got up from dinner every night to "go to work" and never complained when I went to Richmond twice a year. I had fun writing this book because of her gracious attitude and support.

There are too many people to thank for this book. I do, however, especially thank Brian Blount for asking me to undertake this project. I hope I will justify his confidence and his infinite patience. Former presidents Hartley Hall and Louis Weeks have gone over my manuscript and given me their perspectives. Jim Mays graciously read chapter after chapter and made insightful comments while Charles Swezey kept me on track. Their kind words gave me a context to examine my point of view on several issues. My advisory committee of John Kuykendall, Heath Rada, Stan Skreslet, John Trotti, Mark Valeri, and Rebecca Weaver got me started and pointed me in the right direction.

Willie Thompson was the first person to offer assistance, and he was more than generous with his time and notes. His work on antebellum southside Virginia, the relationship of the seminary to slavery, and the Removal formed the basis of my research on those areas of Union's history. In addition, he directed me to Benjamin Mosby Smith's diary (which should be published) and alerted me to other diaries and letters, as well as the impact of Alexander Jeffrey McKelway III. John Trotti generously shared his unpublished history of the library with me and was available for conversations even when he was ill. Hartley Hall also shared his unpublished notes on Union's administrative history.

Don Shriver graciously opened his house to me, and we spent two after-noons discussing Union in the 1950s. He wrote a short paper for me that was critical in understanding biblical theology and its influence. Peter Hobbie was generous in sharing his insights on E. T. Thompson and how much "Dr. E. T." still influences Union.

This book would not have been possible without a lot of on-campus help; it takes five and a half hours to drive from my house in Spruce Pine, North Carolina, to the Thompson House. Whenever I needed something from the library (and they heard from me constantly), no request was ever too much. Paula Skreslet, Rachel Perky, Fran Eagan, and Ryan Douthat never said no. There was nothing they could not find, and Ryan's photocopying made it possible for me to work from so far away. Sheila Mullenax never failed to find a room for me; Janet Swann Shook, Barbie Haberer, and Janet Puckett always made sure my paperwork was correct. Without their attention to detail, the logistics of this enterprise would have ground to a halt. In the Registrar's office, Stan Hargraves and Carolyn Day Pruett were consistently cheerful when I asked for just one more statistic. Richard Wong in Advancement and Lynn McClintock and Laura Lindsay Carson in the Alumni/ae Office were always helpful. Suzan White was more than supportive in the decisions over the front cover. Carson Brisson and Rodney Sadler worked with me to check the translation of the Hebrew in chapter 3 (the students in the 1820s got it right). Lou McKinney could always be counted upon to go above and beyond. At the museum on the Hampden-Sydney campus, Angela Way was cor-dial through many phone calls and e-mails as she steered me to materials in the early chapters. Edgar Mayse gave me a tour of Hampden-Sydney, which gave me a feel for Union's first home.

In Spruce Pine, Leah Hamlyn and Linda Wright typed note cards for me and asked questions to make sure what I was writing would have a wider inter-est. Brian Raymond read several drafts of each chapter and, as a former Eng-lish teacher and army officer, has saved me from much embarrassment. Frank Adkins had a habit of stepping in at just the right time with encouragement: he kept me going when times were toughest.

As someone who has had no experience with publishing, I cannot think of anyone I would rather have guiding me through this process than Hermann Weinlick, my editor. From the very beginning he showed a remarkable patience in reading draft after draft, pushing me for clarity, questioning what didn't "sound right," and encouraging me to keep going. Thank you! At Westminster John Knox Press, David Dobson and Daniel Braden shepherded me as the book came together, and I thank them for their grace.

Sandi Goehring has been indispensable to this book from the very begin-ning. She updated the information concerning directors and trustees, presi-dents, professors, and Sprunt Lecturers from the 1976 *General Catalogue*. This information was originally designed to be included as appendixes, but due to space constraints can now be found on the seminary's Web site. She also found the time to listen to ideas, scan (and rescan) pictures, make excellent sugges-tions, and suggest new ways to approach an issue. She was always upbeat, and I appreciate her support.

From my first history class in 1986 until I finished my dissertation, and indeed to this day, Rebecca Weaver has been an example and inspiration. Her exacting scholarship and care for those around her showed me I could combine my love of history and teaching with the parish. She encouraged me to accept Brian's offer. I hope this book justifies her confidence.

I am grateful to the people of First Presbyterian Church, Spruce Pine. I would travel from Spruce Pine to Richmond twice a year, and they were always interested in what I learned. They always listened to my many references to the history of Union Seminary in my sermons and understood when I closed my office to interview someone.

During the writing of this history, I combed through the entries in the 1976 *General Catalogue* and was constantly amazed at how often my path crossed those of earlier Union graduates, both in churches I visited and in those I had served in Virginia, as well as Spruce Pine. The true history of the last two hundred years of Union Theological Seminary is written in their ministries and in the lives they have touched in the ministry of Jesus Christ. Those who helped me in writing this history made it better; only the mistakes are mine.

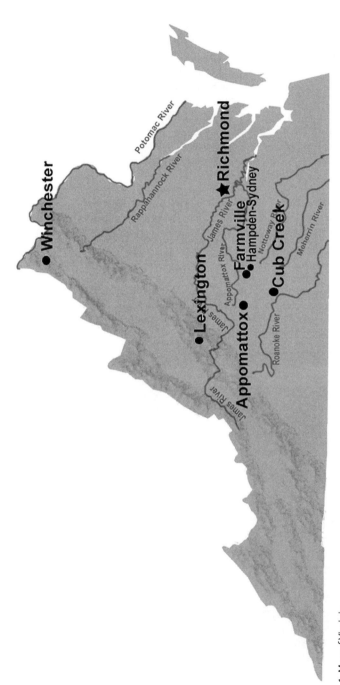

1. Map of Virginia
Lou McKinney, Union Presbyterian Seminary Media Services Department

Chapter One (1706–1806)
The Vacant Congregations Are Perishing
for Lack of Knowledge

From the perspective of two hundred years, it is difficult to imagine the Presbyterian Church without seminaries. The ideal of an educated ministry has been consistent throughout the history of the church. Yet in the seventeenth and eighteenth centuries, population growth and geographical expansion tempted the Presbyterian Church in the American Colonies to abandon its commitment to theological education. Local churches in growing western settlements suggested following the pattern of other denominations and creating various levels of ordained offices so that minimally educated men could enter the ministry. The heirs of John Knox, however, remained adamant. Presbyterians never discarded the Scottish ideal of an educated ministry and would never dilute their high educational requirements just to fill pulpits.

Yet high educational requirements and the desire for doctrinal orthodoxy pressured the church to find enough qualified ministers. The population of the American Colonies doubled every twenty-five years throughout the eighteenth century. With no domestic theological institutions to teach ministerial students, and with education in Scotland becoming more impractical, the church could water down either its theology or its educational ideals. At the same time, Presbyterians wanted to evangelize the frontier. Yet revivals—such as those adopted by other denominations—were theologically incompatible with traditional Calvinism. Consequently the education of ministers became the primary concern and frustration of colonial and post-Revolutionary Presbyterians.

To resolve the dilemma between evangelizing a new country and maintaining an educated ministry, colonial Presbyterians had to decide what their ministerial candidates should know and how they should be taught. In the process of establishing standards, many models would be tried: Scottish universities, log colleges, tutors, church colleges, and cooperative endeavors with the Congregationalists. Presbyterians were so open to educational experimentation because the issue of ministerial education was foundational to how they understood the church. Indeed, the issue of Presbyterian theological education was so important that it underlay every church division and theological controversy in the eighteenth century. The establishment of what came to be Union Presbyterian Seminary was not a systematic, reasoned process. Instead, the founding of Union Seminary evolved out of a series of often incongruous actions in response to the national shortage of ministers and a hostile culture in colonial and post-Revolutionary America.

1

The Desire for an Educated Clergy

On October 27, 1706, seven Presbyterian ministers were on the second day of their meeting in Philadelphia. Although historians would later call this gathering the first Presbyterian General Assembly, these ministers saw themselves merely as "the presbytery met at Philadelphia."[1] According to Francis Makemie, moderator, they had modest intentions: They did not intend to inaugurate a church. Rather, they gathered only "to consult the most proper measures, for advancing religion, and propagating Christianity, in our Various Stations."[2]

On the second day the first order of business was to conduct "Tryals" for a young ministerial candidate, John Boyd. The "Tryals" were extensive: John Boyd "preached a popular sermon [on] Jno. i. 12, Defended his Thesis[,] gave Satisfaction as to his Skill in the Languages, & answered to extemporary questions." The presbytery was satisfied and approved his ordination and call to a church in Freehold, New Jersey.[3]

While hearing candidates preach and asking questions from the floor is a feature of most modern presbytery meetings, Boyd's examination was something new for colonial Presbyterians. Until British North America grew away from the coast, most Presbyterian ministers received their education in Scotland or Ulster, were examined and ordained by their home presbyteries, and were then sent to the Colonies in response to a presbytery or church request. Colonial Presbyterians wanted to make sure their ministers were properly educated in biblical languages, orthodox theology, and proper polity, and the only place to receive that education was in the old country.

Francis Makemie (1658–1708), the Father of American Presbyterianism, is representative of the Scottish university model. Makemie was born in County Donegal, Ulster, probably graduated from St. Andrews, and was licensed by the Presbytery of Laggan (Ulster) in 1681. In December 1680, a Colonel Stevens from Somerset County, Maryland, had asked the Presbytery of Laggan to send a minister to his congregation. The presbytery assigned Makemie to Maryland, where he arrived by 1683.[4] He returned to England in 1704 on a recruiting trip and returned with two ministers.[5] In 1707, on behalf of the newly formed Presbytery of Philadelphia, he wrote to the General Assembly of the Church of Scotland, requesting financial assistance to support itinerant ministers in Virginia.[6]

Presbytery minutes document the stream of ministers disembarking from Scotland and Ireland. As early as 1684, Josias Mackie arrived in Virginia from County Donegal.[7] James Anderson was ordained by the Presbytery of Irvine (Scotland) on November 17, 1706, for settlement in Virginia, but he moved to Delaware within a year.[8] John Henry, ordained by the Presbytery of Dublin, wrote to his home presbytery in September 1710, describing the poor conditions of the Presbyterian Church in Virginia and requesting that ministers be sent.[9]

John Boyd's examination, then, illustrates the promise and the dilemma of colonial Presbyterianism. The ministers gathered in Philadelphia had expected to discuss evangelism because the Colonies were growing and new towns needed ministers to fill the pulpits. The growth of what would become the United States, however, exceeded their dreams. In 1700 the colonial population was twenty thousand; by 1750 it had reached one million; and by 1800 there were four million Americans.[10] The demographics were inexorable: with every new immigrant and every settlement, the need for clergy grew.

An Established Curriculum

Colonial Presbyterians had a definite idea of what an educated minister should know. Drawing on their Scottish roots, they expected their ministers to meet the standards set forth in the Church of Scotland's Book of Discipline (1560). Influenced by his Genevan experience and what he considered to be the low educational level of the Roman Catholic clergy, John Knox had emphasized ministerial education in the Book of Discipline and designed a seamless course of study from undergraduate to graduate theological education.

Knox had mandated a comprehensive educational system for the Scottish church. Each church would have a school. Smaller schools would send qualified students to larger schools, and qualified graduates of the larger schools would attend one of four universities: Aberdeen, Edinburgh, Glasgow, and St. Andrews. Those desiring to enter the ministry would attend St. Andrews, where Knox envisioned a curriculum of two parts: "Tongues" (Greek and Hebrew, with "readings and interpretations" in the Old and New Testaments) and "Divinity" (theology, church history, and polity). The courses leading to ordination would take five years to complete.

Knox placed ministerial scholarship on the same level as law and medicine, so the classes at St. Andrews were not designed for what we would call undergraduates: "None should be admitted unto the class and siege of Divines but he that shall have sufficient testimonials of his time well spent in Dialectics (philosophy), Mathematics, Physics, Economics, Moral Philosophy, and the Hebrew tongue."[11] The Book of Discipline mandated a clear model of theological education: students who had completed their undergraduate work would undertake lengthy, comprehensive courses in Greek and Hebrew exegesis, theology, church history, and polity. Those who had graduated in "Divinity" would then undergo presbytery examinations and, if successful, were only then considered ready for ordination.[12]

This comprehensive educational system gave the Church of Scotland confidence that its ministers could interpret Scripture, defend orthodox theology, and preach.[13] Moreover, there would be no deviation from or exception to the educational requirements. In Knox's view, it would be better for a church to have no minister for a time than to have an uneducated one.[14]

The ministers who gathered for that first presbytery meeting in Philadelphia, then, had clear and specific educational requirements in mind. Yet, as the population of the Colonies increased, it became clear that Scotland and Ulster could not supply the number of qualified ministers a growing church required. As the Colonies grew, the Synod of Philadelphia (encompassing the presbyteries of Philadelphia; New Castle, Delaware; and Long Island, New York) was formed in 1717 to help colonial churches fill their pulpits without help from across the sea. The bonds between the old and new church were loosening with every native birth, and Americans were learning to rely on their own resources. For example, in September 1719 the Synod of Philadelphia "received a letter from the people of Patomoke in Virginia" (now in Maryland), requesting a minister. It is significant that they turned to the synod, not to Scotland or Ulster. The synod responded by sending Daniel McGill.[15]

How Should Presbyterian Ministers Be Taught?

From its very inception the Presbytery of Philadelphia labored to find ways for students to meet the requirements of the Book of Discipline. There were only two colleges in the Colonies before 1700 (Harvard, from 1636; William & Mary, from 1693; Yale was founded in 1701). Since the Presbyterians had no indigenous system to educate ministerial candidates, they were free to innovate. After the examination of John Boyd, the Presbytery of Philadelphia set "tryals" for a candidate named Smith to discuss *an fides solum justificet* (justification by faith alone) and give a sermon on John 6:37. Just two years later, the presbytery tried to figure out how to "advance" David Evan so that he could prepare for his "tryals." They asked him to quit his job for a year and study a curriculum designed by three presbytery-appointed ministers. It is not recorded if he ever took his examinations,[16] but there is never any hint of sending him to St. Andrews. Colonial Presbyterians knew what they wanted their ministers to know, but they needed an institution to educate their own ministers.

In 1726, William Tennent Sr. (1673–1746) thought he had remedied the lack of an educational institution by founding the first log college at Neshaminy (present-day Warminster), in Bucks County, Pennsylvania. Log colleges dotted the colonial landscape, but three were particularly connected with Presbyterians: Tennent's log college (the main source of clergy in the south) at Neshaminy; the log college at Fagg's Manor, Chester County, Pennsylvania; and Robert Smith's log college at Pequea, in Lancaster County, Pennsylvania.[17] Tennent was a graduate of Edinburgh who had migrated from Ireland to America in 1718. After serving pastorates in New York, he accepted a call to the church at Neshaminy in 1726. Like other ministers, Tennent had tutored young men in theology and had prepared four for the ministry before 1735, when he opened his log college.

Many in the Synod of Philadelphia, however, disparaged log-college graduates. Indeed, the very name "log college" was used as an insult. The colleges themselves were simple, just one 20-by-20-foot log building. Even George Whitefield (one of the main figures in the Great Awakening and perhaps the best-known preacher in Britain and America during the eighteenth century), after a visit to Neshaminy, called the college "plain" but said it reminded him of "the school of the old prophets."[18] Presbytery objections to the log college were not necessarily directed toward the education offered. Rather, it was William Tennent's and his son Gilbert's (1703–64) enthusiasm for revivals that gave them pause. The Tennents always held to the curriculum of the Book of Discipline, but they also insisted that a basic theological education must be combined with the power of the Holy Spirit for an effective, "converted ministry." It was the Tennents' support of revivals that caused many Presbyterians to be suspicious of the school.

Log colleges, however, represented a new way of thinking. William Tennent envisioned that his school would cultivate pious men through a rigorous curriculum, and those men would then be tutored as apprentices by experienced, presbytery-approved ministers. In this way the church would be assured of a steady supply of ministers who would meet the expectations of the Book of Discipline. But log-college critics saw these schools as a way to avoid traditional educational requirements, because they were uncontrolled by the presbyteries or synods and suspected as breeding revivalism. Log colleges became the catalyst that divided the church.

Although the presumption that all colonial Presbyterian ministers should accept certain basic theological standards was raised as early as 1727, the debates over the Adopting Act of 1729 laid bare the continuing problem of clerical education. The Adopting Act required all ministers to agree with the Westminster Confession of Faith as the basis of their faith. Before 1728 there were no stated requirements for ordination. Ordination examinations were at the whim of the presbytery. While examinations usually covered preaching, exegesis, and theology, there was no uniform standard of subjects to be examined and no criteria for acceptable answers. In addition, ministers transferred between presbyteries, and from Scotland and Ireland, with no examination: they simply presented testimonials from their previous presbytery and were accepted.

Scotch-Irish ministers (centered in Philadelphia and New Castle Presbyteries) wanted the synod to require all ministers to assent to the Westminster Confession of Faith. In contrast, New Englanders from the Presbytery of Long Island argued that individual conscience could be bound only by Scripture. The Synod of Philadelphia unanimously passed the Adopting Act of 1729 as a compromise, requiring "all the Ministers of this Synod, or that shall hereafter be admitted into this Synod," to declare "their agreement in and approbation of the Confession of Faith with the larger and shorter Catechisms of the assembly of Divines at Westminster," as the basis of all "Christian Doctrine." The Adopting Act became, therefore, the ordination standard.

While ostensibly setting the theological basis for ordination, the Adopting Act intensified questions over what kind of education ministers should receive. On one hand, academic knowledge was important. After all, one cannot agree with the Confession of Faith and articulate Christian doctrine if one does not know the Confession or theology. On the other hand, knowing theological precepts does not mean one lives them.

In 1734, Gilbert Tennent (William's eldest son) overtured the Synod of Philadelphia to "exhort and obtest all our Presbyteries to take Special Care not to admit into the sacred office loose, careless, and irreligious persons, . . . and that they diligently examine all the Candidates for the Ministry in their Experiences of a work of sanctifying Grace in their hearts," and admit none who are not "serious Christians." Tennent, and many like him, saw in the Adopting Act a move toward emphasizing academics over piety. Those opposing Tennent accused him of trying to weaken the educational requirements by accepting testimonies of "sanctifying Grace" in place of academic achievement and favoring emotion over study.

The issue of clergy education occupied the 1738 meeting of the Synod of Philadelphia. While many in the synod were suspicious of a log-college education, the Tennents and others were equally concerned that the synod was advocating training over faith. Gilbert Tennent, supporting log colleges and revivals, was dissatisfied with what he considered insufficient investigation into the piety of ministerial candidates. He and his supporters pushed for the creation of a new presbytery, New Brunswick, in which they were the majority.

In retaliation, the Presbytery of Lewes (Delaware) moved that the synod create two standing committees, one for the north and one for the south of Philadelphia. These two synod committees would remove from the presbyteries the task of examining candidates. Presbyterians who held strongly to the traditional educational requirements (concentrated around the Presbytery of Philadelphia) were becoming suspicious that the Presbytery of New York (formed in 1738 when the Presbytery of Long Island merged with the Presbytery of East Jersey) were too lax, accepting insufficiently educated men into the ministry, which in their view resulted in weak theology, with an accompanying openness to revivalism.

The wording of the overture from the Presbytery of Lewes is instructive, lamenting that "[this] Part of ye world where God has ordered our Lot labours under a grievous Disadvantage for want of ye opportunities of Universities and Professors skilled in the several Branches of useful Learning." The overture then observed that students were not able "to spend a Course of years in the European or New-England Colleges—which discourages much and must be a Detriment to our Church." To prevent this "Evil," the overture proposed the appointment of a standing committee that would set a course of study "in the several branches of philosophy and Divinity and the Languages." The Synod would then administer exams which, upon successful completion, would "in some measure answer the Design of taking a Degree on College."

This overture sought to define what ministerial candidates should know and create a structure to obtain that knowledge "without putting them to further Expences." The synod would also control the content of theological education by requiring that "young men be first examined respecting their literature by a committee of Synod, and obtain a testimonial of their approbation before they can be taken on trial before any Presbytery."

It would be the synod, not the proprietor of a log college, who would "Prevent Errors young Men may imbibe by Reading without Direction." By this plan the synod would "banish ignorance, fill our Infant Church with Men eminent for . . . Learning." The synod would also control the quality of ministers by eliminating examination by the presbyteries.

Resistance was immediate. After the synod adjourned, the Presbytery of New Brunswick licensed John Rowland. The Synod of Philadelphia objected to Rowland's licensing and revoked it in September 1739. The synod was uneasy that Rowland had attended Tennent's log college and claimed that his education did not meet the standards of the Presbyterian ministry. In retaliation, the Presbytery of New Brunswick ordained Rowland the next month, with William Tennent loudly proclaiming that Rowland's education was sufficient. The synod reacted by refusing to accept Rowland as a member.

During the latter part of 1739, George Whitefield made his second visit to the American Colonies, and his revivals discomforted many in the Synod of Philadelphia. The Tennents gladly identified themselves with Whitefield's revivals, and log colleges were fatally tainted by association. The tension came to a head at the 1741 synod meeting when those following the "Old Side" (aligned with the Presbytery of Philadelphia) accused the "New Side" (usually aligned with the Presbytery of New York) of "enthusiasm," not enforcing educational standards, and favoring itinerancy. The church split when the synod expelled the Presbytery of New Brunswick, who formed the Synod of New York with the Presbytery of New York.[19]

Old Side, New Side

At first glance, the controversy would seem to be about the theology of revivalism, but the issues went deeper than that. The church was beginning to recognize the challenge of deism. In general, deism denies the Trinity, the authority of the Bible, and miracles. According to deists, God created natural laws so the world would run on its own, without divine intervention. Thus natural reason alone is sufficient to establish religion, and there is no need for revelation or individual salvation from a personal God. Deism, with its emphasis on reason and education, attracted people of the upper classes throughout the Colonies.[20]

The New Side sought to attack deism on the flank, arguing that the emotionalism inherent in revivals was the antidote to the cold rationality of the deists. Mere education and simple subscription to the Westminster Confession was insufficient to combat the irreligion of deism. William Tennent cried out for a "converted ministry" while Jonathan Dickinson, a New Side leader from Massachusetts, maintained that "acknowledgement of the Lord Jesus Christ for our common head," acceptance of the Scriptures as a "common standard in faith and practice, with a joint agreement in the same essential and necessary articles of Christianity, and the same methods of worship and discipline"—these were more vital to a competent ministry than a traditional education.[21] In contrast, the Old Side held that only an educated clergy could confront the skepticism of the time head-on. The Presbytery of Lewes, when it called for teachers "skilled in the several Branches of useful Learning"[22] in 1738, articulated the Old Side position. Even eighty years later, the 1810 Report of the Presbyterian General Assembly argued that a seminary was needed to combat deism and to address the shortage of ministers in a growing church.[23]

The Old Side–New Side split persisted for seventeen years, from 1741 to 1758, and education remained in the foreground for both parties whatever their theological differences. Neither side questioned the need for educational standards and the basic curriculum for ministerial candidates, only the degree of education that should be required for ministerial candidates. Both the Old Side and New Side parties, however, came to understand that the days of finding candidates who were trained in a Scottish divinity school were over.

The Old Side attempted to establish at least three academies to educate their ministers and remain "stedfast" to traditional educational requirements. "For our Vacancies were numerous and we found it hard in such Trouble to engage Gentlemen either from New-England or Europe to come among us."[24] These schools mostly floundered due to lack of resources, and so there were proposals to send students to Yale to get their degrees. Yale was acceptable to the Old Side because its administration was theologically acceptable; Yale had expelled David Brainerd and fined other students for participating in revivals.[25]

At the Synod of Philadelphia's 1746 meeting, when Gilbert Tennent heard that the synod intended to send students and money to Yale, he "cried out" and accused the synod of ignoring his school. In turn, many accused Tennent of dividing the church: "Mr. Gilbert Tennent grew hardy enough to tell our Synod he would oppose their Design of getting Assistance to erect a College wherever we should make Application and would maintain young Men at his Father's School in opposition to us." Before the synod could dismiss him, Tennent withdrew.[26]

Nevertheless, the Old Side and the New Side never disagreed on the ideal or the necessity of an educated ministry. The disagreement was over *how* to educate Presbyterian clergy. While it is true that the log colleges had few resources, they did fill a need. Before the Presbyterian Church divided in 1741, the Presbytery of Philadelphia had received five men from Tennent's school. In all, twenty-one men went into the Presbyterian ministry from the school at Neshaminy before Tennent died in 1746.[27] The irony of the log-college controversy was that by 1746, standards had fallen so low in the old country that no one took a divinity degree in Scotland that year. Log-college graduates were as well or better prepared than Scottish students of the time.[28] Yet, in the view of the Synod of Philadelphia, Tennent's graduates drew the church away from Calvinism and closer to the revivalist theology of New England.[29]

The College and Tutors

It is paradoxical that while the Old Side accused the New Side of ignoring education in favor of revivalism, those of the New Side were the ones who focused their energies and resources to establish the College of New Jersey in 1746. Although favorably disposed toward revivals, the New Side also keenly felt the need for an educated ministry. Unlike the limited curriculum of the log college, this new college would employ "the Usual Course of Study in the Arts and Sciences now used in the British Colleges." After graduating, ministerial candidates would spend "at least one Year, under the Care of some Minister of an approved Character for his Skill in Theology. And under his Direction shall discuss difficult Points in divinity, study the sacred Scriptures, form Sermons, Lectures & such other useful Exercises as he may be directed to the Course of his Studies."

The Old Side–New Side split ended when the Synods of New York and Philadelphia reunited in 1758 and created the Synod of New York and Philadelphia, with Gilbert Tennent as moderator. Whatever the theological differences between the former adversaries, the shortage of ministers remained a primary concern, and the new synod threw all its support behind the College of New Jersey (now Princeton University). But the reunited synod kept to tradition and would not tolerate an inferior education:

> No Presbytery Shall licence, or Ordain to the Work of the Ministry, any Candidate, until he give them competent Satis[fac]tion as to his Learning, and experimental Acquaintance with [Re]ligion, and Skill in Divinity and Cases of Conscience, and declare [his] Acceptance of the Westminster Confession of

Faith, and Catechisms, [as] the Confession of his Faith, and promise Subjection to the Presbyterian Plan of Gover[n]ment in the Westminster Directory.[30]

Although it had an expanded curriculum beyond what any log college could offer, the College of New Jersey did not educate ministers. The curriculum prepared undergraduates to receive training from a tutor after graduation. The use of the tutors in an apprentice-type model of education was logical to the colonial mind because all professionals learned on the job. From the founding of the Massachusetts Bay Colony in 1630 until the beginning of the nineteenth century, the tutor was the bedrock of the educational system. Indeed, in the eighteenth century the tutor represented the only way to obtain any kind of education. For the church, the goal of undergraduate education was to increase the numbers of qualified ministerial candidates, who would then be assigned tutors. These tutors would prepare their students to pass the ordination exams and fill vacant pulpits. The church, however, quickly realized that relying on tutors for graduate theological education was insufficient in a growing country. Consequently the role of the tutor changed from that of general educator to professional specialist. The careers of Samuel Davies (1723–61) and Moses Hoge (1752–1820) illustrate how the use of tutors evolved in theological education.

Samuel Davies and Moses Hoge

Samuel Davies was born to a farming family in New Castle County, Delaware. Since there was no school in the vicinity, Davies was taught by his mother until he was ten years old, when he went to a boarding school for two years. He returned home to be tutored by a minister for another year, and next attended Samuel Blair's (1741–1818) log college at Fagg's Manor in Chester County, Pennsylvania. Davies studied under Blair for a little over a year and was licensed by New Castle Presbytery on February 19, 1747.[31] Then he was sent to preach to a congregation in Hanover County, Virginia.

Samuel Davies's experience was typical. With a sparse population unable to support many educational institutions, learned persons (usually ministers) taught individual students or small groups in impromptu schools. Tutors with professional experience taught protégés as apprentices. Drury Lacy (1758–1815), one of the most influential ministers of his time, was taught at home, attended a boarding school for two years until his father died, and began to read theology under John Blair Smith, professor at Hampden-Sydney College and future president of the College of New Jersey.[32] Benjamin Holt Rice, brother of John Holt Rice, never attended college or seminary; he was tutored by Archibald Alexander before Alexander became the founding professor of Princeton Seminary in 1812.[33]

By the beginning of the nineteenth century, the tutor's role had undergone a metamorphosis. Elementary education was still conducted by a tutor, but higher education conducted in an institution was now the norm. The education of Moses Hoge, who was president of Hampden-Sydney College for twelve years and the professor of theology who founded what was to become Union Theological Seminary in Virginia, represents the change in the tutor's position. Born on February 15, 1752, in Frederick County, Virginia, Hoge had only a total of seven weeks of formal education before the age of twenty-five. His father, although only self-educated, taught his son, encouraged his love of books, and allowed him to read constantly. Hoge's parents taught him the Westminster Confession and were strict when it came to religious matters.

Although he was a ruling elder in the Presbyterian Church, Moses Hoge's father withdrew from the Presbyterians around 1758 for unknown reasons. While the rest of the family continued to worship at the local Presbyterian church, father and son joined an Associate Reformed Presbyterian Church (from the Scottish Covenanters) in Pennsylvania and traveled more than a hundred miles round trip for the Lord's Supper once a year. Moses Hoge joined the Associate Reformed Church when he was twenty.[34]

In 1777, when Moses Hoge was about twenty-five years old, he entered a grammar school in Culpeper, not far from his home in Frederick County, but was there for less than a year before he volunteered for the Revolutionary militia. It is not documented whether Hoge saw any action, but in November 1778, Hoge entered Liberty Hall (now Washington and Lee University) to study theology under William Graham (1745–99), the rector. Hoge graduated with a solid reputation in May 1780, and on October 25, 1780, the Presbytery of Hanover examined Hoge and received him. The presbytery licensed him in November 1781;[35] he was ordained on December 13, 1782, and called to a church in what is now Hardy County, West Virginia. Like many ministers of the time, Hoge opened a grammar school to supplement his income.

Five years later Hoge was called to Shepherd's Town, Virginia (now in West Virginia), and there he began to build his national reputation. In 1793 he published a defense of Calvinism titled *Strictures on a Pamphlet by the Rev. Jeremiah Walker, entitled The Fourfold Foundations of Calvinism Examined and Shaken.*[36] In 1797, Hoge published a widely read pamphlet, *The Christian Panoply*, in response to Thomas Paine's *Age of Reason*, published two years earlier. He pointed out that Paine had no answer for the problem of evil or the question of existence. "[Will] trigonometry, will astronomy, or natural philosophy . . . resolve the most important problem of human existence?"[37]

When the Presbytery of Winchester was established in 1794, Hoge preached the first sermon and was elected its first moderator. His wife died in 1802, and in November 1803 he married again, to a widow he had met only a month earlier at a Synod of Virginia meeting. He opened his own "classical school" in Shepherd's Town in 1805; two years later Hoge was called to be the president of Hampden-Sydney College, with the understanding that he would tutor ministerial candidates. He moved to the college in October 1807.

By accepting the call to Hampden-Sydney College, Moses Hoge was fulfilling a lifelong dream. Those who knew him remarked that he had an enduring love of teaching. In both of his previous calls he had opened schools, and he dreamed of establishing a college where all, rich and poor, could receive an education.[38] He was well aware that Scottish universities and log colleges could not meet the growing need for qualified ministers. Hoge saw the opportunity to make Hampden-Sydney College into a seminary.

A Shortage of Ministers

By the last quarter of the eighteenth century, it was clear that the College of New Jersey could never produce enough ministers to meet the unrelenting growth of the Colonies. In 1660 there were five Presbyterian churches in the Colonies; by the time of the first Presbytery meeting in 1706, there were twenty-eight.[39] Beginning in 1707[40] and for virtually every year throughout the century, the minutes of the Presbyterian Church contain petitions from congregations and presbyteries pleading for ministers. At least every other year, the Synods of Philadelphia and New York wrote to presbyteries in Scotland or Ireland, begging for ministers to come to the New World. By 1740 there were 160 congregations; in 1761 the synod lamented: "The Church suffers greatly for want of a Opportunity to instruct Students in the Knowledge of Divinity." Between 1716 and 1766, some 200,000 Scotch-Irish immigrated, primarily from Ulster, with the majority settling in the Shenandoah Valley.[41]

The meeting of the first post-Revolutionary Presbyterian General Assembly, in 1789, counted 215 congregations with ministers and 204 without. Recognizing the shortage of ministers, the assembly called for each synod to recommend two members as missionaries to the frontier.[42] The call was repeated at the 1790 meeting.[43] At the 1794 assembly, the church acknowledged the lack of qualified ministers: "We hear with pain that you are peculiarly exposed to visits from men unauthorized by the churches, unsound in faith, and of unholy and immoral lives, who call themselves preachers."[44] The assembly then identified 209 churches with ministers and 126 vacant pulpits (many churches apparently did not report or had closed).[45]

Presbyterians may have argued over the finer points of the Westminster Confession of Faith, but there would be no deviation from educational requirements for ministers, even if it meant a shortage. In 1756 the Hanover Presbytery—in the second year of its existence and deluged with petitions for ministers—examined John Martin. He "delivered a discourse upon Eph. 2:1 which was sustained as a part of Tryal; and he was also examined as to his religious experiences, and the reasons of his designing the ministry; which was also sustained." He was likewise examined in the Latin and Greek languages, and briefly in "Logick, ontology, Ethics, natural Philosophy, Rhetoric, geography and Astronomy; in all which his Answers in general were satisfactory." The Presbytery appointed him "to prepare a Sermon on I Cor. 22–23, and an Exegesis [in Latin] on this question, *Num Revelation Supernaturalist fit Necessarius* [Is supernatural revelation needed?], to be delivered at our next committee."

At the next meeting John Martin preached his sermon and presented his exegesis. "The committee proceeded to examine him upon ye Hebrew, and in sundry extempore Questions upon ye Doctrines of religion and in some cases of Conscience." Martin was then appointed to give a lecture on Isaiah 61:1–3 at the next meeting of the presbytery. After sustaining his trial, the presbytery asked him to preach for the next meeting on 1 John 5:10 and further examined him in "various branches of Learning and Divinity; and reheard his religious Experiences; and upon a review of ye sundry trials he has passed thro; they judge him qualified to preach ye Gospel; and he having declared his Assent to and approbation of ye Westminster Confession of Faith, Catechisms and Directory, . . . ye Presbytery do license and authorize him to preach as a Candidate for the ministry of ye Gospel." The following year, Martin opened presbytery with a sermon and prepared a Latin thesis on *An Mundus Fuit Creatus*[46] (whether the world was created [pure], from Calvin's commentary on Ps. 51:3–6).

In 1782 the Synod of Philadelphia heard a request to relax the educational standards for one candidate, but John Witherspoon (1723–94) took the lead in opposition, and the request was denied. In 1783 the Presbytery of Philadelphia heard an overture "that inasmuch as the shortage of ministers was so serious" and the prospects of securing more clergymen so low, that laymen might lead worship by reading printed sermons. The presbytery, and then the Synod of Philadelphia, could not bring themselves to allow laymen to read printed sermons until 1786. Educational requirements for ministers would not be compromised. In 1785 the synod rebuked the Presbytery of New Brunswick for allowing a candidate to do part of his exegesis in English instead of Latin. At this same meeting, the synod was overtured: "Whether in the present state of the church in America, the scarcity of ministers to fill our numerous congregations, the Synod, or Presbyteries, ought therefore to relax, in any degree, in the literary qualifications required of entrants into the ministry?" The overture was rejected by a huge majority.[47]

The Plan of Government (1789) of the newly formed Presbyterian Church in the United States of America was uncompromising: every candidate for ministry should have a college diploma, "or at least authentic testimonials of his having gone through a regular course of learning." Two years of theological study under the direction of some approved divine were required. As a result, presbyteries and synods began designating certain men to teach candidates and compensating them for their time.[48]

The Plan of Union

Throughout the eighteenth century the Presbyterian Church relied on its own resources to increase the number of ministers. The results of all the squabbles, divisions, and overtures, however, did not solve the problem. It was no longer practical to import candidates from overseas, log colleges had failed, and there were not enough college graduates studying under tutors to fill pulpits. The church needed a new approach. Perhaps combining with another denomination could fill the need. The Plan of Union (1801) is traditionally seen as a model of ecumenical cooperation, yet its genesis came from the shortage of ministers.

In 1801 the General Assembly of the Presbyterian Church and the state associations of nearly all the New England Congregational Churches adopted an agreement to fill the pulpits of the rapidly growing west. This agreement was designed to be a blueprint that their respective missionaries would follow in evangelizing new settlements in the Northwest Territory. In a series of military campaigns from 1778 to 1779, George Rogers Clark had driven out the French, British, and Native Americans from what would become Ohio, Indiana, Illinois, Wisconsin, Michigan, and parts of Minnesota. By 1800, thousands of settlers were pouring into this huge expanse. Both denominations wanted a presence in the region and took advantage of the Land Ordinance (1785) and the Northwest Ordinance (1789), which granted land to organized churches within the township system.[49]

The Northwest Territory increased the size of the United States by almost 70 percent.[50] Since most of the families moving into the territory claimed either Presbyterian or Congregational membership, cooperation seemed logical.[51] New England Congregationalists and Presbyterians had worked against the establishment of a colonial bishop between 1767 and 1776, and they shared a strong commitment to Calvinism. Consequently, it was almost natural for each church to adopt common policies for evangelization and to recognize each other's ministers and sacraments. They formalized their cooperation in the Plan of Union in 1801.[52]

Under the Plan of Union, it did not matter if a particular evangelist were a Presbyterian or a Congregationalist. He was to establish a new church in each frontier community and then allow the congregation to decide for itself which denomination it preferred. Once a congregation joined one or the other denomination, their minister, regardless of his previous denominational affiliation, was eligible for membership in the governing body of the denomination to which the congregation belonged. John Holt Rice was enthusiastic over the prospects of the Plan of Union: "I am very greatly pleased with it. I do delight greatly in witnessing the union and co-operation of Christians in building up the kingdom of our common Lord."[53]

Virginia's Unique Position

Although the College of New Jersey and fraternal relations leading up to the Plan of Union increased the supply of ministers to the north, southern churches continued to face a shortage in their pulpits. In 1775 the Hanover Presbytery included what is now Virginia, West Virginia, Kentucky, North Carolina, Tennessee, and most of Maryland.[54] The presbytery's minutes are filled with requests for ministers. In 1779, for example, the presbytery informed a commissioner from Kentucky that there were not enough ministers, and the presbytery would send pulpit supplies as soon as possible.[55] There is no record of anyone being sent. In 1780 the Hanover Presbytery asked the Connecticut Association (Congregational) if they could help fill vacancies in Virginia. In response, two ministers came from Connecticut in 1782, but they did not stay long.[56] As late as 1792, the Synod of Virginia reported that only sixteen of twenty-five congregations were supplied.

The first post-Independence Presbyterian General Assembly in 1789 recognized the growth of the new country and divided the Synod of New York and Philadelphia into four new synods: New York and New Jersey, Philadelphia, Virginia, and the Carolinas. Hanover Presbytery was put under the Synod of Virginia, and its boundaries were limited to the Commonwealth of Virginia. The General Assembly called for missionaries for the frontier, but two years later the Synod of Virginia reported a bleak picture. The synod concluded that the congregations within their bounds were "perishing for lack of knowledge."[57] The synod further reported that three missionaries had "very extensive circuits assigned to them of seven hundred miles" in the Shenandoah Valley.[58]

The reasons for the scarcity of ministers and the lack of educational infrastructure were the results of geography, politics, and culture. Until the 1730s, the concerns of the Synod of Philadelphia followed population patterns and political realities. Colonial immigration followed specific patterns: New England was primarily Congregational; South Carolina and Virginia were overwhelmingly Anglican. Presbyterians tended to cluster in the Mid-Atlantic region: Pennsylvania, Delaware, New Jersey, New York, and Maryland. These congregations occupied the synod's concern because they were close and contained the majority of American Presbyterians.

Virginia was the largest colony and the largest state until the completion of the Erie Canal in 1825, but the Anglican Church was more firmly established in Virginia than in any other colony. As a result, it was difficult for Presbyterians and other dissenters (non-Anglicans) to build churches, worship without interference, and not pay taxes to the local parish.[59] The Scotch-Irish migrated westward across Pennsylvania and south through the Shenandoah Valley by 1725. These Presbyterians wanted their own churches with their own ministers; often they joined Episcopal parishes, becoming the majority in those congregations because there was no other church to join.[60] In addition, small Presbyterian communities grew outside of Tidewater (the area between Richmond and Norfolk) during the 1740s, increasing the call for Presbyterian ministers in Virginia.[61] The minutes of the Synod of Philadelphia, the Presbyterian General Assembly, the Synod of Virginia, and the Hanover Presbytery up to the 1820s show repeated requests for ministers.[62]

Whereas other colonies largely accepted the right of denominations to coexist, Presbyterians had to establish their very right to exist in Virginia. On May 26, 1736, eleven years before the arrival of Samuel Davies (who was the first non-Anglican minister licensed to preach in Virginia), John Caldwell of Cub Creek requested the Synod of Philadelphia to petition the colonial governor of Virginia to allow Presbyterians to worship under the Toleration Act of 1689. The Toleration Act exempted dissenters from attendance at the parish churches, provided they took an oath of allegiance to the Crown, continued to pay their tithes to the local Anglican church, and attended their own religious services with the regularity prescribed by law. Furthermore, their ministers were required to be "regularly" ordained, accept certain articles of the Church of England, and preach only in registered "places of meeting." In 1699 the Virginia legislature applied the Toleration Act to the colony, exempting dissenters from any penalties as long as they attended their own worship "once in two months." The act did not specifically protect dissenting ministers. In 1711 the English Parliament passed a supplementary act, which allowed properly qualified dissenting ministers "to officiate in any congregation in any county" provided the meeting place was duly certified and registered.[63]

In its 1738 meeting, the Synod of Philadelphia complied with Caldwell's request and petitioned Governor William Gooch to apply the Toleration Act to Virginia. The petition was submitted on behalf of "a considerable Number of our Brethren who are . . . in the remote Parts of Your Government," who are of the "same Perswasion with the Church of Scotland" and have "manifested an unspotted fidelity to our gracious Sovereign King George." The synod read Gooch's reply at its next meeting in 1739. The governor was clear: "You may be assured yt [that] no Interruption shall be given to any Minstr. of your Profession . . . so long as they conform themselves to the Rules prescribed in the Act of Toleration."[64]

Gooch's policy was tested five years later. According to what could be called Presbyterian hagiography, Samuel Morris, James Hunt, and two other Hanover residents refused to worship in the established church in Hanover in 1743 (four years prior to Davies's arrival). The local priest reported their nonattendance to the magistrate, who found them guilty, and they were summoned to Williamsburg to appear before the governor. They had first decided to call themselves Lutherans because they had read some of Martin Luther's works. It is said that one of the party stayed at the home of a Scotsman in Williamsburg, who lent him a copy of the Confession of Faith of the Church of Scotland. After reading it, this man showed it to the others, and they decided they agreed with it. When Governor Gooch asked them to identify themselves, they simply handed him the book.[65] Gooch, an Anglican but also a Scotsman, declared them Presbyterian and therefore tolerated.[66]

In 1751 the Synod of New York (New Side), after reporting that the College of New Jersey was graduating candidates for the ministry, sent Nehemiah Greenman to investigate the "distressing Circumstances of Virginia." Four years later, the synod created the Presbytery of Hanover.[67] The Synod of New York (New Side) clearly expected the new presbytery to support the College of New Jersey, no doubt with the belief that the college would supply Virginia with all the ministers their pulpits required. At its first session in 1755, the Hanover Presbytery heard an appeal from the synod "to all congregations within its bounds to raise a collection for the College of New Jersey." Hanover replied that because of "the present impoverished state of the colony in general and our congregations in particular," any fund-raising effort was "quite impracticable."

On July 12, 1758, seven former New Side ministers and three former Old Siders met in the Cumberland Church to form a new, united presbytery and decided to keep the name Hanover Presbytery.[68] Although Virginia's Presbyterians were now unified they still did not send money to Princeton, and there was still a shortage of ministers. In 1762 the Synod of New York and Philadelphia sent Enoch Green and William Tennent Jr. to Hanover Presbytery to supply churches for six months. Hanover Presbytery asked for more "Supplies" in 1763 and again in 1774. In response, the synod sent John DeBow (under the care of the New Brunswick Presbytery) and Samuel McCorkle (under the care of the New York Presbytery) to the Presbyteries of Hanover and Orange to serve as supplies for one year.[69]

Immigration continued, congregations formed, and the shortage of ministers continued. On the eve of the Revolution, there were thirty Presbyterian churches in the Shenandoah Valley alone.[70] At its October 1778 meeting, Hanover Presbytery, recognizing "the danger of the [extermination] of our churches, unless some speedy and effectual means be adopted to prevent the evil," considered a motion "to shorten and reform the mode of education so as to afford a longer time for cultivating the study of theology, and to make the pulpit more accessible to pious youth who are advanced in years before they have entered on a course of learning." No action on the motion was recorded,[71] but the anxiety was palpable.

Virginia churches needed a reliable supply of qualified ministers. At first they put their hopes on the church's college. At their first meeting in October 1789, the Synod of Virginia "very strongly recommended to each Presbytery . . . that they should do their utmost to promote collections for the New Jersey College,"[72] and the synod appointed agents to solicit subscriptions. There are no records of any funds being remitted to the college.

Virginia Goes Its Own Way

The fund-raising efforts for the College of New Jersey must have seemed too little and too far away for most Virginia Presbyterians. In October 1770, a motion was made to establish an undergraduate school within the bounds of Hanover Presbytery (in Augusta County), but there is no record of any action taken.[73] The discussion concerning a "literary institution" within their bounds and under their care, however, continued through the meetings of October 1771,[74] April 1772, and June 1773. The presbytery made its decision on October 16, 1773: "The Presbytery agrees to fix the public Seminary for the liberal education of youth in Staunton, Augusta."[75]

From its inception in 1755, Hanover Presbytery was concerned with the lack of ministers, and it was clear to all that the College of New Jersey could not supply the presbytery's pulpits. The Synod of Virginia and the presbytery searched for "some plan calculated to educate persons designed for the Gospel ministry."[76] Their solution was to establish two undergraduate schools, one to the west of the Blue Ridge and one to the east. A rector would supervise the education of undergraduates and would also be the theology teacher for ministerial candidates.

Augusta Academy was founded as a "classical school" in 1749 in Augusta County. Educational terms in the eighteenth century were vague. A "classical school," "college," or "seminary" could denote virtually any kind of institution of higher education, such as a preparatory school or college in the modern sense, or a professional institution to train young men for ministry.[77] In 1776, Augusta Academy was renamed Liberty Hall by its Scotch-Irish patrons, to show their support of the American Revolution. In May 1780 Hanover Presbytery moved the campus twenty miles south to Timber Ridge (in Lexington) due to a gift of forty acres, and appointed William Graham as rector.[78] Graham struggled to make Liberty Hall more than just another log college, but his school languished for lack of resources. Although two buildings at Liberty Hall were finished by January 1, 1794, the school's finances were never secure. In some years, Graham went without pay; when it was clear that additional money was not forthcoming, he resigned in 1796. Two years later in Ohio, he died penniless.[79]

In 1790 the Presbyterian General Assembly suggested a three-year theological course for ministerial candidates. While the Virginia presbyteries refused to make this a requirement, it spurred the Synod of Virginia to rethink theological education.[80] In 1791, for the first time, a synod committee recommended something like a seminary education, proposing that two schools be opened "for all youths desiring to study for the ministry." One school would be located in Rockbridge, at the already-established Liberty Hall, under William Graham;

and the other in Washington County, Pennsylvania, under John McMillan. The Presbyteries of Hanover and Lexington were to be trustees of the "Seminary" in Rockbridge.[81] Hampden-Sydney College, founded in 1775, was not mentioned at this meeting.

On October 1, 1791, Hanover Presbytery called William Graham as president of the proposed seminary in Rockbridge. The Synod of Virginia wanted Hanover and Lexington Presbyteries to unite in support of this seminary,[82] but Hanover never really backed Graham's enterprise. On September 27, 1793, the synod praised the Presbytery of Redstone (formed in 1789 in southwestern Pennsylvania, which belonged to the Synod of Virginia at the time) for their fund-raising efforts on behalf of "educating indigent and pious youths."[83] In contrast, the synod criticized Hanover for being behind on their subscriptions.[84] At the presbytery meetings of November 2, 1795; April 21, 1796; October 14, 1796; and April 14, 1797, there were continued calls to support the education of poor and pious youth.[85]

Yet the idea of separating graduate theological education from the undergraduate curriculum had taken hold. While the words academy, college, and seminary were used interchangeably, it is clear from the minutes of the Synod of Virginia and Hanover Presbytery that Graham understood he would teach undergraduates and ministerial candidates in separate courses. The synod was thinking of something new: an undergraduate curriculum followed by a year or two of study under an "institutional" tutor. The institution to educate ministers, however, would stand alone.[86] There would be one board of trustees for the college, and the Presbyteries of Hanover and Lexington would be the trustees for the theological school. The presbyteries would provide funds to make theological education available, examine students, and provide supplies. "In one or other of these institutions [Rockbridge, Virginia, and Redstone, Pennsylvania] it is the desire of the Synod that all youths who intend to engage in the ministry of the Gospel within our bounds shall be instructed."[87]

In truth, the schools in Lexington, Virginia, and Washington County, Pennsylvania, amounted to little more than an addition of religion to an undergraduate curriculum. While the presbyteries did examine Liberty Hall students once or twice and raised a small amount of money, the synod soon lost interest in the project: there is no further mention of the proposed two schools after Graham's resignation in 1796.[88] But the lack of ministers was still urgent, and one school, located in southside Virginia, had ties to the College of New Jersey and was in relatively good shape: Hampden-Sydney College.

Hampden-Sydney College

Although Hanover Presbytery had called on their churches to support "the public Seminary for liberal education of youth in Staunton, Augusta" at their October 1773 meeting, it was not until 1774 that congregations were asked to pledge for it. The presbytery intended the subscriptions to be paid by December 25, 1775. Yet by October 1774 plans had changed; the presbytery reported that Samuel Stanhope Smith, "a Probationer of the New Castle Presbytery, . . . a gentleman who has taught the Languages for a considerable time in the

New Jersey College with good approbation, . . . may be enduced to take the Superintendency of a public seminary in Prince Edward in the upper end of the Cumberland."

By February 1, 1775, ten months before subscriptions for the school in Augusta were due, it became obvious that Hanover Presbytery would never support the school in Rockbridge. Instead, the presbytery reported that "subscriptions needed for establishment of a seminary in Prince Edward have succeeded beyond expectations," with £1300 already subscribed and £400 to be spent on books. The next day, members of the presbytery went to a hundred-acre site at Hudson's Branch in Prince Edward County and agreed to build classrooms, a dwelling for the Superintendent, and other necessary houses. On February 3, 1775, the day after the presbytery voted to construct the buildings, the presbytery called Samuel Stanhope Smith as rector and authorized one assistant.[89] Hanover Presbytery now had their "seminary in Prince Edward: Hampden-Sydney College.

Virginia Presbyterians wanted ministers, but only qualified ministers. The one constant throughout this period, whether in Philadelphia, New York, or Virginia, was the strict educational requirement for ministry. Whether earned in a Scottish university, log college, church college, or from a tutor, the education of a minister was expected to conform to the curriculum set out in the Book of Discipline. The colleges would ensure that candidates had studied dialectics, mathematics, physics, economics, and moral philosophy. Tutors would teach Greek and Hebrew, theology, church history, and polity. And presbyteries would examine candidates to make sure they could apply what they had learned.

The uniformity of educational expectations can be seen in presbytery examinations during the eighteenth century. In 1706, as previously noted, John Boyd "performed tryals," preached a "popular sermon" on John 1:12, defended his "thesis," and answered questions in Philadelphia.[90] In 1777, in Bedford County, Virginia, John Blair Smith presented an exegesis on "judgment" (in Latin), then preached on Romans 3:25, and lectured on Daniel 9:24–27. One year later he preached on 1 John 3:1 and was then approved for ordination.[91] Presbytery examinations were surprisingly uniform: Latin exegesis, a lecture on a passage of Scripture, a lecture on a contemporary topic, and a sermon, usually a year later. In 1789 Hanover Presbytery began to accept a Hampden-Sydney College diploma as part of the exam.[92] Although Liberty Hall and Hampden-Sydney had both been offering classes in theology since 1776 (even though theology was not an official part of the curriculum), Hanover Presbytery's preference for Hampden-Sydney was clear from the beginning.

Hanover Presbytery's confidence in Hampden-Sydney College was due to the reputation of its first president, Samuel Stanhope Smith (1751–1819). Smith was born in Pequea, Lancaster County, Pennsylvania. His father, the Reverend Robert Smith, had immigrated from Londonderry and was the founder of the Pequea Academy. Smith began attending his father's school when he was around six. His father allowed only Latin to be spoken at school, and his son enjoyed reading theological books. He entered the college at Princeton in 1766, when he was sixteen years old, and graduated after two years. Smith taught at his father's academy after graduation and returned to Princeton in 1770 to teach. It was while teaching at Princeton that he began "pursuing a course of theological study with reference to ministry," by studying under John Witherspoon.[93]

The Presbytery of New Castle licensed Smith in 1773. He immediately requested to go south in an effort to improve his poor health. The presbytery sent him to Virginia, and he became the president of Hampden-Sydney in 1775. Smith, however, did not stay at Hampden-Sydney for very long; he became more and more frustrated with the nonchalance Virginians displayed in their approaches to religion. He returned to the college at Princeton in 1779 to teach and succeeded John Witherspoon as president in 1794.

In his short time at Hampden-Sydney, Samuel Stanhope Smith shaped Virginia Presbyterianism through his vision of education. Moses Hoge always remembered a remark made by Smith when he heard Smith speak at Culpeper Academy: "While sanctified learning is the greatest blessing, unsanctified learning is the greatest curse."[94] Smith resolved that his new school would offer sanctified learning on a specific plan. On September 1, 1775, in an advertisement in the *Virginia Gazette*, he stated that the curriculum of the as-yet unnamed "Academy in Prince Edward" would be like that of the College of New Jersey.[95] The College of New Jersey had established a theology department in 1748,[96] and Smith intended for his school to follow that pattern.

The College of New Jersey had a huge impact in colonial Virginia. The Scotch-Irish in the Shenandoah Valley had migrated from Pennsylvania and New Jersey,[97] and transportation routes through the valley allowed them to keep close commercial ties to those areas.[98] As a consequence, they tended to support the College of New Jersey as their own.[99] Of the first six ministers in Hanover Presbytery, five were graduates of the College of New Jersey. Four graduates were on the first board of trustees at Hampden-Sydney College,[100] and two graduates were the first presidents of Hampden-Sydney College. It is no wonder that Samuel Stanhope Smith boasted that Hampden-Sydney's curriculum "will resemble that which is adopted in the College of New Jersey, save that a more particular attention shall be paid to the cultivation of the English language than is usually done in places of public education." The College of New Jersey and Hampden-Sydney College represented an improvement in the education offered to eighteenth-century students, and both schools would face an increasingly hostile culture.

A Culture of Skepticism

Hampden-Sydney College faced an ambivalent, if not antagonistic, culture. The antireligious attitude in Virginia was in part a reaction against living under an established church. Most Hampden-Sydney students came from gentry backgrounds where faith meant performing the required rituals but required no commitment. These students tended to regard "religion and religious persons with contempt and ridicule."[101] In 1795, Archibald Alexander, Hoge's immediate predecessor at Hampden-Sydney, wrote: "Most of our educated men have become Deists or worse."[102]

With memories of an established church still strong in people's minds, Hampden-Sydney College had to walk a careful nonsectarian line. When

Hanover Presbytery announced their new institution, they were careful to calm public fears about the school's goals: there was no mention of training ministers. In 1775, after all, Presbyterians were seen as dissenters, so the less said about religion, the less opposition the new college would arouse. Samuel Stanhope Smith emphasized that "all possible Care shall be taken that no undue Influence by any member of this Pby [presbytery], the Rector, or any Assistant to Byas [bias] the Judgement of any; but that all of every Denomination shall fully enjoy his own religious sentiments."[103]

Yet the college was an institution of the church; the education received at Hampden-Sydney would prepare candidates to study theology under a tutor. In a sermon, the manuscript of which still exists, Smith advocated learning in various branches—languages, science, history, eloquence, all included in the projected curriculum—to equip a minister "to answer the challenges posed by educated and informed critics and foes of the Christian religion" and, more positively, to "open the passage to the heart as well as to the understanding." The challenge posed by deism would be answered by a converted, educated ministry.

In post-Revolutionary Virginia, Hampden-Sydney College had to be intentionally nonsectarian to be accepted, and Smith faced the hostility head-on. He decried any "ambition to distinguish myself as a sectary." In letters to Thomas Jefferson concerning his plan for public education in Virginia, Smith deplored sectarianism, disclaiming "any ambition to be the leader of a sect," and declared that it was "time to heal these divisions, for the honor of religion and to promote the noblest design to which this or any other country has given birth."[104]

Almost immediately after Hampden-Sydney College announced its opening, a letter signed by "Luther" appeared in the *Virginia Gazette* on November 18, 1775. Although Luther acknowledged that "public schools under proper regulations are extremely advantageous," he felt that the "worthy gentlemen-contributors [to Hampden-Sydney] are not sufficiently aware of the evil consequences which may arise from the way and manner it is intended to be conducted." Luther then charged that it is "inconsistent with prudence and good policy to let Dissenters teach in public schools, much less act as president, both of which are intended for Prince Edward academy." He objected to Presbyterian doctrines as "repugnant to the doctrines of the Church of England" and "subversive of morality." He went on to declare, "Every parent with the spiritual interest of his child at heart should determine whether the education of his child should [be entrusted] to those who believe such doctrines."[105]

Luther feared that dissenters would try to replace the established church with their own establishment and urged Anglican subscribers to Hampden-Sydney College to withhold payment of their subscriptions until the school was put under teachers who were members of the Church of England. "If the school has the success Mr. Smith intimates," he wrote, "we may reasonably expect to see in a few years our senate-house and pulpit filled with Dissenters" who might secure a religious establishment in their favor.[106]

Anglicans had reason to be suspicious and bitter. Between 1776 and 1799 Virginians, with Presbyterians and deists in the lead, had struggled over disestablishment—the elimination of the Anglican Church as the official church of the Commonwealth of Virginia, with special privileges and tax exemptions. When disestablishment was effected in 1802, the selling of glebes hit Virginia

Anglicans hard. Glebes were church-owned lands (including the rectory where the priest and his family lived) that had been granted by the colonial government. In many cases these lands had been in the possession of a parish for two hundred years, and they now disappeared overnight. Since glebes were often rented out to support the priest and pay the expenses of the church, priests' families became destitute with disestablishment, and smaller parishes closed. The easy access to influence and the enormous prestige of the Anglican Church evaporated. In reaction, the dispossessed Anglicans vowed that Presbyterians would not establish their own church. In turn, Presbyterians had to prove they were not in favor of any established religion.[107]

Samuel Stanhope Smith took pains to show that his new school was no threat. He reassured *Gazette* readers that Hampden-Sydney and the Presbyterians did not intend to establish a church. He pointed out that although Presbyterian ministers conceived the idea of the academy and cultivated it, they "yield the power of visitation and managing the general concerns to trustees who are chiefly members of the Church of England."[108]

In addition to the fear of an established church, Virginia culture was hostile to any kind of faith that fell under the suspicion of "enthusiasm." Being accustomed to the established church as little more than a cultural decoration, the upper classes of Virginia recoiled at the demands of supporting a church and the perceived excesses of "evangelical" faith. William Hill was a student at Hampden-Sydney College in 1785 and later a major figure in New School Presbyterianism in 1837. He lamented that "among the 80 Students then in college, there was not one who gave the least evidence of seriousness or respect for religion." He felt out of place and miserable because of his faith. "Among such a number of young men from among the most wealthy & respectable families in the community, . . . anyone who shd [should] evince serious impressions on this subject wd [would] be necessarily exposed to incessant sneers of contempt & ridicule." Hill had not read a Bible since he had left home and "could not hear of one in all the College."

Hill related that students would go to revivals for entertainment, and when a classmate, Cary Allen, made a statement of faith after hearing a Methodist circuit rider, Allen was afraid to make his new faith known. Hill then observed: "It is probable that neither Dr. Smith, nor any of the College professors had ever heard that any one in College felt any concern upon the subject of religion until Allens return & professed conversion."

William Hill, along with Cary Allen and his roommates, began to pray in Hill's room, with the door closed. But after they "began singing, tho' with suppressed voices, it was soon found out by the Students what we were about, & the whole College was soon collected at our door, & commenced thumping at our door, whooping & swearing until a perfect riot was raised. This entirely broke up our meeting, & they became so riotous as to require the professors in College to interfere to suppress the noise & riot."

After investigating this incident, Smith was pleased to hear that at least some students were praying, singing hymns, and reading the Bible and invited them to hold their next meeting in his parlor.[109] At the next meeting, Smith's house "was crowded in every part; . . . almost the whole of the students were assembled."

In 1796, soon after coming to the University of North Carolina at Chapel Hill (near Raleigh), Joseph Caldwell complained:

> Religion is so little in vogue, and in such a state of depression, that it affords no prospects sufficient to tempt people to undertake its cause. In New Jersey it has the public respect and support. But in North Carolina . . . everyone believes that the first step which he ought to take to rise into respectability is to disavow as often and as publicly as he can all regard for the leading doctrines of the Scriptures. One of the principal reasons why religion is so slighted and almost scouted is that it is taught only by Methodists and ranters with whom it seems to consist only in the power of their throats, or wildness and madness of their gesticulations and distortions.[110]

Deism and agnosticism were fashionable and prevalent. As late as 1810, Bishop James Madison, the first Episcopal bishop of the Diocese of Virginia and eighth president of William & Mary, wrote: "Infidelity was rife in the State, and the College of William and Mary was regarded as the hotbed of French politics and religion. I can truly say, that then, and for some years after, in every educated young man of Virginia whom I met, I expected to find a sceptic, if not an avowed unbeliever."[111]

Even though Hampden-Sydney College was founded by the Presbyterian Church, its culture reflected the antireligious sentiments of the commonwealth.[112] Indeed, when Thomas Jefferson heard of the revival at Hampden-Sydney, he predicted that parents would have "no taste for religious phrensy" at the college.[113] Smith welcomed the revival, but his passion for religion, along with his absences for preaching engagements, evoked so much criticism that he resigned in 1779 and returned to New Jersey.[114]

The revival of 1787–89 changed the tenor of the college. Nash LeGrand (Class of 1786), "one of the wildest and most dissolute" students, was converted in a revival and spent over twenty years in the ministry. Yet in the eyes of many Virginians, the revival marked Hampden-Sydney as a hotbed of offensive religious enthusiasm and cost the college a number of students. By the 1780s the religious character of Hampden-Sydney College was obvious. According to the bylaws of June 23, 1784, students at Hampden-Sydney were required to attend public prayers every morning and every evening at 5:00 p.m., public worship on Sunday at any church within three miles of the college, and there would be no swearing and no liquor.[115]

This church-related institution, then, had to walk a fine line. Hampden-Sydney (and later Union Seminary) could argue for the philosophical imperatives of faith, but against the emotionalism of revivals. In an ostensibly anonymous 1823 essay, John Holt Rice argued that a Presbyterian revival must keep to "the rule of external decorum," be solemn, "be accomplished by argument and reason," and "must be attended by a conduct worthy of the dignity of man returning his allegiance to his Maker."[116]

When Samuel Stanhope Smith resigned in 1779, Hanover Presbytery called John Blair Smith, Samuel's brother and also a Presbyterian minister, to lead the college. John Blair Smith understood that Hampden-Sydney would be a training ground for ministers who must walk a fine line between revivals and skepticism and still remain able to defend and propagate Calvinism. On October 24,

1780, the presbytery intensified theological education by taking a young Moses Hoge under care and directing "that he shall prosecute the Study of Divinity under care of some of our members."[117]

In June 1783, the Virginia General Assembly granted Hampden-Sydney College a charter, thereby making the college independent of Hanover Presbytery.[118] Incorporation allowed the college to begin granting degrees; the first class of eight received them on September 22, 1786.[119] On April 25, 1789, Hanover Presbytery began to examine Nash LeGrand's knowledge of the "learned languages and the sciences." LeGrand produced his diploma from Hampden-Sydney, and the presbytery accepted it as a substitute for the exam in secular learning; this was the first time a diploma was accepted as a substitute for an exam.[120] In 1790, "Mr. William Hill . . . produced a Diploma from Hampden-Sydney College" and was licensed to preach by Hanover Presbytery after it "examined him in Divinity."[121] At its meeting at Winchester on September 29, 1791, the Presbytery of Hanover reported to the Synod of Virginia that they had "four candidates under trial." Of the four candidates (William Cahoon [Calhoun], James Turner, Samuel Brown, and Moses Waddle [Waddell]), Calhoun and Waddell were graduates of Hampden-Sydney.[122]

After a Century

Throughout the eighteenth century the Presbyterian Church confronted a shortage of ministers as immigration increased year after year. After independence, the new country acquired new lands to the west, and immigrants continued to pour into these new lands. The synods and presbyteries relied on the educational heritage from Scotland as the model of what a Presbyterian minister should know. When the universities of Scotland and Ulster could no longer fill the empty pulpits of British North America and then the United States, the church turned to log colleges, tutors, cooperative efforts with other denominations, and finally their own institutions of higher learning to educate their ministers. These educational models relied on tutors, yet it was becoming clear that a more systematic model of theological education was needed.

At the same time, a skeptical culture questioned the need for any kind of faith. New Side Presbyterians wanted to address the cold logic of deism through revivals, the Old Side through more intensive and rigorous education. After a century of failing to fill their pulpits, Presbyterians were ready to try something new.

Chapter Two (1807–21)
Poor and Pious Youth

Writing to a friend in 1816, John Adams pondered two hundred years of American history and mused that the Revolution was not just a political event, but also a continuum initiated when the Pilgrims landed at Plymouth Rock. As ties with the mother country loosened with each generation, there was a "Revolution in the minds and hearts of the people, a change in their religious sentiments . . . This radical change in the principles, opinions, sentiments, and affections of the people was the real American Revolution."[1] After independence, a new national character began to evolve, and Presbyterians had to find innovative ways to minister to this new society.

In 1790, America was largely Presbyterian, Congregational, Anglican, and Calvinist Baptist. By 1815, the population had become primarily Methodist and Baptist.[2] The denominations preeminent before the Revolution declined either due to disestablishment (for Episcopalians) or the inability to supply their pulpits (for Presbyterians and Congregationalists). To keep their churches in the Ohio River Valley supplied with educated clergy, the Presbyterians and Congregationalists united in the Plan of Union (1801). But as settlers moved into Kentucky (admitted in 1792) and Tennessee (admitted in 1796), and as the Louisiana Purchase (which almost doubled the size of the United States in 1803)[3] was opened for settlement, the Plan of Union just could not produce the number of ministers required by Presbyterians and New England Congregationalists.

A New Idea for Theological Education

A century of clergy shortages had frustrated the church. In 1756 the Presbyterian General Assembly established a theological library at the College of Philadelphia,[4] hoping to attract more tutors and students. There was, however, no increase in ministerial candidates. In 1778 the Hanover Presbytery voiced its concern that without ministers its churches were dying and blamed the shortage on the extensive educational requirements for ordination.[5] Tutors and libraries were not enough.

Beginning around 1800, what came to be known as the Great Revival (or the Second Great Awakening) began in Kentucky and spread into the Carolinas and Georgia. As itinerant Baptist ministers and Methodist circuit riders held camp meetings in remote locations, thousands of people hungry for fellowship and encouragement flooded to their tents. The Cane Ridge, Kentucky, meeting attracted up to twenty thousand people. Eager to give their isolated communities a spiritual center, local congregations began to ordain their own ministers, with no educational requirement. Presbyterians, however, held to the traditional ideal of an educated clergy. They would rather let churches go without ministers than allow uneducated men to fill Presbyterian pulpits.[6] In 1808, churches in Tennessee asked the assembly for the freedom to "license" ministers without education.[7] The assembly refused, and in 1810, Presbyterian churches in Tennessee, Kentucky, and other areas primarily in the West left the General Assembly and formed the Cumberland Presbyterian Church.

By the beginning of the nineteenth century, it was clear that foreign universities, church colleges, and tutors could not supply the number of ministers a growing country demanded. The church needed a new model of theological education. As petition after petition, usually from the West, inundated the General Assembly, and as the threat of Presbyterian churches ordaining their own uneducated clergy became a reality, the assembly began to seek a comprehensive solution. The idea of seminaries dedicated solely to educating ministers gradually began to evolve.

At its 1806 meeting, the members of Hanover Presbytery heard an overture from the previous year's Presbyterian General Assembly, which reiterated the obvious: the Plan of Union was not supplying the number of ministers the church required, and something else had to be done. The 1805 overture had recommended that each presbytery establish a fund to provide for the theological education of "poor and pious youth."

Hanover Presbytery responded in three ways. First, they established a theological library at Hampden-Sydney College. The library would be separate from the college, with a standing committee (including John Holt Rice) dedicated to its management. Second, they established a fund for the education of "poor & pious youth." Funds raised by the committee would be deposited with the trustees of Hampden-Sydney College, but the appropriation of these funds would remain with the presbytery. Finally, they would call a theological professor who would teach ministerial candidates, and the school was to be part of the college.[8]

Hanover Presbytery proposed something new, going beyond the request to establish a fund to educate poor and pious youth. They had a comprehensive plan to change theological education over the long term, addressing the need for ministers, faculty, curriculum, and funding. The presbytery presented the plan to their members, along with a three-point explanation of why they should go beyond the 1805 overture. First, they reasoned, the time was right for a new model of theological education because "we live in a country vast in extent, rich in fertility and growing in population, . . . and the melancholy truth is that Teachers of religion with proper Qualifications are not to be obtained."[9] Second, the church needed a learned ministry: "Nothing is more plainly taught in Scripture than that those who undertake to preach the gospel . . . should have knowledge to communicate."[10] And the presbytery was definite on what constituted an educated ministry: "Original languages, a knowledge of Antiquities, including History, Manners, Customs, Rites and Ceremonies, Apologetics."[11]

Finally, money was now available. For over eight years before the General Assembly overture, the Hanover Presbytery had tried to fund theological education. In 1797 the presbytery had adopted Archibald Alexander's proposal to create a fund to help educate young men for the ministry.[12] The proposal languished, however, because there were no contributions. The situation changed in 1804. Andrew Baker, of Prince Edward County, died and bequeathed £400 in interest-bearing bonds to Hanover Presbytery for charitable purposes. By 1806 the presbytery had decided that one part of the bonds would go to the managers of the fund to educate poor and pious youth, one part would support missionaries, and one part would purchase books for distribution to the poor.[13]

The Library

The precedent for a centralized repository of biblical and theological reference books for ministerial students to borrow had been established by the Synod of Philadelphia at the College of Philadelphia in 1756.[14] Hanover Presbytery seized on this idea and established a theological library at Hampden-Sydney College. On April 30, 1806, the presbytery appointed John Holt Rice as special agent to solicit books and money. Between April 1806 and April 1807 he visited Richmond, Norfolk, and Williamsburg, Virginia, raising $2,500[15] and spending $324 for seven titles in twenty-two volumes to begin the theological library's collection:

> Walton's *Polyglot Bible*, six volumes, folio
> Castell's *Lexicon*, two volumes, folio
> Rabbi Joseph's paraphrase [a targum], one volume, 4to [quarto]
> *An Introduction to the Study of Oriental Languages*, one volume, 4to
> Chrysostom's *Works*, eight volumes, folio
> Tertullian's *Works*, one volume, folio
> Calmet's *Dictionary*, three volumes, Quarto[16]

The original library regulations established in 1806 have been so effective that the original volumes have remained on the shelves throughout Union's history. The rebinding process has removed the markings on some of the books, but eight of these volumes are inscribed in bold pen: Ex libris Bibliothecae Hampden-Sidneni 1807.[17] There are other early gift books in the present rare book collection carefully inscribed with date and donor. One such Latin inscription reads Bibliotheca Theologica Hampden Sidnensi, librum donodedet Robertum Anderson, Jan. 22, 1820. Many others are inscribed in English and have a dollar value affixed.[18]

The theological books were located in a segregated part of the college library, and the presbytery set the rules for their books. Students could use the library for free, but members of Hanover Presbytery had to pay an annual fee of two dollars. No more than two volumes could be taken out at one time, and no book frequently used by students could be removed from the library at all. Also, Walton's *Polyglot Bible*, Castell's *Lexicon*, and Calmet's *Dictionary of the Bible* could not be checked out. The fine on an overdue book was twenty-five cents, and in case of damage to a book, the professor of divinity would estimate the cost to repair the damage or replace the damaged book. The librarian was authorized to require a deposit sufficient to cover possible damage on any book borrowed.

2. Original library desk and books

Money derived from fines, damage fees, or payment for the use of books could be used only for the benefit of the library. Only the professor of divinity was allowed to make marginal notes in the books. The presbytery authorized the theology professor to purchase books and required the librarian to keep a catalogue of the holdings. Each book was to be inscribed with the name of the donor and the book's cost.

The Hampden-Sydney College Board of Trustees supported the presbytery's efforts by making space for the books and hiring a theological professor. On April 5, 1808, John Holt Rice, James Daniel, and Conrad Speece, representing Hanover Presbytery, met with Goodridge Wilson, Richard N. Venable, and Henry E. Watkins, representing the college board of trustees. The six men drafted an agreement under which the presbytery would transfer to the president and trustees of Hampden-Sydney College, and the latter would accept, the books and funds held by the presbytery for theological education. The college agreed to preserve the books and use them as directed by the presbytery. The dividends from the principal of the presbytery's funds would be used to buy books as directed by the presbytery. Both the presbytery and the college committed themselves to educate "poor and pious youth for the ministry of the Gospel," and the college pledged to "employ a teacher of theology for the instruction of such poor and pious youth" as recommended by the presbytery and approved by the trustees. Hanover Presbytery ratified the agreement May 5, and Hampden-Sydney did so on June 20, 1808. The committee of Rice, Daniel, and Speece reported to Hanover Presbytery in October 1808 that the college trustees had ratified the agreement. Moses Hoge, called a year earlier as the college's president, was elected professor of theology.[19] When Hanover Presbytery established the library in 1806, it was known as "The Theological Library and School of Divinity at the College."[20] With Moses Hoge's election, the library was renamed "The Theological Library of Hampden-Sydney College."[21]

The library has always been the best measure of the seminary's vitality throughout its history. Moses Hoge moved the theology books from the college library to his attic. John Holt Rice moved the books out of the attic into the kitchen, where he first held classes, then to shelves in his study, and then to shelves on two levels of the seminary building (present-day Venable Hall at Hampden-Sydney College).[22] The theological library would not have a permanent home for another eighty years, until Brown Library (present-day Winston Hall at Hampden-Sydney College) was built.

Moses Hoge as Theology Professor

Moses Hoge was expected to be a college president, theology professor, and librarian. Yet nothing in his experience had prepared him for these tasks. Although he was well known through his writings and involvement with the Presbyterian General Assembly,[23] he was not a dynamic personality. One observer gently described him as "plain in appearance," while others called his manner "ungraceful, even uncouth," yet with a great intellect and generous nature.[24] William Graham tried to "improve" Hoge but "gave up in despair"; not only was Hoge "destitute of that tact which is necessary for the success of the highest talents," but "no man since Samuel Johnson and especially no popular preacher ever retained so faithfully the incongruities usually lost in intimate association with polished society."[25] One of Hoge's students, W. S. White, remembered Hoge as "an awkward preacher, but able teacher."[26]

Yet Moses Hoge was eminently qualified to be the theology professor. He understood Virginia culture. John Randolph of Roanoke, Virginia statesman and an avowed deist,[27] wrote to Francis Scott Key in 1814:

> There is but one man in all of Virginia who ought to preach, and that is Dr. Moses Hoge. I consider Dr. Hoge as the ablest and most interesting speaker that I ever heard in the pulpit, or out of it. . . . If he has a fault (which being mortal, I supposed he cannot be free from), I have never heard it pointed out.[28]

Randolph went on to say that only two men could bring quiet to the Prince Edward Courthouse yard on Court Day: "Patrick Henry by his eloquence and Moses Hoge simply by passing through it." Moreover, his publications defending Calvinism and criticizing Thomas Paine were well known. Robert Lewis Dabney would later credit him with a long-lasting impact, arguing that Hoge impressed "on the Virginia [Presbyterian] ministry the moderated type of evangelical Calvinism which has since distinguished it."[29]

Moses Hoge
President of the College 1807–1820

3. Moses Hoge, First theology professor

Moses Hoge believed in serving the church. He was the first moderator of the Presbytery of Winchester and preached the sermon at its first meeting.[30] He was a commissioner from the Presbytery of Lexington to the first post-Independence Presbyterian General Assembly on May 21, 1789.[31] Yet, however devoted Moses Hoge was to Calvinism and the Presbyterian Church, the breadth of his theological understanding was wide ranging. His library contained works by the church fathers, Roman Catholics (Loyola, Fénelon), Anglicans (William Law, John Newton, Devereux Jarratt, George Whitefield), German Pietists (Augustus Gottlieb Spangenberg), and Puritans (Samuel Rutherford, John Bunyan, Cotton Mather, Jonathan Edwards, Richard Baxter).[32] Hoge was dedicated to education; he taught school in each of his pastorates.[33] He believed very strongly that learning increased piety, and education strengthened the church against deism; his aim was "sanctified learning," while avoiding the excesses of revivals.[34]

The key to understanding Moses Hoge and his vision for the seminary is found in his expansive view of the body of Christ. His ideal for the seminary was set forth in a report adopted by the Synod of Virginia in 1816:

> As our theological seminary is not intended exclusively for the advantage of any denomination, it seems hardly necessary to observe that party zeal, instead of being fostered and promoted, is to be proscribed and banished from all its offices; that the students are to be taught to distinguish between the essentials of the Christian religion, respecting which the Protestant churches are so generally agreed, and the circumstantials, about which there have been so many worse than fruitless debates.[35]

Hoge and his wife, Susannah, made themselves available to both undergraduate and theology students. They hosted "praying society" meetings in their home, and many students came to think of the Hoges as their spiritual guides. Daniel Baker, a college student, recalled that some professors as well as six or eight students usually attended the meetings, which included singing that "affected many." One student had "a saving and happy conversion . . . at our praying society." William Graham, who was Hoge's teacher at Liberty Hall, observed: "To all pious young men, he and his house were open and he treated them with all the kindness of a father, and with the condescension and familiarity of a friend or brother. . . . He wanted them to obtain a spirit of piety." These prayer meetings were the foundation for the Hampden-Sydney revival of 1814–15.

Hoge did everything he could to encourage "sanctified learning." John D. Paxton, later fired from his pulpit in Virginia for his abolitionist views, said that young men, when preparing for the ministry, "are apt to think their chief business is to acquire knowledge and imagine they can acquire the spirit of the gospel afterwards." Hoge, however, taught his students to cultivate a spirit of piety and develop a talent for religious conversation, to labor to be good and do good.[36]

As part of the ethical demands of faith, Hoge lived a relatively ascetic life and was known as a "Puritan" when it came to morals.[37] He believed that self-denial was one of the marks of "ministerial duty." That is, "the man whose glorious office it is to be the honored instrument of detaching others from the love of this world, must not himself love the world, or glory in any of its possessions." Yet, while Hoge lived and advocated a simple life, he was not otherworldly. His asceticism required action in this world. Individual daily prayer, daily prayer with one's family, frequent meditation, daily Bible reading, reading spiritual books, and keeping journals—all these did not have an esoteric aim but steered the believer into doing what pleased the Lord in this world.[38]

How Many Seminaries?

Moses Hoge was in a unique position to teach the future Presbyterian ministers of Virginia. But he did not have time to settle into his chair before the Presbyterian General Assembly realized that the 1805 overture calling for each presbytery to establish a "fund for poor and pious youth" was too little, too late;

something much more was needed to increase the number of clergy. Archibald Alexander was elected moderator of the General Assembly in 1807; during his sermon at the 1808 assembly, he declared that "the deficiency in preachers is great, our vacancies are numerous, and [they] often continue for years unsupplied, by which means [the churches] are broken up or destroyed. Our seminaries of learning . . . furnish us with few preachers. This state of affairs calls loudly for your attention." He called for a theological seminary in "every presbytery, or at least every Synod."[39]

Alexander was well aware of the founding of Andover Seminary in Massachusetts by Trinitarian Congregationalists angry over the appointment of a Unitarian professor of divinity at Harvard College. Andover offered a model for what Presbyterians could do to meet the urgent demand for ministers and to check the nation's growing secularization. Alexander wanted a school controlled by the denomination, unattached to a college or university, and devoted to educating a professional, orthodox clergy.[40]

Jacob Green had fruitlessly called for dedicated schools to educate ministers as early as 1775; it would be his son, Ashbel, pastor of Philadelphia's Second Presbyterian Church, who would finally see theological education established. In 1805, Ashbel Green pleaded for the Presbyterian General Assembly to "give us ministers" for the frontier, but there were none to send. Nothing more substantial was done until Archibald Alexander addressed the assembly three years later.[41] At that same assembly, when churches in Tennessee asked for the freedom to "license" ministers without education,[42] Alexander argued that Presbyterians needed clergy who could combat the twin dangers facing the church arising from "two opposite points: From what is called Rational Christianity [Unitarianism], and enthusiasm." And only literate, trained men could meet the challenge.[43]

In reaction to Archibald Alexander's sermon, the 1808 assembly sent a memorial (a statement of the issue with a proposed resolution) to each presbytery, asking them to debate and then approve one of three plans for theological education by the 1810 General Assembly. First, one national seminary. Second, two seminaries: one for the North, one for the South. Third, one seminary for each synod.[44]

Since Moses Hoge had been teaching ministerial candidates at Hampden-Sydney College for over a year, Virginia presbyteries wanted to keep what they had. Hoge feared that one large official seminary would result in a deficiency of piety and believed that presbyteries and synods should have the right to establish their own seminaries as they saw fit.[45] Moreover, Hanover Presbyterians were already invested in what Hoge was doing and did not want to send their money elsewhere.[46] Consequently, on April 19, 1810, Hanover Presbytery voted that the Presbyterian Church should have one seminary for each synod.[47]

Ashbel Green and other northern ministers lobbied hard over the winter of 1809–10 in favor of one national seminary.[48] Less than one month after Hanover Presbytery voted, the Presbyterian General Assembly met in Philadelphia in May 1810 and referred the votes of the presbyteries to a select committee chaired by Green. After seeing churches in the West leave to form the Cumberland Presbyterian Church and perhaps fearing more churches would leave, the committee could not afford to let the votes against the national seminary impede their plans, so they disregarded the votes against a national seminary.

> It appears to the committee, that although, according to the statement already reported to the Assembly, there is an equal number of Presbyteries in favour of the first plan, which contemplates a single school for the whole church; and in favour of the third plan, which contemplates the erection of a school in each Synod; yet, as several of the objections made to the first plan, are founded entirely on mis-conceptions, and will be completely obviated by developing details of that plan; it seems fairly to follow, that there is a greater amount of Presbyterian suffrage in favour of a single school, than of any other plan.[49]

The committee decided that those voting against one centralized seminary did not understand the issues and recommended that the General Assembly establish one national, central seminary, whose name shall be "The Theological Seminary of the Presbyterian Church in the United States of America."[50] The 1810 Assembly approved the committee report and appointed another committee, also chaired by Ashbel Green, to prepare a plan for the seminary and report back the following year.

After adjourning, Green wrote a letter to the presbyteries in the name of the General Assembly, announcing the establishment of the new seminary and pleading for support. The letter began by stating that everyone understood the need for qualified ministers: the pulpit was vacant in more than four hundred congregations. The letter then declared that the time had come to increase the number of candidates for holy ministry, and the only way of increasing the number of ministers was through improving local educational resources. Presbyterians could no longer rely on the schools of the old country.[51]

The National Church Establishes One Seminary

The report presented to the 1811 Presbyterian General Assembly was essentially the same as the report given to the 1810 assembly; Green and his committee had been working on the organization of the seminary for a long time. Unlike the log colleges, the new seminary would be owned by the assembly, which would choose its board of directors of fourteen ministers and appoint all professors. Moreover, the board would ensure the orthodoxy "of the professors, especially in regard to doctrines actually taught." If a professor was found to be unsound, he would be reported to the assembly. The school would be unapologetically Presbyterian: "All professors must be an ordained minister of the Presbyterian Church and subscribe to the Confession of faith, catechisms, and form of government." There was no notion of academic freedom. All professors were required to "lay before the board of directors . . . a detailed exhibition of the system and method which he proposes to pursue, and the subjects which he proposes to discuss. In conducting the youth that shall come under his care, . . . he shall make alterations or additions as the board shall direct."

The board was required to supervise the students and report annually to the Presbyterian General Assembly. Green and his committee did not want to repeat the divisive fights over the quality of log colleges in the establishment of the new seminary. This was to be graduate education. "Every student applying for admission must prove he is in full communion with some church [and] has passed through some course of academical study or submit himself to an examination in regard to the branches of literature in such a course."

Student conduct was similarly strict: "Strict temperance in meat and drink is expected of every student, with cleanliness and neatness in his dress and habits; while all excessive expense in clothing is strictly prohibited."[52] Attendance at morning and evening prayers was required, and each student was expected to read Scripture every day. Sundays were special: "The whole of every Lord's day is to be devoted to devotional exercises, either of a social or secret kind. Intellectual pursuits, not immediately connected with devotion or the religion of the heart, are on that day to be forborne. . . . The conversations had with each other are to be chiefly on religious subjects." Moreover, "if a student, after due admonition, persist[s] in a system of conduct not exemplary in regard to religion, he shall be dismissed from the Seminary."[53]

The curriculum was drawn directly from the Book of Discipline (1560); it mandated Hebrew, Greek, theology, church history, and polity, in addition to preaching:

> Every student must be well skilled in the original languages of the Holy Scriptures. . . . He must be able to support and defend the Confession of Faith and Catechism. . . . He must have considerable acquaintance with Natural Theology, Polemic, and Casuistic Divinity [and] defend the Christian faith against deists. . . . [He must study] General History . . . and [have] particular acquaintance with the history of the Christian Church. . . . He must compose and deliver sermons, have carefully studied the duties of pastoral care, and must have studied attentively the form of Church Government.

These courses would be completed in "no less than three years." The Presbyterian General Assembly was tasked to build a library "as a leading object of the Institution" and purchase books to begin the collection. The final part of the section dealing with students contains a pledge that all Union students took at least until the 1990s:

> Every student, before he takes his standing in the Seminary, shall subscribe the follow declaration: . . . Deeply impressed with a sense of the importance of improving in knowledge, prudence, and piety, in my preparation for the Gospel Ministry, I solemnly promise, in a reliance on divine grace, that I will faithfully and diligently attend on all the instructions of this Seminary, and that I will conscientiously and vigilantly observe all the rules and regulations specified in the plan for its instruction and government, so far as the same relate to the students; and that I will obey all the laws and requisitions, and readily yield to all the wholesome admonitions of the professors and directors of the Seminary, while I shall continue a member of it.[54]

The 1811 Assembly adopted the report of the select committee and chose Princeton as the seminary's site. Princeton was thought to be the perfect place to train ministers for the entire church due to its neutral location; northern New Jersey was equidistant from both New Englanders and the South.[55] In an effort to make the seminary truly national, and perhaps to appease sectional jealousies, the committee charged with raising funds for this national seminary included ministers from both North and South. Archibald Alexander, former president of Hampden-Sydney College, was the chair, and the committee appointed agents for each of the seven synods (Albany, New York and New Jersey, Philadelphia, Virginia, Pittsburgh, Kentucky, Carolinas) to raise funds. There were seven ministers, including Drury Lacy, Conrad Speece, John Holt Rice, and Samuel B. Wilson, and two laymen appointed as agents for the Synod of Virginia.[56]

A Seminary in Virginia . . . But Where?

Hanover's reaction to having the General Assembly dismiss their vote for a synodical seminary was muted: there is no record of any kind of protest. There is also no recorded reaction to the assembly's 1810 fund-raising letter or the 1811 plan. Perhaps Alexander's position as chair of the committee and the inclusion of so many prominent Virginia clergy quieted any overt objections. But Hanover Presbytery showed their attitude toward the new national seminary by their nonsupport.

In 1806 the Theological Committee of Hanover Presbytery had been charged with raising funds for the library and for the theology professor at Hampden-Sydney. At first, fund-raising was a success, but once the vote for one central seminary was announced, all efforts ceased. Virginians were afraid that they would be compelled to send their money northward and watch their own school wither. The presbytery dissolved the Theological Committee on May 3, 1809, and heard at their October 11, 1809, meeting that no subscriptions had been received since May. No subscriptions were received for the rest of 1809, throughout 1810, and up to May 2, 1811. On October 11, 1811, the presbytery appointed a committee to purchase books for their library and report on its state.[57] Clearly, the vote for one national seminary had angered Virginia.

There is also no record of protest from the Synod of Virginia concerning the assembly's decision to disregard the votes of their presbyteries. Yet the synod's silence did not mean they were dormant. At its meeting on October 17, 1811, the synod heard that Hanover Presbytery had three congregations without ministers and Lexington Presbytery had fourteen vacancies. The shortage of ministers was greater than the report indicates because there were many more "preaching points" that could not become congregations until they had an ordained minister serving them. Presuming that the proposed seminary could not help their churches, the Synod of Virginia took action. On October 22, 1812, a full two years after the General Assembly vote, the synod appointed a committee to "inquire into the expediency of establishing a Theological Seminary within the bounds of Synod." This committee of seven included Moses Hoge and John Holt Rice, who presumably was still the synod's agent responsible for raising funds for the seminary at Princeton. The next day the committee reported that establishing a seminary within the bounds of the synod would be expedient.

On October 24, 1812, the committee recommended that Lexington, Virginia (meaning Liberty Hall), be the permanent site of the synodical seminary and that "Hampden-Sydney College be the temporary seat of this institution." It was also recommended that a committee be formed to raise subscriptions for the seminary. Finally, the committee recommended that Moses Hoge be appointed professor of theology pro tem in the proposed seminary.[58] This meant that Moses Hoge was both president of Hampden-Sydney College and the de facto head of the seminary in Lexington.

There is no record of any debate over this issue, so it is unknown why the Synod of Virginia would even think of establishing a seminary at Liberty Hall in Lexington when the library and the theology professor were at Hampden-Sydney. Although the members of this committee, including Moses Hoge, were all graduates of Liberty Hall[59] and the synod had already considered establishing a theological school there, the fact remains that Hampden-Sydney was already turning out educated ministers. To complicate matters further, the Synod of Virginia had appointed Hoge as its preferred teacher for all ministerial candidates within the three presbyteries that made up the synod: Hanover, Lexington, and Winchester. The synod, therefore, expected Hoge to supervise a college with a liberal arts curriculum, teach and manage a theology department, and tutor nonenrolled ministerial students from the entire Commonwealth of Virginia.[60]

By 1812, Moses Hoge had become the lynchpin to theological education in the Synod of Virginia. John Trotti, who served the seminary as librarian for thirty years, is fond of saying that books came first, the students came second, the professor came next, and then the seminary.[61] Trotti's observation is accurate and represents the disorganized way the Synod of Virginia finally muddled its way to establishing a seminary. And Moses Hoge found himself at the nexus of conflicting expectations, mutually exclusive roles, and competing demands. Although thirty of his students would become ministers, the conflict between Hoge, the college, and the presbytery would almost destroy theological education in Virginia.[62] Without clear organizational lines, whatever Moses Hoge accomplished would be done without clear authority from either college or presbytery.

Beginnings at Hampden-Sydney

Archibald Alexander left Hampden-Sydney College to assume the presidency of Princeton under a cloud; he thought that the college administration was hindering him[63] and the students were uncontrollable.[64] When Moses Hoge was called to become the sixth president of Hampden-Sydney College on April 10, 1807, he faced extraordinary expectations. The board, students, and surrounding community anticipated that his presidency would be a marked departure from the five men who came before him. He had more experience with students than his predecessors, and many hoped that the addition of a theological school would give more order to college life.

It may be said that the first history of Union Seminary was written as a newspaper article in 1810 by Moses Hoge, Drury Lacy, and Matthew Lyle, published in the *Virginia Argus*. The article reviewed the need for theological education, the logic behind the founding of "our Theological Seminary," and trumpeted the appointment of "the Rev. Moses Hoge" as "Teacher." The wording is instructive: the college saw "our theological seminary" as an integral part of their institution. It stressed that a "Theological School and Library" had been "lately established at Hampden-Sidney College."[65] It seems clear, then, that Hoge advertised himself as the president of a college with a theological department.

Yet Hoge may have seen his college presidency as little more than a necessary evil in order to implement his vision of theological education. He may have thought that his tenure as college president would be temporary, until Hanover Presbytery could raise enough funds for a full-time theology teacher. Indeed, it would not be too much to say that he ultimately saw the college as a mere adjunct to the seminary. In January 1810, his third year at the college, Hoge wrote to a friend: "It was chiefly from a regard to a Theological Seminary lately established at this place that I was induced to accept of the Presidency of Hampden-Sydney College."[66] In May of the same year, John D. Paxton, Hoge's deputy, recorded in his diary: "I have this day arrived at this place [Hampden-Sydney College], invited by Dr. Moses Hoge to assist him in teaching. My chief inducement in coming is the theological school, and the assistance in theology expected from Dr. Hoge."[67]

Hoge saw himself not just as a president or professor, concerned to impart academic knowledge, but also, according to a former student, "to cultivate an ardent piety" in his students.[68] He expected college to be preparation for seminary; education was a way to mold and reinforce a holy life. Being the president of Hampden-Sydney College "would give him special opportunities to train young men for the ministry, something he had been doing routinely for a number of years in the Lower Valley of Virginia."[69]

Although his vision of being president of a college and educating ministers would ultimately clash with reality, at first his ideas seemed to succeed. In February 1808, one year into Hoge's presidency, John Holt Rice wrote optimistically to Archibald Alexander:

> The opinion that Mr. Hoge will succeed very well at [the] college seems to be gaining ground. He is in high estimation with the students. He is very popular among the trustees; and many in the neighborhood who have never been thought friends to the college, have expressed a favourable opinion of him. My opinion is that he is very well qualified to be a teacher.[70]

Hoge had every reason to believe that the college trustees supported his designs for the school as a nursery of piety. One trustee had written to convince Hoge to take the presidency of Hampden-Sydney by emphasizing the school's need for his background in theological education. Another trustee conflated the mission of the two schools in a way that appealed to Hoge: "For some years to come the head of the Theological School must be the President of Hampden-Sydney College. . . . You are called up to take upon you a charge of very great importance, to teach the youth of our land virtue and science, and to train up young men for the ministry." In 1807, Drury Lacy wrote to Hoge, also enticing him to become president, by reminding him he would be initiating a seminary: "You know we have been making some efforts toward establishing a Theological School at the College. I trust this consideration will have some weight in turning the scale in our favor and inducing you to come among us."[71]

Hanover Presbytery also encouraged Hoge to view the college as secondary to the seminary. He was admitted as a member of the presbytery to succeed Archibald Alexander as president of Hampden-Sydney on October 24, 1807.[72] Five days later, the Presbytery of Winchester dismissed Hoge to join the Presbytery of Hanover.[73] With this dismissal the efforts to establish a theological school at Lexington ended. Although the Presbyterian General Assembly voted to establish one national seminary two years later, the only functioning institution for educating ministerial students in the Presbyterian Church before 1812 was at Hampden-Sydney College. Before Princeton or Union were founded, Hoge could boast: "We now have nine or ten who intend to preach the gospel, and about the same number of my alumni are now preaching."[74]

The Theological School and Library at Hampden-Sydney challenged the national church. Indeed, when Hanover Presbytery passed the resolution to establish and raise funds for the Theological School and Library, they showed an unexpected national vision. Fund-raising was not limited to Virginia: the agent, John B. Hoge, son of Moses Hoge, was instructed to collect funds also from states south of Virginia. It may be that John Holt Rice was behind this new strategy of soliciting funds from southern states. He knew firsthand that the synod was divided: Winchester and Lexington supported Princeton, and Hanover Presbytery could not support the institution on its own.[75]

The vision was there, but the money was not. In the 1810 article in the *Virginia Argus*, after recounting the founding of "our Theological School," Hoge publicly admitted that fund-raising had entered into "an unproductive season." Since the theological school's founding, only $3,536.38 had been collected, with just $1,557.88 designated as principal, now earning 6 percent interest.[76] Three years later, at the October 20, 1813, meeting of the Synod of Virginia, the two agents who had solicited funds in the states south of Virginia reported only $16.00 collected. After hearing this report, the synod passed a motion rescinding the previous year's motion making Liberty Hall the permanent site of the seminary, with the proviso that "Hampden-Sidney continue to be the seat of the Theological Seminary until it shall appear to the Synod to be for the interests of the institution to be removed elsewhere." The minutes of the Synod of Virginia mention the "institution established last year."[77] Thus, despite the false starts and indecision, the founding date of what would become Union Theological Seminary is the previous year's meeting, October 24, 1812.

Although the Synod of Virginia established a fund for the education of "poor and pious youth for the Ministry of the Gospel" and urged the presbyteries to give to this fund at their 1813 meeting,[78] the fund for poor and pious youth was never mentioned again. The next year, at the 1814 meeting, the previous motion for an education fund was amended to read that the youth who would receive "the gratuitous education in this seminary" be selected by their presbyteries and not the synod committee.[79] From this time on, all fund-raising would fall on the shoulders of the seminary.

The New School Adrift

Hoge was quickly overwhelmed and demoralized by the demands of his jobs. As early as 1810, he began to complain about a lack of money. His dissatisfaction intensified when the college ran out of money and could not pay his salary.[80] By 1812 he began to despair of his college ever amounting to anything.[81] He openly complained about the workload and problems with student discipline.[82] Hoge announced his intention to resign in summer 1812, relented, and then threatened to resign again in March 1813. In an effort to convince Hoge to stay, the college trustees appointed a vice president, Charles H. Kennan, in May 1813. Kennan took over administrative duties, and Hoge devoted more time to teaching the senior class and divinity students; he decided to remain.[83]

It appears, however, that many in the synod still pined for a school in Lexington. At the synod meeting of 1814, the minutes indicate that many still considered the institution at Hampden Sydney as temporary: "The Synod being desirous to fix the permanent site of the theological school as soon as convenient, resolved, that this be done at their next meeting."[84] The next year the Synod of Virginia finally "resolved, that the College of Hampden-Sydney be the site of the Theological Seminary; but the Synod reserve themselves the power of removing the institution, should such removal become necessary."[85] With the site officially established, Lexington was forgotten, and the synod began to support Hoge's efforts.

At their meeting in 1815 the synod signaled their new resolve to support the seminary within their bounds by two actions. First, they exerted more control over the seminary's management, which until then had been left solely up to Hoge.[86] They appointed fifteen trustees, at least one from each presbytery, directed them to petition the legislature for incorporation, and told them to conduct a curriculum review. Second, the synod formed a committee "to consider whether any, and what measures can be adopted by the Synod to increase the funds of the theological school under its care."[87] In previous years the synod had appointed agents to convince people to subscribe to the seminary, but the synod was ready to try something new. This committee appointed agents, but also called for pastors to establish "societies" within their congregations to support the seminary. Yet at the 1817 synod meeting the committee reported that these efforts produced virtually no results.[88]

On the ground at Hampden-Sydney, however, it seemed as though the rough times had passed and the college's prospects were improving by 1816. With his administrative workload diminished, Hoge devoted more time to teaching. He also began to receive a regular combined salary of $1,200 per year from both college and synod in 1816.[89] Perhaps more important, however, his colleagues began to publicly recognize that he was performing a vital mission. John Holt Rice, who had persuaded Hoge to remain at Hampden-Sydney in 1812 and 1813, publicly commended him for his work. The theological education offered by Hoge, Rice maintained, was "the only school in the southern country . . . The Virginia brethren felt the great necessity of a southern school for southern churches."[90]

Despite the lack of direct congregational support, the Synod of Virginia's agents were finally raising money. At their 1818 meeting, the synod heard a report heralding a new period of growth: $1,334.88 had been received in the previous year, bringing the total in the theological education fund to $4,779.16. For over six years, Hoge had been hoping to be able to hire a second professor, and the synod allocated $4,000 to pay for the second teaching position. The synod redoubled its efforts and appointed twenty-five agents to complete the fund-raising for the new professor. A committee was then appointed to develop a "plan for the organization, government, and general management of the Theological Seminary."[91] The synod also heard that $146.87 had been spent on books.[92]

Yet the hopes for a new era of adequate support were short lived. The 1819 synod meeting report was dismal: virtually no subscriptions had been collected in the previous year. In frustration, the synod once again called for auxiliaries in each presbytery, with associations in each congregation, to raise money for the seminary.[93] As in 1817, the churches did not respond. On the eve of Moses Hoge's death in July 1820, the seminary was almost broke. Nevertheless, there was a curious report in the synod's minutes of 1820: $459.56 had been donated by Alex M. Cowan and $126 by Newton Gordon, both of Massachusetts.[94] With the listing of two donors outside the South, the seminary had a glimpse of future areas of support.

College versus Seminary

By 1812 the Presbyterian Church was united in the view that a seminary education was vital to the church. The indecision concerning the seminary's location and the difficulties in fund-raising were mechanical issues; it was now unquestioned that only ministers with a systematic, comprehensive theological education were competent to serve congregations. Yet the location of where this theological education would take place quickly developed into a conflict between the goals of college and seminary. There was tension between the liberal arts and theology curricula at the college, the perceived inadequacies of Moses Hoge, and the continuing hostility toward non-Episcopalian churches that characterized the Virginia culture.

The founders of Hampden-Sydney College in 1775 assumed that the college would prepare men for ministry. When Moses Hoge was called to be president of the college in 1807, the trustees held the same general expectation. Hoge would be "a suitable person at once to preside over the college and to foster the nascent Theological Seminary."[95] He was a well-known preacher and famous enough from his writings to draw students from as far away as Georgia.[96] But he was not in any sense prepared to teach the scientific curriculum that was becoming the foundation of modern education. Hoge began his presidency with high hopes: important churchmen had encouraged him to stay, but in the end his tenure was not happy.

In 1812 the Synod of Virginia appointed a committee to recommend a curriculum for the new seminary. The committee report, apparently written by

Hoge,[97] was not submitted until October 25, 1816. It is an interesting document. Instead of detailing courses, administrative structure, and goals, it is more theological treatise than curriculum and is unexpectedly defensive in tone. Hoge begins the report by declaring the Bible to be "the true inspired word of God" and argues that a seminary education is only one component of a minister.

> It is not however, indispensably necessary that a Christian minister should be a man of superior mental endowments. Moderate talents in a state of cultivation may, under the influence of divine grace, be very useful in the church. Whereas superior geniuses dazzled by their own splendors, and confident in their own strength prove, not unfrequently, a great determent to the cause they have undertaken to support.

For Hoge, the job of the seminary was obvious; the seminary referred a student to the "Holy Scriptures" and saw to it that "some of the best treatises upon the subject be put into his hands." Moreover, he should be assured

> that it is not an office of worldly endowment, ease, or dignity; that it requires the greatest self denial, the most unremitted exertions, and in many instances, very costly sacrifice; that its object is nothing less than the glory of God in the salvation of perishing sinners; and that for the accomplishment of this great object, no labours should be thought too great, no sufferings too severe.

Then Hoge, following the outline of the Book of Discipline (1560), asserted that his students learned "Biblical history, systematic theology (along with apologetics and preaching), polity, and church history."[98]

By the second decade of the nineteenth century, it was becoming clear that Hoge's idea of a seminary had no place in a modern college. The inclusion of chemistry in the curriculum represented a change in the orientation of American higher education. Until the nineteenth century all American colleges, except the Academy of Pennsylvania (created in 1751 by Benjamin Franklin and renamed the University of Pennsylvania in 1791) were oriented toward the training of ministers. Thus, when Hampden-Sydney was founded in 1775, there was no expectation that classes in the physical or natural sciences would be taught. By the early years of the nineteenth century, however, momentum for science classes was building around the country. At Hampden-Sydney College, chemistry was included in the curriculum by 1820, and the need for a dedicated chemistry laboratory was recognized.

The trend toward studying the physical and natural sciences was initially welcomed by the church, but soon it became clear that education for ministry and scientific instruction were not naturally allied. Indeed, the argument could be made that theological seminaries were founded in reaction to the popularity of chemistry. Four years before he arrived at Princeton, Archibald Alexander, as president of Hampden-Sydney in 1803, had expanded the "science" laboratory and said: "The great extension of physical sciences, and the taste and the fashion of the age, have given such a shape and direction to the academical course, that I confess it appears to me to be little adapted to introduce a youth to the study of Sacred Scriptures."[99] It was now apparent that the interests of church and higher education were diverging.

As students showed more interest in scientific pursuits, the college trustees supported those interests. Moses Hoge did not keep up with the times. Although he was hailed when he assumed the presidency in 1807, his theological interests came to be seen by 1814 as inhibiting the college's mission. Moreover, his methods were criticized as outmoded and inefficient. Hoge taught according to the old tutor model, not by lecturing, but by meeting with two or three students at a time. He apparently did not conduct regular classes but instead would meet with students, assign books for them to read, and talk about the subject matter at their next meeting. Occasionally, "on particular subjects," he told the students his own views. His teaching was thus principally supervisory. Theology student John D. Paxton expressed regret that he did not have the advantage of a theological class. This method of teaching made Hoge vulnerable to charges of negligence.[100] The 1816 synod report was defensive because the expectations of students and trustees had changed: the goals of church and higher education had wandered apart.

Hoge had become an anachronism; he saw undergraduate and graduate theological education in tandem, forming a spiritually sensitive man. Yet, when one attends college to gain scientific knowledge, piety is not necessarily a priority. As Hoge emphasized "religious character" at the college, graduation rates decreased. During Hoge's tenure (1807–20), of the 163 students who could have graduated, only 29 did so; of the 305 enrolled, 243 stayed only one year.[101] Moreover, Hoge was not an enthusiastic fund-raiser, and this lack was criticized by both the college board and the synod.[102]

Combined with pressure from above, there was pressure from below. Student conduct caused Moses Hoge to threaten to resign in 1812 and 1813. In the early 1800s, students entering Hampden-Sydney were usually between 14 and 18 years of age. Alexander and Hoge both complained about the behavior of the students, and dismissals occurred on a regular basis. What did these students do to interrupt "the peace of the college"? Offenses included playing "fives" (an early version of handball) against the buildings, keeping guns and dogs in rooms, ringing the bell at night, stacking wood against a tutor's door so it would fall on him when he opened it, throwing a brick through a window, and firing a pistol on campus.[103] Hoge had expected to spend his time with mature students who shared his interests, but instead he had to deal with immature boys who were interested in other things.

Every president of Hampden-Sydney College prior to Hoge had been a Presbyterian minister. Hoge expected to continue the tradition of training ministers, but the trustees of Hampden-Sydney ultimately expected Hoge to keep the theological curriculum second to the needs of modern undergraduate education. By the time Hoge unexpectedly died on July 5, 1820, the college trustees and some faculty thought that he was devoting too much time to his congregation and the theology department, thereby neglecting what they considered to be his primary role: college president managing a modern, scientific curriculum.

While the college pulled in one direction, Hanover Presbytery pulled in the other. Whereas in 1807 the presbytery expected Moses Hoge to be a tutor, as time went on they also wanted him to be both administrator and teacher. He was in an untenable situation, where the interests of the college and the presbytery would collide. Hoge was asked to manage and teach in the college, with its liberal arts curriculum, while managing and teaching in a separately financed theology department. In 1807, the college's enrollment increased, with a large number of preministerial students. Hanover Presbytery was pleased, but the college trustees felt slighted.[104] The college's attitude can best be seen in their actions after Hoge's death. They immediately chose a resident faculty member to be president. The faculty member, Jonathan Cushing, was from New Hampshire, a Dartmouth graduate, and the first professor of Natural Philosophy and Chemistry.[105] He had no interest in training ministerial students, and it was becoming clear that Hampden-Sydney College would no longer support a seminary.

The Synod Takes Charge

By 1817 the Synod of Virginia recognized that one man, however capable, could not adequately manage the seminary on his own. At the same time, they were frustrated with their own lethargy. Although trustees had been appointed in 1815 to organize the administrative aspects of the school and raise funds, nothing had happened. The synod accused the trustees of "hardly attempt[ing] anything beyond the mere management of the funds." On October 17, 1817, the synod tasked the theological school committee to draw up regulations governing the board and once again directed the trustees to appoint officers and make bylaws. The synod committee was also directed to outline the duties of an additional professor and determine whether the school needed a librarian. Three days later, the committee made three recommendations: organize a seminary board, call another professor in "Biblical Criticism," and give the current theology professor a raise of $200 to $800 per year.[106]

The committee never made a recommendation for a librarian. Instead, they inexplicably criticized the management of the library. There were no indications that books were missing, and they did not order an inventory of the holdings; yet they were concerned that the librarian (Hoge) was lax in collecting fines. The committee imposed a new schedule of fines and demanded that the fines be collected.[107]

The apprehensive tone of his 1816 report shows that Hoge felt beleaguered. He had interpreted the synod's appointment of trustees in 1815 as implicit criticism of his administrative abilities. His report is an attempt to justify his curriculum and efforts. The continued emphasis on trustees and criticism of the library demoralized him. In June 1818 he wrote bitterly to a friend:

> The mystery which has for the space of eight months covered the proceedings of the Synod of Virginia in impenetrable darkness, begins to be the truth. . . . To be suspected of negligence in the discharge of one of the most responsible offices in the world! Had I been charged with suicide, it would have been more plausible at least.[108]

Enrollment in both college and seminary was declining, and public support was diminishing by 1817. The synod may have recognized that Hoge was doing too much and needed assistance. After all, he was president of the college, sole professor of the seminary, custodian of the library, and adviser to the students. Hoge and his wife boarded some students in their home, and he helped some students with his own money.[109]

While Hoge may have been overly sensitive to criticism, there are hints that by 1819 many in Virginia thought their school was a failure and their funds and their students should instead go to Princeton. The synod found it necessary to defend the need for a seminary in Virginia. They reminded their churches that

> a number of liberal minded persons have contributed money for the form-ing of a permanent fund amounting now to between five and six thousand dollars. This money was given expressly for the purpose of founding a semi-nary in this state and it is thought that the Synod has no right to divert it to any other purpose, nor to disappoint the hopes and expectations which they themselves have raised. For that reason the infant seminary at Hampden-Sidney College is regarded with warm wishes for its success and it is thought that the Synod ought not to abandon it; unless compelled by necessity. It may yet flourish and under the smiles of Providence prove a lasting blessing and honour to our state.

The committee then reiterated that "the course of studies in the seminary embrace Biblical Criticism, Systematic Theology, and History and Polity of the church and shall be continued for three years."

With the issue of location out of the way and some wondering why there should be two seminaries in the church, the synod finally took its responsibili-ties for theological education seriously at its 1819 meeting. They exerted their authority over the seminary by limiting the theology professor's prerogatives in three ways. First, the board's composition was changed and localized. After Hoge had been a board member for seven years, the synod decided the presi-dent should no longer be a member, finding it "manifestly unsuitable that men should be called on to vote and determine in their own case." The synod also "suggested" that all board members should live "contiguous to the Seminary,"[110] so as to make it easier to check on the condition of the seminary and students. By locating all board members within southside Virginia, the board could better supervise Hoge, and the synod would be more focused on Hampden-Sydney and less on Liberty Hall.[111]

Second, the theological professor could no longer make independent deci-sions on student admissions and financial assistance. The synod had already created an admissions committee on October 25, 1816,[112] but there was no report from them until three years later, when the synod ruled that "no person shall hereafter be received as a student in the seminary until he shall have completed his classical and scientific education."[113] Since Hoge kept no notes, it is not clear that Hoge always enforced strict admission standards.

Finally, the synod took the management of the fund for poor and pious youth away from Hoge. Apparently he had supported a number of young men out of the charitable fund, but only three had become licensed to preach. Thus it appeared that Hoge had diverted some funds to college students whom the synod had never intended to help. He apparently selected recipients from the fund on his own, just as he made decisions about admission. Consequently, the synod set up the Education Society of Virginia to relieve the professor of theology of the responsibility of deciding who should receive financial support.[114]

Despite fears that his heavy workload at the college and seminary would be injurious to his "constitution," Hoge enjoyed "remarkably good health" for most of his life. Early in 1819, however, he became ill and for some three months was confined to his room. No one can tell how much the charge of negligence hurt him, but the accusations and the clumsy way in which the synod handled him crushed his spirit.[115]

William Hill argued that the lack of a standard curriculum, only one assistant, lax admissions that allowed students to begin studies at any time, and irregular funding—all these left Hoge open to criticism from people who did not understand the conditions. Hill points out that as many as twelve students boarded in the Hoge household, and he never turned anyone away. Moreover, at his own expense Hoge procured substitutes for student draftees in the War of 1812, which was accepted practice at the time.[116]

Sixty years later, John Blair Hoge, grandson of Moses Hoge, wrote that the first years of the seminary were an opportunity lost because

> the Synod never entered, with spirit, into the arrangement of a system of instruction and government. In this chaotic state it was thrown into [Moses Hoge's] hands: and notwithstanding the subsequent appointment of a Board of Trustees, from 1812 to 1820, its management rested chiefly with his discretion, and when Hoge ran into problems, the synod and presbytery only offered criticism.[117]

Moses Hoge gave students a chance, boarded them, taught them, and ministered to them, but still Hampden-Sydney was isolated and behind the times. Conrad Speece arrived at Hampden-Sydney in 1799 from Liberty Hall to teach and stayed two years; he later became one of the most prominent Presbyterian ministers in the state, serving five terms as moderator of the Synod of Virginia. He was not impressed with the location of Hampden-Sydney or with the students. Later he would complain:

> A daily, dull repetition of the same dull exercises of College, like I have seen a weary horse creep round & round in a mill, must be tiresome to any man who has a taste for real pleasures. I could, however, reconcile myself much better to the business of teaching if the students had genius and industry with good moral dispositions. But we find very few such.

And facilities were so limited that "double-bunking" was standard for years. That is, a freshman would share a bed with an upperclassman until he could secure his own furniture.[118]

Legal Limbo

As Moses Hoge, the college, and the theological school contended with the internal frictions of changing expectations, student dissatisfaction, and declining enrollment they also faced external antagonism: the Commonwealth of

Virginia refused to grant the presbytery's school a charter. As long as the seminary did not have a charter, it would always be a creature of Hampden-Sydney College by not being able to hold property, borrow money, or conduct normal business transactions. Consequently, the conflicts inherent between a liberal arts college and a theological school would be institutionalized rather than solved.

The postcolonial Virginia legislature was inherently hostile to any hint of religion in public life. Before the American Revolution, the Anglican Church was more firmly established in Virginia than in any other colony. Indeed, it was not until January 12, 1802, that the Commonwealth stripped the church—by then known as the Episcopal Church—of all land acquired before January 1777 and sold it, with the proceeds given to the poor.[119] Disestablishment was a painful process in Virginia; long-standing churches lost all the property they possessed, communities were divided, and many clergy were impoverished. Supporting an established church was so odious to Virginians that the Virginia General Assembly did not want to give any type of official recognition to any church-related institution so as to be safe from even appearing to establish another church.

When the Synod of Virginia voted "that the College of Hampden-Sydney be the site of the Theological Seminary" at its meeting in the fall of 1815, they also directed the newly formed seminary board of directors to petition the Virginia General Assembly for a charter.[120] On December 13, 1815, the Committee of Propositions and Grievances of the Virginia General Assembly found "the petition of the Trustees of the Theological Seminary of Virginia for incorporation reasonable."[121] In this petition, Moses Hoge was named as president, and John Holt Rice was listed as a trustee.[122] Although a motion was immediately made from the floor of the House of Delegates to reject the petition, the legislators refused and invited John Holt Rice to argue for incorporation before the committee, which he did on January 2, 1816.[123]

Although Thomas Jefferson had once said that Presbyterians had done more for the promotion of learning than any other group,[124] he was deeply suspicious of the motives for wanting a charter. In a letter to a friend he laid his anxiety bare: "[They are] the most intolerant of all sects, the most tyrannical and ambitious. . . . They pant to reestablish by law the Holy Inquisition."[125] Due to Jefferson's opposition and the ingrained suspicions of many Virginians, the Virginia General Assembly denied the petition for incorporation by a vote of 119 to 48 on February 1, 1816.[126] John Holt Rice was disappointed. "This petition has very unexpectedly excited strong sensation & has been the subject of much conversation."[127] He was also offended; he understood that the delegates rejected the bill because they believed that by incorporating the seminary, the Presbyterians were "squinting towards an establishment." But Virginia Presbyterians had always stood against the idea of an established church.

In rebuttal to those who accused the Presbyterians of trying to establish their own denomination as the state church, Rice wrote *An Illustration of the Character and Conduct of the Presbyterian Church in Virginia*. This little book was published early in 1816, during the drive to secure a charter for the theological school, but published too late to influence public opinion or the legislative outcome. Rice argued that Virginia had nothing to fear from granting a charter to a Presbyterian institution. Presbyterian polity and history were evidence of republican tendencies, which had been proved before, during, and after the Revolution.[128] An educated ministry, he argued, was not only necessary for a strong church, but also for a free society, and Presbyterian ministers were educated and not "illiberal sectarians."[129] More important, however, Presbyterians had the interests of all Virginians at heart. "The directors of this institution . . . have never thought of confining the benefits of the institution to believers of their own church merely; on the contrary, acting on the principle of equal liberty, . . . they have opened the benefits of the institution to all persons of all religious persuasions." Presbyterians did not want to establish their church, but only desired that "their ministers should be men of education."[130]

Although the Synod of Virginia authorized an appeal and Rice's pamphlet received a wide hearing,[131] the legislature remained unmoved and refused to take up the issue again. The synod would approach the Virginia General Assembly again in 1826. John Holt Rice again campaigned heavily for incorporation, reprinting "Memorials to the General Assembly of Virginia" in the January 1826 issue of his newspaper, the *Literary and Evangelical Magazine*. This article reprinted several memorials of the Presbytery of Hanover: the 1776 memorial to the Virginia General Assembly, arguing against any religious establishment; the 1777 memorial to the Virginia General Assembly, against a general assessment for the support of any church; the 1784 and the 1785 Presbytery of Hanover memorials to the Virginia House of Delegates against incorporation of the Episcopal Church; and the 1785 memorial supporting "An Act for Religious Freedom"[132]—all in an effort to prove that the new seminary's charter would be no civil threat. The legislature, however, was adamant and overwhelmingly rejected the petition. It would not grant a charter of incorporation until 1867.

Enrollment

Enrollment figures for this period are unreliable; students seemed to arrive, take classes, and depart according to their own schedule, and Hoge's records are haphazard at best. There were at least forty-nine students in the seminary between 1807 and 1822. As might be expected, this student body was somewhat provincial: forty attended Hampden-Sydney, and three came from Washington College; but Middlebury College, Amherst College, and Williams College were also represented, with one student each. The vast majority of students came from Virginia, yet nine called North Carolina home, and Georgia, Massachusetts, New Hampshire, and Vermont claimed one each.

Although Moses Hoge intended his institution to be open "to all persons of all religious persuasions," only one non-Presbyterian can be positively identified: Edward Baptist, who was Baptist. Everyone served at least one church, some as far away as Iowa and Missouri, and most had some involvement with education. Edward Baptist would later found Powhatan Academy, which ultimately became the University of Richmond, and among the graduates there would be an assortment of professors and principals of academies and professors. J. D. Paxton (1812) would serve College Church, go to Syria as a missionary, then hold pastorates in Pennsylvania and Indiana.

The Theological Society and the Society of Missionary Inquiry

While Hampden-Sydney College, Hanover Presbytery, and the Synod of Virginia may have had questions about the leadership of Moses Hoge and the viability of his theological school, the students had no doubts. College, presbytery, and synod records provide a detailed account of the formal administration of the seminary throughout its first years, but only two sources give a glimpse into student life and the evolving identity of the seminary: the Theological Society and the Society of Missionary Inquiry.

In a manila envelope in the archives of the seminary library today, there is a worn volume with the title "The Theological Society Minutes, 1812–1823." The title page of the minute book reads: "Constitution, Regulations, & Proceedings of the Theological Society established at Hampden-Sydney, November 14th, 1812." It is clear that the seminary students thought of themselves as separate from the undergraduates from the very beginning. The purpose of the Theological Society was to promote "improvement in Theological knowledge and practical piety." The preamble to the Theological Society constitution stressed that it was to be a student-run organization. "Considering the importance, the duties, & the responsibility of the sacred Office of the ministry which we the subscribers have either immediately or remotely in view; we are desirous to unite ourselves in a Society, that we may mutually assist each other in making due preparation for that Office."[133]

The Theological Society gathered every other Friday at 7:00 p.m. in a designated room. After an opening prayer and a short business meeting, they would hear a presentation on a previously assigned question. Afterward questions from the audience were encouraged, and a general discussion typically ensued, as in a section discussion today. Students were expected to perform research on their topics and be prepared to answer questions. From 1812 until 1814 the students ran the meetings, and the questions tended to pertain to Christian conduct and ethics. All theological students were expected to attend (with graduates sitting in once in a while), and a student could expect to give four presentations a year.

From 1814 onward, Hoge moderated the meetings, and the questions tended to have a theological or doctrinal emphasis. It is clear that these seminary students were serious and quite unlike the college students that gave Alexander and Hoge so much trouble. Although they were primarily from rural areas and probably had very limited knowledge of the world, these students were anxious to broaden their horizons. The questions they assigned themselves show an eclectic range, usually falling into the categories of theology, Bible, or polity. The first question asked on November 13, 1812, was "What are the most satisfactory evidences of a regenerate state?" Two questions prior to 1814 were "What is the meaning of that charity which is represented as greater than faith or hope, & why is it said to be greater?" and "Is moral inability consistent with command and obligation?"[134]

At the end of 1814, Moses Hoge began to moderate, and each meeting began with a student "oration" on the assigned topic, followed by a discussion among all members present. They tackled wide-ranging topics in theology: "Was Adam created holy? Was there a covenant made with him? If so, what was the nature of that covenant? And what would have been the consequences of Adam's disobedience to that covenant?" "Whether election be a scriptural doctrine. Is it absolute or conditional?" "Is the grace afforded to all the hearers of the Gospel sufficient to enable them to obey the Gospel, that is, to repent and believe?" "Has the doctrine of the final perseverance of the saints a tendency to lead to licentiousness?" (Hoge "delivered some remarks upon" this subject.) "The parity of the Christian ministry; or, Are the bishops mentioned in Scripture any superior to the presbytery?" "Are there three equal persons in the Godhead, the Father, the Son, and the Holy Ghost?" "Is there any provision made in the gospel for the Salvation of the non-elect?"[135]

Questions on Scripture were exegetical: "What is meant by the Spirit witnessing with our spirit that we are the children of God (Romans VIII.16)?" "How are we to understand the passage Thou art a Priest forever after the order of Melchisadec [Heb. 5:6]?" "In what sense is all Scripture said to be given by inspiration of God?" "In what way are the iniquities of the father visited upon the children?" "Are those prophecies which predict the return of the Jews in Judea, to be interpreted in a literal sense?" "Is there any inconsistency between the apostle Paul and the apostle James, on the article of justification?" "Is the character described in the 4, 5 verses of the 6th Chapter of Hebrews, to be considered as one who has been wholly regenerated?"[136]

Polity questions usually focused on the sacraments: "Should the infants of baptized persons who are not in full communion with the church be admitted to baptism?"[137] "How far are baptized children subject to the discipline of the church?"[138] On "the Sacrament of the Lord's Supper,"[139] "should we admit to communion all whom we believe to be real christians?"[140] "What discipline is the church to exercise toward baptized children, after they have arrived to years of understanding?"[141] "What are the qualifications necessary for a christian communicant?"[142] And the ever-popular "Is immersion the scriptural mode of baptism?" (This one was asked at least eleven times.)

Students being students, there were times when things became a bit chaotic. On January 23, 1818, most of the meeting was taken up with "complaints that some members of the society were monopolizing the debate." The issue was resolved with a motion "that no one may speak more than twice on an issue." On January 21, 1820, there were complaints that the orations were incomplete, and the society moved that the moderator appoint two members of the society to "review the orations, and make such critical observations as they may think proper at the next meeting."

The Theological Society evolved into more than a forum for structured discussion. Within a year it began to function as the student government, appointing a committee "to investigate establishing a fund for the purchase of religious books."[143] Although the committee reported back a month later that it would be "inexpedient" to purchase books, by 1817 the society began to assess a fee of 50 cents per semester on all students for the purchase of religious papers. On November 29, 1816, the secretary "was directed to request the Rev. J. H. Rice (of Richmond) to have forwarded to the Society, such religious periodical papers, as he would recommend, not to amount in the whole to more than 10 or 12 $ per annum."

The Theological Society became so important to the seminary that on June 24, 1817, it convened with Moses Hoge as moderator "at request of a majority of the members to investigate the conduct of William B. Wallis, member of said Society." Wallis was accused of "profanation of the Sabbath day, . . . ungentlemanly and unchristian conduct towards members of this Society, . . . improper conduct towards several students of College, . . . palpable lying, . . . [and] delivering before this society an oration, as original, which was selected from *Sturm's Reflections.*" The proceedings were to the point: "After the examination of witnesses and hearing the plea of the accused, it was found that each charge was distinctly & fully substantiated; in consequence of which, Mr. Wallis was expelled from this society." Wallis left the seminary that day.

Six years after the Theological Society began meeting, "a number of the theological students of the Synod's school at Hampden-Sydney College" met at College Church on January 13, 1818, to form the Society of Inquiry on the Subject of Missions, or as it would come to be known, the Society of Missionary Inquiry (SMI). At its demise, the SMI was the oldest continuously running student organization at Union Seminary, holding meetings until 1939. The SMI's goals were simple:

> (1) to promote an interest in foreign missions, with a special view to enlisting foreign missionaries from the theological students who were enrolled in Moses Hoge's classes; (2) to seek financial support from the local church for such missionaries; and (3) to put the same vocational challenge in the hearts and minds of other young people in the local Presbyterian congregation.[144]

Interest in missions was growing during the first part of the nineteenth century, and most denominations worked through the American Board of Commissioners for Foreign Missions (ABCFM). The ABCFM had been founded in Boston by students from Andover Seminary in 1810,[145] so a student-led missionary organization was not unprecedented. Presbyterians were not known for supporting missions, so the organization of the Society of Missionary Inquiry, nineteen years before the organization of the Presbyterian Board of Foreign Missions, represents a wider vision among the students of the new seminary than that possessed by the church.

Although these students were more concerned with temperance and missions to western Virginia and North Carolina than they were in foreign missions, they were interested in the world. They subscribed to the *New York Herald* and the *London Evangelical Magazine.*[146] They set up and stocked the "Missionary Room" with books, periodicals, pamphlets, and filed letters as resources for research. These papers covered missionary work in North America and around the world, including the Bible, Tract, and Temperance Societies, Sabbath schools, and revivals.

The Society of Missionary Inquiry was a completely student-run organization.[147] Each meeting was run like that of the Theological Society, and there is evidence that interested undergraduate students from the college also took part. The SMI met the first Monday of each month, and the students took turns presenting papers concentrating on mission-related topics that reflected both the expansive vision and narrow culture of the students. Debate questions included these: "Should not the Licentiates of our Presbyteries act as missionaries for at least one year?" "Can a preacher of the Gospel best promote the interest of the Church by teaching a school in conjunction with his pastoral labors?" "Can a missionary in a heathen land be more useful in a married or single state?"[148]

The students were also aware of the doubts concerning their institution. In the midst of the Synod of Virginia's deliberations on whether to support Princeton Seminary, the debate question for January 17, 1820, was, "Ought the churches in the south encourage the Theological Seminary at this place, in preference to that at Princeton?" Later on, "Is a pubblick theological school better calculated to prepare a man for the Gospel ministry than private instruction?"[149] "Is it better to spend the usual term of the Theological course exclusively in study, or partly in pubblick exercises?"[150] Recognizing that the prospect for the resumption of classes was not good, the SMI discontinued debating on November 19, 1821. From this point forward, the president asked members to write essays on specific topics to present at the next meeting.

Perhaps the most interesting part of these early minutes of the Society of Missionary Inquiry is the correspondence book. On January 13, 1818, the society directed the secretary to send letters to the students at Andover Theological Seminary in Massachusetts and Princeton Seminary. Over time, correspondence was continued with students at Andover, Princeton, the Episcopal seminaries in Massachusetts and at Alexandria in Virginia, Auburn Theological Seminary in New York, Western in Pittsburgh, and the Dutch Reformed Seminary in New Brunswick, New Jersey. These letters uniformly decry the low state of religion in Virginia and North Carolina; the students saw themselves as the ones to lead "the Sacramental Host against the prince of darkness."[151]

A Leadership Vacuum

Moses Hoge was sick during much of 1819, and his poor health continued during the first part of 1820. The minutes of the Theological Society reflect his illness; he was absent many times, and the society had to name substitute moderators, such as local ministers and college professors. The minutes of the meeting of July 22, 1820, are poignant: R. H. Anderson was appointed moderator, not substitute moderator, because Moses Hoge had died in Philadelphia on July 5. Hanover Presbytery had commissioned Moses Hoge to attend the Presbyterian General Assembly that year in Philadelphia. He first stopped in New York to attend a meeting of the American Bible Society. He took sick a week after arriving in Philadelphia and died on July 5 at age sixty-nine. Hoge is buried in the cemetery at Third Presbyterian Church in Philadelphia.[152] His tombstone reads: "A man of genius, profound erudition, and ardent piety."[153]

John Holt Rice preached Hoge's memorial sermon, which was then reprinted in Rice's monthly periodical, the *Virginia Evangelical and Literary Magazine (and Missionary Chronicle)* (1818–28). Rice described him as a "studious man of uncommon intellectual endowments who exhibited fidelity in all the relations of life, a great believer in religious liberty and reverence for the laws of the land, and entirely free from sectarian zeal." As a teacher, Hoge was averse

> to wire-drawn speculations and metaphysical refinements. It was his opinion that what one called new discoveries in religion, are, for the most part,

obsolete errors revived. The result has been this, that his pupils have gone forth sober thinkers; who raise no disturbance in the church by the use of novel phrases, and the uttering of daring and strange dogmas.[154]

Moses Hoge had educated more than thirty men for the ministry, and at first no one at the seminary was concerned that his death would mean much to the seminary enterprise; most believed that finding a replacement would be easy. Within a month of his death, the Synod of Virginia, Hampden-Sydney College, and Briery and Cumberland Churches all extended calls (in tandem) to entice Archibald Alexander to return to Virginia.[155] Alexander declined in October 1820, and the synod seems to have been stumped as to what to do next. No further action on anything pertaining to the seminary seems to have been taken. Hampden-Sydney College, however, took the initiative and elected Jonathan P. Cushing as president.

By choosing its own president, who was not a minister, the college left the seminary to an uncertain fate, and the students knew it. On July 11, 1821, the corresponding secretary of the SMI lamented: "We are still without a president, nor shall we know until fall who will be put over our heads, or who will be made theological professor in the place of our great and good Dr. Hoge." Fall came and went with no professor. On December 17, 1821, the society correspondence chronicled low morale.

> We are yet without a professor of Theology. The Synod, contrary to our hopes, have referred the re-establishing the theological seminary at this place until their next meeting. The number of young men at this institution who are preparing for the study of theology is thirteen only. Six of our number finished the college course and left here last session. There are some others that are kept from prosecuting their studies.[156]

The students saw the situation clearly: the synod was out of options and was tired of dealing with theological education. After two years of trying unsuccessfully to find a professor, on October 25, 1822, the synod gave the seminary to Hanover Presbytery. The presbytery established the seminary as a separate institution from Hampden-Sydney College, with its own board, and put its funds "in perpetual trust for the education of students in divinity who design to take orders in the Presbyterian Church."[157] The presbytery received $8,756.04 from the synod; they had already taken ownership of the other assets: twelve shares of Farmers Bank of Virginia stock, two shares of Bank of Virginia stock, and $1,115.68 in cash.[158] Officially, the seminary ceased to function.

Many in Virginia, especially in the Shenandoah Valley, began to consider Princeton, under the leadership of Archibald Alexander, as the only viable seminary. Prodded by the Presbyteries of Lexington and Winchester, the Synod of Virginia began to suggest that supporting one national seminary backed by the Presbyterian General Assembly was a wiser investment than trying to keep the synodical seminary going.[159] Valley Presbyterians, due to immigration patterns[160] and transportation networks,[161] had always felt closer to Pennsylvania than Piedmont and Tidewater Virginia. As the synod discussions grew more serious about giving their funds to Princeton,[162] John Holt Rice began to emerge as the leading advocate for the seminary at Hampden-Sydney; he opposed the idea of educating southern seminarians in the North.

Early in 1821, the Synods of North Carolina, South Carolina, and Georgia had agreed jointly to raise $30,000 in five years for Princeton Seminary. This commitment to Princeton prompted Rice to use his newspaper to cajole and shame Virginians into supporting their seminary. Rice, writing under the name "Lucas," in a letter to the *Evangelical and Literary Magazine and Missionary Chronicle* in 1821, complained that Virginia churches were not doing enough to support the education of ministers: "I have looked upon this growing indifference as an exceedingly bad omen for the cause of religion." He lamented that in the entire state of Virginia, there were only sixty-eight Presbyterian preachers. Some churches had worship services only once a month, and some less than that.

The solution was not just more ministers, but more southern ministers. The southern church could not depend on "abroad" or the North: northern churches and schools had their own needs. Lucas declared, "We must help ourselves." He then claimed that there were "fifty pious young [men] within the bounds of the Synod, willing to commence an education if they could afford it." According to Lucas, the solution was simple; appeal to "Christians of our own denomination in particular, and to the pious and benevolent in general, to cast their offerings into the treasury of the Lord, and assist in educating pious and promising young men for the gospel ministry."[163]

Rice failed to revive the seminary for the moment, but he achieved a minor victory. The Synod of Virginia did not send their funds to Princeton Seminary, remitting them to Hanover Presbytery instead.[164]

John Holt Rice had always been insistent on the need for a southern seminary and used his paper to keep the issue before his readers. When it was apparent that the Synod of Virginia was ready to abandon its school and support the Presbyterian General Assembly's institution at Princeton, Rice strenuously opposed the move. He pointed out that graduates of Princeton Seminary could hardly be persuaded to settle in the South and were not equipped to succeed in the South. At the same time,

> the majority of students in the South, will not go to the North. I think this is a settled point. In the state of North Carolina there are twelve or fifteen candidates for the ministry, now studying divinity in the old field school way. And between preachers brought forward in this manner, and those who have better opportunities, there is growing up a strong spirit of envy and jealousy on the part of the former.

A seminary in the South, Rice argued, was essential to the advancement of Presbyterianism.[165] Even after finally accepting the call as theology professor, Rice continued to campaign for southern support for an educated southern ministry. In an 1823 issue of *Evangelical and Literary Magazine*, a "traveler" commented upon southern Virginia, noting that the Episcopal Church had been brought low because the established church never had enough priests. The traveler was afraid the Protestant churches were making the same mistake. He estimated that most people now did not hear a sermon "oftener than once in two or three weeks: in many cases not so frequently," and "the houses of worship are few and unfinished." To make matters worse, "the intellectual character of the preachers of the gospel needs to be greatly improved." The result was that in Virginia "not more than one-third acknowledge a connexion of any sort with Christian society."

The solution, according to this perceptive traveler, was "the location among them of a competent number of truly pious and well educated ministers of the gospel. I am not solicitous as to the denomination to which they may belong. Only let them possess the qualifications just stated, and I shall be satisfied." These ministers could not only preach, but also teach school: "Lower Virginia needs teachers." Then, appealing to his readers' pride, the anonymous traveler pointed out that New England had nine colleges and universities because they had educated clergy to teach their children. If Virginia had educated clergy, Virginia would have more and better schools at every level.[166] Consequently, an educated ministry was not only a theological imperative but also a civic asset.

The Students Save the Seminary

Officially, with the death of Moses Hoge and no replacement, with the Synod of Virginia wanting to give up its funds, and with the growing support for Princeton Seminary, theological education at Hampden-Sydney College appeared to be finished. But the minute book of the Theological Society tells a different story. The students undoubtedly believed, like the Synod of Virginia, that a new theology professor would take office quickly. Yet as the synod's inaction continued, the Theological Society began to serve somewhat as administration in waiting.

On September 2, 1820, there is a curious entry: "On motion, Resolved, that in consequence of the death of Dr. Hoge, certificates be granted by this society, to Messer's D. C. Cochran, Davis, and J. Harris, who are about to leave this place." The seminary, with no charter and no functioning board, could not grant diplomas; so with no other administration, the students themselves began to grant "certificates" to those students they deemed to have earned them. There is no mention of what was required to earn a certificate, only that the students voted to grant them to those deemed qualified. Certificates were granted on September 2, 1820; August 25, 1821; and June 6, 1823, to a total of nine students. They also continued their weekly debates. On August 2, 1822, the society contemplated: "Is a college residence unfavourable to growth in grace?"

Despite the formal leadership vacuum, the students knew what they needed. On August 30, 1822, the Theological Society resolved "that a committee of three be appointed to prepare and read to [the] Society a petition to be presented to the members of the Hanover Presbytery, at their next meeting, requesting them to appoint a Theological Professor at Hampden Sidney College." On September 25: "At a call[ed] meeting, the committee appointed to prepare a petition to Hanover Presbytery read the petition to [the] Society, which when the members had made some observations upon it, was received, and the committee was directed to present it to [the] Presbytery." And finally, on November 30, 1822, it was the students who saw the future of their seminary:

> On motion, resolved, that a letter should be sent, on behalf of the Society, to Dr. Rice, beseeching him to accept the call of the Hanover Presbytery to the professorship of Theology at this place. Mr. Hammond was appointed to

deliver this letter to Dr. Rice. On motion, resolved, that a committee of three
be appointed to draw up a petition to the Trustees of the Theological School,
beseeching them to erect the buildings for that School, at this place. Messer's
Armistead, Metcalf, and White were appointed for this purpose.

The last entry in the Theological Society minute book, and the last mention of the existence of the Theological Society, is the meeting of July 4, 1823.
Although the Society of Missionary Inquiry would meet for another 115 years
and would become the de facto student government, in the beginning it was
the Theological Society that kept meeting and granting certificates in the face of
apathy, indecision, and outright hostility.

The Threads of History

The early 1800s was a time for founding seminaries. Population growth and the
country's westward expansion made the old ways of education obsolete; the
revolution in "religious sentiments" required a new model to train ministers.
Between 1812 and 1834, eight Presbyterian seminaries were founded: Union in
1812, Princeton in 1812, Auburn in 1821, Western (Pittsburgh) in 1826, Columbia in 1828, Northwest/McCormick in 1830, Lane in 1832, and Union in New
York in 1834. Other denominations also built seminaries during this time. The
Moravian Seminary in Bethlehem, Pennsylvania, was established in 1807, the
same year as the seminary at Andover, Massachusetts; the Harvard Divinity
School was organized in 1816; and the Episcopalians founded their southern
seminary at William & Mary in 1821 (which moved to Alexandria, Virginia, in
1823). What would become Union Theological Seminary was the first graduate
theological institution in the South. Indeed, in 1818 the Presbyterian General
Assembly finally saw the merit of a regional seminary and left it up to presbyteries to establish their own schools; that year it authorized the Presbytery
of Central New York to establish what was to become Auburn Seminary.[167]
Presbyterians needed their own resources to combat deism and revivalism and
ensure orthodoxy.

With the call of Moses Hoge as theology professor to the "Theological School
and Library" at Hampden-Sydney College in 1807, it is possible to begin to see
the five themes that run like a red thread throughout Union Seminary's history: defining an educated ministry, the interplay between a "southern" and a
"national" seminary, how Union has engaged the world, the tension between
reform and the status quo, and the influence of Union Seminary on the denomination and theological education.

When Moses Hoge was called to Hampden-Sydney College, the church
accepted that an educated minister should know biblical Hebrew and Greek,
theology, church history, and Presbyterian polity. The Presbyterian Church,
however, did not have a coherent vision or plan for seminary education.
It would be Moses Hoge who would adapt the model of graduate theological education found in the Book of Discipline (1560) to a new context. And it
worked: Before 1807, ministerial students went to college, then studied under

a minister in the parish. After 1807, the church expected theological students to study as a group under a qualified professor while residing at a college.[168]

The Theological School at Hampden-Sydney was a Virginia school. Yet Hoge had an ecumenical outlook; the benefits of his institution would be open to "all persons of all religious persuasions." This outlook has stamped Union throughout its history. While the first students were Presbyterian, except Edward Baptist, and most came from Virginia, Hoge had a vision that included students from other denominations.

Hoge did not see himself as an agent of reform, but he also did not accept the status quo. He took personal action against slavery yet never called for abolition. He aimed to educate pastors who embodied high ethical standards and encouraged his students to defy prevailing cultural norms when accepted custom ran counter to the demands of the gospel. At the same time, Hoge wanted men who could minister to their people. It cannot be said that Union had had much influence on the denomination or theological education. Just by surviving, though, what was to become Union Seminary was setting a foundation for the future.

Moses Hoge was not as effective as he wanted to be because he was not supported, and the clashing expectations of synod, presbytery, and college (and college students) obscured the value of his efforts. Yet it was through his perseverance that systematic theological education was established in Virginia and the vision of an educated southern ministry took root. John Holt Rice would finally make this vision a reality.

Chapter Three (1822–31)
No Ism but Bibleism

By the second decade of the nineteenth century, the idea of a seminary-educated ministry was firmly implanted in the major American denominations. Yet the newly established seminaries were all in the North. Virginia Presbyterians shared the same expectations and desires as their northern brothers and sisters for an educated ministry, yet they also wanted a school in the South. There was a disconnect, however, between the vision of a seminary and the money that dream would cost. During the tenure of Moses Hoge, the synod appeared to have little understanding of how to adequately fund and manage their theological school. Moreover, Virginia Presbyterians did not see how a seminary could stand as an independent institution. When Archibald Alexander declined the call as theology professor (and president of Hampden-Sydney College) in October 1820, the Synod of Virginia seemed paralyzed.[1] If the southern part of the Presbyterian Church in the United States of America was to have a seminary the equal of Princeton, they would have to transform their way of thinking and establish an independent seminary, with its own sources of funding. John Holt Rice would show them how.

A Lay President for Hampden-Sydney

When Moses Hoge died in Philadelphia on July 5, 1820, the trustees of Hampden-Sydney College, needing to keep the college in session, immediately appointed Jonathan P. Cushing as acting president. All previous presidents of Hampden-Sydney were Presbyterian ministers, and many in Virginia considered the college "an appendage to the school of divinity," rather than an institution to teach the liberal arts and sciences. Keeping to the tradition and the attitude that an undergraduate college education should prepare a young man for the ministry, they desired that their next president would be a Presbyterian minister. They first called a minister from New York, and he declined. They then called a minister from Ohio. When he refused, the board reluctantly turned to Cushing, who was already in the job and apparently doing well. The board was hesitant to call Cushing because they assumed that the Synod of Virginia would have to approve his appointment since college and seminary presidencies were seen as one and the same. Moreover, he was not a member of any church when he was elected, although he became a member of the Episcopal Church after a couple of years, and he had no interest in theology. Hampden-Sydney's board thought that they would needlessly damage their relationship with the Synod of Virginia if they elected Cushing as their president.

Cushing had graduated from Dartmouth in 1817 and had begun teaching at Hampden-Sydney in the fall of the same year.[2] From his time in the classroom, Cushing recognized the inherent tension between "scientific" studies and a theological curriculum. After becoming president, he built the first dedicated chemistry lab on campus[3] and proposed that theology courses not be required to obtain a college degree. The board refused to eliminate the theology requirements at first, but it was becoming clear that students did not want to take theology courses, and educating undergraduates in theology was becoming obsolete.[4]

Cushing's insistence on science courses in the curriculum reflected the trend of American education toward secularization and specialization. As a consequence of educational reforms deemphasizing theology, the University of Berlin (present-day Humboldt University) awarded the first doctor of philosophy degree (PhD) in 1814 (in chemistry).[5] Yale awarded the first PhD in the United States in 1861 (for original research in literature).[6] By the 1820s the very definition of what it meant to be educated had changed. In the eighteenth century, the classics were the foundation of a college education. At the beginning of the nineteenth century, the classics were no longer the mark of an educated person. In the eighteenth century, apprenticeships were sufficient to learn medicine, architecture, engineering, and a whole host of other professions. In the nineteenth century, scientific knowledge became the foundation for the modern college curriculum, and professional schools began to develop; colleges had to devote resources to build laboratories and hire science professors with no interest in theology. Moreover, students arrived on campus expecting to learn the latest in scientific advancements, not traditional theology. The addition of scientific subjects to the curriculum and the demand for scientific knowledge transformed all American colleges, including Hampden-Sydney.

The difficulty in calling a theology professor, the changes in curriculum, and the urgent need for leadership caused Hampden-Sydney College to elect Cushing as president on September 26, 1821. Not everyone was sure his election was a good idea. He was elected on a split vote only after a committee reported that student conduct had been exemplary during the previous year.[7] The students concurred. In a letter of December 17, 1821, the secretary of the Society of Missionary Inquiry wrote: "The literary institution here is in more flourishing condition than it has ever been before. Mr. Jonathan B. Cushing, of New Hampshire, has been lately elected president."[8] Cushing was the first layman to lead the college; perhaps his call, with the assumed support or acquiescence of Hanover Presbytery, is evidence of the implicit recognition of the need for a separate college and theological seminary.

The Virginia Seminary in Doubt

While Hampden-Sydney College was moving forward, official support for theological education was stymied. The Synod of Virginia's first choice to lead the seminary declined the call, and there seemed to be no alternative. Moreover, the synod showed no confidence in its school. In fact, the synod gave serious consideration to abandoning theological education and transferring the remaining theological education funds to Princeton.[9] The students tried to fill the vacuum by educating themselves, but they knew their classes were no more than a holding action.

The Synod of Virginia was divided. It could be said that antebellum Virginia was composed of two distinct states: East and West divided by the Blue Ridge Mountains. East of the Blue Ridge, in Tidewater and Southside, the plantation system predominated, with an English culture and a large concentration of slaves. West of the mountains, small farms were the norm, Scotch-Irish and German immigrants were the majority, and only 15 percent of the population was enslaved, the smallest proportion of any place in the South.[10] The Shenandoah Valley was largely settled from Pennsylvania, and the immigrants kept ties to the North open; there was more trade with Pennsylvania than with the rest of Virginia.[11] The close ties can be seen in the fact that candidates for the ministry from Lexington and Winchester usually went to the seminary at Princeton.[12] Tidewater and Southside church regions wanted a seminary in Virginia, but Shenandoah Valley congregations supported the seminary at Princeton.[13] William Henry Foote argues that the East-West split within the Synod of Virginia over what seminary to support froze any positive action concerning theological education for two years.[14]

After two years of indecision, the Theological Committee of the Synod of Virginia reported on October 24, 1822, that their institution had "hitherto enjoyed but [a] very limited degree of prosperity." The report then laid out three alternatives: One, support the seminary at Princeton. This course of action was immediately discarded. Funds had been collected for theological education in Virginia, so there should either be a school in the synod or the money should be returned, and no one wanted to return the money.[15] Two, allow the donated funds to sit, accrue interest, and be used at some future date. This would also violate the premise under which the synod had raised the funds. Three, let Hanover Presbytery manage the seminary since it was within their "land."[16]

The synod adopted the third recommendation and transferred all funds for theological education to Hanover Presbytery in perpetual trust, "that the same shall be forever applied and devoted to the object for which they were raised, that is, to the education of students of Divinity who design to take orders in the Presbyterian Church at the College of Hampden-Sidney or elsewhere within the bounds of the Commonwealth." This action was taken without much enthusiasm or confidence: the synod repealed the standing order to collect funds for the seminary and suspended the Committee on the Theological Seminary after it had submitted its report.[17]

The committee report had revealed the poor state of the seminary: the scarcity of funds, lack of students, failure to obtain a charter, and paucity of support from the synod's congregations. From his vantage point in Richmond, John Holt Rice lamented the dim future of "our piddling school."[18] Despite the long odds against survival, on November 14, 1822, Hanover Presbytery accepted the funds from the synod, appointed a board of trustees for the seminary, and transferred the money to that board.

4. John Holt Rice, founder of Union Theological Seminary in Virginia. Original portrait is at Hampden-Sydney College.

New Leadership: John Holt Rice

The presbytery, though, did more than accept the synod's money and create a board; on November 16, 1822, they called John Holt Rice as theology professor. Coincidently, the College of New Jersey had also called Rice as president the previous September, and Princeton's call was in hand when Rice learned that Hanover had also called him. He did not answer either institution right away. He took sick while Hanover Presbytery was meeting and returned home to Richmond. His recovery was slow, and he made no decision until June 2, 1823.

That both Princeton and Hanover Presbytery wanted Rice to lead their respective institutions speaks to his reputation. He was already an agent for the theological library, a member of the Hampden-Sydney College board, a founder of the American Bible Society, publisher of the most prominent religious magazine in the South, and the successful pastor of First Presbyterian Church, Richmond. He could have stayed in Richmond, or he could have gone to Princeton, where he would have made more money and enjoyed more fame. Instead, he chose to build up a nearly abandoned theological school in a remote part of Virginia. It was his stature, connections, worldview, and energy that gave the new seminary a chance.

By the time John Holt Rice was called to resurrect theological education in Virginia, he was a nationally known figure. Born in Bedford County, Virginia, on November 28, 1777, he was the third of six children. His father, Benjamin Rice, was a lawyer and deputy clerk of Bedford County, but the family had always struggled for money. Benjamin Rice was an elder in the Peaks and Pisgah Presbyterian Church, pastored by his brother, David Rice, who would later be known as the Apostle of Kentucky. Catherine, the mother of John Holt, was a near relative of the second wife of Samuel Davies (the first non-Anglican minister licensed to preach in Virginia and fourth president of the College of New Jersey).

John Holt Rice was plagued with poor health throughout his life, beginning at the age of two, when he nearly died of fever.[19] He was an intelligent child, always interested in the church. His siblings remembered that he often preached to them and to their dolls. He could read parts of the Bible and all of Watts's *Psalms and Hymns* by the time he was four, but his formal schooling did not begin until he was eight.[20] Then Rice's father sent him to a Latin grammar school taught by his uncle John White Holt, an Episcopal priest in Botetourt County. He learned Latin quickly,[21] but the school soon closed due to his uncle's poor health, and he returned home. Thereafter Rice was taught by a succession of tutors.

The happy and peaceful times of his childhood ended with the death of his mother when he was twelve years old. His father quickly remarried the widow of Patrick Henry's brother, and the young John Holt Rice and his new stepmother immediately clashed. She saw no reason to continue his education and wanted him to be apprenticed. To preserve peace in the family, his father sent him to Liberty Hall in Lexington when he was fifteen. Just before leaving home, he made a profession of faith.

By all accounts, Rice was anxious to go to Lexington; William Graham was at the height of his fame, and Liberty Hall was becoming well known. After eighteen months as an indifferent student, however, Rice ran out of money. His father intended to bring him home and probably secure an apprenticeship for him. But George Baxter, who had known Rice at Liberty Hall and had just opened an academy in New London, Virginia, in Bedford County, intervened and invited Rice to his new academy.

After eighteen months of studying under George Baxter, Rice again ran out of money and secured a job tutoring for the Nelson family at Malvern Hill, thirty miles southeast of Richmond. While there, he began his intellectual journey by confronting deism for the first time and debating those who thought the philosophy of Montesquieu, Rousseau, Diderot, and Voltaire would make religion unnecessary.[22] Rice was well regarded by the Nelsons, but tutoring did not pay enough, and after eighteen months he began looking for another position. On a visit to Bedford, he contracted malaria and would suffer its effects the rest of his life.[23]

In 1797, after some months of recovery, Rice saw an advertisement for a tutor at Hampden-Sydney College. He walked seventy miles from Bedford to the college to apply for the position, only to find that it had been offered to the Reverend Robert Logan of Fincastle. Logan had not notified the college whether he would accept the job, so Rice walked to Fincastle, another seventy miles, and learned that Logan did not want the position. Rice walked back to the college and gave the news to the trustees, who hired him on the spot. Rice was just shy of twenty years old and had 12½ cents to his name. Major James Morton, who lived in the vicinity of the college, loaned him the money to pay off a debt in Lexington and buy some clothes.[24]

Rice arrived at Hampden-Sydney a few months before Archibald Alexander was elected president, and the college's prospects were poor. He had only three or four students to teach. He got along well with Alexander and Conrad Speece, another tutor,[25] but Alexander was not impressed with Rice; the new president complained that Rice never finished his assignments. His friends considered him to be a poor conversationalist and a weak public speaker, with a "dry" voice. Others described him as clumsy.[26] During his time as a student and tutor, Rice showed nothing of the scholarship or interest in education that was to come later.

After two years at the college, Rice resigned in 1799 and took charge of a school started by Major Morton to educate the children in the area. By all accounts, Rice did well, but he was restless. Also, Morton's daughter Anne, who was fifteen and Rice's student, apparently rejected his romantic overtures,[27] so after one year as a tutor for Morton, he went to Powhatan to study medicine, intending to go to medical school in Philadelphia. In the fall of 1800, however, Alexander asked Rice to return as a tutor, and Anne Morton, it seems, began to respond more favorably to his romantic interests. He resumed his life at Hampden-Sydney College as a tutor and began to study theology under Alexander. Rice began his home life in July 1802, when he and Anne married.

On September 12, 1803, Hanover Presbytery licensed John Holt Rice to preach; in 1804 he was ordained at Cub Creek Church in Charlotte County, Virginia, and served that congregation for eight years.[28] The call did not pay much, so he ran a small farm, with the help of a few slaves his wife had inherited, and established a school for boys in his home.[29] Under his leadership, Cub Creek Church grew from 58 white and 55 slave parishioners to about 400 white and 100 slave members.[30] It was not unusual for whites and blacks to attend the same church: it was customary for slaves to attend church with their masters.

In 1812—in the aftermath of the grief and outpouring of religious fervor that followed the Great Richmond Theatre Fire on Christmas Day 1811, which killed seventy-two people and was at the time the worst urban disaster in American history—Rice was called to organize First Presbyterian Church.[31] Now in Richmond, John Holt Rice found his voice and became a national presence. He saw First Church grow to 190 members in the ten years he was its pastor.[32] Although he was never a powerful speaker, he became one of the most popular and influential preachers in Virginia.[33] While in Richmond, Rice owned and operated a printing company that produced inexpensive popular Christian literature, and he became known as "The Defender of Presbyterianism."[34] He was instrumental in the founding of the Virginia Bible Society in 1813 and the American Bible Society in 1816, during his first trip to the North.[35] In 1819 he organized the Young Men's Missionary Society of Richmond;[36] Rice became known for his work with other denominations. Princeton Seminary awarded Rice the doctor of divinity degree in 1819, and he was elected moderator of the Presbyterian General Assembly in 1819.

Nothing better illustrates Rice's wide-ranging intellect and popular influence than the *Virginia Evangelical and Literary Magazine*, which he published between 1818 and 1828. Rice had long been interested in publishing. While he was pastor at Cub Creek Church, he wrote a number of articles for the *Virginia Religious Magazine*, founded by the Synod of Virginia in 1805. After establishing himself in Richmond, Rice began publishing the weekly *Christian Monitor*, which he founded in 1815 and discontinued in 1817.[37] In 1818, he established a platform in the monthly *Virginia Evangelical and Literary Magazine* and its successor titles: the *Evangelical and Literary Magazine*, the *Evangelical and Literary Magazine and Missionary Circle*, and the *Literary and Evangelical Magazine*. First in Richmond, then at Hampden-Sydney, Rice's magazines made him a national force.

The *Virginia Evangelical and Literary Magazine* was the first popular periodical in the South to be successful, both in length of life and extent of circulation.[38] Where previous southern mass periodicals had lasted no more than two or three years,[39] Rice's magazine lasted for eleven and had between 900 and 1,000 subscribers.[40] Contemporaries praised Rice's magazine as providing "almost the only gleam of general literature and science that has appeared South of Philadelphia."[41]

The articles in the *Virginia Evangelical and Literary Magazine* reflected Rice's wide-ranging intellect and forward thinking. "On the True Theory of the Universe," "On Conversation," "Remarks on the Study of Natural Philosophy," "On Usury," "On the Manner in Which Some People Spend Their Time," "Probable Moral Effects of the Present Scarcity of Money," "A Review of the Cultivation of Female Intellect in the United States," and "Women Not Unequal to Men"—all show a curiosity not evident in earlier years. One subject that continually preoccupied Rice was education. Nearly every issue carried an article about improving education in Virginia.[42]

Rice also used the magazine to promote his views and projects. He successfully marshaled support to force Thomas Jefferson to withdraw the appointment of Thomas Cooper, a Unitarian, to the first professorship at the University of Virginia in 1819.[43] He also strenuously argued against sectionalism. In 1824, Rice wrote "A Journey in New England," an account of an 1823 fund-raising trip, and he ended the article as follows: "According to my whole observations, there is wanting nothing but better acquaintance between the Northern and Southern people to do away with prejudices and promote the cordiality which ought to exist between citizens of the same country."[44] And Rice used the magazine to generate interest in a southern seminary.[45]

John Holt Rice and an Educated Ministry

As early as 1809, Rice had been calling for an educated ministry. In a widely circulated sermon titled "On the Duties of a Minister of the Gospel," preached on October 11, 1809, he argued that an effective minister should be able to teach Scripture "in both doctrine and manner,"[46] meaning that the minister must have "such acquaintance with ancient languages, history, laws, and customs, that he can justly interpret" Scripture. Only when he has a full understanding of the Bible can he "comfort the afflicted, instruct the ignorant, and assist the poor and needy. He will, like an angel of peace, enter the abodes of want and sorrow, pouring the 'oil and wine' of consolation into the wounded heart of the widow, and drying up the tears of the orphan."[47]

John Holt Rice was one of the last members of the Revolutionary generation. From his vantage point in Richmond, he lamented that political independence had led to a decidedly un-Christian society. Only a seminary, a southern seminary, could raise the low state of religion in the South through training educated, competent ministers to confront the hostile culture. Just as education was the key for Americans to secure their political freedom, so education was necessary if the church, like Paul in Athens at the Areopagus (Acts 17), were to address an indifferent or antagonistic society.

Indeed, it may be said that Thomas Jefferson and John Holt Rice were the central figures in overcoming Virginia's cultural lethargy. Both Jefferson and Rice were convinced that personal autonomy and political freedom could only be preserved through education. They also strongly believed that America could survive only with an intelligent electorate, and Virginia society could only be made more equitable through education.

Rice knew from experience that the old system of education would not work in a republican society; private tutors, "Old Field Schools" (neighborhood schools that charged tuition), and apprentice schools (where masters were required to teach the three Rs and the rudiments of Christianity)—all these favored the aristocracy and perpetuated the class structure of colonial Virginia. Rice, Hoge, and other Presbyterian ministers usually opened schools in their churches, and these schools taught all who could pay. Presbyterians were the most active educators in Virginia during the seventeenth century. Remembering that two of Virginia's first three colleges, Hampden-Sydney and Liberty Hall, were Presbyterian (with William and Mary firmly Episcopalian), Jefferson remarked that Presbyterians "had done more to promote education than any other branch of the Church in the South."[48]

In the pages of his magazine, Rice consistently deplored the low state of "religion" in the South and the inability of the church to make its voice heard. In 1820, out of the forty-nine counties within Hanover Presbytery, only ten had Presbyterian churches.[49] In 1821 there were only fourteen candidates for ministry in the whole region from Maryland to Texas.[50] In 1825, Rice estimated that only "one-fifth of the population from the Potomac to the Mississippi acknowledges a connection with the Church of Christ in any form. And of this fifth, more than three-fourths are under the guidance of extremely ignorant preachers." With the Cumberland split in 1810 and the frontier moving further westward, Rice argued that the growth of Presbyterianism in the South would be undermined by the dearth of qualified ministers. When the Synod of Virginia hesitated over continuing its own seminary and considered throwing its support to the seminary at Princeton, Rice despaired: "I am satisfied that if we do not raise our own preachers, we shall go without them. Besides, our genius and habits suit the Southern country best."[51]

An educated ministry was a constant theme in Rice's writings. In 1822, under the pen name "Holem," he argued that "the religious character of a people is very intimately connected with the character of the ministers of religion among them."[52] "People," he observed, "commonly are in the business of life, and the cares of the world, [and] their opinions are, in a great degree, regulated by the expositions of divine truth heard from their teachers, and their thoughts and feelings are moulded by those to whom they look for instruction." Thus it is vital for society to have educated ministers who can apply the principles of religion to everyday life.[53]

If American society, however, was to achieve a responsible and thoughtful faith, the mediocrity of the American clergy had to be replaced with academic excellence.

> In sadness of heart I do believe that other professions are running before the clergy of the country. I foresee the evils which will result from this state of things; and, in my humble sphere, am labouring to prevent them. . . . Let none imagine that we can, in this age, safely dispense with ripe and sound scholarship in the church.[54]

Only a seminary could give ministers the scholarship and professionalism needed to appeal to a modern world and prevent disunity in the church. In an 1823 letter to Archibald Alexander, Rice argued:

> In the state of North Carolina, there are twelve or fifteen candidates for the ministry, now studying divinity in the old field school way. And between preachers brought forward in this manner, and those who have better opportunities, there is growing up a spirit of envy and jealousy on the part of the former. This is so much the case, that among Presbyterians there is actually now an undervaluing of that sort of education which we think very important. And things are likely to get worse and worse. But my plan is, if we can succeed here, to take Princeton as our model. . . . [We will do] all that can be done to bind the different parts of the Church together.[55]

For Rice, educated ministers were the only ones who could combat "modern" heresies. In his 1825 pamphlet, *The Injury Done to Religion by Ignorant Preachers*, Rice argued that an ignorant ministry relies on "religious excitement" to make its influence felt. By contrast, seminary-trained clergy would guard against the "nonsense and frothy declamation of unlettered enthusiasts"[56] and address all classes of society.

According to Rice, only graduates of a seminary located in the South could effectively minister to Southerners and combat the deism and revivalism that afflicted southern culture. On May 27, 1823, just weeks before accepting the call to Hanover Presbytery's theological school, Rice wrote to William Maxwell that some missionaries from the North had finished their assignment to southern churches and would soon return home, "scampering off from us, in the way I hope soon to hear of the French scampering off from Spain," even though they "were entreated by the people to stay, with the promise of more than missionary pay." If there were to be a southern church, Rice asserted, "we must have a school."[57]

John Holt Rice Reestablishes the Seminary

By early 1823, Rice was almost in despair: "The Presbyterian cause is sinking in Virginia,"[58] and only a seminary would save it. He refused the call to Princeton so that the South could have that seminary. As he explained to Archibald Alexander:

Here my nominal salary is $2,000, my real one is $1,600, very irregularly paid, and my expenses are beyond my income. At Princeton I should get $2,500, punctually paid, and should have less company. People would say, "Northern gold has brought him." And my influence in the South would be destroyed. . . . I am convinced that a theological Seminary in the South is a necessary, and that if there is not one established before long, the consequences will be very deplorable.[59]

Rice was concerned for the South, but he was also a nationalist. If a southern seminary strengthened the southern church, the cause of Jesus Christ would be strengthened everywhere.[60] Robert Burwell, a member of the first class that entered the seminary in 1824, remembers Rice arguing for a southern seminary:

Dr. Rice earnestly advocated this idea, not from any hostile feeling towards the North, or from any want of confidence in Princeton or Andover. So far from this being the case, Dr. Rice had warm personal friends in the North, who gave substantial proof of their good feelings for the South and of their esteem for Dr. Rice. He advocated the establishment of a Seminary, on the ground that it would best prepare young men for laboring in the South where the circumstances were peculiar, and thought it would increase the number of candidates for the ministry, and also give an impetus to the work of domestic missions and make the Southern churches more aggressive.[61]

Rice would always insist that "we are not indifferent to the success of Princeton . . . and [will] support [it] to the extent of our abilities."[62] Rice saw his theological institution as complementing the school at Princeton: a southern school serving the national church, and a national church that would grow so large so as to be able to support two theological schools.

In an 1822 article, Rice tried to shame Virginians into supporting the failing seminary at Hampden-Sydney by writing about the seminary at Andover. He gave a glowing account of the Andover seminary's history (founded in 1808, from the academy established in 1788—a remarkably similar pedigree to Hampden-Sydney College) and its robust endowment ($20,000). The article excitedly reported the enrollment (132), number of graduates (312), professors (4), and buildings (2); it described the library (5,000 volumes) and the curriculum (familiar to Presbyterians).

Rice concluded that the South needed a seminary like Andover because "in order to render religion respectable, its ministers must be learned and respectable." He observed, "The Holy Spirit employs human instruments in carrying on his gracious purposes. . . . Accordingly he chooses instruments adapted to the ends proposed. When the ignorant are to be taught, well-instructed men most clearly ought to be appointed teachers."[63] Over the next four years, the *Virginia Literary and Evangelical Magazine*, under the guise of letters written by "Rusticus," regularly reported on the condition of other seminaries around the country. The stories always concluded that the South needed more and properly educated ministers.

Rice's support for Moses Hoge and his plea for Archibald Alexander to return home from Princeton were based on his ambition to see a southern seminary producing educated ministers for the southern church.[64] His greatest fear echoed Thomas Jefferson's complaint:

> We see our youth flying to foreign countries (Yale, Princeton, and other Northern colleges) to obtain that of which they are deprived at home: a liberal education. . . . There is one thing very common among young men who receive their education abroad: . . . they fall into the habit of thinking everything foreign excellent, everything native odious and detestable. I have seen [that] many young Virginians, who had finished their education at Princeton, Yale, etc., appeared to have conceived an incurable disgust against all that was Virginian, and nothing could be heard from them but censures of the laws, the politics, the manners and customs of Virginia.[65]

Rice wanted to educate southern ministers in the South to preserve southern culture. Yet even though he had decided to stay in Virginia, he knew good intentions were not enough.

Rice did not immediately accept the call from Hanover Presbytery to become the theology professor, and there may have been more to his hesitation than sickness; there may also have been an unwritten understanding to hammer out. On September 25, 1822, a committee from the Theological Society presented Hanover Presbytery with their resolution "requesting them to appoint a Theological Professor at Hampden-Sydney College."[66] The individual to be appointed, however, is not named. The presbytery extended the formal call to Rice on November 16. He did not respond immediately but asked the presbytery to commit more support to the seminary. The presbytery promised to answer him at their next meeting and appointed a committee.

The presbytery probably gave Rice assurances of financial and organizational support before he accepted the call. The Synod of Virginia had already issued a detailed report on the dreadful state of the seminary; everyone knew there were problems.[67] Two days before issuing the call to Rice, on November 14, and without any formal committee work, Hanover Presbytery appointed a new board, accepted the funds from the synod, and transferred all funds to the new board. No action had been taken for two years, yet now the presbytery acted in a purposeful rush and created a new institution, perhaps meeting Rice's specifications. The name of the new institution was simple and showed who was in control: "The Theological Seminary of the Presbyterian Church under the care of the Presbytery of Hanover."[68]

The news traveled fast. On November 30, 1822, the students at the newly named seminary weighed in: "On motion, resolved, that a letter should be sent, on behalf of the Society, to Dr. Rice, beseeching him to accept the call of the Hanover Presbytery to the professorship of Theology at this place."[69] Over the next several months the presbytery appointed agents to receive and raise funds and appropriated money to hire a librarian. Rice, with a board in place, a fundraising apparatus, and student support, then believed the presbytery was serious. He accepted the call on June 2, 1823.[70]

Whereas Hoge had been criticized for his lack of fund-raising, Rice knew that money would be as important to the new school as teaching. Moreover, he was experienced at raising money. He had raised money for his magazines, and in 1806–7 he had served as an agent in raising money for Hanover Presbytery's theological library at Hampden-Sydney and the "poor and pious youth" fund. He knew that his school had to have a firm financial foundation, and southern Virginia was not the place to look for money. For the six months between the time he formally accepted the presbytery's call and his inauguration in January 1, 1824, Rice was raising money in the North. In the nine years between accepting the call in 1822 and his death in 1831, he made four fund-raising trips to the North (primarily to Philadelphia, New York, and Boston).[71] Rice knew that Northerners would support his school. For example, Jonathan Little of New York had already donated $2,500 for the endowment of a scholarship on November 14, 1822, seven months before Rice accepted Hanover Presbytery's call.[72]

Rice's trip to the North in 1823 showed his wide range of contacts. Negotiating the Plan of Union made him well known to the northern part of the church. Through knowing Rice, Northerners felt comfortable supporting a southern seminary and sending students to his school (in 1823 and 1824, up to a third of the new school's students came from New England, Pennsylvania, and New Jersey).[73] On his 1823 trip, he visited Albany, Saratoga Springs, Schenectady, Boston, Salem, Andover, Philadelphia, and Baltimore.[74] Professors from Andover expressed "their cordial approbation of the design of establishing a Theological Seminary in Virginia" and "their entire satisfaction with the character and qualifications of the man who has been appointed to the office of Professor; and their earnest wishes for the success of the Institution." In Boston, on September 30, 1823, William Phillips, the former lieutenant governor of Massachusetts, donated $200, and Daniel Webster gave $25. Rice raised a total of $1,340.96 in Massachusetts.[75] By the time he gave his inaugural address on January 1, 1824, the school had $25,000 in subscriptions.[76]

Rice valued cooperation. In 1819 he wrote, "Protestants of different denominations endeavored for ages to sustain and advance the Truth by controversy, and they have well-nigh disputed vital religion out of the world. . . . It is by zealous cooperation that the glorious things foretold in the Bible are to be accomplished." He lamented the inability of Christians to work together:

> O! that there were a spirit of union among all the followers of Christ! But I fear that the day of perfect peace is yet far distant. . . . The spirit of controversy is like to be wakened up; and we shall see how Unitarianism and Universalism, and other heresies, will triumph on account of the quarrels of orthodox Christians![77]

Cooperation was the only answer: "The cause of real religion is one undivided and invisible cause; and its prosperity affords abundant occasion of rejoicing to all who love the Lord Jesus Christ in sincerity."[78]

Seminary education was not an end in itself; educated ministers had a goal: evangelization. From the pages of his magazine, Rice called for missionaries to go to rural areas.[79] On his deathbed Rice wrote an overture, asking the Presbyterian General Assembly to declare that "the Presbyterian Church in the United States is a Missionary Society; the object of which is to aid in the conversion of the world, and every member of the Church is a member for life of said Society." His students followed his example. In 1832, the year after his death, the

Society of Missionary Inquiry reported that two of their members would apply to the ABCFM for assignment as a missionary in foreign lands, and others were considering it.[80]

Rice's view of Christianity, while expansive, had its limits. When the Episcopal Bishop John S. Ravenscroft of North Carolina claimed that the Episcopal Church was the only valid church with the only valid ministry and the only valid sacraments because Episcopalians had bishops in the line of apostolic succession, the usually irenic Rice answered in the *Evangelical and Literary Magazine*. The true Christian, Rice insisted, is tolerant of differences in others, but "it will always be his duty to oppose those arrogant claims, and exclusive pretensions, which, in pursuit of a hopeless uniformity, break up the fellowship of Christians, prevent their co-operation, and place stumbling blocks in the way of others."[81]

Not everyone shared Rice's cooperative spirit. While he urged Presbyterians to support and join the ABCFM, the Presbyterian General Assembly rejected cooperation with the Congregationalists.[82] In 1846, James W. Alexander wrote of Rice: "Some of his warmest admirers did not hesitate to avow their belief that his dread of controversy was excessive." And he adds: "As a Theological Professor, he was a thorough Calvinist, opposed to all the innovations in Divinity which were then beginning to show themselves; yet ready to go all lengths in forbearance towards the persons of dissentients."[83] Yet, if Rice was too accommodating for some, it was because he realized he could not build and sustain a seminary without the assistance of the entire church.

The Plan for the Future

On January 1, 1824, John Holt Rice ascended the pulpit at the Brick Church at Hampden-Sydney to give his inaugural lecture. Standing in that pulpit, he could count only three students, an endowment of $10,000 plus $25,000 in pledges, and a contingent fund of $1,000.[84] His inaugural address is the DNA of Union Seminary. It contains both the aspirations and the tensions that make Union Seminary unique, and his speech highlights the five threads that run throughout the history of the school. He defines an educated ministry, seeks to resolve the tension between a "southern" and a "national" institution, and addresses how the seminary should engage the world and how far it should support the status quo or push for reform. It also addresses the influence a seminary should have on the denomination and theological education.

Rice began his address with an exegesis of 2 Timothy 3:16–17: "All Scripture is given by inspiration of God," and in good Presbyterian fashion he defined the Greek words "given by inspiration" (θεόπνευστος) and "doctrine" (διδασκαλίαν). After explaining these definitions, he declared: "Our business, as inquirers, is to ascertain what the Bible means. This being done, inquiry is at an end; for we then know what God requires, and nothing remains for us but to believe, and obey."

Defining an Educated Ministry

For Rice, the seminary curriculum could only be based on the Scottish Book of Discipline. According to the Plan, the curriculum would consist of biblical criticism ("original languages of the Old and New Testaments"), Christian theology, ecclesiastical history, church government, and preaching. The curriculum was orthodox: "the doctrines taught in the Seminary shall be in conformity with those of the confession of faith of the Presbyterian Church."[85] And there was only one textbook: "Our Seminary shall be based on the Bible; and we will know no isms there but Bibleism. I am sure that the Bible will afford good support to sound Presbyterianism, and if it will not, why, let Presbyterianism go."[86] An educated minister, however, was one who not only knew the Scriptures but was "acquainted with the enemies of the Church, their forms of attack, and the most successful method of repelling their assaults . . . He is a man of extensive knowledge, yet not vain; a man of taste, yet not fastidious; a man of study, yet not a recluse; a man of deep thought, yet plain and simple in his mode of teaching."[87]

Rice's vision was straightforward; he intended his students to have solid biblical knowledge and an awareness of the world. He did not want "young men [who] know nothing of the spirit of the times. We want men all on fire, and at the same time so acquainted with the state of the world that they will be ready to take hold at the right place of any work of Christian love that Providence may set before them."[88]

For Rice, an educated minister would be part of a profession on par with the other professions:

> It is a matter of very great importance, that as Science advances, and the range of human thought is extended, the ministers of religion should be able to keep an even pace with the best taught of their fellow-citizens. . . . When intellectual men constantly witness ignorance and inferiority in religious teachers, they will rarely fail to think of religion itself with contempt.[89]

When he accepted the call as professor of Christian theology, the tutor model was discarded, the log college no longer had a place in Presbyterian education, and the relationship between college and seminary was irrevocably altered. Individual tutorials would give way to classrooms; students would have a firm undergraduate foundation, preparing them to study theology; and the seminary would be a place of postgraduate education. Competent, educated ministers could come only from seminaries because "there is an accumulation of means of excitement and improvement which cannot be procured in any other way."

If it was the business of the student to learn what "to believe and obey," the job of the teacher was similarly straightforward:

> The great duty of a professor of Theology, is to imbue the minds of his pupils, as thoroughly as possible, with the knowledge of revealed truth. The Bible ought to be the great text book; and the whole course of study should be so laid out, as to enable the student to understand and explain the sacred volume.

A Southern versus National Institution

Once Rice had defined an educated ministry as those who learned the traditional curriculum taught in a classroom, he argued for a "southern" institution "to rear her own ministry." There were three reasons a southern seminary was needed. First, practicality: the lack of ministers could not be filled by one national seminary. Rice admitted that Princeton was a good school, but the church needed at least fifty new ministers a year, and Princeton could only provide twenty or thirty.

Second, seminary education should be personalized, and thus seminaries should not be large. Professors must have personal contact with students "to prevent heresy, wild speculations, and unprofitable theories." The seminaries at Princeton and Andover were large enough already. Finally, a seminary must be local to have influence; it should not be remote from the people it serves. It was up to southern Presbyterians "to educate their own young men, for their own people."

In Rice's view, only a southern seminary could confront both the emotionalism of revivalism and the skepticism of deism that infested southern culture. The only way to challenge both extremes was to make seminary education truly liberal and comprehensive, by rising

> above all party feelings; above the minute differences that prevail among evangelical men; it ought to discard the metaphysical subtleties, and impalpable distinctions of system-making, and support the common doctrines of Christianity, that were handed down by the apostles, and revived at the Reformation. At the same time, it ought so to attend to the progress of science, and the prevalent literature of the age, as to make it interesting to men of letters. A work like this is most urgently demanded by the times.[90]

"Our Theological Seminary," Rice declared, "is not intended exclusively for the advantage of any denomination." Rather, "party zeal" would be "proscribed and banished from all its offices—the students are to be taught to distinguish between the essentials for the Christian religion . . . and the circumstances about which there have been so many warm and fruitless debates." His seminary would welcome all Christians and encourage all ministers to cooperate. "We must hold to the great and precious doctrines of the gospel, and at the same time let little things pass for little things."[91]

Rice's seminary would be the classroom where ministers learned cooperation because their primary goal was evangelization. Cooperation would be vital if American Christians were to fulfill the Great Commission. "But if we cannot, separately, do the good which the Bible tells us must be done; we can do it collectively. . . . And all the knowledge, the wisdom, the energy of our best men, ought to bear on this mighty subject of co-operation, among American Christians for evangelizing the world."[92] Throughout his life Rice maintained, "It is particularly the duty of American Christians to enlist and combine their energies for evangelizing the world."[93]

Engaging the World

Having defined an educated ministry as those who learned the traditional curriculum taught in a classroom, and arguing for a southern institution to

serve the wider church and to combat the extremes of deism and revivalism, Rice maintained that seminaries are beneficial to society as the agents of
reform and improvement. He saw a culture that was afflicted with an unchal-
lenging faith, a lack of learning, and too much alcohol. These factors led to
backwardness, which left the South behind the rest of the country. An educated ministry would raise "the standard of moral character . . . [and] promote peace and order in the community." More than that, "with enlarged and
liberal views, they give the weight of their character to all plans of general
improvement."

Influence on the Denomination and Theological Education

Rice's seminary would influence theological education. He foresaw his graduates entering into the world of scholarship with their unique point of view.
"Literature," according to Rice, "is either an efficient enemy or a useful auxiliary to religion." He lamented that contemporary American Protestant theology was too dependent on Europe "for works on Theology as well as on
almost every branch of human science. Philosophy, History, and Poetry, must
be made to feel the influences and subserve the interests of evangelical truth,
or they will be placed in direct hostility to it." His seminary would produce
scholars to challenge what he called "German" scholarship.[94] From his point of
view, "German" scholarship referred to the new generation of commentators
who advocated a break with the traditional understanding of biblical study.
Whereas previous generations read the Bible devotionally, by the middle of
the eighteenth century, scholars centered around the University of Tübingen
analyzed the Bible according to the principles of any other historical document.
Rice believed it was important to stress the divine, inspired nature of Scriptures
in the academic debates. Near the end of his life, he wrote that "it was necessary
that there should be a change in our theological literature."[95] Each generation
would need the faith explained to them, and it was up to Presbyterians to make
sure the scholarship was faithful and sound.

> We have English books, Arminian and superficial. We have metaphysico-
> theology from other sources. . . . If there should be no change, sound Presbyte-
> rian doctrine will be destroyed by the very books which are brought into our
> Theological Seminaries. Now, I want Presbyterians to form better Lexicons,
> better Commentaries, better systems, and better Ecclesiastical Histories than
> any other denominations; and so much better that the people will be glad to
> get them; and even be obliged to use them.[96]

A competent ministry, however, was above all else worshipful. "It being the
great object of the Seminary to furnish to the Church, ministers of the Gospel
thoroughly qualified for every good work, improvement in vital piety shall
be steadily aimed at, through the whole course of instruction." As a result
Rice specified two times of worship each day, at which "a suitable portion of
Scripture shall be read with a special regard to practical improvement, a hymn
shall be sung and prayer be offered." In addition, "the Sabbath shall be wholly
employed in exercises, suited to produce a pious and devout frame of mind;
and such other measures as may be approved." And the students, reflecting

the seriousness of their call, would "carefully avoid all levity and every thing inconsistent with the sacred vocation."

Rice ended his inaugural by reviewing the short history of the school. He lamented the struggles; he rejoiced that Hanover Presbytery, from their "zeal, prudence, and fraternal love," had called him to the office he now filled. He stood at the pulpit and looked into the future; he saw the seminary as "a copious fountain of living water, sending out streams in every direction, to fertilize the land, and make glad the city of our God."

The Rev. Clement Read then charged John Holt Rice. Where Rice's words were idealistic and far-reaching, Read's stayed practical and close to home. "The object of this Theological Seminary is to furnish the church, and especially the southern part of it, with a useful and successful gospel ministry." For Read, useful and successful meant orthodox:

> We want, Reverend Sir, a useful, not a splendid ministry. . . . How great soever the acquired abilities of the theological student may be, if he be master of Greek and Hebrew languages, if he be deeply acquainted with oriental literature, if he be well versed in all history and all science; yet if he be heretical in his principles, he will be a curse to the church.

There was only one standard of orthodoxy: the Westminster Confession of Faith. And such a seminary, "professedly erected under the patronage of the Presbyterian Church, should teach no doctrines but such as are agreeable to this standard" because "the gospel ministry, to be useful, must be pious as well as orthodox." Thus, Read concluded, "To promote piety in this Seminary, Reverend Sir, should be your principal care."[97]

The Synod of Virginia minutes simply recorded that the seminary had opened in January, Rice was inaugurated, and three students began class. The minutes also note that $3,000 was added to the permanent fund and $2,000 was to be spent on a building for the professor and his family. Rice hired James Marsh, who taught at Hampden-Sydney College, as temporary assistant teacher in original languages.[98]

There was no housing at Hampden-Sydney for Rice and his family, so Cushing, the college president, had invited them to live in his house. Cushing occupied a large downstairs room, where because of his health he often held his classes and in which he kept his chemical "apparatus." The larger of two small rooms downstairs was used as a parlor and dining room, and the smaller, which had no fireplace, was occupied by Rice's niece, Harriet Minor. John and Anne Rice lived in an attic room with a fireplace, and they had to vacate this room every morning because Cushing used it as his study. Another attic room had been equipped with shelves to function as a library. A servants' room adjoining the kitchen was converted into Rice's study and classroom.[99]

The First Class

With three students present on January 8, 1824, one week after his inaugural address, John Holt Rice convened the "school of the prophets" in the kitchen of Jonathan Cushing's house.[100] The students who sat facing Rice that Thursday morning were, in many ways, representative of the students to come. Jesse S. Armistead, from Cumberland County, Virginia, was twenty-eight years old and a second-career student. He had been a merchant and after a conversion experience decided to become a minister, so he enrolled after graduating from Hampden-Sydney. Thomas P. Hunt, a stepson of Moses Hoge, was twenty-nine years old and had been taking classes with the Theological Society for two years, so he spent only one year taking classes under Rice. Although he did serve a church after finishing in 1824, he became a well-known temperance lecturer in 1830 and ultimately became wealthy through coal investments. And Robert Burwell, from Dinwiddie County, Virginia, was twenty-one years old and had graduated from Hampden-Sydney. He had also taken classes with the Theological Society the previous year.

Burwell had accompanied John and Anne Rice on the three-day trip from Richmond to Hampden-Sydney when they had moved to campus. Writing in 1894, Burwell provided one of the rare existing descriptions of John Holt Rice. Burwell related that Rice was tall, good natured, and made everyone feel at ease, but also he could be moody, with a sarcasm that could "sting." "His Catholic spirit was well known. A Presbyterian by birth and conviction, he was no bigot, but cordially received as his brethren all who loved the Saviour. He was emphatically a man of peace, but when the truth was assailed, he girded his armor and gave stunning blows."

While not in a class with the "Germans," according to Burwell, Rice was a "learned" man who loved books.[101] He read Calvin in Latin.[102] As a teacher, he "manifested a deep interest in his students." Rice stressed being prepared in the pulpit, and his lectures "dwelt on pastoral duties, of which he knew so much from his own experience."[103] As a preacher

> he was plain, and always aimed to be understood. . . . Dr. Rice had the power of going down to the level of his audience so as to be understood by all. The common people heard him gladly. But in his preaching he never used slang words, never told anecdotes to cause a sensation or provoke a smile. He had no clap-trap device to attract and stir a crowd.

Classes met Tuesday through Saturday, and the times seem to have varied week by week. There were no individual books; all reading assignments were from books in the library, which had to be shared. Burwell remembers that the 300-page book for church history was particularly difficult reading. Learning Greek and Hebrew was basically memorizing vocabulary, and there would be daily recitations of what was assigned the day before. James Marsh taught Hebrew, while Rice taught Greek in the mornings, daily. Rice also lectured on New Testament three times a week, on church history twice a week, and on the confessions three times a week. This was the only theology course, and it took a year to cover the Westminster Confession.[104]

The admissions requirements of the new school were minimal, there was no charge for instruction, and there were no grades, diplomas, and graduation.[105] The Plan of the Seminary specified only that every student admitted be "of good moral character, and of full communion in the church of Christ." In addition, students must possess a diploma "from some college of established reputation, or wanting this, shall undergo an examination before the committee of the Board."[106] The Plan called for the presbytery to appoint the board of the seminary, and the board was responsible for hiring professors, raising funds, approving courses, maintaining facilities, making regulations for student conduct, and examining students at the end of the term.[107] In reality, however, it was Rice who admitted students, raised funds, maintained facilities, and conducted examinations. Graduates did not receive diplomas. Rather, according to the 1828 board minutes, "At the close of the third year the students who shall with approbation have gone through the whole course prescribed and shall have maintained a conversation free from reproach, shall receive a testimonial of Approbation signed by the president of the Board and professors."[108]

The Plan of the Seminary followed the plan approved by the Presbyterian General Assembly for the national seminary in 1811, with one important difference. Whereas the General Assembly supervised the seminary at Princeton, Hanover Presbytery was charged with "general superintendence of [this] . . . Seminary," which included hiring teachers, fund-raising, and "whatever may be necessary for its due regulation and prosperity." Although the presbytery was required to report annually to the synod and General Assembly, it was the presbytery who appointed the trustees: seven clergy and five laypeople in three classes. Yet the board was required to examine students at the close of each term, "see that the professors do their duty," and act as an admissions committee.[109] There is no evidence the presbytery-appointed trustees ever really fulfilled their jobs.

It quickly became clear that the planned relationship between the board and the school was unwieldy. The board had appointed an Examinations Committee on December 12, 1823, "to examine and admit into the Seminary any students who may apply for admission as directed in the plan of the Institution";[110] yet according to the minutes of 1828, members of the committee were usually absent or expended only minimal time examining students. Committee members did not want to fail anyone because they were afraid of offending the presbyteries. At the same time, Rice complained that presbyteries were sending unqualified students, and the board did nothing to see that they had enough training in music, reading, composition, and public speaking.[111]

Ironically, Rice's biggest challenge was keeping the presbyteries from stealing his pupils. After the first year, a student was eligible to "place himself under the care of the Presbytery of Hanover, or the Presbytery to which he most naturally belongs, in order to [obtain] his licensure."[112] The presbyteries, starving for ministers, enticed students to serve churches rather than return to the seminary after their licensure. Consequently, many students never returned to seminary after their first year, not because they failed or rejected their call, but because their presbytery offered them a full-time call. The school waged a constant battle to keep students in seminary for the entire course of study.[113]

Building an Institution

Although formal strategic planning is a relatively modern concept, it is clear that Rice had three primary goals for his school that would make it a viable institution for the future: first, become independent from Hampden-Sydney College; second, establish a consistent and dependable source of fund-raising; and third, build a physical plant.

Once installed Rice moved quickly to sever the seminary's formal connection with Hampden-Sydney: "We find it will not do to leave [the seminary] connected with [an institution] of a literary character. They interfere. Jealousies are excited. The Trustees of the College require more power over us than we think is safe to give." As long as Hanover Presbytery had supervisory control over the seminary and the college trustees held the money, the seminary would never control its own affairs. Rice planned to seek incorporation once again and convince Hanover Presbytery to return the institution to synod control, with an eye toward "paternal superintendency" by the Presbyterian General Assembly.[114]

Just as with the effort eight years earlier, incorporation was an immediate failure. The Commonwealth of Virginia was still too sensitive to its history with an established church, and the Virginia Constitutional Convention of 1829 flatly refused to permit the incorporation of a theological seminary.[115] Rice wanted incorporation so that the seminary could hold its own funds. Since incorporation in Virginia was not possible, Rice turned to the Presbyterian General Assembly so that his school would not be beholden to either college or presbytery.

Rice desperately wanted a secure connection with the General Assembly for two reasons. First, he wanted to ensure equality with the national seminary. A seminary was in the church's "common interest." As such, "the highest Judicatory of the church, ought to exercise a paternal superintendence over all such institutions. The whole church ought to help to build it up, and to keep it sound and healthful. . . . The Assembly [should have] such power over this School of the Prophets as that body can beneficially exercise." Second, and perhaps more immediate, was the hope that such a connection "would enable us to cover our money with their charter; and thus keep us independent of any mere worldly body of men." The Presbyterian General Assembly, incorporated by the Commonwealth of Pennsylvania, could act as trustees in place of a charter, giving donors confidence that their money would be managed properly and giving the seminary administration freedom of action.

While he was working on the legal means to hold funds, Rice needed to have sufficient funds to stay in business. There was very little money, not many students, no buildings, and even less privacy. On March 18, 1825, Rice wrote to Archibald Alexander:

> The State of things here is such that I have every thing to discourage me. . . . There is nothing like united, active exertion to build up this institution, and I often fear that the effort will fail. Had I known what I know now, I certainly would not have accepted the office which I hold. But now I have put my hand to the plough, and am not accustomed to look back. There is, however, a sea before me, the depth of which I cannot fathom, and the width such that I cannot see over it.[116]

The one bright spot was from some donors in New York, who provided funds for the Rev. Hiram P. Goodrich to assist in the fall,[117] but these funds were lost in the Panic of 1837.[118]

Perhaps alarmed at his friend's pessimism, Alexander visited Hampden-Sydney in June 1825. He preached at his former congregations, and Rice was able to collect $14,000 from donors in Charlotte and Prince Edward Counties for an endowed chair.[119] It was during this visit that Rice first revealed his goal to his friend: three professors, a hundred students, homes for professors, support by the Synods of Virginia and North Carolina (and South Carolina and Georgia if they would abandon plans for their small school), and General Assembly support.

Throughout 1824–25, Rice campaigned for the Synod of Virginia to manage the seminary. Although the synod was willing to supervise the school, Rice quickly found that Virginia Presbyterians were no more anxious to give money to the seminary than in Hoge's time. He continued to send letters to his northern supporters, appealing for funds. In 1825 he wrote to a friend in New York: "Do, my dear Brother, continue to pray for us; and urge all our friends in New York to do the same. We greatly need your prayers, and all the aid you can give us. Our people here are doing something; but they are feeble, and need encouragement."

Donations from the North, however, would not be a permanent solution to the seminary's financial needs. Rice had to "enlist all the churches of the state, and of North Carolina, in the support of the institution." In order to raise funds from Virginia and North Carolina, Rice claimed, it would be helpful to transfer the school "from the care of the Presbytery of Hanover . . . to the care of the Synod of Virginia, and afterwards, to place it under the jurisdiction of the two Synods of [Virginia and North Carolina]; and perhaps also of the Synods of South Carolina and Georgia."[120]

Union Theological Seminary in Virginia

In October 1826, after two years of speeches and meetings, the Synod of Virginia agreed to replace Hanover Presbytery in managing the seminary and overtured the Synod of North Carolina to join them.[121] Rice understood that Virginians could not support the seminary on their own and therefore intended to include North Carolina to lighten the burden. Joseph Caldwell presented an obstacle to Rice's plans.

Caldwell was born in Lamington, New Jersey, on April 21, 1773. After a strong Presbyterian-influenced education, he entered Princeton in 1787 at age fourteen and graduated in 1791. He began tutoring boys at Elizabethtown in northern New Jersey and studying for the ministry on his own. Then he returned to Princeton as a tutor in 1795 and continued theological studies under John Witherspoon, being licensed by the Presbytery of Brunswick the same year. In October 1796, Caldwell was elected professor of mathematics at the new University of North Carolina. He became its first president in 1804, resigned in 1812 to teach, assumed the presidency again in 1816, and held the post until his death in 1835.[122]

Caldwell envisioned the University of North Carolina as a citadel of learning for all knowledge. Like Thomas Jefferson, who designed the University of Virginia, Caldwell conceived his school on a quadrangle. Unlike Jefferson,

Caldwell wanted science buildings on one side and philosophy and theology buildings on the other. Whereas Jefferson rejected religious influence, Caldwell wanted each denomination to have its own building flanking the quad. The North Carolina legislature did not approve of his plan,[123] but Caldwell still wanted the Synod of North Carolina to establish a seminary at his university.

Rice knew Caldwell's plans would limit the influence and support of his seminary and so began cultivating members of the Synod of North Carolina. He was assiduous in courting the North Carolinians "for the purpose of awakening an interest . . . in our Seminary."[124] Rice attended meetings in Greensboro and Charlotte, urging North Carolina Presbyterians to share in the election of trustees for his Virginia school.[125] On August 29, 1826, he invited the Rev. Samuel L. Graham to meet him at Charlotte. He argued that if both synods established their own seminaries, neither school would be strong, but "if the brethren of North Carolina will but drop local feelings, and come into the plan, we may have a Seminary that will do honour to the Southern churches, and exert a mighty influence in building up the kingdom of the Redeemer."[126]

John Holt Rice and Joseph Caldwell appeared before the Synod of North Carolina with their respective plans in November 1826, soon after the Synod of Virginia accepted control of the seminary. Caldwell presented his case, but Rice had outflanked him; there were only two dissenting votes in supporting the theological school at Hampden-Sydney.[127] Rice's letter to Alexander on November 14 was generous but triumphant:

> The proposition made to the Synod of Virginia was unanimously adopted; as I hear, with great good feeling. That to North Carolina had several difficulties to encounter, Dr. Caldwell, who has more influence than any other man in the state, had set his heart very much on having a Seminary in North Carolina. He is a very able opponent. The subject was debated for two days. At length the Doctor yielded. When Dr. Caldwell found that the majority was against him, and felt that he was totally defeated, instead of showing offended pride, he yielded with all the grace of a gentleman and a Christian. He certainly raised himself much in my estimation and affection.

If North Carolina had not accepted his plan, Rice would have resigned.[128] Instead, he had succeeded: his school had become a separate institution with its own fund-raising base.

Although it is unclear how the name of the new seminary was chosen, William Henry Foote argues that Rice wanted a name symbolizing North Carolina's and Virginia's equal commitment to the school. In speaking with individual members of the Synod of North Carolina, Rice assured them that the seminary would not be a "Virginia" school, but an institution of both states. The best way to avoid showing partiality to either state and to give both synods the pride of ownership would be to bind them together in the name of the school. Thus "The Theological Seminary of the Presbyterian Church under the care of the Presbytery of Hanover" was renamed "The Union Seminary of the General Assembly under the care of the Synods of Virginia and North Carolina."[129]

When South Carolina and Georgia declared that they would support their own institution, rather than join with North Carolina and Virginia, Rice was disappointed.[130] Still, he was sanguine that the "South Carolina plan" would fail.

"Any who try the experiment," he predicted, "will find that to build up a Seminary is not so 'easy a job,' and experience of the difficulties will change views and inclinations of many who have set out with high hopes, and great ardour."[131]

With the new arrangement, the Presbyterian General Assembly assumed boardlike control by managing the permanent funds and reserved the right to veto the appointment of any professor or trustee, to dismiss any professor who taught a doctrine contrary to Presbyterian standards, and to appoint visitors. Hanover Presbytery was required to report annually on the condition of the seminary.[132] The seminary's funds were removed from the college trustees. The General Assembly did not have power to originate administrative measures for the operation of the school, but it had the power to ensure the seminary's orthodoxy.

If the establishment of the theological school in 1812 came out of the desire for the Synod of Virginia to organize ministerial education, the refounding in 1823 had the effect of enforcing orthodoxy. Whereas Hoge had taught for three years without supervision, Rice had a board from the start, and he sought General Assembly oversight. Hanover Presbytery was to inspect the faculty for orthodoxy and report to the synods. Professors were required to present an "Exhibition of the System" they taught. Hoge had not conducted regular classes, but gave his students books to read and then examined them. Rice set class schedules and wanted professors to give regular, expert instruction.[133] Thus the "union" of the Synods of Virginia and North Carolina was not only evidence of John Holt Rice's political acumen and vision; it also set the outlines of future instruction and management.

On April 30, 1827, Hanover Presbytery accepted the General Assembly action to take control of the school. The presbytery, however, asked that the permanent funds remain in the state of the institution for which they had been raised. The General Assembly accepted the reservation about the location of the funds that May.[134]

After creating a place to hold seminary funds, Rice had to raise those funds. Perhaps because of his business experience, or his time on the Hampden-Sydney College board, or as agent for the theological library—financing was never far from Rice's thoughts; nearly every letter from 1824 until 1831 involves raising money. But Rice did more than just fret. In July 1825 he hired Robert Roy from Nottoway as the agent, or professional fund-raiser, for the seminary. The strategy was simple; Rice would continue to travel in the North, while Roy would travel around the South.

> He is going on the plan of finding first in the South, and then elsewhere, fifty men who will bind themselves each to pay one hundred dollars a year, for five years. He is also to find one hundred men who will agree, each, to pay fifty dollars a year for the same period. This will endow two professorships. Besides this, he carries a third paper on which he receives subscriptions and donations for any sum from two hundred and fifty dollars down to twenty-five cents. On this plan our agent has already obtained about eight thousand dollars.[135]

Robert Roy was effective: through his efforts the financial aspect of the seminary became secure for the first time. According to Burwell, Roy's "activity and energy and his pleasant manners accomplished much in a short time, but the personal influence of Dr. Rice was more effective. A gentleman used to say that Dr. Rice held the sheep while Rob Roy took the fleece."[136] By October 1825, Rice could report, "Mr. Roy still goes on successfully."[137]

Seminary and College Part Ways

With adequate funding, Rice could finally begin to construct buildings. From the day of Rice's arrival until his death, relations between the college and the seminary were uneven, at best. At first, Rice and Cushing were close. It was Rice who had persuaded Cushing to go to Hampden-Sydney and wrote a letter recommending him for the teaching position at the college in 1817. Cushing gave up his house for the Rice family and for seminary classroom space and persuaded Martin Saylor to give 4 ⅜ acres for the site of the seminary in December 1823.[138] Just as the college and the seminary had different goals, however, so Cushing's and Rice's interests diverged into inevitable conflict. Cushing believed Rice betrayed him when Rice supported Jefferson's efforts to receive funding from the state legislature for the University of Virginia in 1824, while Hampden-Sydney got nothing because of its church affiliation.

The land on which the seminary building was built was "hallowed ground" for Rice: that plot was where Hampden-Sydney students had gathered to pray during the 1787 revival.[139] He also wanted to purchase a site from Cushing for a professor's house, but Cushing would not sell unless the seminary would buy the entire tract of land. Rice was offended because he felt that Cushing was trying to take advantage of the seminary. The Rices moved out of Cushing's house after only eighteen months, moved into the recently completed first floor of the seminary building, and remained there until their house was finished in 1829.

At the end of 1827, the seminary board instructed Professor Hiram Goodrich to buy the bell currently used by the seminary, but owned by the college, for fifty cents a pound. Cushing wanted more money, and the fruitless negotiations dragged on for more than a year. After talks finally broke down, the seminary board instructed Goodrich to buy a bell in New York, at a price not to exceed $55. The bell was finally installed in 1830.[140]

Out of all this friction, a consciousness developed that the seminary and college were two separate institutions.[141] Indeed, when James Marsh left Hampden-Sydney to become president of the University of Vermont in 1826, Cushing and Rice agreed that there would be no more faculty appointments between schools.[142] But frustrations remained; the Hampden-Sydney board was so irritated that in 1829 they asked the seminary to move to another location.[143] The seminary board rejected the idea as "injurious to the welfare of the seminary and a violation of good faith to its benefactors: and that it deem(ed) it not expedient to regard it as a subject of future consideration." The seminary remained at Hampden-Sydney College for the time being.

It would not be until April 1831, five months before Rice's death, that the Hampden-Sydney trustees would deed any property to the seminary, and the deed was not recorded until 1887. The deed was important to the seminary's future. Without a charter, Hampden-Sydney College, which still owned the land, also legally owned the structures thereon, which included the Seminary Building, Boston House, North Carolina House, and their outbuildings.[144] This was an emotional point for the seminary; with Cushing's help, Rice had laid out the plot for the first seminary building (now the college's Venable Hall).[145] Dabney Crosby, who is believed to have worked with Thomas Jefferson in creating the University of Virginia, designed and supervised the construction of the first wing of the seminary building. The rest of the original seminary buildings (present-day Penshurst, Middlecourt, and the rest of Venable Hall at the college) were built by Reuben and John Perry, who also built Monticello, the first buildings of the University of Virginia, and Jefferson's retreat at Poplar Forest.[146]

Building a Seminary

Rice not only knew how to raise funds; he also knew how to get around the presbytery. In August 1824 the presbytery approved a plan for a 50-x-40-foot *one-story* wooden building with basement, purposefully designed as the east wing of a future building. At a called meeting later that year, Rice convinced the presbytery to enlarge the original plans to a 40-x-38-foot building with *two* stories.[147] Disregarding his previous presentation and ignoring the need for further presbytery approval, he promptly ordered that the new structure be built with brick instead of wood and expanded the plans to make a 52-foot wing. So instead of spending $5,000, Rice spent over $6,000, and eventually $8,000, and got a building with two stories.[148] Hanover Presbytery responded by criticizing him for building large buildings so that he could entertain lavishly.[149] He shot back in a letter to Samuel L. Graham, a member of the board from North Carolina: "And why should not the Board, in boldness of faith, take a high ground, and enter into large plans of operation without delay? In this age, great enterprises which fill the mind, and excite a powerful interest, succeed; while little timid schemes fall through."[150]

Despite the presbytery's grumbling, construction proceeded. The first floor of the seminary building was completed in August 1825, and the Rice family moved in immediately. Classes were held with about ten students while the second story was completed. Student Benjamin Mosby Smith was impressed with the new building, although it was basically just one large room serving as chapel, lecture room, and library with about five hundred volumes.[151] When the two-story building was completed in July 1826, the books were moved to the hallways.[152] In his junior year, Smith "had already developed that interest in libraries which he was to display during the long period of his professorship at the Seminary; . . . in spite of [the] pressure of his other activities, [he] spent much time and hard labor in arranging and cataloguing the library."[153]

The original campus at Hampden-Sydney is a road map of Rice's fundraising trips and his belief in a united church set in brick and wood. By 1830 its outline was complete. The first house built on seminary property, where John and Anne Rice ultimately made their home, was called "Boston House" (present-day Middlecourt on the Hampden-Sydney College campus) because the funds used to build it came entirely from Massachusetts.[154] Boston House also included a cottage for Rice's slaves (present-day Coleman Cottage).[155]

The second house was "North Carolina house" (present-day Penshurst). This southern school would be supported by the entire church working together. The Seminary Building (present-day Venable Hall), with library, chapel, lecture rooms, and professor's residence, was completed in 1830. The road between the seminary and college campuses became known as the Via Sacra. Rice envisioned a seminary campus with a main building that would house 100 students and contain a library, a chapel, lecture rooms, and living spaces for three professors.

Although buildings were going up, money was always a pressing concern. Rice spent a large proportion of his family's $20,000 fortune, mostly from his wife, supporting the seminary.[156] He appeared to have some problems in keeping his personal funds separate from seminary funds and keeping endowment accounts for buildings and faculty separate. Rice's financial difficulties and perhaps an effort to avoid the appearance of impropriety[157] caused him to sell his library to the seminary in 1824, for $8,000.[158] In June 1827 he complained, "I have sacrificed my little estate . . . so that I have found it very difficult work to live through the year." He then pleaded, "If some one could be prevailed on, by a donation of ten or twelve thousand dollars, to fill up the partially endowed professorship which is now affording me 'half' a living, it would be a relief from present embarrassment, of the most important character."

Although the "New York professorship" was fully endowed by January 1828, Rice's trips to the North apparently caused him problems with his constituency. In a letter in the same month, Rice related, "One excellent brother told me that he suspected me for being too much of a Yankee." For raising money the next month, Rice had to defend his decision to go to New York rather than Charleston. He argued that by going to New York (by way of Baltimore and Philadelphia) he had raised "somewhere between thirty-five thousand and forty thousand dollars." He knew where he could find the money he needed: "I do not know what would have been the result if I had gone to Charleston."

Northerners, though, could be as difficult as anyone else. In a letter dated March 31, 1829, Rice replied to a letter sent to him by B. B. Wisner and John Tappan. They had been helping Rice raise money in Boston and reported that they were having difficulty collecting subscriptions pledged on Rice's previous trip. All Rice could do was lament:

> When it was known that I had ventured to make this contract, the people who knew my circumstances, asked me on what I relied to raise the money. I replied "on the faith of my friends in Boston—their promise is as good to me as money in the bank, to be drawn next June." Now, in the present state of things, I would not, for the value of the money, have it known that I was disappointed in the confidence placed in the Boston people.[159]

Fund-raising may have been made more difficult because doubts persisted about the South's willingness to support a southern seminary. Throughout 1826 and 1827, Rice wrote letters and articles defending southern seminary education. In 1826 a letter sent to the editor of the *Literary and Evangelical Magazine*, signed only by "Iota," complained that there were seminaries at Princeton in New Jersey, Auburn in New York, Prince Edward County in Virginia, Maryville in Tennessee, Western Theological Seminary in Pittsburgh, and two planned for

South Carolina. Iota argued for one national seminary to counter "local feel-ings."[160] Rice countered by arguing that one seminary could not supply enough ministers for a growing population.[161] And for those who doubted the scrip-tural authority for a seminary education, Rice reminded his readers that Scrip-ture does not forbid an educated ministry. The apostles taught, and there were schools of the prophets.[162]

Rice also had to remind his readers that college and seminary were not the same. Hampden-Sydney was a "Literary Institution." Union Seminary was "in every way separate and independent" from the college and therefore needed help "to place this Southern Seminary on anything like an equality with North-ern Institutions."[163] It was a tough sell.

> The great difficulty heretofore has been to waken the interests of Southern Presbyterians and induce them to cooperate. . . . We have enemies to encoun-ter, and opposition to put down in the South. Infidels and Sectarians are very jealous of us, and watchful against us. . . . I am more than ever convinced of the importance and necessity of our institution. The South needs it greatly, and it must be built up. . . . Our Seminary is the only one South of Princeton, between the Atlantic and the Pacific. . . . We therefore feel that we have the claim which brotherhood gives us, on all who love the Presbyterian church, and the cause of the Redeemer in this land of desolation.[164]

Rice did have some support. On June 1825, Hanover Presbytery called on "Southern Presbyteries" to cooperate . . . in building up and supporting this institution,"[165] and Orange Presbytery recommended that the seminary receive its support.[166] The presbytery also appointed an agent (probably Robert Roy) to visit the Synods of North Carolina, South Carolina, and Georgia.[167] In the fall of 1829 the Presbytery of Winchester established the second endowed scholar-ship, worth $2,500, called the Winchester Scholarship, and named the recipient. This is the first evidence of concrete support from west of the Blue Ridge.[168] In 1829, Rice tried for one last time to appeal to the Synod of South Carolina and Georgia, but they rejected his offer in the fall of 1830.[169]

The Plan of Study

No document better illustrates Rice's thoughts and goals than the so-called Plan of Study. Drawn up for the board of trustees in 1827 by Rice himself, it was published in the *Virginia Evangelical and Literary Magazine* in 1828 and is also in the board minutes. Recognizing that not everyone still supported the idea of a seminary, the Plan began with a civil and social justification for an educated clergy. Rice argued that "religious teachers" can enforce the "obligation of jus-tice," "strengthen the authority of civil law," and "secure the peace and order of society."

Many times Rice asserted that an educated ministry is necessary for the church. "It is not sufficient, however, that the preacher should know, and be able to state what religion is. He must also be able to prove it—but this he cannot do, by retelling his own experience." A minister must be able to prove "the true meaning of the Bible" and teach the doctrine that "Christ taught his apostles." Rice accused Roman Catholics of taking Scripture away from the common people, which the Reformation then "restored." In turn, modern scholarship "bound and hid" the Bible "by Theology closer to philosophy than Scripture." Therefore, "the Bible is to be in the Union Theological Seminary, the great subject of study; and the only source of authority." And in order to achieve a correct understanding, the Bible must be studied in the original languages.

> The Professor of Christian Theology, then, has two [*sic*] great duties to perform: 1st, By a careful induction to establish the theological facts recorded in the Bible, 2d, To give them a clear scientific arrangement. . . . 3d, But . . . it is entirely proper that the professor in this department should present a distinct analysis of [the] Confession, that the student may compare the received doctrines of the church, in which he expects to minister, with the Bible, which alone has authority to bind the conscience.

Just as in the Book of Discipline (1560), the Presbyterian General Assembly's Plan of 1811, and Hanover's seminary Plan of 1824, Rice mandated the five traditional parts of the curriculum: Greek and Hebrew, "Sacred Criticism" (biblical interpretation), Theology (basically the confessions), Ecclesiastical History, and Church Government (polity). Rice also wanted some additional subjects in his curriculum: singing, writing, and public speaking. In a report to the board, he made the case for music:

> Through the whole Southern country, sacred music is very much neglected; and the value of it, as a means of doing good, is greatly underrated. . . . It is very important, then, that candidates for the ministry should cultivate their voices and acquire skill sufficient to enable them to perform well a service. . . . It is therefore recommended that the Board pass an ordinance, requiring every student in the Seminary, unless prevented by physical impediments, so to study and practice singing, as to be able to lead the tune, when called on to pray in the chapel or lecture room.[170]

Adding music to the curriculum, however, was a short-lived experiment. In 1829 the Examinations Committee recommended that composition, reading, and public speaking be stressed.[171] But music was asking too much:

> It is difficult to convince those who have little or no taste for music and who have never felt its power, of its importance as an instrument in the hands of a preacher of the gospel [for] doing good. A society for singing has indeed been formed; and has during the greater part of the session been kept up by weekly meetings. But only a small part of the students have attended; and it cannot be said that any general improvement has been made.[172]

The Plan called for four professors: one in Greek and Hebrew, one in biblical literature (exegesis), one in Christian theology, and one in church history and polity. There were no electives, and the Plan set a course of study that any Union student would recognize. First-year students took Greek and Hebrew, biblical criticism ("Classes and Character of Manuscripts and Rules for ascertaining the True Readings"), biblical literature ("History and Character of those Books" and "Sacred Geography"), and biblical interpretation ("Practical

Interpretation of the Hebrew and Greek Scriptures, with daily Recitations and Monthly Reviews").

Second-year students would take Christian Theology in two parts: Natural Theology ("The Existence and Attributes of the Deity" and "Nature of Man, and his Duties"), Revealed Theology ("Evidence that the Bible is the Word of God, with an answer to the various objections of Infidels of all classes"), analysis of the Confession of Faith, and pastoral theology ("including the composition and delivery of sermons, and the other duties of the Pastoral office").

Third-year students would take church history ("History of Theological Doctrine" and "History of the External form of the church"), church polity ("the Principles of Ecclesiastical Polity"), and rhetoric ("Exercises in speaking, and composition, according to the discretion of the Professors").[173]

By 1827, Rice was feeling better about the prospects for the seminary. On November 26 he wrote:

> We are going on with increasing prosperity. There are now twenty students in the Seminary. Two more are expected to arrive every day, and others after a while. Our influence is extending. We have got full hold of the hearts of ministers in the "Valley" and reach into the state of South Carolina. If we go on this way, the Lord will get to himself a name, and a praise in this Southern region.
>
> Our students too are in a fine spirit; they are growing in holiness. I hope a revival is beginning among them.
>
> Our Board has met from Virginia and North Carolina. It was a lovely meeting. Every thing as kind and fraternal as could be wished. And they went home praying for us, and feeling more than ever.[174]

The 1827 board meeting voted to enlarge the seminary building. The 1827 Synod of Virginia meeting acknowledged the "New York" professorship and voted to consider hiring another professor.[175]

Union Becomes a National Seminary

On his preceding trip to the North, Rice had raised $30,000 in New York, enough for the endowed chair, $10,000 in Philadelphia, and $20,000 in Virginia.[176] But Rice understood that more was needed. He left Hampden-Sydney in May 1827 for the Presbyterian General Assembly meeting in Philadelphia and continued onward to New York, Albany, and Troy. On this trip Rice began to complain about asking for money: "Being a beggar goes strongly against my Virginia feelings."[177] For the first time, apparently, he did not meet his goal. Although he reported to the General Assembly in 1828 that he had $75,000 in subscriptions,[178] he had to return to the North in December 1827 to collect overdue money.[179]

As Rice saw it, whatever problem there was with fund-raising was due to division within the church, not dissatisfaction with the seminary. Throughout his trip he reported that people wanted to know if the new seminary would follow Auburn or Princeton, or the New Englandism of Old Presbyterianism.[180] Rice condemned this newly emerging partisanship: "I will acknowledge as brethren those who love the Lord Jesus, of all parties, and I will cooperate zealously and heartily with any who aim to promote the truth as it is in Jesus."[181]

By 1828, two professorships were fully endowed: Rice's chair in theology and the "New York" chair in Oriental Languages. These professorships were the core of his design to succeed where Hoge had failed. Rice believed that Hoge was burdened by his teaching and administrative load. The Plan called for a division of labor so that one man would not be burdened with administering an entire seminary; an agent would raise funds while three professors would teach. But Rice had to be politically astute lest his hiring decisions alienate his constituents. As a consequence, he purposefully selected Hiram Goodrich, of Albany, New York, and a graduate of Andover, to be the professor of Oriental Languages and librarian[182] because Rice thought a New York man should fill the New York professorship. After all, he reasoned, "Why should we not add a fourth professorship; and let it be the professorship of South Carolina and Georgia; and let that Synod appoint their man."[183] By the time Rice died, he would have subscriptions in hand for a third professorship, church history and polity, which was filled by Stephen Taylor from Massachusetts in 1835. By 1829, in the pages of the *Literary and Evangelical Magazine*, Rice could boast that the Plan of 1827 was in place.[184] There were two professors, Rice and Goodrich, and the full curriculum was taught on a regular schedule. Moreover, under the care of Goodrich, the library began to function.

The Library

In 1827 the seminary's board of trustees appointed a Library Committee "to inquire into the present state of the Library, its preservation and increase." That same year, Rice and Goodrich arranged the books with a three-letter arrangement—one letter for the alcove, one for the case, and one for the shelf (such as A-D-I). The alcoves were intended to hold subject matter together, and the cases were ordered by more specific refinements. The letters A, D, and I can still be seen on older books in Union's collections, and many books show as many as three different locations over the years. In 1829 the library held more than 2,000 books, though it lacked many standard reference books. Fines totaling $1.75 were collected that year. The board voted to hire a student librarian, who should be paid "not more than 50 cents per hour." For Goodrich, the responsibility was considerable, and personal: "The Treasurer is directed to charge the former librarian with the value of the books which were lost during his time of service."[185]

Enrollment

From the moment Hanover Presbytery voted to establish a theological library at Hampden-Sydney College in April 1806, it would be easy to summarize the history of Union Seminary as one of struggle. While it is true that institutional interests, financial needs, personal jealousies, ecclesiastical politics, and sectional feelings often collided, students were learning and creating a life together in the midst of it all. In 1828 the Examinations Committee reported:

> The Junior Class was examined on the Principles of Interpretation, the Greek Testament, and the Hebrew Language and Archaeology; the Middle Class on the Greek Testament, Biblical Theology, patriarchal and Jewish, and the Hebrew Language; the Senior Class on Systematic Theology and Ecclesiastical History. The entire course of study here pursued to prepare men for the ministry of the gospel, the sacred principle is incessantly and intensively indicated that the Bible and the Bible alone is the authoritative code of our religion. Your committee believes that in proportion as the Servants of God shall give honours not to their own theological systems and speculations but to the inspired Word, . . . his blessing will render effectual their labours for the destruction of heresy, the healing of divisions among Christians, and the conversion and salvation of a perishing world.[186]

Between 1823 and 1830 there were sixty-five students—all Presbyterian, except for three Congregationalists. Although students from Virginia and North Carolina predominated, there were students on campus from the West (Tennessee and Kentucky), from the North (six from Pennsylvania, three from New York, two from New Hampshire and Massachusetts, and one from Vermont), one from South Carolina, and one foreign student, from Scotland. While all graduates had a first call to a parish, their careers followed many paths. At least ten ended up working for tract publishers and temperance societies, and several became professors and principals of academies. Drury Lacy (1831) became president of Davidson (N.C.) College.[187] Isaac Cochran (1823), who hailed from Vermont and graduated from Middlebury College, was the first graduate to publish. In the 1830s he wrote *The Influence of Missions on Literature and Civilization.*[188] In 1849, William Spottswood White (1826) wrote *The African Preacher* about a slave preacher, Uncle Jack, and his ministry among the slaves of Nottoway County, Virginia.[189]

This decade saw the beginning of a wave of graduates becoming missionaries. Daniel Lindley (1831) became a missionary to the Zulus, serving with the ABCFM. John Agnew (1831) began his career as a missionary to the Indians. Stephen Foreman (1830), who was born in the Cherokee Nation in Georgia, spent most of his career as a missionary to the Cherokee Nation. The first graduate to become a foreign missionary was Thomas Johnson (1832), who sailed for Turkey in 1833, where he labored in Constantinople for twenty years. In 1834 three men and their new wives went to what was then known as the Transvaal Republic in South Africa.[190]

At the board meeting on July 12, 1826, the trustees voted to charge students "occupying rooms at Seminary" $12 annually as rent. In addition, each student would be charged $1 for using the library and be able to produce his receipt at the beginning of each session before being allowed to enter the library.[191] In 1827 the board was concerned that students get more exercise, perhaps by working in a vegetable garden, which was authorized in 1828.[192] At this same meeting, two students reported that they had spent $100 of their own money to furnish their rooms; they asked the board to repay them $40, and the board complied.[193]

Enrollment skyrocketed during Rice's tenure. He faced three students at his inaugural lecture, and by 1830 there were forty-one students enrolled. Near the end of his life he was concerned that the seminary was sacrificing quality for unqualified quantity by admitting underqualified students. In 1830 he reminded the board that it was not up to the seminary faculty to make up deficiencies in literature reading or science just because presbyteries approved all students.[194] And at this same meeting, in recognition of the burgeoning student population, the board hired a manager to handle boarding issues. This was the beginning of the intendant position. The intendants were usually students, and one of the first was Benjamin Mosby Smith.[195]

The first faculty meeting was held on December 23, 1828. The faculty (Rice and Goodrich) saw themselves as the seminary administration, so they decided on some general policies: chapel would be conducted by members of the senior class in rotation, the faculty would conduct evening prayer in rotation, classes would be held until Saturday at noon, and students would not be permitted to preach from a manuscript.[196] The faculty also functioned as the admissions committee, and the faculty minutes record all admissions, as well as students who did not return from the summer, and those who left in the middle of the year. At this first meeting, Rice and Goodrich decided that the admissions process would consist of requiring a written account of a student's religious experience, providing a certificate of church membership, and proof of educational qualifications.

The class schedule was set at the beginning of each yearly session. It was also recorded that professors were obliged to conduct examinations because the Examinations Committee did not usually show up. On November 18, 1830, Rice and Goodrich set the daily schedule: the bell would be rung at first light, morning chapel would be held at sunrise, evening chapel would be held an hour and a half before sunset, and Dr. Rice's clock would be the standard for time. Also, every student would be responsible for the fixtures in his room. In addition, they clarified an admissions requirement. Several prospective students had been denied admission due to "deficiencies" in Greek and Latin. Thus the faculty made it a policy that examinations would be given in Latin and Greek prior to admission.[197]

Student Life

It is difficult to imagine life in the early nineteenth century, let alone life at Union Seminary. Student organizations, however, offer us a glimpse. The Theological Society, which had continued meeting after the death of Moses Hoge, dissolved on July 4, 1823, after Rice accepted the call to the seminary. With a new professor finally on his way, the student members of the Theological Society apparently saw no need to continue meeting; moreover, they saw no need to compete with the Society of Missionary Inquiry. By 1824 the Society of Missionary Inquiry had become the student government, fraternity, and continuing education department all rolled into one. From its minutes and correspondence, a picture of student life emerges.

The minutes reflect the routine of ordinary life. The students formed committees to coordinate magazine purchasing with the Literary and Philosophical

Society of the college so that there would be no duplications. They complained that the other society was not contributing their fair share of candles and were misusing the reading room. In September 1826, Joseph Edie married, and the society expelled him as "unworthy."[198] The students took up collections for the ABCFM and advertised summer jobs for students with Bible societies in Prince Edward and Lunenburg Counties of Virginia and Granville County of North Carolina. At the end of the school year in 1830, there were accusations that the society's finances were "irregular." The SMI president appointed a committee, and the issue was resolved.[199]

Students shared Rice's attitude that Union would be a southern seminary serving a national church. The minute and correspondence books of the Society of Missionary Inquiry (SMI), a nationwide organization appearing on at least eight other seminary campuses, show that Union students wanted to participate in the wider world; they exchanged letters with other societies at Princeton, Andover, Ohio University at Athens, Auburn in New York, Western Seminary in Pittsburgh, and a new seminary in Columbia, South Carolina. They also subscribed to the *New York Herald*, the *London Evangelical Magazine*, and the *Cherokee Phoenix*, a newspaper published by the Cherokee Nation.

First formed on January 13, 1818, the SMI first met on Tuesday mornings, changing to Monday mornings in 1824. Formally, the society met once a month to conduct a debate. Informally, members seemed to have gathered every Monday morning to read letters and just talk. The practice of debate was canceled on November 19, 1821, and thereafter the president would ask members to write essays on specific topics to present at the meetings.[200] On December 15, 1823, the society welcomed John Holt Rice. "The meeting was attended by Rev. Dr. Rice, who made an appropriate and highly interesting [talk] on the subject of missions. On motion resolved that Dr. Rice, the Rev. Wm. Marsh, & Paxton be appointed honourary members of this society."[201] Rice seems to have attended about a third of the society's meetings during his tenure.

After grumbling about the length of the meetings, the society voted on February 4, 1828, that "no speech or essay prepared by order of this Society, shall be allowed to exceed fifteen minutes in length."[202] Limiting the length of speeches did not seem to work. One year later, on February 2, 1829, it was moved that students no longer suggest subjects on the floor; rather, a committee would preapprove topics. And one year later, the society voted to have one essay read at each meeting instead of two.[203]

The SMI's debates show a surprising openness. "Ought a missionary to preach up the peculiar doctrine of his sect, when itinerating?"[204] "Do the Scriptures justify us in believing that the Jews will all be Christianized and then restored to their original Country?"[205] Later the subjects were chosen by the committee: Revivals of Religion, Pastoral Labors, Foreign Missions, Domestic Missions, Education for Ministry, Sabbath, Temperance, Colonization, Prisons, Jews, Different Denominations of Christians, and the Cause of Seamen.[206]

Slavery

Although the subject of "Colonization" may seem innocuous, just one more subject among others, the reports on this subject reveal how the students, the seminary, and indeed the nation wrestled with the institution of slavery. Years before his students thought about the condition of African Americans, Moses Hoge struggled to make sense of and cope with a system that enslaved fellow human beings. He represents the conflicted social conscience that has marked Union throughout its history.

Although he did own slaves for a time,[207] Hoge's pietism ultimately led him to reject slavery. He had not owned slaves until he married his second wife, Susannah, in 1803. She had inherited several slaves after her first husband died and used them to work her farm in Charlotte County. Yet the couple quickly became uneasy with the immorality of slavery. They were disturbed by the deplorable housing slaves endured, how slaves were overworked, and the casual way slave families were ripped apart. They often spoke out against the abuse of slaves even when the offending owners were neighbors. They also used their own money to reunite slaves who had married and were subsequently separated.[208] Hoge sat with sick and dying slaves, was available to talk with them, and welcomed slaves into his home for communion.

Moses Hoge also took more public action. Sometime before 1810, he freed his slaves because, as his brother-in-law wrote, Hoge believed that "all were one family and the responsible subject of one God, he could not consent to hold them in slavery."[209] In 1817 he founded southside Virginia's only chapter of the American Colonization Society (ACS). The Society for the Colonization of Free People of Color of America, better known as the American Colonization Society, was founded in 1816 in Washington, D.C., in reaction to the 1800 slave uprising in Richmond, Virginia, known as Gabriel's Rebellion. The ACS wanted emancipated slaves and freed blacks returned to Africa. The society founded the colony of Liberia in 1821, with the capital city Monrovia (named after President James Monroe). Liberia became independent in 1847, but colonization was ultimately a failure: by 1830 only 259 freed slaves had been settled in Liberia.[210] Still, belonging to the society, especially in southside Virginia, was a liability; both Hoge and John Holt Rice were charter members of the American Colonization Society when it was founded in 1816,[211] and both were criticized for their liberalism.[212]

In 1805, Hoge's son James had moved to Ohio, a free state, because of his opposition to slavery. The father later wrote to the son: "My objections to the slavery of this country have always been strong & are becoming more so. . . . If you continue in Ohio, I wish your brother to settle there also; and in that case should my life be prolonged, I would wish to spend my last days in that country."[213] James's brother, Samuel Davies Hoge, settled in Ohio shortly afterward. Moses Hoge's grandson, Moses Drury Hoge, received slaves from his wife's estate and freed them. He also once bought five slaves, relatives of his hired servants, "whose position was uncomfortable," and emancipated them. His stepson, Thomas Poague Hunt, who graduated from Hampden-Sydney in 1813, freed the slaves he had inherited and devoted his life to promoting temperance and abolition.[214] Sometime between 1814 and 1820, one of Hoge's students freed his slaves after many months of conversation with his professor.[215]

The Theological Society first mentioned slavery directly in their debate on July 10, 1819: "Does fidelity require the ministers of the gospel in slave states to enjoin religious instruction to the slaves?"[216] Thereafter, slavery and colonization were constant subjects of debate and reports. Through these debates, students began to question the society in which they lived, tackling questions such as "Ought we to give every encouragement to the colonization society?" "Are we under greater obligation to evangelize native Americans, than foreigners?" "Do the Scriptures justify us in believing that the Jews will all be Christianized and then restored to their original Country?"[217]

Since there are no records reporting the resolution of the debates or copies of the essays presented, the society's correspondence gives the clearest view into the students' thinking. On April 9, 1828, in a reply to Princeton Seminary's SMI, which had apparently talked about slavery in their letter, the secretary crafted a reply "for the purpose of correcting some ruinous views sustained by many persons residing where this melancholy evil does not exist." The letter went on to argue that most people were "ignorant of the real state of things in the South" and immediate emancipation would be a disaster for the slaves because "the negroes are not prepared for liberty: It would intoxicate them and stand itself in deeds of uncontrolled and incontrollable licentiousness."

Gradual emancipation would not work either, the letter argued, because "while they retain the color of their skin, they can never [live] in the land of whites, be admitted to all the privileges of citizens. The free blacks are in a condition much worse than that of most of the slaves: many of the slaves themselves think so, and prefer their own situation." The only answer, then, was "the African Colonization scheme." The letter ended with assurances that slavery was not as bad as widely believed:

> With regard to the actual condition of slaves there is a mistake in the minds of many, who have formed them from partial and discolored information. Cruelty of treatment, stinted food, and merciless exaction of labor, are associated in the minds of many, with Virginia slavery. It cannot be denied that this is true in some cases. But these cases are to be considered as exceptions: for, in general, the negroes are comfortably clothed and fed, comfortably attended to in sickness and old age, and are given to do no more work than they are able to perform.

The secretary assured the students at Princeton that the slave trade was "regarded with detestation" in the South. He declared that since all sections of the country agree to condemn "the business of moving negroes from one state to another for sale," there was no reason for sections of the country to be divided on this issue.[218]

John Leith has argued that the theology taught by Moses Hoge, John Holt Rice, George Baxter, and Samuel B. Wilson was dedicated to preserving an unyielding Calvinism by rejecting the insights of science and the modern world.[219] This theology shaped and reinforced a unique cultural consensus. And it was the institution of slavery that defined this consensus and how the church would confront the culture.

From the moment the first slaves arrived at Jamestown, Virginia, in 1619, slavery defined American ethics. Although the Constitution prohibited the foreign slave trade after 1808, slavery was largely left up to the states. By 1804 virtually every state north of the Mason-Dixon Line and north of the Ohio River had abolished slavery. With labor-intensive plantation economies, southern states did not feel they could survive without slavery, and it became an integral part of the southern economy.[220]

Slavery was embedded into the fabric of southern life, including religious life. In 1765, for example, Briery Church (near Hampden Sydney in south-central Virginia) raised £308 to "purchase servants," who would then be hired out to raise money "to support the Gospel."[221] The church purchased three more slaves in 1768, six slaves in November 1774, and sold them in 1819.[222] Cumberland Church (also in south-central Virginia) owned approximately sixty slaves between 1774 and 1820, and it used the money made from renting them out to pay the minister's salary.[223]

Slave labor was part of college life; some students used their servants to pay off tuition. In 1784, Francis Watkins, a college trustee, hired out Agg, who belonged to his nephew Robert Watkins, a student at Hampden-Sydney, to Henry Jones for £20, which was the amount Jones charged Watkins for a year's board. The college used slave labor, hired by the steward, to cook and clean rooms. On January 1, 1803, the college trustees paid £14.19.3 for the hire of James Morton's slave. Around 1810 the college purchased a servant named William (Billy) Brown from Col. Daniel Allen, who later purchased his freedom from tips. By 1810, however, the college seemed to have decided to rent servants from slaveholders rather than purchasing slaves outright. A man named Lewis, who belonged to Jonathan Cushing, was rented from his owner for $10 per month in 1836.[224]

Although the subject of "enslaving the Negroes" was brought up before the Synod of New York and Philadelphia as early as 1774,[225] no action was taken until 1787, when the synod voted to "recommend in the warmest terms to every member of their body and to all the Churches and families under their care, to do everything in their power consistent with the rights of civil Society to promote the abolition of Slavery."[226] In 1796 the Presbyterian General Assembly declared that slaveholders should be admitted "to Christian communion" with those not owning slaves, but asked that all Christians "render the state of those who are in slavery as mild and tolerable as possible." In 1815 the General Assembly called for gradual emancipation.[227]

The statements issued by the General Assembly were vague enough to allow each individual to decide what to do. And since slavery was interwoven into society, local custom prevailed.[228] Thus in 1815, when George Bourn, a Presbyterian minister in Rockingham County, Virginia, demanded that the church expel slaveholders because slavery was theft, Lexington Presbytery could expel Bourn with no qualms. And when Bourn appealed to the Presbyterian General Assembly, the General Assembly could uphold the expulsion.[229] Three years later, in 1818, the assembly ended its indecisiveness and called for colonization: "We consider the voluntary enslaving of one portion of the human race by another as a gross violation of the most precious and sacred right of human nature; and as utterly inconsistent with the law of God."[230]

The issue of one human being owning another pricked the consciences of ordinary Christians. In 1799, for example, David Rice (John Holt Rice's brother) wanted the Presbyterian Church to prohibit members from holding slaves.[231] Since the prevailing southern culture would not contemplate abolition, many in the church found themselves in a dilemma. How could Christians care for souls and accept an immoral institution? The answer for many was to justify the current situation as temporary, advocate for education, and work for gradual emancipation with the aim of repatriation to Africa. Many in the church tried to preserve ecclesiastical peace by navigating between continuing the "particular institution" and immediate emancipation.

John Holt Rice and Slavery

John Holt Rice embodied the contradictions of living in a society dominated by slavery. During the eight years he was pastor of Cub Creek Church (1803–11, in Charlotte County, Virginia), Rice owned and used slaves he inherited from his wife's family to work his farm. He traded his slave named Randolph to the Cumberland Church for its slave Sampson. In at least one instance, he employed another man's slave. When Benjamin Mosby Smith arrived at Hampden-Sydney for college in 1825, he brought the family's servant, Wilson, to work at John Holt Rice's home to defray the cost of his room and board.[232] At the same time, Rice supported the ACS and tried to be a conscientious minister to slaves. His congregation at Cub Creek numbered 400 whites and 100 blacks by 1811.[233] Indeed, from 1806 to 1811 the Presbyterian General Assembly commissioned Rice to work with slaves. When a large portion of his black congregants were sold to a plantation thirty miles away, Rice made it a point to ride the sixty-mile round-trip to administer the sacraments to them.[234]

Rice knew the "particular institution" intimately from both sides and hated it. He published many articles denouncing slavery in his magazines, but there are two for which he is best known. He published "Thoughts on Slavery" in the *Virginia Evangelical and Literary Magazine* in 1819, and "The Influence of Christianity on the Political and Social Interests of Man" in the *Evangelical and Literary Magazine* in 1823. Rice was clear: "It is to be generally admitted that slavery is the greatest . . . evil which has ever entered the United States."[235] And in 1823 he lamented, "Would to God that I could enumerate among the achievements of religion, the universal and complete abolition of a practice so detestable and so horrid."[236]

But for Rice, immediate emancipation was out of the question, "and perhaps domestic emancipation will always be impracticable." He believed that the long-term goal should be repatriation of slaves to Africa because "we never can give them here rights of citizenship."[237] A prosperous colony in Africa could be funded from the sale of federal land: "a proportion of the money arising from the sale of those lands" could be used to purchase slaves for immediate return to Africa, blessing native Africans with the "arts, the religion, and the civilization of this country."[238] For Rice, religious instruction, treating slaves like human beings, and "manifesting a proper regard for their welfare" should be the policy of the country.[239] "We may for a season still hear the sighs of the captive and the clanking of his fetters," he grieved, "but they must cease. We will pray for it; we will labour for it."[240]

Rice believed he could persuade slaveholders to recognize their common humanity with their slaves and awaken masters to their Christian duty to educate and then emancipate human beings who were really their brothers and

sisters. This was not a job for meddling abolitionists but "a subject of great deli-
cacy and difficulty—a subject which ... demands most mature deliberation and
the wisest councils."[241] In 1816, writing in the *Christian Monitor*, Rice appealed
to patriotism for abolition:

> In this world, where all things are prone to deterioration, the worst of all doc-
> trines is, "that evil will cure itself." On the contrary we must make exertion to
> procure amendment. It is folly to delay. ... Let the attention of the people then
> be at once turned to this great matter; let the collected wisdom of the nation
> be brought to operate, ... and let us wipe away the reproach which rests upon
> us. He who will devise and carry into effect a measure of deliverance from
> this evil will deserve to stand next to the father of his country—the immortal
> Washington.[242]

In a letter of 1827, he declared: "I am most fully convinced that slavery is the
greatest evil in our country, except whiskey; and it is my most ardent prayer
that we may be delivered from it." But he was against quick measures, believing "it was not the design of divine inspiration to abolish slavery in a premature manner."[243] The answer lay in colonization:

> The existence of a prosperous colony on the western coast [of Africa], will
> of itself do more for the cause of emancipation, than all that any, or all of us,
> now can effect by speaking of [immediate abolition]. So fully am I convinced
> of this, that I deplore every movement that raises any thing like opposition to
> the [American Colonization] Society.[244]

If slavery was evil, and if the solution was not emancipation, the only
humane alternative was to combine support for colonization with the energetic
Christian education of blacks to prepare them for freedom. But for Rice, this
issue was not a matter for the church. Like most whites, Rice feared immediate emancipation, believing that slaves could not handle freedom and that
white society would be damaged if the slaves were freed. He believed the pulpit could prompt the consciences of slave owners to do the moral thing given
enough time.[245]

Rice never saw a place for the church in debating the slavery question. He
accepted that the slave was property and that the New Testament either sanctioned chattel slavery in the American South as comparable to classical slavery
or said nothing about it. When slaves are considered property and not human
beings in the fullest sense, Rice believed that the Christian ethical attitude
toward enslaved people should be one of benevolence in this life and the assurance of salvation in the life to come. To speak of salvation in this life would be
construed as supporting abolition.

> The reason why I am so strenuously opposed to any movement by the church,
> or the ministers of religion on this subject, is simply this. I am convinced that
> any thing we can do will injure religion, and retard the march of public feel-
> ing in relation to slavery. I take the case to be just this: as slavery exists among
> us, the only possible chance of deliverance is by "making the people will-
> ing" to get rid of it. At any rate, it is this or physical force. The problem to
> be solved is, to produce that state of the "public will," which will cause the
> people to move spontaneously to the eradication of the evil. Slaves by law are

held as property. If the church or the minister of religion touches the subject, it is touching what are called the rights of property. The jealousy among our countrymen on this subject is such, that we cannot move a step in this way, without wakening up the strongest opposition, and producing the most violent excitement. The whole mass of the community will be set in motion, and the great body of the church will be carried along.

Under this conviction, I wish the ministers of religion to be convinced that there is nothing in the New Testament which obliges them to take hold of this subject directly. In fact, I believe that it never has fared well with either church or state, when the church meddled with temporal affairs. And I should—knowing how unmanageable religious feeling is, when not kept under the immediate influence of divine truth—be exceedingly afraid to see it brought to bear "directly" on the subject of slavery. Where the movement might end, I could not pretend to conjecture.[246]

What came to be known after the Civil War as "the spirituality of the church" had deep and wide roots. "The evil," Rice argued, "was originally none of our own seeking, but was forced on us. We are not, then, under the impulse of a vague feeling of benevolence, to rush into measures equally ruinous to ourselves and our bond-men." Rice was persuaded that "slavery is lawful so long as necessity requires the continuance of it, and no longer." He feared that premature emancipation would be worse than slavery: "reason does require us to emancipate a people, whose emancipation would bring ruin on themselves and upon the whole society with which they were connected."[247]

Rice advocated a peaceful, middle way to solve the problem of slavery. He believed he could fashion a compromise that would result in both abolition and peace. He argued sincerely, "We are no advocates of slavery. God forbid that we should be." Rice earnestly declared, "We cherish the hope, we do most devoutly pray that the time may come, when such privileges as 'American citizens' enjoy, will be the portion of all of every colour on the face of the earth." But he was also apprehensive:

> It would be easy now to produce a feeling in the holders of this sort of property, which would bring back former [harsher] modes of treatment. It would be easy to excite a feeling among our bondsmen, which would render "recession" necessary as a measure of self-defence. It is most obvious that immediate emancipation would be madness. It would be turning loose on society fifteen hundred thousand lawless, ignorant, and depraved beings, who have never been accustomed to reflection or self-government. . . . We do, then, most earnestly entreat those who take a lively interest in this thing not to be rash; to use no intemperate expressions; to abstain from irritating language; and above all to make themselves well acquainted with the actual state of things, before they recommend particular measures for producing a total change.[248]

Colonization was seen as the only reasonable way to end slavery peacefully. Rice was not alone; in 1818 the Presbyterian General Assembly endorsed the American Colonization Society: "We recommend to all our people to patronize and encourage the society lately formed, for colonizing in Africa, the land of their ancestors, the free people of colour in our country."[249]

In 1787 the Presbyterian General Assembly only "recommended in the warmest terms . . . to promote the abolition of Slavery."[250] But in 1818 there was no equivocating:

> We consider the voluntary enslaving of one part of the human race by another, as a gross violation of the most precious and sacred rights of human nature; as utterly inconsistent with the law of God, which requires us to love our neighbor as ourselves, and as totally irreconcilable with the spirit and principles of the gospel of Christ.

Gradual emancipation, however, was the prescription to ensure the "safety and happiness of the master and slave."[251]

An Era Ends

John Holt Rice was traveling to raise money, supervising the building of a campus, teaching classes, writing articles, and participating in the leadership of the Presbyterian Church, the American Bible Society, and the American Colonization Society. The slavery issue seemed intractable, but his efforts and hopes for the seminary came to fruition in 1827. After months of politicking, Rice finally persuaded the Synods of Virginia and North Carolina to overture the Presbyterian General Assembly to "superintend" Union Seminary, which the General Assembly approved in May; the board voted to enlarge the seminary building, and Rice made two trips to the North, one in May and one in December 1827. Although he should have been elated, the exertion began to wear on him. On November 14, he wrote, "My labors are excessive, and I feel that I am sinking under them."[252]

Possibly in an effort to lighten his teaching duties yet still keep his students current, Rice had a hand in forming the Philological Society on March 1, 1828. This organization is unique, with its antecedents perhaps going back to the Theological Society of 1812–23. The Philological Society was organized "to investigate Subjects of Biblical Literature." The society met every other week "on Friday evening at early candle-lighting," and lasted "no more than 90 minutes." The president of the society would be "one of the professors in the seminary," and Rice and Goodrich assembled a list of topics for discussion, which was adopted at the first meeting. All Union students were members of the society.

Meetings were analogous to seminars: "Each meeting will have a presentation on a topic concerning Biblical literature. Students will be chosen on a regular schedule to write essays on specific topics and present them at the assigned meeting." Furthermore, "the essays shall be written on papers of the same size and quality and carefully preserved for the use of the society."[253] The Philological Society, then, was a seminar designed to supplement the biblical studies course taught by Rice, which may indicate that he was unable to teach on a regular schedule. Because the society met on Friday nights, Goodrich could fill in for Rice, and as long as the professors chose the subjects for research, Rice could be sure real learning was accomplished. Moreover, the Society of Missionary

Inquiry discontinued the practice of students choosing their own themes. On February 5, 1829, it assigned eighteen standardized subjects, much more detailed than previous topics and presumably also chosen by Rice and Goodrich.

Any Union student of any era would recognize the assignments. There were 112 questions on the docket covering Greek, Hebrew, and biblical criticism. A quick sample is revealing: An exposition of βασιλεία τῶν οὐρανῶν as it occurs in the New Testament.[254] An excursus on the phrase δόξα τοῦ θεοῦ, and a "philological dissertation" on the meaning of the Greek word αἰώνιον.[255] There were essays on the words χάρις,[256] δίκαιος, δικαιοσύνη,[257] דָּבָר,[258] נֶפֶשׁ,[259] ὑπέρ,[260] and an excursus on the phrase τὸ ποτήριον τῆς εὐλογίος ὃ εὐλογοῦμεν (1 Cor. 10:16).[261] There were essays on "Grisbach's Classification of the Greek Manuscripts of the N. Testament,"[262] "the history of the gospel of St. Mark, with a view to its interpretation,"[263] "a history of the translation of the Septuagint,"[264] and "the nature and use of the ancient Jewish Cabballa [Kabbalah]."[265] In the archives are three complete essays from the Philological Society: an exegesis of ἱλατήριον from Romans 3:25 (January 8, 1830), a "Critical Exercise" based on 1 Corinthians 11:10 (no date), and "On the Value of the Oriental Languages in the Interpretation of the New Testament" (November 26, 1830).

The minutes end on December 17, 1830. In September 1830, Rice had gone on a fund-raising trip to New York State and reported that he had caught a cold. Not wanting to cut his trip short, he returned by way of Princeton, Philadelphia, and Richmond, arriving at the end of November. He preached in College Church and then took sick on December 15; never able to leave his bed, he died on September 3, 1831.[266]

Hiram Goodrich made a simple entry in the faculty minutes for September 3, 1831:

> This evening at 9 o'clock, John H. Rice D.D. Prof of Theology was summoned to the eternal world. He has been confined by illness since the 15th of December 1830. His last hours, like his whole life, exhibited Christian thoughts and feelings of a high order. Almost the only desire exampled was that the "principles of the seminary might be maintained."

In a letter to the SMI chapter at Western Theological Seminary in Pittsburgh, the Union SMI secretary lamented, "Not only ourselves but [also] American Zion harken to mourn the death of a great and good man whom we loved and revered, and with whose life, not only the best interest but almost the very existence of this seminary appeared to be most intimately connected."[267]

The Threads of History

With the creation of Union Theological Seminary, John Holt Rice solidified the idea of an educated ministry in the South. The curriculum for a learned ministry had been defined fifty years earlier, and Moses Hoge institutionalized John Knox's curriculum in 1812; yet it was not until Rice's tenure that Union Theological Seminary made the ideal of an educated ministry permanent. He wanted the ministry to be on par with other professions and Presbyterian ministers to navigate between the extremes of deism and revivalism. From 1807 to 1820 about thirty students studied under Moses Hoge. While Rice taught forty,[268] only ten more, the way they were taught set the model of seminary education that predominates to this day: buildings and faculty in an independent institution, providing a professional education.

Even though the national church threw its weight behind Princeton Seminary, John Holt Rice saw room for Union Seminary on the national stage. Union would be a national seminary, but one that served the national church by providing ministers for the South. He collected a large part of Union's funding in the North, and northern students were enrolling. Union Seminary's first catalogue, released in 1830, is the publication of a national school. This catalogue contains a list of students since 1823, the towns from which they came, and their colleges—predominantly southern, to be sure, but with at least a third of the students from outside the South.

"Our Theological Seminary," Rice declared, "is not intended exclusively for the advantage of any denomination." Rather, "party zeal" would be "proscribed and banished from all its offices—the students are to be taught to distinguish between the essentials for the Christian religion . . . and the circumstantial about which there have been so many warm and fruitless debates." His seminary would welcome all Christians and encourage all ministers to cooperate. "We must hold to the great and precious doctrines of the gospel, and at the same time let little things pass for little things."

Rice called for the seminary to engage the world through evangelization, which called for cooperation with other denominations. Although he was proudly Calvinist and never thought of modifying the curriculum, Rice was determined to avoid "party zeal." He welcomed Baptist and Congregational students in fulfilling the Great Commission. A year before his death and after his trip to the North, John Holt Rice sadly noted that the Presbyterian and Congregational churches were further apart than ever before: "We are dividing, and disputing, and strengthening local feelings, and cherishing sectarian jealousies and letting sinners go to perdition!"[269] By stressing the commonalities among all Protestants and welcoming students of other denominations, he manifested his hope that seminaries could unite the body of Christ.

John Holt Rice tried to resolve the contradiction between Christian ethics and slavery through peaceful compromise. But the Revolutionary era was over. There would be no goodwill compromises or half measures on slavery. The alternative was to cope with the untenable assumptions of the "particular institution" by keeping the church from commenting on social issues, which would ultimately lead to war.

Rice believed Union Seminary would show the Presbyterian Church the value of theological education. When he accepted Hanover Presbytery's call as theology professor, support for a Virginia seminary was in doubt. Within three months after Rice died, George A. Baxter was appointed theology professor. The seminary was now seen as a necessity. Readers remember that Rice wanted Union Seminary to influence the Presbyterian Church and the theological world by producing faithful scholars. These men would combat "German" influence by writing lexicons and commentaries, systematic and pastoral theologies, and church histories that would explicate the Reformed tradition and make faith understandable in each generation. This aspect of his educational vision would have to wait for over a century.

Rice's legacy is the fact that the Presbyterian Church now expected its ministers to have a seminary education. When he began classes in his kitchen in January 1824, he faced 3 students. Seven years later, there were 47 students (20 of them from outside of Virginia and North Carolina),[270] 3 instructors, a substantial administration building, and 2 faculty residences. When he was inaugurated on January 1, 1824, the endowment was $10,000, with a contingent fund of $1,000; when he died, the endowment was $50,000.[271] The expansive vision that drove John Holt Rice to establish Union Seminary endures, but it would be challenged by sectionalism, schism, and war.

Chapter Four (1832–65)
Our Southern Zion

John Holt Rice died at the same time as the nationalism and conciliatory out-look that had defined the Revolutionary generation was fading out. Southern-ers and Northerners began to see themselves in a new light, with conflicting interests. While these divergent points of view could be analyzed economically, socially, and politically, the disintegration of the United States was rooted in the obstinate and unyielding positions on slavery. Rice's goodwill and impulse toward cooperation were overcome by calls for further repression and violence. The church, and Union Seminary in particular, instead of being an advocate for the simple humanity of all human beings and an agent of peace, became a foun-dation of intransigence and sectionalism. The hardening of political positions that led to war was foreshadowed by the Old School–New School split, which was led by George A. Baxter, Rice's successor.

Less than three months after the death of Rice, George Addison Baxter chaired the faculty meeting on December 10, 1831, "having commenced the duties of his office a few days since."[1] Seven months earlier, Thomas McAuley and John McDowell had been called to teach church history. McAuley refused the call, and McDowell had not been released by his synod.[2] Baxter, of Lexing-ton, had then been called as professor of ecclesiastical history, and the board appointed him theology professor upon Rice's death.[3] The new theology pro-fessor, as de facto head of the seminary, would go on to shrink Rice's expansive dream of Union as a national seminary into a regional school speaking to the southern church alone.

The Culture of Slavery

Rice had departed from Hampden-Sydney on his last fund-raising trip to the North in September 1830. He was weak, and his trip would not just be his last: it would also symbolize the end of the unified, post-Revolutionary era. States were deciding what laws they would obey. The Nullification Debates, deciding if South Carolina could declare the Tariff of 1828 null and void within its ter-ritory, began on March 9, 1830. The executive branch decided it could ignore the Supreme Court. Ignoring the court's order, President Jackson ordered the forcible removal of the Cherokee, Chickasaw, Choctaw, Muscogee-Creek, and Seminole people from their lands on September 27, 1830, beginning the Trail of Tears. Jacksonian America not only divided politically; it also morphed from a fragmented agricultural way of life to a crowded industrialized culture, where technology conquered distance. In 1830 there were no railroads in the United States; yet 3,200 miles of rails appeared by 1839. Regular transatlantic steamship travel began in 1838.[4]

For a moment it seemed as though the slavery question would be solved. William Lloyd Garrison began publishing *The Liberator* in January 1831, and his calls for abolition seemed to make some headway. The Virginia General Assembly inconclusively discussed the issue of emancipation in its 1831 session. The western delegates voted to end slavery, the eastern part of the state wanted to keep the status quo. Nat Turner's Rebellion, however, squelched any possibility of abolition.

On the night of August 21, 1831, Nat Turner, a slave who was also the foreman on a plantation in Southampton County, Virginia, gathered perhaps as many as seventy enslaved men from neighboring plantations. In a little over two months, they killed about sixty white people, mostly women and children. By the time he was executed on November 11, the notion of gradual emancipation had completely disappeared. The slave rebellion hardened attitudes. In 1827, Rice could deplore slavery as "the greatest evil in our country, except whiskey" and hold out hope for some type of calculated abolition. After 1831, however, all talk of emancipation in the commonwealth ceased. Slavery was no longer a problem to be solved, but an institution to be managed. For many in the South, slavery came to be seen as economically necessary, ordained by Scripture, and a permanent part of southern society.

Until 1831, slaves in Virginia enjoyed limited freedom of movement. After Turner's rebellion, the fear of insurrection resulted in the "Negro Codes," which constricted the lives of slaves and free blacks alike. In 1828 the Society of Missionary Inquiry could confidently declare a "favorable change of public sentiment," which would make gradual emancipation and colonization a peaceful reality.[5] By 1833, the society recorded:

> The Legislature of Virginia, fearing that it might lead to insurrections, passed a law to prevent coloured people from meeting together for the purpose of being taught or instructed any way except by licensed white men. To meet this difficulty the Synod of VA, at their last Sessions, authorized the Sessions of the churches under their care to license lay men to instruct the coloured people. Under this provision five or six of the students of this institution have taken license, and are engaged every Sabbath in instructing them; . . . we hope that it will be very beneficial to the slaves of our country.[6]

In 1833 the elders of Cumberland Presbyterian Church made a one-year appointment of two students from Union Seminary. Their assignment was "to give oral instruction to the colored population within the bounds of Cumberland Congregation."[7]

Even Sunday instruction for slaves was thought to be too dangerous; in class they might have the opportunity to conspire, and they might be tempted to learn how to read. Two years later the Society of Missionary Inquiry lamented that it was "a sad disappointment, but a painful necessity, not to provide religious instructions to slaves."[8] The seminary trustees were told that theological students could not conduct separate classes and worship services for slaves. Slaves could attend religious instruction only if the classes were held at "the regular services of their masters."[9] Rice's successor would reorient Union Seminary; Rice's vision of gradual emancipation would dissolve as Union supported the institution of slavery.

George Addison Baxter

George Addison Baxter was born on July 22, 1771, in Rockingham County, Virginia. His father was successful in business and local politics and served as an elder in the Augusta Church. George was the third child and second son; his father was able to hire good tutors to educate his eight children. His earliest memory was learning the catechism. George fell from a tree when he was about five and walked with a limp the rest of his life. Baxter attributed his lifelong love of books to his inability to play with other children. In 1789, when he was eighteen, he entered Liberty Hall, studied under William Graham, and tutored John Holt Rice (who was six years younger than Baxter).

While a student at Liberty Hall, Baxter made a profession of faith and sometime thereafter was licensed by Lexington Presbytery to preach. He apparently overcame a pronounced stutter as he preached at small churches in the mountains.[10] In 1793 he took charge of the New London Academy in Bedford, Virginia, and invited Rice to teach. After Rice assumed his duties, Baxter spent the next six months preaching in Maryland and Virginia, raising funds for his school, becoming well known throughout both states. In 1798 he was elected professor of mathematics at Liberty Hall and left Bedford for Lexington. When William Graham died a year later, Baxter became rector, overseeing the transformation of Liberty Hall into Washington College in 1813 and becoming its first president. During this time he also pastored New Monmouth Church.[11]

When Baxter chaired that faculty meeting on December 10, 1831,[12] he was an experienced educator and well-known churchman. He had received a DD from the University of North Carolina in 1812.[13] Baxter taught Samuel B. Wilson, who would later teach theology at Union, and Drury Lacy, who would become the president of Davidson College. He also taught the future president of Centre College, Kentucky; governors of Virginia, Mississippi, and Kentucky; senators of Kentucky, Mississippi, South Carolina, and North Carolina; and the presidents of Washington College and East Tennessee University.[14] His views on slavery were also well known. In the spring of 1818, before the Presbytery of Lexington, Baxter led the committee that argued against the Presbyterian General Assembly's pronouncement condemning slavery, maintaining that slavery was in accordance with Scripture.[15]

When George Baxter stepped into the pulpit at College Church on April 11, 1832, to give his inaugural address as Union Seminary's theology professor, he faced an apprehensive community. The economy, feeling the first effects of the Panic of 1832 (when President Jackson refused to renew the charter of the Second Bank of the United States and transfer federal funds to the state banks, causing 800 banks to close and unemployment to rise to 10 percent, the highest since the Revolution), was descending into recession and endangering the endowment. About half the students from the previous year had departed. Nat Turner's Rebellion and calls for abolition had created fear. The terms "Old

5. George A. Baxter, Professor of Theology, 1831–41

School" and "New School"—describing where each party stood on revivals, cooperation with other denominations, and slavery—were well understood, having been first used by the *Christian Advocate* in 1824.[16] Baxter anticipated the growing rift between the emerging Old and New Schools of Presbyterianism. Yet, instead of seeking to make Union Seminary an agent of reconciliation, he struck a partisan tone.[17]

He began his inaugural address by emphasizing the need for ministers. "Few parts of what may be called the Christian world," he declared,

> exhibit a more melancholy appearance of moral and religious destitution than can be found in the regions by which we are immediately surrounded. The two Synods connected with the Seminary contain within their bounds a population of about two millions—nearly one-sixth part of the whole population of the Union. The number of religious teachers, of all the evangelical denominations in this region, is entirely insufficient. There are numbers in almost every part of our country, who attend no church, and who hear no voice of salvation; and if there be none to break the bread of life, how shall the church of God be fed?

Yet instead of calling for more ministers, Baxter implied that it would be better for pulpits to be vacant than to allow ministers who would tolerate the creed of the church to be "broken up, or trampled under foot." Ministers, Baxter argued, must "study to promote religion, without exciting fanaticism."[18] The contrast was clear. John Holt Rice rejected partisanship: he wanted his students to be able to "hold to the great and precious doctrines of the gospel, and at the same time let little things pass for little things."[19] George Baxter saw his job as winnowing out the unorthodox.

For Baxter, revivals were at the heart of the problem, and he used the rest of his inaugural address to make his case. This emphasis is somewhat surprising. Baxter learned to preach and minister in a revivalist culture, and he was known as an emotional speaker. By the 1830s, however, revivals were becoming emblematic of an uneducated ministry and as incubators of abolitionism. Cumberland Presbyterian ministers, according to the Old School stalwarts, relied on the emotionalism of revivals because they themselves were uneducated. At the same time, the New School was becoming abolitionist; the revivalist emphasis on self-improvement and reform began to be expressed in calls for emancipation. In his inaugural address, though, Baxter did not mention the burgeoning antislavery movement, but presented his objections to revivals in purely theological terms. Baxter argued that revivalist theology was misleading because it was Pelagian, convincing the believer "to do every thing for himself" and so effect his own salvation. For Baxter, revivalist theology was nothing more than the old heresy of innovation: historical amnesia allowed people to see revivals as something new, unique, and positive. These innovations were a "cloud" that seemed like "the smoke of a cottage," but would only grow and destroy the church.

After Baxter stepped down from the pulpit, William Hill gave the charge to Baxter in much more conciliatory language. Hill challenged Baxter to produce "a new race of ministers" who would teach the orthodox faith for a new time. Baxter's job would be to hand on the "rich legacy from their fathers." Hill proudly noted that the southern part of the church was pure and united,

> while many of our northern brethren have acquired either an extravagant rage for innovation, or an indiscreet zeal for orthodoxy—[they] have been classed as belonging either to the new school or to the old school, and have become zealous partisans. . . . [While] we have stood aloof, and wondered and grieved at their indiscretion, . . . we have happily preserved the unity of the spirit in the bonds of peace.[20]

According to Hill, the "old race" of ministers failed because they did not address their times and misunderstood that not all parts of the creeds are essential. He admonished Baxter:

> Of all stupidity, orthodox stupidity is the most dreadful. It ought to be remembered that ice palaces have been built of orthodox as well as heterodox materials. And when the creed, which is but the handmaid of religion, is regarded [as] more real than religion itself, then the reign of high church and creed idolatry has begun.[21]

Hill charged Baxter to see to it that "our southern clergy" would not be drawn into the "vortex of contention." Whereas Baxter saw historical amnesia when it came to revivals, Hill saw that same amnesia when it came to blindly applying orthodoxy. "Be assured, my Brother, we have fallen on times other than the church of Christ ever saw before—The intellect of man has waked up to new activity. Old foundations are broken up, and old prejudices, and principles, and maxims, are undergoing a thorough and perilous revision."[22]

The tension within the church was manifest for all to see, and the theology professor at Union was in a position of enormous influence. The theology professor was the senior member of the faculty and the public face of the school. "Senior" was not defined in terms of age or length of service; the senior member was whoever occupied the faculty position in theology.[23] In this position, Baxter set the course for nineteenth-century southern Presbyterian theology. He argued that while Scripture is the infallible guide, the creed is the best exposition a fallible church could give of the Scriptures. Thus ministers must make the confessions the "bond of union" in their theological thinking.

Baxter and Rice were almost polar opposites. Rice was thin, and Baxter was heavy—almost three hundred pounds. Rice's lectures were almost conversational and usually related the material to pastoral duties, but Baxter's style of teaching was catechetical.[24] He would "kindly" cross-examine students "as a lawyer would cross-question a witness, until he made [the student] wind himself up completely and so discover his error."[25] Rice's preaching was plain and conversational, while Baxter was emotional. One student remembered Baxter's face "bathed with tears"[26] during a sermon. Students would also remember that "often in the midst of a logical passage, his cheek would flush, his face quiver, and great tears would flow down his manly face."[27]

In his inaugural address, Baxter observed that the church, as in the days of John Holt Rice, still faced a shortage of ministers. In 1816 approximately 540 pulpits were vacant throughout the church. By 1826, the number of vacant pulpits had risen to 860, and by 1830 the number of vacant pulpits had increased to 970. Some leaders considered these figures and declared that the Plan of Union was working; without cooperating with the Congregationalists, the scarcity of ministers would have been much worse. But others believed the Plan of Union was benefiting the northern Presbyterian and Congregationalists only.[28] Rice had supported the Plan of Union; Baxter saw the Plan of Union as the problem.

A New Provincialism

Baxter's focus was always on the South. He never went northward to raise money and consistently advocated the southern position on slavery. His views must have been well known; most of the northern students left when it was known he would be the theology professor.[29] Moreover, in 1828 Columbia Theological Seminary was founded in Lexington, Georgia (and moved to Columbia, South Carolina, in 1830), and undoubtedly attracted some southern students who would otherwise have journeyed to Hampden-Sydney. A southern partisan as theology professor and a competing seminary led to a precipitous drop in enrollment. There were 47 students in 1831, Rice's last term. Two years later, in Baxter's second year, there were 34, then 20 in 1835, and 38 in 1836, but only 22 in 1838.

Funding was an immediate concern; the Panics of 1832 and 1837 devastated the national economy and Union's endowment. The board had intended to hire a third professor by 1832, but the panic depleted the endowment and made the hiring of a professor impossible. In the summer of 1833, Baxter began raising funds; he did not go to the North, but spent his time in Richmond and Petersburg. Since Baxter's fund-raising was not as successful as anticipated, the board appointed both Baxter and Hiram Goodrich as agents of the seminary. Operating funds remained short, and in 1835 the board decided to pay them 5 percent of all money they collected. The board also found it necessary to borrow for the first time: $2,000 to pay off a contractor to finish a building.[30] By the end of 1835, Baxter and Goodrich had raised $7,000, which was enough to hire the third professor, and Stephen Taylor was elected the professor of ecclesiastical history and polity.[31]

In 1828, John Holt Rice had complained that people wanted to know if his seminary would follow Auburn or Princeton or the New Englandism of Old Presbyterianism.[32] Rice condemned this newly emerging "party spirit." But the "party spirit" was not due to theological categories alone; the church had not found a way to heal the festering sore of slavery. While Presbyterians first officially considered the "the subject of negro slavery" in 1774, the Synods of New York and Philadelphia, after "much reasoning on the matter," took no action. In 1787 the Synod of Virginia "earnestly" directed members of the church who held slaves to provide "such good education as to prepare them for the better enjoyment of their freedom." The General Assembly of the Presbyterian Church in the United States of America, at its first meeting in 1789, repeated the synod pronouncement on education and called for slaves to be allowed to purchase "their own liberty at a moderate rate." Presbyterians hoped that gradualism would "procure eventually the final abolition of slavery in America."[33] The Presbyterian Church took a stand against slavery in 1818, when the General Assembly condemned "the voluntary enslaving of one portion of the human race by another as a gross violation of the most precious and sacred right of human nature; and as utterly inconsistent with the law of God."[34]

Despite the indecisive pronouncements, the church began to choose sides, and the first hint of schism—along with the solidifying of the Old School and New School positions—came in 1826, when the Synod of Pittsburgh informed the Presbyterian General Assembly that they would not accept ordained ministers from other denominations who had not assented to Presbyterian doctrines. This was in direct opposition to the Plan of Union, negotiated in 1801. In addition, the synod noted with disapproval that some members were enthusiastically supporting voluntary benevolent associations, instead of church boards, as the vehicles for conducting the work of the church. The controversy simmered under the surface until 1830. On April 20, New School members, after their beliefs were belittled at a church meeting in Lynchburg, Virginia, withdrew and petitioned the presbytery to form their own congregation. Only one of the elders in the congregation remained with the Old School party.[35]

The seminary was not immune from the trouble beginning to roil the church. In 1834, Hiram Goodrich offered to resign as he faced accusations that he was not orthodox. Although a motion was made to accept his resignation, the board voted to affirm full confidence in Goodrich, and he withdrew the resignation.[36] Apparently some students had complained of a division within the faculty, but there are no extant records of any specific accusation against

Goodrich or divisions on campus. Yet it is not difficult to see where conflict lay. Baxter, Union's titular leader, was uneasy with the Plan of Union (of which Rice was so proud) and supported slavery. Goodrich, hired by Rice, was from New York. Stephen Taylor, who taught history, was also a Northerner and graduate of Andover, although he had taught school in Boydton, Virginia, and served congregations in Halifax County, Virginia, and in Richmond.[37]

In 1834, after a contentious debate, the Presbyterian General Assembly refused to abrogate the Plan of Union. In response, 2,075 commissioners signed "The Act and Testimony," deploring the "unchristian subterfuge" by which outside agencies attracted Presbyterian support and weaken the church. The signers then called for a preconvention meeting of all those who agreed, to be held before the next General Assembly in May 1835. The group that gathered before the 1835 assembly was composed of 47 ministers and 28 elders, representing 49 presbyteries, with no representatives from Virginia or North Carolina. This preassembly convention formulated a resolution to terminate the Plan of Union. The overture failed.[38]

Old School/New School

The "cloud" that seemed like "the smoke of a cottage" grew into a storm at the 1836 General Assembly. A Presbyterian minister in New Jersey was tried for heresy. The minister, Albert Barnes, was a popular Christian writer and had been ordained in 1825 in Elizabethtown, an area connected to the Tennents and the original log college. According to Barnes's accusers, his widely read *Notes on Romans* (1835) denied original sin and taught that humanity had to cooperate somehow in the atonement. During the course of the trial, it became evident that a great number of northern ministers not only supported Barnes's right to continue working within the Presbyterian Church; they actually agreed with him on many doctrinal issues.[39] Many in the church were dismayed; if the General Assembly could not find Albert Barnes heterodox and would not abrogate the Plan of Union, it seemed as though the polity and theological core of American Presbyterianism was being destroyed.

Baxter saw his opportunity to step forward as a national leader. He and members of the seminary board had been following national events; they were dismayed at the high level of support for the Plan of Union and began preparing for a denominational split. On April 12, 1836, the board passed a resolution recognizing that "apprehensions have been entertained and expressed that the Presbyterian church may be soon divided" and formed a committee to withdraw all seminary funds held by the General Assembly.[40] The next day the committee reported that all real estate held by the seminary was located in Virginia and North Carolina, $13,000 in bonds was held by the board's treasurer, $27,000 in stocks was held by the trustees of the General Assembly, and $11,000 for the New York professorship was held by Knowles Taylor of New York City.[41] Under the terms of the General Assembly trusteeship, the seminary could withdraw funds at any time as long as one year's notice was given to the Synods of Virginia and North Carolina. No further action was thought necessary.[42]

After the 1836 Presbyterian General Assembly, however, Baxter saw a division in the church as a foregone conclusion and took two actions that solidified his denominational influence. First, he secured his base. In September 1836, at the first board meeting after the 1836 General Assembly, he convinced the seminary directors to ask the General Assembly trustees to return (to Union) the stocks they had been holding for the seminary, even though John Holt Rice had placed these funds with the General Assembly in 1827 as an expression of confidence.[43]

Next, he employed his influence to control the General Assembly voting. He realized that if southern presbyteries did not attend the General Assembly and vote together, the New School would predominate. Throughout the next year he worked tirelessly to ensure Southerners would attend the 1837 General Assembly. When the Old School convention met prior to the 1837 General Assembly, they counted 120 commissioners from 65 presbyteries. Their goal was simple: to put an end "to these contentions which have for years agitated our Church." The New School had held a majority in the 1836 General Assembly, but Baxter made sure the Old School presbyteries were now in control.

George Baxter was elected the president of the Old School convention. With southern presbyteries strongly represented for the first time, Baxter was determined to turn the church his way. He was instrumental in the convention's resolution, which was designed to punish the New School presbyteries.[44] Moreover, if the assembly would not abrogate the Plan of Union, he was prepared to lead the Old School presbyteries to secede.[45]

When the General Assembly met on May 11, 1837, Baxter was ready with an Old School majority. By a vote of 143 to 110, the Plan of Union, in effect for 36 years, was abrogated, but during the debate Baxter realized that any measure punishing New School synods would fail. So on the evening of May 29, he rounded up the Old School delegates and masterminded another strategy. After three days of debate, by a vote of 132 to 105, the 1837 General Assembly dissolved the Synod of Western Reserve, since it was a product of the Plan of Union. The next day the General Assembly dissolved all the presbyteries created under the Plan of Union (Utica, Geneva, and Genesee—all in New York State),[46] all strongly New School in theological orientation and hotbeds of abolitionism.[47] The Old School accused the New School of an

> ever restless spirit of radicalism, manifest both in the church and in the state,
> . . . [transmuting] our pure faith into destructive heresy, our scriptural order
> into confusion and misrule. It has crowded many of our churches with igno-
> rant zealots and unholy members, . . . filling our churches with confusion and
> our judicatories with conflict.[48]

The historian William Warren Sweet declared: "No religious body ever took such measures to rid the church of what was considered heresy as did the Presbyterian body in 1837. Without hesitating a moment, four synods, and eventually 533 churches and more than 10,000 members and all their ministers and church elders were read out of the church by a strictly party vote."[49] In 1801, after working for passage of the Plan of Union, John Holt Rice had declared that he was pleased and delighted in witnessing how Christians cooperate. That plan was now anathema.

On the surface, the primary issues of the Old School–New School split were based on polity and theology. Many in the Presbyterian Church struggled to decide whether to support denominational missionary and educational boards or national voluntary societies. At the same time, legitimate doubts about the Plan of Union arose. In numerous instances, ministers who had been denied ordination in the Presbyterian Church were then ordained in the Congregational Church, and thus entered the Presbyterian Church through the Plan of Union. Ministers who had never subscribed to the Presbyterian polity and confessions were able to vote in presbytery. Some presbyteries in New York State that had been founded on the basis of the Plan of Union sent commissioners to the General Assembly who were not even ordained in the Presbyterian Church. Although the South was largely untouched by the Plan of Union, many Southerners viewed it as a "Trojan horse," introducing into the church "many who were unfriendly to its doctrines and government."[50]

From the official Old School point of view, the New School embraced revivals and interpreted the confessions more broadly, and its polity allowed and encouraged cooperation with interdenominational voluntary societies. New School Presbyterians saw themselves as combating the antiseptic logic of the Enlightenment and addressing the needs of the continuing westward migration in the United States.[51] Yet beneath the revivalism, the confessional liberalism, and the ethic of cooperation lay the real issue: the New School was absolutely in favor of abolition.[52] As a result, the New School remained largely a northern phenomenon; only 15 percent of its membership was in the South.[53]

The Old School adherents portrayed themselves as antirevivalist, but their main objection was how revivals were conducted. Revivals were the most important aspect of American religious life between 1800 and 1865.[54] Around the 1830s, Old School Presbyterians began to criticize revivals because of their lack of "comeliness and decorum."[55] Presbyterians valued "orderly, learned, and reverent" worship.[56] Old School Presbyterians believed that orderly revivals would reinforce a strong Calvinistic theology, which would call attention to the need for an educated ministry and not interfere in the institution of slavery. Orderly revivals were emblematic of an orderly church. If revivals got out of control, then the revivalist notion of personal perfectibility could lead to the notion of a perfect society, which could lead to abolition.

The word was rarely mentioned, but behind the theological accusations and debates over polity, slavery was never far from anyone's mind. Baxter was well aware of the New School's abolitionist leanings.[57] The basic position of the Old School on the issue of slavery was simple: slavery was an institution founded in the providence of God, and the church could not judge the morality of slavery, except to counsel the slave owner to instruct his slaves on religious matters, because slaveholding was legal. The Old School, therefore, became the party of slavery. At the Old School convention that preceded the 1837 General Assembly, Joshua Wilson of Cincinnati was questioned about bringing up the issue of slavery on the floor of the assembly. He replied: "I believe that I shall let the Southern brethren manage their own concerns."[58]

It cannot be denied there were real theological issues involved in the Old School–New School split. Southern presbyteries were generally in favor of church-controlled boards rather than independent, cooperative societies.

Moreover, they prided themselves on their unwavering adherence to the Westminster Standards. Yet it is also true that not until some in the New School branded slaveholding as a sin did Southerners began to unite against the New School. Since the Declaration of 1818, the slavery question was consistently brought before the General Assembly by memorial, petition, or reference. Although the assembly just as regularly declined to act, southern commissioners were forced to listen again and again as their fellow churchmen questioned their morals and faith.

Theodore Weld, who more than any other person was responsible for the religious crusade developing in the North against slavery, attended the 1835 General Assembly as a lobbyist for "immediatism," and he arranged antislavery meetings with the commissioners. When the assembly closed, Weld reported that the number of commissioners "decidedly with us on the subject of slavery"—that is, those who believed slavery was a sin and immediate emancipation was an obligation—was "nearly one fourth part of the Assembly!" Between the 1835 and the 1836 General Assemblies, abolition sentiment grew rapidly, particularly among the New School Synods of Ohio, Western New York, and Pennsylvania. "It looks as if the Presbyterian Church were becoming an Abolition Society," wrote an observer.

In 1836, at the same General Assembly that refused to convict Albert Barnes on charges of heresy, a report was submitted to the floor declaring that since slavery was "inseparably connected" with state laws, since there existed "great diversity of opinion . . . in the churches represented in this Assembly," and since "any action on the part of the Assembly . . . would tend to distract and divide our churches, . . . Resolved, That it is not expedient for the Assembly to take any further order in relation to this subject." A minority report, however, offered by a single member of the committee, set off the alarm bells: "Resolved, . . . That the buying, selling, or holding of a human being as property, is, in the sight of God, a heinous sin, and ought to subject the doer of it to the censures of the church." Most of the support for this resolution came from New School commissioners.

After a long and acrimonious debate, James Hoge, a son of Moses Hoge who had moved to Ohio because of his opposition to slavery and had become a pioneer in the antislavery movement, wanted to calm the charged atmosphere. He moved that the whole matter be indefinitely postponed on the ground that no church judicatory had any right to make laws binding the conscience, and the time limits on the assembly would not allow the deliberation necessary to arrive at a judicious decision. This motion, which pleased neither the southern commissioners nor the abolitionists, carried 154 to 87.[59] In essence, any action condemning slavery was blocked. Despite his well-known abolitionism, Hoge clearly hoped that some kind of delaying action would result in a compromise. But the time for concession and conciliation was over: there was no going back for the church or the seminary. Tensions were so high that the General Assembly even decided not to republish the church's 1818 position on slavery because those moderate words were considered too divisive.[60]

Nothing changed a year later. Baxter ensured that the 1837 Assembly would not issue a pronouncement on the subject of slavery. Although the church was clearly split, Baxter and William Hill "were resolved on some third course yet to be found out" and met after the 1837 General Assembly. According to William Foote, Baxter was willing to accept the solution on slavery offered by James Hoge: just don't talk about it. Hill agreed.[61]

The time had passed, however, for a "third course" compromise. Before the 1838 Presbyterian General Assembly, both Old and New School commissioners met in their own special conventions. On the evening of the first day's sessions, a committee from the New School commissioners, of which William Hill was a prominent member, presented to the Old School convention a series of resolutions "to open a friendly correspondence for the purpose of ascertaining if some constitutional terms of pacification may not be agreed upon." The Old School understood this to mean a return to 1835, thus reinstating the Plan of Union and readmitting the exscinded synods and presbyteries. Baxter felt Hill had betrayed his trust. The Old School reply, drafted by a committee chaired by Baxter, rejected the terms out of hand.

When the 1838 Assembly met, the majority, led by Baxter and the Old School commissioners, refused to enroll the commissioners from presbyteries in the four exscinded synods. New School commissioners, acting upon legal advice, thereupon took the floor, elected a moderator and clerk, and adjourned the assembly to the First Presbyterian Church. The Old School commissioners organized their own assembly, electing W. S. Plumer of Richmond as their moderator. There were now two General Assemblies, each claiming to be the true Assembly of the Presbyterian Church in the United States of America. The matter ultimately came before the Supreme Court of Pennsylvania, which decided that "the Commissioners from [the excluded] Synods were not entitled to seats in the Assembly, and that their names were properly excluded from the roll." But both Assemblies remained in existence, one, the New School, terming itself the Constitutional Assembly; and the other, the Old School, identifying itself as the Reforming Assembly. The split was complete and official.

Baxter would later say that one of his motives for convening the pre-Assembly conference was to satisfy himself regarding the positions on slavery in both Old and New Schools. He found the New School to be abolitionist almost to a man; the Old School, with few exceptions, was "reasonable and prudent on the subject of slavery." Writing a little later in the *Watchman of the South*, Baxter charged that the New School had attempted a twofold revolution: "to change our creed, and to pour a flood of abolition into the bosom of the Presbyterian church." Amasa Converse later recalled a private conversation in which Baxter justified the exclusion of the four New School synods on the ground that "if we had not exscinded them, they would have exscinded us for slaveholding."

Union Becomes a Southern Institution

The 1837 and 1838 General Assemblies made George Baxter a national leader. One would expect the seminary and college communities to rally behind him. Instead, the church's rupture drove a wedge between colleagues and friends at home. One Hampden-Sydney College trustee and elder in College Church, Samuel C. Anderson of Prince Edward Courthouse, made the motion in Philadelphia to exclude the Western Reserve Synod. College president D. L. Carroll withdrew from Hanover Presbytery to join one of the exscinded synods. Carroll was also publicly critical of Baxter's role in the split.[62]

Within the next few years, three New School congregations formed in the immediate area around the seminary: Douglas, organized from Briery Church; Harris Creek in Appomattox; and Prince Edward Courthouse, just north of the village of Worsham. Elisha Ballantine, who taught Hebrew, became pastor of the Douglas and Prince Edward Courthouse churches. William Hill, who had tried to find a "third way," became a New School leader in Virginia.[63] The vast majority of southern Presbyterians, however, remained Old School.[64]

Richard McIlwaine, Class of 1857 and president of Hampden-Sydney College from 1883 to 1904, remembered the atmosphere at Hampden-Sydney College during the split as "unseemly and bitter." In 1837, Benjamin Franklin Stanton, a native of Connecticut and the minister at College Church, preached on 1 John 2:19, "They went out from among us," and launched into "a heated diatribe against all who differed from the Old School position." A large majority of the church got up and walked out "with utterances of disapproval."[65] William Hill lamented that the Old School–New School division had wounded "our bleeding Zion."[66] By 1837, New School supporters had ceased to support the seminary, while Old School supporters were suspicious of perceived New School influence at Union. Over 140 years later, Herbert Bradshaw would observe: "In 1837 and for years afterward, good Christians, followers of Calvin, hated each other as bitterly and reviled each other as roundly as ever Puritans hated the surplice or the Anglican priests reviled the followers of Wesley."[67]

When the 1837 General Assembly's actions become known, the synods put pressure on the board of directors. In September, the Synod of North Carolina not only affirmed the General Assembly's actions and Baxter's leadership of the Old School; it also ordered the seminary professors either to concur with the General Assembly's actions or "dissolve their connection with said seminary."[68] Although a copy of the order was sent to the professors, the board, meeting a few days later, stated that simple disagreement with the last General Assembly action would not be sufficient reason for resignation.[69] On October 5, the Synod of Virginia affirmed the actions of the General Assembly but did nothing more.[70]

Although the faculty remained intact during the winter of 1837–38, the tension was unbearable. At its April 1838 meeting, the board reported that three of four faculty members were opposed to the General Assembly's actions. Union was in a precarious position: "Indeed it is plainly manifest that in the present state of things neither portion of our church has sufficient confidence in the institution to patronize it in good earnest." The best indicator of turmoil was declining enrollment; students were resolving to leave the seminary if nothing was done to resolve the tensions on campus, and "it was only by private persuasion of individual members of Synod that the present students of the Seminary had been induced to remain, and a proper supply of students cannot be expected from the parts of the two Synods which concur in the assembly action until something is done to inspire confidence and interest." The board sadly reported: "The number of Students has not been so great as in some former years: but this is principally to be attributed to the agitated state of things in our Church."[71] The faculty reported only nineteen students on campus.[72]

With declining enrollment and deteriorating synod support, the board had to act. At its September 1838 meeting, the September 1837 action of the Synod of North Carolina was brought up again. With the professors present, the board debated and concurred with the North Carolina resolution. They then asked the professors if they could comply with the will of the Synod of North Carolina. Goodrich replied that "he could not hold his sentiments in silence, but must disseminate them." Taylor concurred: "The resolutions of the Synod of North Carolina had induced him to express through the press his sentiments, that neither they nor his positions would be doubtful."[73]

The board, "in order to secure the confidence of this Synod and its cordial cooperation in building up and sustaining the Union Theological Seminary," asked the professors to concur with the actions of the assembly. When they stated they could not concur, both resigned, along with the board's secretary, Rev. James H. C. Leach (a New School pastor). The board gave the professors three months' pay and allowed them to live in their houses until other arrangements could be made.[74] Elisha Ballantine also resigned from teaching Hebrew. The students were affected by the resignations; Goodrich and Ballantine had been especially popular.

There is a revealing letter in the Society of Missionary Inquiry's correspondence book, from 1839, addressed to "the Rev. A. L. Holladay, Missionary to the Nestorians in Persia," reporting on conditions at the school. Holladay, an 1836 graduate, had earlier inquired about classmates and the state of the seminary. The secretary informed Holladay: "Circumstances connected with the unhappy controversy in our Church seemed to render it desirable that the connection of Professors Taylor and Goodrich, and of Mr. Ballantine with the seminary should be dissolved." The letter continues with a melancholy benediction of victory: "Amputation is painful—but amputation is preferable to death. In separation for its own sake, we have no delight; but separation is better than ceaseless contention; and ceaseless contention better than a sacrifice of principles and conscience."[75]

Stephen Taylor, a graduate of Williams College and Andover, had been called as professor of history in 1835. Although he was from Massachusetts, Taylor had served churches in the South and was seen as "no partisan." The board had believed that Taylor would "neither head a party, nor follow a party." Yet when Baxter engineered the exscinding of the synods and presbyteries, Taylor publicly disagreed, questioning the constitutionality of the act. He interpreted this division as detrimental to the fulfillment of his evangelical task: "I will never permit Denominationalism, as such," he is remembered to have said, "to prevent my preaching Christ to a dying world."[76] He seemed to agree with the basic Old School argument that purity of doctrine had to be preserved, but he found the exscinding of synods and presbyteries too extreme. "Are we not bound by the principle of christian charity," he asked, "to put the best . . . construction . . . upon the words and actions of our brethren?"[77]

Elisha Ballantine was known for his antislavery sentiments. When the issue of gradual emancipation was debated before the Virginia State legislature during its 1831 session, he had opposed Benjamin Mosby Smith. The question was straightforward: "Shall the State of Virginia immediately set on foot measures for the gradual emancipation and removal of our slave population?" Ballantine, then a 22-year old seminary student from New York State and a graduate of Ohio University, argued in the affirmative. Smith, then a 20-year-old first-year seminary student from Powhatan County, Virginia, argued in the negative.[78]

In his inaugural address, George Baxter had predicted the coming turmoil of the church. Within six years, those who disagreed with him were gone. Going forward, Union Seminary ceased to be a national seminary; it was now a southern seminary, dedicated to preserving the Old School ideal of orthodoxy and committed to silence on what the church and culture considered to be social issues. The symbol of this regional emphasis and identity was made manifest for the next century: only men who were born and educated in the South would teach at Union Seminary. This southern exclusivity did not change until 1938, when Howard Kuist of Illinois joined the faculty, but he finished his career at Princeton Seminary. He was followed in 1943 by Donald Miller, a native of Pennsylvania, who was later called as president of Pittsburgh Theological Seminary from 1962 to 1970. The first Northerner to stay at Union Seminary for the length of his career was Donald Dawe, who was called in 1969.

After receiving Goodrich's and Taylor's resignations, the board called the Reverend S. L. Graham of North Carolina to teach ecclesiastical history in 1838. When the board changed Graham's duties to teaching biblical literature, they elected the Reverend Francis S. Sampson, of Goochland County, Virginia, to teach ecclesiastical history and polity after N. H. Harding of North Carolina declined the position.[79] Under John Holt Rice, the seminary had drawn faculty and students from other sections of the country. Now Union Seminary was quite literally an institution representing two Southern states, Virginia and North Carolina. Moreover, after 1838 there were no more fund-raising efforts in the North until after the Civil War.[80]

With only the Synods of Virginia and North Carolina to depend on, the board saw a bleak financial future. On April 10, 1838, the faculty lamented "the drying up of some of the sources from which the institution has been accustomed to derive its money" and how the division within the church hurt the seminary financially.

> It is well known to the Board that a difference exists in the bounds of the two Synods on the subject of the measures of the last General Assembly. This difference has already had the effect of causing those who are opposed to the action of the last Assembly to withdraw almost entirely their support from the Seminary. Individuals have refused to pay their installments pledged some years ago, and societies which have for years given decent aid have of late entirely ceased to do so.

At its 1838 meeting, the board concluded that finances were so bleak that a fourth instructor could not be hired and all faculty would be asked to raise money.[81] Indeed, Harding may have declined the call to Union because he thought he would be doing more fund-raising than teaching.[82] The board further requested that the synod "ask Pastors and churches under their care to take up collections for aid of the Seminary."[83] In 1838 the seminary had a deficit of more than $1,700. Desperate, the board recommended that the seminary's financial trouble be published in the newspapers, urged ministers to speak of it to their congregations, and passed a resolution to collect $8,000 due in subscriptions for the New York professorship. At this same meeting, the board voted that all funds and property would be held by its treasurer.

At the fall 1838 meeting, the board prevailed upon the synods to have the General Assembly transfer Union's stocks to the care of the seminary board.[84] The Synods of Virginia and North Carolina concurred,[85] and by the spring meeting of 1839 the stocks had been transferred,[86] signaling the complete break with the national church and the New School. While there were many who were pleased to see the northern students and professors depart, the feeling of joy was not universal. On April 9, 1839, Anne Rice wrote a letter deploring "this lamentable party strife."[87]

The atmosphere on campus was ugly. The board's 1838 report to the General Assembly stated: "The students almost unanimously are determined to leave the institution unless something is done to remedy this state of things."[88] Upon Baxter's return from the 1838 General Assembly, the students asked him to give a lecture defending his position.[89] No notes of the lecture remain, but the students seemed to accept his explanation. The faculty recognized the tense atmosphere on campus and, in an effort at reconciliation, issued an invitation, "that the Professors & Students unite with the Congregation in the College Church in observing the 13th of this month [December] as a day of 'humiliation, thanksgiving, and prayer' according to the act of the last assembly."[90]

The decline in enrollment, division in the church, and the dreary economy prompted the board to question the viability of Union Seminary. In the fall of 1839, the board proposed uniting with Columbia Seminary, founded just a decade previously, in an effort to ameliorate the financial hardships at both institutions.[91] The Union board thought that with the South solidly Old School, this would be a propitious time to realize Rice's dream of one southern seminary.[92] Just days after the board appointed their committee, the Synods of Virginia[93] and North Carolina[94] concurred. While both Union and Columbia agreed that one large southern seminary would be advantageous, neither wanted to move to the other's location, nor could they agree on a neutral site. Suggestions for a merger were broached again in 1841 and again in 1842. Everyone agreed on the concept but not the location.[95]

The Specter of Slavery

However one dressed up the debate with theological or ecclesiastical concerns, the issue of slavery drove the widening divide between North and South, Old School and New School, and came to define southern culture. From 1830 to 1861, the Society of Missionary Inquiry regularly answered letters and held discussions on that particular institution. On April 4, 1831, Professor Goodrich had cautioned against involvement in the colonization cause, causing Union students to decline an offer to cooperate with students from Andover in supporting colonization efforts,[96] but the issues of colonization and the education of enslaved people were brought up at least once a year between 1830 and 1861.

Ironically, students were concerned with Africans in Africa, but not Africans in America. In 1834 the Society of Missionary Inquiry observed: "Of all parts of the heathen world, Africa has the strongest claims on Amer. & especially

Southern Christianity. Would that we do something to cancel the immense debt we owe her by pouring into her Groans the blessings of the gospel!" At the same time, the SMI lamented that only a few ministers gave "instruction to our poor blacks" and "in one at least of our churches—in the Valley of Va.—small classes of young blacks receive instruction from the ladies." The society had high praise for the one of their number, a Northerner, who was interested in the education and salvation of enslaved people.

> There is in this State one missionary at least who devotes his time exclusively to this class of our population. We mean Bro. Van-Ransellaer, who is now laboring in Halifax County, amongst a large population of slaves. The dear bro. from the North who is a son of Gen. Van-Ransellaer of Albany, so well-known for his wealth and beneficence,—has exhibited a spirit of self-denial & devotion which shall rouse a generous emulation in our mind.[97]

And in 1839, while writing to a missionary in West Africa, the SMI secretary optimistically predicted, "The injuries [Africa] has received at our hands no doubt will be repaid by sending her the gospel with its precious blessings."[98] Yet by 1841 there was no pretense of optimism; interest in African missions had waned, and all instruction of slaves had ceased. "Our congregations," they wrote, "neglect the heathen at home and also those abroad."[99]

Other issues related to slavery were debated, such as "Should the Servants of believers be baptized on the faith of their master and under what circumstances?"[100] And "Is it at present, the duty of the Christian Church in Virginia, to establish generally Sabbath Schools for the oral religious instruction of the negroes of this Commonwealth?"[101] One particularly incisive question for debate appeared: "How can the church best discharge the debt she owes to the negro population of the South?"[102] And one debate concluded by lamenting "the deplorable state of ignorance among the black population of our country & expressing a hope that a better day would soon come when servants would be taught to read the word of God & thus receive a saving knowledge of the gospel."[103]

In the South, and at the seminary, any questioning of slavery was suspect. On January 19, 1844, Captain Samuel McCorkle of Lynchburg accused William Cochran, a student from the North, of "sentiments in relation to slavery and its abolition which were highly offensive and pernicious." Professors Wilson and Graham spoke to Cochran and concluded:

> He [Cochran] was opposed to slavery, but would do nothing to distract the peaceful relations of Master and Servant: on the contrary, that should he ever speak to Servants his principles would [have] him to inculcate obedience and submission to their Master: and that he did not believe the holding of slaves to be inconsistent with piety, though he could not, consistently with his view of propriety, hold them himself. They then advised him to write to Captain McCorkle and explain more fully his meaning and views. He promised to do so: and here the matter was at that time dropped.[104]

Yet rumors persisted that Cochran continued to hold abolitionist sentiments and spoke about them publicly. Although he did write Captain McCorkle as instructed, Cochran was summoned to a faculty meeting on January 23. The faculty drew up a "paper" and "submitted [it] to Mr. Cochran to ascertain whether it impressed his sentiments in relations to slavery. After some alterations and . . . [unreadable], it was assented to, but at his own request, he was allowed to take it for further consideration—and the faculty adjourned."[105] Two days later Cochran signed the paper.

> I hold that slavery is an evil though not in all cases and necessarily sinful; that all unlawful attempts to change the relation of Master & Servants would be disorganizing and inconsistent with gospel principles. I would not meddle with the relation between Master and Servant; but should I be called in any way to speak to Servants concerning it, would maintain the duty of obedience to Masters,—the same as of children to parents. I was born and raised in a state where Slavery does not exist, but I never did belong to an abolition society.
>
> (Signed) W. C.

The statement was then circulated within the seminary, Captain McCorkle was informed, and the faculty resolved to take no further action.[106] Cochran, however, left the seminary at the end of the school year.

William E. Thompson has found that not only did the faculty own slaves, but the seminary may also have owned slaves: faculty minutes before the Civil War refer to "servants of the seminary."[107] Mrs. Thomas Miller kept the refectory in Steward's Hall for the theological students. She was often angry about her "back-biting" household slaves, and there is one entry where Mrs. Miller continued to read her Bible in order to block out the screams of a slave she had directed to be whipped.

The Campus Is Completed

Amid the increasingly acrimonious divisions over abolition, the Old School–New School split, and a poor economy, George Baxter was able to finish building the seminary and purchase seventeen acres of land during the 1836 recession. This land had belonged to Cushing and was offered to Union by a supporter, J. D. Wood, on the same terms at which he bought it at public sale.[108] In 1837, therefore, the campus and physical plant of Union Theological Seminary were set, except for a library. The Seminary building contained the chapel, library, classrooms, and faculty and student rooms. Boston House, North Carolina House, Westminster Hall, and Eastcourt surrounded the Seminary Building.[109] In 1839 the board purchased 25 buckets, 2 ladders, and 2 fire hooks and directed the faculty to organize students to fight fires.[110] In an effort to save money, the board allowed nonstudents to rent dorm rooms in September 1840, and in 1841 it allowed ministers to use the seminary's library for a fee.[111]

Student Life

With the physical plant set, the students wanted their own space for meetings. They applied for permission, but faculty members resisted granting them a room for their own use until the board ordered them to "appropriate some convenient rooms for the use of the [Society of Missionary Inquiry], and also for a reading room."[112] With this seemingly innocent action, the society became the de facto student government. As the only functioning student organization, the society was asked to invite speakers to graduation ceremonies, which were first held in 1848.[113] Apparently graduation was not well attended. In an effort to ensure that all graduates would attend, the faculty required every member of the 1849 graduating class to speak during the ceremony.[114] The policy was reiterated the following year.[115]

Despite the controversies of the time, student life had a settled routine, and the students expressed satisfaction with their "Southern Zion."[116] But the board minutes frequently contain criticisms that student rooms were messy. Indeed, in 1847, Dr. Sampson talked in chapel about the cleanliness of student rooms, including an admonition against throwing trash from the windows.[117] There were also regular reports about students not attending classes. In 1848 the faculty voted to begin taking attendance at all classes and in chapel.[118] Students had to cut wood for heat, but the intendant complained that students broke up their furniture and burned it because they were too lazy to chop wood.[119]

At the beginning of the 1830s, the SMI had subscribed to newspapers as diverse as the *Richmond Whig*, the *New York Spectator*, the *Charleston Observer*,[120] and the *New England Spectator*;[121] but by 1838, southern newspapers predominated. In 1838 the SMI cancelled the *Boston Recorder* and *Philadelphia Observer* and began to subscribe to the *New Orleans Observer*.[122] In 1838 the society also voted to "return every avowedly abolition news-paper that may be sent to the society." They then voted that a recent issue of the *Western Presbyterian Herald*, published in Louisville, Kentucky, "be returned to the editor with the article on abolition marked."[123] In 1844 the SMI subscribed to the first Presbyterian newspaper west of the Mississippi, the *Herald of Religious Liberty*, published in St. Louis, Missouri.[124] In 1846 the society's newspaper subscriptions were canceled due to lack of funds, but after instituting dues of $1.75 per year in 1848,[125] newspapers once again were available in the reading room. On June 7, 1849, the librarian reported that the SMI was receiving eight newspapers, all reliably Old School, and five "monthly pamphlets," only one of which was a denominational publication.[126]

Some in the SMI tried to keep a wider worldview through their correspondence. They communicated with students from Andover Seminary; Jefferson College, Pennsylvania; Centre College, Kentucky; Hanover College, Indiana; the Episcopal seminary in Alexandria, Virginia; Brunswick Seminary in New Jersey; Columbia Seminary; Princeton Seminary (which sent a catalogue of their library holdings); and Western Seminary, Pittsburgh. Beginning in 1833, the SMI kept a consistent correspondence with foreign missionaries: Cape Palmas (present-day Liberia), Ceylon (Sri Lanka), Singapore, Greece, Northern India, West Africa, and Calcutta (Kolkata). They also received or heard reports from missions to American Indians and missions in Greenland, East Africa, Brazil, Greece, the Madeira Islands, Persia, and Madagascar.[127]

Modern students tend to think that their predecessors were pliant and silent. Union students, however, have always spoken their mind. The desire to have a say in their education and protect "their" time led to the first student protest in Union's history. On November 3, 1832, the Society of Missionary Inquiry, which met formally on the first Monday morning of the month and gathered informally on other Mondays, formed a committee "to petition the faculty to omit recitations on the first Monday of the Month."[128] Four years later, faculty members were concerned that students were not using Monday mornings wisely. They noted on November 11, 1836, that while the first Monday of the month was understood to have been set aside for fasting and prayer, "and has not been generally used; therefore Resolved, that the regular Lecture and Recitation of the seminary proceed on the first Monday as on any other Monday of the month."[129]

Student reaction was immediate. Two days later, on November 13, the students formed "a committee of three . . . to present the views of the Society in regards to a recent order of the Faculty requiring recitations on the First Monday of the Month; and that this committee report at a subsequent meeting of the Society." The committee met and promptly drew up a memorial that in effusive language expressed "deep regret as well as surprise" that the faculty would take away such a long-standing part of the schedule as Monday morning. The SMI also pointed out that "we have never understood that the first Monday of the Month was originally set apart as a day of fasting." Rather, Monday was a time for students to meet under the auspices of the SMI "to awaken the affirmation of candidates for the Gospel Ministry to the Spiritual destitution of the world, and to enlist their feelings, their prayers & their energies in the great Christian enterprise of Consoling Mankind with allegiance of the True God." The SMI was worried that classes meeting on Monday morning would undermine the Great Commission.[130]

Faculty members were taken aback by the student body's strident initiative. They met on November 22, read the petition, and adjourned until the next day, deciding how to reply. On November 23, they sent a resolution to the SMI stating that while the faculty "are still of opinion that as but a small proportion of the students are occupied in preparing reports," they were "ready to adjust the times of the Lectures & recitations, so as to give appropriate opportunities for the meeting of the Society of Inquiry & also the monthly concert."[131]

The students were not satisfied. On November 25, after reading the faculty resolution, the students objected that the meetings of the Society of Missionary Inquiry were not occasional "indulgences at the request of the students," but an integral part of their education. The faculty offer not to schedule lectures and recitations on an irregular basis did not help the society or the cause of missions. The students voted to suspend the SMI's meetings "until such arrangements shall be made as this Society may deem suitable for resuming them."[132] In other words, they went on strike.

The faculty responded with a conciliatory gesture. On December 21, the SMI read a faculty resolution "that the first day of every month be devoted to the cause of missions, & to transacting the business of the Society of Inquiry, & that whenever the first day of the month shall fall on the Sabbath the Saturday proceeding shall be so appropriated."[133] The students accepted and the faculty affirmed this compromise on December 26.[134] The first day of every month was now officially reserved for the formal meetings of the Society of Missionary Inquiry.

But students were still students. Regular complaints appear in the society's minutes about lengthy meetings because some people talked too much. On June 1, 1840, the SMI voted that "no member shall be permitted to speak longer than 10 minutes, nor oftener than twice, & the whole discussion shall be limited to one hour & thirty minutes."[135] The minutes record numerous complaints about students removing newspapers from the reading room and scores of ideas for instituting a system of fines, but it seemed that nothing worked. On December 1, 1850, the society decided that "the members in their turn alphabetically [would] make the fire & ring the bell for meeting."[136]

The society's debates fell into four general categories: professional, polity, public policy, and theological. The professional outlook produced wideranging topics:

- What are the best means of evangelizing the lower classes of our country?
- What are the comparative advantages and disadvantages of extemporaneous and written prayers?
- Should members of the Presbyterian Church be permitted to go out as Missionaries under the care of any association which will not allow them to organize churches on Presbyterian principles?
- Is it right for Missionaries among Pagans, to induce them to adopt Christian Customs before their conversion, in order to remove their prejudices & prepare them for the cordial Reception of the Gospel?
- Does the domestic field present stronger claims upon us for missionary labor than the foreign?

Polity topics centered on the organizational responsibilities of the church:

- How may the church most effectually increase the number of Candidates for the Ministry?
- How can the Church prevent the entrance of inefficient men into the Ministry?
- Should Instrumental Music be allowed in the public worship of the Christian Church?
- Does the Multiplication of benevolent Societies have a tendency to lessen individual efforts to do good?
- Ought Presbyterians to support their own Boards of Missions in preference to others?

Public policy questions reflected the times:

- Is it expedient for the Presbyterian Church to adopt a system of Parochial Schools, as recommended by the General Assembly?
- To what extent should Ministers participate in the political affairs of the nation?
- What is the proper course for Protestants to take with regard to Roman Catholicism in the U. States?
- May the downfall of Popery be soon expected?
- Is there reason to believe that the prohibition of the liquor traffic in Va. would have a good effect on the cause of temperance?

The theological area called forth wide-ranging topics:

- Is it probable that the Jews will be returned to Palestine?
- Can it be proved independently of the Bible that the human race had but one origin?
- Do Theological Seminaries tend to check or cherish the Missionary Spirit in their students?
- Ought a Minister to take a decided stand against dancing among the young of his congregation?
- Is the student's life in the Seminary any indicator of the future character of his ministry?
- What is the most profitable manner in which a Theological Student may spend his vacation?
- Does Geology contradict the Mosaic Account of Creation? [The discussion of this question went on so long that it was continued at the next meeting.]
- Should Christians abstain entirely from intoxicating drink except for medicinal reasons?[137]

Romanism, Sabbath schools, temperance, revivals, and "Evangelization of foreign countries nominally Christian" were also popular topics. On December 31, 1842, a new subject appeared: "Ought the Mohammedans to be made the object of Foreign Missions in the present state of the world?"[138]

Even if Baxter was freezing Union into a theological ice palace, and as the Old School–New School split was tending to turn Union Seminary inward and provincial, yet these debates show that there was still a strong desire among students to confront the world around them. Moreover, instructors began to realize that the world was bigger than southside Virginia. During this time, traveling to Europe for what we would call graduate education began. Elisha Ballantine was the first instructor to have studied in Europe, doing advanced work in Oriental Languages in Berlin in 1834–36. Although he resigned due to the Old School tilt of Union Seminary in 1838, the school was proud of his efforts: "We shall rejoice when the fruits of German research shall pass into evangelical hands & be consecrated to the advancement of pure Christianity."[139] After B. M. Smith graduated in 1834, he became an assistant instructor for two years. He was ordained in 1836, but instead of taking a church right away, he studied church history and Semitic Languages at the University of Halle (Prussia, now Germany) from June 1836 until August 1838.[140] Francis Sampson studied in Berlin and Halle from July 1848 until August 1849, just before he was appointed full professor of Oriental Literature.

As his organization of the Old School delegates indicated, Baxter was an able administrator. At the first faculty meeting of his first full year as theology professor on November 6, 1832, he discussed giving diplomas to graduates (which would not happen for another fifty years) and standardized the school day for the first time: morning prayers were conducted by students at sunrise (changed to 8:30 a.m. in 1856), evening chapel was conducted by faculty one and a half hours before sunset, and Sunday evening was spent discussing religious topics with the faculty.[141] He also continually experimented with the school calendar; in 1845 it was finally set, with two terms, the year beginning in August and ending the second week of June, and each term followed by a vacation of six weeks.[142] In 1848, students and faculty petitioned the board to end the spring term in mid-May, and the board agreed.[143]

Despite politics and calendar changes, the curriculum remained constant. The first class schedule was printed in the 1833–34 Catalogue and would be recognizable to any Union Seminary student of any era.

First Year	Second Year	Third Year
Hebrew and Greek	Psalms and Isaiah	Christian Theology
Jewish "Archiology"	Chaldee (Daniel)	Bible
Sacred Geography	The Epistles	Church History
Biblical Criticism	Natural Theology	Prophets and Proverbs
Canon of Scripture	Christian Theology	Church Government
	Church History	Pastoral Theology[144]

The curriculum was demanding, but admissions standards were lax. The only requirement for admission was a faculty interview, and in the early days only nine potential students were denied admission. The professors constantly complained of the low standard of "literary attainments" of their students,[145] and graduation was no certification of competence. In 1836 the board noted that the committee charged with examining students "had failed to discharge that duty."[146]

Students were difficult to control. On March 31, 1835, the faculty decreed that classes must be taken in order and preaching must be done without a manuscript.[147] The faculty repeated this admonition at regular intervals. Students had to be reminded to show up for evening prayers, that "no sermon shall exceed 30 minutes in length,"[148] and that "no wood be deposited in front of the seminary or cut within its walls."[149] In 1836 the faculty asked the board to take action to discourage "premature marriages" on the part of the students. The board declined to act, "however much they may regret the occurrence of such events in all ordinary cases." In 1894, Walter W. Moore observed that "about fifty years later the Faculty made exactly the same request, with exactly the same result."[150]

One of the more entertaining problems found in the records was related to farm animals. In 1836 the faculty passed a motion: "Resolved, that it is inexpedient that any live stock run in the seminary yard."[151] "For sixty years," Moore observed, "we have been working at this problem. Even the passage of the stock law did not solve it. The Seminary has neighbors who do not regard the law of Exodus xxii. 5 either as interpreted by the Authorized Version or the Revised as binding."

The predecessor of the present Intendent (apparently assuming that cows which had been coming to the Seminary so long could read) is said to have posted a notice at each of the entrances, to the grounds, beginning as follows: "All cattle are hereby notified," &c. But the cows and hogs continued to come in, regardless of this considerate and earnest appeal. We believe, however, that the days of their depredations are numbered. The present Intendent, evidently determined not to be out-generaled by a lot of illiterate cattle, has adopted a simple and familiar mechanical device, which we trust will prove effectual.[152]

Another strategy for managing unruly behavior, not of animals but of students, was the financial penalty. The church believed that a seminary education ought to be provided by the church, so the seminary charged no tuition. Rent, however, was charged for the student rooms; from 1824 to 1851 the rent was 25 cents a year. In addition, from 1839 to 1851 each student paid $2.50 per year into a seminary "expense fund." In 1840 the board warned the students that "whoever deposits ashes in any part of the Seminary buildings shall be subject to a $5 fine for every such offense." Moreover, anyone who removed a "fender" (fireplace screen) would also be charged $5. New fenders had been purchased the previous year.[153]

The board was concerned that an uncaring student body was eroding the physical plant. The 1847 intendant's report was detailed:

Every part of the building bear[s] marks of extreme neglect and abuse. The conditions of all the passages and many of the rooms are filthy in the highest degree. One or two of the rooms are likely to sustain very serious injury from being used as Bath Rooms, and the plastering throughout the building has been shamefully mutilated by carelessness in carrying up wood and throwing it down at the doors. The steward has also appropriated rooms to his own use not allowed by his contract.

In response, the board resolved that

the Intendant keep all vacant rooms locked; that no room be used for bathing except one in the basement allotted by the faculty; that each student provide a box for fuel and be charged for repairing any plaster he breaks; and that every student be enjoined to a conscientious regard to the preservation and cleanliness of their quarters, and the faculty take oversight.

In 1849 the intendant wearily reported,

Furniture moved around and panes broken at [the] first of the session—still that way; two feather beds and one hair bed injured by moths. One pitcher and bowl broken and value collected from breakers. The proper key of Nottoway room has been lost by Mr. Wm. B. Tidabill who occupies that room. Tops of foot posts of the bedstead in Wilmington room occupied by E. L. Cochran have been sawn off.

The intendant proposed

that rooms in basement used for keeping wood be rented yearly to students and furnished with lock and key; . . . that the steward be held answerable for any damage and annoyance from college students boarding with him—such annoyance as running in the passages, ringing the seminary bell, and tying or untying the bell-rope.[154]

Recurrent gripes included students spitting tobacco juice on the floors and walls of the seminary building, hitching their horses in the front yard of the seminary, and continuing to chop up their furniture for firewood. Students regularly complained about the food in the dining hall.[155] In 1849 a student was fined $5 for letting his chimney catch fire.[156] Students had to be continually reminded to show up at the beginning of the school year, and the board was concerned about the "state of religion" on campus. In 1849 the board forbade students to preach at Sunday night services; students could preach during the week, but faculty should preach on Sunday night, and students should be in attendance.[157]

Intendant

Francis Sampson became the Hebrew teacher in 1838, after Ballantine resigned. He was the first professor who was a Union alumnus, and the first with no pastoral experience.[158] He was born in 1814 in Goochland County, Virginia, and received his early education from tutors. In 1830, Sampson attended a boarding school in Albemarle County, Virginia, and one year later was baptized in the Presbyterian Church in Charlottesville. He studied at the University of Virginia, graduating with an MA in 1836, and entered Union Seminary that fall. Sampson excelled at languages, which was why he was chosen to succeed Ballantine. He was ordained by East Hanover Presbytery in 1841.

By all accounts Sampson was an excellent teacher. In October 1848, he was elected professor of Oriental Literature and Languages, but his life and work were cut short when he died in 1854 at age thirty-nine. Robert L. Dabney, who would teach at Union from 1853 until 1883 and was a defining influence on southern culture, wrote of Sampson in glowing terms in 1898: "Having set under the teaching of several of the most learned and able professors, who ever appeared on this side of the Atlantic, I am compelled by the truth to declare that Dr. Sampson's instructions were more valuable to me than those of any other living man."[159] Sampson also had the makings of a good administrator. He understood the value of alumni and was largely responsible for the establishment of the alumni association in 1847. Although he was paid less than other members of the faculty, Sampson was asked to serve as agent, librarian, and intendant.[160]

During Sampson's tenure the intendant became an important position. The job was first recorded in 1830 as the person who managed the practical, routine operations of seminary life. From the board's point of view, the intendant was the board's representative to the students. The intendant was sometimes a student or a recent graduate, but more often a faculty member and occasionally a local member of the board. The intendant was responsible for housing, building maintenance, collecting student fees, supervising food preparation, garbage disposal, student deportment, and cattle.

Chairman of the Faculty

Another development for the seminary came to pass in April 1841, at the death of George Baxter. Baxter had donated land for the cemetery; when he died, he was buried on that land.[161] Since that time all tenured professors and spouses have had the option to be buried in the cemetery. Baxter's successor, Samuel B.

Wilson, was unanimously elected professor of theology[162] and began his duties on June 28.[163] Wilson was from Lincoln County, North Carolina, and graduated from Washington College, in Maryland. He was serving a church in Fredericksburg, Virginia, before his appointment as the theology professor,[164] and he remained at Union Seminary for twenty-eight years.

By all accounts Wilson was an adequate theology professor but a failure as an administrator. The board recognized his shortcomings and devised an unusual leadership plan in 1859, creating the position of Chairman of the Faculty. This position rotated on an annual basis to each member of the faculty in turn. Wilson continued to teach and serve as faculty chairman in his turn for another ten years, until he died in 1869. As Hartley Hall pointed out, the practical result of alternating the position of Chairman of the Faculty was to leave the seminary virtually leaderless. Since rotation was automatic, without regard to individual administrative interest or ability, the lack of continuity created an administrative vacuum. There was a low level of leadership initiative; the goal was not improvement, but maintaining the status quo.

During this time of rotating chairmanship, the position of Clerk of Faculty remained permanent and therefore grew in importance—a fact that was to have administrative significance when R. L. Dabney occupied that post in the decades following the Civil War. In addition to the clerk, there was a librarian (also a faculty member), a steward (who appears to have been a jack-of-all-trades sort of handyman), and the intendant.[165]

Declining Support

Student enrollment in the 1840s continued to decline; from 30 in 1841–42 to 13 in the 1848 school year. Between 1823 and 1850, total enrollment was only 250.[166] In 1846 the board minutes mentioned the small number of students and asked: "Shall the Seminary be abandoned, or allowed to continue in this state until forced to do so?" The board then asked the synods to complete the endowment so that the seminary would not have to "subsist on irregular, demeaning, and unpredictable annual offerings."[167] The synods agreed to complete the endowment for the third professorship in June 1847, but raised only $20,000 of their $35,000 goal by 1850.[168]

Operating funds were a constant worry; in September 1843 the board members had a "free discussion . . . concerning the pecuniary embarrassment of the seminary," and the board issued a plea for funding from the synods.[169] In 1845 the shortage of cash forced the seminary to pay faculty from the endowment, but that move only delayed the crisis. In September 1846 the treasurer reported an operating deficit of $920 and a total debt of $2,000. Graham was not given a salary; instead, he received the interest, not to exceed $1,200, on $20,000 worth of stock. In addition, the board ordered two lots in Brooklyn, New York, apparently left over from the New York professorship, sold to reduce debt.[170] In 1847 the synods began to be receptive to the idea of providing the seminary with endowment funds to allay the yearly shortfalls, but their intentions were not enough. There was not enough money to pay Francis Sampson during his first two years of teaching.[171]

The seminary did not just rely on the largesse of the synods. Susan Bott of Petersburg, Virginia, made and sold wax-flower arrangements in the late 1840s, contributing some $7,000 to the seminary.[172] Some of these wax flowers are in the rare book room of the library. In 1848 the board appointed an agent to raise $25,000 and paid him $200 a year more than a faculty member made. These were the funds used to hire Sampson, and by 1848 the number of faculty was equal to the number prior to the Old School–New School split a decade earlier. In 1850 the Synod of Virginia, concerned about the lack of students, recommended that professors spend as much time as possible visiting and corresponding with churches so as to encourage men to enter the ministry.[173]

In the 1824 Plan of the Theological Seminary, Rice envisioned giving certificates to all students who had completed the full course of study. According to the faculty and board minutes, however, there were not many who qualified to receive a certificate. At the fall 1838 board meeting, a certificate was approved for only one student who "had passed through the full course of study." The next day, the faculty reported that more students did not earn completion certificates because presbyteries scheduled their meetings during the seminary's semiannual examination periods.[174] Eight students were awarded certificates in 1843.[175] Both faculty and board complained about student absenteeism, and they laid the blame squarely on the presbyteries.[176] Indeed, student absenteeism in order to attend presbytery meetings was so serious that the Synods of North Carolina[177] and Virginia[178] asked the presbyteries not to schedule their meetings during seminary exams.

The board accused the presbyteries of undermining the seminary's efforts in two ways: First, presbyteries would send men who were not properly prepared and then license them before they finished the course of study. In 1844 the Synod of Virginia enjoined their presbyteries to take special care to ensure that their candidates were well grounded in their elementary education, and particularly in knowledge of the Greek language, before they entered the seminary.[179] This lack of preparation was particularly frustrating for the board since, by 1843, Presbyterians had forty-three colleges east of the Mississippi, more than any other denomination.[180]

Second, presbyteries seemed to discourage students from completing the full course of studies. They would often license students to preach after a year or two at Union, so students saw no reason to spend three years studying; graduation had little or no bearing on their continuing in ministry. In 1838 the Synod of North Carolina echoed the board's request that presbyteries not license seminary students until they had completed the course of study, and the presbyteries ignored both pleas. In 1842 the obviously frustrated faculty voted to award certificates to students "with the approbation of the Faculty, though they may have been absent from one or more of the regular examinations for reasons adjudged to be good by the Faculty."[181] The faculty evidently thought that awarding certificates to those who missed some exams would keep them in school longer, but it did not work. In 1849 the board expressed regret that the entire senior class went to their presbyteries for licensure and failed to return to complete the course and take the examinations.[182] The Synod of Virginia made the same request in 1854,[183] but the appeals did no good. The entire Class of

6. Susan Bott's wax flowers

1854 was called away by their respective presbyteries for licensure and failed to receive their certificates.[184]

While the board and faculty complained that students left school when they felt like it and accused the presbyteries of complicity, part of the problem lay in the conflicting requirements set by the Presbyterian General Assembly. According to the original Plan approved by the 1810 General Assembly, the board was responsible for examining students and expected presbyteries to use these examinations in granting admission to the presbytery. By reserving the right of examination to the presbyteries, the General Assembly made seminary examinations superfluous: students knew where the real power lay and saw no need to be examined by the board. The board itself was also partly responsible. There was never an instance when the entire examination committee was present for the exams, and in 1860 not a single board member was present on the first day of exams and only one managed to get there for the second day.[185]

By the late 1840s it was clear that Union Seminary was trying to reestablish a degree of institutional self-confidence and even enthusiasm. Sampson had established the Alumni Society in 1847. The first public commencement and first alumni meeting were held in June 1848. Perhaps as a result of Baxter's death in 1841, northern students began to return. In the 1840s five students were admitted from northern states, and during the 1850s, eight were admitted.

While this was not a large number, it indicated that Union Seminary was once again becoming a more national institution.

Influence of Alumni

Between 1831 and 1865 there were 309 alumni. Since certificates were largely ignored and diplomas unknown, prior to the 1890s a student who had completed enough classes to receive a call (even if he had attended for only two years) was considered a graduate of Union Theological Seminary. The careers of Union alumni were uniform during this era. Everyone served at least one church and then followed one of four paths if they did not serve a parish: missions, education, mass communications, or denominational offices. Twelve alumni went into the foreign mission field, at least six of whom went with the ABCFM (American Board of Commissioners for Foreign Missions) and one under the New York Presbyterian Mission Board. They served in South Africa, India, Turkey, Greece, Liberia, Persia (Iran), and Siam (Thailand). Austin Hazen Wright (Class of 1838, from Vermont) served as a missionary to Persia in 1840–60 and translated the Psalms and the New Testament into Syriac. Four alumni served as home missionaries: one to the Creek Nation, one to the Cherokee Nation, one to Native American people in Pennsylvania, and Courtland Van Rensselaer (Class of 1833, from New York) to enslaved people in Virginia (1833–35). The Old School–New School split, however, intervened here as well. Only one alumnus entered the mission field after 1838: Thomas Spencer Ogden served on the island of Corisco, off the coast of Equatorial Guinea, from 1857 to 1861 and died there. In 1835 a letter to the students at the Episcopal Seminary in Alexandria declared: "Our field is the world; . . . whether in China, in Africa, or at home, we all belong to the same company—are one household."[186]

The society's correspondence books are filled with letters from missionaries abroad, both alumni and those the students did not know personally. In 1834, Thomas Pinckney Johnston (1832) wrote from Turkey after forty-five days at sea: "I am permitted at last to address you from missionary ground. We used to read and talk about the conditions of the heathen, and the labour of the missionaries in foreign lands, . . . but now I have seen with my eyes a little of what we then knew only by the hearing of the ear."[187] Occasionally missionaries on furlough visited the campus and spoke.

Union Seminary alumni had a huge impact on education in the antebellum period. During this time nine alumni served either as professors or college presidents, including three presidents of Davidson, one president of Lafayette College (Pennsylvania), and one president-elect of Hampden-Sydney College (who died before he could assume the office). Before the Civil War, there were only seventeen institutions of higher education in the United States that admitted women. Of this number five were colleges, and the rest were denoted as female seminaries or institutes, which offered only a limited liberal arts education. Union graduates served as presidents, principals, or teachers at ten of them, all in the South. Thomas Morrow (1833) served as the first superintendent of public schools for Morgan County, Alabama, from 1856 to 1869.

Throughout the nineteenth century, virtually every denominational newspaper in the South had a Union graduate as editor or a member of the editorial board. Four alumni began the trend: George Leyburn (1834), editor of the *Presbyterian Witness* in 1858; William Brown (1836), editor of the *Central Presbyterian* in 1860 as well as 1870; William T. Richardson (1845), editor of the *Central Presbyterian* from 1879 to 1895; and Daniel Blain (1861), editor of the *Southern Evangelist*, the *Montgomery Messenger*, and the *Home Church* in the 1880s.

Before the Civil War, three alumni served on the denomination's Board of Publications, and William Brown (1836) served as permanent clerk to the General Assembly of the PC(US) in 1865–84. There were four General Assembly moderators who were connected with Union: John Holt Rice and Courtland Van Rensselaer (1833) served as moderators of the Presbyterian Church in the United States of America (in 1809 and 1857, respectively), John Lycan Kirkpatrick (1837) as moderator of the Presbyterian Church (CSA) in 1862, and Stuart Robinson (1837) as moderator of the new Presbyterian Church in the United States in 1869.

There were several graduates who, after serving a congregation, worked for a time in parachurch organizations, as temperance agents, colporteurs (selling religious books in the 18th and 19th centuries), and agents for the American Tract Society, the American Bible Society, and the American Colonization Society. One Union graduate served as an agent for Austin College.

Robert Lewis Dabney and Benjamin Mosby Smith

The two professors who would define the irony of Union Seminary's history, and perhaps represent the two sides of southern culture into the twentieth century, were elected as professors within a year of each other in the 1850s. Robert Lewis Dabney was elected to the chair of Ecclesiastical History and Polity in 1853, and Benjamin Mosby Smith was elected to the chair of Oriental Literature in 1854. From outward appearances, Dabney and Smith were bookends. Both were native Virginians, both attended Hampden-Sydney College and Union Seminary, and both received university training outside the church, Dabney at the University of Virginia, where he earned a master's degree, and Smith at the University of Halle. Moreover, the two men served as copastors of College Church for sixteen years.[188] Yet these two men approached life, southern culture, and the institution of Union Seminary in entirely different ways.

Benjamin Mosby Smith was born in Powhatan County, Virginia, on June 30, 1811, the middle of five children. The family was known for its piety. When Smith was a boy, his family had morning and evening worship in the house with their slaves.[189] John Holt Rice was a regular visitor to Montrose, the family plantation, and encouraged the educational pursuits of the Smith boys.[190] Benjamin's father believed that education was important for his children and established a school for them. But when he was just eight, his father died and regular schooling came to an abrupt halt as the family became almost destitute. Smith was only able to continue his education in fits and starts: he had five tutors in five years and then attended a substandard boarding school.

7. Robert Lewis Dabney, Professor of Ecclesiastical History
and Polity, 1853–69; Adjunct Professor of Theology, 1866–69;
Professor of Theology, 1869–83.

Recognizing the financial difficulties of the Smith family, John Holt Rice
offered to take Benjamin and his older brother Joe into his home and prepare
them to enter Hampden-Sydney College. After about a year, Rice thought
Smith would be ready to take the exam to enter Hampden-Sydney. He passed
the entrance examination, but the college's president, Jonathan Cushing, had
to lend him the money for matriculation; Smith was fourteen years old. He
lived above Rice's study and grew close to the family. Smith graduated from
Hampden-Sydney in 1829 and worked as the headmaster at an academy in Milton, North Carolina, for two years. He entered Union in 1831 and, after graduating in 1834, was appointed assistant instructor in Semitic Languages for two
years. Smith was ordained in 1836, but instead of taking a church right away,
he went to the University of Halle.[191] On his return from Europe, he then served
churches in Danville (1838–40), Tinkling Spring and Waynesboro (1840–45),
and Staunton (1845–54), all in Virginia. In 1854 he was appointed the secretary
of the Board of Publication in Philadelphia, then elected to the faculty at Union
Seminary.

Seventy years later President Benjamin Rice Lacy called Smith the man who
"saved Union Seminary in her hour of desperate need."[192] Most reminiscences

8. Benjamin Mosby Smith, Assistant Instructor of Oriental
Literature, 1834–36; Professor of Oriental Languages,
1854–89

from the late nineteenth century remember Smith as a man of expansive vision
and generous politics, far beyond the tenor of the times. But he was still captive
to his time. His slave worked off his board with the Rice family while Smith
was in seminary, and he publicly argued against emancipation.[193] Indeed, when
Smith moved to Hampden-Sydney to join the Union faculty in 1854, he was so
indignant over the activities of the Free Soilers, who advocated abolition, that
he thought it might be wise for the southern states to secede from the Union
right then.[194] He owned slaves until the Emancipation Proclamation, although
he was known as a "kind and wise master."[195]

Perhaps Smith's most important legacy at Union is the library. In 1835, while
an assistant instructor, he was appointed librarian. Smith took his duties seriously; he was the first to systematically catalogue the holdings. He campaigned
for more money and space, was concerned about misuse of the library, and
was known for admonishing "some young ladies whom he thought too much
disposed to novel reading."[196] In 1834 his inventory showed there were three
thousand volumes in the library.[197]

Beginning in 1835, presumably at the prompting of Smith, the Library Committee of the board began to be more active, offering recommendations, for

example, that the librarian sell off duplicate books, lock up "rare or curious books" in the library desk, and place "suitable locks" on the library doors.[198] Samuel Graham was appointed the first permanent librarian in 1848.[199] When Francis Sampson took a leave of absence to study abroad, he purchased books for the library, the first substantial increase in the library holdings since the purchase of John Holt Rice's library.[200]

Robert Lewis Dabney was born in Louisa County, Virginia, on March 5, 1820. His father was a lawyer and church elder. He began his formal education when he was seven at a small log school near his home. Dabney learned Latin from an elder brother and later began to study Greek. After attending at least two more schools and studying under a tutor who specialized in mathematics and algebra, Dabney entered Hampden-Sydney College as a sophomore in June 1836. His father had died in 1833, and the Dabney family fortunes declined thereafter. Dabney spent just one year at Hampden-Sydney; he left in September 1837, returned home to assist his mother, and taught two terms at a local school. In the fall of 1839 he entered the University of Virginia, graduating in 1842 with a master's degree.

Dabney was undeniably brilliant and was disappointed in Hampden-Sydney: "This place is not very remarkable for anything at all except poverty, for the college [Cushing Hall] stands in the middle of an old field full of gullies and weeds, and the cows of the neighborhood come up to the very windows with their bells, making such a noise that I cannot study." He thought the other students were messy and refused to socialize with them.[201] He did not have a high opinion of his professors: "I do not think that I learn any more of Latin or Greek than I could learn by myself, for our professor of languages is so indifferent that he does not teach us anything."[202]

Right before he left for home, Dabney made a profession of faith at a revival in September 1837,[203] which he later identified as a turning point in his life. After stabilizing the family fortunes, he entered Union Seminary in 1844, graduated in 1846, and became a home missionary in Louisa County. After ordination in 1847, Dabney served the Tinkling Spring Church in Augusta County, Virginia, and married Margaretta Lavinia Morrison in Rockbridge County, Virginia, on March 28, 1848. Of the six Dabney sons, three died as children. Dabney became Union's best-known professor until the 1880s.

One of the most fascinating documents in Union's history is Dabney's inaugural address: "Uses and Results of Church History" (1854). According to Dabney, the primary aim of theological education is piety through study of doctrine.[204] But this education should be expansive; Dabney argued that seminary students must possess a knowledge of "secular history, geography, chronology, and political institutions." The student must be concerned with "causes and relations" and not merely "multitudes of facts." He must have an ample knowledge of the philosophies that have influenced the world. Thus seminarians should study history because it gives them an "arsenal" to discuss issues involving institutions, ideas, and ethics.

Dabney insisted on using original documents: "Nor can he [the scholar] seek his witnesses only among compilers and professed historians. He must ascend to the contemporary sources of information: he must know the literature and the spirit of the age he studies." The student must then incorporate "the most operative elements of social, national, and religious welfare," to understand the tensions and tenor of the times. Thus church history is the fundamental theological discipline: "The most instructive and profitable way to study theology is to study the history of theological opinions" and in that way break "the unconscious shackles of local prejudice and sectional modes of thought."[205]

When Dabney joined the faculty in 1853, Samuel Wilson's inept leadership was coming to an end. In 1854 the board appointed Dabney as intendant, and when the board acted to rotate the faculty chairmanship in 1859, Dabney managed to have himself appointed clerk. It was a position that he would occupy almost continuously until he left Union Seminary to settle in Texas in 1883. In 1869, when Samuel Wilson finally died, Dabney succeeded him as professor of theology. Over the years, therefore, Dabney managed to accrue a great deal of institutional authority.

An Isolated Campus

Dabney's and Smith's organizational abilities, fund-raising efforts, and reputations reversed the decline in enrollment at Union Seminary in the 1850s. But Hampden Sydney was still a lonely place in Virginia. The most prominent memory of nineteenth-century students was the isolation and the difficulty of getting to the campus. In 1835 the B&O Railroad finished a line from Richmond to Washington, and by 1838 the Richmond & Petersburg Railroad connected Richmond to southern Virginia.[206] There was, however, no railroad to the west as yet. After reaching Richmond, students had to take a boat on the James River to Cartersville, then a stagecoach to Farmville, and finally a carriage to Hampden Sydney. Richard McIlwaine remembered that his first trip to campus in 1848 took 1⅓ days from Petersburg (75 miles).[207] It took Joseph McMurran, from Jefferson County (now in West Virginia), four days to reach Hampden Sydney in 1850, on two trains, a riverboat, and a stagecoach.[208] The 1848 catalogue wistfully predicted that the seminary would "in a short time be easily accessible by the Richmond and Danville Railroad."[209] In 1852 it took a student from Baltimore four days to reach the college, riding on two trains, two riverboats, one stage, and the mail carriage (for which he had to pay a "good price").[210] The first train did not arrive in Farmville until 1854.[211]

And once the students arrived, they were not impressed. In the fall of 1851, Alexander Pitzer, who traveled three days from the Shenandoah Valley, pronounced the Hampden Sydney landscape as "dreary beyond description." Again and again student accounts told of overgrown fields, horrible roads, and cows and hogs running around. Joseph McMurran was despondent when he first saw Hampden-Sydney College in the fall of 1848: "Nothing but pine barrens, red clay soil, Chinquapin bushes, and scrubby oak groves greet the eye of the new comer. Even the buildings of the campus present nothing to relieve the surroundings. There is nothing in nature's surroundings here to stir the heart to make the orator, nothing to excite the imagination to make the poet."

The amenities were basic. To take a bath, students went to the pump between the seminary building and Boston House, pumped water into buckets, and carried them to a stove in the basement of the seminary building, where it was heated and poured into a wooden tub. Because this task was so time consuming, the same tub of water was used by more than one student. The six outhouses for the seminary were located behind Penshurst; when a privy pit reached capacity, another was dug nearby, and the outhouse was moved over it. Light was provided by oil lamps.

In the winter months, fire was the main source of heat. Each room had a fireplace, and students were responsible for chopping and transporting their own wood. Students carried the wood to their rooms in a V-shaped trough, which could hold about ten pieces of wood at a time. They were prone to stack firewood on the porch, and the faculty complained that it was an eyesore. There were no serious fires, even though the Philanthropic Literary Society stored phosgene on the third floor for use in its elegant gas lamps.[212]

The tracks of the South Side Railroad that reached Farmville in 1854 changed everything. The line was just seven miles from Hampden-Sydney College, and telegraph lines accompanied the tracks. Instead of taking three days to travel from Petersburg and Richmond, it now took just four hours. Newspapers published in Richmond, Petersburg, and Lynchburg could be in Farmville the next day.[213]

Relations between the college and seminary students were cordial, in general. Richard McIlwaine remembered that the college and seminary boys would go to Farmville 2 or 3 to a buggy, 12 to 15 in a wagon.[214] In addition, college and seminary students ate together and sometimes rented rooms in the same houses.[215] McIlwaine described his classmates with respect:

> Of all the men with whom I was associated at the Seminary, there were only two who were triflers or something worse. They were not natives of Virginia or the South and my impression is they never got into the ministry of the Presbyterian Church U.S.A. The others were God-fearing, in earnest to fit themselves for the duties of life and careful in their conduct and conversation, with whom it was a privilege to be in fraternal association.[216]

Growing Stability in the Last Days of Peace

The decade between 1850 and 1861 was a time of growing identity and stability. In the 1850s, college students began to refer to seminary students as "seminites."[217] Francis Sampson and S. L. Graham, who had been teaching since 1838, were inaugurated in 1850, and both their inaugural addresses were published, indicating a developing institutional consciousness.[218] Enrollment shot up from 12 students in the 1850–51 school year to 39 at the beginning of 1860. Despite the growth and efforts to raise money, seminary professors seldom received their entire salary, so they kept cows and pigs, grew gardens, and took in boarders to make ends meet.[219] In 1851 the seminary board abolished room rents, which were 25 cents a year. Instead, they instituted a $5 annual fee for all students. Twenty years later, Walter W. Moore would consider this assessment, still in force, "a reproach to the institution and the church." He believed that seminary education ought to be paid entirely by churches through the synods.[220] The board also approved a limit on the number of books a student might check out of the library: five.

9. The UTS campus in 1858

In 1853 the board began work to establish a fourth professorship, which was finally accomplished in 1856.[221] William Hoge, younger brother of Moses Hoge and native of Ohio, was named the fourth professor (of biblical literature and the interpretation of the New Testament) and served until 1859. R. L. Dabney did not have a high opinion of Hoge's scholarship or teaching ability; Dabney convinced Hoge to accept a call as copastor with Gardiner Spring at the Brick Church in New York City. At the seminary, Hoge was succeeded in 1859 by Thomas Peck as professor of ecclesiastical history and polity, when Dabney became the theology professor.

Peck, a native of South Carolina from a Presbyterian family, studied under James Henley Thornwell at the College of South Carolina (later the University of South Carolina). Thornwell was a Presbyterian minister who had become one of the leading theologians of the time, defending Old School Presbyterianism and slavery in the Old School–New School division. Peck entered college when he was just fourteen and was considered to be a brilliant student. He became Thornwell's protégé and then friend. After a conversion experience, Peck decided to become a minister and finished his undergraduate work. After learning theology and languages from Thornwell, Peck was ordained and served two small churches near Columbia, South Carolina. In 1845, Second Presbyterian Church of Baltimore called Thornwell, but the College of South Carolina refused to release him. He recommended his friend to fill the pulpit, and Peck moved to Baltimore in 1846. After twelve years he was called to Central Presbyterian Church in Baltimore, but only remained there a year. In 1859, Thomas Peck was called to Union Seminary.

Students remember Peck as giving "the impression of a rather forbidding austerity. But he had, in fact, a lively sense of humor and a spirited wit."[222] Peck's anti-Catholicism was something new for Union Seminary. In 1855 he wrote, "Obedience to God is eternal enmity to Rome." It is not clear whether Peck believed abolition or immigration was a greater threat to the country. As Irish immigration increased during the 1850s, he was afraid the nation was being driven "nearer, every day, to the decision of the great question which must be decided, sooner or later, whether Protestantism and liberty, or popery and despotism, shall rule this country."[223]

The only physical addition to the campus around this time was Dabney's house, Westmerton. Standing apart from all the other buildings, a quarter mile down Roxbury Road to the west, it was built in 1856 and designed by Dabney. He considered himself an architect and designed not only College Church but also the Tinkling Spring and Farmville churches.[224]

Documents from these days show very few instances of serious student misconduct; students not showing up to ring the bell seems to have been the most prevalent offense. In fact, students were so unreliable in their bell ringing that the board authorized the intendant to hire a bell ringer, who may have been a "servant."[225] There is one incident that surfaces in a cryptic notation in the faculty minutes. On November 30, 1854, Willis L. Miller was dismissed "out of a difference of opinion between him and the Professors, as to the propriety of his retaining in his family a female nurse of reputed bad habits, in the Seminary Buildings."[226]

The year 1854 was a turning point for the seminary. The rail line reached Farmville, Benjamin Mosby Smith came on the faculty (preceded by Dabney in 1853), there were twenty-three students (twice as many as the previous year), and the fund-raising campaign for the fourth professorship was launched. In 1853 the board reported to the synod that Princeton and Alleghany Seminaries had four professors. Moreover, Kentucky, with only a third of the congregants of Virginia and North Carolina, had raised $60,000 for a seminary and college (Danville Seminary in Kentucky opened in the fall of 1853). The board's question was simple: Why can't we raise $40,000 for a fourth professor?[227] Not to be outdone, the Synod of Virginia launched a fund-raising campaign in 1854. There was "substantial progress"[228] from the very beginning, and fund-raising for the fourth professorship was completed by 1856.[229] Moreover, professors' salaries were being paid on time. The board also had enough money to purchase nine acres adjacent to the campus to shield itself from undesirable neighbors, enlarge the graveyard, and buy a storehouse to rent to the steward.[230] From 1857 to 1860 the endowment increased by $40,000, passing $110,000 in 1861.[231] Professors' salaries increased from $1,350 a year in 1857 to $1,500 in 1860. Gold from California was increasing the prosperity of the nation, and Union Seminary saw some of the benefits. In 1856 there were three scholarships; by 1860 there were seven.[232] Indeed, in 1860, times were so good that the board thought they could try to collect funds in New York.[233]

Worship was a central part of student life. There were daily morning and evening chapel services, and prayer meetings among the students at least once a week. Students were expected to attend Sunday morning worship, which was in College Church if the student had no church nearby, and faculty conferences with the students on important topics were held on Sunday afternoons. The 1854 catalogue describes the "conference" as being like a colloquium "on questions which are pastoral or experimental. The plan of the Seminary requires the Professors to act as pastors to the students."[234] The board noticed a revival of religion at the college and seminary in the spring of 1854, which resulted in "a more elevated tone and pious feeling, and the hope is expressed that it would also result in an increase in candidates for the ministry."[235] Richard McIlwaine remembered that Davy Ross, a slave belonging to the college, was converted at this revival.[236]

Since there was no formal preaching and worship class, students were expected to learn by doing: "Every student of the Seminary is required to preach a sermon, of his own composition, four times during each session, in the presence of the professors and students, and such other audience as may assemble on the occasion." The students preached their sermons at the Wednesday night service, where "a very respectable audience generally attends; and after the audience is dismissed, the whole service is criticised by the Professors, in the presence of the students. The students are also frequently engaged by the Session of the College Church, to preach to the Blacks of the neighborhood."[237]

For students in midcentury and the late nineteenth century, preaching on Wednesday night was sheer terror. In 1856 the Synod of Virginia required students to preach half of their trial sermons without a manuscript, and the no-manuscript rule had a huge impact. Two students would preach in front of the professors, the student body, and anyone from the community. After the service, everyone would leave except for the professors and the two students who had preached. Richard McIlwaine remembered that when he was scheduled to preach second, the first student lost his place and just sat down. McIlwaine then rambled on for forty-five minutes, during which everyone got up and left except for the faculty and a few students. Dabney, who had been whittling a stick, offered just one criticism: "Mr. McIlwaine will do well to take a lesson from nature; it doesn't thunder all the time." Dabney criticized another sermon by saying it was Episcopal in nature: "There is nothing at all in that sermon to edify or instruct anybody."[238]

The Synod of Virginia wanted trained preachers but deplored the practice of students preaching before licensure, except as an academic exercise. They asked professors to dissuade students from taking a text, preaching a regular sermon, and pronouncing the apostolic benediction.[239] The board complained that students continued to preach from a manuscript.[240] In 1861 the board tried to compel student attendance and participation in formal public debates. These debates were designed to improve extemporaneous speaking, but students did not regularly attend.[241]

The 1854 treasurer's report recorded that the Episcopal Seminary in Alexandria had obtained a charter during the most recent session of the Virginia General Assembly.[242] Mindful of earlier attempts to incorporate, the Synod of Virginia, at the board's urging, appointed a committee to apply for a charter. This charter, however, would only allow the seminary board to hold up to $250,000 for twenty-one years; property was not even mentioned.[243] On December 20, 1855, the Commonwealth of Virginia granted the seminary this limited charter. However, a problem was recognized at the first board meeting convened under the new charter in May 1856. The original wording of the charter as submitted to the Virginia General Assembly had said that the "Directors" of the seminary would procure replacements and manage funds under synod supervision. But the wording of the charter granted by the legislature said that the trustees would choose their own replacements and manage money on their own.[244] Neither the Synod of Virginia nor of North Carolina approved the wording of the new charter, and in 1857 the synods voted not to accept the charter until it specified their overall management.[245]

The conflict was resolved by vote of the synods in 1860: the synods created two boards made up of the same members.[246] No funds were ever transferred, though, because the Civil War broke out, and incorporation in 1869 would render the problem moot. Nevertheless, the seminary was hopeful that a full charter was in the offing. Indeed, the 1856 catalogue erroneously bragged: "The property of Union Theological Seminary is held and managed by a Board of Trustees, who are incorporated by the Commonwealth of Virginia, for this purpose."[247]

The 1854 catalogue is the first extant one later than 1830. Only one student was from the North, a graduate of the University of Michigan, and the curriculum had not changed from 1830. In 1854 there was no tuition, board was $10 per month, wood was $2 to $2.50 a cord, and washing 75 cents to $1 per month. The catalogue reported that students could "generally find some employment as teachers, with families in the neighborhood." But the seminary knew it was isolated. The 1854 catalogue put Hampden-Sydney in a positive light by reassuring prospective students that Union was

> situated in a rural, Christian community, which affords a circle of the best Southern society. The region of country, and especially the immediate vicinity of the Seminary, are noted for their healthfulness; being free from local causes of disease at all times, and affording, in fall and winter, a genial and pure atmosphere, which has often been found salutary by those who had suffered from more severe climates. The place has been long celebrated as possessing as great an immunity from disease as the most favored spots in the Southern country. The Seminary is between the South-Side and Richmond & Danville R. Roads; being seven miles from the former, and ten miles from the latter. The traveler may now easily breakfast in Richmond or Petersburg, and dine at the Seminary; and, after a few months, when these railroads will be completed, the same statement will be true of Lynchburg and Danville.[248]

Entrance requirements were straightforward:

> Every candidate for the ministry in the Presbyterian Church must produce satisfactory testimonials that he possess good natural talents and is of a prudent and discreet deportment; that he is in full communion as a church-member; and that he is proficient in such branches of literature as are required of candidates by the constitution of the Presbyterian Church; or, wanting these, he shall submit to an examination on them by the Faculty.
>
> But any member of any other evangelical denomination of Christians, who is seeking the ministry in his own Church, will be admitted to all the privileges of the Institution, upon his presenting satisfactory evidences of his church-membership and Christian character, and complying with the regulations of the Seminary.[249]

Union was good to its word. In 1857, Matthew Lyle Lacy, who was under the care of the Second Presbytery of Philadelphia (New School), was admitted from Douglas Church, a New School church in Prince Edward County.[250] He was later one of the first ministers ordained by the New School Hanover Presbytery.

The seminary library became more important in the 1850s. Until Samuel Graham was appointed the first permanent librarian in 1848, the library was managed by a student appointed by the board. As a result, there were virtually no book acquisitions. Once Graham conducted an inventory, he requested that "some duplicate or unneeded volumes might be sold and new books bought." The board gave permission, provided the names of the donors of the old books would be transferred to the new books bought with the funds from the sale. A permanent "Library Fund" was approved by the board in 1850, but no fund-raising was done until 1854.[251] Until the 1880s, requests for donations to the Library Fund were found in every catalogue, along with a count of the holdings.

A New Curriculum

Perhaps the most important program development before the Civil War and the best indication of Dabney's influence was the reorganization of 1856. Dabney was apparently the force behind the departmental restructuring of the school, and he published a pamphlet announcing the changes. Publicity was something new: Union had never thought it necessary to announce what it was teaching. Dabney, however, believed that publicity would help with raising money for the fourth professorship and with drawing students away from Columbia Seminary by showing that Union was a modern institution.[252]

The 1856 "curriculum" retained the traditional subjects, while the seminary was now formally organized into four distinct departments.[253] The Bible was still the center of the seminary: "This institution was intended by its great founder, Dr. Jno. H. Rice, to be a school of Biblical Theology."[254] Old and New Testament, with the appropriate languages and "interpretation," were the first two departments. The third department was Systematic and Pastoral Theology, including Mental and Moral Science, Natural and Revealed Theology, Sacraments, and the Pastoral Epistles. The fourth department was Church History and Polity, where the book of Acts was taught.[255]

This was not an era of specialization. In general, faculty members would decide what chairs they desired—usually chosen on the basis of seniority—and the board concurred. Wilson was 72 years old in 1855 when he was released from teaching polemical theology to teach pastoral theory. B. M. Smith was transferred from biblical criticism to teach polemical theology, while Harrison taught biblical criticism. In 1858 some board members wanted Wilson to resign. Dabney opposed forcing Wilson to resign and agreed to help him teach theology. In 1859, Wilson's teaching load was reduced to just one class: pastoral theology. Dabney was then appointed adjunct professor of theology, and he ended up teaching all other theology classes.[256]

Secession

By the mid-1850s the Old School–New School divisions were set: the younger students could not remember a united national church. An improving economy and the growing national consensus to accept slavery, but confine it to the

South (resulting in the Kansas-Nebraska Act of 1854), made attending seminary in Virginia more palatable. Union's reorganization into a modern seminary and the growing notoriety of both Dabney and Smith foreshadowed the possibility that Union was becoming more than a regional seminary. Yet, beneath the veneer of compromise and optimism, national politics intruded on Union and circumscribed its horizons.

In the late 1850s, Benjamin Mosby Smith had offers of pastorates in Philadelphia, Baltimore, and Louisville. He refused these calls because he owned slaves. In his diary he confided:

> I am utterly astonished that I should ever come to Virginia to live after having had the opportunity to live in Pennsylvania, but one's inconsistencies are amazing. Oh, what trouble—running sore, constant pressing weight, perpetual wearing, dripping, is this patriarchal institution! What miserable folly for men to cling to it as something heaven-descended. And here we and our children after us must groan under the burden—our hands tied from freeing ourselves. December 21, 1858.
>
> I am more and more perplexed about my negroes. I cannot just take them up and sell them though that would be clearly the best I could do for myself. I cannot free them. I cannot keep them in comfort. . . . I am determined now to avail myself of the first clear opening to move out. . . . What would I not give to be freed from responsibilities for these poor creatures. Oh, that I could know just what is right! December 31, 1858.[257]

In 1860, Princeton Seminary offered Dabney a professorship in theology, and he was also called as pastor of the Fifth Avenue Presbyterian Church in New York City. He turned both down because he owned slaves; the refusal of some northern states to enforce the Fugitive Slave Act meant that he would not be able to take his slaves north with him.[258] An act of Congress could not answer the basic morality of slavery. In a letter of March 19, 1859, Anne Rice lamented that some people had lately declared slavery to be a positive good, describing it as the best institution that could be devised, thereby completely relieving their consciences of the moral issue of enslaving a fellow human being.[259]

While Anne Rice repudiated slavery and Smith privately struggled over the issue, Dabney's ideas moved in another direction. Paradoxically, when he was twenty, Dabney wrote a vigorous criticism of slavery, describing it as economically impracticable, politically indefensible, and inconsistent with the ideal of the kingdom of God. He argued that if the abolitionists had left the South alone, emancipation would have come gradually.[260] Prior to 1850, Dabney did not write extensively on slavery, but he did express misgivings and anxiety over the morality of slavery and voiced fears that the institution would inevitably result in a tragedy for the South. After 1850, however, he (and many others in the South) began to follow James Henley Thornwell's argument that abolition was wrong because the Scriptures justified slavery. Moreover, the church was positively prohibited from commenting on social issues and so could not have a voice in the slavery argument.[261]

In 1847, while some voices—like Ruffner in Virginia and Breckinridge in Kentucky—were calling for gradual emancipation, Thornwell argued: "We stand upon the platform of the Bible. God's word recognizes the relation of master and servant, as a relation that may lawfully subsist." Furthermore, he argued, the church as a spiritual body

> has no right to interfere directly with the civil relations of society. Whether Slavery shall be perpetuated or not, whether arrangements shall be made to change or abolish it, whether it conduces to the prosperity of States or hinders the progress of a refined civilization,—these are questions not for the Church but the State, not for Ministers but statesmen. Christian men may discuss them as citizens and patriots, but not as members of the Church of Jesus Christ.

This argument was powerful for Dabney; he would employ it after the war when he tried to make sense of the conflict and define the church's place in society.

Union's professors, Dabney, Wilson, Smith, and Peck, were originally against secession. They made sure their views were widely known by publishing them in the *North Carolina Presbyterian*, the *Central Presbyterian*, the *Presbyterian Herald*, and the *Christian Observer*. In a letter of January 1861, Dabney went so far as to condemn South Carolina:

> I have considered the state of Northern aggression as "very ominous" for many years, . . . but I do not think that Lincoln's election makes them at all more ominous than they were before. . . . Hence, I consider Lincoln's election no proper "casus belli," least of all for immediate separate secession, which could never be the right way, under any circumstances. Hence I regard the conduct of South Carolina as unjustifiable towards the United States at large, and towards her Southern sisters. She has, in my view, "worsted" the common cause, forfeited the righteous strength of our position, and aggravated our difficulties of position a hundred fold; yet regard to our own rights unfortunately compel[s] us to shield her from the chastisement which she most condignly deserves.

Dabney argued that the United States government had a right to defend its federal forts but not to take any aggressive action against South Carolina. But if such action were taken, other Southern states should say, "Hands off, at your peril."

Daniel Blain, a Union student, expressed a somewhat similar sentiment in a letter written after Mississippi, Florida, and Alabama had seceded:

> War seems inevitable, but a merciful providence may yet avert it. . . . The spirit of madness and fanaticism seems to have seized all parties—north and south. I trust old Virginia will rear her massive front and quell the storm. She can save us if she's cool and decided. But if we are delivered over to the tender mercies of such Godless, heaven defying states as South Carolina and those who follow in her lead we are doomed to pass through one of the bloodiest wars that ever cursed any land. I'll fight for old Virginia and her rights, but not one finger would I raise to defend one inch of South Carolina soil. I would as soon think of defending that vile sinkhole of isms and "personal liberty bills," New England. I consider one as much in the wrong as the other.[262]

Up until the shelling of Fort Sumter on April 12, 1861, Dabney wanted it both ways. He tried to justify slavery and wanted to avoid armed conflict. As war drew near, Dabney traveled through the South, pleading passionately against any resort to arms on the grounds that Christian brethren could not conceivably settle their differences in such fashion. Even after southern states began to secede, he continued to assert that war must be avoided. When South Carolina attacked Fort Sumter, Dabney was indignant. He railed against South Carolina as "the little, impudent vixen [that] has gone beyond all patience. She is as great a pest as the abolitionists, and if I could have my way, they might whip her to their hearts' content, . . . only do it by sea and not pester us."[263]

One month after Fort Sumter fell, and with nine states having already declared they were no longer in the Union, the Old School Presbyterian General Assembly met in Philadelphia. There were very few southern delegates present, but the atmosphere was hopeful under the leadership of Charles Hodge from Princeton. In January 1861, he had argued that although the southern states might separate from the Union and form their own country, such an act would not necessitate "the secession of the Presbyterians in those states from our General Assembly." He reasoned that a united church would be helpful in restoring good relations between North and South after the "excitement" had subsided.[264] The leadership of the 1861 General Assembly carefully avoided making political pronouncements. Indeed, a delegate from "Bleeding Kansas" was denied the time to report on the condition of his state so controversy would not break out.

The atmosphere changed, however, when James Henley Thornwell's letter explaining his absence was read to the assembly. He ended his letter by praying that harmony and goodwill would soon be restored "between your country and mine." Many on the floor of the assembly reacted with shock and derision at his choice of words.[265] On the third day of the assembly, Gardiner Spring, copastor with William Hoge (who had taught at Union Seminary until he accepted the call to Brick Church the previous year), introduced a resolution:

> That this General Assembly, in the spirit of that Christian patriotism which the Scriptures enjoin, and which has always characterized this Church, do hereby acknowledge and declare our obligations to promote and perpetuate, so far as in us lies, the integrity of these United States, and to strengthen, uphold, and encourage the Federal Government in the exercise of all its functions under our noble Constitution; and to this Constitution in all its provisions, requirements, and principles, we profess our unabated loyalty.
>
> And to avoid all misconception, the Assembly declare that by the terms "Federal Government," as here used, is not meant any particular administration, or the peculiar opinions of any particular party, but that central administration, which being at any time appointed and inaugurated according to the forms prescribed in the Constitution of the United States, is the visible representative of our national existence.

Trying to define what they meant by "Federal Government" was futile; everyone understood that the Presbyterian General Assembly was calling for loyalty to the Lincoln administration and obedience to the call for volunteers issued two days after the shelling of Fort Sumter. Charles Hodge led the opposition to the resolution, declaring that the General Assembly had no right to decide "to what government the allegiance of Presbyterians is due," nor "to make that decision a condition of membership in our Church." His arguments, however, had little effect; the Gardiner Spring Resolution passed 156 to 66, after twelve days of debate in a politically charged moment, on May 16, 1861. Virginia had already seceded on April 17, five days after Fort Sumter, and Arkansas and Tennessee seceded on May 6 and 7, respectively.[266]

It was ironic that Gardiner Spring would introduce this resolution. Pastor of Brick Church since 1810, he had close ties to the southern states and especially to Union Seminary. In 1858, Dabney had convinced Spring, whom he considered a good friend, to make the trip from New York City to Hampden-Sydney so that Spring could offer the associate's job to William J. Hoge. During the visit, Spring preached a week of special services at College Church and stayed with the Dabney family. Spring even preached at the Sunday evening worship service at the New School church at nearby Prince Edward Court House. Hoge accepted the call, but the times were against him. He resigned under pressure when he refused to take a stand against secession and moved south.[267] He gave his final Sunday sermon on July 21, 1861, while the Battle of Bull Run was being fought just south of Washington.[268] The exodus went both ways. A son of Charles Hodge, A. A. Hodge, who had served for six years as pastor of the Presbyterian Church in Fredericksburg, Virginia, and was beloved by his congregation, was "sorrowfully" dismissed by his presbytery, "with no word of recrimination."[269]

Virginia was reluctant to secede. Lincoln was elected on November 6, 1860. South Carolina seceded on December 20; by February 1, 1861, Florida, Mississippi, Alabama, Georgia, Louisiana, and Texas all voted for secession. Lincoln was inaugurated on March 4, 1861. On April 4, Virginia voted against secession 88 to 45. On April 12, South Carolina fired on Fort Sumter, and on April 15 Lincoln called for two million volunteers. In response, the Commonwealth of Virginia voted to secede 88 to 55 on April 17, 1861, and North Carolina seceded on May 20.[270]

War

Like the Commonwealth, once Fort Sumter was fired upon, Benjamin Mosby Smith threw his support behind secession as the only way to defend the South against northern subjugation.[271] Dabney agreed: "This mountainous aggregate of enormous crime, of a ruined constitution, of cities sacked, of reeking battle fields, of scattered churches, of widowed wives and orphaned children, of souls plunged into hell; we roll it from us, taking the Judge to witness . . . that the blood is not upon our heads."[272]

Dabney volunteered immediately. He received a commission as a chaplain in the Prospect Rifle Grays of the 18th Virginia Regiment from April through September 1861, and he was present at the first Battle of Bull Run. Some students enrolling after the war report that they felt their call to ministry after hearing Dabney preach.[273] After serving for five months, however, he thought he could do no more and returned to Hampden-Sydney.

However reluctant the Commonwealth of Virginia was to take up arms, the students at Hampden-Sydney were enthusiastic, if not prepared, to fight the North. Abraham Lincoln was elected on a Tuesday, and by Thursday college and seminary students had formed a militia and were drilling. The students voted to name their unit "The Hampden-Sydney Boys" (Company G of the 20th Virginia Regiment),[274] which had been the name of the student company that fought in the Revolutionary War.

On Thursday, April 18, 1861, the day after Virginia voted for secession, the Richmond's *Daily Dispatch* reported on the mood at Hampden-Sydney:

Glorious Demonstrations in Prince Edward
Hampden Sidney College, Va., April 16, 1861

Secession is triumphant at last. Speeches were made yesterday (Court Day), at the Court-House, by Col. Bouldon, in favor of rebellion in Eastern Virginia, if necessary: by Messrs. Asa Dickinson, Booker (member of the House of Delegates from the county). T. T. Tredway and others, all out and out Secessionists; and every word in regard to the glorious attitude of the Southern Confederacy . . . fairly rent the air. At night about 80 or 100 of the students turned out to serenade the prominent men on the hill. At the U. T. Seminary, Prof. T. E. Peck was called out, and paid a high tribute to South Carolina, the land of his birth; then we next serenaded Dr. F. B. Watkins, who had heretofore been the strongest Union man in our midst.

In his speech he declared that it would be madness and folly, disgrace and cowardice, to remain in the Union, and said that our destiny was with the South. His effort was a fine one, and showed that, though the grey hairs had covered his head, yet he still had the vigor and spirit of youth. We next found ourselves in front of the residence of Rev. Ro. L. Dabney, D. D., who came forward and made a speech, a speech which would make the abolition horde quake and fear. Our spirits burned within us. It was a grand speech and I wish that every man in Virginia could have heard it. Afterwards, Prof. Charles Martin, of H. S. C., spoke, declaring his intention to carry arms against the North, where he was born, and also from Mr. Smith, a Seminary student from Pennsylvania, to the same effect. Messrs. T. Walker Gilmer, W. Houston, [undecipherable] Lyell, Hugh A. White, [undecipherable] Darnall [Darnell,] and Harvey Gilmore, of the seminary, made speeches. There is to be a company of students organized in a few days, with Rev. J. M. P. Atkinson, President of the College, as Captain, and we will be ready to go at the first sound of the bugle.

Attached to the same article was a small notice: "Lincoln was burnt in effigy . . . amid a 'calithumpian' serenade." The writer's pseudonym, Sumter, shows his sympathies.[275]

The seminary board met on May 13. Ten of the thirty-nine students had already left because "they judged that the situation of their parents and friends, or duty to their states, justified them in leaving their studies for the remainder of the session."[276] In a burst of patriotic enthusiasm, the board then invested seminary funds in Commonwealth and Confederate bonds.[277] The Synod of Virginia was concerned about seminary students serving in the armed forces and advised those who were preparing for the ministry to ponder carefully the question whether they were really needed by the country as soldiers or in performing other equally important duties. The minutes of the synod include

Jefferson Davis's warning on "grinding the seed corn" and thus imperiling a future harvest.[278]

Benjamin Mosby Smith wrote: "We are in the midst of preparations for war. Dr. Atkinson [president of Hampden-Sydney] has raised a college company and my dear boy [Morrison, his eldest son] has come home to join it. . . . The enthusiasm of the people is without bounds. Companies are forming everywhere." Zeal, however, could not replace competence. It is said that Atkinson instructed his boys to march by directing: "Raise the right leg until the thigh is perpendicular with the body. Then raise the left leg alongside it." There is also a story that once after initiating a march, he could not remember the command to turn his troop, and they all marched into a fence. When the 20th Virginia Regiment received their orders to what is now West Virginia, B. M. Smith, who had probably seen these maneuvers, sighed: "I have felt from the first that nothing but God's special providence can save our little army out there. They are poorly commanded and have had no time to be fully prepared for this hard service."[279] In contrast, Tazewell McCorkle, third lieutenant in the Hampden-Sydney Boys, described the optimism and enthusiasm in the 1906 *Kaleidoscope*:

> The sweet moral atmosphere that had always pervaded the homes and hovered over the altars, and was an inspiration to all who entered the classic halls of "Union" or "Hampden-Sydney," seemed now charged with electricity of war. Grave "Seminarians" were leaving the reading of Turretin's [views on] Natural and Revealed Theology, and were ready to use the leaves of hymn books for "wadding" if need be to force bullets to the hearts of the enemy.[280]

Smith was right to be concerned. On July 9–11, 1861, Union forces crushed the 20th Virginia Regiment and the Hampden-Sydney Boys at the Battle of Rich Mountain in Randolph County, West Virginia. Almost everyone (including Atkinson and Smith's son Morrison) was captured and paroled on July 13.[281] Granting paroles was common on both sides in the early years of the war. Those paroled surrendered their arms, gave their solemn word that they would fight no more, and were sent home. Unless they were "exchanged" for enemy troops, both sides expected them to keep their vow and not reenter the war.

John Trotti, Union's librarian for thirty-six years, has reported that surprisingly few references to the war appear in the official records of the seminary. Presumably everyone knew what was going on, so there was no reason to mention it. The faculty minutes of September 9, 1861, at the opening of the 1861–62 school year, however, tell the story. "On this day, appointed for the opening of the session, only Dr. Wilson and Rev. Mr. Peck, of the Faculty, and a very few of the students were present, in consequence of the disturbed condition of the country, and other causes. It was determined by the professors present, to postpone the exercises of the Seminary until a full attendance was secured."[282]

As the war progressed, Confederate General Stonewall Jackson (a staunch Presbyterian) was concerned for the safety of his wife, Mary, who had been staying with his minister's family in Winchester, Virginia. When Union forces began their Shenandoah Valley campaign, Jackson feared that his wife would become a target. In early spring 1862 he sent her far from any anticipated action to Hampden-Sydney, alternating living between her two second cousins, Mrs. Dabney and Mrs. Smith.

Jackson, knowing Dabney through his wife, was impressed with Dabney's views on predestination, which were similar to his own. On March 29, 1862, Jackson wrote to Dabney, offering to make him his aide-de-camp. On April 8, after Jackson's adjutant was called back to Richmond, Jackson offered to make him his adjutant general, with the rank of major.[283] Jackson made it clear that Dabney would not be a chaplain: "Your duties would be such that you would not have an opportunity of preaching, except on the Sabbath." Dabney was unsure because he had no military training, but Mrs. Jackson "urged Dr. Dabney to accept the position offered by her husband."[284] After some hesitation, Dabney accepted the commission in March 1862. Whatever his rank, he never made a military impression. Professor Frank Bell Lewis described Dabney's military bearing:

> Dr. Dabney was still protesting that he was not a soldier but a man of peace and refused to wear a uniform. Instead, he wore a long black Prince Albert coat, a high beaver hat, and in lieu of a sword he carried an umbrella. He was obviously somewhat of an apparition as he rode down the ranks of Jackson's army. And it is reported that the men offered comments—"Come down from out of that umbrella, Major Dabney, we know you're in there, we can see your feet hanging down."[285]

Jackson required Dabney's presence immediately. Although the seminary bylaws called for advance notice, Dabney wrote a letter to the board of trustees on April 21, 1862, justifying his decision to leave without adequate notice. He explained that Stonewall Jackson had called him to serve on his staff and the call of the Confederacy superseded his seminary duties.

> The exigencies of the country are so unprecedented and tremendous, every thing that makes our heritage as a people precious, our altars, our homes, our sanctuaries and our Seminaries are so obviously at stake in this crisis, that it appeared to me all other duties shrank into insignificance, beside the duty of rendering aid to our bleeding country, resting upon those who have power to do so. If any modern nation can possibly be placed in the situation of Judea when oppressed by Antiochus, when the Maccabees, although priests, judged it their religious duty to take up the sword, our people are now in a case equally urgent. But my main object, as I need hardly say, is to exercise a religious influence among my brethren and fellow-citizens now acting as defenders of our country; while at the same time there seems to be providentially offered a post, in which I can do no more, with my capacities, in the course of public defence, than perhaps in any other situation.[286]

Dabney contracted "camp fever" in June, however, and was back at the seminary by October. His health was so poor that he could barely teach or preach. Indeed, he was too ill to attend the founding meeting of the PC(CSA).[287]

Enthusiasm for the war remained high for the first years. In 1862, Moses Drury Hoge wrote a letter to Dabney:

I have all along differed from those who think this will be a long war, and I venture the prediction that it will be over by the first of January, 1863. . . . As soon as we drive the enemy from our territory, and, in fact, as soon as we break his lines sufficiently to enable us to make the attempt, I want our armies to invade the United States. I am in favor of fighting on, year after year in case the Northern armies do not make overtures for peace, . . . until the North is scourged and scarred, so as to retain the mark for generations.[288]

But with the losses mounting, enthusiasm began to give way to apprehension as the specter of total war became a reality. The faculty reported to the board on May 12, 1862:

We deeply lament and deplore the necessity which has compelled most of the students to suspend their studies during a part of the past session, in obedience to a demand of our government, to engage in the defence of our invaded country and our dearest rights. And we do most earnestly hope, and will continually pray that under his most wise and holy providence, God will soon cause this unholy war to cease, and peace be restored in all our borders, that our land may no longer be polluted with blood, or the interests of Zion hindered.[289]

The minutes of this same board meeting record that no members of the examinations committee were present, no students were examined, two professors were absent, and only four students were enrolled—and these were parolees from the Battle of Rich Mountain. All students had left in February after the Confederate government called for troops to defend Richmond.[290] All the board could do was pray "that it may please him [God] to spread over our cause his sheltering wing, that he may have under his holy keeping the beloved professor and brethren who have gone from the Seminary to the army, and in his own good time and way, vindicate our righteous cause, and bless us with enduring peace."[291]

Throughout 1861 and 1862 many in the South believed that they could withstand any hardship and force a stalemate as a worst case. Northern victories at Vicksburg (May 18–July 4, 1863) and Gettysburg (July 1–3, 1863) divided Confederate forces and deprived the South of use of the Mississippi to move forces and supplies. These two losses convinced Dabney that the South must be prepared for greater sacrifices if it were to maintain its independence. This sacrifice, he argued, was unthinkable just a year earlier but now was absolutely necessary: gradual emancipation. As he saw it, the South had the choice of emancipating by its own act, gradually and prudently, or continuing to fight until the Confederacy was exhausted and lost the war.[292] He knew how desperate life was on the home front. Professors seldom received their salary, so they kept animals and grew gardens to eat.[293] When B. M. Smith's horse died in 1864, he did not have the money to purchase another one: his former congregation in Staunton presented him with a replacement.[294]

Fighting and survival made education superfluous. Only fifteen students were present at various times during the 1861–62 school year. In March 1862, the Confederate government called for more troops, and all seminary students departed except the four parolees. At the end of the school year the paroled students were exchanged, and they returned to the army. At the opening of the session of 1862–63, the seminary had no students.[295] One student enrolled in the autumn of 1863 and two early in 1864. During the last year of the war, only one student, who had been exempted from military service because of physical disability, was in attendance.

On August 23, 1862, the faculty received a letter on behalf of Columbia Seminary faculty, "requesting that the faculty of Union Sem. concur with them in petitioning the Congress of the Confederate States to exempt students of Divinity from military duty."[296] The Union Seminary faculty responded by appointing a committee and asking Columbia Seminary to send a copy of the petition. The faculty minutes for September 8, 1862, note: "There being no students present at the opening of the session, the faculty held no meeting on that day." They then signed the petition.[297] On January 20, 1864, William Bailey, apparently unfit for the army, "presented himself for classes."[298] B. M. Smith sadly noted that "all [students], or nearly all, [are] in the army." Despite having only one student, with two more who would show up later, the board determined "to keep the seminary open as long as providence permits."[299] There was concern about the property deteriorating, not from battle damage but from disuse.

Only three board members—William H. Foote, C. C. Read from Virginia, and E. Nye Hutchinson from North Carolina—showed up for the board meeting in May 1863. They noted that Anne Rice, John Holt's widow, was considering moving, and the board offered her free room and board for life. Inflation caused them to raise professors' salaries by $300 a year—$150 Confederate was now worth $3 in silver, and its value was falling[300]—and ordered the intendant to sell any extra articles of clothing and furniture.[301] They directed that the uninvested endowment be placed in Confederate bonds.[302] The board also tried to show faith in the cause:

> The Board [members] have directed the faculty to open the Seminary at the usual time, and if any students appear, to conduct regular exercises of the course. They hope that during the war, a few students whose service in the field is not needed by our country may be prepared to meet the prospective destitution of ministers: and they deem it important to prevent the disorganization of the institution by the separation of the faculty; in order that, at the return of the peace, it may be prepared at once for full usefulness.[303]

By the middle of 1864, the effects of the war were all too clear: the board failed to meet in May. The Synod of Virginia, which met in Lexington in October, ordered the board to meet to consider how to support the professors, but nothing was done immediately.[304] On that December 14, the board met for the first time in eighteen months, and the atmosphere was desperate. They voted that all interest derived from the permanent fund not otherwise appropriated and all contingent funds be split among the four professors, not to exceed $4,000 total. In addition, the board asked the churches where the professors preached to pay them more, and they authorized the faculty to rent the seminary buildings to other parties. Perhaps more telling, the board authorized a special subscription to take care of Anne Rice and told the professors to get other jobs. "It was resolved, that until further ordered, the professors shall be left to their own discretion as to any engagements for labor elsewhere which they may deem it expedient to make, provided they make such arrangements as they may agree upon among themselves for the instruction of any students who may come to the institution."

Another Beginning

The war ended just thirty miles from Hampden Sydney, at Appomattox Court House on April 9, 1865. The seminary property was untouched by the conflict. Thomas Peck, the intendant, informed the board: "United States soldiers visited the premises on the 7th and 11th of April, but did no damage to the property of the institution. Naturally the army passing through took clothes, blankets, furniture, and food."[305] B. M. Smith later remembered:

> We had throngs of the enemy here Friday [April 13, 1865: this date differs from those Peck gave], and that night we did not go to bed. The campfires and noise of the army were perceptible all around us. On Tuesday [April 17] while at breakfast, I was sent for to see Mr. Samuel Anderson, dying. I returned to find my premises crowded with soldiers who carried off all my corn and other feed. Simon [his slave] had, with Peter B. [another slave,] secured and saved my horses. We got through the turmoil and devastation better than we expected.[306]

Approximately 12,500 infantrymen of the Army of the Potomac's Fifth Corps spent the night of April 7–8 on and around the college and seminary campus. Fearing the soldiers would loot and destroy the college, seminary, and adjacent houses, Hampden-Sydney College President Atkinson sent a messenger to General Sheridan at the Court House, requesting that guards be assigned to protect Hampden-Sydney. A son of a former Hampden-Sydney College math professor, Henry Snyder, a pro-Union sympathizer who had resigned from the college in the summer of 1861, was within earshot of the messenger's voice. Because the young Snyder had been raised there and was acquainted with its occupants, he volunteered to lead a company to protect the buildings. The soldiers left for good four days after the surrender on April 9, and there was no property damage.

College Church's oldest ruling elder, Samuel Anderson, nearly seventy-seven years old, was walking near the Prince Edward Court House the evening of the surrender, which also happened to be Palm Sunday. Committed to the southern cause, Anderson had made the motion to expel the New School presbyteries at the 1837 General Assembly. As he walked across the courthouse lawn, a messenger galloped by, shouting that Lee had surrendered to Grant at Appomattox Court House. On hearing the news, he collapsed with a stroke. Anderson lingered in a coma until early the following Saturday morning, April 15, 1865, succumbing at exactly the same hour Abraham Lincoln died in Washington, D.C., two hundred miles away.[307]

Richard McIlwaine recalled that the news of Lincoln's assassination was received in Farmville with regret. The Union commander asked McIlwaine for permission to use Farmville Presbyterian Church for a memorial service in honor of the slain president, and McIlwaine, as pastor, agreed. McIlwaine and the clerk of session were the only people from Farmville present for the service.[308]

As directed by the board, the seminary remained open. On Monday, May 8, 1865,

> at the hour appointed by the constitution, divine service was celebrated in the chapel of Union Theological Seminary, Prince Edward. The sermon was preached by the Rev. Henry Foote, D. D., first Vice-President of the Board of Directors (and the only member present), from Isaiah XXXV.10: "And the ransomed of the LORD shall return, and come to Zion with songs and everlasting joy upon their heads; they shall obtain joy and gladness, and sorrow and sighing shall flee away."

Foote preached to four professors and one student.[309] The exercises of the seminary were then adjourned, to recommence on the second Thursday in September 1865. Foote died in November 1869, after serving more than thirty years as a director.[310]

Union Seminary provided 32 chaplains and 44 line troops for the Confederate Army, and one chaplain for the Union Army. Seven alumni and students were killed in action, including one chaplain. Morrison, the son of B. M. Smith who had enlisted in the Hampden-Sydney Boys after Fort Sumter, contracted a fever in July 1864 and died shortly after the surrender.[311]

One strange incident occurred within days of the surrender: the librarian reported that a package of books "on the Swedenborgian system of belief" had been received, yet without any note of explanation.[312] The books are still on the library shelves. Indeed, Union preserved its academic treasures during the war; in his 1868 catalogue, B. M. Smith reported that all twenty-two of the original volumes in his 1833 catalogue remained on the shelves: not one volume was missing.[313]

The fall 1865 board minutes list returning members of the Class of 1860–61 as if they were coming back after summer vacation, but this effort to ignore the events of the last four years was only wishful thinking. The seminary was bankrupt. The board had invested $46,000 in Confederate States and Commonwealth of Virginia bonds and bank stocks. All were a total loss. The Commonwealth vowed to repay its bonds, but there was no income in 1865. As a consequence, the intendant did not collect the usual $5.00 fee from each student, and he recorded that the rooms had no furniture.[314]

When the Presbyterian Church in the Confederate States of America was formed on December 4, 1861, it had 47 presbyteries, almost 1,100 congregations, and more than 75,000 members.[315] Whatever the circumstances of its creation, the church did represent the aspirations of its people. And the scars of fratricidal bloodletting would preclude reconciliation. The 1865 Northern General Assembly meeting in Pittsburgh ordered every presbytery, north and south, to examine every minister or layman seeking admission to the church to ascertain

> whether he has in any way, directly or indirectly, of his own free will and consent, or without external constraint, been concerned at any time in aiding or countenancing the rebellion and the war which has been waged against

the United States; . . . he shall be required to confess and forsake his sin in this regard before he shall be received.

The northern church would not recognize a separate denomination:

This Assembly regards the civil rebellion for the perpetuation of Negro slavery as a great crime, both against our National Government and against God, and the secession of these Presbyteries and Synods from the Presbyterian Church, under such circumstances and for such reasons, as unwarranted, schismatic, and unconstitutional.[316]

Quite naturally, Southerners objected to this attitude and responded with defiance. Historian Shelby Foote has described the developing southern consciousness after the Civil War as the "Confederacy of the mind." That is, Southerners had to deny that slavery was the cause of the conflict and maintained they were only defending a level of purity in culture and theology abdicated by the North. On November 2, 1865, the Central Presbyterian printed a letter signed only "H," but probably written by Moses Drury Hoge:

We shall, with God's blessing, maintain our distinct Assembly, and we will proceed to "restore the Churches, South, to their former status" with such means as the Lord may afford us out of our own recuperating resources. All that the Presbyterian Church in the United States has ever suffered, and all that it now suffers, has come of the New Englandism [by] which it has been so carefully inoculated. Now that the Southern Church is happily separate, let us keep aloof from that element. Let us have a happy, pure, free, "Presbyterian" Church.[317]

Just as the Old Side had complained of "enthusiasm" and "New Englandism" on the part of the New Side in 1741, and the Old School had complained of the "revivalism" and "New Englandism" on the part of the New School in 1838, the old arguments were now employed in a new cause. And Union Seminary would once again take a leading part in defending that cause, continuing the course set by George Baxter.

The Threads of History

Union Theological Seminary was now a southern school. But it remained dedicated to the five subjects in the traditional curriculum taught in a departmentally organized seminary. Rice's ideal of a seminary-educated ministry was secure. Churches and presbyteries now expected their ministers to attend at least two years of seminary. More important, however, the supporting synods and presbyteries began to care about the future of their theological institution.

Baxter, however dedicated he was to the ideal of an educated minister, led Union away from John Holt Rice's ideal of a southern seminary serving the national church. By masterminding the Old School faction that divided the Presbyterian Church and investing in a theology that defended slavery, he had turned Union into a southern institution. Although three faculty members had studied in Germany during this period, Union had still not fulfilled Rice's dream of American Presbyterian scholarship answering German critical study. Indeed, John Leith, who taught at Union Seminary from 1958 to 1990, observed that the first four theology teachers were dedicated to the church more than to their academic disciplines.

> The four professors of theology during this period were not self-conscious theologians. They were ministers out of the church, and teaching was a way of fulfilling their ordination vows. They had little formal education, but they were effective human beings and intellectually bright. Their theology was biblical, designed to mediate God's grace to people, and grounded in the Westminster Confession.[318]

Although Union professors had early doubts about secession, they considered their country to be Virginia and approved of using arms to defend it and its peculiar institution. Union students passionately took up arms for the South.

Through this period, Union students remained eager to engage the world. Despite Hampden-Sydney's remoteness, students in the 1830s enthusiastically embraced world and home missions, but ignored the plight of slaves. The Old School–New School split dampened the missionary spirit, and the threat of abolition caused them to narrow their horizons. Yet Union graduates were nurturing embryonic social change; they served as agents for various temperance and Bible societies. Graduates upheld the idea of an educated ministry, while participating in "reasonable revivals."

Union's influence on the denomination became formidable. Union graduates served as moderators of the Presbyterian General Assembly, presidents of colleges and institutes, and principals of academies and female seminaries. Although destitute as the result of war, the faculty kept the doors open. George Baxter may have retreated from John Holt Rice's vision, but the vision remained.

At the end of volume 1 of the Faculty Minutes are fifteen pages of signatures preceded by the oath:

> Deeply impressed with a sense of the importance of improving in knowledge, prudence, and piety, in my preparation for the gospel ministry, I solemnly promise, in a reliance on divine grace, that I will faithfully and diligently attend on all the instructions of this seminary, and that I will conscientiously and carefully observe all the rules and regulations specified in the plan for its instruction and government, so far as the same relate to the students; and that I will obey all the laws and requisitions, and readily yield to all the wholesome admonitions of the professors and directors of the seminary, while I shall continue a member of it.

This oath first appeared in the 1811 Plan of a Theological Seminary, written by Ashbel Green, and the 1824 Plan of the Theological Seminary, written by John Holt Rice. The signatures begin in 1823 and continue through 1859, and volume 2 holds thirty pages of signatures covering the years 1859 to 1892. Whatever the politics of the day, the national upheavals, the personal opinions of the students, or the theological fashions then current, the curriculum remained true to the 1560 Book of Discipline, and the students continued to do their best to answer their call. From the subjects they learned and their efforts to apply what they learned in their congregations, the foundations of the future of the Presbyterian Church were set, guided, and supported by Union Theological Seminary.

Chapter Five (1866–97)
Fighting Yankees and Moving to Richmond

Barely one month after Lee surrendered, about thirty miles away, the Rev. Henry Foote declared to four professors and one student that "the ransomed of the LORD shall return." Over the next thirty years, Union Seminary would not just return to its former preeminence as a southern seminary; it would also position itself to become a national leader in theological education. In a culture that was continually and obstinately looking backward, Union became known for its innovation in teaching methods, progressive educational philosophy, and commitment to the urban South. Walter W. Moore stressed hands-on education, introduced Christian Education into the curriculum, and understood that Union would have to address a newly urbanized South. And he finally decided that Hampden Sydney was too small and isolated a place to put his ideas into practice. So he relocated the campus to the city of Richmond, in what became known as the Removal.

The Civil War had been fought primarily in the South; the maritime blockade, constant foraging by the armies, and destruction of the industrial base devastated the Confederacy. Unlike many places in the South, the students returning to Hampden-Sydney College did not find the campus destroyed, but it was dilapidated. Although the war had not touched the seminary, the buildings were shabby due to lack of maintenance. The roofs leaked; buckets had to be put in the garrets when it rained.[1] In 1870 a student wrote to Rocky River Church, which apparently had furnished his room: "The room itself is a comfortable one; . . . the floor abounds in cracks, which are particularly valuable in contributing to the ventilation of the room, in which, so far, no one has ever died of suffocation." He noted that the carpet was made "principally of holes," and the beds, "made of shucks, and no doubt many years ago were very luxurious. At present, however, they abound in ridges, interspersed with knots and other like contrivances that remind one of a chopped sea, or the bed of your own Rocky River, and consequently are very mortifying to the flesh."

William Stephens Tucker complained to the secretary of the board of trustees: "The employees of the Cook's department empty the slops from the cookroom into a ditch right in front of our window. The stench is such that I have had to endure the absence of air. I have remonstrated again and again to no effect with the cook. I, as a last resort, appeal to you." Disgusted that nothing was done, he quit UTS and joined the Baptist Church. There was a petition signed by nineteen students (including Joseph Anderson Vance [1888], a future moderator of the northern church) protesting the shortage of water during the fall months "by reason of the cisterns not being large enough to supply the demands with winter water, but must be filled with summer water, which is not palatable."[2]

There was no money. During the war the seminary's board of directors had invested $46,000 in Confederate securities, about $20,000 in bank stocks, and $102,035[3] in Virginia and North Carolina State bonds. The Confederate securities and bank stocks were a total loss. Although the state bonds would ultimately be repaid, the payment of interest was suspended for three years.[4] Between 1865 and 1869, not one cent of income came from the endowment.[5]

Enrollment was chaotic. The fall 1865 board minutes list the 11 members of the Class of 1860–61 as returning, plus 4 new students. Faculty reports, however, show the admission of the 4 new students but give a total of 24 attending. The general catalogues show a total of 11 students in attendance. There is no way to reconcile these discrepancies; faculty minutes show that students enrolled and departed arbitrarily at various times. Returning veterans enrolled whenever they could return to Hampden-Sydney, and students already in class had to leave to look after family affairs (such as spring planting).

At the end of 1865, the intendant reported that the usual tax of $5.00 on each student for the Contingent Fund had not been collected, "for a reason too obvious to need to be mentioned," and the rooms had been robbed of a good deal of furniture. He added that the kindness of friends "had supplied the deficiency in part," the largest donation being twelve army blankets from a friend in Baltimore.[6] Returning Confederate veterans wore their uniform tunics with the buttons covered in black: it was illegal to wear "Rebel" buttons.

The 1866 Catalogue says it all. It is only four pages in length and to the point: Tuition, "gratis"; matriculation, $.00; rooms and furniture, "gratis"; board, $17 per month; wood, $2.50 per cord; washing, $1.50 per month. The buildings are described as "handsome and commodious for seventy students; climate excellent." The curriculum remained intact, with five courses offered: Pastoral Theology and Evidences, Systematic and Polemic Theology and Sacred Rhetoric, Oriental Literature, Ecclesiastical History and Polity, and Biblical Introduction.[7]

A Southern or a National Seminary?

Just fifty years earlier, John Holt Rice had a vision for a national seminary. He raised money in the North for his school of the prophets and made sure the General Assembly, representing the national church, would care for his vision. George A. Baxter retreated from Rice's aspirations by leading the Old School split. With the war over, Union had a choice: return to Rice's expansive vision or remain a sectional institution. This is the irony of Union's history. In the last half of the nineteenth century, Union saw itself as a southern seminary, but one that depended on the Northerners for survival; a bulwark of southern conservatism, but producing students who undermined this conservatism.

The paradox of Union's history is personified by Robert Lewis Dabney and Benjamin Mosby Smith. While Dabney sought to reinterpret and preserve traditional southern culture against the intrusions of the modern world, he did very little for Union Seminary as an institution. It was B. M. Smith who pulled the seminary through the postwar years. His fund-raising efforts in 1865–66 gave the seminary a future. When Lee surrendered at Appomattox in April 1865, Dabney commenced his own emotional war to defend what he saw as the southern birthright. Smith went north to raise money, and it was northern support that allowed Union to stay open.

In June 1865, Mrs. Harmon Brown traveled from Baltimore to Hampden Sydney with a donation of twelve army blankets for the students, and $100 and cloth (for making clothes) for each of the professors. For the Brown family, Union's rebuilding was an act of faith on several levels. Thomas Peck, professor at the seminary, had been the Browns' pastor from 1857 to 1860, and Mrs. Brown did not want to see her former pastor in distress. Moreover, she came to see Union as a symbol of the South that must be restored. After delivering her gifts, she asked if one of the professors could return with her to raise money. B. M. Smith immediately left with her for Baltimore, hoping to raise perhaps $400 or $500. After two weeks in Baltimore, he met with such success that he decided to go to New York for two more weeks. He returned to Hampden Sydney with $4,000 in cash and another $4,000 in pledges, which allowed classes to resume.[8]

Having seen a wealthy land untouched by combat and knowing that the South was too impoverished to support the seminary, Smith persuaded the board to reestablish relationships with their "friends" in the North. On his own initiative, he began a correspondence with the industrialist Cyrus McCormick, appealing for his assistance, and McCormick responded with a gift of $30,000.[9] By 1869, the endowment had increased to $90,000, including a $30,000 gift by Henry Young, a stockbroker in New York City.[10]

Besides cultivating his own northern contacts, Smith persuaded the board to launch a drive to raise $100,000. They began the campaign by publishing a small pamphlet, *Address to the Christian Public*, in 1866. Undoubtedly written or edited by Smith, this was more than a fund-raising device; it was Union's declaration to be a seminary for the entire church:

> The institution welcomes to its advantages all who seek instruction in the word of God as interpreted and set forth in the time-honored standards of the Presbyterian Church. . . . All ultraisms in doctrine, and all subjects connected with political government, and questions that engender strife, are carefully discarded from the topics of discussion and instruction in the Seminary.[11]

This brochure also assured the reader that "no student has died within the walls of the seminary."[12]

The pacific and conciliatory language contained in *Address to the Christian Public* was quickly contradicted by Robert Lewis Dabney. He published two books shortly after the war. The first was the *Life and Campaigns of Lieut.-Gen. Thomas J. Jackson*, published in 1866. The second was *A Defence of Virginia (and through Her, of the South) in Recent and Pending Contests against the Sectional Party*, written prior to Jackson's biography, but not published until 1867. Thus *Address to the Christian Public* is sandwiched between them.

Although Dabney's biography of Stonewall Jackson was popular, his *Defence of Virginia* may be one of the most influential books in American history. Indeed, throughout the next century Southerners would define tradition in his terms and employ his reasoning to defend the "southern" way of life as segregation and resistance to change. It is through *A Defence of Virginia* that Dabney became known as one of the leading theologians of the South and the southern Presbyterian church, along with James Henley Thornwell in South Carolina, who developed the doctrine of "the spirituality of the church," and Benjamin Morgan Palmer of New Orleans, whose 1860 Thanksgiving sermon influenced Louisiana to secede and who was the first moderator of the PC(CSA).

Dabney's argument in *A Defence of Virginia* is simple: since the enslavement of Africans by Europeans was permitted by the curse of Noah upon Ham, slavery was justified by Scripture. It was England who had forced slavery upon Virginia. In God's providence, slavery had actually turned out to be in the best interests of the Negroes, the South, and the nation as a whole. Abolitionists (whose ancestors had made money on the slave trade) only became self-righteously opposed to slavery when it had ceased to be profitable. The South, therefore, was innocent in the war, only protecting itself against tyranny. In the end, however, God permitted the South to be defeated "for our sins towards him."[13]

While Dabney was just beginning his tirades against the Yankees, B. M. Smith was cultivating Yankee donors. His correspondence with Cyrus McCormick, whom he met at the 1859 General Assembly, is instructive. Cyrus Hall McCormick was born in 1809 in Rockbridge County, Virginia, and by the time of the Civil War his reaping machine had made him one of America's wealthiest men. McCormick was a devout Presbyterian and had opposed the trend toward abolition in the New School Assembly. He was anxious for the Old School General Assembly to rescind the Gardner Spring Resolution of 1861, paving the way for the reunion of the northern and southern churches. When the 1865 Old School northern General Assembly refused, McCormick believed it was up to him to undertake his own efforts to bind the wounds of the war, even if he had to pay for it himself.

In 1848, McCormick had paid for the Seminary of the Northwest to be relocated from New Albany, Indiana, to Chicago, where it was renamed McCormick Theological Seminary. He took pride in his eponymous school. During the war, however, McCormick was increasingly disappointed to see control of the seminary pass to those he considered "radical." In 1865 he contributed $1,000 to the emergency fund being collected for Union Seminary. B. M. Smith noticed. On May 12, 1866, he wrote McCormick and hit just the right note in the tradition of John Holt Rice:

> We have never had "isms" and fanatical men. . . . I am utterly opposed to all sectionalism. I go for a national church. We may now be poor and despised— but with the truth and God's blessing, we will grow and strengthen, and the remnants of Old School Presbyterianism in the north, when their convulsions shall have subsided, will be with us.[14]

McCormick had promised to pay $100,000 when the Seminary of the Northwest was established in Chicago. Although he had already paid $75,000 of the pledge, he now refused to pay the final $25,000 when a man of whom he disapproved was elected to the faculty.

Smith saw his chance. On May 31 he wrote another long letter, reminding McCormick that "the effect of the action of the A[ssembly] and the prospect of a union of the Old and New School leaves our Seminary (except Columbia, which is too crippled to do much) the institution around which all old-fashioned sound Presbyterians over the whole land must rally." McCormick immediately promised $30,000.[15]

As 1866 came to a close, Smith was optimistic about Union's future. In an exultant letter to McCormick on December 11, after his return from his fund-raising expedition to Louisville, St. Louis, and the PCUS General Assembly at Memphis, he wrote:

> From all I could see & hear, I am more than ever convinced of the wisdom of those, who founded this Seminary and of others, who like yourself, have made it the object of a large & liberal charity. In the progress of things, we may look for the present instability north & south to subside. . . . Already the Missouri & Kentucky men are saying —"We shall look to you." It would never do for us to remove one inch to the south, nor to the west. The strong Virginia feeling in Kentucky, Missouri, Tennessee & Arkansas—will turn the men & churches there to us. We have every reason to believe, that in a few years, perhaps not over ten, this Institution will deserve, & will have, the "first place" in the confidence & affection of all sound conservative Presbyterians, throughout the country.[16]

On May 14, 1867, Samuel B. Wilson presented to the board of trustees what should be considered the first history of Union Seminary. The previous year, the board had asked Wilson, as its secretary, to write a history to give some context to their present situation. In his sixteen-page history Wilson found inspiration in Moses Hoge and John Holt Rice, virtually ignoring the immediately preceding thirty years. Wilson seems to be arguing that Union should return to Rice's original vision and consider itself a national seminary.[17] For the moment, it seemed as though Union could reclaim that expansive heritage.

Vestiges of War

Despite the positive outlook brought about by northern support for Union, McCormick's fears of "radicals" in both North and South were justified. At the May 1865 Old School General Assembly in Pittsburgh (held in an emotionally charged atmosphere just a few weeks after Lincoln's assassination), the northern church refused to recognize the southern Presbyterians as a legitimately organized Christian denomination, stopping just short of labeling the Southerners heretical. The Pittsburgh General Assembly stipulated that they would only receive southern congregations and ministers into a "reconciled" denomination if southern presbyteries and church sessions would sign a "penitential pledge," acknowledging that their views on states' rights, slavery, and the Confederate government had been sinful.[18] At the December 1865 meeting in Macon, Georgia, the first General Assembly of the Presbyterian Church in the United States (PCUS, refashioned from the Presbyterian Church in the Confederate States of America) rejected the northern terms of reunion.[19]

Cyrus McCormick and the faculty of Princeton Seminary spoke out forcefully against the northern church's actions.[20] McCormick also launched his own personal crusade within the northern Presbyterian church to repeal both the

1861 Gardiner Spring Resolutions and 1865 "sin pledge." His support of UTS can be seen in the light of his desire to see the church reunite as equal partners. B. M. Smith crystallized the southern position in a letter to McCormick: "We are as much disposed to a united, harmonious National Church as ever. But the view implied in speaking of our 'returning' to the Church is not the correct one. We have never gone away."[21]

Any thought of reunion remained stalled for four years. Although the southern New School and Old School General Assemblies united in 1861, the northern New and Old School Assemblies did not combine until 1869. Once the northern churches reunited, the drive for joining northern and southern churches reignited. The first General Assembly of the reunited northern churches unanimously resolved to "heal all unnecessary divisions" and to establish cordial relations with the southern Presbyterian church "on terms of mutual confidence, respect, Christian honor, and love." In good Presbyterian fashion, they appointed a special committee to negotiate with the PCUS, if that body should appoint one also.[22]

The opening was presented the next year, in 1870, when Dr. Henry Van Dyke, a noted conservative Northern Presbyterian minister and friend of many Southerners, came with a delegation to the PCUS General Assembly in Louisville, Kentucky, moderated by Robert L. Dabney. Van Dyke suggested that at the least a fraternal exchange of representatives might be established between the two General Assemblies.[23] Dabney replied: "I hear brethren saying it is time for forgive. Mr. Chairman, I do not forgive! I do not try to forgive! What! Forgive these people, who have invaded our country, burned our cities, destroyed our homes, slain our young men, and spread desolation and ruin over our land! No, I do not forgive them!"[24] While Dabney's uncompromising stance carried the day, B. M. Smith went against his colleague and advocated at least talking to the northern delegation.[25] Smith understood that by rejecting the northern overtures, fund-raising in the North would come to an end. He was right: financial support from the North was virtually nonexistent by 1872.[26]

Although Dabney was married to Smith's wife's sister and they were copastors of College Church, their differences were out in the open by 1870. They sometimes exchanged "sharp words" in public.[27] Smith frequently traveled to the North, both before and after the war, while Dabney never went north after 1860. Smith could also not abide the developing theology of the spirituality of the church, which held that the church could have no say on political issues. Before the war he took a public stand against dueling,[28] and in 1859 he publicly criticized James H. Thornwell because Thornwell opposed a resolution commending the work of the American Colonization Society on the grounds that the church was a spiritual body and had no temporal functions. Smith replied that the spiritual body of the church has temporal functions, as shown by the institution of deacons. So the church diaconate should materially assist the American Colonization Society in their work. Besides supporting at least talking to delegates from the northern church, Smith advocated for fraternal relations with the Dutch Reformed Church and the Cumberland Presbyterian Church.

Dabney fought intensely against public education (which had been mandated by the postwar Virginia constitution). He believed that education was the responsibility of the parents, not the state. In contrast, Smith spent his adult life working to establish public schools for all children, regardless of race. In 1838 he wrote to Virginia Governor David Campbell, proposing to organize Virginia's public schools on the Prussian model. In 1869 he publicly called for the state to assume full responsibility for the education of all children[29] and to support the schools through public taxes.[30] He helped William Henry Ruffner (1846), his longtime friend, establish a statewide public education system for both races in Virginia. He then volunteered to chair Prince Edward County's first public school board from 1865 to 1881 (serving as the Superintendent of Schools for Prince Edward County for eleven years), and helped several surrounding counties establish their school systems.[31]

Dabney's and Smith's conflicting legacies can be summed up in a story that illustrates how they were seen by contemporaries:

> During the war, when the pressure on the people at home for the means of sustenance had become stringent and universal, the writer of this sketch, then living some forty or forty-five miles distant, happened to meet some one from the neighborhood of the Seminary and inquired how the professors were getting on. "Well," said he, "Dr. Dabney is fighting the Yankees, Dr. Smith is hunting for provisions, and Dr. Peck is trusting in God."[32]

Smith's legacy was administration, not theology. He saved UTS after the war, yet he never had the influence of Dabney. It was Dabney who became the most influential theologian in the PCUS and indeed the South in the last half of the nineteenth century. Indeed, until the 1930s his successors used Dabney's *Syllabus* as their textbook.[33]

Yet even Thomas Cary Johnson, professor of Church History and Polity at Union at the end of the nineteenth century, and author of Dabney's first biography, admitted that Dabney "was at war with much in his age." It is clear that by the end of his book, even Johnson is uncomfortable with Dabney's implacable racism, hatred of the North, and resistance to change. He became an embarrassing anachronism to almost everyone. In the seventieth-anniversary history of Union Seminary, Walter W. Moore emphasizes those whom he considered important to the seminary. He goes to some length to highlight Rice and Smith, but Baxter and Dabney are virtually ignored. In his autobiography, Richard McIlwaine also ignores Dabney, and he compares Smith to Rice.[34] Indeed, when the death of B. M. Smith was reported on March 31, 1893, the faculty minutes paid tribute to him: "The outward prosperity of the Seminary is more indebted to him than to any other man since the death of its founder Dr. J. H. Rice."[35]

Keeping the Reformed Tradition

While B. M. Smith was courting northern donors, the board was able to create an organization to guide the future of Union Seminary. Although the seminary had received a limited charter in 1855 (which only allowed it to hold money), Virginia's Reconstruction constitution allowed for the incorporation of theological schools, and Union Seminary was finally incorporated in 1867 (fifty-two years after John Holt Rice first approached the Virginia General Assembly), and the Constitution and Plan was published in 1869. Without incorporation, Union's subsequent actions would not have been possible. With a charter of incorporation, the seminary could make its own decisions about land, personnel, and administration without interference. Beginning with the 1886 catalogue, and continuing until 1976, Union made its independence clear:

> The Seminary is under the care of the Synods of Virginia and North Carolina. The Board of Directors is composed of twenty-four members, twelve from each of the Synods to which the Board reports. The General Assembly of the Presbyterian Church in the United States also has a right of general superintendence, may advise and commend, but not originate, measures for the management of the institution.

The Union Seminary constitution (both the 1869 version and the 1892 revision) not only allowed the board of trustees to administrate the seminary's business affairs; the board would also ensure orthodoxy. Each professor was required to accept "the Scriptures of the Old and New Testaments to be the word of God, the only rule of faith and practice," and to "receive and adopt the Confession of Faith of the Presbyterian Church in the United States as faithfully exhibiting the doctrines taught in the Holy Scriptures." More important, each professor promised "not to teach anything that appears to contradict any doctrine contained in the Confession of Faith, nor to oppose any of the fundamental principles of the Presbyterian Church government." The faculty members were required to "introduce their lectures and recitations with prayer," as well as hold two "daily seasons of prayer (excepting Saturday and Sunday), on which all the students and at least one Professor shall attend."

The 1869 Constitution and Plan set "the regular course of instruction and study in this Seminary" at "not less than three scholastic years." Moreover, "every student of the Middle and Senior Classes shall be required to preach in the presence of the Faculty and students and any other persons twice every term, or oftener; one such sermon to be delivered without notes, and one with manuscript."[36] The Plan also required every student, "before entering on his studies," to affirm the pledge first found in the 1810 General Assembly Plan, obligating himself to "diligently attend on all the instructions of this Seminary, . . . observe all the rules and regulations specified in the plan, . . . and readily yield to all the wholesome admonitions of the professors."[37]

The curriculum remained intact. Although the names had changed somewhat, the Plan mandated the traditional five courses: (1) Oriental Literature and Biblical Interpretation; Greek and Hebrew, plus Chaldee (Aramaic) in the second year; (2) Systematic and Polemic Theology, and Sacred Rhetoric—apologetics and homiletics; (3) Pastoral Theology and Evidences—a study of the Pastoral Epistles to "store the memory with facts and arguments" to defend the faith; (4) Ecclesiastical History and Polity; and (5) Biblical Introduction—a combination of English Bible and theology as it pertained to inspiration and revelation. As William Oglesby has pointed out, the course offerings did not deviate from the Reformed ideal.

It would be possible, with little disruption, to reprint the course designations of the 1830s to the 1880s and conclude that the life of the seminary moved along at about the same pace with about the same emphases at any given point. Primary emphasis was still given to the Bible in the original languages, to systematic theology, to church history and polity. The actual function of the minister in day-to-day activity received little curricular attention with the exception of the preparation of sermons.[38]

Dabney, however, thought the curriculum was outdated and submitted a Memorial on Theological Education to the Committee on Seminaries at the 1869 PCUS General Assembly. He recommended reorganizing the seminary curriculum "to keep abreast of advances in the sciences in order to answer their objection to faith." In addition to more classes in apologetics, he argued against setting a specific number of years to gain an education. Rather, "a standard of proficiency should be fixed," and students should be allowed to proceed at their own pace.[39]

Smith, however, fought back by arguing that an emphasis on apologetics would diminish the traditional prominence of biblical languages. He wanted Union students, in their preaching and teaching, to appeal "to the word of God, as he revealed it, and not to a version, however generally faithful." A facility with scriptural languages, he argued, would make a better preacher, "with clear perceptions and fullness of scriptural thought, and a style enriched by scripture language and imagery."[40] The General Assembly rejected Dabney's memorial.

Although the 1869 General Assembly refused to entertain his Memorial on Theological Education, Dabney saw the future. Charles Darwin published *On the Origin of Species* in November 1859. The challenge was obvious: if natural selection was responsible for all life, the Creator was superfluous. Dabney's proposed curriculum would prepare ministers to confront Darwin's challenge. Glenn T. Miller points out that the debate over Darwin shifted the focus of American theology from the exposition of traditional theology to the discussion of the contemporary questions before the church.[41] As a result, many questioned the need for biblical language training. In 1873 and 1881, overtures reached the PCUS General Assembly challenging the language requirement as outmoded. Yet biblical languages would continue to be the cornerstone of Union's curriculum.

In 1859, Columbia Seminary appointed James Woodrow (uncle of future president Woodrow Wilson) as the first Perkins Professor of Natural Science in Connection with Revelation: he was given the optimistic charge "to envince the harmony of science with the records of our faith, and to refute the objections of infidel science." Dabney, the guardian of orthodoxy in the southern Presbyterian church, objected, fearing that Woodrow would be led to "naturalistic and anti-Christian opinions." In 1875 he published a broadside against Woodrow, warning him not to be "dazzled by the fascination of facts and speculation." He dismissed evolution by noting the unbridgeable gap between the mentality of man and animals.[42]

In 1884, the year after Dabney left Union, Woodrow published a pamphlet titled *Evolution*. In it he insisted, "The Bible does not teach science; and to take its language in a scientific sense is grossly to pervert its meaning." He further argued that creation was not a six-day affair, but a series of "gradual processes by which the Creator had brought [the earth] into its present condition."[43] Woodrow's essay created a firestorm, and Dabney led the attack. In

1886, Columbia Seminary's Board of Directors asked for Woodrow's resignation. He refused, and the board fired him. At least nine synods, twenty or more presbyteries, and five General Assemblies from 1884 to 1888 had the case before them. In the end Dabney won: Woodrow lost his job.

Effects of the Woodrow case were to last for more than fifty years. Woodrow was fired "because he taught doctrines opposed to the traditional interpretation of Scripture and the Standards of the Church." Seminary and denominational professors were not to question the accepted understanding of both Scripture and the Westminster Confession, but only to transmit it. Southern Presbyterian scholarship went into the doldrums. Dabney ensured that southern scholars would not depart from "the Tradition."[44]

Turning away from the World

Dabney's legacy is one of sad insularity. He constructed an inflexible theology and nurtured a seething hatred for the North. It was his all-consuming racism, however, that seared his view of life. Immediately after the war, he was alarmed over the freedmen in the Mercy Seat community adjacent to the Hampden-Sydney campus. He could not stand to see former slaves become landowners and prosperous, and his solution was to leave. At various times between 1865 and 1880, he thought about emigrating to Australia, New Zealand, Mexico, Venezuela, British Honduras (present-day Belize), or Brazil.[45] In August 1865, Dabney wrote Moses D. Hoge:

> It appears to me that there are only two prospects for the South. Parts of it will continue under the present paralysis, until they sink permanently into the condition of Jamaica. . . . Other parts will again see material prosperity; but only by being completely Yankeeized. . . . I fear the independence, the honor, the hospitality, the integrity, the everything which constituted Southern character, is gone forever. . . . The only chance to save any of the true Christianity of the South is to transplant it as quick as possible.[46]

On January 2, 1867, he again wrote to Hoge: "Either the Negro must move, or the College and Seminary must move."

However repulsive Dabney's racism may seem to us, his views are representative of nineteenth-century culture. Dabney was not the only one to feel anxious about the increasing ownership of land by freedmen. Both seminary and college felt under siege, especially when freedmen owned land adjacent to the south edge of the seminary grounds. The board minutes of 1876 describe plans to form a land company to purchase land to prevent "an undesirable population in the vicinity of the Seminary."[47] In the minutes of the 1877 spring board of directors meeting is a paragraph titled "Colored Population": "Resolved, that Dr. J. D. Eggleston be requested, on behalf of this institution, to aid the faculty in any feasible plan of preventing the settlement of an undesirable population in the vicinity of the Seminary."[48]

In 1874 the faculty ordered that the students and "the Seminary servants" be informed "that no freedmen can be admitted to the Seminary, for service, except those regularly connected with the Intendent's department, and the messes."[49] By the 1880s, the seminary professors and trustees were concerned about declining land values.

Racist attitudes, however, were obscured by the pervasive paternalism, which led whites to believe that they were the best friends of blacks. In the 1850s, for example, when Dabney discovered that the architect's design for a new College Church had not included plans for attendance by slaves, he literally tore them up and made his own blueprint, which included separate slave seating and entrance because he believed slaves should be in church.[50] In 1917, G. Nash Morton (1866), a longtime missionary to Brazil, remembered that Smith and Dabney had a small Sunday school for Negroes in the College Church.[51]

By the 1880s, Mercy Seat Baptist Church, within sight of the seminary, was one of the few institutions owned and governed by blacks, and relations appeared cordial. Seminarians conducted a Sunday afternoon education and worship program at the church, and Walter W. Moore collected clothes and food for blacks and frequently preached at Mercy Seat Baptist on Sunday nights. However, when he preached at white churches, Moore used to tell "funny stories in the Negro dialect, to which he could impart the genuine Virginia flavor."[52]

But even benevolence had its limits. In 1867 three African American ministers organized an independent presbytery (Knox), later received into the northern Presbyterian church. The three ministers argued that they had to be separate because, being deprived of seats on the floor of the presbytery, they would never be equal. Their position was confirmed that fall when the question of ordaining freedmen came before the Synod of Virginia. Dabney took the floor and spoke against the ordination of freedmen with "every force of argument, emotion, will, and utterance"[53] and carried the day.

Dabney was the first person to advocate moving the seminary when in 1867 he recommended it because of the presence of freedmen. He never had the resources to follow through, however, and nothing was done. When Walter W. Moore, the senior faculty member, raised the issue of moving at the 1892 board meeting, the stated reason was fund-raising and facilities. Yet beneath the veneer of Christian brotherhood shown by Dabney, Smith, and Moore, Union was still a nineteenth-century southern institution, and the benign paternalism could turn vicious. In 1939, Randolph B. Grinnan (1885) remembered events surrounding the 1876 presidential election. He relates that in the 1876 election, "the Negroes voted solidly for the Republican ticket, and there was considerable feeling between the whites and blacks. Under bad leadership, the Negroes were quite insolent. One student, hearing a group of Negroes who were quite insolent and noisy on the Via Sacra, called several "college boys and Seminary students" and gave them guns; they surrounded the blacks who were celebrating the Republican victory. "The Negroes were guarded and held in a cellar room of the Seminary building and taken to Farmville the next day and handed over to the county officers."[54]

In the early 1880s, paradoxically, College Church developed a small outreach to the local black community through a Sunday school chapel for freedmen. Robert Lee Telford (1890) and other concerned seminary students convinced B. M. Wilkinson, a young black man from southside Virginia who had studied at Stillman Institute in Tuscaloosa, Alabama (the only PCUS school for the training of black ministers), to help them with their Sunday school. The students had been holding Sabbath school classes for local African Americans, and these classes became so popular that they thought these classes would develop into a full-fledged congregation. Wilkinson began in 1883, but his work only lasted a year.[55]

In 1883, Dabney's health broke: his kidneys were failing, and he was going blind. His doctor advised him to live in a warmer climate, so he resigned from the seminary and moved to Texas. For the next fifteen years, he taught philosophy at the new state university and would organize the theology department, which later became Austin Theological Seminary. Later in his life, Dabney looked back on his resignation from Union and acknowledged that his health was not the only factor in his decision:

> The introduction of the railways and the fall of the Confederacy left the Seminary in an undesirable location, no longer on a grand thoroughfare as when Dr. Rice placed it near Hampden-Sydney College, but isolated and in the middle of the "black belt," and without the excellent society of country gentlemen, once so congenial a society for it, doomed to extirpation by the conquerors.[56]

Dabney spent his last days pining for the imagined past of a southern Elysium in Virginia and doing all he could to keep the seminary from moving to Richmond. Southerners, he scornfully wrote, had become "debauched and befooled by Northern literature." He finally concluded that the South had succumbed to northern ways, and Southerners had become "well adapted to make good spaniels."[57] He died in Victoria, Texas, on January 3, 1898. Dressed in his old Confederate uniform (in accordance with his instructions), his body was shipped to Hampden Sydney for burial in the Union Seminary cemetery.

On Thursday afternoon, January 6, 1898 (nine months before the seminary moved to Richmond), six students met his remains at Farmville and accompanied the casket to Hampden Sydney. The entire student body had planned to meet the hearse a mile from the campus and accompany it to College Church, but the telephone message notifying the campus of the casket's arrival was not delivered.[58] Beginning at 8:00 a.m. the following day, as seminary students stood as honor guards in one-hour shifts, a constant line of mourners filed past. Four ministers presided at the afternoon funeral.[59] Everyone knew an era was over: "the great Southern theological triumvirate has been Thornwell, Palmer, [and] Dabney,"[60] and now all were gone.

Dabney served on the faculty for thirty years (Smith served for forty-three), and his theological influence was undeniably enormous, but consistently negative. He never thought of himself as an original thinker, but as the transmitter of tradition. Each lecture in his Systematic and Polemic Theology course was based on two primary sources: the Confession of Faith and Turretin's *Elenctic Theology*. Swiss theologian Francis Turretin (also known as François Turretini, 1623–87) was probably the greatest of the Reformed scholastics. Both Charles Hodge at Princeton and Dabney used Turretin as their text. It would not be too much to say that Turretin set the character of American Calvinism until the mid-twentieth century. Indeed, both Karl Barth and Paul Tillich paid tribute to the high quality of Turretin's scholarship.

At the same time, Dabney's scholarship was surprisingly comprehensive. In every lecture he used an unexpectedly wide range of sources, including extensive use of Thomas Aquinas. His first lectures analyzed natural theology (the proof for the existence of God), and the last lectures covered "Religious Liberty and Church and State"—seventy-four lectures in all. He devoted an entire lecture (Lecture III) to criticizing evolution by saying Darwin's theory of natural selection relies on chance. He criticized Roman Catholicism by stating that Protestant faith is intelligent, while the "Papist" is trapped in a closed system that is not rational, despite his own use of Aquinas. His theology relied on the plenary inspiration of Scripture: "All the statements and doctrines of Scripture, so far as they come within the scope of man's consciousness and intuitions, are seen to be infallibly true."[61]

Balmer Kelly argues that Dabney saw himself as fighting for civilization itself against the "great apostasy in Germany." For Dabney, there was "no middle ground between believers and infidels." Dabney's confessional theology, undergirded with a belief in biblical inerrancy, bequeathed to Union (and the southern Presbyterian church) an unyielding view of Scripture. For example, Thomas E. Peck, who succeeded Dabney, declared in a sermon: "Every word of Scripture is the word of God, just as much as if spoken in an audible voice from the throne, without the instrumentality of man or angel." A generation later, in 1900, Thomas Cary Johnson held that "the writers of Scripture are so superintended by the Holy Ghost that their writings as a whole and, in every part, are the word of God to us. . . . The original autographs of these writings were absolutely infallible when taken in the sense intended."[62]

Spirituality of the Church

A belief in southern particularism, strict confessionalism, biblical inerrancy, and opposition to modernity incubated the theology of "the spirituality of the church."[63] Although first advocated by James Henley Thornwell as early as the 1850s, it was Dabney who made the spirituality of the church emblematic of southern theology. The doctrine of the spirituality of the church held that the civil and ecclesiastical spheres of life were absolutely separate, to the point that one could have no comment on the other. Civil rights, for example, was considered political and therefore outside the boundaries of church pronouncements. It was thought that Christians, hearing the Word of God rightly preached every Sunday, would make up their own minds and institute godly policies.

Southern Presbyterians justified the spirituality of the church on the foundation of *jure divino* Presbyterianism, first set forth in the Second Book of Discipline of the Church of Scotland (1581). The theory of this divine-law Presbyterianism rested on the belief that God had set forth his law for the church in his infallible Word. The church had an obligation to teach and do all that was commanded by Scripture; it was implicitly forbidden to teach or do anything that was not commanded, or that could not be drawn from it by deduction.[64] In this way a "pure" church, speaking the Word of God, would purify society. So *jure divino* Presbyterianism became the hallmark of Union Seminary. Thomas Peck, professor of ecclesiastical history and polity, taught Senior Class History and Polity from 1860 to 1893, and he was insistent that *jure divino* Presbyterianism be the norm.

The Doctrine of the Church, as an essential element of the Gospel, is specially inculcated, with careful exposition of the errors of Papists, Prelatists, and Ana-Baptists.

As to polity, a *jure divino* Presbyterianism is taught, with the largest charity to all of every name, who love the Lord Jesus Christ. Particular pains are taken to expound the relations of the civil to the ecclesiastical power, and to vindicate the absolute independence of the Church and State in their respective spheres.[65]

In 1892, Thomas Cary Johnson was elected professor of ecclesiastical history and polity. In his 1893 inaugural, titled "The Tenent of *Jure Divino* Presbyterian Polity," he defended *jure divino* Presbyterianism. He contended that *jure divino* Presbyterianism protected southern Presbyterian orthodoxy. The boundaries of *jure divino* Presbyterianism kept the church from going beyond the express commands of Scripture in polity, theology, worship, and mission. It demanded a rigid confessionalism and freedom from contamination by the secular world, and prohibited any voice on "social" issues; the church could comment on "moral" issues alone. Johnson argued that *jure divino* polity was the best way to support the spirituality of the church and the proper political organization of the state.[66] In his charge to George Baxter during his installation in 1832, William Hill had warned Baxter against constructing "ice palaces" out of orthodox theology. Those ice palaces were now standing.

The Library

While Dabney was constructing the theoretical foundation of the past, B. M. Smith was preparing for the future by constructing a new library. Brown Library symbolized an intellectually curious school and was the capstone of Union's revival. Smith had always been interested in the library. He had conducted the first cataloguing in 1835, when he was a student. The library, located in the seminary building, held around 3,000 volumes before the war, and growth was agonizingly slow. The only major book acquisitions between the purchase of Rice's library in 1824 and the Civil War were the books purchased by Francis Sampson while he was studying in Europe in 1849.

Smith was appointed librarian in 1855, and he quickly tried to increase the library's holdings. In 1857 the book collection numbered 4,443. He reported to the board of trustees that while "the character of the books we have in our library compares favorably with those of other institutions; in respect to number we are behind them and especially deficient in the more recent publications of the day."[67] In a bid to improve the collection's quality and quantity, he established the library's own endowment, which yielded about $50 per year by 1860.

In the first librarian's report after the Civil War (in 1869), Smith reported the results of the second recataloguing. He declared that the library held 5,000 volumes. Moreover, "it is gratifying to state that during a period of about 35 years since the printed catalogue was prepared by me, I find that not over two or three volumes have been lost, and those of no great value."[68] Yet Smith was dissatisfied: he wanted a new library building. He complained that "the cases built against the wall were full," and he described the remedy: "a special building of suitable dimensions—permanent in structure, fireproof, with suf-ficient light not only by windows but [also] sky-lights, and well-ventilated." Recognizing that he was probably the only one who thought a new library was important, he took the initiative and (as he reported to the board), "I applied to Mrs. Brown, of Baltimore, who, with characteristic promptness and generosity, responded by a cash donation of $10,000."[69] This donation grew to $18,000 by 1879 and allowed the library to be built.[70]

After Smith's report, mentions of the library regularly appear in the cata-logues for the first time. The 1870 Catalogue boasted: "Each Student is also entitled to draw two volumes at once, to be used in his room, returnable or renewable every two weeks; and, besides, may take out on the opening of the session two volumes, a Text-Book and some other, as a commentary, which he can retain (or their substitutes) all the season." Each later catalogue contains a plea for donations to the library endowment and a report on the number of books on the shelves: in 1870, the library held 6,000 volumes, growing to 7,500 in 1873, to 10,000 in 1876, to 12,000 in 1886, and over 15,500 in 1896.[71]

On September 1, 1879, the cornerstone was laid for the Brown Memorial Library (present-day Winston Hall at Hampden-Sydney College), named for Mr. Harmon Brown. B. M. Smith gave a surprisingly defensive keynote address. He observed that some questioned the need for any library, let alone such a magnificent structure. In reply, Smith pointed to the excellence of Rice's own library and his hopes that his seminary would be a center of academic excel-lence. He then emphasized the generous gift of $9,000 from the Rev. Urias Pow-ers in 1869. Rev. Powers, Smith reported, believed the seminary "only need[ed] a larger library to give the reputation of a first-class institution." He defended the need for a library by reasoning that the reference room would increase the amount of time students could spend on their studies, thus making their educa-tion more valuable to the church. Interestingly enough, he pointed out that the extensive holdings would allow students to read other theologies and compare them.[72]

The building of Brown Library declared that Union had recovered from the war. It also signaled a change in theological education. The seminary was no longer devoted to catechetical instruction, but was becoming a place of research. The library was now an important part of the curriculum, holding books that would enlarge the horizons of those who availed themselves of its resources. Yet, after the library was built, everyone discovered they missed something: for the first time students were going to a library facility located away from where they lived. In the year following the library's opening, a multiseat privy was built somewhere behind the library, and it was informally referred to by students as "a reading room."[73]

Walter W. Moore

The year 1883 is as important to Union as 1821. In July, Robert L. Dabney left for Austin, Texas. In September, Walter W. Moore arrived, and a new era began. At their spring 1883 meeting, the board of directors called Walter W. Moore (just two years after his graduation) to help B. M. Smith (who was in failing health) teach Hebrew.[74] Moore was born in 1857 in Charlotte, educated at a private academy in Lenoir, North Carolina, and graduated from Davidson (N.C.) College in 1878 (one of the first Union students from Charlotte and Davidson). He entered Union in the fall of 1878 (at twenty-one) and graduated in 1881, excelling in biblical languages. After graduation, Moore spent one year as a stated supply (filling a pulpit in a church for a specific period of time, whereas installed pastors serve a church without a specified limit) in Swannanoa, North Carolina, and then as pastor of the Millersburg, Kentucky, Presbyterian Church in 1882–83. Moore remained with the seminary until his death in 1926, for forty-three years.

Dabney's departure was bitter. According to his recollection, he submitted his resignation to an adjourned meeting of the board in July, and they accepted it immediately, with no protest. Dabney would later lament: "I had gone to the extreme in maintaining my loyalty to the seminary, almost to the verge of indirect suicide." He accused the board of being unappreciative: "The seminary seemed to experience no check from my withdrawal—a circumstance well-calculated to teach us how unimportant we are in the course of events and to humble our egotism." Yet Thomas Cary Johnson, history professor at Union and Dabney's biographer, would point out that both the board and the Presbytery of West Hanover had adopted resolutions expressing appreciation for his service and regret about his departure.[75]

Whatever the emotions surrounding his departure, Dabney and Moore could never have coexisted; times were changing. Dabney represented the Old South of the "Lost Cause," ever looking backward to a time which never really existed. In contrast, Moore represented the New South, forward looking, with new possibilities and a national outlook. Moore became a national figure through his association with William Rainey Harper, who would ultimately become the first president of the University of Chicago in 1891. Harper became famous for his "inductive" method of teaching Hebrew. Although the "inductive" method has never been clearly defined (and Harper's class notes have not been preserved), the inductive method of teaching languages appears to be the foundation for the way languages are now taught. Instead of students learning endless vocabulary words, Harper had each student learn enough vocabulary and grammar to read a text, then progress to a more complex text, building on what they had previously learned.

Right after Moore was called to the faculty in 1883, he went to Morgan Park, Illinois, to study under Harper, and they quickly became colleagues (Moore was 25 years old, Harper 26). While Francis Sampson and B. M. Smith had studied Hebrew in Germany more than thirty years earlier, Moore was the first Union Seminary graduate to do postgraduate work at a U.S. institution—and this institution was in the North.[76] In later years, Harper and Moore collaborated in a "Summer School of Hebrew," held several successive years at the University of Virginia.[77]

Moore became one of the few southern churchmen well-known outside the South. He spoke at Dwight L. Moody's encampment at Northfield, Massachusetts.[78] In 1884, Harper organized the American Institute of Hebrew, and Moore was a charter member.[79] In 1885, Harper became the principal of the Chautauqua Summer College of Liberal Arts, and he regularly sought Moore's assistance. On more than one occasion, Harper publicly introduced Moore as "the finest Hebrew teacher in the country."[80]

What became known as "Chautauqua" was an adult education movement first organized in 1874 on the shore of Chautauqua Lake in New York State. Although first designed as a retreat for Sunday school teachers, it began to cater to the emerging middle class who could afford to travel. Expanding from its strictly religious intent, Chautauqua offered entertainment and culture, with speakers, teachers, musicians, entertainers, and preachers whom people could not hear at home. Theodore Roosevelt regarded Chautauqua as "the most American thing in America." Drawing from all over the country, Chautauqua brought Moore into regular contact with some of the leading educators in the country and gave Union unprecedented national exposure.[81]

Professionalism in Seminary Education

Glenn T. Miller has argued that Walter W. Moore was one of the first to understand the primary tension in late-nineteenth-century theological education: as the nation was becoming industrialized, urban, and exposed to new ideas, the seminary and the church remained resolutely rural and parochial. Many ministers did not comprehend either the methods or the conclusions of modern science. Congregational life pulled the minister away from engagement with modern intellectual currents; church life was largely unchanged from the early nineteenth century. The only way to bring the church into the modern era was to change the nature of the seminary. The church needed professionals on par with physicians, lawyers, and scientists. William Rainey Harper advocated for the seminary to adopt the university model for education—research, course electives, and practical experience.[82] Moore would introduce these ideas into the South.

One of the most important aspects of professionalism is specialization. Like every other professor at Union, Moore was not a specialist; he taught Church History, Old Testament, New Testament, Homiletics, and Pastoral Care. But Moore, besides wanting to teach languages more effectively, saw that theological education itself had to be overhauled to produce specialists in ministry. The first step would be to institute "practical experience" into the curriculum. He wanted his students not just to preach to professors, but also to fill the pulpits in local churches, teach Sunday school, and visit parishioners. Yet in the Hampden-Sydney area, especially with pulpits filled by professors, there was no chance for developing any kind of sustained, meaningful fieldwork. The only practical training at Union was preaching for professors and one ministry course, a semester exegeting the Pastoral Epistles. It may have been the opportunities for practical education that caused Moore to consider a move to an urban area.[83]

With Reconstruction over, cities were growing and southern life was changing. Moore grasped the tenor of the times and feared that Union Seminary was falling behind. Indeed, even before he arrived on campus, the board and professors were concerned that students could not speak effectively in public.[84] In 1877 the board ordered that an elocution instructor be hired to improve the students' public speaking. In 1881 the Union Catalogue advertised public speaking classes for the first time: "The seminary provides, without expense to students, the best professional instruction in elocution and public speaking. This is additional to the course of rhetoric and exercises given by the faculty itself."[85]

By the 1880s enrollment seemed to be stagnating, and the curriculum took the blame. The PCUS General Assembly believed its seminaries did not offer courses that fit the needs of the modern church and in 1882 urged the teaching of English Bible. The Union board did not hesitate and immediately hired an agent to raise funds for the fifth endowed chair, in English Bible and Pastoral Theology. In 1884 the board took unprecedented action by calling James Fair Latimer, a South Carolinian, as professor of ecclesiastical history and polity, the first professor with a PhD. A graduate of Columbia Seminary, he earned his PhD from the University of Leipzig in 1880. He had minimal pastoral experience (as pastor of Second Presbyterian Church in Memphis for one year when called), but had taught philosophy, German, and Greek at Davidson College in 1872–83. He died of consumption in 1892, and a professor with a PhD was not called again until 1915. The board, therefore, was open to new ideas when it called Moore.

In an organization devoted to seniority, Moore (the youngest member of the faculty) quickly became the de facto leader. In the classroom, he changed the way languages were taught. Outside the classroom, he made sure the facilities met expectations. For years students had complained about the lack of recreational amenities. In 1884 the board built a baseball field and "playground," but lamented that there was no money for a gym.[86] Dissatisfied with the board's halfway measures, Moore used his own contacts to raise the money for building a gym just two years later.[87] He understood that Union's facilities had to be unmatched to attract students in a quickly urbanizing, newly wealthy society.

Walter W. Moore represented not only something new for Union Seminary; he also brought a new professionalism in seminary life. Theological education before 1870 was confessional, focused on interpreting denominational confessions to a post-Enlightenment world. Between 1870 and 1970, however, ministerial education had to respond to new demands. The historical-critical method, Christian education, and pastoral care required specialized knowledge as these fields developed their own theories and methodologies.

Most important, though, the nature of education changed. The average undergraduate education was no longer based on the classics. College graduates had a more comprehensive education, which included the natural and physical sciences. Ministers, who no longer automatically majored in religion as undergraduates, had to confront questions and attitudes that were unimaginable a generation earlier. Indeed, the entire context of ministry changed: the dynamics of an industrial society, the development of urban areas, and the rise of the middle class required different skills than the country preacher ever had to possess. Church congregations expected a "professional," a man who could interpret this new world and administer a growing church organization.[88]

Moore also wanted faculty policies to reflect the new field of personnel management. He was originally called to Union to help B. M. Smith teach Hebrew, but Smith was so frail that Moore was soon doing all the teaching. Moore also knew that Dabney only began to teach theology when Samuel B. Wilson became feeble. Both Wilson and Smith remained on the faculty well past their effectiveness because, like ministers, seminary teaching was considered to be a lifetime appointment. B. M. Smith retired to Petersburg in 1889 and died in 1893.[89] At Moore's urging, in 1894 the board instituted mandatory retirement when a professor reached age seventy. The board, however, had the option to renew the contract yearly. Mandatory retirement was not popular. In his retirement letter to the board in 1930, Thomas Cary Johnson, church history professor and Dabney's biographer, was bitter at being forced to leave what he loved: "I am not able to rejoice at being considered unfit any longer to discharge the duties of a full chair in the Seminary."[90]

Union Seminary Magazine and the New Professionalism

Moore wanted Union Seminary to train professionals. His energy, imagination, intellect, and drive for professionalism can be seen most clearly in the pages of *Union Seminary Magazine*. Although Rural Free Delivery (RFD) was not instituted until 1896, for over a decade its advocates had been pushing for expanded mail service. With mail delivery to the entire country, Moore envisioned a seminary periodical reaching a national audience as both a marketing tool to enhance Union's reputation, and a forum to lead southern scholarship away from Dabney's rants. The first issue was October 1889 and represents a return to Rice's vision: a southern seminary serving the national church.

Union Theological Seminary was no longer going to be a backwoods school in Prince Edward County: Moore's seminary would have national impact. *Union Seminary Magazine*, dedicated to "Religious Thought, Sermon Literature, [and] Missionary Intelligence," was more than just a publicity organ for the seminary. Although issues did contain "Local and Alumni Notes," professors' obituaries, convocation and commencement speeches, and pleas for funds, there were also articles on a wide variety of subjects that set the standard in biblical and theological studies, not just for southern Presbyterians, but also for the entire South. *Union Seminary Magazine* was the only serious theological journal in the PCUS for decades.[91]

Although all UTS professors wrote articles, contributors came from all over the world. The articles reflected the best of current scholarship. Moore, for example, regularly contributed articles in biblical studies, including "The Passing of Ussher's Chronology,"[92] which caused a minor stir and began to shake the foundations of biblical inerrancy. Other articles included "The Psychological Aspects of the Conversion of the Apostle Paul,"[93] "Textual Emendation and Higher Criticism,"[94] and "Some Impressions of Radical Old Testament Criticism."[95] There were always articles on biblical archaeology and, surprisingly, frequent articles on Judaism, Islam, Buddhism, and Shintoism, plus one article on the Baha'i faith.[96] Archaeological finds were regularly reported, explaining how recent discoveries did not contradict the Bible but buttressed the Bible's credibility. There were always warnings about "German scholarship." In 1899 "The Bugle from Berlin: The Retrocession of Harnack" cautioned that German research deriving from the work of Adolf von Harnack undermined biblical scholarship and faith.[97]

After biblical studies, articles on theology were the most numerous. Most of these were apologetics for the southern Calvinist tradition, but also showed a deep awareness of contemporary theological currents. In 1900, Professor G. B. Strickler wrote a four-part series titled "The New Theology,"[98] in which he argued that the "New Theology" was based on the same ideas as "Higher Criticism" and mixed natural and spiritual laws. Thus, while it stressed God's immanence, it led people away from time-tested truths. In "The Bible and Science,"[99] Strickler argued that while the Bible does not teach the laws of science, Scripture contributes to the understanding of science.

In 1900, William Caven's article "Biblical Theology and Systematic Theology" called for a new kind of theology. In a glimpse of the future of theology at Union, Caven (a professor from Knox College, Toronto) argued that systematic theology was insufficient for the modern world. It relied on the outmoded concepts of philosophy and hence was too removed from everyday life. In contrast, "Biblical Theology" kept its eyes on Scripture, not allowing biblical knowledge to be harmonized or modified, and applied its principles directly to life.[100]

Union Seminary Magazine became a surprisingly open forum; the notion of the spirituality of the church did not keep writers from tackling social issues, and not always in accordance with PCUS pronouncements. By the time the campus moved to Richmond in 1898, race was a consistent topic. In 1900, Booker T. Washington contributed "The Relation of the Races in the South,"[101] in which he described the agricultural courses at Tuskegee Normal and Industrial Institute and how these classes contributed to positive race relations. This article may seem quaint to us, against the background of Union students beginning their urban ministries in Richmond. Yet Washington's observations concerning how whites must change their views of blacks foreshadowed the change many students would undergo as they worked in the "colored" sections of Richmond. Another article, "Colored Labor in Relation to the Prosperity of the Southern Farmer," concluded that African American farmers were no threat to white farmers.[102]

Modern ministers needed to be prepared to confront a new world, and *Union Seminary Magazine* would help prepare them. Intellectual currents were important features. Evolution was a recurring topic, with stories such as "Evolution as It Stands Related to Christian Faith"[103] and "Evolution as a Science and a Philosophy."[104] Frequent articles explored contemporary philosophy, as in "Some Impressions of Philosophy in a French University."[105] Regular features posed ethical questions; examples engage economics: "Is the Church Meeting the Changed Conditions in the Social and Business World?"[106] (the writer answered no); and Christian living: "The Christian and the Theatre"[107] (Christians should not attend, according to the writer).

Union Seminary Magazine also tackled curricular and professional issues. In 1897, Thomas Cary Johnson declared, "The seminary should beware of coming to regard itself as a Moody Institute on the one hand or a theological university on the other." In 1897[108] and again in 1902[109] the magazine took a stand for eliminating the Latin thesis, or exam, as part of the trial for licensure. The magazine regularly upbraided presbyteries for allowing unprepared and unqualified men to come to seminary:

The truth of the matter is that some men come to seminary totally unprepared for their work, some of them having never even looked into a Greek or Latin text-book; and as for the English language, it is butchered unmercifully. The fault of all this lies with the Presbyteries, and upon them must rest the blame of our having men who shall not be able to divide aright the world of truth.[110]

Professional advice was also a regular feature. "A Clinic in Homiletics" appeared in many issues, as well as "Books Which Every Preacher Ought to Have." Pastoral care concerns appear consistently after 1900 with such articles as "First Principles in the Relief of Distress."[111] Liturgical matters (such as "The Lord's Supper—A Plea for Its More Frequent Observance"[112]) were frequently discussed, as were articles on Sunday schools. Each General Assembly was reviewed, and questions of polity were regularly discussed.

Every issue had at least two articles on world and home missions and book reviews, which gave readers a glimpse on a wider world. At the same time, *Union Seminary Magazine* reflected the provincialism of the time. While the magazine advocated working with the YMCA before the General Assembly did, cooperation had its limits; Roman Catholics and northern Presbyterians were the enemy. Articles such as "Romish Obstacles to Mission Work in China"[113] and criticisms of the new "Romish University at Washington, D.C.," reflect the anti-Catholic prejudice common in late-nineteenth-century America. Theological articles before World War I usually contain digs at the "badly mixed" theology of the northern church,[114] and in a book review there is a rant against "our self-appointed censors and social-equality negrophilists in the North."[115]

At the same time, the magazine gives a glimpse of a new generation and a burgeoning ecumenical outlook. Union hosted the Inter-Seminary Missionary Alliance on March 11, 1892,[116] and there were annual reports from students who attended Student Volunteer Movement and Inter-Seminary Missionary Alliance conventions all over the country. The report from the Detroit conference in 1894 showed genuine surprise. At the convention were 1,187 student attendees from 294 educational institutions in the United States (plus 35 in Canada), with 35 student representatives from the southern Presbyterian church. The Union students were impressed: "The people of Detroit opened their hearts and their homes to us, and showed us that our own dear Southland hasn't all the good people in the world."[117]

Moore's professional approach is also seen in the new look of Union's catalogues and a new emphasis on statistics. Before his arrival, the contents of the catalogues are haphazard, course descriptions are sporadic, and in many years it is unclear what classes are to be taken in what order. After 1884, each course is fully described, and the texts, except for those taught by Thomas Peck, are listed. Before 1884, statistics are nonexistent; after 1884, each catalogue contains a list of students, their hometown, college, and presbytery. Union issued a General Catalogue in 1884 containing the name of every professor and graduate (and each position they held) from 1823 to 1884.

Moore was conservative in a new way; he was a devoted scholar who understood the need for questioning. He cautiously supported the methods of higher criticism and building bridges to northern Presbyterians. Moore also believed that the southern church should redefine what was "essential" and "non-essential" in its doctrine.

> We must have more liberty in our church, . . . or there is going to be an explosion which will astonish some. . . . It is better not to have the explosion. It is better to profit by the experience of our church in Scotland and in the North than to have an experience of our own. . . . In my judgment there is nothing more certain, as to the future of our church, than that we must allow a subscription to the system of doctrine without trying to tie men down to every statement of detail.[118]

As William E. Thompson has pointed out,

> In an age that was already moving into conflicts over the claims of Biblical criticism, the theory of evolution, and other theological controversies, Walter Moore represented a spirit of conservatism that was solid without being rigidly doctrinaire. Faculty and students, as well as supporting laity across the church, recognized [Moore] as an open-minded, progressive person open to intellectual changes, yet one who clearly "kept his head on his shoulders." He and his institution could attract their financial support and interest with hardly any qualifications.[119]

Enrollment

Students responded to Moore's reputation and initiatives. Although enrollment increased somewhat after the war, there was a decline in enrollment between 1875 and 1885. After he began to institute his changes on campus and in the classroom, enrollment exploded; 46 students were enrolled in 1870, then 50 in 1880, and 72 in 1890. Union remained, however, an institution rooted in the South. Between Appomattox in 1865 and the relocation of the campus to Richmond in 1897, the vast majority of students were from Virginia and North Carolina. Between 1870 and 1879, there were 224 students; 1 from Indiana (who joined the PCUS), 1 from Pennsylvania (who remained in the northern church, formally known as the PC(USA)), 1 from Scotland, 1 from Ireland, and 2 from Canada (Ontario and Quebec). During 1880–89 there were 235 students, all from the South and border states, except for 1 student who was the son of Chinese missionaries, and 1 student each from Scotland and Ireland. During 1890–97 there were 221 students, with 1 from New York, 2 from Scotland, and 1 from Ireland. An average of 5 students per class did not have a college degree.

Admissions standards remained consistent from 1865 through 1897:

> Any young man, who is a communicant in any Christian church of evangelical faith, being a graduate of any respectable college, or presenting satisfactory testimonials of possessing such literary qualifications, especially in the [ancient] languages, as would entitle him to enter the Senior Class in any such college, may be admitted to the privileges of the Seminary.[120]

Student Life

Despite the growth of southern cities, a growing economy, and improved transportation, which transformed southern culture, student life at Union still moved at an antebellum pace. Throughout the nineteenth century, the calendar remained constant. The 1879–80 school year is typical. The session began on August 13 and ended on the second Wednesday in April 1880, with no breaks, except one day at Christmas. Beginning in 1885, though, students received a week's break at Christmas.[121] Before the war, the students did not even get Christmas Day off. In 1875, the faculty proposed a new design for the school year. The proposal called for a four-year course of study, with a six-month school year. Classes would convene for half the year, then during the other half year, students would supply churches. Like the Student in Ministry (SIM) year a century later, it was argued that this calendar would give students a more practical education and provide the home presbytery a greater opportunity to judge the candidate.[122] The board, however, rejected the proposal.

The curriculum remained consistent, except for the addition of Greek in 1892 (recognizing that students did not prepare for seminary as in the old days) and English Bible in 1895. The 1885 Catalogue presents a course of study familiar to any UTS student:

First Year	Second Year	Third Year
Homiletics	Systematic & Polemic Theology	Systematic Theology
Acts	Exodus	Pastoral Theology
Luke	Paul's Epistles	Psalms & Isaiah
OT History	History of the Reformation	Romans
Hebrew	OT Geography & Anthropology (life, occupations, architecture, & government of the ancient Hebrews)	Polity

Until September 1893, classes were scheduled from Monday at 10:00 a.m. to Saturday at noon. Like students almost sixty years earlier, students convinced the faculty that fall to schedule no classes on Monday, and the faculty consented.[123] The board was also concerned about course load. In 1869, the board ruled that all courses were to occupy an equal amount of time in order to prevent departmental "favoritism."[124]

Classroom teaching was built around the lecture. Dabney's theology class was typical. According to Thomas Cary Johnson, Dabney spent two class meetings on each topic, separated by an interval of two days. At the close of the second meeting, he placed on the blackboard a syllabus of the next topic to be taken up, with reading references for the students to consult. The leading textbook was Turretin (in Latin). The students were also required to write a paper on each topic, which Dabney read and corrected before returning them.[125]

The 1888 Catalogue mentions a type of postgraduate study for the first time: "Students who wish to prosecute their studies for a longer period" could take a "post-graduate course" of electives under the supervision of a professor.[126] Formal electives appear for the first time in 1894, under the heading "Fourth

Year." There was, however, only one elective: a class in Old Testament Biblical Criticism that met two hours a week.

Official relations between Hampden-Sydney College and Union Seminary had always been close. The first six college presidents had direct ties to Union, as did Richard McIlwaine (Hampden-Sydney, 1853; Union, 1857), president of Hampden-Sydney from 1883 to 1904. Yet, while official relations were cordial, at least until Union moved to Richmond in 1898, rapport between college and seminary students was not always close. In 1907, Hampden-Sydney graduate Louis B. Johnson (who did not attend seminary) remembered that a third of college students after the war were candidates for the ministry, and everyone else resented their influence.[127] Turner Wharton (1886) remembered that "the college boys loved the seminary students fully and devotedly as Maltese cats love stray dogs."[128]

John Leighton Stuart (Hampden-Sydney, 1896; UTS, 1902) remembers Union as "almost like a graduate school to the college." But he also agrees with Johnson and Wharton: "In the main the spiritual atmosphere was earnest and sincere. We students did not admire the scholarship or social origin of most of the ministerial students, nor in all cases their moral behavior. The compulsory Bible courses were deadly dull, the chapel and Sunday services none too inspiring. But this was not thought of with impatience or protest."[129]

Stuart was, however, impressed with the faculty:

> On the other hand the Seminary professors without exception, and notably [Walter W. Moore] were men of unquestionable sincerity, piety, scholarship and broad human sympathies. They had been chosen largely as having been successful pastors, and were interested in training useful preachers rather than in polemical theology. The preparation for classes did not require very much time, and I tried to keep the evenings free for reading from the excellent library, selecting chiefly the newer books on religious, scientific and related issues. This helped me to reconcile even the form in which the doctrines were taught with what seemed to me the essential truth in their sometimes unconvincing or even repellent statements and proofs. There was thus a minimum of tension within myself and in my ecclesiastical relations.[130]

There are numerous recollections of pranks and "raids" that the college students and seminites played on each other. These included wrestling, snowball fights, and stealing bathtubs and water buckets. And the seminary students gave as good as they got. Clarence Wallace (Hampden-Sydney, 1880) remembered in 1916: "I have a lively recollection of a burly West Virginia Seminite, who grappled with me and rolled me mercilessly in the snow. In my memory he resembles a dismounted Cossack."[131] Practical jokes were popular; the campuses were so far from Farmville that students played tricks on one another as a form of entertainment. But all was not pranks and competition. The *Hampden-Sydney Magazine* of December 1893 describes that year's Christmas party held in the college gymnasium (the center of present-day Cushing Hall) for the children of College Church families:

> After each child had been made happy by the presentation of a remembrance, which the lavish hand of Santa Claus—in the shape of a "Semie"—dealt out

to them, the crowd present indulged in the old time game of blind man's bluff, in which the usual number of mistakes occurred.[132]

Life, in all its forms, intruded into seminary life. On September 19, 1876, Arebie C. Dalton, a junior, died due to "some obstruction of the alimentary canal." Services were held in the chapel.[133] Another time, students requested a recess from classes to attend the 1876 "Exposition at Philadelphia," the first World's Fair held in the United States, since faculty would be at the Synod meeting. The faculty replied that they had no power to grant a recess, "save one day at Christmas."[134] In 1879, a student was accused of being intoxicated in Farmville. He appeared before the faculty and repented, but the faculty wrote to his presbytery and home church to determine how they wanted to handle the matter.[135] The student was allowed to remain because his presbytery said they would "guard" him.[136]

In 1897, *Union Seminary Magazine* commissioned a questionnaire to be distributed to the students of Union Seminary. The purpose was to show life as it was in Hampden Sydney. The results were reported in *Union Seminary Magazine* with the following introduction:

> Few people have a clearly defined idea of seminary life. Many wonder if it is one round of prayer meetings and praise services. Some suppose that long faces and mock dignity may be found in every room. And many a good mother in Israel would be shocked to suppose that tennis courts, the gymnasium and football have attractions for any of the students. Such surmises and speculations are very far from the facts. Life here is as many sided as man's nature. All work would kill a man. An unbroken solemnity would destroy his reason. Unremitting idleness would render him a nuisance. Work is a duty; sobriety is a grace; and relaxation is a necessity. Let us look then at the seminary life from the sides which perfect manhood demands, of "work, spirituality, and relaxation."[137]

According to the survey, students spent an average of 9.2 hours per day "over the books." The library was well used; 88 percent of students used the library during the year, and half of them read the newspapers in the reading room. These newspapers included the *Baltimore Sun, Richmond Dispatch, Charlotte Observer,* and several denominational newspapers.[138] Students were also able to use the library for recreational reading; in 1886, the board left it up to the faculty whether fiction could be included in the library's holdings.[139]

Worship opportunities were numerous and mandatory: Morning chapel was conducted by one of the professors, every class meeting began with prayer, there was a weekly class prayer meeting, and each Wednesday night two students preached before the faculty, students, and the so-called Hill people—those who lived around the Hampden-Sydney campus. Monday morning was reserved for the Society of Missionary Inquiry, and Sunday night for the volunteer band to practice. Everyone attended Sunday morning services, and half participated in Sunday afternoon religious work.

The average age of students after the Civil War was between 25 and 29, and sports were important to them. Tennis became popular in the 1880s, and everyone seems to have played horseshoes. "Every form of exercise is adopted. The jingle of the bicycle bell from 5–6 keeps the pedestrian in constant fear. The gymnasium, with a regular instructor, is freely used."[140] College and seminary teams played against each other in baseball. On Saturday, September 20, 1884, Hampden-Sydney defeated Union, 18–16. "The evening was very fine for playing, with the exception of the heat. More ladies than usual attended the game. The game was called by the umpire at the end of the eighth inning on account of darkness."[141]

Seminary social life revolved around the faculty. There was a practice known as "calicoing." Faculty would open their homes one night a week, and students would drop in for light snacks and conversation. It was thought bad form for seminites to visit only one house, so they visited as many as they could.[142] Many remember that "promiscuous seating" was not allowed in College Church: men were supposed to sit on one side, and women on the other. The pews had a partition separating the men's and women's seats on the center pews. This divider, apparently, was not too high to thwart an informal and approved community custom. Courting couples could scramble over other people on their respective "gender sides" in order to claim adjacent seating on either side of the dividing partition. In this way courting couples could comfortably share hands on a single hymnal when they stood to sing. It had become something of a congregational spectator sport to see exactly which young people would be sitting beside one another "at the divide," and how many Sundays that particular "hymn-singing twosome" would last.

Daughters of boarding-house families and seminary professors married newly minted ministers. Lucy Taliaferro, Mary Friend, and Natalie Friend, whose families boarded Seminites, married new graduates. Benjamin and Mary Smith had five daughters, and they all married Union men. Thomas and Ellen Peck had seven daughters, only three of whom survived into adulthood, and all three married seminary graduates. By the time the seminary was preparing to move to Richmond in the late 1890s, the three daughters of Thomas and Lila English all married Union graduates. Givens and Mary Francis Strickler had two daughters, but only one of them married a seminarian.[143]

Prior to the Removal, attendance continued to bedevil the faculty. Catalogues from 1854 to 1897 contain notices to remind students to show up for the school year on time. Every catalogue after 1870 reminds students to stay until the last day. In 1877 only half of the senior class was present to receive certificates from the faculty showing completion of the full course of study and of passing the final exams.[144] In 1872, grades were introduced to monitor student progress more objectively, with results forwarded to the student's presbytery. Just as before the war, only half of the students completed the three-year course; the rest left early to be licensed. Again and again, the trustees vainly petitioned the General Assembly and presbyteries to change their meeting times to accommodate the seminary calendar. Daily attendance also remained problematic. In 1871 the board authorized the faculty to call the roll "at such exercises the faculty deems proper." In 1874 the trustees cracked down even harder, requiring roll to be taken in every class and prayer hall.

The growing trend toward certification, a mark of professionalism, led to an emphasis on testing and grades. Consequently the board and faculty developed a carrot-and-stick approach to exams. The board began requiring both oral and written exams in 1876.[145] In 1877 the board permitted the faculty to conduct "intermediate" exams. In 1879 the board required students to pass the intermediate exams. Diplomas were first awarded in 1885.[146] Only those students who completed their final exams were eligible for diplomas; the rest received certificates. In 1892, grading was refined. Grades of "distinguished" and "excellent" would merit a diploma; grades of "mediocre" or "low" were given a certificate. In 1892 the board heard that boisterousness was on the rise, and appropriate student conduct was made a criterion for graduation.[147] In 1895 the faculty, concerned that UTS was becoming too concerned about academic grades at the expense of developing the skills needed for ministry, asked the board's permission to suspend the grade system for a year.[148] Grades were reinstituted in 1897, with 60 percent being the lowest mark a student could receive and still graduate with a certificate. In 1898 the seminary charter was amended to allow for the awarding of degrees, which was first done in 1900. The granting of a degree, the bachelor of divinity, made Union an academic institution as well as a school of the church.[149]

The student reaction to these new regulations was not positive. In 1874 the students protested having their presence at prayer recorded, and the board acknowledged their point.[150] The students also protested grades.[151] They argued that according to the Book of Order, only presbyteries had the right to pass on the qualifications of candidates. In response, the faculty argued that higher education demanded examinations: "When compared with the examinations which are now almost universally introduced into colleges and universities, . . . ours are almost ludicrously perfunctory."

From the late 1870s the faculty and board showed continuing concern for student "deportment." In 1880 the faculty reported to the board,

> For several years past there has been apparently a growing lack of uniformity and grave and serious deportment so eminently becoming candidates for the ministry. It is by no means alleged that such a demeanor necessarily envinces a low state of purity. Still it is respectfully suggested that some dedicated expression of the views of the Board and the necessity of watchfulness and diligence in a course of life becoming their high calling may be peculiarly appropriate and useful.[152]

In 1892 the faculty informed the board that most students "have maintained a consistent walk and conversation as Christian men." Yet they went on to complain that "a very small minority of our young men . . . have manifested at times a boisterousness and levity of manner ill becoming of prospective ministers of the Gospel." The faculty reported that they were trying to instill in all students "the difference between innocent recreation, a cheerful piety, and happy service of God on the one hand, and on the other that thoughtless, loud, and even half contemptuous tone and manner, trenching at times hard by the verge of irreverence." Yet "some have shown a persistent indifference to duty, absenting themselves at will from the classroom, neglecting their proper studies, and spending this time either in idleness and vain jangling or in the prosecution of favorite secular studies."

We can catch a glimpse of student life from the rules the intendant felt compelled to publish in the 1870s:

The student is expected to provide bed linen as well as towels, at his own expense.

The throwing out of the window of slops, water, fruit rinds and parings is prohibited. Ashes must not be deposited in a wooden vessel.

The students are earnestly requested not to put their feet on the mantle-piece [mantel-piece] or the chimney-jamb. They are also entreated not to spit tobacco juice on any floors or walls of the building.

Games of croquet, lawn tennis, or any other, such as will injure the grass, are not allowed on the lawn of the main building or the yard of the former Mess-Hall.

The grazing of horses or cattle, and the hitching or staking of such in the front yard of the Seminary or former Mess-Hall, at any time, is positively prohibited.

As late as 1891, the intendant repeated these rules virtually word for word.[153]

Student Organizations

Student organizations took on a new role after the war. The Society of Missionary Inquiry (SMI) reorganized itself on January 6, 1866, and continued to function as both the de facto student government and a seminar on missions. They invited speakers to commencement and subscribed to magazines and newspapers. But the basic aim of the society was to study missions and encourage students to enter the mission field. The society formally met on the first Monday of each month in the morning, to hear reports from one of nine standing committees appointed to report on missionary activity around the world.

In addition to the Society of Missionary Inquiry, however, a new student organization was formed on October 25, 1872, and it continued to meet until 1894: the Rhetorical Society, whose purpose was to improve students' research and public speaking skills by functioning like a debating society. In general, the debates of the Rhetorical Society were complementary to the reports given in SMI meetings. The Rhetorical Society debates were chaired by a faculty member or visiting minister. Two previously chosen students were chosen for each side of the question, and the prevailing argument was decided by vote. In addition, each speaker was critiqued by another student, chosen by the president before the meeting. All meetings were held on the first and third Fridays in the chapel, usually at 7:30 p.m. These meetings were very well attended: almost the entire student body was present at most meetings.

The SMI correspondence with missionaries was lively; letters from the field were read at virtually every meeting. Returning missionaries, either on leave or going to a stateside church, addressed the society. The students heard from missionaries to Greece, Mexico, Brazil, and Japan. Letters from other seminaries, however, were sparse compared to the antebellum period. Princeton Seminary and Columbia Seminary were the only two regular correspondents.[154]

The SMI reports and the topics for the Rhetorical Society debates show a growing awareness of the world around them, especially after 1880. Along with the traditional concerns for foreign missions, reports on urban missions begin to appear, such as "What are the best means for reaching the Masses in our

Cities?" One report in 1896 advocated for "shorter hours, child labor laws, and pastors who visit." They also deliberated on policies governing missions, such as how quickly native pastors should be trained. The society also thought that all missionaries should have medical training before entering the field.[155]

Union students wholeheartedly supported the Student Volunteer Movement (SVM) and the Inter-Seminary Missionary Alliance.[156] According to the *Union Seminary Magazine*, Union sent representatives to every SVM and Inter-Seminary Missionary Alliance national convention from 1886 onward, and reports from the conventions were always read to packed houses.[157] Moreover, Union hosted the Inter-Seminary Missionary Alliance national convention on March 12, 1892.[158] It might be said that the convention was a coming-out party for Union. Although specific figures are not available (only one program is retained in the archives), speakers and delegates from all over the country descended on Hampden-Sydney. The convention was held on a Saturday, and the students were excused on Friday to make final preparations. Local churches were also pleased to host so many visitors, probably over a hundred.[159]

The minutes of the Society of Missionary Inquiry and the Rhetorical Society mark a subtle shift from Dabney's bitter reactionary nostalgia to Moore's forward-looking conservatism. One of the most consistent topics both societies tackled had to do with race. The relationship between "the church of Christ, in the South, to the colored people" came up regularly over the next twenty years.[160] There were also concerns that the church would "have better results in evangelizing Africa by educating the Negroes of this country as Missionaries, than by sending White Missionaries there." Yet the only time domestic race relations were mentioned was under the topic "The Pastors duty toward the Negroes in his field." The speaker concluded, "Before we actively engage in work among them, we should remove the prejudices in the minds of our own people."[161] Removing those prejudices would take time. The Rhetorical Society repeatedly upheld "separate church courts organized for the negroes,"[162] and (after being debated "with great vigor") students gave an affirmative answer to the question "Does the Spirit of the Gospel sustain us in placing the negro in separate churches?"[163] The students also confronted government policies concerning Native Americans. In 1887, one report declared that "if the money spent in taking the Red man's blood had been given to his religious education, he would have been, long ago, a helpful friend. . . . But while the government was drawing his blood, it was hard for the missionary to persuade him that the white man's God would bless him."[164]

The SMI and the Rhetorical Society also addressed what we would call polity issues:

Should we have Rotating Eldership?" (41-1 against)

Can the duties of a Deacon be performed by an Elder? (12-6 affirmative, abstain 24)

Should Ruling Elders be chosen as moderators of our church courts? (20-14 affirmative, abstain 20).

Should our students preach during their vacations & previous to licensure? (a resounding "Yes").

Should a church suspend a member who persists in selling ardent spirits as a beverage? ("Yes," unanimous)

Worship and professional concerns were popular topics and affect us still: "What are the best methods that a pastor may employ to make his weekly prayer meeting attractive?" Students debated, Is it "right for Christians to have instrumental music in connection with the public worship of God?" (Settled in the negative three out of five times.) They also decided that ministers should visit more and should not sanction Sunday school picnics. Students were also aware of the downside of ministry as they discussed, "A pastor's encouragement during a fruitless ministry." Recognizing the growing southern economy, Union students affirmed it was right "for Christians to expend large sums of money in the erection of handsome churches," but it was never right for churches to raise money by sponsoring "festivals, tableaux, concerts, and the like." They also decided that the "litho-law" (copyright) did not apply to the church.

What we would call Christian ethics addressed personal behavior and public-policy issues. In 1875 and 1878, the students decided that "dancing in all its forms" should be "positively prohibited by our church courts." In 1886, however, the students decided that there was nothing wrong with dancing. The students thought that reading novels was "injurious," and Christians should stay away from "the theatre." They declared themselves opposed to insider stock trading, as it was a "breach of the eighth commandment [against stealing] to take advantage of the private knowledge of a sudden rise in the price of any article of trade." And in 1872 the students decided that "the principle of Slavery" is wrong.

One of the more interesting discussions concerned life insurance. In 1874 the question "Is it proper for a minister to insure his life?" was debated for the first time. Dabney spoke for 47 minutes on the subject, and the question was decided in the negative, 29-18, with several undecided. In 1879 and 1881 the debate question was "Should the Presbyterian Assurance Company be encouraged?" Again Dabney spoke for the negative, and again the question was decided in the negative. For Dabney, the issue was simple: a Christian who had life insurance was placing his trust in the insurance company, rather than in the Lord, to care for his family after his death.[165] But in 1886, after Dabney had departed, the students approved of life insurance.

The students discussed other religions. The question "Is Mohammedanism losing ground?" was discussed "with much interest." Increasing immigration from southern Europe sharpened anti–Roman Catholic attitudes. In the 1870s, the students saw the Roman Catholic Church as a front for Satan or a foreign power, and they decided that it was better for a community to have no church, than just a Roman Catholic Church. In the 1880s the Rhetorical Society affirmed that "the Baptism of the Romish church should not be acknowledged as Christian Baptism." And in 1896 the SMI heard a speaker declare that the church of the "Romanists" was nothing more than "the head of the world forces against the true church, [which was] spoken of in the Revelation."

Other Reformed and Protestant denominations fared little better. Although the SMI subscribed to the northern church's "missionary journal," they voted against any sort of relationship with the northern Presbyterians the six times it came up for debate. Moreover, they condemned "the Presbyterian Church (North) [for] petitioning Congress on the Liquor traffic" because a church should have no comment on a political matter. The students also disapproved of any type of union with the Dutch Reformed Church or any type of official or unofficial contact with the Pan-Presbyterian Council, and they held that "Presbyterian ministers and people [should] refuse to participate with the Methodists in the accustomed methods of conducting their protracted meetings." They also decided that there should be no cooperation with lay evangelists "such as Moody." In 1880, before Moore's arrival, they voted that there should be no participation in the Chautauqua Sunday school movement.

What we would call questions concerning the relationship of church and state were also important and contradictory. "Ought ministers to take an active part in Temperance and other such reform movements?" was a constant theme. Students thought the church should not encourage temperance societies because that would involve the church in politics, but they were consistently in favor of Prohibition. They also tried to determine how far the government could go in supporting the church in enforcing the Sabbath. They were against Sunday mail delivery and in favor of the state enforcing Sabbath laws.

Union students were in favor of nonsectarian public education that included both sexes. They were against Chinese immigration, in favor of a protective tariff, against a minimum wage, in favor of American efforts to obtain the Panama Canal, and in 1886 supported home rule for Ireland. Women's issues were not as cut and dried as we might suppose; they could not decide if it was proper for "Deaconesses" to be elected in the church, but they were certain, after a "spirited debate," that there should be no universal suffrage.[166]

Reconstruction was the bane of every white Southerner. From being coerced to sign loyalty oaths in order to vote, to living under state constitutions that had been imposed upon them, to seeing federal troops enforce the law—many white Southerners in 1865–77 believed they were living under occupation. In the election of 1876, Samuel Tilden (Democrat) defeated Rutherford B. Hayes (Republican) in the popular vote, but Hayes led Tilden in the Electoral College by 184 to 165, with 20 votes disputed. After the bosses from both parties got together in "the smoke-filled room," they reached what became known as the Compromise of 1877. In return for removing all federal troops from the South, congressional Democrats agreed to vote for Hayes. Congress awarded the 20 disputed electoral votes to Hayes on January 31, 1877, and the Republicans began to dismantle Reconstruction.

Before the compromise was reached, however, the South was concerned that the North would manipulate the Electoral College to manufacture a Republican victory and continue the onerous Reconstruction laws. The tension can be seen in the January 12, 1877, Rhetorical Society debate: "If the Republican party should seat Hayes directly in the face of the Law, should a revolution be justifiable?" The question was decided in the affirmative. Feelings of aggrievement died slowly. As General Lee was considering surrender at Appomattox in 1865, some of his staff officers suggested conducting a guerilla campaign against the Union forces. Lee not only disagreed but vowed to fight against anyone who prolonged the war. In 1884 the Rhetorical Society debated: "Would it have been morally right for the Confederate government to have fought under the black flag?" (black flag being a euphemism for guerilla war). This session was the first time Moore chaired a debate, and the minutes describe the discussion as "extended." The question was decided in the negative by only two votes, 13-11, with six abstentions.[167]

The reports and debates on biblical studies and theology show how modern biblical scholarship was slowly being accepted, and traditional notions of biblical inerrancy were becoming anachronistic. Four times the Rhetorical Society debated: "Was the world created in six days of 24 hours each?" They voted in the affirmative in 1873, in 1880, and in 1883, but decided in the negative in 1887. Union students were well aware of the theories of Charles Darwin and voted that it contradicted the Scriptures; yet Darwin's theories did not disprove the existence of God. In 1888 the students held that former Columba Seminary professor James Woodrow's comments on evolution did not contradict the Scriptures.

Although we tend to think that focusing on curriculum is a modern preoccupation, beginning in the 1870s there were a surprising number of debates concerning grades, electives, and seminary education in general. In 1873 the Rhetorical Society voted against any kind of grading system, and the students did not want electives. They were against changing the academic calendar from "three years of eight months to four years of six months, and thus enable the candidate to spend more time in the public work." And reflecting the concern that Presbyterians did not have enough ministers, the students debated relaxing "our requirements for Collegiate or Seminary Training" or radically changing "Church Methods of Ministerial education." Any proposed changes were always voted down.

Students had definite ideas about the curriculum. In 1880 the Rhetorical Society debated: "Would it be expedient or advisable to ostracize Francis Turretin from the Theological course in the Seminary?" The minutes record that the debate "was unusually good & interesting" and that "Dr. Dabney spoke." Although the question was decided in the negative, 24-13, with six abstentions, it is surprising that the vote for getting rid of Turretin was not larger, given Dabney's presence.[168] Throughout the last third of the 1800s, students had requested a class in missions. In 1895 the students again petitioned the board to add a course that would give a "Systematic Study of Missions." They even submitted a suggested outline for the course and recommended that Thomas Cary Johnson, the history professor, teach it; the board agreed.[169]

Despite the continual cycle of reports and debates, the routine irritations of life were always present. There were constant complaints that the reading room was messy and students were removing newspapers from the reading room.[170] In 1890 the treasurer was instructed to address "the students in a mass meeting, that the papers are not to be taken from the reading room."[171] But just as before the war, the complaints had no effect. In the records are motions upon motions that reports are to be no longer than four pages in length and debates should last no longer than ninety minutes. Numerous pleas ask the moderator to declare certain motions out of order, such as those that are off the subject or are a veiled personal attack, and there are consistent protests that students are always arriving late or leaving early. Even the meetings themselves were not always conducted decently and in good order (cf. 1 Cor. 14:40): "The Censor gently admonishes the young gentlemen who occupy the 'favored' seats in the

S.E. corner of the hall that one speaker at a time is all the rules of the Society permit."[172]

We gain a view of student life from the letters of Turner Wharton from Texas; he had intended to go to Princeton Seminary after graduating from the University of Texas. After spending a few days in Greensboro (N.C.) with his family, he left for New Jersey but decided to stop by Hampden-Sydney to catch a glimpse of Union. He remained at Union only after meeting his future wife. Although he grew to love Union, he hated it at first. "Hampden-Sydney was literally in the wilderness" and the seminary was a "jail-like structure" appended to the college. He was also dismayed that he had to "carry my daily supply of coal and water up three flights of stairs" and decided "the conveniences and modern comforts of these institutions were notably marked by their total absence." Wharton loved the afternoons, however, when he could hunt turkey and quail, and the cooks would dress and prepare them. But his worst memory was preaching for the faculty: "I do not know why the Spanish Inquisition neglected to use this exquisite means of torture."[173] Indeed, in 1893 the senior class requested that they not be required to preach on alternate Sabbath nights, but the faculty rejected that plea.[174]

Alumni

Between 1866 and 1897 virtually all graduates served at least one church, and nine graduates were elected as moderators of the Presbyterian Church in the United States (PCUS). Joseph Anderson Vance (1888), who grew up in a northern Presbyterian church in Tennessee, was the moderator of the PC(USA) in 1935. The number of Union graduates on General Assembly boards is too numerous to list. Late-nineteenth-century alumni also had an impact on American higher education. During the years 1865–97, forty-eight graduates headed fifty-nine separate institutions for varying periods. These included colleges, seminaries, academies, and "female seminaries" (most of which have ceased to exist). Some of the colleges and seminaries headed by Union graduates include Southwestern, Austin College, Agnes Scott, Queens, Converse, Hampden-Sydney, Davidson, and Columbia Theological Seminary.[175] Thornton Rogers Sampson (1874) was the first president of Austin Seminary. He was the son of Francis Sampson (Hebrew professor in 1839–54) and was born in North Carolina House (present-day Penshurst).

Although each issue of *Union Seminary Magazine* contained articles on home and foreign missions, southern Presbyterians did not conduct home missions among the newly freed blacks. They also objected to the missionary efforts of the northern church among the blacks as "jurisdictional interference."[176] Thus the primary stress was always on foreign missions, but there were at least four graduates who worked among Native Americans, including one in South Dakota. In 1898, Thomas R. English, professor at Union, reported that of 28 PCUS missionaries currently in the field, 24 "had gone out from her walls." In addition, "Since the Civil War 45 of her alumni have been engaged in the foreign field."[177]

In an age of communication conglomerates, where newspapers, television, and radio are controlled by a few corporations, it is difficult to imagine the multiplicity of magazines and newspapers in late-nineteenth-century America. The expansion of rural mail service and introduction of steam-powered printing presses lowered the price of magazines; now Americans could have the world brought to their mailbox. Denominational and religious periodicals were especially popular. Of the nineteen Presbyterian-oriented newspapers in the South between 1837 and 1900, virtually every one had a Union graduate serving either as editor or a member of the editorial board. These papers carried news of synod and General Assembly actions, reported on educational issues, followed well-known personages, and enthusiastically supported missions. And with almost no exception, they anticipated stands taken in the Progressive Era (beginning in the 1890s): they inveighed against child labor, argued for the eight-hour day, condemned the use of private detectives to break strikes, advocated for the minimum wage, promoted temperance, and called for the passage of the Pure Food and Drug Act. While they never addressed racial issues and commonly avoided women's suffrage, it is still curious that some of the students who studied under Dabney and imbibed his influence would reject the doctrine of the spirituality of the church and instead speak out on social issues.

Isolation

The Society of Missionary Inquiry and the Rhetorical Society, as well as the dorm and boarding houses (and later the gymnasium), were the primary places where students formed their social lives. But no matter how many times the societies met and no matter how many pranks the students played on each other, there was no getting around the fact that the Hampden-Sydney location was remote. Officially, the seminary was easily accessible; every catalogue from 1870 to 1897 assured the reader that Hampden-Sydney was surrounded by sophistication and was healthy.

> The Seminary is about six miles S.S.W. from Farmville, a station on the Lynchburg and Petersburg (South-side) railroad whence a daily stage runs to the Seminary, and thus is easily accessible from all parts of the country. It is within one-eighth of a mile of Hampden-Sydney College, in the midst of a community proverbial for intelligence and morality, and with a climate celebrated for the mildness and sanitary influences on those of feeble health. No student has ever died within its walls.

The reality was that the Union campus was isolated and behind the times. By the last quarter of the 1880s, central heating, hot water, and gas or electric lights were commonplace features of many schools, even in the South. No such conveniences, however, ever came near this seminary: the students had only outhouses and hand pumps. They bathed by carrying buckets from the pumps to the basement of the Seminary Building; the buckets were then heated on two wooden stoves, and the water was poured into a round wooden tub, which was emptied out the back door after the last man had

10. Seminary Building, Hampden-Sydney, 1890

taken his bath. Dormitory and classrooms were heated with fireplaces and woodstoves. Students were expected to split their own wood from a huge woodpile behind the seminary and lug the logs up to their rooms. Extra woodcutting time was required each Saturday afternoon, since no wood-chopping was allowed on the Sabbath.[178] Telephones arrived only in 1884,[179] electricity between 1888 and 1892, and the college, but not the seminary, had indoor plumbing by 1895.[180]

Despite the optimistic tone of the catalogues, it was becoming obvious that southside Virginia was confining and inadequate. As Moore became widely recognized, he attracted an increasing number of students. Paradoxically, Moore's fame posed a dilemma for the board of directors: a well-known president would bring in more students, but more students required more facilities and thus more money. In addition, a widely known president would be pursued by other seminaries. The board responded to these dilemmas by spending more money.

In 1883, Cyrus McCormick had tried to entice Moore to his new seminary in Chicago. Recognizing their need to keep him, the board built a spacious modern Victorian house (present-day Maples at Hampden-Sydney College) for Moore and his family. The new house was equal to what other seminaries could offer and was a dramatic change from their cramped quarters in Boston House, constructed in 1829. Students were next. As Moore's reputation increased enrollment, housing became a pressing issue. There was a tremendous upsurge of students in the late 1880s and early 1890s. In 1891 the board directed the faculty to spend each summer visiting congregations in North Carolina and Virginia raising funds and recruiting students. The board was specific: they wanted capital funds rather than general operating expenses.[181]

The Removal

The relocation of the campus from the Hampden-Sydney campus to Richmond, in what became known as "the Removal," was initiated by the lack of student housing. Following the board's directive, Moore spent almost the entire summer of 1891 raising $10,000 for the construction of two new dormitories. They were completed in 1892 and are located at the intersection of College Road and Via Sacra. Moore named these new dormitories "Geneva" and "Edinburgh." Although he had raised enough money to build the new dormitories, when he reported to the trustees in 1892, it was obvious that a new era was dawning. He reported that it was becoming difficult to raise money for the seminary because donors were dissatisfied with Union's location and did not want to contribute their money to erect build buildings in the "wrong place."

> Many of our private members, as well as many of our ministers and ruling elders, seem to think that the officers of the Seminary have been blind to the changed conditions of the country since the war and have not recognized the vital importance of planting our principal training school for ministers in some center of population and business influence, where its property would accumulate and increase rapidly in value, where its accessibility and metropolitan advantages would commend a much larger patronage, where the best methods of Christian work could be seen in actual operation, and where the contingent of picked men reinforcing the pastors in their Sunday Schools and mission would make Presbyterianism a colossus instead of a pigmy among the Christian denominations of the future. The church cannot afford to ignore the concentration of modern life and influence in the cities. These great centers must be seized by us as they were seized by the apostles of old. They are the vital strategic points of the future. If the Seminary remains in the backwoods, it is doomed to inevitable decline. No power on earth can save it. Therefore it is unwise to throw out any more anchors in the form of buildings.[182]

Moore was not just suggesting a different location: he was proposing to look at theological education in a completely different light. The first salvo in the Removal had been fired.

Although we tend to see the Removal as a dramatic transformation in Union's life, Moore presented moving to Richmond as the end result of an evolutionary process that had already been in motion. Walter Lingle agreed: moving the seminary was inevitable due to the transformation of the South after the Civil War. He remembered that no one "ever wanted to leave [Hampden-Sydney]; . . . it was a matter of necessity. Conditions were rapidly changing. Our share of students were not coming. The young man raised in the city preferred not to go to the country for his seminary course." But the church also had new expectations:

> The church at large was at the same time demanding that the Seminary should train her students along practical lines of work. The facilities for such training could be found only in the city. For these and other reasons too numerous to mention, the Board felt the necessity of removing the Seminary from the hallowed spot on which it had stood for more than three-quarters of a century.[183]

Moore advanced five principal arguments for moving to Richmond: (1) difficulty in raising funds from North Carolina; (2) declining enrollment; (3) deteriorating physical plant; (4) Hampden-Sydney's isolation; and (5) theological education required practical education, which could only be achieved in an urban setting. Moore's first point was simple: raising funds for Union would soon become impossible. The difficulty of fund-raising was the theme of his 1892 report, and he would continually remind the board and the synod of that fact for the next three years. North Carolina donors did not want to give their money to a declining physical plant in a rural area that showed little future.[184]

Moore's second argument was declining enrollment. On the face of it, the numbers do not support his argument: enrollment was actually increasing throughout this period. He claimed, however, that there could be more students on campus; those who went to other seminaries would have gone to Union but for its unfavorable location.[185] Columbia, for example, was making a play for North Carolina students, and they could offer a location more accessible than Hampden Sydney.[186] Not only was Columbia Seminary recovering as South Carolina came through Reconstruction, but Cyrus H. McCormick also was pouring money into his seminary in Chicago. Moreover, the PCUS Synods of Kentucky and Missouri began to organize their own seminary in Louisville.[187] And after he left the Hampden-Sydney setting in 1883, Dabney had organized what was to become Austin Theological Seminary. The monopoly on southern seminary education that Union enjoyed for seventy years was coming to an end, and the school had to address the changed circumstances or die.

Moore's third argument was self-evident: the physical plant at Hampden-Sydney was deteriorating. At the seventieth-anniversary celebration in 1894, Moore painted a dismal picture of the seminary's infrastructure. He complained that as early as 1876 the board had ordered that arrangements be made for ventilating the lecture rooms, "especially the one occupied by the Trustees at their meetings," and in 1878 they had ordered that "the lecture-rooms be refurnished with more comfortable accommodations." "But," as Moore reported in 1894, "things are never done at Hampden-Sidney in indecent haste. So it was not until 1891 that these instructions were carried out." He also noted:

> The eastern end of the main building [was] occupied as a residence first by Dr. Rice, and last by Dr. Alexander. . . . The two largest apartments were converted into lecture-rooms and furnished with convenient desks [in 1891]. Incredible as it may seem, the students before that had had no facilities whatever for taking notes.
>
> The two ancient stoves which had so long disfigured the Chapel and mocked the desire of its shivering occupants with promises of warmth which were never fulfilled, were now relegated to the lumber-room, together with the excruciating low-backed benches which had for years tortured Protestant students of theology as though they had been Romish ascetics doing penance; and also that long counter, with its faded red curtains, which did duty for a pulpit, and over which so many torrents of sacred eloquence had been poured on Wednesday nights; and instead of these, a furnace was placed in the basement with registers for heating the chapel above; opera chairs were substituted for the benches, a modern reading stand for the archaic counter

aforesaid, and pulpit chairs for that vast horse-hair sofa, so strongly sugges-
tive of the iron bedstead of Og, king of Bashan.

Moore disparaged the water; two cisterns replaced numerous wells in 1876,
"but the supply of water is still of uncertain quantity, and sometimes of indifferent quality." Also, "some system of heating, too, less primitive, less dangerous, and less expensive than that now in use, has long been needed, and the
same thing is true of lighting. To speak plainly, the Seminary has no 'modern
conveniences' whatever, and it is the only Seminary known to us of which this
is true."[188]

A year after Moore gave his report to the board, on July 12, 1893, Frederick
Jackson Turner stood at the podium of the World's Columbian Exposition (also
known as the Chicago World's Fair) and declared that the American frontier
had disappeared; there were now more people living in cities than in rural
areas. Turner was worried that without the wide-open spaces, the democratic
dynamism of American society would disappear. What Turner deduced from
the 1890 census, however, Walter W. Moore felt in his bones. And where Turner
was pessimistic that America would lose its egalitarian and innovative drive,
Moore saw the rise of cities as an opportunity for the church. As William E.
Thompson has pointed out, Moore's letters show his fascination with the speed
and ease of train travel.[189] The South was becoming industrialized, urbanized,
and connected by rail; it was not the Old South of Dabney, but the New South,
a forward-looking land equal to the North. And Moore wanted Union to be
part of that future.

But Union could only be a first-class, national institution if it had access
to railroads. Railroads dominated American life in the nineteenth century the
way interstates are inescapable to us now. In 1865 the nation had 35,000 miles
of track, then 93,000 miles in 1880, some 164,000 in 1890, and 254,000 by 1916.
Without railroads, organizations like the Student Volunteer Movement (SVM)
would not have been possible. Founded at Dwight L. Moody's 1886 student
conference at Mount Herman, Massachusetts, its motto was "evangelization of
the world in this generation." Their optimism was possible only because modern transportation put the mission field within reach. Because of the railroads,
students could travel to conferences, and the SVM was represented on the vast
majority of the country's campuses, including Union.

Transportation made it possible for seminaries to relocate to cities. In the
last third of the nineteenth century, the Southern Baptist Seminary, located in
Greenville, South Carolina, relocated to Louisville, Kentucky. Southwestern
Baptist Seminary moved from Waco, Texas, to Fort Worth. Northern Baptists
moved Morgan Park Seminary to Chicago. And Methodists moved to Evanston
and Boston.[190] In an address on the twenty-fifth anniversary of the Removal, Dr.
R. F. Campbell pointed out that Union began to realize that modern students
"would not come and go over muddy roads in a stuttering hack, when they had
opportunity to ride in swift and comfortable railway coaches to Columbia or
Louisville; to Princeton or to New York."[191]

There was no direct railroad connection to anywhere from the Hampden-
Sydney campus. Indeed, because so many other places were now within reach
by rail, Hampden-Sydney was more remote than it was in 1800. Stage lines had

always gone through Prince Edward Courthouse, only a mile from Hampden-Sydney. When the Southside Railroad between Petersburg and Lynchburg was planned in 1854, it was originally engineered to follow the stage routes. But the tobacco warehouse owners in Farmville literally bribed the railroad to run through Farmville, eight miles away.[192] A train trip to Hampden Sydney from Virginia and West Virginia took a day; from Charlotte, Raleigh, or Greensboro took most of one day; and from Wilmington or Fayetteville in North Carolina, it could take two days.[193] And at the end there was always that trip across the "Red Sea" (the red-clay road from Farmville to the Hampden-Sydney campus); one to two hours in good weather, up to four in bad.[194]

Finally, Moore argued, Union's rural location resulted in the lack of opportunities for practical education. Just as tutors and log colleges gave way to seminaries, isolated seminaries producing ministers for a rural society now had to give way to urban seminaries educating professionals in a fast-changing, mobile, and diverse culture. Moore was always blunt on this point:

> This institution should be moved to some center of population and influence, where the students could have the benefit of participating during their period of training in every form of actual Christian work, and where the institution could be set in the full current of the Church's life, and where its needs could be recognized and met, and where it would be enabled to do its appointed work for the Church on a continental scale instead of a parochial scale.[195]

Moore was adamant. He insisted that "fieldwork education" be a part of every student's seminary training.[196] There was no possibility of large-scale fieldwork in southside Virginia because there were not enough churches. Ultimately, Moore saw theological education in a new way:

> The Protestant idea of a divinity school is not monasticism but ministry, not monkish seclusion from the world, but genial, helpful, Christlike mingling with one's fellowmen. With the changing conditions of modern life, our former location exposed us more and more to the danger of sending out from our Seminary helpless abstractionists, who did not know how to deal with men and whose first year in the ministry had to be devoted to throwing overboard untried and unworkable theories, and adjusting themselves to practical conditions.[197]

Moore prefaced his arguments for moving with an appeal to antiquity. The supporters of the Removal cited the October 20, 1813, Synod of Virginia minutes declaring that "Hampden-Sydney continue to be the seat of the Theological Seminary until it shall appear to the Synod to be for the interests of the institution to be removed elsewhere."[198] They also recalled the 1829 invitation to move by the Hampden-Sydney trustees.[199] Thus, the argument went, in their earliest statements the Union Seminary's founders had implied that this "school of prophets" might be moved sometime in the future. The implication was clear: the time had come. Even Thomas Cary Johnson declared in a conversation with Moore in 1894: "Union Seminary must be removed to Charlottesville, Richmond, or some other location more favorable to its growth."[200]

In the *Union Seminary Magazine* issue of 1895, an editorial claimed that the removal of the seminary to Richmond was not a new idea: it had been suggested immediately after the Civil War and supported by the faculty ever since.

> For the last thirty years it has been evident to many of the friends of the Seminary, especially those most closely identified with its work, that, by reason of the changed conditions of the country since the war, the institution would have to leave its present location, sooner or later, and seek a more central and accessible site. Otherwise it could not hope for any large and increasing measure of usefulness in the future. The first public advocate of some change was an eminent and honored servant of the church, then a professor in the Seminary, who, shortly after the war made a powerful speech on the subject to the Synod of Virginia, not indeed advocating removal to a city but stating with great force the disadvantages of the present site and demonstrating the necessity of seeking another. The professors and directors generally agreed with him, but the movement took no practical shape at that time because of the impossibility of securing the necessary means to effect such a change. Dr. Peck, however, another member of the old faculty, who survived all his former colleagues but one, continued to the last to insist that the Seminary must be moved. The members of the present faculty have always been equally positive in their conviction about it, and in the spring of 1894, when the Board of Directors received the overtures referred to in the following action, the faculty presented a unanimous memorial in favor of the proposed removal.[201]

After Moore addressed the board in May 1892, and despite recognizing that their present location was untenable, the board did nothing. Moore apparently decided that if the seminary would not move, he would, so he submitted his resignation to the board in May 1893, hoping he could force a decision. Moore's resignation was not an idle threat, and a new house would not be enough to keep him this time. Two years earlier, in 1891, just when he was raising money for two new dormitories and running into resistance, the organizers of the new Louisville seminary had offered him the job of president. He was evidently somewhat interested and visited Louisville to see the campus.[202] A year later, Southwestern Presbyterian University had offered him a professorship. In 1893, Nettie McCormick, the widow of Cyrus, again asked Moore to lead McCormick Seminary.[203] The offers from Louisville and McCormick were not conducted in the hushed tones of a contemporary search committee. Rather, both offers were public, reported in church publications and the Farmville papers.[204]

There were no surprises: the board, Moore, donors, student body, and the public knew who had made offers and the consequences of their actions. It appears that in 1893 Moore was again considering moving to Louisville. The board, however, refused to release him, citing a clause in the seminary's constitution requiring any professor who resigned to give at least a three-month notice before the annual board meeting in May. (When Dabney had resigned without notice a decade earlier, the board could have enforced the resignation clause. They did not do so, perhaps because they were happy to see him leave.)

Moore accepted the board's rejection with good grace. He insisted that he had not known about the resignation clause and counted the "discovery" of the clause as a sign that God wanted him to stay at Union. But everyone understood Moore's strong position. Some suspected Moore of leveraging his offers from other seminaries to force the board into action. Indeed, Moore's closest friend on the Louisville faculty, Dr. Charles R. Hemphill, would later write that "he and others in Louisville took a certain degree of pride in the fact that their offer to Dr. Moore had ultimately been the catalyst that set in motion the move of Union Seminary to Richmond."

Whatever gamesmanship was going on, it was also clear to everyone that it was time to act. In the 1892–93 academic year, several Virginia ministerial candidates had chosen to go to Louisville, and Moore feared that this was a "portent of things to come." Whatever Moore's intentions, whether he seriously considered going to Chicago or Louisville, it is undeniable that by the middle of June 1893, he "had been left in the strongest possible position to get almost anything he wanted, and he wanted the seminary to move."[205]

The Fight for Removal

In the spring of 1894, four out of five faculty members voted in favor of moving. Clement R. Vaughn, a distant relative and neighbor of Richard McIlwaine, president of Hampden-Sydney College, was the lone dissenting vote.[206] Moore had hinted about the difficulties of fund-raising in 1892, and the board (composed of equal numbers of Virginia and North Carolina Synod members) took no action; but now they had to act on the faculty resolution. At its meeting in May 1894, the seminary board considered three motions, all calling for a move.[207] No specific site was mentioned, and the board appointed a committee to study the issue.[208]

The idea of relocating the Union campus could no longer be kept quiet. Six weeks after the Union board meeting, the Hampden-Sydney trustees met, and McIlwaine was furious. He claimed he knew nothing of the seminary's intentions until the Union board voted to relocate. However, since Vaughn and McIlwaine were neighbors (as were McIlwaine and Moore), McIlwaine's claim that he did not know of Union's plan until the summer of 1894 can be seen as little more than a disingenuous ploy for sympathy. More seriously, McIlwaine accused Union of not caring if their plans left a wrecked college in its wake.

> The authorities of the Seminary in dealing with this question seem not to have considered the interests of the college at all, nor to have recognized any obligation of courtesy towards it by reason of the fact that the Seminary is its daughter or because of their close association and interdependence for over seventy years. Certainly the removal of the Seminary would place the college in a critical position.[209]

Richard McIlwaine, Hampden-Sydney College, and College Church now became the center of opposition to the Removal. The prevailing opinion at both the college and the seminary was that the Synods of Virginia and North Carolina would have to approve a move. It was generally accepted that North Carolina would vote to move. Indeed, Colonel Martin, chairman of the faculty at Davidson, had already given his public support for relocating.[210] North Carolinians hoped the seminary would move either to North Carolina[211] or to a city where rail connections would make travel more convenient.[212] Votes in the Synod of Virginia, in contrast, were much less certain. Many in Virginia wondered why they should spend money just to satisfy Tar Heel interests. The strategy of those opposing the Removal was simple: influence the vote at the next Synod of Virginia meeting in 1894 to keep Union Seminary at the Hampden-Sydney campus. They understood that three-fourths of those voting at the meeting would be from rural churches. Consequently they hoped to show that if Union relocated to the city, the church would end up abandoning small churches in isolated areas. If they could secure rail access to Hampden-Sydney, they could demolish the most obvious part of Moore's argument; and if they could scare Virginia's rural churches into thinking that the seminary would abandon them, they could divide the Synod of Virginia's votes, and the seminary would stay put.

On July 14, 1894, six weeks after the college's trustees met, a letter signed only by "Layman" appeared in the Farmville paper. It encapsulated all the arguments against the Removal. While Layman professed his utmost respect for Dr. Moore and recognized him "as the prince of pulpit orators and one of the leading scholars of the day," Layman felt compelled to answer Moore's reasons for wanting to relocate. Layman recounted Moore's primary arguments: (1) urban students had more opportunities to visit churches, Sabbath schools, and other religious assemblies; (2) Hampden-Sydney was without water, gas, municipal authority, or pavement; and (3) Hampden-Sydney was miles from a railroad, and therefore the cost of living was higher.

Layman's reply showed the gulf between the traditional view of theological education and the transformation proposed by Moore. First, Layman argued, students should be "hitting the books" and not visiting Sabbath schools and other religious assemblies. Shouldn't "the D.D.'s on the Hill" be able to teach men how to be preachers? Second, Layman found the idea of going from Hampden-Sydney to Richmond to find water ludicrous. The water "of Hampden-Sidney is so pure that though the college has now been in operation for more than 100 years, not more than two students have ever died there from the effects of disease." Besides, there is plenty of "pure water [in Hampden Sydney], and not a drop of whiskey." More ominously, city conveniences meant city life: "there are no 'strikes,' nor riots, nor rows, nor city thieves, nor city disturbances . . . [in] quiet, dear, orderly, literary Hampden-Sidney." Layman also dismissed the need for pavement, which caused corns, and the lack of a railroad connection just meant there were not as many temptations to lead innocent seminarians astray. Layman concluded: "The leading spirits of this and every age were trained in the quiet of the country, rather than in the unrest of the city."

For his part, McIlwaine hammered the rural-versus-urban arguments at every opportunity. In the Farmville and Richmond newspapers, he challenged Moore on his views of theological education in southside Virginia.

> Neither Oxford nor Cambridge, in England, nor a number of German universities, are in large cities. Neither Princeton College nor Seminary is in a city, but in a college town created by them; nor Central College, nor Danville Theological Seminary, nor Central University, nor the universities of Virginia, North Carolina, Georgia, Missouri, and Mississippi; nor Washington and Lee University, nor Randolph-Macon, William and Mary, Roanoke, Emory and Henry, and scores of other colleges and universities throughout the country.

McIlwaine declared that moving was betrayal: "The people of the vicinity had contributed to the original buildings at the seminary with the notion that the institution would always be there in their midst, exercising its benevolent spirit over the surrounding area." It was unthinkable for the seminary that it should treat its "mother" in this manner.[213]

The five months between the seminary's board meeting in May and the Synod of Virginia's October meeting in Danville were critical. However, Moore came down with a severe case of mumps, so those opposing the Removal had the field to themselves. Moore did address Richmond churchmen in July, but his health broke again, and he made no public statements until the synod meeting in Danville in October.[214]

Whatever the emotions, the real arena where the Removal would be fought was not the board room at Hampden-Sydney, but the Synod of Virginia. Travel to the synod meeting was not easy, but the meeting in Danville had the largest number of registrants ever recorded. On the second day, October 24, 1894, McIlwaine introduced a resolution to suspend any action on moving until the citizens of Prince Edward County had voted on a railroad bond issue, in the election to be held the next month. If the voters approved the bonds, then the seminary trustees should cease any investigation about moving and instead take measures to ensure an adequate water supply "and such other conveniences as shall put their institution on a footing with other similar schools."[215]

After a long series of parliamentary maneuvers, McIlwaine opened the debate by arguing that the seminary was located on "holy ground," similar to Mount Sinai. After a dinner break and communion service, Moore took the floor "and observed that Mt. Sinai was indeed holy ground, sanctified by the very presence of God: But, Mr. Moderator, the day came when the Lord said: 'Speak to the children of Israel that they go forward,' and they turned their backs upon all the holy memories of Sinai and faced toward the Promised Land."

The synod exploded into applause.[216] Moore acknowledged that Hampden-Sydney was "a place of hallowed memories and inspiring traditions," but he also pointed out that if the seminary did not move, in a few years "the buildings will be here, but the students elsewhere."[217] According to J. Gray McAllister, Moore's biographer, Moore's ninety-minute speech was the greatest of his life. James R. Sydnor, retired professor at PSCE, recalled that when his minister father was a student at UTS, his teacher Thomas Cary Johnson described Moore's performance to his class two days after the debate with McIlwaine: "First he lathered him well, . . . and then he shaved him clean."[218] On the first Sunday after his return home from Danville, McIlwaine greeted Mrs. Moore at church and declared half-humorously, "I tried to down the Doctor, but I couldn't."[219]

The debate continued until 11:00 p.m. the next day, but in the end the synod voted to take no action. The synod's indecision was a victory for Moore because it left him free to pursue his plans. The Synod of North Carolina, meeting at the same time as the Synod of Virginia, likewise voted to take no action. But the North Carolinians voted to make George Watts their representative on the UTS board of trustees.

If McIlwaine had lost, he viewed it as only a temporary setback: he could still make his case. For Moore, however, his victory was really no more than a holding action; he had received permission only to explore the possibilities. During the synod meeting, Dr. Murkland of Baltimore voiced the feeling that if Moore had at least $150,000 in guaranteed building funds, then the synod would be more likely to approve a move.[220] Thus Moore had to raise enough money, and the Prince Edward County voters had to reject the bond issue before the synod would vote for Removal.

Moore devoted himself to raising money for the rest of 1894 and most of 1895. Richard McIlwaine had once snidely remarked that Moore "could smell money," and Moore now proved it. After the synod meeting in Danville, Moore announced that an anonymous patron had promised a gift of $50,000 to enable the move, providing that $50,000 more could be raised from the Presbyterian constituency. Meetings for soliciting pledges had already been held during the preceding summer in several potential cities, testing the possibilities of financial support. The Richmond meetings, chaired by Moore, had a promise of $25,000 for a new library from W. W. Spence of Baltimore, a northern Presbyterian.[221]

McIlwaine claimed that Union could not leave its present location due to property obligations. He argued that Martin Saylor, who originally owned the land upon which the seminary sat, had made land available for the seminary and no other entity. According to McIlwaine, the college actually had been the legal receiving agent of the property (because the seminary could not incorporate), so a later generation of seminarians did not have the right to abrogate Saylor's transaction. The charter granted to Union by the Commonwealth in 1867, however, clearly settled the property issue. McIlwaine's property argument was desperate, but it still had huge emotional appeal; Saylor's third-generation relatives still lived around Hampden Sydney.

Once Union's trustees announced their intention to move, there were many who thought the college should move with the seminary. McIlwaine, therefore, not only had to convince the synod to keep the seminary at Hampden-Sydney; he also had to reassure his supporters that the college would never leave. He always claimed that Hampden-Sydney's rural location was an asset. But after the inconclusive Danville vote, Removal opponents had to find some way to improve transportation connections and neutralize one of Moore's most effective arguments. Colonel Henry Stokes of Green Bay, Virginia (a member of the college's board, elder in College Church, and member of Prince Edward County Board of Commissioners), initiated a petition to issue bonds for building a railway between Farmville and Keysville. Rural paradise or not, a railway was critical to keeping the seminary.[222]

By late July 1894, Colonel Stokes had gathered enough signatures to put the railroad bond issue on the ballot. In August, the editor of the *Farmville Herald* came out in favor of the bonds. The paper highlighted the fact that many people were linking the fate of Hampden-Sydney with that of Union: "We cannot afford to lose Hampden-Sydney nor Union Theological Seminary."[223] More than that, there were those who were afraid of what would happen to the vacant seminary buildings: "Shall the Seminary buildings be sold to the State for the purpose of—what the State now needs—a lunatic asylum for the Negroes? God forbid!"[224] When the Methodist school Randolph-Macon left Boydton, Virginia, for Ashland, Virginia, in 1867, the northern Methodist church purchased the buildings and started a black Methodist College. The Hampden-Sydney community was afraid that the northern Presbyterian church (active in the African American communities in Amelia and Charlotte Court House) would do the same thing.[225]

Opponents of the Removal characterized Moore's desire to relocate to an urban area as criticism of rural life. McIlwaine prophesied that seminarians would be corrupted by city temptations, and urban-trained ministers would not want to serve rural churches. Moore replied that "the church must seize an urban environment, lest it be captured by secular forces in the same fashion that the infidel Turks had now captured Jerusalem."[226] The rural-versus-urban argument resonated in southside Virginia. At the 1894 Synod of Virginia meeting, the Rev. T. P. Epes, pastor of the Blackstone Church, developed an extensive argument to show that the city originates heresy, while the country perpetuates orthodoxy.[227] Emotionally, it was almost impossible for anyone to conceive of Union Theological Seminary anywhere other than at Hampden Sydney, Virginia. On May 2, 1894, the Union Board of Trustees announced that it was prepared to consider offers for a new site, but only if there was a $100,000 guarantee. On May 12, 1894, an editorial in the Farmville paper quoted a Richmond newspaper article: "The Richmond Presbyterians and other citizens are talking of trying to locate the school here. The Farmville editor answered: Oh, no, brother, it were as possible to remove Willis' mountains from Buckingham as Union Seminary from old Prince Edward."

Letters to the Farmville paper accused the current generation of seminary students of being "soft." They could not endure the rigors of the slow, bouncing wagon ride to the seminary, and simply "had to have" more convenient bath facilities than their ten-gallon wooden tubs in the basement of the seminary building. Such fainthearted ministers would not share the values of rural families, nor would they be willing to serve country churches.[228] The hysterical arguments show that the move to Richmond was more than geographical. By ridiculing the students, southside Virginians were resisting the urbanization of the country.[229]

The bond election was set for November 18, 1894, and McIlwaine wrote an editorial for the Farmville newspaper on November 10, stressing the importance of passing the bond issue to improve and preserve the way of life in Southside. Not only did they need a railroad to keep Union Seminary: "A vote for the railroad is a vote for new life and vigor within our border, for the introduction of values, for the permanence and growth of our educational centre, and for the added prosperity and comfort of our whole people." But there was also another reason for keeping the seminary. "The Christians will abandon College Hill and let the negroes go in and occupy."[230] The editor then added his own opinion. "Let the railroad be finished to Hampden-Sydney, and Union Theological students and Hampden-Sydney College boys will continue to use it for ages to come. We will continue to guard well the quiet country places, and when the country contingent comes in contact with city life, it will help and not hurt it."[231]

Just by looking at the newspapers, it would appear that public opinion was solidly behind the $30,000 in bonds. But once the votes were counted, it failed, 718-545. The bond issue needed 60 percent of the 1,263 votes cast, but only received 56.84 percent, thus 40 votes short. The Farmville paper reported: "The election . . . resulted in a great surprise to everyone."[232] Surprise is really too mild a word: people were stunned. The entire strategy of the anti-Removal forces had been based on the assumption that the bond issue would pass.[233]

Removal opponents underestimated the changes in society and the force of Moore's vision. Moore wanted to be part of the transformation in theological education. As he traveled around the country, he saw the need for practical education. And it was also clear that Hampden Sydney was not the place for a modern seminary. Roads were poor, there was no rail access, the seminary's physical plant was deteriorating, the population was sparse and rural, and the rest of the South—especially North Carolina—seemed to have emerged from Reconstruction with optimism, a future-oriented outlook, and money. These were attitudes and resources not found in southside Virginia.[234]

Richmond

While editorials were being written, speeches given, letters sent, and votes counted, the committee charged with finding a new site for the seminary was quietly working. At the board meeting on May 2, 1895, they reported:

> Two sites have been offered near the city of Richmond; one of them is on the Brook Turnpike, about one mile from the limits of the city, and contains 11.3 acres. The other is on the line of the Chesapeake and Ohio railroad, near the city, and contains 10 acres. A site has been offered near the city of Lynchburg, known as the Miller Park Place, containing about 16 acres, and within a few hundred yards of the city limits. Either of these sites, in the opinion of your committee, is well suited as a location for a theological seminary. But, in the opinion of your committee, no proposition for the removal of the Seminary can be considered unless, besides the offer of a site, this Board can be assured of not less than $100,000, either from the offerers of the site or others.

Union Seminary Magazine devoted a lengthy editorial in the November– December 1895 issue that is the official history of the Removal. The editorial argues that the site selection was transparent. The editor complemented the "Directors in pursuing the course which they saw to be necessary, and also of the deliberation and caution with which they have proceeded." They approvingly reported Moore's proposal that if people of Richmond would raise $50,000 to bring the seminary to their city, he would raise an equal amount outside of Richmond. The editorial then describes how much the people of Richmond wanted the seminary:

> Rev. Dr. Robert P. Kerr, pastor of the First Presbyterian Church of Richmond (of which Rev. Dr. John Holt Rice, the founder of the Seminary, was the organizer and first pastor) had already been appointed chairman of a committee to secure sites and subscriptions in Richmond; and in spite of tremendous odds in the way of hard times and a general incredulity as to the practicability of the enterprise, he succeeded in getting the sum of $60,000, besides a handsome site of about 12 acres in the beautifully improved Northwestern suburbs of Richmond, lying on the ridge which constitutes the watershed between the James River and the Chickahominy, 18 feet higher than the hill on which the

capitol stands, and where the conditions of health, quiet, and accessibility are all perfectly met. Dr. Moore also was able to report that he had exceeded his promise, having secured two subscriptions amounting to $75,000. Of this amount Mr. George W. Watts, of Durham, N.C. gave $50,000, and Mr. W. W. Spence, of Baltimore, $25,000.

The editorial goes to great pains to show how the process was open and above board. The story relates how the "Rev. Dr. A. C. Hopkins, president of the Board of Directors and Trustees, called a special meeting of the board in the lecture room of the First Presbyterian Church, Danville, Va., on Friday, October 18th, 1895, to consider and act on the whole question of removal." The report was to the point:

> That a lot containing eleven and three tenths acres, in the northwestern suburb of Richmond, bordered by the Brook turnpike, has been offered as a gift; and that in addition to this site, subscriptions aggregating $125,000 have been secured for a building fund. The committee therefore recommends that, in case removal is decided upon, this offer of a site and subscriptions be accepted.[235]

There was, however, more to the Brook Road site than civic goodwill. Major Lewis Ginter's real estate development of "Ginter Park" was in trouble and needed an anchor tenant to attract other buyers and save his investors. Indeed, by the time the board decided on Richmond, Mr. George Washington Watts, North Carolina's new lay representative on the seminary's board of trustees, and the business manager of the Duke Tobacco Company of Durham, had personally promised Moore an outright gift of $50,000 to help guarantee the move. This gift was not made public while the process of studying all the suitable areas was still in process.[236]

In 1894, Major Lewis Ginter was seventy years old and the wealthiest man in the Commonwealth of Virginia. He had made and lost at least two fortunes before purchasing a major share in the John F. Allen Tobacco Company, believing that a quality cigarette could be fashioned from the bright leaf tobacco of Virginia and North Carolina and that tobacco would ensure the prosperity of the South. Cigarettes, at this time, were manufactured from foreign tobacco and were regarded as a product for women and Europeans; real American men chewed plugs and smoked pipes and perhaps an occasional Cuban-wrapped cigar. Understanding the value of packaging and publicity, Ginter used colorful lithograph pictures and eye-catching lettering on his boxes; he offered premiums and trading cards with each pack; and he was one of the first to employ personalities to endorse his product. He was creating a market, and the sales of Allen and Ginter cigarettes exploded after the public saw their display (designed by Ginter) at the Philadelphia Centennial Exposition in 1876.

Lewis Ginter became the chief rival of Washington Duke, his three sons, and their major partner and business manager, George Washington Watts. George W. Watts was born in Cumberland, Maryland, in 1851 and educated in Baltimore. His father's wholesale tobacco business survived the Civil War intact. Watts attended the University of Virginia from 1868 to 1871, then worked as a salesman for his father for the next seven years. Sometime in the early 1870s, Gerard Watts (George's father) visited Durham, North Carolina, seeking exclusive rights to sell Duke products in Baltimore. He saw a company with a good product, but poorly run. Seizing an opportunity, Gerard Watts purchased 20 percent of the Dukes' company with the understanding that his son, George, would move to Durham and manage it. George was so successful that seven years later W. Duke and Sons became W. Duke and Sons and Company; George Watts was the "and Company."[237] All three Duke sons had reputations as playboys. In contrast, George Watts was seen as "a man of clear intelligence, sound judgment, systematic habits, steady industry, and inflexible integrity." Indeed, it is said that Watts's example prompted the Dukes toward a greater benevolence in medicine and education, which helped to move a small Methodist college to Durham in 1892. This college ultimately became Duke University.[238]

Watts understood that the new Bonsack cigarette-rolling machine would revolutionize the cigarette industry. With so many cigarettes produced by so many different companies throughout the 1880s, cigarette manufacturers began to cooperate and fix prices in order to corner the market (which ultimately led to the passage of the Sherman Anti-Trust Act in 1890). George Watts and Lewis Ginter formed the American Tobacco Company in 1890 (it would be broken-up in 1913 in one of the first successful suits filed under the Sherman Anti-Trust Act). Ginter served as American Tobacco's first president (owning $3.5 million in shares) and Watts as its first secretary-treasurer (owning $2.5 million). Watts succeeded to the presidency of American Tobacco precisely at the time he was coming onto the seminary's board of directors in 1894.

By the time the American Tobacco Company was organized, therefore, Lewis Ginter and George Watts knew each other well. But they were a study in contrasts. Both were astute businessmen, but while Ginter was known as generous to civic causes and individuals in need, he was a nominal Episcopalian, more interested in the church as a cultural institution. Like Ginter, Watts was one of Durham's leading philanthropists, but he was also a devout Presbyterian. Watts was a longtime member and elder of First Presbyterian in Durham. He lived an active faith, sponsoring chapels, Sunday schools, and prayer meetings throughout the city.[239] Watts was also one of the first North Carolina industrialists to offer good wages and proper housing to a significant African American workforce. At the time of his death in 1897, Lewis Ginter paid more personal taxes than anyone else in Virginia; at the time of his death in 1921, George Watts was the largest individual taxpayer in North Carolina.[240]

During his later years, Ginter dreamed of developing America's first suburb: Ginter Park. He first conceived the idea when he visited Australia in 1888. He was struck by the number of Melbourne businessmen who worked downtown and then returned by carriage to spacious, manor-type houses that had a rural feel. Ginter Park was to be Lewis Ginter's monument; he planned his community down to the placement of the shade trees and hedgerows, ensuring there would be broad asphalt avenues, land for schools, and sewers.

Ginter invited his friends and associates to put their money into this new kind of community, and Watts was an early investor. Initial public response to Ginter Park was, however, disappointing. Attitudes changed when James

11. George W. Watts, influential in the move to Richmond

Power Smith purchased a house, and the surrounding publicity increased sales. Smith was well-known throughout the South; he had been a Presbyterian pastor in Roanoke and Fredericksburg, was editor of the *Presbyterian of the South*, served for over fifty years as stated clerk of the Synod of Virginia, and was the last surviving member of Stonewall Jackson's staff. He had lain beside the mortally wounded general, singing hymns as Jackson died.[241] The Presbytery of the James now occupies his house.

Contradicting the official history of the Removal, the Rev. Robert P. Kerr (1873, then pastor of First Presbyterian, Richmond) remembered that the seminary's board of directors sent him to approach Ginter in late 1894.

When I first called on Major Ginter and asked him for a site for the seminary, he told me he did not remember ever to have heard of it before, but, when he understood what an important institution it was, he said he was glad to donate land for its future home near Richmond. He offered a choice between two tracts, but neither of them (suited). . . . So I asked him to give us the block on Brook Road immediately opposite Mr. Joseph Bryan's residence ("Laburnum"). He said: "Why, that is about the best piece of land I own." "Yes," I replied. "I think it is. . . ." He took a few days to consider and then made the gift, freely.[242]

Ginter wanted Union Seminary in his development; the school would give an air of permanence and respectability to his suburb. Also, he must have known that Watts had committed $50,000 for the erection of the seminary's initial structures. Construction began two years later, and Ginter died three years later.

In the Gilded Age, that was the way business was done—through interlocking friendships and conflicts of interest. Indeed, Moore never mentions Ginter's offer in his writings. He attributed the campus site to the "active leadership of the Rev. R. P. Kerr, D.D.," and claimed that "the people of Richmond gave a beautiful site of twelve acres, now valued at $30,000, and contributions of money, materials, and land, aggregation about $50,000" for the new seminary. In the 1907 Centennial General Catalogue and in the General Catalogue of 1924, the people of Richmond are credited with donating the land for the campus. Ginter's donation was not widely known until McAllister's biography in 1939 and E. T. Thompson's narrative in the 1976 General Catalogue.[243] And it was not until William E. Thompson's own study under the direction of Dr. James Smylie in 1992 that the silent business connection with George Watts was affirmed.

Richmond, though, was an easy sell. The city was the New South, "glowing with both the supreme confidence of the manufacturing and transportation accomplishments of the Gilded Age and the powerful forces of the Lost Cause."[244] Moore had his site and money in hand; now all he needed was synod approval. The meeting would be in Charleston, West Virginia, in October 1895.

A few weeks before the 1895 synod meeting, Robert Lewis Dabney weighed in from 1,500 miles to the south. His article "Do Not Remove Union Seminary" appeared in virtually all the church papers and was reprinted in the Farmville Herald of October 5, 1895, just before the synod meeting. His article was well received in Hampden Sydney. The pastor of College Church, James Murray, read it aloud to his congregation one Sunday evening.[245]

Dabney could not resist his "I told you so" moment. He reminded his readers that he wanted to leave right after the war and of his fruitless efforts to form a land company in 1876 that would have guaranteed "a cultured residence village of the best white families" instead of "that village of free negroes" which had formed on the very borders of the seminary. He then addressed those who worried that seminarians would not attend a rural seminary and would leave for a rich northern seminary. Dabney opined:

Let them go. We should be well quit of them. These self-indulgent men are not fit for the work. To my apprehension there is no manifestation of character more contemptible than this, to see a young fellow, most probably poor and plainly raised, demanding these luxuries, as essential to his wants, while professing to enlist the hard and rough warfare of Christ.

He prophesied that the softness of city life would render men unfit for rural churches and the mission field.

> She [the church] has taught each young minister to say: "I am bound to have my streetcar conveniences, my hydrant water, my bathtub and my city luxuries; and I can't go where these are not." How much good will one of these clerical dudes ever do, with his exclusive luxuries, among plain farmers and laboring men who do not and cannot have them?[246]

Dabney also predicted that the new campus would not be as beautiful as the Elysium of Hampden-Sydney.

> You will get for the Church buildings possibly half as good, tricked off with some leaky Queen Ann Turrets and taudry ornaments devised by some pretender to architecture according to some (what shall I call it?) Tuckahoe modification of modernized, bastard Byzantine style which the dudes will pronounce awfully pretty, but which good taste will despise as contemptibly fussy.

James Appleby, speaking a hundred years later, agreed with Dabney: "No dudes [will] pronounce our architecture as 'awfully pretty' but rather just 'pretty awful.'"[247] And Jim Smylie would often call the building design "Halloween Gothic."

Prior to the Synod of Virginia meeting in Charleston, West Virginia, Moore sent a letter to all attendees, outlining the specific proposal and arguing for the advantages of Ginter Park over Hampden-Sydney.[248] In addition, the seminary board met at a called meeting in Danville on October 18, 1895, four days before the synod meeting. The board adopted a resolution attesting to the synod that they had secured a site and enough money, and they asked the synod for permission to move.

The Synod of Virginia met on October 22, 1895. The Removal debate lasted from Thursday afternoon to Friday at 11:30 p.m., with every vote recorded in the minutes. Removal won 100 to 67. The Synod of North Carolina was meeting at the same time in Fayetteville and, after a short debate, voted 110-3 in favor of the move. Moore ensured that the North Carolina vote was telegraphed to Charleston.[249]

Many people believed that the margin was larger than expected because McIlwaine was so vicious that he alienated the uncommitted vote.[250] McIlwaine's arguments became vitriolic personal attacks, which offended many. In contrast, Moore's graciousness was widely commended. While people admired McIlwaine's perseverance, in the end they did not particularly admire the man himself, and much of his overall effectiveness as a churchman was diminished by his manner.[251] But there was more than personality at stake. As the historian John Luster Brinkley stated, the New South won.[252] The symbolism was too obvious to miss: McIlwaine was in his early sixties, he had been a Confederate soldier, he was stooped: he represented the past. In contrast, Moore was thirty-six, tall, handsome, a scholar, and nationally known: he represented the future.[253]

Interregnum

From the first time Walter W. Moore stood before the trustees in May 1892, it was understood that the desire to move was an implicit criticism of southside Virginia. Once the vote was taken, some way had to be found to repair wounded feelings. *Union Seminary Magazine* would editorialize in 1895: "We are glad that the change was ordered by so large a majority, for this secures the general concurrence of all the friends of the Seminary in the transfer."[254] It was not just Union Seminary that was concerned with hurt feelings. Before the debate, Moses D. Hoge introduced a resolution committing the synod to support UTS whatever the outcome.

> The Synod of Virginia gratefully recognizes the fact that both those who favor the removal of the Seminary from its present location, and those who oppose its removal, are actuated by motives equally conscientious and pure. Remembering also, that because of the infirmities of our humanity, unless controlled and conquered by divine grace, it is possible that the disappointment of either party in the attainment of its aims might alienate some of the former friends of the seminary.
>
> Resolved, That the members of this Synod, in reliance on the aid of the divine Spirit of peace, do pledge themselves not to abate their loyal efforts for the prosperity of this beloved institution whatever the final decision may be.

This resolution was seconded by Moore and McIlwaine, and it was unanimously adopted by a rising vote.[255]

Hard feelings, however, remained. The local Farmville paper claimed that Southside had been cheated out of its birthright. On November 9, 1895, the paper sarcastically reported: "The Hotel Jefferson has opened its doors. Most delightful resort it will be for Seminary students who want to learn of high life in the city in order to do better service for Christ." In the same issue, the paper reported that the "old Randolf-Macon College buildings in Mecklenburg County are used as a colored school. What will be the fate of the deserted buildings of Union Seminary?"[256]

If Moore stated he wanted to move to a "better" location, the implication was that Hampden-Sydney was substandard. Feelings were bound to be hurt. Richard McIlwaine became president of the college at the same time Moore arrived at Union and lived next door to him for fifteen years. Yet, in his autobiography, McIlwaine mentions 381 people, and Moore is not among them. He remained bitter over the Removal until the day he died.

> Perhaps, however, the most serious blow came from the removal of Union Theological Seminary and especially from incidents connected therewith. In order to pacify the Presbyterians of Virginia and reconcile them to this step, it was thought necessary to vilify and abuse its locations and surroundings in Prince Edward. This, of course, reacted on the College. . . . An intelligent citizen of Prince Edward told me he heard of it ad nauseam in Richmond and overheard a lady say to a friend, "I intended to send my son to Hampden-Sydney, but if that is the kind of place it is, he certainly shall not go there."

Although McIlwaine acknowledges "there were restrictions and draw-backs" to the Hill, he insisted that Hampden-Sydney "was an ideal place for both" the college and the seminary. The real problem was that the seminary, like the Egyptians who had forgotten Joseph, was an "ungrateful foster-child." He sadly concludes: "The Presbyterian Church in Virginia and the South owes [Hampden-Sydney College] a debt of gratitude which it ought to be forward to pay, but can never fully repay."[257]

Immediately after the Synod of Virginia vote, construction began on Union Seminary's initial eight buildings, and land sales boomed in Ginter Park.[258] Moore noted that "well-known business men and ministers kindly consented to serve on the Building Committee and have from the very beginning directed all the complicated affairs connected with the planning and erection of the buildings with accurate judgment, admirable taste, and unflagging zeal."[259] He was rhapsodic in describing the new campus:

> The buildings are handsome and solid structures of dark red pressed brick, trimmed with red sandstone and terra cotta, and covered with heavy slate roofing. They are all constructed of the same materials, so as to make a harmonious group in appearance. The chief stress has been laid on the qualities of durability, convenience, and adaptation to the actual uses of a working Seminary. All the buildings are provided with bath-room conveniences, are heated with steam, in addition to open grates, and are lighted with gas or electricity. [There are] also five substantial residences for professors.[260]

Moore's expectations were limitless: "With such advantages of location and equipment, and with the continued blessing of God, the Seminary may well be expected to do a great work for the church throughout the future."[261]

There was one more piece of business; like ending a bad marriage, the assets had to be divided. The seminary offered to sell its buildings to the college, but the college refused to pay the asking price of $20,000. Two years later Major Richard Venable of Baltimore (Hampden-Sydney, 1857) purchased the seminary buildings and land for $10,000[262] and promptly donated them to his alma mater,[263] doubling the size of the college physical plant. And Union needed the money. It would ultimately cost $133,000 to build the eight new buildings in Richmond (Watts Hall, $50,000; Spence Library, $25,000; Westminster Hall, $20,000; and the five faculty homes, $38,000). The move left the seminary $30,000 in the red.[264] The final valuation of the land given to Union Seminary was $20,000. The chapel was added to Watts Hall in 1900, entirely paid by a gift from George W. Watts.[265]

The Move

The biggest physical challenge in relocating from Hampden-Sydney to Farmville was how to move the library books. In the summer of 1898, the library held almost 16,000 bound volumes and 5,000 unbound pamphlets. Their weight would have been much too heavy for wagon axles and the clay road of the Red Sea. Consequently, Walter Lingle, who was a graduate assistant at the time, and

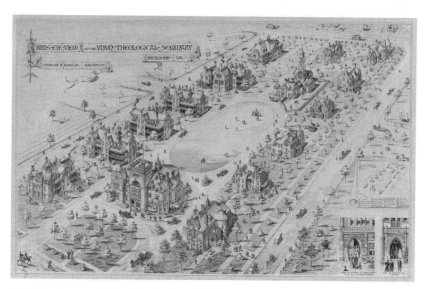

12. Original campus design. Note the laundry and stable in the center of campus.

a student team packed the entire collection into thirty waterproof tobacco hogs-heads (large wooden barrels) with sawdust for cushioning.[266] The hogsheads were then rolled down the Via Sacra (the dirt road in front of the old seminary) to Buffalo Creek, where they were loaded on flatbed barges. The barges were poled several miles to the Appomattox River, where they were then poled one mile farther eastward and were unloaded just a hundred yards north of the Farmville freight depot (at the present-day Green Front Furniture Store). They were then rolled up to the landing dock and onto a Richmond-bound freight train.[267]

When the hogsheads were unloaded in Richmond, they were put onto dray wagons, one hogshead to a wagon, and transported to Ginter Park. When they arrived at the campus, the books were unpacked, dusted off, catalogued, and properly shelved —"a task that Lingle remembered clearly as long as he lived and referred to often with a humorous gleam in his eye."[268] Lingle, however, did not move with the seminary. He left that year to pastor a church in Dalton, Georgia.

Union sold the buildings at Hampden-Sydney, but two other things remained. The college owned the original portrait of John Holt Rice, and it did not make the move. And at the end of Via Sacra, the land that George Baxter donated for the cemetery stayed intact. The cemetery is reserved for professors, senior administrators, and their maiden daughters. Meandering among the graves and reading the headstones is a walk through the nineteenth-century history of Union Seminary. Yet no one was buried there after 1898. Feelings over the Removal were so hard that no seminary faculty member dared to exercise the burial privilege until Mrs. Emma White Lacy passed away in 1947. Semi-nary President Benjamin Rice Lacy buried her in Hampden Sydney, and with that peacemaking gesture, other seminary burials occurred there ever since.

Walter W. Moore is buried in North Carolina's old Salem Cemetery, amid his wife's Moravian ancestors; at the time of Moore's death in 1926, many southside Virginians considered this gesture to be his final insult to the Hampden-Sydney institution.[269]

The Removal reflected the way the South was moving. Although it wasn't until 1910 that southern property values equaled 1860 values, 1880 is the dividing line for economics in the South. Textile output doubled between 1870 and 1880, tobacco began to be exported, and coal production exploded from 6 million tons in 1880 to 26 million in 1890. Between 1865 and 1875, most southern towns doubled in size, and by 1883, railroads connected every major city in the South with each other and with the North.

Presbyterians, however, seemed ill equipped to meet the challenge of growth. In the 1870s, Baptists and Methodists were growing faster than Presbyterians. The reasons given by various General Assembly committees were that Presbyterians did not sing hymns in line with "the popular taste," pew rents kept people of modest means away, and the unyielding requirements of theological education constricted the supply of ministers. The General Assembly could do nothing about congregational singing or stewardship, but proposals to change the shape of theological education came from all quarters.

The *North Carolina Presbyterian* blamed Presbyterian seminaries for putting "a little too much bent on respectability." The paper complained that "Methodists and Baptists let their young men preach while they were still full of enthusiasm, while the Presbyterian candidates for ordination were required to go first to college and then to the seminary," draining away his "fire and vigor." Is there not "some middle path between an educated ministry and an over educated one?" The *Christian Observer* took up the call and seemed to be calling for more practical education: "The young graduates of the seminary know everything except how to manage a congregation. They can tell about Greek verbs and Hebrew roots, about supra-Lapsarianism and sub-Lapsarianism, but they know little about human nature."[270] If Presbyterians were complaining that they needed more ministers (as they did in 1706 and 1806) and ministers who could "manage a congregation," Walter W. Moore was determined to make sure Union Theological Seminary would meet the need in the Presbyterian way. In his mind, a resurgent South demanded a professional seminary.

The March–April 1898 issue of the *Union Seminary Magazine* (published five months before the Richmond campus opened) reflects the contradiction between Union's past and its anticipated future. The entire issue is both a benediction for southside Virginia and an invocation of a new creation in Richmond. It is a historical analysis of what the seminary accomplished in confined, isolated Hampden Sydney and a call to imagine what the seminary will become in a cosmopolitan, modern city.

Walter Moore recalled that UTS had educated over 1,125 ministers in the previous 86 years; two-thirds since 1860. Over 50 percent of PCUS missionaries were UTS grads, as were 75 percent of Synod of Virginia ministers, and 50 percent of Synod of North Carolina ministers.[271] Thomas Cary Johnson celebrated that the alumni had a huge influence on the denomination as pastors of large churches, college presidents and professors, editors of religious newspapers, authors, and executive officers of the church—proudly noting that all graduates had been pastors of small churches. Moore called Union to be conscious of its influence; he viewed Union's history at Hampden-Sydney as a prelude to greater things. This viewpoint is echoed at the end of the issue by R. L. Wharton, who announced that this issue would be the last one published in Hampden Sydney.

> As we go to Richmond next year, of course, that means "good bye" to Hampden Sidney. The Staff has urged me to be specially pathetic in this part of my valedictory. I don't know how to do that, yet I suppose there is not a student in the Seminary but that regrets to leave the place. The Faculty of the College has been a source of inspiration. For each of that Faculty we wish to express our highest regard. The people of the Hill have been genial, courteous and hospitable. We regret to leave them all. Yet as we turn our faces to the future and see our beloved Seminary located in its new home, with a greatly enlarged sphere of usefulness, we cannot but rejoice that it has thus been transplanted after seventy four years of work among the good people of Hampden Sidney.[272]

The Threads of History

The definition of an educated ministry in 1866 differed little from that of 1766. Until the Civil War, a minister was expected to be able to explain the confessions and teach the Bible in a supportive culture. Yet between Appomattox and the Removal, the ideal of an educated minister was transformed. An educated minister was now defined as one who could dispute the theological implications of the theory of natural selection in an urban, industrialized culture and manage church programs. The curriculum, however, remained true to the tradition. Although English Bible was added in the 1890s, languages remained the foundation.

Union embodied John Holt Rice's aspirations for a southern seminary serving the national church. Students and professors ironically thought of Union as a southern seminary, yet one that depended on the North for support. As B. M. Smith turned north to raise money, Dabney stoked southern bitterness and denounced northern influences. As in the antebellum era, Union continued to engage the world by long-distance connection; students studied about missions (and some went onto the mission field), and they debated current events, but there were precious few ways for hands-on learning. Although graduates staffed the faculty and administration of many southern schools, filled denominational boards, and influenced religious editorial boards, some began to call for reforms that would be prominent in the Progressive Era. Union was still a thoroughly nineteenth-century institution, willing to live with the contradictions of race.

Because Union has always kept the traditional curriculum at its center, it is sometimes difficult to detect the tradition of innovation. Seminary education itself was a unique advance in theological education in the early nineteenth century. Just seventy years later, Walter W. Moore saw the future of theological education and ensured that his seminary would be at the cutting edge; Union would not be a rural monastery, but a center of education in the new urban landscape. As the new century dawned with all its hopes, Union Theological Seminary would renew itself for a new world.

Robert Burwell (1826) knew Rice personally. He was asked to speak at the seventieth-anniversary exercises in 1894, but was too frail to be at the ceremonies (he died the next year). Instead, he sent his remarks to be read. He was certain of Union's future.

> We have been looking back on the last seventy years, and what a record do you see. What a contrast between January 1st, 1824, and January 1st, 1894. Truly God has done wonderful things for us. Let us be glad and rejoice. Seventy years hence, in 1964, another will stand here to tell the story, and what a glorious history will it be of the mercy and truth and faithfulness of our Covenant God and Father through Jesus Christ.[273]

Chapter Six (1898–1926)
Conservatism in Doctrine,
Progressiveness in Methods

Despite the politicking, real estate deals, fund-raising, planning, and hogshead rolling, the 1898–99 school year would not begin on time. After three years of construction, delays in building faculty housing postponed the opening of the new campus and the convening of classes by one month. Faculty families began to move from Hampden-Sydney into their new houses along the quadrangle during the third week of September. Students began to arrive around October 4. Classes were set to begin on October 10, after two days of dedication exercises on October 5–6. From the first moment the seminary's move was announced, the Richmond papers enthusiastically reported on each phase of construction:[1] everyone was ready.

There was, however, more to the Removal than new buildings in a new location. Walter W. Moore would introduce "practical" education into the curriculum for a new kind of professional minister. This minister would not only be proficient in the traditional subjects, but would also have a firm grounding in Christian education and modern management methods; he would be able to function in an urban environment and explain faith in an increasingly empirical world. Yet it would be the students who would transform Union Theological Seminary from a provincial, regional seminary to an institution that would challenge their culture and its assumptions derived from the doctrine of the spirituality of the church.

The New Campus

On Wednesday, October 5, at 11:30 a.m., George W. Finley (the board president) and George W. Watts gathered the assembled dignitaries and professors in the lobby of Spence Library and led them under a gray drizzle to a packed house in the "main hall" of Watts Hall. The crowd included the governor of Virginia, Hoge Tyler, who was a Union Seminary trustee. Services began with the reading of Psalm 115. Then S. H. Hawes, chair of the Building Committee, reported that all work had been completed and handed the new door keys to Finley. At noon, Dr. Theodore Cuyler, the featured speaker, rose to the podium. At first glance, Cuyler was a curious choice to address this convocation. He was a native New Yorker, a Princeton graduate, and pastor of Lafayette Park Presbyterian Church in Brooklyn (the largest church in the northern denomination).

Cuyler introduced himself by stating that when he was a student at Princeton, he was received into the Presbyterian Church at a service preached by

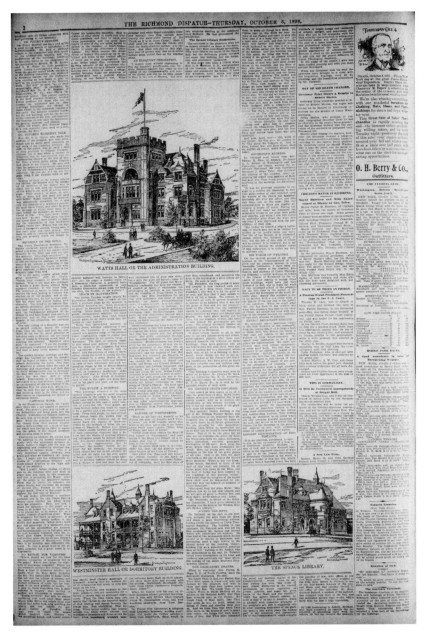

WATTS HALL OR THE ADMINISTRATION BUILDING.

WESTMINSTER HALL OR DORMITORY BUILDING.

THE SPENCE LIBRARY.

13. *Richmond Times-Dispatch*, October 6, 1898, 2

John Holt Rice. "So you see," he observed, "if I am not Virginia born, I am Virginia bred—in theology." His speech addressed the challenges of ministry and theological education in the modern world—what one would expect. Near the end of his remarks, however, he talked about Union and Princeton, linking them as members of the same team, if in different denominations. He congratulated Union on holding fast to the traditional curriculum and the Westminster Confession, respecting the inerrancy of Scripture, training ministers to care for souls, and speaking with eloquence in the pulpit. He ended his speech by "expressing my heartfelt gratification that Virginia Presbyterianism has come to the Capital of the Commonwealth" and is now confronting the modern world. He concluded:

> God grant that these new and beautiful edifices, founded on the Rock of Ages, may ever stand as a grand Gibraltar of orthodoxy, until the first rays of the Millennial Dawn flash on their towers, and these walls echo and resound with the acclaim, "Hallelujah, Hallelujah. The Lord Jesus Christ Omnipotent reigneth. Amen, Amen."

Union was no longer a parochial, rural, southern seminary; Moore's school had made an entrance onto the national stage. At 4:00 p.m. Spence Library and the faculty residences were dedicated.[2]

Union Theological Seminary's eighty-sixth session opened at 11:00 a.m. the next day. Thomas Cary Johnson was the principal speaker, and he faced the largest student body in Union's history: eighty-eight students. He made it clear that while Union had changed location, the school had not changed its mission. Although he had applauded the introduction of English Bible six years earlier, he now took this opportunity to defend learning biblical languages. "This is a Bible school, my brethren," he began, and argued that learning the original languages is the only way to combat "Germany's unregenerate scholars." The move to Richmond meant that Union would claim a preeminent place in American theological education and give southern Calvinism a place in the modern conversation.[3]

After the opening exercises ended, the attendees broke for lunch on the quad and reassembled at 5:00 p.m. in front of Watts Hall. The Covenanters was the citywide umbrella organization of Presbyterian youth groups, and they had been active in raising money for the seminary. Their gift was last on the agenda. As the crowd of about 200 left the quad and came around the corner of Watts Hall, they discovered about 120 boys standing in front of them. After some short words of introduction and a prayer, the boys presented a Covenanter flag to the seminary: a gold St. Andrews cross on a blue field. At a signal, the flag was unfurled atop Watts Hall. It was a moving sight; the Covenanter flag flying over Watts Hall was used as the cover of early catalogues after its removal. "As the banner first waved from the mast, there was great cheering."[4] Union Seminary was now home in Richmond.

As the spectators, faculty, and students departed from Watts Hall, they could see Walter W. Moore's vision before them. There were eight buildings around the quadrangle: Watts Hall (without the chapel), Westminster Hall (containing the refectory), Spence Library, and five faculty residences. The campus was surrounded by open fields. There were no houses on what is now Seminary Avenue

14. The new campus from Westwood Avenue

15. The view from the Quad, 1899

and very few on any other street in Ginter Park. Brook Road was a turnpike; a tollhouse stood in the middle of the road between the campus and Westwood, not then owned by the seminary. There was no electricity. The buildings were designed to be illuminated by gas, which was to be supplied by a main line constructed by the city. But the line was never built; according to Dr. Moore, "There were no electric lights in the community then, only a few arc lights along the line of the street railway. The campus was in absolute darkness."[5]

Charles H. Read Jr. designed Watts Hall, Westminster Hall, Spence Library, and the faculty houses. His father was pastor of Richmond's First Presbyterian

Church for fifty years. He was educated at the Virginia Military Institute and fought at the Battle of New Market on May 15, 1864. After the war he attended the University of Virginia and worked as a draftsman for Tredegar Iron Works. Sometime in the 1870s, he left Richmond for Washington, D.C., to work in the Office of the Supervising Architect of the United States. This office designed the Smithsonian "castle" and other public buildings, which gave late-nineteenth-century Washington a Gothic flair. He returned to Richmond in 1889 and was considered the most prominent southern architect in the late nineteenth century.

Once Union moved to Richmond, it was thought that Hampden-Sydney would also move, despite McIlwaine's assurances. The Medical College of Virginia had already moved from Hampden-Sydney the year before, and "there was a hope at one time to get the rest of Hampden-Sydney here and form a Presbyterian University that would counteract the pernicious influence of the Baptists at the University of Richmond." Inspired by the notion of a Presbyterian university, Read patterned the campus after the University of Virginia; Union's quadrangle is exactly the same size as Thomas Jefferson's quadrangle.[6]

The campus was meant to be a landmark. Watts Hall, the first building to be constructed (finished in 1896), has the largest gargoyle in Richmond on its top.[7] The chapel was in the original design, but not added until 1901.[8] The second building was Spence Library—the first library building in Richmond.[9] Read used the color red in every building, including the brick and mortar and the terra cotta tiles with Tudor roses, because red was associated with intellect. The campus has a vague military look; Watts Hall and Spence Library have turrets, the doorways are off-center, and windows and wings are placed in uneven positions. The Gothic influence is meant to convey strength and permanence. The deodar cedars (*Cedrus deodara*) are in the same family as the cedars of Lebanon. The cast-iron balconies on Westminster Hall were among the last to be installed in Richmond. Read also indulged his Victorian love of octagons. The chapel, library, and living rooms of many of the residences are octagonal. Symbolizing Moore's philosophy of theological education, the campus was designed to be open and not inward: the seminary is not a cloister.[10] And the wider world was convenient: electric trolleys ran on both Brook Road (fare was five cents) and Chamberlayne Avenue (fare was ten cents).

Watts, Westminster, and Spence Library are reminders of the dawn of the twentieth century. In 1898 the United States had forty-five states; the U.S.S. *Maine* exploded and sank in Havana harbor on February 15, initiating the Spanish-American War; Hawaii was annexed; Pepsi-Cola was invented; John D. Rockefeller organized Standard Oil Company, controlling 84 percent of America's oil; and one of the last battles of the Indian Wars was fought on October 3, when the Ojibwa defeated army troops in the Battle of Sugar Point in northern Minnesota. The battle was reported on the front page of the *Richmond Times-Dispatch* right next to the story of Union Seminary's dedication.[11]

The October–November 1898 issue of *Union Seminary Magazine* contained a glowing account of the new campus and seminary, which had moved from "the ancestral oaks." The editor observed approvingly that the architectural style of Watts Hall "impresses one with its durability and immovability, giving prospect of long residence in the land."[12] The article also admitted that the school needed a chapel. By 1900, the magazine could report, "The contract for

16. Building Watts Chapel, 1900

17. The new campus, 1901

18. Watts from the Quad, 1901

the building of the chapel has been awarded, . . . and work upon it has already been begun. It is to cost fifteen thousand dollars." The article concludes: "The chapel is the gift of Mr. George W. Watts, of Durham, N.C., and is an annex to the handsome main building. . . . It will have a seating capacity on the main floor and in the gallery of about five hundred. . . . The interior will be neat and attractive, without anything that is gaudy. There will be a belfry, with a place for a large clock."[13] Progress on the construction was reported in every succeeding issue.[14]

The *Union Seminary Magazine* stated that the "upper portions of Watts Hall are used for dormitory purposes, chiefly for the incoming class, perhaps on the principle that the children should always be put safely away upstairs out of harm's way." And the editor boasted that the building is heated throughout by steam and lighted by gas: "two features which every Seminary should have, in order that those of the brethren who shall leave for the rural districts and foreign lands never to return, may for once in their lives have the comfort and joy of using these two modern conveniences." Then there was Westminster Hall. "The lower portion is devoted to dormitory purposes as in Watts Hall; the upper part contains the refectory."[15] The story pled for a gym and another dormitory building: "Are there not other persons, friends of the Seminary, who will provide the money for a much-needed gymnasium and another dormitory building for student's rooms?"[16]

19. Students in Spence Library, 1900

Just as the building of Brown Library at Hampden-Sydney announced that Union had recovered from the Civil War, so Spence Library declared that Union would be the equal of any seminary in the country. Moore had insisted that the library would be one of the first buildings constructed on the new campus. In 1865, Mrs. Harmon Brown of Baltimore had given blankets and the funds to build the Brown Library at Hampden-Sydney. In Richmond, the "Baltimore connection" came into play again. W. W. Spence, an elder of the First Presbyterian Church in Baltimore, donated the entire cost of the new library, "the peer of any theological building in America."[17] The 1898–99 Catalogue describes Spence Library in some detail, including a sketch, and proudly claims that the collection contains 16,000 bound volumes and 5,000 unbound pamphlets.[18] Spence Library was one of the first libraries in the South to be completely fireproof.[19] There was a large fireplace on the west end of the stack room with a wooden mantle, upon which was inscribed, "There is but one book."

In keeping with the idea that professors could do several jobs, Walter Moore was appointed librarian in 1903. The board believed he could run the library with three student assistants, just as at the Hampden-Sydney location. But the increase in enrollment and more patrons attracted by an outstanding facility made part-time management impractical. In 1902, the library budget was $305.57, with 72 books purchased, and the doors were open only 16 hours a week. It quickly became apparent that Moore could best be employed to raise money, so the board appointed Thomas Cary Johnson as librarian in 1905, and he served until 1930. Although he was suspicious of most of the modern world, Johnson kept the library up-to-date. In 1908 he placed bookshelves in the classrooms and set up faculty-centered special collections. Some of the old "located" books in the library today have an inscription, such as "Dr. Johnson's Classroom."[20] And like B. M. Smith before him, Johnson complained that the "Reading-Room [is] the leading attraction of the Seminary," especially with young ladies.[21]

Moore made sure that funding was available for a first-rate library. In 1907 the library held 18,906 volumes and 5,000 unbound pamphlets.[22] By 1912 three student assistants had increased to eight, and by 1913 the library held 25,000 volumes. With the inventory increasing every year, Johnson began to realize that the cataloguing system used in the Hampden-Sydney library was now unworkable. In 1915, after noticing that "despite our best efforts a good deal of inconsistent and illogical cataloguing has been done," Johnson selected the Library of Congress system to classify the library's 28,077 volumes and 12,000 unbound pamphlets. By 1916 he reported that many of the old handwritten catalogue cards had been redone in the Library of Congress style.

Moore and Johnson wanted the best theological library in the South, if not the whole country. The creation of the graduate department in 1915 gave them the opportunity to transform the library from supporting a one-degree denominational school to enlarging the collection to match any respected research institution. Offering graduate degrees meant the library had to provide in-depth resources in a number of fields. Despite his personal opinions, Johnson ensured that there would be a broader collection of foreign-language materials and a wider range of books representing viewpoints other than that of the faculty or of the PCUS.

Johnson was proud of the library. In 1922 he called for an expansion of the building, now crowded with 30,068 volumes, plus 1,912 holdings in manila binders, 1,353 bundles of material, and 4,710 pamphlets. In 1925, the library was open 27 hours a week: 1:45 p.m. to 6:00 p.m. and 7:00 to 9:00 p.m. daily (except for Sundays and Wednesday nights). In 1925 the seminary made an effort to share duplicate books with missionaries overseas, a precursor to the International Book Project. Just as with the introduction of computers, the library was also the herald of new technology: typewriters. Beginning in 1925 the faculty minutes are typed, and the librarian's reports from 1902 forward are transcribed from handwritten pages to typed pages. Typewriters were used for routine work by 1926: typed cards began to replace the handwritten ones.[23]

Life in Richmond

With the Removal, life changed in Hampden Sydney. On the last Sunday in September 1898, College Church attendance was down; not nearly as many couples were scrambling to sit beside one another at the midpew barricades.[24] McIlwaine may have sulked, but most college students were glad to see Union go. In 1895 one student wrote to the *Hampden-Sydney Magazine* that he was glad to see the seminary decide to leave because too many people, when they heard the name Hampden-Sydney, thought first of the seminary and considered the college a mere adjunct; what was worse, some visitors mistook college students for "Seminites."[25] In another editorial, the writer argued that since the "earnestness" of the ministerial student was "dangerous to the peace of mind of young girl-collegians," now would be an ideal time for the college to admit women, and the seminary facilities could be used to house the females.[26]

Robert Fishburne Campbell (1885) remembered how life also changed for seminary students. A friend of his

> arrived in Richmond tired and travel-stained, went to the Lexington Hotel and ordered a bath for which he paid a dollar; got something to eat, and then took a car for the Seminary, only to find that all he had paid for was at his disposal for nothing. The 10-gallon round wooden tubs at Hampden-Sydney had been replaced by "sure-enough" bathtubs in Richmond.[27]

An urban location also meant city manners. Early student handbooks had to remind those who were used to the rural informality of the Hampden-Sydney site:

> Cuspidors are provided in the halls, and the students are requested to use them so far as necessary, and in no case to turn carpet, floor, fireplace, or windows into a spittoon. The cuspidors must not be removed from the halls into the rooms. Any student who wishes to have a cuspidor in his room may provide it at his own charges, but it must be regularly cleaned.
>
> Students who wish to employ a servant to care for their rooms and polish their shoes can secure a suitable man for this purpose by applying to the Engineer. The regular charge for this work is 50 cents per month in Watts Hall and 75 cents per month in Westminster Hall.
>
> The students are requested to exercise all possible care in the use of the lavatories, and especially to throw no matches, slops, newspapers, or other obstructive matter into the waste bowls of the water closets. Toilet paper will be put in place, and no substitute will be allowed.
>
> Any student who wishes extra electric lights placed in his room can have it done by applying to the engineer. The charge for each extra light is 60 cents per month. Students are requested to turn out their lights when leaving their rooms at night for supper, evening service, etc.
>
> The athletic grounds at Westwood afford ample facilities for outdoor games, and all ball playing on the campus is forbidden.
>
> Furnished rooms in Westminster Hall, with water and lights, are rented to students wishing to remain during any part of the summer vacation at $1.00 per week, or 25 cents per night for shorter periods than a week.
>
> No cooking in the dormitories is allowed. [Bicycle racks were located in the basement of Watts Hall, and there was a 25¢ fine for a bicycle in a room.]
>
> Do not turn on the electric lights when standing in the metal bath-tubs.[28] [The campus was fully electrified by 1903, and this warning continued until 1920.]

Seminary students were excited to be in Richmond. The Removal opened up a new world. As one incoming student recalled, a quarter of a century later:

> It was a sore trial to me to leave Hampden-Sydney. My five sessions on "The Hill" had greatly endeared the place to me, and I would not take the choicest pastorate in the Assembly for the memory of pulling through the red mud of Prince Edward, the exhilarating exercise of splitting and carrying my own firewood, and the tantalizing endeavor of taking a weekly bath in a washtub.

. . . [But] somehow, when we went to Richmond all life took on a new meaning. I seemed to see things in a broader way, to feel more keenly and to study
more purposefully. . . . We were vitally in touch with the great throbbing
world about us. The very atmosphere we breathed imparted faith and confidence and consecration. We all realized from the first that in its eastward
migration the Seminary had journeyed toward the sunrising, that a new and
larger life had come to her. And this I say, "not that I love Caesar less, but
Rome more."[29]

City life was cushy. The first ten-day Christmas holiday was given in 1900.
Prior to this, the only holiday was Christmas Day.[30]

Criticism from Caesar was remembered, though. In every seminary catalogue until World War I, there was an emphasis on health and seclusion, perhaps answering the charges that Richmond would not be as healthful as bucolic
Hampden Sydney. Just as catalogues after the Civil War assured prospective students that no one had ever died on the Hampden-Sydney campus, so the first
catalogues of the twentieth century bragged about the Richmond location: "The
climate is equable and salubrious, not being subject to the extremes of heat or
cold." The reader was assured that "the official statistics prepared by Surgeon-
General Wyman, of the United States Marine Hospital Service, gave Richmond
a preeminent position in point of health among American cities." The campus
was located "above the level of the highest points of the city," with pure artesian
water and a fine sewage system. Moreover, the campus was secluded, but close
to the city, "being but twenty minutes' ride by the electric cars to the business
center of Richmond at the intersection of First and Broad Streets."[31]

Union Seminary Magazine editorialized: "The close of the first quarter of this
century witnessed the establishment of Union Theological Seminary at Hampden-
Sydney, Virginia; the close of the last quarter witnesses the re-establishment
in the city of Richmond, Virginia." Yet the editor still found it necessary to justify the Removal by pointing out that the church must recognize increasing
urbanization: "the church in fulfilling her mission must come in contact with
the world and know it."[32]

The magazine reassured its readers that moving to Richmond was the right
decision. Students, the editorial claimed, worked harder at their studies because
there was no wood to chop or water to carry: "The average preparation of the
students now in the Seminary is far above that of the men of two years ago, and
hence they are better fitted for the course of study." Moreover, students had the
opportunity to hear the ministers of Richmond and learn ministry by hands-
on participation, "not that we would advocate regular preaching by students
during the session, but [only] occasional preaching and regular Sabbath-school
work." The editor also reported that health advantages had been realized:
"With one exception there have been no cases of serious sickness within our
ranks; and we believe that we can honestly say that that one case mentioned
was not due primarily to the climate of Richmond, but to grip[pe] settling on
the lungs."[33] Union's geographic, cultural, theological, and emotional isolation
was over.[34]

Once the seminary's initial eight buildings began to take shape, land sales
boomed in Ginter Park; Union's impact on the neighborhood and the city was
immediate. Emma Davidson Poole, a seminary neighbor, remembered that
"Ginter Park was a hot bed of Presbyterians."

We went to church and Sunday School on the seminary campus; used the classroom in Watts Hall and the church in Watts Chapel. . . . In the hot summer we went to church fanning, perspiring, and fighting the flies that came in the open windows. . . . Later on Schauffler Hall replaced Watts Chapel (for Sunday services). Seminary President Dr. Moore and his wife made their stately progress down the aisle to a front pew. Dr. Moore wore formal morning attire, as did Gov. James H. Price when he came later.[35]

Union Seminary saved Major Ginter's development. After the Richmond papers announced that Ginter Park was to be the site of the new seminary campus, lots began to sell. Union's move to Richmond was more than just a new start for the school. The city considered Union's move to Ginter Park as validation. Richmond had never really recovered from the Civil War; it was poorer in 1900 than in 1860. Moreover, the city's leaders focused on racial issues at the expense of attracting industry.[36] The poll tax and literary tests instituted by Virginia's 1902 constitution had the desired effect: 1900 found 6,427 African Americans registered to vote; 1902 had only 760.[37] In the eyes of Richmonders, Union's selection of Ginter Park meant that the seminary and the church believed in them and would help them keep their traditions while moving into the new century. Construction on the campus was always news, as were the gifts that the seminary received. The *Richmond Times-Dispatch* put the dedication ceremonies on the front page and also devoted its entire second page to the "consecration," with beautiful engravings of the new buildings and a transcription of Cuyler's speech.[38] Beginning in 1898, in editorial after editorial, Richmond papers lauded UTS for advancing Richmond's civic, intellectual, and religious life.[39] The seminary would also, however, bring new influences to challenge the old capital of the Confederacy.

Official Richmond expected the students at the new seminary to buttress the developing southern culture devoted to the Lost Cause and racial segregation. But these students quickly saw how conditions in Richmond contradicted the gospel, and they began to undermine the doctrine of the spirituality of the church. First articulated by James Henley Thornwell before the Civil War in an attempt to keep the church from commenting on slavery, Robert Lewis Dabney became the foremost advocate of the doctrine after the war. The doctrine of the spirituality of the church, which held that the church could have no say on political issues, depended on a belief in southern particularism and a worldview wedded to an agricultural, rural, and hierarchical mind-set. Once in Richmond, Union's students would lead the church and the South to confront an industrial, urban, democratic world. Much of the South reacted to modernism by retreating into fundamentalism or uncritically embracing whatever was thought to be modern. Union would seek a middle ground: conservative but not fundamental, progressive but orthodox.

The seminary's influence was, however, indirect at first. Oddly enough, the first issue that Union confronted was how Richmonders would address revivals. "Tent meetings" were a feature of eighteenth- and nineteenth-century America, but Presbyterians were of two minds when it came to revivals, especially the growing ranks of the professional revivalists of the twentieth century. On one hand, Presbyterians were uneasy with the emotionalism and revivalist theology that seemed to exalt human agency and belittle the sovereignty of God. On the other hand, everyone in the eighteenth and nineteenth centuries (including

Moses Hoge, John Holt Rice, George Baxter, R. L. Dabney, B. M. Smith, and T. C. Johnson) had positive experiences with revivals in their backgrounds. Yet Virginians (especially Richmonders) distrusted extroverted public expressions of faith. Moreover, they felt that professional revivalists, such as Billy Sunday, were coarse and sensational, and that their personal organizations undermined the effectiveness of the local church. The suspicions about mass revivals were so pervasive that no revivals were held in Richmond between 1894 and 1909. Attitudes changed, however, at the conclusion of the 1909 Chapman-Alexander revival. Wilbur Chapman (1859–1918) was a curious person to change the minds of Virginians toward revivals. Born in Indiana and a graduate of Lane Seminary, he pastored seven Reformed churches before engaging in full-time evangelism. Although he preached with Dwight L. Moody beginning in 1893, and Billy Sunday thought highly of his campaigns, Chapman did not enter into full-time evangelism until 1907.

Chapman was, however, thoroughly Presbyterian. In 1895 he was appointed Corresponding Secretary of the northern church's Committee on Evangelism, and in this position he began to realize the importance of working through local churches. In 1905, John H. Converse, a wealthy Presbyterian philanthropist, offered to underwrite Chapman's expenses if he would become a full-time evangelist. Chapman accepted and joined forces with popular gospel singer Charles McCallon Alexander: they launched the "Chapman-Alexander Simultaneous Campaign in 1907."

Although a Northerner (and moderator of the northern church in 1918), Chapman endeared himself to southern churchmen in general by working through local churches and to southern Presbyterians in particular by supporting their efforts to establish the Bible Conference Center at Montreat, North Carolina. Southern Presbyterians praised Chapman for "his plain, practical preaching and dignified manner," and his "tasteful use of worshipful music." Chapman insisted on the inerrancy of Scripture, but instead of hectoring those who disagreed with him, he organized debates. Marshaling his considerable intellect and seeking experts from outside his organization, his reasoned discussions attracted the educated middle class. While in Richmond in 1909, he took time to speak at UTS, emphasizing the importance of a seminary education. Union, therefore, was seen as an institution that could mediate between excesses. Indeed, Billy Sunday also visited UTS during his revival in 1916.[40]

Toward a Professional Clergy

John Holt Rice and Walter W. Moore were separated by almost a century, but they stood on a continuum. Rice understood that an educated clergy could provide an alternative to revivalism and skepticism. In the early twentieth century, Moore wanted his graduates to answer both fundamentalism and liberalism. In the nineteenth century it was enough just to attend seminary; in the growing professionalism of the early twentieth century, standardized credentials were required. Glenn T. Miller argues that by the beginning of the twentieth century, seminaries were anxious to establish the "scholarly" character of their profession. The new world of the professional rendered the old icon of the preacher-teacher obsolete. The new image was the religious professional. And the way to certify professionalism was the standardized degree. A bachelor's degree objectively defined what "professional," "educated," or "trained" meant. Above all, seminaries "wanted for their graduates and for themselves the high status that Americans gave to the expert, to the person who knew what needed to be done and how to do it. The minister should at least be as skilled in the cure of souls as the modern physician was skilled in the cure of bodies."[41]

Grades and diplomas were necessary to obtain these credentials. By 1898, grades at Union were a firmly established fact of life (despite student protests). As the next logical step, Union introduced the BD degree in 1898, which led to stricter entrance requirements. From that time onward, anyone desiring to study at Union had to have an undergraduate degree or "shall have pursued a literary course that may be fairly considered the equivalent of the A.B. course," which would be shown by a diploma or written exam given by the faculty.[42] The days of a presbytery recommendation and minimal faculty interview were over. The BD declared that a seminary education was a legitimate educational endeavor. The *Central Presbyterian* boasted: "The requirements for the degree of bachelor of divinity are now exactly the same as those of the professional schools of the University of Virginia for degrees in law and medicine."[43]

By 1915, however, Union recognized that by requiring a BD for graduation, the school was exceeding what the church required. In response, three distinct "Courses of Study" were introduced: the "Regular" course, leading to a bachelor of divinity degree; a "Special" course, leading to a diploma without a degree; and the "Post-Graduate" course. The "Special Course in English Leading to a Diploma without a Degree" was exactly the same as the course of study required for the "Regular" course leading to a BD except that the "Special Course" lacked Greek and Hebrew. These students studied "in English all those portions of the Holy Scriptures which are studied exegetically in the Greek and Hebrew by the regular candidates for the degree Bachelor of Divinity." No student was allowed to take the "English diploma course" without the consent of his presbytery. "The object of this course is to provide for those students who cannot possibly meet the requirements of the regular course a full, rich, well-articulated three-year course, which shall give them a thorough, practical training for their great work."[44]

In an effort to help students meet the stricter admissions standards, UTS began to cooperate with area colleges. In 1916, Union worked out an agreement with Richmond College that allowed Union students to complete their undergraduate degree by attending afternoon classes at the college.[45] William & Mary became part of this degree program in 1924.[46]

A bachelor of divinity degree alone, however, would not give Union the national profile Moore wanted. It was necessary to offer a graduate degree. Since students arrived at Hampden-Sydney in 1806, the most significant change in Union's educational mission, and perhaps its self-image, was the introduction of graduate degrees. Only by offering a graduate degree could Union enter the ranks of nationally important seminaries.

Walter Moore, as James Smylie has argued, embraced the "university model" of graduate education. In contrast to Union's traditional model of ministers-professors as generalists, whose main aim was teaching, the university model required specialists, academic professionals whose main goal was research. Moore believed that the university model would produce ministers and scholarship in a credible alternative to both the historical-critical method and biblical literalism. The price paid for gaining this credibility was a curriculum not necessarily controlled by or for the church. The dilemma in adopting this method would be seen within a generation: would seminary professors serve the church or academia? Indeed, the growing status of specialized professional societies detached from the interests of the church heralded the decline of denominational influence.

Professional societies around the country were organized in the late nineteenth and early twentieth centuries, and they began to replace denominations as the supervisory agencies of American seminaries. For example, the Society of Biblical Literature was founded in 1880, the American Society of Church History in 1888, and the American Academy of Religion in 1909. If the PCUS was going to have a credible voice in American scholarship, it had to offer a credible graduate degree. The degree's credibility, however, would come not from the church but from the academy.[47]

Moore understood the new educational dynamic. By the early twentieth century, just as medicine, engineering, architecture, accounting, law, and the other professions had their own special subdisciplines and were no longer learned by apprentices, so theological education was becoming less generalized. To be a modern institution, Union Seminary needed to offer specialized, meaning graduate, courses of study. Union's graduate program, however, grew in fits and starts. As early as 1897, "postgraduate students" were admitted to unspecified undergraduate classes.[48] In 1898, ministers were invited to come to the seminary for "a month or two" to "refresh and enlarge their acquaintance with special subjects." The catalogue listed the classes available to them, which were basically second- and third-year electives.[49] The Moses D. Hoge fellowship for graduate study (first awarded in 1901 to J. Gray McAllister) represents the first attempt to distinguish undergraduate from graduate education. Recognizing the need for a more systematic graduate curriculum, the faculty introduced identifiable graduate classes in 1902.[50] Yet without a graduate studies department, there was no way to manage or organize a program leading to a degree. Consequently, interest in graduate instruction was spotty. In 1914 the first graduate diploma was awarded to Benjamin Rice Lacy Jr., the Hoge Fellow for that year.

Graduate study did not become a distinct part of the seminary curriculum until 1916, when Union began to offer the DD degree, with specific graduate classes leading to the degree. Entrance into the program required a seminary degree. The DD degree itself required three years of classes (the final three months spent in residence) and a declared major;[51] candidates had to pass written exams and write a thesis.[52] There were seven majors leading to the DD: "Systematic Theology, Old Testament Interpretation, New Testament Interpretation, English Bible, Christian Sociology, Church History, and Sunday School Work and Organization."[53]

The DD program was widely advertised, and it was obvious that the time was right; 150 prospective students submitted their applications. Perhaps not fully understanding the commitment of resources, Union admitted 25 DD candidates, and 18 men took up residence. The additional classes added to a workload already burdened by increasing enrollment.[54] The board became concerned about faculty overwork and temporarily suspended the DD after only one year. The board wanted to preserve the faculty's primary emphasis of teaching undergraduates.[55]

To centralize graduate course administration and equalize the workload, the board established the Graduate Department in 1917. Edward Mack, who had been called in 1915 as the Old Testament professor, was appointed dean, a position he held until he retired in 1939.[56] A son of a Presbyterian minister born in Charleston, South Carolina, Mack graduated from Davidson College in 1886 and Princeton Seminary in 1889, then studied at the University of Berlin for one year. He was the first minister ordained by Albemarle Presbytery and served churches in Charlotte, North Carolina; St. Louis, Missouri; Norfolk, Virginia; and Shreveport, Louisiana—all this before being called as professor of Old Testament at Lane Seminary, Cincinnati, Ohio, in 1904. While at Lane he earned his PhD from the University of Cincinnati and was the only Lane faculty member with a PhD at the time. He was elected moderator of the PCUS General Assembly in 1939.

Mack immediately revised class schedules and restricted entry into overcrowded areas. Although students were making progress—three DD degrees were awarded in 1920, with three more by 1924—he realized that the program was too large for the school. In 1920, requirements for entry into the graduate program were revised. Certain requirements remained: diplomas "of full graduation from standard seminaries," three years of classes or research time (with the last three months in residence), passing a written examination in each subject area, and an approved thesis "exhibiting independent research on some special subject." However, admission to the graduate program would be limited to "ministers of not less than five years' ministerial service."

Besides organizing the graduate program, Edward Mack also created what could be called Union's first attempt at continuing education. Beginning in 1920, he designed an annual midwinter "semester." These courses were designed for ministers who could return to Richmond for a short, intensive period of study. The catalogue advertised the "special courses of lectures for the benefit of ministers and missionaries who wish to put themselves abreast of current theological discussion, to study the various 'isms' of the time, and to freshen up on modern methods of religious work." A course on public speaking was also included.[57]

By 1925 the graduate program was firmly established, and Mack brought Union's graduate degrees in line with those of other seminaries. Traditionally, the Hoge Fellowship functioned as a kind of postgraduate diploma. In 1924, Union introduced the master of theology (ThM) degree as an independent study degree, to be completed in one year and supervised by a professor.[58] By 1925, two students were in the ThM program, and seventeen were working toward a DD.[59] Since the earned DD was often confused with the honorary degree, the degree of doctor of theology (ThD) degree was instituted in 1930; the last earned DD was awarded in 1933.[60]

Some leaders questioned the need for advanced degrees. Several board members were concerned that any resources devoted to graduate education

20. Walter W. Moore, president, 1904–26

would shortchange Union's primary mission of educating men for the pastorate. They argued that the time professors spent with graduate students would be time taken away from undergraduates preparing for the parish. Moreover, the library would need to spend more money to obtain works to support the research required for the DD, and later for the ThM and ThD degrees.[61] Thus, until the 1950s, pursuing an advanced degree was not necessarily encouraged. Even by 1925, for example, Edward Mack was still the only faculty member with an earned doctorate.[62] The only way to answer these objections was with more money.

A New Organization for a New Time

Moore personally raised the funds to move Union from Hampden Sydney. Once in Richmond, he needed all his skill to raise money for the new programs that would make his vision of theological education a reality. But the old ways would no longer suffice. Until 1904, there was no official head of the seminary. Different members of the faculty, in order of official seniority, served as chairmen of the faculty for a year at a time. The plan had obvious weaknesses in that there was no continuity. A modern organization demanded clear lines of authority and consistent management. There was really only one man who could represent Union before the church and public and transform the very idea of theological education. Accordingly, the trustees elected Dr. Walter W. Moore first president of Union Theological Seminary in Virginia in 1904.[63]

President Moore's inaugural address is not visionary, but more of a philosophical statement of the relation of the church to theological education. He singles out "the able and learned and pious men with whom I have been associated in this faculty" by citing B. M. Smith, but not Dabney.[64] He then argues that the seminary can only have a subtle, generational influence on the church. The church sends students to the seminary, and the church becomes "largely what her authorized teachers are, and that her teachers are chiefly what their theological training makes them."[65]

The new president pointed toward the modern ideas of corporate organization. He emphasized that the seminary needed both professors and skilled administrators: there was no turning back to the simple days of Hampden-Sydney. The move to Richmond initiated a new, larger set of financial responsibilities, which required more concentration on fund-raising; spending the summer visiting tobacco barons was no longer a feasible strategy. When the board established the office of president, they were direct: "It is hoped and believed that this change will increase the endowment of the seminary." The president's annual salary was $2,500. And with a president, an organization followed. In 1907 the board relieved the president from daily responsibilities by creating the office of proctor, a position filled by retiring faculty member C. C. Hersman. In 1915, William R. Miller was named the seminary's treasurer, and he functioned as the chief executive.

President Moore embodied the stereotypical Scotch-Irish Presbyterian when it came to management. His classroom and office furniture were "a hodgepodge of all sorts of benches in various states of dilapidation." His office chair was "a cane bottom chair with three slats in the back that did not cost $1.50." He thought a telephone and a secretary were luxuries and took it upon himself to trim the hedges around the campus. It was not until 1924, and then only through a gift, that he hired a personal secretary.[66] "Year after year Dr. Moore scrutinized every expenditure and audited every bill personally." For all of his careful management, however, he was known as approachable and had a sense of humor.[67]

Once the board relieved President Moore of the daily routine of running a large organization, he could concentrate on finances. Raising money for the Removal was largely done on Moore's initiative and George Watts's generosity. The Centennial Fund, started in 1907, was the first systematic fund-raising initiative. Through targeted efforts and extensive speaking engagements by the new president, the Centennial Campaign raised $322,000 by 1911. But funds were always short. In 1919 the Synod of Virginia complained: "It is most deplorable that the distinguished faculty of the seminary must be kept forever on the edge of despair over the depressing problem of making ends meet."[68] In 1925, UTS and Columbia explored the idea of merging, but these talks were scuttled when Columbia moved to Atlanta in 1927.[69]

Moore's assumption of the title of "president" suggests that Union now looked at itself differently. A modern seminary could not be run by one person from his kitchen. The successful seminary needed a president with a vision and the resources to carry out that vision.[70] He saw his school as going beyond John Holt Rice's dream. He wanted Union to be a southern seminary, not only in service to a national church, but also to a universal theological endeavor.

Consequently he saw himself as the preserver of an institution within a particular tradition. For President Moore, this tradition was larger than the spirituality of the church or *jure divino* Presbyterianism. The "tradition" in which Union Theological Seminary in Virginia stood was intellectual Calvinism, and Union graduates would help the average believer understand it.

Scholarship at Union: Conservative, not Fundamentalist

Walter W. Moore's idea of scholarship gradually took hold. On January 17–19, 1900, the Rev. P. P. Flournoy of Philadelphia gave a lecture series titled "When Were the Gospels Written?" The answer given by the Tübingen school, according to Flournoy, was simple: "Long after their reputed authors were dead." Flournoy, however, gave the orthodox answer, "By their reputed authors and in the latter half of the first century."[71] The faculty at UTS approved of the lectures. But then in December 1902, Moore moved past the traditional definition of biblical literalism by criticizing Ussher's chronology. Moore argued that since calendars change, and the Bible did not give specific time frames, Ussher's opinion was only a fallible human interpretation, not gospel. Only the gospel is the gospel.[72] His article signaled that Union would now challenge both modern "German" higher criticism and fundamentalist scholarship.

Moore, as both professor and president, set the tone for scholarship at Union. Perhaps remembering Dabney's tirades, he wanted debate, not attacks. "It has made us sick at heart," he wrote, "to observe how most of those who have undertaken to speak in the popular periodicals for the conservative side . . . have, by their want of discrimination and their violent and abusive tone, injured our cause and fostered a timorous view of truth."[73] He wanted to use the tools of science to support faith. Moore argued, for example, that archaeological evidence helped to prove the historicity of Jonah,[74] established the scriptural view of early Hebrew history,[75] and bolstered traditional views regarding the authorship of Daniel and Isaiah.[76] Edward Mack, who followed President Moore in the Old Testament chair (1915–39), "remained to the end an eloquent foe of the higher criticism which rejected the Mosaic authorship of the Pentateuch and accepted the theory of the two Isaiahs. He ended his teaching career insisting that the most recent scholarship had rendered the findings of the higher critics untenable."

Union had begun to address the issues of modern textual criticism at Hampden-Sydney, but Richmond presented a larger stage. The primary issue at stake for southern Presbyterians was the inspiration of Scripture. Henry C. Alexander (New Testament professor in 1869–91) summarized the traditional view by arguing that the Christian faith depended on the absolute inerrancy of the original autographs. He applied "the remorseless maxim, *falsus in uni, falsus in omnibus* [false in one point, false in all]."[77] It was all or nothing.

Thus, however intellectually curious Union's scholarship became under President Moore, Union saw itself as the conservator of a tradition. Beginning with the October–November 1900 issue of *Union Seminary Magazine*, G. B. Strickler presented a four-part series titled "The New Theology." He defined the New Theology as depending on higher criticism and dismissing anything that was not confirmed by science. He dismissed new theology as the old heresy.[78] The "New Theologian" professed "to find the Scriptures pervaded by elements of error, historical, scientific, chronological, ethical, and religious."[79] The only defense against the new theology was sound, doctrinal preaching. "If Calvinism is not preached, and its great doctrines are not constantly explained and vindicated, the people are left to learn almost all they know about them from the enemies of those doctrines, [and] nothing else can be expected but that they will soon be renounced."[80]

Again, however, conservative never meant fundamental. Whereas fundamentalism depended on a cultural consensus based on a uniform interpretation of the King James Version, Union's conservatism was rooted in an intellectual Calvinism circumscribed by the confessions. Wedded to studying Scripture in the original languages, Union students were more aware of the Bible's ambiguities than were fundamentalists. Thus premillennialism, Prohibition, and the status of women were merely opinions, albeit fiercely held ones. Union Seminary could be conservative and yet educate women to assist missionaries, send students into the city, advocate against child labor, and question prophecies of the end times precisely because it was understood that many so-called biblical imperatives were human interpretations. What was not questioned was the Reformed tradition as understood by the PCUS.

As a student of T. C. Johnson's, Ernest Trice Thompson remembers that his revered professor "did not teach us anything about any theological developments after the Westminster Confession and the scholastic theologians." He further complained that Johnson "just drilled us" with Dabney's theology and discouraged student questions, which led to a limited theology.[81]

> Thomas Cary Johnson gave as his standard assignment in theology twelve pages of Dabney a day. Dabney's text was to be mastered. One student remembers the famous A to H assignment on moral responsibility. Dabney had listed these, numbered A to H, on the Calvinist position followed by Arminian or Pelagian interpretations. Johnson expected his students to know the Reformed doctrine of moral responsibility A through H.[82]

Even T. C. Johnson, though, would not fit into the fundamentalist mode. He acknowledged his belief in a form of theistic evolution, affirming only that the "original manuscripts" of the Bible were infallible, and rejected a literal interpretation of Scripture. Edward Mack was also opposed to biblical literalists. He argued that "the manner and degree of the unfolding" of God's truth "changed and advanced with each age," and he called such progressive revelation "a scriptural reality." In a series of talks delivered at First Presbyterian Church and later published as a book, Mack faulted both liberal interpretations and "extremely literal interpretations." Although the *Union Seminary Magazine* occasionally took jabs at German scholarship and northern Presbyterian theology, the editor could never entertain a fundamentalist viewpoint.

In the wake of World War I, fundamentalists absorbed premillennialism, with its perceived signs of the second coming of Jesus. In 1918, President Moore attacked premillennial theories as mere "products of times of persecution and calamity." He accused premillennialists of forcing "these arbitrary and literal interpretations onto figurative passages of Scripture" and indulging in "precarious interpretations of passing events." In the same way, Mack regretted that the prophetic passages of the book of Ezekiel had been "turned to all manner of fantastic and fanatical uses." He described Armageddon as "not a single local struggle, but an age-long conflict, involving all nations" with a final consummation in "the land of Israel."[83]

For E. T. Thompson, E. C. Caldwell (Old Testament professor in 1914–15; New Testament professor in 1915–32) was a glimpse of the future. Caldwell had no interest in buttressing the old Calvinistic system: "He shared his own independent convictions quite fearlessly with his students and compelled them to think for themselves. He widened the horizons of a generation of students and was responsible for some of the new currents of thought that soon made themselves felt within the church." Thompson remembers Caldwell as ready "to re-examine old traditions . . . and throw off the dead hand of the past."[84]

Despite his willingness to confront both liberal and fundamentalist viewpoints, President Moore clearly understood that he was president of an institution that relied on the goodwill of donors. He had to consider the reputation of his school and his relationship with every part of the church, from industrialists to farmers. His goal was to build Union Seminary into a first-class institution, and he needed the church's support to realize his dream. In 1915, Dr. Harris E. Kirk had delivered the Sprunt Lectures, titled "The Religion of Power." Balmer Kelly, who taught theology at Union, characterizes Kirk's lectures as a "strong, clear, and beautifully written exposition of Pauline thought with particular reference to the contemporaneous religions of the Roman Empire." On the basis of his lectures, Kirk was invited six years later to teach "courses" at the seminary, possibly an indication of an intention to call him to the faculty. In the meantime, however, Kirk had made a lecture tour though some of the mission stations in China. In casual conversations, he made comments about evolution and William Jennings Bryan that offended the ultraconservatives of the Southern Presbyterian Mission. Their protests, published in the *Sunday School Times* and the *Christian Observer*, caused considerable concern among members of the board of trustees; undoubtedly under their pressure, President Moore withdrew Kirk's invitation to teach.[85]

The line was clear. No matter how modern the campus appeared, no matter how professional the students and faculty, and no matter the scholastic aspirations—the move to Richmond could not distance Union from its commitment to Dabney's interpretation of Calvinism. Union's allegiance to Dabney would last as long as the spirituality of the church kept the PCUS from engaging the world. Union could leave Hampden-Sydney behind, but during this period the doctrine of the spirituality of the church restricted the range of Union's intellectual life.

Spirituality of the Church

In his magisterial three-volume history of southern Presbyterianism, *Presbyterians in the South*, Ernest Trice Thompson identifies the spirituality of the church as the distinctive doctrine of the PCUS. Thompson argues that Dabney popularized the doctrine after the Civil War, and that Givens Brown Strickler

(1870) translated this doctrine for the New South. Strickler was born in 1840 in Rockbridge County, Virginia. He entered Washington College in 1859 and enlisted in the Confederate Army (Liberty Hall Volunteers) in 1861, rising to the rank of captain. Captured at Gettysburg, he returned to Lexington after the war, graduated, and was an instructor at Washington College until 1868, when he entered Union Seminary. He pastored the Tinkling Springs church and in 1883 was called to one of the most important churches in the denomination, Central Presbyterian Church in Atlanta. Strickler was elected moderator of the PCUS General Assembly in 1887, and Union called him as professor of systematic theology in 1896. He was regarded by many as the most powerful preacher in the southern Presbyterian church, and the doctrine he preached was good old-fashioned Calvinism.

E. T. Thompson reports, however, that Strickler never preached on ethical concerns. Strickler was not blind to social issues, but only addressed them indirectly. As he once declared:

> We are in the most effective way, preaching [on matters of moral reform] all the time. We are seeking to bring them under the power of the Gospel; we are seeking to implant in them by regeneration the principles of righteousness and holiness, and if we can do that, then moral reform in all the directions in which it is desired, in temperance, in politics, in business, will follow as the certain and inevitable result.

E. T. Thompson (who would do the most to demolish the concept of the spirituality of the church) would write a generation later that Strickler's silence on social issues reflected his time:

> Dr. Strickler's mistaken assumption that moral reform is the automatic fruit of regeneration, belied by the evidence all about him, and the whole of Christian history, was shared by the vast majority of his contemporaries. Southern Presbyterian ministers preached the evangelical gospel convicting men of sin, pointing them to Christ, confirming them in the faith, comforting them in sorrow, strengthening them for the battles of life, setting before them high personal ideals, planting seeds which would bring forth "the fruit of the Spirit," but not a gospel which pricked the conscience regarding the deeply entrenched wrongs of Southern society.

The southern Presbyterian minister was expected to ignore the growing Jim Crow mentality, child labor, disenfranchisement, and lynchings—thus to preach "a dateless religion, one that is the same yesterday, today and forever."[86] When Givens Strickler argued that the church was preaching most effectively about moral reform when it was sticking to "the power of the Gospel" and implanting "the principles of righteousness and holiness," he was acknowledging the doctrine of the spirituality of the church. Givens B. Stickler made Dabney's legacy palatable to the sensibilities of the New South, and Thomas Cary Johnson would carry it into the new century.

Thomas Cary Johnson (1887) was born in Monroe County, West Virginia, in 1859, near the village of Alderson. His father was a large landowner and never thought education was important: his son would be a businessman. When Thomas was seventeen, the Rev. H. R. Laird accepted a call to the Presbyterian church in Alderson, and Laird ignited Johnson's love of the classics and history. He entered Hampden-Sydney College when he was twenty and graduated with honors in 1882. In his sophomore year, Johnson had a religious experience, joined College Church, and began to think about the ministry. After graduation, however, he returned home to teach in the school Laird had founded. After teaching for one year, Johnson went to the University of Virginia and took graduate-level courses in Latin, Greek, and Mathematics. Feeling confirmed in his call to the ministry, he entered Union in 1884 without accepting a degree from the university.

His scholarship caught the eye of the newly arrived Hebrew teacher, Walter W. Moore. In 1887, Johnson attended William Rainey Harper's Hebrew School at the University of Virginia, and he followed Harper to Yale. He continued his Hebrew studies but also took several classes in psychology. In 1888, Dabney invited Johnson to teach Greek, Hebrew, and Biblical Introduction in Austin. When Dabney took ill in the fall of 1890, Johnson also taught his courses in Philosophy and Systematic Theology. He did so well that he stayed on for another year and taught these courses while Dabney convalesced. Once Dabney was able to teach, Johnson accepted a call to a church in Louisville, Kentucky, but after one year was called to Union.[87] Johnson's two years in Austin convinced him that Dabney was the intellectual center of modern Calvinism and southern Presbyterianism.

Union became the transmitter of Dabney's theology. Thomas Peck, who succeeded Dabney (history and polity professor, 1860–83; and theology professor, 1883–93), Clement Read Vaughan (1893–96), Givens Brown Strickler (1896–1913), and Thomas Cary Johnson (1913–30)—all followed Dabney's *Syllabus* and drilled it into successive generations of students paragraph by paragraph. In 1913, *Union Seminary Magazine* declared that "the spirituality of the church can never be outgrown" and the church "has no right" to speak on any issue not directly addressed in Scripture.[88] Not every student accepted the spirituality of the church, however, and some began to chip away at it.

Alexander Jeffrey McKelway III (1891) is perhaps the best example of those who began to awaken the church's conscience. He was born in Sadsburyville, Pennsylvania (between York and Philadelphia), in 1866. His father, a Presbyterian minister, accepted a call to Charlotte Court House, Virginia (near Hampden Sydney), in 1870. He graduated from Hampden-Sydney College in 1886, and after seminary graduation accepted a call to First Presbyterian Church, Fayetteville, North Carolina, in 1892. It was in Fayetteville that McKelway witnessed children as young as nine working twelve to sixteen hours a day for almost nothing.

In 1898, McKelway became the editor of the *North Carolina Presbyterian*. Here he found his voice and became known as a crusader for child labor reform and Prohibition.[89] He turned the regional *North Carolina Presbyterian* into a denominational publication (the *Presbyterian Standard*) in 1899, with Walter W. Moore on the editorial board. Wanting to reach a larger audience, he served as interim editor of the *Charlotte Evening News* for eighteen months. In 1904 he became the southern secretary of the newly formed National Child Labor Committee (which also included John Dewey, Jane Addams, and Walter Lippmann).

McKelway's job was to orchestrate state campaigns to abolish child labor. He investigated the conditions under which children worked and lobbied legislatures to pass labor regulations. By 1907 the National Child Labor Committee began to work for a federal bill outlawing child labor, and McKelway became a force in national politics. In 1909 he met with Woodrow Wilson at the northern church's General Assembly,[90] and in 1912 he advised Wilson on electoral strategy for the southern states. In 1916 he may have written as many as twenty of the twenty-eight planks in the Democratic Party platform.

McKelway never hesitated to speak to Presbyterian ministers and urge them to use their influence to pass laws abolishing or limiting child labor. To those who complained that his advocacy compromised the purity of Presbyterianism, he responded:

> There is certainly no more effective way of building up the Kingdom of God than by tearing down the opposing kingdom of Satan. And we believe that many a man of God is hampered by tradition from taking hold of a civic evil that is the worst enemy of his church. . . . If our ministers fail to lead our people along ethical lines in the solution of these problems, who shall do it?[91]

He was so effective that the 1908 PCUS General Assembly passed a resolution against child labor, and by 1910 all southern states had enacted minimum wage laws.[92]

While Alexander McKelway went from the church to the world, Walter Lee Lingle (1896) remained in the church and set in motion the forces that ultimately destroyed the doctrine of the spirituality of the church. Indeed, Lingle represents the lost opportunity of southern Presbyterianism. In 1909, when Lingle was pastor of Atlanta's First Presbyterian Church, he was glancing at the magazines in the Carnegie Library and came upon an article by Ray Stannard Baker. Baker's essay dealt with Christianity and the nation's social problems and mentioned a new book by Baptist theologian Walter Rauschenbusch, titled *Christianity and the Social Crisis*. Lingle was so impressed with Baker's glowing review that he located the book and read it that night. On the twentieth anniversary of that discovery, Lingle delivered the Sprunt Lectures (titled "The Social Teachings of the Bible") and recalled: "Since that time, I have read many volumes on the same general subject, but no other book has so stirred my soul as that first one."[93]

Inspired by Rauschenbusch, Lingle proposed that Atlanta's Sunday School Union buy ten acres of land with a recreation center, tennis courts, baseball diamond, croquet grounds, swimming pool, and picnic facilities in 1908 to show that the Sunday schools cared for the "social and physical welfare of its members as well as for the spiritual." He also dissuaded his congregation from selling their downtown site and moving to the suburbs. Although Lingle came late to the "race issue," he ultimately became a leading advocate of desegregation.[94]

When Union relocated to Richmond, the General Assembly wanted their educational assets to be near their flagship seminary. A. L. Phillips, the newly appointed general superintendent of Sabbath Schools and Young People's Work, moved to Richmond in 1901,[95] and the PCUS Committee of Publication followed in 1904. In 1911 the PCUS General Assembly recommended that its seminaries "adopt and teach a brief, practical course in Sociology." Within a month A. L. Phillips wrote to Lingle confidentially, but obviously with President Moore's approval, asking him if he would teach a class on "Christian Sociology." Phillips had heard that Lingle advocated for social issues "with great force and conviction" from the pulpit and knew he would be acceptable to both the school and the church.

In an atmosphere hostile to social concerns, Lingle had credibility because he was seen as a loyal herald of the New South. Born in 1868 in Rowan County, North Carolina, he was a Davidson graduate. After graduation from Union, he was an assistant instructor of Hebrew and Greek until 1898. Instead of following the seminary to Richmond, however, he was ordained and accepted a call to Dalton, Georgia, from 1898 to 1902. He then served First Presbyterian Church, Rock Hill, South Carolina (1902–7), and First Presbyterian Church, Atlanta (1907–11). He wrote columns for the *Presbyterian of the South* and the *Christian Observer*. He was elected moderator of the Synod of North Carolina in 1912 and moderator of the General Assembly in 1920. He served as the program chair of Montreat in 1910–24 (ensuring that social questions were prominently discussed) and was on the PCUS Executive Committee of Home Missions and the International Sunday School Lesson Committee. In 1924 he assumed the presidency of the General Assembly's Training School for Lay Workers (ATS) in Richmond (founded in 1914). In 1929, at the request of the students, Lingle was invited to deliver the Sprunt Lectures, titled "The Bible and Social Problems." The lectures were published and had a huge influence on the church.[96] That year he resigned to become the president of Davidson College, a position he held until his retirement in 1940.

Although originally called to teach Hebrew, Lingle immediately included a short course on "Christian Sociology" in his schedule. By the time he was appointed professor of Christian History and Missions in 1914, his sociology class was a semester long, and he also taught an elective study of Francis Peabody's *Jesus and the Social Question*. His class was the most important addition to the curriculum in the first century of Union's existence. It was offered only to the senior class and sought to apply the biblical ethic to daily life. "The purpose of this course is to acquaint the student with the great social movements and problems of to-day, and to point out the ethical teachings of Jesus and the Holy Scriptures which are especially applicable to these present-day social problems and conditions."[97] Lingle rejected isms of the twentieth century: individualism, socialism, and communism; he was searching for a new Christian ethic, to "translate into life the social and ethical teachings of our Lord."

Students flocked to his lectures, the only class on social ethics in any southern Presbyterian seminary. Successive generations have remembered his lectures and influence as formative. Indeed, the ministers who were in the forefront of changing attitudes in the PCUS attributed their own awakening to Walter Lingle. His genius was that he could apply the social gospel movement (whose primary concern was for the city) to rural communities.

Although the General Assembly authorized the teaching of Christian Sociology, Lingle found himself opposed by a broad spectrum of the church: by conservatives who believed that Christianity contained no social message, and by liberals who found nothing in the Bible except a social message. He proposed a middle position, arguing that ministers had a prophetic duty to emphasize the earthly aspects of the kingdom of God and that all Christians were called to be personally involved. President Moore believed that the seminary could help the church face the complexities of modern life, and he supported his professor against criticism.[98] Lingle did receive numerous letters of support. One Presbyterian minister declared: "I might even hazard the suggestion that it would do more good for the Kingdom for the young theologue to know something about the housing conditions of the Richmondites than to be intimately acquainted with the family life of the Hittites; the Richmondites being still alive, and the Hittites having been a long time dead."

Many more letters were negative, arguing that sociology was involvement in politics, while others were just confused with this innovative idea:

> The most interesting reaction to the announcement of a course in the Seminary on the Social Teachings of the Bible was that of a fine Christian woman, who had a half-dozen charming daughters. She remarked that she was so glad that I was to give a course on "The Social Teachings of the Bible," as her daughters were starting out into society, and she was not clear in her mind as to what they ought to do about cards, theatres, and dancing, and now she was so glad that I was going to clarify what the Bible had to say on these subjects.[99]

But a former student, Willis Thompson (1912), wrote to Lingle, expressing the thoughts of many. Lingle had inspired Thompson to minister in the coalfields of Kentucky and Tennessee, and he hoped that more would listen to him. "I had intended to write of what a real stimulus your influence at the Seminary afforded me. . . . It would not be heresy to say that I look eagerly for the modern viewpoint among the brethren in hope that it is with[in] them to invigorate the healthy conservatism of our church; but my watching is very discouraging at times."[100]

Lingle became Moore's heir apparent, and the president had such confidence in him that he appointed Lingle as editor of the *Union Seminary Magazine* in 1913. Up to this time the editor had been a student appointed every year. While Lingle had already been informally working on the magazine since his return, the public face of Union Seminary would now have a new point of view and boldly state it to the church.[101]

Lingle changed the name of the *Union Seminary Magazine* to the *Union Seminary Review* when he became editor. He wanted the name change because "our old name gave the impression to many that our magazine was similar to the usual College Magazine." But this journal would have a voice: "We want to widen the scope of our publication somewhat, and make it more and more a review of our church's work and of living questions in the religious world."[102] The magazine gradually became a platform for the social gospel.[103]

Lingle understood that for the PCUS to embrace the social gospel, he had to redefine it for the South.[104] Articles like "The Social Message of Micah"[105] appear scattered throughout issues prior to World War I. After 1919 there is a new section titled "Sociology," which covered issues such as labor and the reason for strikes, race relations, housing problems, juvenile justice, immigration, and Prohibition. Although each of these articles could conceivably have caused controversy, what ultimately would cause Lingle to resign from the seminary was the subject of reunion with the northern church.

A False Start for Reuniting Two Churches

In the burst of nationalism following the Great War (World War I), many in the northern and southern churches thought it was time for Presbyterians to forget the Civil War. Walter Lingle devoted the entire January 1918 issue of the *Union Seminary Review* to the subject of the northern and southern Presbyterian churches, PC(USA) and PCUS, reuniting after fifty-seven years. Of the seven articles dealing with reunion, two suggested some type of federal union, and five (one of these written by E. T. Thompson's father) called for organic union as soon as possible. Lingle wrote an innocuous piece comparing the "northern" and "southern" versions of the Westminster Confession. He concluded that there was virtually no difference between the doctrines of both churches.[106]

As Peter Hobbie has argued, Lingle's seemingly inoffensive conclusion and the general positive tenor of the issue supporting reunion (or some federal-type of relationship) disappointed and alienated President Moore.[107] Reunion was the one thing the president could not countenance. He had not put his life into Union Seminary to have his school become just another theological institution in a homogenized denomination. He wanted Union to serve the church universal as an excellent southern seminary. His estrangement and loss of confidence finally became too much, and Lingle resigned from UTS in 1924, accepting the presidency of the General Assembly's Training School.

Just as Robert Lewis Dabney and Benjamin Mosby Smith offered two competing visions of theological education and church life in the nineteenth century, Thomas Cary Johnson and Walter Lee Lingle presented two alternatives in the twentieth. Johnson kept the mantle of Dabney and the spirituality of the church alive, constantly urging the church to look back for inspiration. Lingle was the catalyst that brought the seminary from the rural nineteenth century into the industrialized twentieth, from the nostalgia of Reconstruction to the promise of modern America. Their differences can be seen in their respective histories of the Presbyterian Church (US). Shortly after his inauguration as the professor of church history in 1892, Johnson was asked to write *The History of the Southern Presbyterian Church* as a part of the American Church History Series, a thirteen-volume set about American denominations, edited by Philip Schaff.

Compared with the other generally irenic and ecumenical volumes, Johnson's historical analysis of the thirty-three-year-old denomination was combative. He concluded that all denominations, except the PCUS, had strayed from the gospel truth of the "Non-Secular Character of the Church."[108] He then reviewed actions taken by the northern church since 1861 that, because they deviated from *jure divino* Presbyterianism, made any kind of organic union with the more orthodox southern church impossible. Johnson accused the northern church of involving itself in political questions, opening the "floodgates of politico-religious syncretism and fanaticism";[109] he thought that the "Northern Pharisees would dictate terms of intercourse between the Christians of the two races, South, which would lead to race amalgamation if followed out."[110] Reconciliation between Presbyterians would never be possible, in his mind. In contrast, Lingle's history (published in 1928 and reissued at regular intervals) is generous and sees the PCUS as having a place in the family of denominations;[111] he never mentions *jure divino* Presbyterianism or the spirituality of the church.[112]

The fact that Lingle gave the 1929 Sprunt Lecture, one year before Johnson's retirement and at the specific request of the students, shows the depth and range of his influence. His years of teaching had prepared students to challenge the doctrine of the spirituality of the church. His lectures were published as a book, *The Bible and Social Problems*. The chapters are unlike anything Thomas Cary Johnson or Givens Strickler ever uttered from the pulpit: "The Bible and Money," "The Bible and Poverty," "The Church and Social Reform." Lingle called for ministers to study the social problems of their communities and then preach about those problems from the pulpit. He urged them not to engage in partisan politics but to apply the social and ethical teachings of Christ. "I have a deep and abiding conviction that one of the greatest needs of the present time is that Christians should translate into life the social and ethical teachings of our Lord. They are the only solvent for the world's social problems."[113]

The Centennial

When Walter Lingle joined the faculty in 1911, Union Seminary was anticipating a bright future: student-run ministries were flourishing, plans for graduate education were proceeding, fieldwork was a reality, classes in Christian sociology and Christian education were being offered, and the seminary felt at home in Richmond. The year 1912, however, was Union's centennial: students, faculty, and alumni took a moment to consider what the last century had meant. There were two celebrations: Sunday, October 13, 1912, for the seminary community; and Wednesday, October 16, for commissioners from the Synods of Virginia and North Carolina. On Sunday, President Moore and Lingle addressed the seminary. The president's speech was titled "The First Fifty Years," and Lingle spoke on "The Last Fifty Years." The speeches were triumphal; they traced the inexorable march of Union Seminary to prominence, but also differentiated the school from its provincial past.

On Wednesday the Synod of North Carolina chartered a special train to Richmond; it began in Goldsboro and picked up commissioners as it moved up eastern North Carolina, something not possible just fifteen years earlier. There were about 1,000 representatives from both synods, with an additional 1,500 spectators. As the commissioners disembarked from streetcars, automobiles, carriages, and busses, students handed them souvenir badges with a picture of Watts Hall attached to blue and white ribbons, badges embossed with the words *vivat, crescat, floreat seminarium* [The seminary lives, springs up, and flourishes].[114] On a mild, sunny day, the crowd gathered on the quad in front of Watts Chapel. A succession of speakers described the various aspects of Union's influence on the church, refreshments were served in the refectory (now located in Richmond Hall), and the campus was illuminated from 5:00 to 6:00 p.m. At 8:00 p.m. two speeches were delivered to a packed house in the City Auditorium; the Rev. Egbert W. Smith (1886) spoke on "Union Seminary in Home Missions," and the subject for Rev. James I. Vance (1886) was "Union Seminary in Foreign Missions."

Egbert Smith delineated Union's impact on PCUS home missions. In the Synod of Virginia, 90 percent of workers, executive committee members, and all superintendents had been UTS graduates. In the Synod of North Carolina, 66 percent of all workers, 5 out of 6 on the executive committee, and all Superintendents (except 2) were from Union. In the Synod of Missouri, 50 percent of the leadership in home missions were alumni. Each summer UTS sent 75 students to work in the mission field.[115] James Vance then explored Union's influence on foreign and domestic missions as a portent for the future. He pointed out that Union students formed the Society of Missionary Inquiry in 1818, 19 years before the General Assembly organized the Presbyterian Board of Foreign Missions. He told the crowd that 50 percent of all foreign missionaries in the PCUS were "Union men."[116] By 1912, Union had produced 900 active ministers,[117] and the Centennial celebrations were a testament to their impact. Indeed, it was undeniable that Union was important to the southern church. President Moore observed that 75 percent of pastors in the Synod of Virginia and 57 percent of pastors in the Synod of North Carolina were from Union.[118] Indeed, 38 percent of all PCUS ministers had graduated from Union, and 55 percent of the 128 largest churches in the PCUS had pastors who were "Union men."[119]

Union was also accepted as an equal around the country: Columbia, Austin, and the Divinity School of Southwestern University (in Clarksville, Tennessee) sent compliments; also, Princeton, McCormick, and Western Theological Seminary (in Pittsburgh), and Union (NY) sent letters of congratulations. Virtually every other major seminary in the United States, regardless of denomination, sent greetings. Southern colleges and universities such as Washington and Lee, Richmond College, Davis and Elkins College, Johns Hopkins, Davidson, the University of North Carolina (Wake Forest), and North Carolina State Normal and Industrial College (Greensboro, North Carolina) also sent their best wishes.[120] Just as John Holt Rice had received some of his first donations from the North, these letters confirmed that Union was a national institution.

Yet the most insightful work produced for the Centennial was not a speech, but an article written by Theron H. Rice (1892) in the celebratory issue of the *Union Seminary Magazine*. In an introspective essay, "Union Seminary in Theological Education and Religious Thought," Theron Rice places Union in the landscape of American theological education. Over a decade before the first systematic study of American seminaries and twenty years before the very idea of accreditation was broached, Rice explores Union's strengths and weaknesses.

Theron Rice argues that Union's personality was formed by John Holt Rice, who conceived Union as a school grounded in the Bible and dedicated to producing ministers for southern churches. Dabney gets a fleeting mention, but Theron Rice calls President Moore the "second founder" of Union for relocating the school to the site of the church's next challenge: the city. Union's influence on the church, Rice insists, is enormous but indirect—through the parish. In contrast, Union's impact on scholarship is negligible.

The professors at Union have not so much attempted to write books as to make men. They have poured themselves into their students and written themselves on their characters and lives; their method has followed that of Jesus with the Twelve. As a consequence Union Seminary has not influenced religious thought so much by her output of books as through her training of living voices for Christ.

Although Rice does list all the books written by UTS graduates and professors, it is clear that he sees the field of academic scholarship as one Union has yet to conquer. After all, one of John Holt Rice's goals in establishing his school of the prophets was to answer "German" scholarship, and thus far no professor was considered a nationally known scholar, except perhaps for Walter W. Moore. Theron Rice finishes his article by listing UTS graduates serving as professors and presidents in other seminaries (all southern): "Drs. McPheeters, Reed, and H. A. White of Columbia; Dr. J. Gray McAllister, of Louisville; Drs. Rosebro and Somerville, of Clarksville; and Drs. Vincent (the president), Sampson, and Caldwell, of Austin."[121] The reader is left to ponder what Union's influence would be like if scholarship had been stressed.

If the Centennial was a time for celebration and introspection, it also saw the expansion of Union's influence. The Synod of West Virginia joined with the Synods of Virginia and North Carolina on the board in 1914, and the newly formed Synod of Appalachia joined in 1915.[122] West Virginia and Appalachia could have opted to support either Louisville or Columbia, but they chose Union. The faculty expanded as well. In 1862 UTS had 4 faculty members, 5 in 1898, up to 7 in 1912,[123] and 8 in 1926 (when President Moore retired)—to accommodate not only an increasing student body but also graduate education.[124]

Practical Education

If graduate education represented President Moore's intellectual goal for Union, practical education was the heart of his vision. The acceptance of practical education in the PCUS was, however, indirect and unplanned. The 1882 General Assembly had questioned the need for learning Latin.[125] The issue was revisited each year until 1891, when the assembly received thirteen overtures against the language requirement. Although the assembly, browbeaten by Dabney at his vociferous best, refused to act, it was clear the church was ready for more practicality in theological education.[126]

The controversy over the Latin requirement revealed a churchwide concern for practical education, which resulted in General Assembly approval for a required English Bible course in 1882. Once the funds were raised, Union did not hesitate to add English Bible to the curriculum (the only change in curriculum between the Civil War and the Removal)[127] and call a fifth professor. Thomas Cary Johnson (1887) was elected professor of English Bible and pastoral theology in 1891. He acknowledged that the English Bible course signaled the church's recognition of the value of practical education. Indeed, English Bible was "one of the best things in the spirit of the age."[128] But President Moore had bigger plans than just one class.

Union led the effort to abolish the "Latin thesis." In 1903, Lingle argued that the typical thesis "consisted of copious quotations of Turretin and the Vulgate bound together with a few sentences of dog Latin." The requirement "had become a farce, a delusion, a snare, and a weariness to the flesh." Opponents argued that the Latin thesis was necessary to uphold the standard of a liberal classical education. That is, if Latin were discarded, why keep Greek and Hebrew? "The gravest objection to this change," wrote one minister, "is that it will be a change. . . . We are too much given to change." Following this line of reasoning, the 1903 General Assembly voted to keep Latin. In 1914, however, the PCUS amended the Book of Church Order to permit presbyteries to accept either an English or Latin thesis. The Latin requirement was not completely removed until 1945.[129]

Union continued to institute practical courses. In 1908 the Curriculum Committee issued its first report, calling for greater emphasis on English Bible and Practical Theology, for elocution to be established as a required course (begun in 1913), an elective course in vocal music to be offered, and a senior-year course to be offered in sociology (which Lingle started in 1911).[130]

What seemed like curricular chaos to many in the church was welcomed by President Moore. In the early 1900s the YMCA issued a series of booklets on the ministry in America. John Mott (president of the YMCA and the World Student Christian Federation, and presiding officer of the 1910 World Missionary Conference, who would receive the Nobel Peace Prize in 1946) was the general editor and reprinted the individual pamphlets as a book titled *The Claims and Opportunities of the Christian Ministry*, with a foreword by Theodore Roosevelt. President Moore, the only southern contributor, wrote chapter 4 (first published in 1909), "Preparation of the Modern Minister." From the vantage point of thirty years of observation and experience, he argued that preparing for ministry was more than an academic exercise. Besides "exegetical theology" (biblical studies), "historical theology" (church history, "what Christianity has done in the world and how it has done it"), and "systematic theology" (the comparison of schools of theology), seminarians must be thoroughly trained in "experimental theology" (examining their own faith experiences) and practical theology, which applies the first four areas to modern life.[131] He also saw practical theology as a way to explain the Calvinist tradition, as interpreted by the southern church, to the twentieth century. He never expected his students to change the tradition. The fact that Union students and graduates began to question that tradition was the greatest unintended consequence of the Removal and the emphasis on practical theology.

Student-Run Missions

The transformation of the Society of Missionary Inquiry indicates how the change from rural to urban affected the students. Until the Removal, the SMI functioned largely as a graduate seminar, studying and reporting about missions and theological topics. By the end of the first year in Richmond, however, the SMI became the management agency that organized the students to actually work in local missions. Beginning in 1899, the society's minutes no longer assigned topics for discussion. The society still met every Monday evening for "prayer, conference, and inquiry concerning missions throughout the world"; they also met on the first Sabbath evening in each month to hear addresses delivered by returned missionaries, representatives of the Student Volunteer

Movement, and other specialists in missions work.[132] These addresses, however, were quickly eclipsed by the society's real mission.

After just one year in Richmond, the SMI was no longer hosting lectures and refereeing debates. The students were leading missions study classes and managing local missions. Missions study classes were usually three-week seminars led by a student (sometimes with a faculty member present). The student leaders would choose their own subjects, and there were different classes every semester, so students were exposed to a wide range of topics. The annual report for 1917 is a good example of how missions study classes were organized.

> For the purpose of informing ourselves concerning Missionary work in the world today—we have four mission study classes, conducted by leaders selected from the Student Body. During the past year we have studied the following books—
>
> > *The South Today*—John M. Moore
> > *South American Neighbors*—Homer C. Stuntz
> > *Jesus, the Missionary*—Hugh W. White
> > *Rising Churches in Non-Christian Lands*—Arthur J. Brown
>
> During the past year 55 men were enrolled in these classes. On the first Sunday night of each month, we have the privilege of hearing an address by some speaker who is in close touch with the Missionary Situation in the world.[133]

Other topics included "Negro Life in the South," "Korea in Transition," "The Chinese Revolution," and "The Challenge of the Country."[134]

While missions study classes were conducted on campus, local missions got the students into the new world of urban Richmond. Beginning in 1900, it became standard practice for the society's first meeting of the year to be devoted to assigning volunteers to local missions: students were now doing missions and not just hearing about them. The society's meeting on September 22, 1913, is typical:

> The first regular meeting was called to order by the president, and after appropriate words of welcome and explanation, for the benefit of the new men, the various mission works engaged in by the students were presented:
>
> > Penitentiary
> > Rail Road Shops
> > City Home
> > Soldiers Home
> > Seventeenth Street Colored Mission
> > Hospitals[135]

In the 1916–17 school year, the City Jail, Street Preaching (Dr. Lingle in charge), and the Colored Children's Industrial Home became part of the city missions.[136] Students were also available for "occasional supply work for absent city pastors of all denominations."[137]

Missions were important. On March 19, 1923, the Society of Missionary Inquiry issued the following report of their mission activities for the previous month:

Sermons preached.. 200
Sunday-school classes taught.. 135
Visits to Pine Camp (consumption sanatorium) 27
Visits to Seventeenth Street (negro section of city) 62
Visits to Confederate Soldiers' Home...................................... 20
Visits to State penitentiary... 9
Talks at factories (noon hour)... 12
Talks on missions to Christian Endeavor Societies, etc......... 48
Boy Scout meetings held.. 15
Stereopticon [stereo slide projector] Lectures given............... 6
Pastoral visits.. 150
Bible study classes led... 6
Visits to Old Ladies' Home... 3
Prayer meetings conducted.. 8
Led singing—Sunday school, etc 9
Led singing during special evangelistic meetings........17 days

There were 577 services conducted or aided by the students, besides 150 pastoral visits, all in the space of four weeks. This was not possible in Hampden Sydney. Moreover, about 25 students served churches on the outskirts of Richmond, in the eastern edge of West Virginia, and in eastern North Carolina. One-half of these communities were within fifty miles of Richmond, and the others were reached by train, so absences from class were reduced to a minimum.[138]

The missions were always student-run and done on the students' time. Bill Oglesby, future professor of pastoral care, was impressed that such undertakings rested on the students alone.

> When I arrived at the seminary in 1937, it was assumed that I would engage in [local missions], although there was no effort for organizing the students on the part of the faculty or assisting in reflection on what was being done. The truth of the matter is that the responsibilities were passed from student to student. I was urged to work in the Hoge Memorial Church, which was in a deteriorating section of the Shockoe Valley and made up largely of persons living on Church Hill not too long before there was a complete racial turnover in the area. My work was with the youth, although I assisted in worship from time to time on Sunday evening.[139]

These student-led missions had an impact; they led to the organization of the Overbrook and Fairfield Presbyterian Churches.[140]

Union's arrival in Richmond was like releasing a steam valve: the students established over forty different missions around Richmond. They had an expansive outlook that could pit them against the values of the culture in which they lived. Less than a decade after Virginia discarded the Reconstruction constitution in favor of the constitution that institutionalized the "separate but equal" Jim Crow laws (while the denomination kept African Americans at arm's length), Union students began a mission to the residents of the segregated neighborhood known as Hell's Bottom. In a 1922 article for the *Union Seminary Review*, Cothran Smith (BD, 1923), who had worked in the mission, wrote a history of the Seventeenth Street (or Hell's Bottom) Mission and its impact. Hell's Bottom was an aptly named place, which most people tried to avoid.

> For almost a mile, the C. & O. R. R. Yards run parallel to a little creek that the city has converted into an open sewer. In the ravine carved out by this stream lie huddled the buildings that serve as homes for seven hundred Negro families. The air of the place is tainted by fumes from the stream and soiled by smoke and cinders from the locomotive works and its switch engines. In this sordid atmosphere, between the factories and shops, their children grow up in much grime and blackness and sin.[141]

Smith's description is an accusation against the church. "There within range of a church bell, were eight hundred children who played and fought in the streets all Sunday afternoon, because they had nowhere else to play and nothing else to do." Although his article is tinged with the paternalistic attitudes reflective of the times, he and other students would not isolate themselves on campus, away from the larger Richmond community, because of any feelings of racial superiority.

In the fall of 1911, three students—Thomas Sheldon (BD, 1923) from the UPC, Tom Ruff (BD, 1914), and Arch McKinnon—convinced the Presbyterian League of Richmond to pay $8.00 a month to rent an abandoned chapel on Seventeenth Street. In November, the students moved in and opened a Sunday school. The school had twelve charter members, and during the course of the winter grew to an average attendance of thirty pupils. After graduating from Louisville Seminary, McKinnon served as a missionary in the Congo until 1950.[142]

Matt Grey (BD, 1914) then volunteered to become the superintendent and remained its head until 1916. His classmates recall that he worked on weekends from 6:00 a.m. to 11:00 p.m., visiting people's homes, distributing clothes and food and fuel. Grey taught children in the late morning and afternoon, memorizing catechism and Scripture verses. He bought a stamping outfit, laboriously printed hymns on "roller charts," and literally papered the walls with those scrolls. He also organized a sewing class for the girls and taught the boys to weave baskets and to repair cane-bottom chairs. Under his leadership, Sunday school enrollment grew to 176; in 1925 it was 250.[143] Grey was superintendent of the Seventeenth Street Mission for four years and then took a position with the YMCA when he resigned.

Enthusiasm was consistently high for the Seventeenth Street Mission. In 1919, J. K. Hobson (BD, 1920; superintendent of the mission for 1919–20, missionary in the Congo from 1920) raised money to build a playground. In 1921, the Presbyterian League gave $20,000 to build a modern Sunday school building. In 1922,

> the Sunday school during the winter months has averaged three hundred attendants. The teaching staff has been doubled and has been thoroughly reorganized by departments. During the week twenty volunteers from the Assembly's Training School and from Union Theological Seminary visit in the homes." Smith relates that their efforts bore fruit in the most unlikely places.
>
> Some time ago, one of our boys was arrested on the suspicion that he had been raiding a fruit stand. The judge asked the boy point blank whether or not he had taken the fruit.
>
> "Before God, Boss," he said, "I didn't do it."

"What do you know about God?" was the Judge's next question.

The boy braced himself with a long breath and replied, "God is a Spirit, infinite, eternal, and unchangeable, in His Being, wisdom, power, holiness, justice, goodness, and truth."

"Where did you learn that?" the magistrate asked.

He stated that he had learned about God at Seventeenth Street Mission. His case was promptly dismissed.

The Police Department has taken notice of this district that it has been with Jesus and has been able to materially reduce its force of patrolmen in the neighborhood of the Mission. The fruits of the Spirit are love, joy, peace— and against such there is no law. The streets, in daylight at least, are safe for women, and business [is] less liable to the depredations of thieves. A coal retailer in the vicinity of the mission says he has had less coal stolen lately than in previous years. . . .

[Smith then concludes:] The enterprise must of necessity grow until it has adequately met the challenge of a class of people who have been persistently denied the right to live upright lives.[144]

The Seventeenth Street Mission was the first systematic attempt by any part of the PCUS to evangelize "the Negro race in Richmond."[145] And it was important to the students. Cothran Smith estimated that by 1922, "two hundred of Richmond's Christian teachers and young people have been connected with [the Seventeenth Street Mission's] services as Sunday-school teachers, officers, musicians, etc." In that year the Presbyterian league budgeted $900.00 annually for the mission.[146] In the 1921–22 school year, there were twenty volunteers from UTS and ATS working at the mission.

Ministry is a long-term proposition, and the lessons learned at Seventeenth Street Mission lasted. Ralph Buchanan (Certificate, 1941) grew up in the mountains of North Carolina and was never exposed to many African Americans. After graduating from King College in Bristol, TN, he went to Union, and "just like everyone else," he signed up for missions. Although he was more interested in conducting Bible studies for tugboat crews, in local factories, and at the colored and white penitentiaries, he also worked at the Seventeenth Street Mission on several occasions. There he met "Brother Bullock," who as a young boy before the Civil War saw his mother sold south.

Ralph lived to be a hundred years old and never forgot Brother Bullock. He was president of the Anderson, South Carolina, Ministerial Association in 1963 when they voted to integrate the community Thanksgiving service. Many other ministers retracted their votes when their churches threatened to fire them, but Ralph, although he and his family received death threats, never backed down. He remembered Brother Bullock. However surprised Walter W. Moore may have been to have his students chip away at the doctrine of the spirituality of the church, and however we may look back and shake our heads at their faults, they dug the wells from which later generations would drink.

Institutionalizing Practical Education: ATS, Sprunts, and Schauffler Hall

The student-initiated local missions were a by-product of the Removal. But the Assembly's Training School, the Sprunt Lecture Series, and Schauffler Hall

21. The Seventeenth Street Mission with UTS students

22. The Seventeenth Street Mission with ATS students

were the organizational monuments to President Moore's confidence in practical education.

The Assembly's Training School

In 1907, Annie Wilson (a member of Grace Covenant Church in Richmond) had volunteered and been appointed to assist in a mission in China. To prepare herself, she applied to take classes in Bible and other subjects for one year. The faculty assented and allowed her to attend lectures, but not matriculate.[147] The experiment was a success, and in 1908 the faculty began to offer a two-year course for women preparing for foreign and home missions, headed up by Lingle.[148] By 1909 the enrollment reached twenty-three, and the General Assembly was taking notice; the idea of a lay training school in Richmond with a two-year curriculum began to germinate. Some members of the faculty and public were concerned, however, that this school would draw resources away from Union's primary mission. Moreover, some thought the presence of women would draw the men's attention away from theology. There were also accusations that the president was bringing attractive and suitable women on campus as a source of wives for future ministers. But he never wavered: he insisted that both males and females have access to the education they needed to serve the church.[149]

Doing anything for women would be a hard sell. Following Dabney's long-standing admonition that the public preaching of women was "an assault on the fidelity of God's truth and Kingdom" and was "part and parcel of French Jacobinism, that travesty of true republicanism, which caused the Reign of Terror in France, and which disorganizes every society which it invades"—southern Presbyterians restricted women's work in the church. In 1899 the Synod of Virginia, in its Report on Women in the Church, for example, declared that women were in a divinely decreed subordinate position to men. In 1911, however, five synods proposed to create the position of "General Secretary of Women's Missionary Work in the Presbyterian Church, U.S." and appoint a woman to this position. Thomas Cary Johnson thundered: "These noble women are unconsciously assuming the position of advisors of the Lord as to how he should have his people do their work." Johnson was not alone; the Women's Missionary Society of the Waynesboro, Virginia, church reported being confident that the great majority of southern Presbyterian women were also opposed.[150]

The church, therefore, expected Annie Wilson and those who followed her to be under the direct supervision of an ordained male. The only problem with those expectations was that with so many Union-trained women wanting to enter the mission field (both foreign and domestic), and with a corresponding lack of ordained male superiors, women were left on their own. One Presbyterian minister observed, as he saw his daughter preach at the mission she ran in Breathitt, Kentucky: "Some say that this is irregular; true, but if the work cannot be accomplished in a regular way, it must be done in an irregular way." While pastors and students (always male) would preach to remote congregations infrequently or only during the summer months, the women were with the congregations year-round. After one of his sermons, when the Reverend R. P. Smith explained that Presbyterians did not have enough ministers to assign them to the mountains on a regular basis, a mountain man responded:

We like to hear you fellows preach, and I am not saying anything again ye, but if we can't git both, send us the women teachers. These women teach our children books and good manners during the week and on Sunday they teach all of us a lot of what is in the Bible. Tell your folks to send us the teachers, we can get along mighty well for a good while yet just with them doing the work.[151]

Union responded to the need. The 1909 Catalogue mentions "Courses for Lay Workers" for the first time.[152] The idea was so popular that the 1910 Catalogue needed a supplement titled "The Training School for Christian Workers," listing twenty-three students, all women. The school, however, was open to all "Christian men and women of all denominations, who wish to become better fitted for usefulness as teachers in Sunday Schools, secretaries of Christian associations, assistants to pastors, visitors of congregations, workers in city missions and country missions, or missionaries to foreign lands."

The curriculum was completely practical.

First Year

    I. The English Bible
    II. The History of the Christian Church
    III. The Fundamental Truths of the Christian Religion
    IV. An Introduction to the Study of the Sacred Scriptures
    V. The Principle and Practice of Foreign Missions
    VI. The Religions of the Non-Christian World
    VII. A Course in Teacher Training
    VIII. Pedagogy—The Science of Teaching
    IX. Sunday-School Methods and Work
    X. A Bird's-Eye View of Home Missions in the South

Second Year

    I. English Bible
    II. Church History
    III. The Fundamental Truths of the Christian Religion
    IV. Foreign Missions
    V. Home Missions
    VI. Teacher-Training
    VII. Pedagogy
    VIII. Geography of the Holy Land
    IX. Individual work for individuals
    X. Hospital work[153]

The General Assembly had previously established a Training School for Unordained Christian Workers in 1895 in Atlanta. It closed within two years due to lack of support. In 1909, however, when the General Assembly heard about the two-year course Union was offering, they appointed A. L. Phillips to chair a committee to investigate establishing another training school under General Assembly authority and funding. In 1912, Phillips recommended establishing another school, but the General Assembly was unsure and set formidable requirements to create another educational institution: the site had to be free; dormitory, classroom, and dining hall space had to be provided for three years at no cost; and three years' worth of operating expenses had to be on hand (the General Assembly would assume expenses after that time).

President Moore had always believed that the purpose of the seminary curriculum "is not to make accomplished scholars and specialists in the various departments of theological science, but to make good ministers of Jesus Christ, who will serve Him and His church with increasing efficiency year after year." In his mind, serving the church of Jesus Christ included women serving. Since southern churches were reticent about the place of women in the church, President Moore found his model in the Kennedy School of Missions, recently established at Hartford Seminary. He saw at Hartford a "school [that] is organized in precisely the same way that is proposed for our school in Richmond." He seemed to suggest that Union and the proposed school for unordained workers become two coordinate institutions, sharing resources and personnel. This plan would allow him to placate southern proprieties while achieving his larger purpose. President Moore got to work and a year later reported that the Presbyterian League of Richmond had raised enough the money to begin the school, and he convinced the board to offer the use of seminary property.[154] The General Assembly, however, created the Assembly's Training School as a separate institution under their tutelage.

The Sprunt Lecture Series

Along with helping the Assembly's Training School come into existence, the establishment of the Sprunt Lecture series also shows how President Moore sought to apply the intellect to the practical work of ministry. He had long hoped for a lecture series featuring prominent scholars and personalities who would address contemporary issues. The possibility of a lectureship was first broached in 1883 (one year before Moore arrived),[155] and he had brought several lecturers to Hampden-Sydney, usually under the auspices of the Society of Missionary Inquiry. Complicated travel and the small potential audience, however, could never sustain a continued program. Once the seminary moved, however, Walter W. Moore saw his chance.

As part of the Centennial Fund campaign, he approached James Sprunt of Wilmington, North Carolina. Sprunt was born in Glasgow, Scotland, in 1846 and served on three blockade runs during the Civil War (and was shipwrecked for eight months in the Bahamas). After the war he founded a trading company in Wilmington, North Carolina, with twelve bales of cotton. By 1900 his company was one of the largest in the South, employing over eight hundred, with branches in Boston, Houston, Liverpool, Le Havre, and Bremen. Sprunt was also a Presbyterian elder and taught Sunday school.[156]

Believing in the need for an educated ministry, Sprunt gave $30,000 to Union in 1911 to endow an annual lecture program. In the first years, three speakers appeared at Union every year.[157] The Sprunt Lectures immediately became the most prestigious lecture series in the South. One of the most notable early lecturers was William Jennings Bryan in 1921. He had run for the presidency three times and had also served as Wilson's secretary of state (until he resigned in 1915 over Wilson's handling of the *Lusitania's* sinking). When he spoke at Union, Bryan was at the height of his popularity; four years later, in the famous

Scopes "Monkey" trial, he argued against Clarence Darrow and assisted in the prosecution of John Scopes, accused of teaching evolution—then against the law in Tennessee public schools.

Bryan turned the Sprunt Lectures into a national event. Up to this point, all Sprunt lecturers had been ministers (except for the archaeologist Sir William M. Ramsey), speaking mainly to ministers and scholars. William Jennings Bryan, however, was invited "to present an argument for Christianity which would appeal strongly to those who in our time have been disturbed and confused by current scepticism and who are sometimes none too ready to listen to professional teachers of religion."[158] Bryan gave nine lectures. The first and the last were scheduled for the public and in the City Auditorium. The fifth lecture was intended for students and given in Watts Chapel. The rest were delivered in Schauffler Hall. All of Bryan's lectures were well attended: those who did not come early found only standing room. Bryan also dined with students one day and had dinner with the governor the next.[159]

Bryan's lectures were later published in a book titled *In His Image* because, he said, "God made us in His image, and placed us here to carry out a divine decree."[160] In his lectures he dismissed Darwinism as "guesses strung together," but admitted that evolution did not deny the existence of God. Yet he argued that the idea of natural selection put God at such a distance from humans that there was no reason to believe in any Supreme Being. What was left was a vicious "survival of the fittest." Bryan cited Friedrich Nietzsche as a disciple of Darwin and blamed German militarism and the "bloodiest war in history" (World War I) on Darwinism. He accused evolution of reducing men to brutes. On the verge of launching his campaign for a law against evolution, and perhaps foreshadowing his participation in the Scopes Trial, Bryan then suggested that only true Christians—meaning those who repudiated evolution—should teach in public schools.[161]

The lectures were a sensation and the book a best seller; four editions were issued within the first six months.[162] The Sprunt Lectures never shied away from controversy. Other speakers during this period included John Gresham Machen in 1920 and Robert E. Speer in 1925, involved on opposite sides of the fundamentalist-modernist controversy then raging in the northern Presbyterian church.[163]

Although President Moore did not intend for the Sprunt Lectures to undermine PCUS Calvinist orthodoxy, over the years these addresses brought wider views and even opposing ideas onto campus. Balmer Kelly has observed that early lecturers supported the most extreme positions of biblical conservatism. Yet, as he notices, by the 1930s the Sprunt lecturers, especially from the fields of systematic theology, church history, and pastoral studies, were introducing ideas that were new to the students and the denomination.[164]

Schauffler Hall

The construction of Schauffler Hall was the culmination and completion of Walter W. Moore's vision. Until the twentieth century, religious education had been mostly informal and centered in the home. As the country became urbanized, children attended school away from home, and parents worked in shops and factories, rather than on the farm. Family life was becoming decentralized, and religious education faltered. The church realized it had to make Christian education an institutional concern. A need arose, therefore, to understand how to apply the new theories of education to the church. Schauffler Hall was designed to serve as a model Sunday school and place of worship, under the direction of the seminary.[165]

Schauffler Hall was not in the original campus plans, and a faculty residence had to be torn down to make way for it.[166] The genesis of Schauffler Hall and the Christian Education curriculum can be found in the first conference that Union Seminary hosted after the move to Richmond. Although Union had hosted the Inter-Seminary Missionary Alliance national convention at Hampden-Sydney in 1892,[167] complicated travel arrangements and inadequate local facilities made future conventions and conferences impractical. Once the Richmond facilities were available, however, Union began to reach out. The first public event was held in 1903, when the seminary hosted lectures by furloughed missionaries. These lectures were such a success that the next year UTS hosted the first Sunday School Institute ever held in the southern church. The institute was a resounding success, attended by 75 delegates from 19 churches.[168] With this conference, many in the church began to ask why its seminaries did not do more to stress religious education. President Moore also understood that with Union's convenient location and resources, the seminary was a natural host for conferences. In 1904 the Eastern Conference of Young Men's Christian Associations in theological seminaries met at Union with over "186 delegates representing 26 different Seminaries of nearly every evangelical denomination."[169] Union's national presence was growing, but it would need a specialized building to teach religious education and host conferences.

Ginter Park Presbyterian Church had been meeting in Watts Chapel since 1907, with seminarians teaching Sunday school, preaching on Wednesday nights, and assisting in pastoral duties. Although Walter Lingle had been advocating for a Sunday school department for years, it was not until A. F. Schauffler gave six lectures in March 1911 that the impetus to consider religious education as a separate discipline took hold. Later that year, Lingle was able to organize a Sunday School Department, but without real funding. It was only after Schauffler returned to give the 1914 Sprunt Lectures that the board established a Christian Education chair. In 1915 the board viewed the first plans for Schauffler Hall and heard of its intended use as a "laboratory" for students.[170]

In 1916–17 the board of trustees reported to the supporting synods:

> We are now prepared to announce a . . . great forward stride in the matter of providing for the best scientific study and expert training in all phases of Sunday School organization, equipment, and instruction, including teacher training and field extension. A generous friend has offered to give the institution $100,000 for the erection, equipment, and maintenance of a model Sunday school building, up-to-date in every particular, where "laboratory work" will be done year round.[171]

George Watts endowed the chair for "Sunday school work" in 1918, and UTS in 1919 became the first southern Presbyterian seminary to establish a separate department for Sunday school work.

President Moore's relationship with Schauffler shows how willing the president was to adapt the ideas of others, even from the North. A. F. Schauffler was born in 1845 in Constantinople, where his father (from Germany, mother from Massachusetts) was a missionary. After graduating from Williams College in 1863, he entered Union Theological Seminary in New York in 1868, but transferred to Andover after one year. He served a Congregational church in Brookfield, Massachusetts, for a year after graduation and then accepted a call as a city missionary in New York and director of Student Work at UTS(NY) in 1872–76. His work in the city convinced Schauffler of the importance of Sunday school work. He became president of the New York City Sunday School Association and began to hold seminars on how to organize and teach Sunday school. He became nationally known. In 1896, Schauffler was appointed to the International Sunday School Lesson Committee along with Walter W. Moore. Through this joint effort, Moore and Schauffler became friends and colleagues. In his dedication speech, President Moore declared that Schauffler did more to popularize Sunday school in the United States than anyone.[172]

Mrs. John S. Kennedy of New York (Schauffler's sister) donated the money (adding $50,000 to her original gift, with an additional $50,000 from George Watts), and construction on Schauffler Hall began in 1919. At the dedication service in 1921, President Moore proclaimed that Schauffler Hall would facilitate "the scientific study of all phases of school organization, equipment, management, and instruction including teacher training and field extension."[173] It was also large enough to host conferences and became the home of Ginter Park Presbyterian Church.

No speech more clearly explains Walter W. Moore's thinking and vision than his dedicatory address. He would be gone in five years and saw in Schauffler Hall the completed foundation for the future. He opened his speech by saying that Schauffler Hall concretely symbolized Union's way of approaching theological education: "conservatism in doctrine and progressiveness in methods."[174] In this declaration one can hear John Holt Rice's "no isms, but Bibleism," and B. M. Smith's pledge to Cyrus McCormick: "no ultraisms."

President Moore reviewed the history of Christian Education at Union. He stated that students organized a Sunday school class when the seminary first moved to Ginter Park in 1898, and out of these efforts the Ginter Park Presbyterian Church was organized and first met in the chapel, with Sunday school in the classrooms. In the process the church became a training ground for students. He reviewed how Lingle detached "Sunday School work" from the Department of Pastoral Theology to form its own department in 1911. In 1919, Union had called William Taliaferro "Tolly" Thompson as the first professor of Christian Education in the first Christian Education department in the South. With evident pride, President Moore called Schauffler Hall "a modern Sunday school building."

It took a decade for Christian Education to find its place in the curriculum. In 1912, it was offered to seniors in the second term of the senior year, and the emphasis was on the "practical methods of organizing, equipping, grading, and conducting a Sunday School."[175] By 1923, Christian Education was a yearlong class offered during the junior year and went beyond the Sunday school. Topics such as preaching to children, the preparation of children for church membership, and the conduct of the daily Vacation Bible School received extensive study. Whereas a generation earlier the organizations outside the church were viewed with suspicion, Christian Education classes in the 1920s encouraged ministers to partner with groups such as "The Young People's Society of Christian Endeavor, Boy Scouts, Girls Scouts, Camp Fire Girls, [and] the Christian Citizen Programme of the Y.M.C.A.," among others.[176]

As Walter W. Moore rode trains and saw the country grow up around him, it seemed as though the church had no answer for the modern world. The Assembly's Training School, Sprunt Lectures, and the Christian Education classes taught in Schauffler Hall were the harbingers of the specialization that seminaries would employ to address the modern world. The Sprunt Lectures would keep ministers abreast of the latest developments in theology because revivals were no longer enough in an urbanized, industrialized world. The Assembly's Training School would assist an educated ministry to teach in a way people could understand. Schauffler Hall would be the laboratory where students could not only experience modern congregational life, but also learn how to teach.

Ginter Park Presbyterian Church

In 1907 the Presbytery of East Hanover appointed a committee, which included Thomas Cary Johnson, "to canvas the neighborhood (around the seminary) to organize a Presbyterian church." Response was favorable; the new congregation began meeting in Watts Chapel, and Johnson was called as their first pastor in 1908 (and served until 1926). The church moved into Schauffler Hall in 1921 and remained there until 1954. In 1921, the church had 300 members and a Sunday school enrollment of 275. The children of the congregation provided some comic relief for the staid seminary. Thomas Cary Johnson was an imposing figure for the students (and the faculty and denomination, for that matter). Sensitive about his bald spot, he was never seen without a black skullcap squarely on his head. The children constantly begged for him to take it off or sneaked around, trying to catch him without it on. "We children sat at the window, trying to see the top of his head as he switched from his hat to black skullcap; . . . we never could!"[177]

Westwood Tract and Mission Court

Westwood tract, the final addition to Union's property, was part of the campus by 1910. Dr. Hunter McGuire's farmhouse, "Westwood," the country home of the McGuire family, stood diagonally across Brook Road from the campus. McGuire had served as Stonewall Jackson's personal physician during the Civil War and was with Jackson when he died. The house is probably best known for its ghost. The following story was recounted in *Reader's Digest*, November 1942:

> My mother went with my sister to live in Richmond, Virginia, while my brother was studying there for the ministry. They rented a large, rambling old

house. During the two years of her residence in this house, there frequently appeared before my mother an officer of the Confederate Army whose left sleeve had a band of crape on it. (He wore a black crape band around his left arm for some years as a symbol of mourning for the general.)

She told my brother and sister of seeing the figure, but they teased her about it. Later she told me, because I was a more sympathetic listener. She said that one day, tiring of his repeated appearance, she remarked to him as if he were human, "Oh, why do you bother me so? I wish you would go away and leave me alone." He looked at her, sadly shook his head, vanished out of the dining-room door, and never returned.

Several months later, in some museum or art gallery, my sister was look-ing over the catalogue. Suddenly she said to my mother, "Here is a picture of your ghost." My mother's description of the apparition had been so accurate that my sister had recognized it immediately; and there, too, on the left sleeve was a band of crape. The catalogue said that the soldier in the picture was Dr. Hunter Holmes McGuire.[178]

McGuire died in 1900, and his 34-acre lot was placed on the market for $17,000—an enormous sum. The seminary was already in debt for buildings and running a small annual deficit. But President Moore understood how the original eleven-acre campus would hem in future growth. It is unclear who came up with the idea, but twelve seminary supporters organized the West-wood Land Company in 1901 and purchased what is now known as the West-wood tract. Their avowed object was to hold the property till the seminary could buy it at their purchase price, but they would allow the seminary to make full use of it in the meantime. By 1910, however, nearly all the stockholders had donated their stock to the seminary.[179]

Although Mission Court is torn down now and was never an imposing pres-ence on campus, its construction is an interesting footnote in Union's history. While the denomination and some members of the faculty had reservations about the organizational and financial abilities of women, the Women of East Hanover Presbytery had no such qualms, and the idea of Mission Court grew out of support for a Persian student. Isaac E. Yohannan was born and grew up in Urumia, Persia. Educated by a Presbyterian missionary, the Presbytery of Urumia licensed him to preach, and he came to the United States in 1897 to attend UTS. He graduated in 1901, was ordained by East Hanover Presbytery, supplied churches for two years, and then returned to Urumia as a mission-ary in 1904 (dying in Russia during World War I).[180] Before Yohannan returned home, however, the Women's Foreign Missionary Union of East Hanover Pres-bytery decided to raise funds for books, which he would then carry home. At the same time, the longtime president of the group, Avis B. Stewart, also pro-posed to collect money to build a house for furloughed missionaries.

Despite raising thousands of dollars by 1916, the Synod of Virginia refused to approve the project because it was managed by women. The Women's Foreign Missionary Union of East Hanover Presbytery refused to budge and held the money in trust, "hoping to build a Virginia home some day." Presi-dent Moore heard of their predicament and advised the synod that "nothing would afford as much needed relief and help to our wearied and straitened missionaries" as a house. He also thought that missionaries living on campus would have a positive effect on students. Moore backed up his comments with a concrete offer: to lease the land on which Mission Court would be built to the Women's Foreign Missionary Union of East Hanover Presbytery for $1 a year.[181] The women continued raising money, and in 1920 the first of two Mission Court buildings were completed.[182]

The Curriculum Expands

With new classes in Christian Sociology and Christian Education and new facilities on Westwood tract, some wondered if the curriculum needed updating as well. Urbanization and industrialization made Americans question the old philosophies and relationships. Disillusioned by World War I, many Americans sought comfort in the old ways and the old faith to ameliorate their anxieties, while others wanted to reject tradition altogether. The controversy over evolution, for example, can be seen as a "collision between the secular orientation of an urban-based intellectual elite and the traditional morality of rural, small-town Americans, steeped in the traditional morality of evangelical Protestantism."[183] Before the war, secular and sacred could exist in their own spheres. After the war, mass communication compelled everyone to face new ideas.[184]

President Walter W. Moore, Thomas Cary Johnson, Walter Lingle, and Union Seminary saw their mission as bridging the chasm opening in American society through promoting a constructive, healthy Calvinism. While Johnson urged the church to cling tighter to the spirituality of the church, he could never accept the mindless strictures of fundamentalism. At the same time, Walter Lingle wanted the church to confront the future and replace the isms of the twentieth century with a realistic Christian ethic. He could not accept that the Bible had nothing to say to the modern world. Johnson and Lingle coexisted and even thrived as colleagues and wanted their church to do the same. President Moore saw Union as the area of ideas, faithfully argued, in the service of the church. Their conservatism was neither fundamentalism nor liberalism. Indeed, the Sprunt Lectures included a range of viewpoints designed to lead people to consider other points of view. While Moore acknowledged his own conservatism, he declared that he was "agin' the policy of trying to secure copper-plate similarity among thinking men by the terrors of presbyterial examinations."[185] Their students would begin to discard the old choices and face a future of new possibilities.

Critics had argued against the Removal by warning that the enticements of urban life would distract the students from their studies. In reality, the move to Richmond increased the opportunities for mission and the range of courses offered. Public speaking had also been a concern since the 1880s, and a speech, or elocution, class was first offered in the fall of 1901. It was taught by Miss Eugenia L. Anspaugh, a graduate of the Boston School of Expression. Forty enrolled, and more took individual instruction.[186] She could be considered the first female instructor at Union. This class became the required public speaking course in 1913. Mr. A. B. Curry was appointed the instructor in vocal music in 1910.[187] In 1923 the class in vocal music became a class in church music, "so that the students may be able to sing the hymns accurately and with proper expression . . . and to select with discrimination the hymns for the various demands of worship, and the tunes adapted to express and interpret them."[188]

The 1910 World Missionary Conference (also called the Edinburgh Missionary Conference of 1910) issued a call for more professional training of missionaries. In 1898, Union Seminary and the Medical College of Virginia had already entered into an agreement whereby seminary students "who expect to become foreign missionaries, and who wish to pursue medical studies in addition to their theological furnishing for their work," would be eligible to attend MCV and take medical classes for only $5[189] (this arrangement lasted until 1914). In addition, President Moore had made it possible for women to prepare themselves for the mission field. The next step was to establish a professorship for the study of missions.

In 1895 the student body had voted to petition the trustees "to so arrange the course of study that a definite place may be given to the Systematic Study of Missions." They described in detail the course they wanted, and the trustees responded positively. The students requested and the board selected Thomas Cary Johnson, professor of ecclesiastical history, to teach the missions courses. By 1914 he had a wide range of course offerings,[190] which were augmented in 1915 when Walter Lingle was appointed "Professor of Church History, Pedagogy, and Missions."

As President Moore began to raise money for a chair in Christian Education, he realized the time was right to establish a chair in missions. The 1910 World Missionary Conference's call for better missionary training had prompted many seminaries to add chairs in missions studies. By 1917, professorships in missions had already appeared at Yale, Southern Baptist, Drew, Candler, Princeton, and Union Seminary in New York.[191] Union in Richmond could not fall behind: Frank Sheppard Royster of Norfolk, who had the largest fertilizer business in the South, endowed a chair of missions in 1917.

In 1923 there was a new class: "Pastoral Theology." Although a course of the same name had been offered in Hampden Sydney, this class (offered only to seniors) acknowledged how the parish had changed:

The modern Minister is a Preacher, an Administrator, and a Pastor. This course prepares the Minister for the work he must do exclusive of his actual preaching. In considering the Minister as an Administrator, the whole subject of Church Efficiency is studied in a practical way. Such subjects are discussed as the Church Program, church Organization, Church Finance, and Church Publicity. The men are introduced to those methods which are being used successfully by the leaders in the Church.

The conduct of Public Worship is given careful attention, and the evening service and the prayer meeting, with the problems they present, are dealt with thoroughly.

This course is largely a lecture course, although discussion is encouraged. The students are sent out to study firsthand the work of some of the Churches in Richmond. Reports on their surveys are made to the class. They are required also to read several books and to present papers in class covering their assignments. Every effort is made to equip the Minister for the work as he finds it today.[192]

Enrollment

The students went to class and fashioned a new life on campus: living in new buildings with electric lights and metal bathtubs, seeing women in the classroom, debating the social gospel, and working in local missions. From 1898 to 1926, there was a steady increase in the number of students: an indication of the Removal's success. The average annual number of students attending the seminary for the 25 years preceding the move to Richmond was 43. In 1899, attendance was 88 students, an all-time high up till then. During this era the average attendance was 77 per year, with 158 in 1925–26. The first time 100 students were enrolled was 1911. During this time students came from 26 states, 7 countries, and 57 educational institutions.

Between 1898 and 1926 the student body was 93 percent southern, with over 80 percent of Southerners coming from Virginia and North Carolina. West Virginia and Tennessee were the next most numerous, but students from every state in the South could be found on campus during this time. Students from states and possessions outside the South came from California, Iowa, Kansas, Maine, New Jersey, New York, Ohio, Oklahoma (formerly the Indian Territory), Pennsylvania, and Puerto Rico. In addition, sons of missionaries came from Brazil, Congo, Cuba, Japan, Korea, and Mexico—plus international students from Canada, Czechoslovakia, Denmark, the Netherlands, Persia, the Philippines, and Syria—together giving other voices to campus discussions. The first two Korean students were admitted in 1924. Hyung Chai Kim (special student, 1927) was admitted as a special student (undergraduate) in "teaching and mission work" and received his certificate in 1927. He returned to Korea and worked at the Mission Academy in what is now Pyongyang, Democratic People's Republic of Korea. The first Korean graduate student (and the first Korean to earn a doctorate) was Namkung Hyuk (DD, 1929). After returning home, he taught at the Presbyterian seminary in Pyongyang for fifteen years, edited a theological journal, wrote biblical commentaries, helped translate parts of the New Testament, and was elected moderator of the Presbyterian Church of Korea in 1932. The Japanese occupied Korea from 1910 to 1945 and his Christianity and high profile made him a target for the occupation authorities. He escaped to China during World War II but returned to Pyongyang after the Japanese surrendered. Huyk was arrested after North Korea invaded the south in 1950 and was never heard from again.

During this era virtually every southern institution of higher learning was represented in the student body, with 35 percent coming from Davidson and 11 percent from Hampden-Sydney. Students from the North and other countries were more prevalent after World War I. Although Francis Sampson had started an alumni association in 1847, it did not survive the Civil War. The first post-Appomattox mention of an organized alumni association was in 1907,[193] growing out of an alumni meeting at the May 1906 PCUS General Assembly in Greenville, South Carolina.[194] Alumni association meetings continued to be held at General Assembly meetings until 1954. During 1920–32, reunions were held at commencements, then in later years during times of the Sprunt Lectures. The system of five-year reunions was instituted in 1934, and it was at the 1934 reunion that Dr. J. L. Sherrard was honored as the oldest living graduate.

He was a member of the Class of 1877, ninety-one years old, and had served in the Confederate cavalry.[195]

The directions for getting to the campus in 1898 were a change from crossing the "Red Sea" (of clay):

> Students arriving in the city by any railroad or steamboat line may take any street-car "going up town" from any station or wharf, and ask the conductor for transfer to the "Lakeside cars." These cars go direct to the Seminary. By surrendering their checks for baggage to the agents of the Richmond Transfer Company, who are to be found on all in-coming trains, students can have their trunks delivered at the Seminary at twenty-five cents apiece.[196]

By 1925 steamboats no longer docked at Richmond, and all students had to do was take any streetcar going to the center of town from any station and ask the conductor for a transfer to cars for Ginter Park.[197] "The dormitories are always open. Students arriving in Richmond either day or night should come directly to Richmond Hall, at the Seminary and avoid unnecessary hotel bills."[198]

The Student Community

The students who arrived on campus in September 1898 realized that they needed something to help them navigate the new campus and environment. The first Student Handbook was available to students as they walked onto campus in September 1900. This handbook shows how anxious Richmond was to have the seminary in town. Page after page of advertising tried to lure a new group of customers to clothing (suits cost $20), "general merchandise," and bookstores. There are also numerous advertisements for barbershops, jewelry stores, pharmacies, bicycle shops, and dentists. The handbooks list faculty and class members (with class officers: president, vice-president, secretary, and treasurer). There is also always a list of churches of all denominations, and synagogues are included.[199]

With increased enrollment in the teens of the century, student policies had to cover a wider range of eventualities. By 1910, dorm rules were published in the Student Handbook. A student government was formed in 1915, and the Student Body Constitution was printed in that handbook. One of the most important duties of student government was to establish dorm policies. These policies confirmed that the campus was now surrounded by an urban area.

> Laundry for the washerwomen is to be brought to the cloak room in Richmond Hall Tuesday morning before 9 A.M. Clothes must be in a laundry bag with tag containing sender's name and washerwoman's name. Washerwomen will return bag Friday evenings and Wesley will deliver it to your rooms. On no condition will washerwomen be allowed to go to any other place on the premises.
>
> The shoe men may receive work on Wednesday morning between 8 and 9 in cloak room of Richmond Hall, same to be returned Thursday between 6:30 and 7:30 P.M. to cloak room, where they may collect for their work.
>
> The Broad Rock Water man is to leave water on the first floor of the buildings. Empty bottles to be brought down by users to first floor for the driver.

The apple man will not be allowed in any building. Those desiring apples can carry same to their own rooms.

Advertisers in the *Seminary Magazine* may make calls on students, soliciting their patronage. But work for them will be received in the regular way.

Each student should consider himself a committee of one to question any stranger seen on a dormitory floor, and if not making repairs on the building, he is to be ordered out of the building, and the case is to be reported to Mr. Miller. Exception: If the stranger is calling on a student, show him the courtesy of taking him to the student's room and helping him to find the desired party.

Wesley, Garnett, and Charles have a right to go through the buildings.

Wesley shall act as agent for the washerwomen to collect for work done, and he shall be paid five cents per month per man for his work.[200]

Students had to be reminded how to deal with the servants. "Students should be very cautious about lending to the servants . . . and should not in any way give them occasion to come to rooms in the Seminary buildings"; this admonition was repeated regularly until the 1930s. Also, servants at the refectory were prohibited from pressing clothes for students.[201]

Class schedules were always listed in the handbooks, and the daily routine had not changed with the move. The traditional curriculum was intact in 1900, with the only addition being that of English Bible and English composition. Classes were held from Tuesday through Saturday, 10:00 a.m. through 2:00 p.m. Any Union student would recognize the 1900–1901 schedule (Ch. = Church; Pl. = Pastoral):

DAY	CLASS	10–11 a.m.	11 a.m.–12 p.m.	12–1 p.m.	1–2 p.m.
TUE	JUNIOR	Hebrew		Ch. History	Homiletics
	MIDDLE	Ch. History	Hebrew		Epistles
	SENIOR	English Bible	Epistles		Theology
WED	JUNIOR	Hebrew		Ch. History	Gospels
	MIDDLE	English Bible	Epistles		Theology
	SENIOR	Ch. History	Theology	Hebrew	
THUR	JUNIOR	Hebrew		Homiletics	Gospels
	MIDDLE	English Bible	Hebrew		Theology
	SENIOR	Ch. History	English		Hebrew
FRI	JUNIOR	Hebrew		Theology	Homiletics
	MIDDLE	Ch. History	Hebrew		Epistles
	SENIOR	Pl. Theology	Ch. History		Theology

DAY	CLASS	10–11 a.m.	11 a.m.–12 p.m.	12–1 p.m.	1–2 p.m.
SAT	JUNIOR	Hebrew		Ch. History	Gospels
	MIDDLE	Ch. History	Theology	English Bible	
	SENIOR	Pl. Theology	English		Hebrew[202]

Prayer was woven into the daily routine. All students were expected to attend morning prayer at 9:40 a.m. ("Sunday and Monday excepted") and the Wednesday evening meeting in the chapel. Every lecture and "recitation" was opened with prayer.[203] The whole student body held "a prayer and praise service every evening immediately after supper in Richmond Hall," and each class also had a prayer meeting of its own once a week. In addition, the members of the faculty held "occasional conferences with the students on subjects connected with their spiritual life." On Sundays, students were expected to teach Sunday school and attend worship in the chapel (later Ginter Park Presbyterian Church in Schauffler Hall), with worship at 11:00 a.m. and Sunday evenings at 8:00 p.m., or at another local church.[204]

The Pledge, first found in the 1810 General Assembly Plan and repeated throughout the years, is listed in all the handbooks. Moreover, extracurricular activities (such as the choir), required dates for student preaching, the schedule of collections in chapel, and seminary policies (such as reports to presbyteries) were delineated in the handbook. Practical information, like streetcar schedules and the president's office hours (9:30 each morning to see anyone who wanted to see him—discontinued in 1914) were always listed in the handbooks. And there is always the note:

Attendance on Exercises
All students are under obligation to attend regularly and promptly all the regular exercises of the Seminary, including Morning Prayers and the Wednesday Evening Chapel Exercises, as well as the Class-Room Exercises.

Written excuses for absence from the class-room must be given to the professor in whose department the absence occurs, and in case of failure to do so, the absence is recorded as unexcused. When one is unavoidably tardy and fails to answer at roll-call, the fact of tardiness and the reasons therefore should be stated to the professor verbally at the close of the recitation. Students are expected to obtain permission from a professor if necessity arises for leaving the room during the progress of a recitation.

The early student handbooks reveal just how far "out in the country" the campus was located (Ginter Park was not annexed until 1914). The city of Richmond did not provide a fire company for Ginter Park until 1922, so the students organized themselves into four companies (one for Watts and one for Westminster Hall; one "Engine" company, to bring the hoses; and one "Hook and Ladder" company, to provide the tall ladders), with a chief, assistant chief, and a fire inspector. Since there was no alarm system, the bell was rung to signal a fire: 1 ring for Watts Hall; 2 rings, Westminster Hall; 3 rings, Spence Library; 4 rings, Campus.[205]

Admissions were more intentional. Every year "deputations" of faculty members and students would visit Presbyterian colleges in the synod and, as Gus Summers (BD, 1925) remembers, "present very eloquently the call to ministry." He was a junior at Davidson when he heard their presentation, and "after much prayer I decided to join the large group of the ones preparing to preach."[206] Louisville and Columbia also sent representatives to Davidson, but most students preferred to go to Union.

Food looms large in the life of any student. In Hampden Sydney, each student made his own arrangements with the boarding houses around campus. In Richmond, dining was centralized on the second floor of Westminster Hall when the campus opened in 1898. The refectory was moved to Richmond Hall at the beginning of the 1907–8 school year. During the week, breakfast was at 8:00 a.m., dinner at 2:00 p.m., and supper at 6:30 p.m. On Sunday, dinner was served at 1:30 p.m., supper at 6:00.[207] Seats were assigned in the dining rooms according to seniority.

> The Treasurer of the Refectory has charge of the seating in the Dining Room. At the beginning of the Session, temporary seating is provided, and arrangements are made by which part of the students move at stated intervals from table to table. The object of this is to make it possible for everyone to get acquainted in a short time. When those moving have made the circuit of the tables, the permanent seats are taken. The old men have the privilege of retaining their old seats and of inviting others to fill up the vacancies at their tables.[208]

It was through the refectory that students became included in the policy-making process. In 1902 the board required student representation on the committee supervising the refectory. Similarly, in 1900 the board invited faculty to board meetings when it was convenient.[209]

One of the consistent student memories was the fellowship at mealtimes. "I was in a local fraternity at Davidson which gave me pleasure, but it was nothing like the fellowship at Union." Even after seventy years, alumni remember their tablemates who became lifelong friends. Just as when new people sit in the "wrong" pew, however, there was some consternation when the Treasurer tried to break up groups of students who were eating together. "Because of the criticism, we added [tablemates]; . . . they wanted the fruit basket to turn over."[210]

When the Society of Missionary Inquiry became the clearinghouse for local missions, students still felt the need to discuss current and professional issues. They held a "mass meeting" on Thursday afternoon, February 19, 1914, in Room "A" of Watts Hall to see if there was interest in a "rhetorical" society. There was a great deal of interest, so a committee was elected to write a constitution. On March 9 they voted to form a society "to promote, by public discussion, knowledge pertaining to our Church and Seminary, and to train its members in public speaking."[211] The students named the society in honor of Givens B. Strickler, who had recently died. While the seminary was in session, the Givens B. Strickler Society met on the second and fourth Monday evenings "for the discussion of living questions of interest to the Church and the Seminary for practice in parliamentary procedure."[212]

The society's president chose judges to decide who prevailed in the debate. The president also appointed a critic to give his opinion on each speaker's ability and areas where he needed improvement. The students debated topical issues, such as "organic union of the Southern Presbyterian Church and the United Presbyterian Church" (decided in the negative); whether "our church should adopt the plan of rotary eldership" (settled as no); and "that our church should amend the book of church order, Chapter VI, Article IV (Par. 132), to the effect that men who have the degree of B.D. from any one of our Five Seminaries be exempt from the Thesis, Lecture, and Sermons" in examinations before presbytery (no).

There were debates on social issues, such as establishing and maintaining Parochial Schools" (no); should "Sunday amusements, passenger and freight traffic be discontinued by Christian people?" (yes); and the students thought that "the Protestant Churches of America should seek to cooperate with the Roman Catholic church." They also debated professional questions, voting "that only unfermented wine should be used in [the] Communion service," "immersion should be allowed as an alternate form of Baptism in the Southern Presbyterian Church," and "that sales, suppers, bazaars, etc." should not be used to raise money for the church. The students voted that it was appropriate for churches to pay people to sing in the choir, and they heard reports on church advertising (methods, why churches should advertise, and the most effective advertising).

Perhaps because women had been taking classes on campus since 1907, the students seemed more open to women working in the church than they had in the past. They heard reports "on the scope of women's work in Old Testament times, New Testament times, in the mission field, and in the southern Presbyterian church,"[213] and they unanimously voted that a "Woman's Auxiliary is a valuable adjunct to the Church." The students heard portents of the future on February 8, 1915, when four students gave reports on "the present European War" (no vote was taken). The war in Europe had been going on for nearly seven months, and it would be about two years before the United States declared war on Germany. The last meeting of the Givens B. Strickler Society was January 22, 1917, three months before Congress passed the war declaration on April 6. There were no more debates until after the armistice. After the war, formal debating resumed for at least three years. Students held a referendum during the League of Nations debate in 1919 and unanimously supported the League.[214]

Student costs in Richmond were generally comparable with what students paid when the campus was at Hampden-Sydney; Presbyterians had always believed that educating their ministers was the responsibility of the entire church. No tuition or rent was ever charged during this period. The only charges were an annual fee of $5 (to be paid at the opening of each session), food ($7–12 a month until World War I, $14 a month until 1930), and textbooks (which were subsidized).

In 1906 the faculty requested that the board issue a statement explicitly opposing student marriages. The board, however, would only institute a policy to withdraw financial aid if a student married without his presbytery's approval.[215] The wider church recognized the changes in society and presbyteries were more than willing to approve student marriages. Hanover Presbytery, for example, had a called meeting on December 18, 1916, and gave a candidate permission to marry during his senior year. Union finally had to acknowledge the fact that some students were married; the availability of married housing for thirteen families (apartments in Samuel Davies and Francis Makemie Halls) was advertised as available for the first time in 1916. Married students paid rent on a sliding scale depending upon student income (usually from a part-time job—almost always in a church, presbytery support, or even the wife's employment).[216]

World War I

As it did the rest of the country, World War I changed life at Union. When war was declared, 9 students dropped out to join, and 95 alumni served in the armed forces. Union men usually served in ambulance units and as chaplains; 16 renounced their ordination and served in infantry companies and artillery batteries.[217] Lieutenant Lee Tait, Co. E., 354th Infantry, intended member of the Class of 1919, died on November 13, 1918, of wounds received in action on November 2. The veterans on campus established an American Legion Post (No. 91) in 1920 and named it in his honor.[218]

The feeling of a common enemy gave the South a more national outlook. Drawing on memories of Reconstruction, there were articles in the *Union Seminary Review* about how the PCUS could assist in the reconstruction of Europe and the reintegration of veterans back into civilian society.[219] The war made the United States a creditor nation for the first time in history and brought a new level of prosperity to the entire country. Americans were also becoming used to modern conveniences; after the war, there were no more warnings about standing in the bathtub while turning on the electric light and no more pleas to use the cuspidors. Instead, telephone procedures are explained; the first telephone was installed in 1920.

> The telephone is in a booth under the steps on the first floor of Richmond Hall. The number is Boulevard 611. It is there for the convenience of the students. The students take turns in being responsible for answering the telephone, two students living in the dormitories being on duty each day. On every day except Monday, the hours for which they are responsible are from dinner till 8:30 P.M. On Monday they are on duty all day. Those on duty may divide the time between them as they see fit, and they are expected to get someone to take their place if they cannot act that particular day.

Missions continued and even expanded after the war. In the 1921–22 Student Handbook, "City Mission Work" was still under the supervision of the Society of Missionary Inquiry, and each student was expected to participate in one mission. The missions that year were the Seventeenth Street Colored Mission, City Jail, State Penitentiary, Laurel Reform School, Street Preaching, Factory Work, Beaumont Farm, Pine Camp and West Brook (juvenile reformatories), Bon Air (new church), and the Soldiers' Home. In addition, seniors still preached on Wednesday nights, and all students were assigned preaching duties on Sunday night.[220]

But modernity took time to seep into the culture. E. T. Thompson remembers that, as late as the 1920s, some students continued to walk three or four miles to their mission appointments rather than ride the trolley on the Sabbath.[221]

The athletic association was formed in 1905, and the big sports were football, basketball, baseball, and tennis. Before World War I the games were mostly intramural or against teams in the immediate neighborhood.[222] After World War I, however, Union teams began to travel, and they were not usually a threat. Football was a sometime proposition; teams were not fielded every year. Randolph-Macon, William & Mary, and Hampden-Sydney College regularly beat the seminarians in football, but Union did defeat Randolph-Macon once. Basketball was little better, only defeating the churches on the schedule and always getting thrashed by college and athletic club teams. Baseball teams were lucky to be above .500, but tennis dominated in 1922 (the only year it did so), defeating both the University of Richmond and William and Mary. T. H. Spence and E. A. Woods won the cup in the Middle Atlantic Intercollegiate Doubles Tournament.[223]

Missions and sports were not the only extracurricular activities. The seminary had a Glee Club (which included ATS students) for about half the years between 1898 and 1926. They were in demand throughout the school year at churches and "evangelistic events" in Virginia and North Carolina. In the 1920s, ATS and UTS students alternated in hosting a monthly "shindig." Union and ATS students also invited each other to their respective dining halls on a regular basis, events eagerly anticipated and wonderfully recollected.[224] Union and ATS students also regularly put on skits and plays.

As personal income grew and durable consumer goods came within the reach of more people in the 1920s, students acquired cars and could drive them on campus. Automobiles are mentioned for the first time in 1926. The present walkways around the quad were originally designed as carriage paths (with the stable and a laundry in the middle of the quad).

> The Seminary has been able to provide a limited number of stalls on the Sunnyside tract for automobiles. These are under the supervision of Mr. Leland N. Edmunds, Assistant Sub-Intendent, to whom application should be made for their use. The charge is $1.00 per month.
>
> Under no circumstances is it permissible to park cars constantly on the campus. Care should be taken, even when parking temporarily, not to interfere with free passage to and from the buildings, nor to encroach on the lawns.
>
> The roads are also used as foot paths, and being narrow and curved, should be used by automobilists with usual caution. This applies with special emphasis at the corners of buildings.
>
> To avoid noise and danger and to protect the privacy of their homes, families of the professors would appreciate it if automobilists would not use the private roads between their houses.
>
> The garage floor is drained into the sewer. Sewers will not convey either mud or grease. The cost of a new sewer the past summer was as much as the combined charges for all the stalls for a session. Crank cases must not be emptied into the drain.[225]

There was an atmosphere of receptivity to new ideas after the war. Besides the traditional five subjects, English Bible and Religious Education now had endowed chairs. After W. T. Thompson became the professor of religious education in 1920, some of the older members of the faculty were a little fearful that his "emphasis" on psychology might lead to a depreciation of the work of the Holy Spirit.[226]

But new ideas came to campus anyway. Bill Oglesby tells the story about his uncle Stuart's dissertation defense.

> My father's twin brother, the late Stuart R. Oglesby, was the first student to take a doctoral degree under the direction of W. T. Thompson. His doctoral dissertation was entitled "Jesus and the New Psychology." Since we do not use the term "new psychology" any more, let me remind us that it referred to the psychology of Freud, Jung, Adler, and others as differentiated from experimental psychology, which dealt with laboratory devices, learning curves, and reflex arcs. Freud was little known from a firsthand perspective in many theological circles, and the impression was widely noised abroad that his therapeutic methods were atheistically based and that he was obsessed with sex. In either event, and others that now seem fairly irrelevant, a doctoral dissertation at UTS making use of Freudian concepts and relating them to Jesus or vice-versa was suspect on its face; moreover, the professor who had approved the subject and the process was also suspect. The story goes, probably somewhat apocryphal, that when my uncle was asked the first question by a member of the faculty, Dr. Thompson asked permission to clarify some implications of the question; and thereupon began a debate between Dr. Thompson and the faculty in which he "defended" his field over considerable time. As the story concludes, the faculty, being somewhat satisfied that Dr. Thompson had acquitted himself well, turned to Stuart and said, in effect, "Oh, yes, Mr. Oglesby, your examination is sustained!"[227]

The 1925–26 school year was a watershed for the curriculum: a wide variety of electives were offered for the first time. The core curriculum had always been thought sufficient for the training of a Presbyterian minister. Ministers were now, however, looked upon as professionals, and specialists should be able not only to preach but also to manage a church by organizing a Sunday school and counseling parishioners. Electives were the way to make them more "expert."

The faculty was intentional in designing electives that would "hold as closely as possible to the 'major disciplines' of our historic and standard theological training, and at the same time to fit men according to their varying talents for the much more diverse fields of Gospel service now calling for our young ministers." The 1925–26 Catalogue lists thirty-two electives. Although the emphasis was on Bible and theology courses, some of these subjects were unimaginable just a decade before:

Intertestament[al] History and Literature
Biblical Theology of the New Testament
Rise of Modern Religious Ideas
The Missionary Teachings of the Bible
The History of Missions
The Religions of Mankind
Methods and Problems of Mission Work
Psychology of Religion
The Preacher's Use of His Materials

The Country Church and Rural Religious Conditions
The Country Church and Methods of Efficiency
The Training of the Speaking Voice
The Delivery of the Sermon
Church Music

With all these program and curricular changes, and with the arguments over "higher criticism" and evolution raging in the culture (such as the Scopes "Monkey Trial" in 1925), President Moore thought it was necessary to assure the church that no matter how progressive its methods, Union was still conservative. For the first time in its history, Union had to state the centrality of Scripture in its educational philosophy. The 1925–26 Catalogue assures the reader, "The Bible is the center of the whole curriculum at Union, and there is no theological seminary or Bible school or training school where the Bible is more honored and where the students are required to study it more diligently."[228]

Reminiscences from this era stress the closeness of the community on the quad and the lifelong friendships formed. Yet "we had our problems." Gus Summers remembers that the faculty encouraged students to be single. At a time when the average American male was married at twenty-four years of age and seminary students were expected to be examples of virtue, life could be lonely. One student was found to be gay. "Most of us had never heard of such," Summers recalls, but "Dr. Tolly Thompson had knowledge about it" and helped the student transfer to another seminary. Gus Summers also recalls another student who claimed to be from Canada, to possess MD and DDS degrees from the University of Toronto plus an MDS from the University of Edinburgh, and to have attended Gordon Bible College in Boston. This student was popular on campus; he "wowed us with stories of his adventures in the Canadian wilds." He was licensed by the Cherokee Presbytery in 1923; but in 1925 during the call process to a church in Oklahoma, it was discovered that he actually had no degrees at all.[229] He was never ordained, and the General Catalogue lists him as a "public speaker, naturalist, and explorer."

Alumni

Walter W. Moore could look on Union's alumni since the Removal with pride. Between 1898 and 1926, he saw 2,762 students pass through Watts Hall (with a 3 percent dropout rate), and 95 percent of all graduates served at least one church. The PCUS mission field was dominated by 101 graduates who served in China (27), Korea (19), Congo and other parts of central Africa (13), Brazil (12), Japan (11), Mexico and Central America (8), Cuba (4), Persia (2), Home Missions (1), Indian Territory (1), and Argentina (1). "Union Men" were well represented at the PCUS General Assembly and synods; eleven were elected as moderators of the General Assembly, and numerous alumni served as synod executives, superintendents of mission work, and directors of religious education.

Besides the local parish, Union's biggest influence was on education. During this period, 45 alumni taught at the high school level, 6 served as principals, 11 were college presidents, including Edgar Gammon (BD, 1911), president of

Hampden-Sydney College from 1939 to 1955; and G. T. Gillespie (BD, 1911), president of Bellhaven College, Jackson, Mississippi, from 1921 to 1954. Serving as professors at colleges across the South were 43 graduates. Daniel Freeman (BD, 1924) was superintendent of Mountain Orphanage, Asheville, North Carolina; and William Smith (BD, 1924) was superintendent of Grandfather Orphanage, Banner Elk, North Carolina. At least 3 became prison chaplains, and 2 were directors of mental health clinics and mental health organizations.

Over 50 graduates went into other occupations after serving a church. John Leighton Stuart (Hampden-Sydney, 1896; UTS BD, 1902), was a missionary in China, the president of Yenching University, Beijing, from 1919 to 1946, and was the last U.S. ambassador to China (1946–49). Richard Dodge (BD, 1913) served as parole superintendent for the state of Florida; and Matt Grey (BD, 1914—who was a superintendent of the Seventeenth Street Mission) was superintendent of public welfare for Mecklenburg County, Virginia, for many years. Of the students who graduated during this time, 41 transferred to the northern church, 7 Northerners transferred to the PCUS, and 6 went back and forth. Two alumni transferred to the Congregational Church, two became Roman Catholic priests, two transferred to the PCA, and one transferred to the United Church of Canada.

A New Era

Times had changed. As the 1925–26 school year opened, the campus was complete: the buildings around the quad were set, the graduate school was established, "practical" education (in the form of local missions, Christian Education, and Sociology) was ensconced in the curriculum, electives were offered, the library was first-rate, both modern culture and fundamentalism were being challenged, and—perhaps most important—the traditional curriculum was untouched. But there was one more change.

At the annual meeting of the board of trustees in commencement week of May 1926, Dr. W. W. Moore presented his resignation as president. The board felt constrained, with keen regret and intense sorrow, to accept Dr. Moore's resignation because of the critical state of his health and the desire of the board to prolong his life by lifting every possible burden from him. Dr. Moore consented to remain with the seminary as president emeritus and lecturer on Old Testament literature. But on June 14 the board, faculty, students, and friends of the seminary were bereaved, and the entire church was saddened by his death. At that board meeting in May 1926, the Rev. Benjamin Rice Lacy Jr., DD, was unanimously elected Dr. Moore's successor as president of the seminary.[230]

The future was unfolding in other areas as well. Lingle resigned his chair in 1923, and Ernest Trice Thompson succeeded him in 1925. A new era was beginning.

J. Gray McAllister (BD, 1901), Walter W. Moore's biographer, called him the "First President and Second Founder" of Union Theological Seminary.[231] This is an accurate description of Moore's impact on Union and theological education in the United States. Under President Moore's leadership, the campus moved from rural Hampden Sydney to Richmond. The original buildings cost $155,000.[232] By 1926 the campus was valued at $1,260,000 (including 10 more buildings and the Westwood tract). The faculty increased from 5 to 8; the endowment quadrupled from $309,000 in 1898 to $1,218,672; and enrollment increased from 56 in 1882 to 127 by 1926.[233] In 1898 the library held 16,000 bound volumes and 5,000 pamphlets; by 1926 the collection held over 32,000 bound volumes and 10,000 pamphlets.[234] Walter W. Moore had indeed recreated Union Theological Seminary.

The Threads of History

When Walter W. Moore moved the campus to Richmond, an educated minister was one who was indoctrinated into southern Calvinism. When he died, Union saw itself as educating students in a wide range of disciplines and aware of other points of view, albeit still upholding the southern Calvinist tradition centered on a specific understanding of Scripture. Nevertheless, Moore established a course in Christian Sociology, a Department of Christian Education, chairs in Church History and Polity (the John Q. Dickinson chair) and Christian Missions (the F. S. Royster chair), the Sprunt Lecture Series, and the graduate program.[235] By expanding course offerings (while maintaining the primacy of the traditional subjects), President Moore redefined the minister from that of a solo country pastor to an executive—the head of an organization that would be a force in the community. The modern pastor would have to understand business methods, maintain church records, attract members, develop leaders, organize Sunday schools, and run youth organizations. And then preach an interesting, insightful, and inspiring sermon on Sunday in a worship service with beautiful music.

Union remained a resolutely "southern" institution. At the same time, however, there is no denying that as the school moved to Richmond, it began to enter a wider theological conversation. The nationwide reputation of the Sprunt Lecture series and the influence of the *Union Seminary Review* gave Walter W. Moore's southern school a national impact. As a result of local missions, students began to question, if not challenge, the doctrine of the spirituality of the church through the relationships they made outside of campus.

Instead of retreating from the world, as Dabney had counseled, President Moore engaged the new world of the professional. Union's elective offerings and graduate program embodied his vision for the future of seminary education. Moreover, he made sure that independent fund-raising would ensure Union's preeminence despite the inability of presbyteries and synods to comprehend the resources required by modern theological education.[236]

As a consequence of the Removal, Union students faced the tension between reform and the status quo head-on. As they participated in local missions, they faced the implications of urbanization, segregation, and mass communications while their church tried to turn away. More important, by supporting ATS, Walter W. Moore and Union Seminary advocated for women in church leadership when most Presbyterians denied that women had any capacity for management of the church or in business.

Throughout this period, Union alumni had a huge impact on the denomination and American theological education. By instituting chairs in Religious

Education and Christian Sociology, UTS was ahead of its time and ministering in innovative ways to a newly industrializing and urbanizing South. Walter Lingle's course in Christian Sociology was the first in any PCUS seminary. The Union alumni who taught in colleges, universities, and seminaries throughout the South left their leavening influence for the next generation. As graduates served on denominational boards and religious newspapers, and became involved in politics, Union stood squarely for the eight-hour day, against child labor, and for the reform of society.

In 1914, President Moore published an interesting little book titled *Appreciations*. Intended as a retrospective for the centennial, this little book contains short biographies of important ministers in the history of the PCUS and his centennial oration, "The First Fifty Years of Union Seminary." In summing up Union's history, he identifies three things necessary for a successful seminary: suitable location, a pecuniary base, and qualified professors who enjoy the confidence of the church.[237] By these three measures, Moore's tenure was a success.

Yet the thread that runs through *Appreciations* is innovation. President Moore was not afraid to meet challenges and borrow ideas. His goal was to keep Union up to date. Pioneering courses, the introduction of electives, the stress on practical education, and modern buildings were really just a means to an end: to prepare ministers for the local parish. Moses Hoge taught about 30 students; John Holt Rice taught 40. From 1812 to 1926, students passing through Union's classrooms numbered 2,103. Walter Moore taught 1,399 of those students.

The Removal made Union a modern seminary. Yet Walter W. Moore did more than just build buildings. He transformed how the seminary and its students saw themselves. Now Union was not just a place to conjugate verbs or learn how to preach: the seminary also became an incubator for applying faith to life, and it would teach students how to make an impact on society through their witness to Jesus Christ. On the twenty-fifth anniversary of the Removal, Robert Campbell Fishburne concluded his speech by observing:

> But great endowments, handsome buildings, and books without end do not in themselves make an institution great. Nor does an increase in the number of professors and students necessarily imply a better seminary. Bigness and greatness are not synonymous. The acid test is found in the character and efficiency of the living product turned out by the institution.[238]

Chapter Seven (1927–46)
A First-Class Seminary

Just as Walter W. Moore brought Union Seminary out of the nineteenth century by relocating the campus and instituting innovative ideas, his successor Benjamin Rice Lacy put Union at the forefront of twentieth-century theological education. Through the Depression and World War II, he prepared Presbyterian ministers to meet the needs of a changing South, a consumer culture, and a more democratic society. On campus, he intentionally sought specialized faculty (even from outside the South), emphasized graduate studies, and began to break the barrier of segregation. Lacy made Union a force in the wider theological conversation by supporting the journal *Interpretation*; he encouraged international faculty and student exchanges and defended professors who criticized the cultural status quo. Under his leadership and in the tradition of Walter W. Moore, Union became the center of the biblical theology movement, which advocated studying the Bible as a whole, rejecting both the clinical skepticism of the historical-critical method and the unquestioning biases of inerrant literalism. In the process, Union Theological Seminary led the PCUS away from the bitter conservatism of the past.

Toward a National Seminary

A native of Raleigh, North Carolina, Benjamin Rice Lacy (BD, 1913) was born in 1886, three years after Walter Moore arrived in Hampden Sydney. He had solid roots in Union's history. John Holt Rice was his paternal great-uncle. Lacy graduated from Davidson in 1906, was selected as a Rhodes Scholar, and graduated from Oxford in 1910. During his time at Union, he became known for his affable manner and sharp mind. He impressed Moore; upon graduation he was awarded a Moses Hoge Fellowship and spent an extra year on campus.

After his year of graduate work, Lacy served as an assistant pastor at First Church, Raleigh, for a year; then he pastored a multichurch field in rural North Carolina for two years, until war was declared. In 1917 he was commissioned as an army chaplain and served in the 113th Field Artillery Regiment of the 30th Division. He became known as "The Fighting Parson" and earned several battlefield decorations for actions on September 14, 1918, near Thiacourt, France, and on September 26, 1918, at Bois du Avocourt. In these two battles, Captain Lacy saw wounded soldiers exposed to enemy fire, left his position, and dragged them back to safety. At Thiacourt, while being targeted by snipers, he directed artillery fire on German positions when the forward observer was wounded.

23. Benjamin Rice Lacy, president, 1926–56

After leaving the army in 1919, he pastored Central Presbyterian in Atlanta. With Moore's assent, the board called Lacy as vice president in 1925.[1] Moore resigned as president in May 1926, and the board elected Lacy as the second president of Union Theological Seminary in Virginia. Moore passed away less than a month later. Just as John Holt Rice's inaugural speech set Union's course in the nineteenth century, President Lacy's inaugural laid out his plans to make Union a leading national seminary in the twentieth.

His ideas on theological education had two immediate sources. First, in 1920 the Interchurch World Movement of North America surveyed the major denominational seminaries in the United States and Canada, as part of a larger report on the general state of the church. The authors concluded that seminaries were underfunded and unprofessional. A seminary education, they argued, should be on par with those of other professions and provide graduate-level programs equal to that of any university.[2]

Second, the Institute of Social and Religious Research published a three-year study in 1924. In this groundbreaking work, Robert Kelly compared 161 theological schools in North America, including Union. His conclusions were scathing: "The machinery and the methods used in educating Protestant ministers were inadequate."[3] American seminaries neglected religious education, the psychology of religion, social service, and "clinical work." Prerequisites for admissions were not on par with other graduate schools, and most seminaries did not provide opportunities for continuing education.

Most seminaries, Kelly observed, claimed that their programs were conducted at the level of a university professional school, but they were deluding themselves. Seminaries tended to be isolated from the broader contemporary intellectual debate, shackled by confessional theology, and using outmoded forms of pedagogy. Seminary faculty were generalists, who often preached, lectured, or pastored as well as taught, and this took time away from research. More specialization was needed if seminary education and research were to be respected in modern scholarship and the value of seminary education recognized by the academy.

Kelly applauded the introduction of electives because they represented an engagement with "the expanding worlds of knowledge," but he saw many parts of the seminary curriculum as hopelessly outmoded. Although he may not have called for an outright removal of biblical languages from the general seminary curriculum, it is clear that he thought those languages were for the specialist, not for the pastor. Moreover, he concluded, seminaries failed their students by not offering structured fieldwork. Just as medical students worked as interns under experienced doctors, so student pastors should have the chance to learn under more experienced ministers.[4]

President Lacy used the conclusions of both studies as a road map. He began his inaugural address by restating Kelly's primary argument: seminary education must be equal to other professional schools. As such, Union graduates had to understand the tandem challenges to modern faith. First, biblical criticism had weakened the authority of the ministry. Second, psychology seemed to make faith irrelevant by explaining away miracles and reducing the need for God to no more than an emotional crutch. Just as Rice wanted to counter deism and revivalism, he saw the job of Union Seminary as answering the more extreme conclusions of the historical-critical method and the modern psychological view of human beings in relation to God.

President Lacy declared that Union could only become "a first-class seminary" and combat modern skepticism by emphasizing research and producing books equal in scholarship to "more liberal centers." He announced that Union would do away with one-size-fits-all education by offering more electives. Lacy also intended to initiate a program of continuing education. Union would be a graduate school with quality graduate standards, specialized (and more) faculty, and a library second to none. In the past, he observed, the minister was the best-educated man in town. But twentieth-century mass media disseminated ideas that questioned "the soundness of the preacher's scholarship." There were, therefore, three areas Union Seminary must address to provide the graduate education that the modern church required: fund-raising, facilities, and faculty.[5]

The Walter W. Moore Memorial Fund

Just as John Holt Rice had raised his own funds to build the seminary, and Moore had raised his own money to move from Hampden Sydney to Richmond, so President Lacy immediately initiated a fund-raising campaign to enlarge facilities, hire more faculty, and promote research. Within months of his inauguration, the seminary published a booklet (48 pages on thick parchment-like paper) titled *Walter W. Moore and Union Seminary*. The first half of the book is Moore's biography, and the last half is a prospectus initiating the campaign to raise $1.12 million for the Walter W. Moore Memorial Fund. Although the seminary had consistently announced its independence from the PCUS General Assembly in every catalogue since 1886, the Walter W. Moore Memorial Fund was a concrete statement of autonomy. As the first systematic attempt at public fund-raising, the Memorial Fund would give President Lacy the resources to implement changes in the curriculum and faculty without depending on General Assembly support.

The pages of *Walter W. Moore and Union Seminary* envision a "great theological university" with a minimum enrollment of two hundred, and (using common facilities with ATS) providing study space and housing for first-degree students, graduate students, and ministers and missionaries on sabbatical. The Westwood tract was the centerpiece of this dream. Administration and classroom buildings would remain around the quad, as would the old dormitories and faculty housing, and ATS would remain in its location. The Westwood tract, however, would contain an athletic field, new dorms, a new dining hall, a spacious gym, and a huge library.[6] This library, managed by a professional librarian, was vital if Union was going to be a renowned research institution. The map of the new campus and the renderings of the new buildings show that Union no longer saw itself exclusively as the guardian of a provincial tradition, but a participant in and shaper of the modern theological conversation.

A more specialized faculty was critical to this vision. For President Lacy, the doubts sown by biblical criticism could not be challenged by ignoring modern scholarship or retreating into a fundamentalist-inspired cocoon. Rather, he advocated that Union acquire research-level professors to train ministers who could explain and apply orthodox Presbyterianism to the modern world. He reported that while UTS had 8 professors for 148 students, Princeton had 15 for 222, and the Nanking Seminary in China had 14 for 129. Since "Union Theological Seminary is the most important institution in our Church,"[7] the seminary needed more professors to give students the tools to confront the culture. "We have to admit," he declared, "that for many a decade our beloved church has produced few books of real learning and scholarship which have affected the currents of religious thought outside of our own communion."[8] John Holt Rice wanted to combat "German scholarship," and Walter W. Moore's successor now took hold of his dream; the church required highly trained scholars to maintain its credibility.

The dream would be deferred, however; the Walter W. Moore Memorial Fund campaign was a disaster. Due to the Black Friday stock-market crash about eighteen months after the campaign's launch, only 15 percent of the goal was met.[9] President Lacy, however, was undeterred. While facilities and faculty needed money that just was not there, Union could offer professional courses without straining available resources. Although classes in "Hospital Work" (called Pastoral Care in the 1950s) were not formally instituted until 1946, he encouraged the Society of Missionary Inquiry to include hospital visitation as

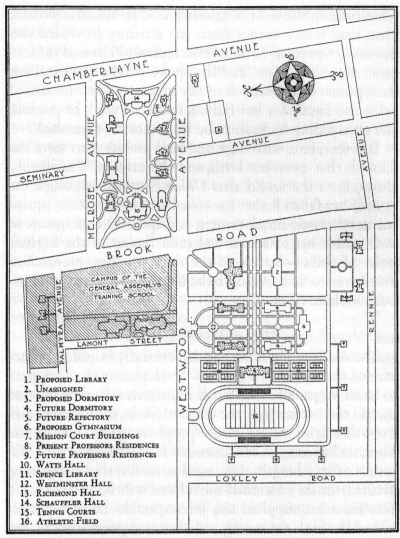

1. Proposed Library
2. Unassigned
3. Proposed Dormitory
4. Future Dormitory
5. Future Refectory
6. Proposed Gymnasium
7. Mission Court Buildings
8. Present Professors Residences
9. Future Professors Residences
10. Watts Hall
11. Spence Library
12. Westminster Hall
13. Richmond Hall
14. Schauffler Hall
15. Tennis Courts
16. Athletic Field

Drawing showing the Proposed Development of the "Westwood" tract and its relation to the existing Seminary buildings, the Assembly Training School and Mission Court

24. Moore Campaign: Proposed campus development

Proposed Latta Hall

THE SECOND STEP

25. Moore Campaign: Proposed dormitory, Latta Hall

Proposed Gymnasium

26. Moore Campaign: Proposed gymnasium

Proposed Library

27. Moore Campaign: Proposed library

a local mission offering as early as 1928. Moreover, he kept as many electives as possible in the curriculum and supported William T. "Tolly" Thompson's efforts to expand offerings in religious education—from one class in the senior year to a yearlong sequence in the junior year by 1935.

President Lacy also expanded the seminary's intellectual horizons beyond traditional southern Calvinism through established programs. He invited prominent scholars (who did not always hold views compatible with southern Presbyterians) to give the Sprunt Lectures, teach elective and January courses, and give the occasional "Special Address." "Sprunts" were always covered by the local press, yet not always in a favorable light. In 1930, the Rev. R. F. Campbell argued against the popular notion of biblical infallibility. He maintained that "the guidance the Bible gives is not like that of a map; no mere man has ever found in it infallible guidance in every detail of faith and duty. . . . The guiding principles are there and are infallible principles. But principles must be interpreted and applied by the reason and moral nature."[10] The *Richmond Times-Dispatch* could only shake its editorial head.

In 1935 the *Richmond News Leader* applauded Union for inviting Karl Heim, "the greatest living representative of the Tübingen school of religious thought," to give the Sprunt Lectures. "The seminary has honored Virginia by bringing Dr. Heim to our state and has conferred high privilege on Richmond by opening to the public the chapel where he is to speak Sunday and daily thereafter for a week." Heim titled his lectures "The Church of Christ and the Problems of the Day." The *News Leader* was laudatory: "Thoughtful persons, especially those who are interested in current trends in religion, scarcely realize what opportunities are offered them by this scholarly institution."[11] Some of the "Special Addresses" of this period were "Christianity and Social Problems," "The Work of Our Church among the Negroes,"[12] and "Youth in War-Torn China."[13]

Accreditation

Although President Lacy did not have the money to construct buildings or hire new faculty, he could begin to influence a change in attitude demanded by the Great War. After the Treaty of Versailles, the European powers were exhausted: their colonies began to demand independence, Marxism was on the rise, and the United States emerged as the dominant economic power. World War I had destroyed confidence in the civilization that spawned the slaughter of the trenches, and the new emphasis on "scientific" analysis led people to question faith as they never had before. As Glenn T. Miller has argued, "The World War marked the beginning of a religious depression that would hold America in its grasp until the revival that followed the Second World War." In an effort to professionalize theological education, 53 theological schools of 15 denominations met at Harvard Divinity School in 1918 and founded the Conference of Theological Schools.

This conference sponsored or encouraged the seminary studies of 1920 and 1924. In 1934 the Institute of Social and Religious Research reexamined seminary education a decade after its previous study and found no improvements: American theological schools remained inferior. In the wake of the 1934 study, the schools belonging to the Conference of Theological Schools began formal discussions on ways to improve theological education. In 1936 they decided that the starting point for establishing the integrity of a seminary degree would be to enforce uniform requirements for curriculum, facilities, and faculty.[14] The conference changed its name to the American Association of Theological Schools (AATS) in 1934[15] and set standards for accreditation. President Lacy made sure that UTS was a founding member and would be part of the drive for high standards and common requirements.

During the previous two decades, the studies of theological education prompted reflection at all its levels. The PCUS General Assembly adopted AATS recommendations for admission. The 1936 Catalogue lists a "Proposed Minimum Pre-Seminary Curriculum" approved by the General Assembly, which was recommended by AATS. Reflecting the decline in religion majors, specific prerequisites were required for admission for the first time: at least one course in psychology and a natural science, two classes in the social sciences (economics, sociology, political science, or education), and a foreign language.[16] The 1936–37 Catalogue also included the first application form: a one-page postcard detachable from the last page of the book.

In 1938 the AATS granted accreditation to UTS. The AATS accreditation standards allowed "extraordinary" admissions, but the definition was initially vague. Union already admitted "extraordinary" students without a college degree, but with an entrance exam, as provided by the Book of Order. In later years, however, as AATS required stricter admissions for accreditation, Union would follow the national policies. From this point onward, it would be AATS, and not presbyteries or the synods, setting academic policies.[17]

Accreditation changed not only admissions but also the degree structure. The AATS recommended the BD degree as the first theological degree, with an option for a diploma or certificate for those who did not desire to take biblical languages; a ThM for the level of a master's degree, and a ThD degree (to be given by seminaries not affiliated with a university) for the doctoral degree.[18] President Lacy aligned Union's degrees with the national standards. The board recommended that the DD degree be converted to the ThD in 1929, "in keeping with the practice of other theological seminaries," and in 1945 the board allowed those holding the DD degree to exchange their diplomas for a ThD for five dollars.[19] There was one area, however, in which Union resisted. The AATS noted that many seminaries substituted electives in more contemporary subjects for "older studies such as biblical interpretation, church history, and theology." Union, however, kept the traditional curriculum intact.

Building a Specialized Faculty

The need for specialized faculty drove President Lacy. One of the conclusions of the 1934 study was that seminary education was inferior because seminary professors were not educated at a level comparable with other professional schools. While 89.1 percent of seminary faculty in America had a BA, only 62.6 percent had a BD, just 56.6 percent had an MA, and a mere 33.3 percent possessed a PhD. Moreover, the study reported, many professors in Presbyterian schools were prevented from research, which "appears to contradict Presbyterian doctrine or oppose any principles of Presbyterian government."[20]

President Lacy understood the issue all too well. He could look at Union's faculty and see the dearth of graduate degrees and even the lack of consensus on their desirability and usefulness. Throughout the nineteenth century, the seminary had only one PhD degree among its faculty: John Latimer, who arrived in 1884. Edward Mack, who joined the faculty in 1915, also had a PhD. Yet many in the church thought an advanced, specialized degree was superfluous, if not dangerous. Consequently, President Lacy had to be cautious in his pursuit of faculty; the fundamentalist-modernist controversy tearing apart the northern church cast suspicion on all scholarship outside the PCUS.

The fundamentalist-modernist controversy is usually associated with the 1920s and 1930s, but its roots lay in the late nineteenth century. While Dabney was leading the charge against James Woodrow in the PCUS in 1884–88, Charles Augustus Briggs was arguing for a new view of Scripture based on the historical-critical method. Briggs was appointed as professor of biblical theology at Union Theological Seminary in New York in 1891. In his inaugural address, "The Authority of Holy Scripture," he argued that Moses did not write the Pentateuch; Ezra did not write the book of Ezra, Chronicles, or Nehemiah; Jeremiah did not write 1 Kings or 2 Kings or Lamentations; David only wrote a few of the psalms; Solomon did not write the Song of Solomon or Ecclesiastes and wrote only a few lines of Proverbs; and Isaiah wrote less than half of the book of Isaiah. In the final analysis, the Scriptures were riddled with errors, and the doctrine of scriptural inerrancy taught at Princeton Theological Seminary "is a ghost of modern evangelicalism to frighten children." Moreover, the Westminster Confession was wrong: the Bible could not be used to create theological absolutes.

As might be expected, his speech provoked condemnation. The 1891 northern General Assembly vetoed Briggs's appointment, but the faculty of UTS (NY) refused to remove him, contending that his removal would violate "scholarly freedom." In October 1892, UTS (NY) withdrew from the denomination. After two heresy trials in New York Presbytery, the 1893 northern Presbyterian General Assembly declared Briggs guilty of heresy. He was stripped of his ordination but was later ordained as an Episcopal priest. For the next several years the northern church was rent by two major heresy trials.[21]

The PCUS watched the Briggs proceedings with dismay and not a little glee, but when the northern church ratified several modifications of the Westminster Confession of Faith in 1904, northern Presbyterianism became completely unacceptable to the South. As a result of the earlier James Woodrow case and the northern views on race, southern biblical scholarship would reject contemporary biblical scholarship as tainted by "northern" influences. When three ministers in the Presbytery of New York refused to assent to the virgin birth in 1909 but were ordained anyway, it made no difference that many in the northern church protested. Consequently, when the Federal Council of Churches was formed in 1908, there was no way the PCUS would join.

After World War I the northern Presbyterian church flirted with the idea of uniting with seventeen other denominations. After Harry Emerson Fosdick preached his famous sermon "Shall the Fundamentalists Win?" in 1921, the northern church split. Fosdick argued that those who accepted the findings of the historical-critical method were sincere Christians who only wanted to reconcile new discoveries in history, science, and religion with the Christian faith. He depicted fundamentalists as intolerant, refusing to deal with these new discoveries, and arbitrarily drawing the line as to what is off-limits in religious discussion. Fosdick proposed that different points of view could exist within the church, but only if conservatives allowed the different perspectives to coexist. The fight over church union was so bitter that J. Gresham Machen, New Testament professor at Princeton, eventually founded the Orthodox Presbyterian Church and Westminster Seminary in Philadelphia.

Throughout the 1920s and 1930s, Union Theological Seminary in Virginia was a bemused spectator. The Sprunt Lectures served as a pulpit for both sides: Machen (1920), William Jennings Bryan (1921, who used the Sprunt Lectures to begin his antievolution campaign), Francis L. Patton (1923, president emeritus of Princeton Seminary), Robert E. Speer (1925), Maitland Alexander (1926), John R. Mott (1938), and John Mackay (1939, president of Princeton Seminary)—all spoke on campus about the controversies raging in the North, while the PCUS congratulated itself on its calm orthodoxy.

Yet the southern church realized that their scholarship was not immune to controversy. In 1929, Herbert S. Turner (BD, 1917; DD, 1922), a pastor in Staunton, Virginia (and an able Old Testament scholar), published an article in the *Union Seminary Review* in which he pointed out that critical conclusions regarding Old Testament literature were now well established in scholarly circles. He proposed that capable, faithful scholarship should be able to "find a bridge between a sane and temperate criticism and a sane and liberal evangelicalism."[22] His article was bitterly resented by Dr. Mack, his former mentor. Turner had hoped to succeed Mack in the Old Testament chair, but his liberal views put the position out of reach. Moreover, many in the church and some on the board began to question the need for students to encounter new, potentially damaging ideas.[23]

With presbyteries having less to say about theological education, Union began to see itself differently. From just another denominational school training students for the traditional parish, President Lacy aspired to transform UTS into a top-level research institution, educating students to address the intellectual challenges of the twentieth century. A graduate program was necessary for the church's flagship seminary, and teaching graduates required specialized scholars, not generalists. As the Scholastic Committee recognized, "It is universally understood that men in the learned professions cannot keep abreast . . . without the inspiring and expansive influence of graduate contacts and studies."[24]

Union's graduate program was in demand from its inception. There was just one student enrolled in the graduate program in 1914 (the Moses D. Hoge Fellow). In 1917 (the first year of the formal graduate program), 25 students were enrolled, and in 1920 the first 3 DD degrees were awarded, as was the first ThM. By 1930 there were 51 students enrolled, then 106 in 1942, and 158 in 1947.[25] Graduate students changed the atmosphere on campus: Parts of the library were reserved for them (much to the dismay of some). Beginning in 1935, the Executive Committee wanted faculty and students to wear gowns at commencement exercises.[26]

As he was nurturing the graduate program, President Lacy was determined to break the "inbred" quality of the faculty and hire professors with earned doctorates trained at other universities and seminaries. Howard Tillman Kuist represented the first step in this direction. Called in 1938 (then accepting a call to Princeton Seminary in 1943), he received his BD from Biblical Seminary, New York, and his PhD from New York University. John Bright (BD, 1931), with his PhD from Johns Hopkins University, was called in 1940; Balmer Kelly (BD, 1939), with his PhD from Princeton, was called in 1943; and Donald G. Miller (BD from Biblical Seminary, New York), with his PhD from New York University, was called in 1944.[27] From now on, pastoral experience was no longer a prerequisite for teaching: a graduate degree was.

The calls of Kuist, Bright, Miller, and Kelly mark the beginning of modern biblical studies at Union.[28] President Lacy had wanted a professional faculty to "loosen the grip of doctrinal theology in favor of applying Biblical principles to ministry." He was really just following his mentor. Moore saw Union as conservative in theology but progressive in methods. Conservative, however, did not mean fundamentalist. James Mays has stated that while the Union he knew as a student was conservative, there was no hint of fundamentalism or inerrancy. John Bright's predecessor in the McCormick chair is said to have argued that Moses wrote the Pentateuch, claiming, "He could have, he would have, he did." That attitude was ending by the 1940s. The Bible was no longer seen as supporting a doctrinal system, but as a theological discipline in its own right.

The unique mix of Union graduates and "outsiders" began to form the distinctive theological outlook that would come to be known as "biblical theology." Howard Kuist and Donald Miller had a common background and made similar contributions to the character of the Biblical Department. They were both reared in the northern, classical evangelical tradition; both graduated from Biblical Seminary in New York and New York University. Biblical Seminary taught what was called "inductive biblical study." It was a way of setting aside questions of higher criticism on the one hand and the preoccupation about inerrancy on the other, in favor of examining the text itself.

The approach that Kuist and Miller brought to biblical study fit the paradigm President Lacy was fostering.[29] Balmer Kelly (BD, 1939; ThM, 1940) also fit into this school of thought. Born in 1914 at Wytheville, Virginia, Kelly was nurtured in the PCUS. Educated at King College, Bristol, TN, he taught fifth, sixth, and seventh grades (in one room) in Cripple Creek, Virginia, after college graduation. Although conditions were primitive, with no indoor plumbing, it was here that he fell in love with teaching. After one year, the school was consolidated, and he went to work as an antique dealer in Bristol. He decided to "try" seminary because he wanted to teach and chose Union because everyone he knew went there.[30]

After receiving his BD and ThM, Kelly returned to King College to teach from 1940 to 1941. President Lacy encouraged him to attend Princeton for doctoral study, which he did from 1941 to 1943. Then President Lacy invited him to return to Richmond to join the faculty and teach Old Testament, while John Bright was in the army. He finished his dissertation while in Richmond, earning his PhD in 1946. The president, however, kept him on the faculty when Bright returned from his army service, shifting Kelly to New Testament, and he served Union for thirty-four years (some of them as acting president), until he retired in 1977.

John Bright (BD, 1931) was Kelly's counterpoint. Born in 1909 in Chattanooga, Tennessee, Bright was also bred in the PCUS. He graduated from Presbyterian College (Clinton, S.C.) and Union, and then received his PhD from Johns Hopkins, where he studied under William Foxwell Albright. Bright approached the Old Testament texts on the basis of their history discovered through archaeology. The theme of his research was to show that the biblical books were grounded in and represented real history in a way that supported their authority as a witness to the faith.[31] Although he was called to Union in 1940, he served as an army chaplain in 1943–46, returning to teach Old Testament until his retirement in 1975.

The influence of Miller, Kelly, and Bright can hardly be overstated. Balmer Kelly and Donald Miller founded the journal *Interpretation* and were the first coeditors.[32] Bright wrote the groundbreaking *A History of Israel*. It was Kelly who developed the course in Biblical Theology. The class was originally designed as an introduction to the Bible, with an overview organized in a somewhat literary and topical way. The result was that students had two surveys of the Scripture: one from Bright, viewing the Bible as theological history; and one from Kelly, teaching "the theology of the Bible."[33] Kelly also edited the twenty-five-volume Laymen's Bible Commentary.

The hiring of faculty from outside the South had not been done since the 1830s, and faculty without congregational experience was unprecedented. From Howard Kuist onward, professors would have a PhD. President Lacy began to use fellowships to identify graduates who showed promise for scholarship and ensured that they received an excellent graduate education. For example, in 1933 John Bright's Walter Moore Fellowship allowed him to attend Johns Hopkins University, and President Lacy encouraged Balmer Kelly to attend Princeton.

The fact that he could identify promising students and give them support shows his power and influence. Indeed, in 1943 the president's report was included as part of the board's official minutes for the first time—signaling that the president would now play an integral part in board meetings. The president was not constrained by search committees or job descriptions. Rather, he had the confidence of the board to pursue the faculty he wanted. When he prepared to call Donald Miller, he read to the board a description of his "unusual ability." The board required nothing else, and Miller was hired.[34] The change in faculty was dramatic. Whereas Edward Mack was the only faculty member to hold a PhD at the end of the 1930s, the inaugural addresses listed in the 1940–41 Catalogue were given by John Bright, PhD (associate professor in the Biblical Department); John Thomas, PhD (theology); James Bear, ThM; and Howard Kuist, PhD.[35] This was the first time all the inaugurated professors had advanced academic degrees.

Even into the fourth decade of the twentieth century, however, Union professors were still generalists. E. T. Thompson is an excellent example of the traditional Union professor. After Thompson's one year in the pastorate, Moore asked Thompson to assist Theron Rice in teaching English Bible, due to Rice's poor health. Thompson only accepted Moore's invitation out of a sense of duty; he really wanted to be a pastor. Rice, however, died before the beginning of school, and Thompson became the English Bible professor by default. He found he enjoyed teaching and decided he wanted to stay. In May 1925, after three years of teaching English Bible, he was moved to the recently established John Q. Dickinson Chair in Church History without being told.[36] When the board appointed him to teach Church History, he originally thought of rejecting the job, but then he remembered that Union graduates never learned any theology but Dabney's Calvinism. He resolved to teach a history of doctrine so that students would know of theological developments after the Reformation and be able to apply their theology to ordinary life.[37]

Thompson changed the way students looked at history. They would no longer recite facts to buttress their heritage. Rather, the past actions of the church universal would inform current ethics. In the 1927–28 Catalogue, he stated that students in his American church history course would study the "attitude of the Church toward public wrongs."[38] But the Bible remained foundational. Although technically in the Church History Department, Thompson continued to teach courses on Acts, the Gospel of Mark, and Amos. James Mays remembers entering UTS as a student in 1946 and not thinking twice about E. T. Thompson teaching New Testament and Donald Miller teaching Revelation. "All faculty drew on Scriptural material as sources for instruction in their discipline."[39]

While his courses were naturally not courses in social justice and ethical responsibility, students throughout the years single out Thompson's innovative use of Scripture as one of their primary inspirations to work for change in the church and culture. His insights into applying biblical principles to life spurred his students to see their role in in an entirely new light. Thompson's expansive view of teaching, ministry, and the Christian life was what President Lacy wanted for Union. Walter Lingle (by teaching Christian Sociology) and Eugene Caldwell (who introduced the historical-critical method to New Testament studies) set the foundations. E. T. Thompson built on what Lingle and Caldwell began, fashioning a new way of thinking that destroyed the doctrine of the spirituality of the church.[40]

Whatever E. T. Thompson's impact, his call represented the ending of an era: he did not have an advanced degree. In his own inaugural, President Lacy had ruefully observed that "for many a decade our beloved Church has produced few books of real learning and scholarship." He then pledged that Union would devote the resources necessary "to develop young men who can do original study and produce great books." This "original" study, however, would entail asking potentially uncomfortable questions. If Union's faculty was to be on par with other professional schools, its members needed to be able to teach and conduct research without interference. In turn, the president would have to protect the faculty's independence.

Ernest Trice ("E. T.") Thompson (BD, 1920) arguably had more impact on southern Presbyterianism than anyone else in the twentieth century. Born in Texarkana, Texas, in 1895, he was the son of a Presbyterian minister. As a child living in West Virginia, he remembered seeing northern and southern Presbyterian churches virtually across the street from one another and wondering why there were two separate churches. He retained his irenic, ecumenical outlook throughout his life.

While a student in high school, he read *Christianity and the Social Crisis* by Walter Rauschenbusch. This book opened up new dimensions on how to live the Christian life and was a lifelong influence. After graduating from Hampden-Sydney in 1914, Thompson (inspired by Rauschenbusch) attended Columbia University to study sociology; he wanted to understand the world and how ministry related to it. His time in New York, however, confirmed his call to ministry; after graduating with an MA in 1915, Thompson entered Union with the intention of serving as a pastor.[41]

Union was a rude awakening for Thompson. Thomas Cary Johnson thought that Union graduates should know only one theology: a scholastic Calvinism that reinforced the spirituality of the church. When he entered Union in the fall of 1915, what struck him was the contrast between T. C. Johnson and Walter Lingle. As he remembers the scene, "[Johnson] taught Dr. Dabney's theology— just drilled it in us. He did not invite questions, did not teach us anything about any theological developments after the Westminster Confessions and the scholastic theologians, discouraged questions, [and] . . . just sort of said, 'My task is to teach you one theology, the right one.'"

In contrast, Lingle's Christian Sociology class prodded students to consider the social teachings of the prophets and Jesus. While some enthusiastically embraced the theology taught by Johnson, exposure to conditions in local missions caused others to become conscious of shortcomings in the church's

28. Ernest Trice Thompson taught English Bible, 1920–26; church history professor, 1926–64

theological outlook.[42] Influenced by Lingle, Thompson challenged his students to consider that the doctrine of the spirituality of the church was inadequate for the modern world. He also admired New Testament professor Eugene Caldwell. Caldwell was conservative yet concerned with what the Bible taught. He encouraged his students not to be dogmatic, but to think for themselves.

When war was declared in April 1917, Thompson dropped out (in his second year) and joined the army. Although he did not want to fight, he felt he could not speak to the men of his generation if he did not serve. He volunteered to become an ambulance driver and served several months, but then was ordained and commissioned as a chaplain. Thompson went to France, was attached to an artillery company, spent three months at the front, and then was assigned to a military hospital. The army exposed E.T. to parts of life he had never previously experienced, and he realized that faith was not just a scholastic exercise. The church could not just talk "at" people, but must talk "to" people.[43]

After his discharge he returned to Richmond and found a changed campus. Returning veterans refused pat answers, and Thompson would later recall that Thomas Cary Johnson's conservatism and orthodoxy, which had impressed students in the preceding decade, no longer commanded a following. For

Thompson, the reason was obvious. "The student body had changed and John-son had not."[44] He graduated in 1920 and began serving the Manhattan Pres-byterian Church in El Paso, Texas. After only fifteen months, President Moore called him to teach English Bible in 1922. He served as professor of English Bible from 1922 to 1925, and professor of church history from 1925 to 1964. Thompson was elected moderator of the Synod of Virginia in 1931 and 1940, moderator of the General Assembly in 1959, and served on numerous church boards. He wrote the three-volume *Presbyterians in the South*, the definitive his-tory of southern Presbyterianism, and was the author of numerous other books and articles. He was an editor of the *Presbyterian Standard*, *Presbyterian of the South*, and the *Presbyterian Outlook*.

When Thompson returned to campus to teach in 1922, Union was still encased in the amber of Robert Lewis Dabney. Robert McNeill (BD, 1942) remembers: "We were to preach on temperance but not prohibition, justice but not politics, greed but not economics, prejudice but not segregation." He remembers that by the late 1930s it was difficult to get classmates to volunteer for the Seventeenth Street Mission.[45] The historical-critical method was gain-ing acceptance around the country, but the PCUS and its seminaries remained bastions of conservatism. Dabney's *Syllabus* was still Union's primary theologi-cal textbook. It was first published in 1871 and went through six editions, the last one dated 1927.[46] Indeed, John Leith argues that theology at Union did not move away from Dabney until 1940, when James Porter Smith taught the sub-ject.[47] Smith, who succeeded Thomas Cary Johnson as professor of systematic theology in 1931, finally replaced Dabney as the primary text and used Augus-tus H. Strong, a thoroughgoing Calvinist, but a Baptist. From that time onward, students were exposed to a wider range of theological thought.[48]

Thompson began chipping away at Dabney's influence, recognizing the con-tinuum in southern church life between seminary and congregation. Scripture and the Shorter Catechism provided a common vocabulary in the PCUS. The aim of teaching theology at Union was not to stimulate theological speculation, but to train students to communicate the Christian faith in the tradition of the PCUS to ordinary people. Professors were very much aware that the seminary was an agent of the church to train ministers. They were preparing students for the parish, not for advanced theological study. Thus, until the 1950s, learning theology meant mastering one basic text (be it Turretin, Dabney, or Strong) as a ready reference for the minister to answer any question.[49] The price for sticking to one text, however, was an inability to articulate an ethical voice to confront the problems facing the church and society. Ernest Trice Thompson gave Union and the church that ethical voice.

Academic Freedom

In February 1924, at the age of twenty-nine, Thompson began to write a weekly essay on the International Sunday School Lessons for the *Presbyterian Standard* (continued later in the *Presbyterian of the South*). The choice of papers was ironic; the *Presbyterian Standard* was one of the most backward papers in the denomi-nation (Thompson admitted he had never read it when he accepted the job), but he enjoyed writing the lessons.[50] In fact, he loved writing Sunday school lessons so much that he wrote over 3,000 lessons, working into his nineties. He used these articles to introduce southern Presbyterians to biblical criticism and apply Scriptural ethics to social conditions in the South, particularly the race issue. This approach caused Thompson to become controversial. From Prohibition to the Scopes "Monkey Trial" in 1925, to the nationwide growth of the Ku Klux Klan, the 1920s was a tense time, when some people fought to keep modernism at bay even as life changed around them.[51]

Thompson was becoming known for his Sunday school lessons and was appointed book editor of the *Union Seminary Review* in 1930. As editor, he recommended books that brought southern Presbyterians into contact with a wider range of scholarship and ideas. In January 1931 he wrote an article in the *Review* titled "Is the Northern Church theologically sound?" His answer: "Our sister denomination is fundamentally sound in faith, and is just as likely to remain so as our own. . . . Differences of interpretation undoubtedly exist and some 'liberal' views. But they also exist in our own church, and will always exist."[52] Just as Walter Lingle was criticized for his conciliatory attitude toward the northern church a generation before, Thompson also faced condemnation for his positive attitude toward northern Presbyterians. This time, however, the censure came from outside the seminary, and it was the president who would protect him.

Thompson's article was widely read; besides the *Presbyterian Standard*, it was reprinted in the *Christian Observer*. John M. Wells (editor of the *Presbyterian Standard*, former moderator of the General Assembly, and former president of Columbia Seminary) wrote an editorial in late February questioning Thompson's orthodoxy. Thompson defended himself, and by the end of May it was all over. Although President Lacy had serious reservations about church union and the Federal Council of Churches, the president would not impose his beliefs and refused to muzzle or dismiss Thompson.[53] Nevertheless, the suspicion lingered that Thompson was unsound because he defended the northern church.[54]

The five-month-long public dispute with Wells, however, obscured an ongoing private correspondence between Thompson and William M. McPheeters that would cause the entire denomination to take sides. In December 1927, Thompson published a Sunday school lesson stating that some modern scholars viewed demonic possession as the biblical understanding of mental illness. McPheeters, a retired Old Testament professor at Columbia Seminary who opposed Thompson in the 1929 General Assembly debate on church union, fired off a letter to Thompson, objecting to Thompson's dismissal of the biblical depiction by saying it led people to question the literal interpretation of Scripture. Thompson disagreed, and nothing more was said. In February 1929 (in another Sunday school lesson), Thompson argued that "the human factor plays a part in the style, the language, the thought" of the Scriptures. McPheeters protested again and intimated that the rumors he had heard about Thompson teaching unorthodox, if not heretical, views in his classroom must be true. Letters between the two continued throughout the summer of 1929, with no resolution.

In the fall of 1929, Thompson wrote another Sunday school lesson (again questioning demon possession), and McPheeters complained to the editor of the *Presbyterian Standard*, James R. Bridges (1880). Bridges, however, took no formal action. In March 1931, as the public dispute with Wells was winding down, McPheeters realized that President Lacy and the Union board would take no action against Thompson for supporting reunion or questioning biblical inerrancy. Deciding to initiate action himself, McPheeters sent a seven-page single-spaced letter to President Lacy, detailing Thompson's supposed heretical views. When the president did nothing, McPheeters sent his letter to four board members, and they supported their professor with no reservation. McPheeters then circulated a memorial among Union alumni that characterized Thompson's teaching as "dishonoring to Christ, and suited to do irreparable harm" to the church. When President Lacy learned of the memorial, he wrote to the president of Columbia, asking him to intervene. McPheeters, however, refused to recant and even offered to surrender his Columbia Seminary pension. By May 1933, however, McPheeters (who was 78 and in declining health) was hospitalized, and most people hoped the controversy would just wither away.

At this point, Tom Glasgow (a nephew of McPheeters) asked the board to consider the memorial sent to alumni. Glasgow, a businessman and elder in Charlotte, North Carolina, was a well-known defender of "the older views of inspiration" and was "strenuously opposed to any approaches to union with the Presbyterian Church in the U.S.A.," as well as any social pronouncements by the church and membership in the Federal Council of Churches. President Lacy and the board, however, stuck by Thompson; on May 9, 1933, they declared him "sound in the faith and worthy of the confidence of the Church."[55]

The issue seemed to disappear. At the 1940 General Assembly, however, Glasgow led the fight to abolish the assembly's Permanent Committee on Moral and Social Welfare, of which Thompson was a member. He also asked the General Assembly to investigate what its seminaries were teaching. The General Assembly retained the Permanent Committee on Moral and Social Welfare and refused to investigate its seminaries. As a protest in August 1940, Glasgow mailed the pamphlet titled *Shall the Southern Presbyterian Church Abandon Its Historic Position? A Plea for Common Honesty; Exposing the Attack of Dr. Ernest Trice Thompson, of Union Theological Seminary, upon the Standards of the Presbyterian Church in the United States* to all PCUS ministers. He charged that Thompson "openly and actively supports doctrines and interpretations of Scripture which are foreign to our interpretation of the Faith" and called for his removal from teaching.[56]

The pamphlet reached ministers on the eve of the respective meetings of Synods of North Carolina and Virginia. But Glasgow's tactics backfired; there was a groundswell of support for "Dr. E.T." and Union. The Synod of North Carolina elected W. Taliaferro "Tolly" Thompson (Union's professor of Christian education) as its moderator and adopted resolutions deploring attacks on the character or orthodoxy of ministers and agencies of the church from pulpits or by pamphlets. It called upon those who had charges to pursue the orderly processes clearly set forth in the Book of Church Order. The Synod of Virginia adopted similar resolutions and, as a token of its confidence, elected Thompson as its moderator.

The Synod of West Virginia unanimously disapproved the character of the attack and directed that a letter be sent to Dr. Thompson expressing the synod's confidence in him. The Synod of Appalachia, the seminary's fourth supporting synod, referred the pamphlet to the seminary's board of trustees for appropriate consideration. More important, however, President Lacy opposed any effort to discipline any professor for his teaching, arguing that any such investigation should be made either by the boards of the institutions or by the presbyteries to which individual members of the faculty were responsible.[57]

Recognizing the need to clear his name, however, Thompson petitioned East Hanover Presbytery and the trustees to hear his case in September 1940. In late November, East Hanover vindicated him.[58] The Presbytery of East Hanover's report was circulated though the church, and Glasgow replied with a second pamphlet titled *Glasgow's Reply to the Report and Action of East Hanover Presbytery*. He dismissed the presbytery's conclusions as a whitewash and urged again that Thompson be dismissed. *Glasgow's Reply* had its intended effect; the pamphlet caused second thoughts in the denomination. Three presbyteries (Mecklenburg, Central Mississippi, and Roanoke) overtured the 1941 General Assembly to appoint a committee to investigate Thompson's teaching and report back to the assembly.[59] President Lacy defended his professor from the floor, and the General Assembly supported Thompson.[60]

Just as James Woodrow had been accused of supporting evolution against the inerrant view of Scripture in 1884, some fifty years later Glasgow accused Thompson of teaching the same error. While it might seem that nothing had changed, Thompson himself observed, "Freedom from the dead hand of the past, from the assumptions . . . that a theological professor must not teach anything contrary to the Standards of the Church or the traditional interpretation of those Standards, had been upheld."[61] As John Leith has pointed out, Thompson's exoneration by the presbytery was "of incalculable importance to the life of the denomination."[62] More important, though, President Lacy's defense of Thompson was a stand for academic freedom in a general sense, but also a statement that Union would be a genuine professional school unafraid to conduct research wherever it led and move beyond regional considerations.[63]

Library

In his inaugural, President Lacy argued that specialized faculty and a professionally run library were vital if Union was to become a research institution. The new president declared that only a minister "who has frankly and fearlessly faced the questions raised by criticism" could address the doubts raised by biblical criticism.[64] He could ensure that Union offer elective courses, protect academic freedom, and cultivate "homegrown" faculty because these actions did not cost money. But there was one expensive resource Union needed if it were to become a respected school, even in the Depression: a library.[65] For President Lacy, the library was the foundation of what he wanted to accomplish; without "a full-time librarian who would keep the library open for ten, perhaps eleven hours per day," there was no hope for attracting the best faculty and the brightest students.

Right after launching the Walter W. Moore Fund campaign in 1927, President Lacy asked Dr. Louis Rounds Wilson (the librarian of the University of

North Carolina) to evaluate the library for two days in November 1928 and two days in February 1929. There are no records as to the planning of the consulta-tion or how Wilson's services were secured. Wanting to support the drive for professionally run libraries, Wilson donated his services and asked reimburse-ment only for his expenses (which totaled less than $25 for each two-day trip, including hotel, meals, and travel). The chair of the Library Committee of the board of trustees paid the expenses himself.

Wilson submitted his fourteen-page report on February 20, 1929. He indi-cated that the building was adequate in size, but poorly equipped and orga-nized. One of the exhibits in the report is a drawing showing how the library can be reorganized. Wilson recommended a librarian's office and a circulation desk. He also observed that the stack room was poorly lit, needed painting, and was cluttered with museum cases and artifacts. Wilson advocated putting tables and chairs in the stack area and opening it up to students (heretofore restricted to one reading room only).

While saluting Dr. Johnson and diplomatically choosing his words, Wilson was criticizing Union's library as inadequate for a graduate research institu-tion. He made the case for a full-time professional librarian to institute a stan-dardized classification system, recatalogue the collection, and revise the reserve and circulation systems. Moreover, he emphasized, the librarian should acquire books that are reflective of the field, not the opinions of the professors. Presi-dent Lacy understood that Wilson's recommendations would require money, but with Wilson's report he could at least describe to the board and donors the kind of library Union required.

Thomas Cary Johnson, the librarian since 1905, took the report as a personal insult and criticized Wilson's report point by point in a long letter to the presi-dent. Where Wilson stressed the need to maintain current periodicals, Johnson replied that periodicals were superfluous: "The Librarian would err in judg-ment if he enticed students to read periodicals in the time needed for the mas-tering of daily assignments by their professors." Wilson recommended opening the stacks to students, but Johnson countered: "A great objection to the use of the stack room as a study for the students of the Seminary and Training School will be a considerable abuse of the books. . . . Look at the dog-eared books in the Reading Room now." Recataloguing would be a similar waste of time. He reported that students had been working on subject cataloguing since 1916. It would save money to stick with the system he instituted.

Johnson, however, did support employing a full-time librarian, but he insisted that his primary training should be in theology rather than library science. While some technical training would be advantageous, the librarian should be "a man of wide, deep [theological] reading. He should not make the Library as such his greatest end, or aim." Apparently President Lacy was inclined to Johnson's point of view and suggested hiring a Union graduate then engaged in doctoral work in Edinburgh. He asked Wilson if such a bright young man might not get enough "technical training" in the summer before starting as librarian in the fall. Wilson responded by urging the president to hire a techni-cally trained librarian. There is no documentation of the subsequent discussions between the president, faculty, and the Board of Trustees Library Committee. It is clear, however, that just as the Brown Library announced recovery from the

Civil War, hiring a librarian and constructing a new library would declare that Union had become a "first-class seminary."

Money for a new position was found just one year after Wilson submitted his report, and Henry M. Brimm was called as librarian in 1930. Although a ruling elder and the son of a Presbyterian minister, many eyebrows were raised when he was called because he was a layman; the first on the faculty. He was a graduate of Presbyterian College and held a BA in Library Science from Columbia University. He had worked in the Presbyterian College library (1923–25) before Columbia, and after graduation he was the assistant librarian at the University of South Carolina (1928–30).

In his first report to the board in 1931, Brimm listed the changes he had already instituted. In 1930, there was only one librarian and eight students who kept the library open 48 hours a week. He increased the operating hours to 66 hours a week and opened the stacks for student use and study. The collection numbered 42,240 volumes, with 171 registered borrowers, and 3,613 books circulated. Brimm, however, saw that the library could do more. He called for a new library building and proposed an extension service to mail resources to pastors. Brimm began writing articles in the *Union Seminary Review* and denominational papers, recommending books and inviting pastors to use the extension services. He was effective; from virtually no extension mailings in 1933, there were 2,000 in 1941.

Brimm's 1938 report to the board gives a glimpse of the future. He reported that the library was out of room (it held 62,000 volumes, including those stored in the basement of Richmond Hall) and gave another extended argument for a new building. Although the board was receptive, there was no money to proceed.[66] There was, however, unused money from the 1927 Walter W. Moore campaign. The board investigated and in 1939 found that the Latta bequest, which had been earmarked for dormitories in 1927, could be applied toward building a new library.[67] In 1940, Brimm finally put T. C. Johnson's cataloguing project to rest and, borrowing from Union Seminary in New York, reclassified the entire collection from the Library of Congress to the Pettee Classification System.[68] Julia Pettee, the chief cataloger of the Union Seminary (NY) library from 1909 to 1939, developed a unique classification system dedicated to theological books in the 1920s. By 1947 over fifty theological libraries in the United States adopted her classifications. Recognizing that Brimm was putting the library in the forefront of modern libraries, the board promoted him to faculty status.[69]

Between 1939 and 1943, Brimm designed a library addition and began construction by using the $100,000 bequest from Edward D. Latta of Asheville, plus $25,000 from Mary Stamps Royster of Norfolk, and $25,000 from Webster Rhoads of Richmond.[70] Despite the shortage of steel and other materials due to the war,[71] construction on the Latta addition began in 1943 and was completed in 1944. According to E. T. Thompson, the biggest change in the seminary in the twentieth century was the library. Before the 1930s, Watts Hall was the center of the campus, and the library was an afterthought. After 1944, the library became the nexus of campus life. With Brimm as the full-time librarian, the library was open 14 hours a day and became a natural meeting point, especially when it was air-conditioned in 1946. There was a new emphasis on research (with 75,000 volumes in 1944), and library usage increased as well; in 1930 circulation

29. Circulation desk, Latta Addition, early 1950s

was 13,012 volumes, with 620 borrowers; in 1948 it was 22,635 volumes, with 912 borrowers.[72]

The library addition was dedicated on May 8, 1944, and was heavily reported, taking up the entire front page of section IV of the *Times-Dispatch*. The story began with an account of Union's history, listing the first books and highlighting how Presbyterians had always stressed education. The library was seen as emblematic of the tradition of an educated ministry. The last quarter of the story contained an extensive description of the library itself.[73] The story ends with the dedicatory address by John Alexander MacKay, president of Princeton Theological Seminary.

MacKay's presence as the principal speaker at the Latta Extension's dedication was symbolic; something more than just the opening of a new building was going on. Union was now entering the ranks of top-flight research institutions. MacKay observed that graduates of both Princeton and Union shared the same heritage and were serving the same cause: Reformed Christianity. It was Reformed Christianity that took the lead in the War for Independence, but the Civil War rent their unanimity. The only way for American Presbyterianism to regain its influence, MacKay insisted, was for the two churches to reunite.[74]

Whereas Lingle lost his standing with Moore because he held favorable views concerning reunion and E. T. Thompson always believed that his accusers resented his positive attitudes toward the northern church,[75] MacKay's

30. Card catalogue, Latta Addition, early 1950s

31. Newspaper lounge, Latta Addition, early 1950s

32. Reference room, Latta Addition, early 1950s

comments advocating reunion were greeted with muted but enthusiastic support within the seminary community. The Latta Addition to the library was Union's mark that it was joining a wider world.

Union Seminary Review

The *Union Seminary Review* mirrored Union's increasing engagement with the contemporary theological conversation. While the *Review* continued to be published in Richmond, in "cooperation with the students and Faculty of Union Theological Seminary," by 1928 the masthead also claimed the assistance of the "professors in the Austin, Columbia, and Louisville Theological Seminaries, and in the General Assembly's Training School." The journal was one of the most important voices of southern Presbyterianism and the only quarterly theological journal in the Presbyterian South.

Although the *Review* tried to be more scholarly, it remained too conservative to be on the cutting edge of theological discussion and debate.[76] Indeed, the noted Christian educator Lewis J. Sherrill bemoaned the lack of scholarly activity in the southern Presbyterian church in his article "The Barrenness of the Southern Presbyterian Pen" (1931).[77] While the *Review* continued to be one of the most important voices of southern Presbyterians during the 1930s and 1940s, many of the articles were not written by PCUS ministers, but by ministers and educators of "sister churches" outside the South.[78]

The last decade of the *Review*, under the editorship of J. Gray McAllister (1932–46), is probably the most significant period in the publication's history.

Through the pages of the *Review*, the southern Presbyterian pen began to bear fruit, according to John H. Grey's "The Rediscovery of the Southern Pen" (1936).[79] That same year the *Review* published Ernest Trice Thompson's "Southern Presbyterians: What We Can Learn From the Past."[80] In 1942, Allen Cabaniss authored "Liturgy in the Southern Presbyterian Church,"[81] and Rachel Henderlite contributed "The Need for Theology in Religious Education"[82] in 1945.

Addressing the wider theological context, the *Review* published several noteworthy articles on neo-orthodoxy and the political situation in Germany. In 1935 a special issue devoted to "Dialectic Theology" contained Karl Barth's "Miserable Lazarus," a sermon on Luke 16:19–31[83] and Emil Brunner's "The Absoluteness of Jesus."[84] Alexander Christie wrote three articles on "The Doctrine of Holy Scripture in Calvin and Brunner" in 1940–41.[85] In 1938–39, Adolf Keller wrote two prescient articles, "A Battle of Life or Death in European Protestantism"[86] and "Totalitarian Faith on the European Continent."[87] In 1945 the *Review* published Wolfgang Schweitzer's article "The Confessional Church in Germany."[88] The *Union Seminary Review* was no longer just a mouthpiece for southern Calvinism.

Enrollment

In his inaugural address, President Lacy mentioned that he had attended the Class of 1927 graduation banquet and saw an Asian, a Persian, two Methodists, a Disciple, and one northern Presbyterian. He remarked that he would have never seen such diversity in his student days. Their presence had reminded him of the church universal, and he had been moved by the variety within the student body.[89] Before World War II, Union Seminary continued to attract students from around the country and the world. The 1930–31 school year attracted one student from France, then two, plus one from England the next year. But Union remained a southern institution: there was never more than 1 percent of the student body from the North until World War II.[90]

Total enrollment, however, reflected the times. The eve of the stock market crash in 1929 found 155 students registered. By 1935 the number had dropped to 127, although 197 students were on campus right before the draft was instituted in 1940. By 1942, only 101 were enrolled, and in 1945 just 94. With the end of the war and demobilization, students returned to class: 115 were enrolled in 1947. Throughout this period, 40 percent of all students came from Davidson and 14 percent from Hampden-Sydney. The number of graduate students fluctuated between 55 and 70, and they represented the greatest geographical range, with at least 25 percent coming from the North.

President Lacy was aware that Union's urban location and presence in the denomination's larger pulpits could make the school seem remote from smaller, country churches. He intentionally reached out to rural parishes by encouraging both UTS and ATS students to work in country churches during the summer. Moreover, when the General Assembly advocated a plan to yoke rural churches, President Lacy and James Appleby (who was later director of fieldwork and professor of evangelism) started the Town and Country Ministers' Institute in 1937 to support rural ministers, especially those in yoked fields.

With a student body made up of almost all PCUS students, it is not surprising that Union had a huge influence on the denomination. Records for 1937 show that 43 percent of active pastors in the PCUS were UTS grads; 83 percent were UTS grads in the Synod of Virginia, 76 percent in the Synod of West Virginia, 66 percent in the Synod of North Carolina, and 63 percent in the Synod of Appalachia.[91] By 1937, the seminary's 125th anniversary, UTS had trained 2,500 ministers and 156 missionaries; over 50 percent of white PCUS missionaries were UTS graduates.

First Steps toward a New South

While President Lacy was proud of Union's increasing diversity, he was also aware of its limits. On November 19, 1934, the Society of Missionary Inquiry met to discuss a petition from "a group in the student body, with reference to having colored delegates to [the] Inter-Seminary Conference as our guests under our roof." After some discussion among themselves, the minutes record that President Lacy had already stated that "Negroes should stay at Virginia Union University." Some students then wanted to open the dining room to the Negro delegates. While it was recognized that they "would have separate tables, . . . our students would eat with them if they liked." The students finally recognized that there was no legal or cultural way to host the Negro delegates. The matter was then dropped, and the students asked the administration "to approach Virginia Union University officially with reference to making arrangements for housing the colored delegates to the Inter-Seminary Conference."[92] Although student disappointment was palpable, state law specifically prohibited any integration of the races in any Commonwealth school.[93]

About one month after the SMI meeting, a letter from Samuel Govan Stevens (ThM, 1937) landed on President Lacy's desk. Stevens was born in Augusta, Georgia, in 1907. After graduating from Haines Institute (a high school sponsored by the northern Presbyterian church) in 1927, he attended Lincoln University in Philadelphia. While at Lincoln, Thurgood Marshall, Langston Hughes, Cab Calloway, and Kwame Nkrumah (the first president of Ghana) were his classmates. He graduated with a BA in 1931 and then attended Lincoln's seminary, graduating with a bachelor of sacred theology (STB) in June 1934.

In July 1935, Stevens was called to First United Presbyterian Church (now Woodlawn), then at the corner of Monroe and Catherine Streets. Seeking advanced studies, he wrote to President Lacy: "I have noticed that the Seminary plans to give a special course for ministers during the month of January, that will lead toward the degree of master of theology. I am wondering if it will be possible for a Negro minister to take this course. I desire very much to work toward the degree of master of theology."[94] He immediately forwarded the letter to Edward Mack, dean of graduate studies. President Lacy doubted that the seminary at Lincoln College was "anywhere near equal our B.D. work," but "I am very anxious indeed to help this man in any way that we can."[95]

Mack recommended accepting Stevens for the January class,[96] and (although the records are incomplete) he was apparently considered a good student and

Samuel G. Stevens
A.B., S.T.B., D.D., Th.M.,
S.T.M.
Assoc. Professor of Religion

33. Samuel Govan Stevens, first African American
student. Courtesy of Lincoln University.

was admitted to the ThM program. He graduated in 1937, the first African American graduate of Union Seminary. Samuel Govan Stevens would always remember his time in Richmond fondly. President Lacy helped him obtain housing at Virginia Union University (a historically black college founded in 1865, which also had a seminary), about a mile and a half away, and a table was made legally available for lunch in the UTS dining hall, at which classmates would join him. Moreover, if he had to study late at the library, classmates with cars would drive him to his room at Virginia Union, so he would not need to walk through a white neighborhood at night. He left Richmond for Pittsburgh in 1940 and returned to Lincoln University in 1951 as professor of practical theology and homiletics. At one time he had taught every African American minister in the northern church. The experience with Stevens showed President Lacy that by working with Virginia Union, UTS could open its doors to African American graduate students. When Joseph Tyler Hill (ThM, 1945), Allix B. James (ThM, 1949; ThD, 1957), and Edward D. McCreary (ThM, 1951) applied for the ThM program in the 1940s, the dean of graduate studies could assure them that housing was available at Virginia Union, "and you can attend classes here on perfect equality with other students."[97]

In 1938 the SMI voted "to invite the men from [Virginia] Union University to our first S.M.I. meeting, and perhaps later to have discussion groups, led by members of each school." In 1939, students voted to "participate in a joint reception with the Training School, sharing the expense equally," and that "overtures of friendship be made toward Virginia Union University." Although nothing ever really came of these initiatives, the president and the faculty agreed with both proposals. Students were beginning to reach beyond their culture.

Student Community

When President Lacy was inaugurated, the United States was rich and confident; the future seemed unlimited. The embryonic consumer society, however, frayed the traditional seminary community. Throughout the late 1920s, there were continual reminders from president and faculty that attendance at Sprunt Lectures and other campus activities was required. The students themselves openly worried about declining attendance at prayer meetings, vespers, guest lectures, and chapel.[98] There were also concerns that not everyone was signing up for local missions and continual laments in the SMI minutes that functions with ATS had virtually disappeared. The general consensus seemed to be that as more students arrived on campus with cars, the campus community suffered.

While the administration and student government complained that it was becoming a chore to require student attendance at Sprunts, prayer meetings, and special lectures, sports remained popular. Until 1937, basketball, baseball, and tennis seasons were eagerly anticipated. As in previous years, the teams were terrible. In the 1927 season, for example, the UTS basketball team went 1-11, losing to Randolph-Macon (twice), Davidson, the Charlotte YMCA, the Medical College of Virginia (twice), the Richmond YMCA (twice), the YMHA (the Young Men's Hebrew Association), the University of Richmond, and Hampden-Sydney. Union beat the company team from the Federal Reserve Bank. The baseball team went 2-5, and the tennis team went 4-3.[99]

The Depression changed life at Union. Until 1933 there was no charge for tuition or rent, and students paid only for their food, which averaged about $3.50 per week. That same year, tuition was first instituted (and thought to be a temporary measure) at $50 per quarter, and scholarship aid was offered to all eligible students. By 1938, food costs increased to $5.00 per week, a "Medical Fee" of $5.00 per year was assessed, and all students were required to pay "student Body Dues of $5.00." In 1934, non-Presbyterian students paid a "sustaining fee" of $25.00 per year, and graduate students paid $25.00 in tuition. Even these costs were prohibitive for some, and the refectory manager was authorized to "make small loans to students who are in desperate need." In 1934, scholarship students were assigned work in return for their financial aid, such as cutting lawns, helping with building maintenance,[100] and light clerical work, such as answering phones. By 1940 the yearly cost of attending Union (the combination of room rent and registration fee) climbed to $250[101] (when the average yearly wage was $1,900); in 1948, tuition became permanent and rose from $50 to $75 per quarter.[102]

Money was tight. In 1935, students began to complain about the costs of supporting sports teams, and intercollegiate athletics were eliminated in 1937.[103] Student Handbooks before 1935 were professionally printed booklets that fit in the shirt pocket. Beginning with the 1935–36 school year, the Student Handbook was just mimeographed on 8½ x 11 sheets of paper and stapled together; there was no advertising. In the minutes are mentions of some students not wanting to pay for the meal plan; in 1938, for the first time, students are warned not to cook in their dorm rooms.[104] It was expensive to keep the two primary student organizations running. In 1930 the Society of Missionary Inquiry voted to merge with the "Student Body Organization." They united on March 30, 1930, and the SMI formally dissolved.[105]

The Depression exposed divisions on campus. In 1935 the executive council of the SMI was concerned that students were segregating themselves in the dining hall according to social class. Their remedy was to "rotate" tables in the dining hall. That is, students would be required to sit at different tables so that they would get to know more people and build community.[106] Seating in the dining hall, however, remained a problem. Robert McNeill (BD, 1942) remembers that when he entered Union in 1939, the tables in the dining hall were like fraternities. The upperclassmen would choose what "acceptable" juniors they wanted at their table. "The whole thing reminded one of the old eating clubs at Princeton." The "snob appeal" bothered him at first, but he did nothing "because I was a beneficiary of the system." By the time he graduated, however, he had helped institute a true rotation system. McNeill credits his experience with abolishing the inequitable way tables were assigned with his future activities in the civil rights movement.[107]

The lack of money changed expectations. Beginning in 1900, the two lower classes traditionally hosted a reception for the graduating class. The reception was discontinued in 1932 due to cost. Prayer meetings increased in popularity. By 1938, vespers were held "every evening in the week, with a man on each hall appointed by the Director of Spiritual Life to initiate the meetings," and a "Day of Prayer" was held each October, beginning in 1931. But the hard times took their toll. Both the student body executive board and President Lacy continually asked students to help "Juniors and others being homesick, discouraged, financially distressed, etc.," and urged the upperclassmen "to endeavor to aid such men."[108]

Students found ways to make their own fun, and relationships were renewed with the students "across the Brook" at the General Assembly's Training School. In 1938, James Sydnor formed a choir with students from ATS and UTS (and later included students from the School of Theology of Virginia Union University [STVU]).[109] Until the late 1950s, ATS and UTS students would gather in the lounge at Watts Hall (at ATS) every Sunday night for a hymn sing. The film star Katharine Hepburn visited ATS in the late 1930s with her father, Dr. Thomas Norval Hepburn. Dr. Hepburn had previously known Natalie Lancaster (the ATS dean of women) in Ashland, Virginia. Katharine Hepburn signed autographs and posed for pictures with the ATS students. Some ATS students phoned UTS friends and told them to come over. No one did: they thought it was a joke.[110] In 1937 the student body voted to have a Thanksgiving party, charging 10¢ per man and 60¢ per guest (with the vast majority of guests coming from ATS).[111] Ralph Buchanan (Certificate, 1941) remembers that at the beginning of each term, UTS students would invite ATS students to dinner. The women wore gloves and hats, and the refectory would serve a special meal. In 1946, UTS and ATS students opened their classes to each other.[112] Union students and "Training School" students gave plays for each other on a regular basis.[113]

The first Calvin Bowl was probably first played in 1932 (with the cheerleaders from ATS). Some of the students who had planned to attend football games over Thanksgiving had to cancel their trips because money was tight, so they decided to establish their own football game (sometimes flag and sometimes touch) and christen it the "Calvin Bowl."[114] In succeeding years, students scrupulously kept the Calvin Bowl tradition: each class formed its own football team at the beginning of the year, played each other in a small schedule, and had the top two teams meet in the Calvin Bowl. In later years, the "Calvin Ball" dance was added.

Students continued to be students. The SMI minutes record continual complaints of radio noise coming from Richmond Hall. It was also suggested that "walking about in improper attire [in] Richmond Hall be called to their attention." "Golden Rule Week" was scheduled for December 11–18, 1935, because the student leadership was concerned about the lack of community and charity on campus. An "epidemic" of athlete's foot appeared on campus in 1933. The students refused to get their feet examined, however, until they could vote on it. The vote was duly taken, and they got their feet examined.[115] Carl Stark remembers that in the spring of 1940, Dr. McAllister's three-story house caught fire; once the alarm was sounded, students left class and poured from Watts Hall. They ran to his house (just south of campus on Seminary Avenue) and rescued its contents.

Whether students could work outside of school was perhaps the most contentious issue throughout this period. During the 1930s, students ushered at local theatres, especially the Mosque and Lyric theatres, to earn extra money. These jobs, however, were not sanctioned by the seminary: "Students are advised not to engage during the term in teaching or other occupations with a view to self-support, as such avocations interfere with proper attention to study, and are rendered unnecessary in most cases by aid which may be received from the sources above mentioned."[116]

The SMI minutes duly record the annual official criticism of part-time jobs taken by students. The faculty contended that scholarship funding from seminary, church, and presbytery was sufficient to support a student on campus. Students, they argued, should be devoting all their time to their studies, and jobs outside of school interfered with study time. The students responded that seminary aid was inadequate, and their presbyteries and churches were incapable of giving the additional support the seminary assumed they were receiving. In 1936, President Lacy felt it necessary to call a special meeting of the student body to remind students that presbyteries and the faculty did not approve of outside jobs. After the president spoke, "the student body expressed its appreciation to Dr. Lacy for coming to talk the matter over with them." After some discussion, a student moved that "the appreciation of the student body be expressed to the Faculty for their fraternal advice."[117] No further action was taken, and students continued to usher.

Ralph Buchanan and Robert McNeill remember the years prior to World War II as almost living in a cocoon; some students participated in pacifist lectures around Richmond, but for most students (as for most Americans), Europe was far away, and they were more concerned with making a living.[118] In 1936, one student was allowed to show "antiwar talkies to the students." But international events did intrude. A Mr. Kim, a graduate student from Korea, was accepted to study at Union in 1932 but needed funds to travel from Korea (occupied by Japan since 1905). Perhaps remembering Hyung Chai Kim and

Namkung Hyuk, the executive council of the SMI voted to provide him with $300 for travel from Korea in 1933, but Kim was never allowed to leave the country.[119] In the early 1930s, the Japanese made Christianity illegal, closing churches and seminaries, and began enforcing worship of the emperor.

The rhythms of seminary life remained constant. Senior sermons remained the ultimate terror: seniors preached every Thursday morning at 8:30 and Thursday night at 7:00.[120] Balmer Kelly (BD, 1930) remembers Dr. Richardson's comment on his senior sermon: "Your sermon was both interesting and original. Unfortunately, the original part was not interesting, and the interesting part was not original."[121] In the midst of the drive for graduate education, however, there were those who believed that Union was deemphasizing preaching. In 1939 a member of the Scholastic Committee wrote to the faculty, arguing that preaching class should teach students "to produce a conviction of sin in the hearts of their hearers and move their hearers to live in a more Christ-like way." Moreover, the committee wanted preaching to be taught in a way in which a student might "get acquainted with his own voice and not be scared of it."[122] But the students were ahead of the board. In 1938 some students began to explore the possibility of airing "a thirty-minute weekly broadcast over one of the local stations."

Bookstore

Perhaps the Depression's most drastic effect on the student body was the failure of the American Bank & Trust Co. Students had operated the campus bookstore since 1899 with minimal help from the administration; they deposited their funds at the bank. The PCUS Committee on Publications provided substantial assistance, helping with book ordering and advising student managers, who were elected. The bookstore was purely a nonprofit enterprise; books were sold at a discount, and snacks were sold on the honor system (with continual complaints that the payment jar was short). In 1933 the American Bank & Trust Co. failed, and the bookstore lost every cent: $415.42. The student body voted to add 3 percent to book prices to make up for the lost funds. It quickly became apparent, however, that the bookstore could not survive as a student-run enterprise, and the students voted to let the Committee on Publications manage the bookstore. The students, however, would still be able to elect a student as the assistant manager.[123]

Merger Talks

The Depression and World War II caused many in the church to rethink the triumphal attitude of the first decades of the century. In 1936, Union Seminary and Columbia Seminary restarted merger talks from the previous decade, and both schools agreed to the principle of a merger, but neither wanted to move. In 1943, UTS invited Louisville Seminary to move to Richmond. Louisville was jointly managed by trustees from the southern and northern churches, and Union's board voted to make room for Louisville's trustees from the northern church. The merger would be a complete consolidation of the seminaries' assets with a new name: Louisville-Union Seminary.[124] The possibility of a merger with a Richmond location made front-page news.[125] Indeed, interest was so high that in 1943 the board convinced the Virginia General Assembly to alter the incorporation law to allow the merger. When everything looked ready to go forward, however, Louisville's supporters in the northern church stopped the negotiations.[126]

World War II

The fall of 1941 was a dreary time. Although the New Deal had created thousands of new jobs and had boosted the country's morale, the economy was flat, and unemployment was still hovering around 15 percent. The war in Europe was far away, and seniors were anxiously thinking about getting a call after graduation. Most students remember listening to the radio on December 7 while they were studying or having "bull" sessions in the dorm; it was just another Sunday afternoon. Some were returning from their churches in the Shenandoah Valley. As usual, the radio was on, and at about 2:30 p.m. the announcer broke in to give the news of the Japanese attack on Pearl Harbor. No one was sure where Pearl Harbor was located, and students ran to find an atlas. Students returning from the Valley heard the news in the railway station. The students were allowed to keep the radio on in the refectory during supper, to hear reports that were coming in by the minute. There was total surprise; although everyone had already registered for the draft in 1940, students assumed that a war, when it came, would come from Europe.

The world changed in an instant. Between 1940 and 1946, enrollment dropped by 52 percent. Many college students who intended to enter the ministry dropped out to "join up," while some college graduates took commissions, intending to continue on to seminary after the war. Those in seminary had deferments that exempted them from military service. To keep their deferments active, however, they had to remain in school year-round. Before 1942, Union students were off for the summer, and they usually worked in a church or in some other "practical" capacity for a church organization. In any event, they were not graded. The Selective Service ruled that if students were not graded, then they could not be considered as attending school, and their deferments would lapse. In 1942, Union responded by establishing the first summer program, consisting of "practical" courses in evangelism, religious education, and hospital visitation. The next year, however, the navy expressed reservations about the "practical" summer education courses. They wanted regular courses taught to speed up the education process and release chaplains into wartime units.

Union, however, resisted being told how to manage the curriculum. Early in 1944, the faculty told the board that they did not see the necessity of teaching regular courses over the summer and hoped practical work would enable students to keep their deferments. But the government did not listen to the faculty. In April 1944, the Selective Service informed Union that students who did not matriculate during the summer could not maintain their deferments.

In response, the faculty rushed to implement a summer course for incoming students that would qualify as academic: Introduction to Greek was offered that summer as a required course.[127] To equip future military chaplains, Union confronted religious pluralism for the first time. The 1943–44 Catalogue lists courses on Mormonism, Christian Science, Spiritualism, and "The Theology of Emil Brunner." Classes in Comparative Religions and Buddhism were offered in 1946.[128]

By the end of the war, 122 alumni had served in the armed forces; 110 were chaplains, with 1—First Lieutenant Thomas Edward Johnson, Chaplain, USA (BD, 1937)—dying in a plane crash in the North Atlantic in 1943. Two Union students disenrolled and enlisted (1 in the navy and 1 in the marines), while 2 were commissioned as line officers in the navy, and 8 were commissioned in the army. Captain William Monroe Wicker, USA (BD, 1941), was killed in action during the North African landing in November 1942.[129]

Postwar Enrollment and Student Community

Enrollment remained relatively steady during the five years of mobilization, with an average of 98 students on campus between 1941 and 1946 because seminary students had deferments. Enrollment increased slowly after demobilization, with 115 enrolled in 1947, but the students were different. Postwar students were older and married. The stereotypical young, single, and naive seminarian was a thing of the past. Indeed, life had changed so much that permission was no longer required for students to get married, and married students became eligible for scholarships and fellowships.[130] Union was also slowly becoming a national institution. Before the war 1 percent of the student body was from the North, and then 5 percent were from the North in 1941–47.

The administration made a special effort to welcome the older, married students, whose life experiences had matured them beyond the typical prewar seminary student. In an effort to bring some cohesion to the seminary community, the first student-faculty retreat was held at the beginning of the 1947 school year, and faculty advisers were formally appointed for each student for the first time.[131] The 1945–46 Catalogue included a "Note to Veterans," recognizing their experience and potential needs:

> First, we wish to assure you of an understanding and warm welcome. Several of our faculty served in World War I, and one has been a chaplain in World War II. A number of Veterans are already members of our student body. We are grateful for the service you have rendered our Country, and we shall be happy, indeed, to have you with us as you prepare to serve the Church.

In an unprecedented move, veterans were allowed to enter "at the beginning of any quarter." If a student had not taken the AATS recommended courses, he was required to take tutorials (usually at the University of Richmond) to make up his deficiency. "No one without his college degree will be admitted except in an extraordinary case, and then only after having successfully passed an entrance examination."[132]

After the war, tuition officially became permanent because veterans could only spend their GI Bill educational benefits on tuition. President Lacy understood that the supporting synods and PCUS General Assembly, hobbled by the postwar inflation and the demands of an expanding church, could not support the traditional commitment to a no-cost education. The administration made tuition permanent to capture the funding made available to returning veterans. What was considered an emergency measure to defray costs during the Depression now became an accepted part of the cost structure. This new source of income was needed. In 1945 it cost $469 per year to attend Union; tuition was $150 per year (raised to $225 per year in 1948), room rent was $90 for the year, meals were $224, and the medical fee was $5. Reflecting the postwar inflation, it cost $636 per year to attend Union in 1947. Even with this high cost, total enrollment for the 1947–48 school year was 225 (including 10 from the PC(USA)), plus 69 graduate students.[133]

Postwar Curriculum

Immediately after World War II, the biggest curricular change was the addition of hospital visiting and fieldwork courses. Although these courses had antecedents in the student-run missions of the 1930s, both hospital visiting and fieldwork now had faculty assigned, and the yearlong classes were required of all students. The 1945–46 Catalogue lists "Hospital Visiting" and "Field Work" for the first time.[134] The course in hospital visiting required students to visit patients at the Medical College of Virginia Hospital one afternoon a week, attend lectures and complete readings (which were discussed in sections), and present verbatims (a summary of their patient conversations) to the class on a regular basis. Bill Oglesby wanted students to realize that their job was to listen; what they had to say was not as important as what their parishioners had to say. Pastoral Counseling was introduced as an elective in 1947.[135]

President Lacy had been waiting for over a decade to insert a practical education course into the course offerings. The postwar economic boom meant that money was finally available. He named James Appleby as director of fieldwork in 1945. What was informal and student-led activity in 1915 was now part of the curriculum. Student-led initiatives gave way to a full-time professor who would "correlate the practical experience of the students in the field with their classroom work so that the former will be more efficient and the latter more meaningful."[136] All students (whether Presbyterian or not) were expected to engage in some sort of fieldwork, usually serving a church as a student intern for at least two years of a normal seminary course and for two summers. As before the war, if students could not secure a church to serve in the Richmond area, they were assigned churches in the Shenandoah Valley or eastern North Carolina. The rail and bus lines offered reduced rates on tickets for students holding "clergy permits," which were issued from the president's office.[137]

The optimism following victory in World War II resulted in a new willingness to cooperate. For Richmond-area undergraduate and graduate schools, it made sense to combine resources. The 1946–47 Catalogue mentions the

Richmond Area University Center for the first time. The seven white institutions of higher learning in the Richmond area committed themselves to an "exchange of professors and students between the cooperating institutions and a pooling of library facilities, including those of the City and State Libraries."[138]

One thing that did not change, however, was the class schedule. Classes were 55 minutes, held from 9:00 a.m. to 4:40 p.m. (with chapel from 8:45 to 9:00 a.m.) Tuesday through Friday, and Saturday from 8:45 a.m. to 12:23 p.m. (with no chapel). Senior preaching was less public, however. Seniors preached to the entire school, faculty and students, on Thursday morning from 8:45 until 9:30 a.m. The preachers and faculty then adjourned to a classroom for faculty criticism (which was not remembered to be as colorful as in previous generations).[139]

If UTS was to be a modern institution, it would require modern expertise and competitive salaries. Reflecting the growth of mass communications, the board hired a public relations officer for the seminary in 1946. In 1946 the faculty received a 10 percent raise to $4,400 per year (the first one since 1933), and in 1950 their salaries were raised to $5,000. At the same time, President Lacy encouraged the faculty to be more public. In 1944 (for the first time) he informed the board of the faculty's extracurricular work—books, articles, and speaking engagements—and his plans to keep them in the public eye.

If the seminary were to meet the increasing demands of postwar life—such as larger enrollment, married students, and new courses like hospital visitation and fieldwork—then the seminary would need to raise funds in a more systematic manner; relying on the church constituency just would not work anymore. In 1941, for example, total synod contributions were $10,000, down from $20,000 in 1939.[140] President Lacy knew that he could not fund a first-class seminary with the current budget. He initiated a campaign to raise $150,000 in 1944, after the Latta Addition to the library was completed. By 1945, however, the campaign was stalled at 50 percent and never raised more than $80,000.[141] It was clear that more attention would have to be given to fund-raising; cutting the budget and raising tuition year after year would no longer work. To provide for more consistent fund-raising, he organized the Friends of the Seminary in 1945[142] and appointed Fred Stair as his assistant in 1948 to concentrate on fund-raising by managing the Mid-Century Campaign.[143]

A new curriculum, classes in hospital visitation, systematic fieldwork, cooperating with other educational institutions, and professional fund-raising—all these would mean nothing, however, if Union had nothing to say to the postwar world. Just a generation before, MacKay's speech calling for reunion would have been rejected out of hand. But the shared sacrifice of World War II made the old divisions, traditions, and theology irrelevant. The old arguments against dancing and evolution had nothing to do with the atomic age. The challenge of making sense of the Holocaust, the growing awareness of inequalities in American society, and the rise of consumerism—all fractured postwar America. Before the war the church could address the culture, counting on a coherent point of reference. After the war the church needed to construct a theology with which to address a society that questioned the very foundations of faith. Union Seminary would try to address that society and provide theological understanding through a new journal: *Interpretation*.

Interpretation: A Journal of Bible and Theology

Postwar America was a time of rapid change and confusion. The Cold War, postcolonialism, mass communications, electronic technology, and civil rights reshaped people's view of the world. The discovery of the Dead Sea Scrolls and the Nag Hammadi Codices, the threat of nuclear annihilation, and scientific advancements caused many to question their faith.[144] Not since the theory of natural selection a century earlier had the church been faced with trying to interpret so much new knowledge and answer such fundamental challenges.

With much fanfare Reinhold Niebuhr founded *Christianity and Crisis* in 1941 (it ceased publication in 1993), and it quickly became the mouthpiece for liberal Protestantism. Niebuhr sought to show how liberal Christianity could address the problems of the mid-twentieth century. J. Gray McAllister, editor of the *Union Seminary Review*, was retiring at this time, and Balmer Kelly and Donald Miller wondered whether to continue the *Review*, or replace it with an entirely new journal. Since 1889 the *Union Seminary Review* had served only the southern Presbyterian church. They wondered if the seminary could create a new journal that would be a credible alternative to *Christianity and Crisis*.

> As we three at Union tested the thought-trends of the 1940s, we sensed that no other theological publication was filling the need for the kind of journal we had in mind. We became convinced that new and widespread interest in the Bible needed a voice to give it expression and leadership. As if spontaneously, the name *Interpretation* sprang to the mind of Balmer Kelly, apparently quickened by Bunyan's picture of the House of the Interpreter in *Pilgrim's Progress*. When, therefore, the faculty of Union was forced to determine the future of the *Union Seminary Review*, we three who had been dreaming of a new journal had the task of selling our dream to the rest of our colleagues.[145]

The three professors thought that UTS needed a new journal to reflect Union's unique contribution to the modern theological conversation and reply to Niebuhr's effort.

Miller argued that the critical approach to the Bible had not been adequate either to understand Scripture or to release its power in life. For him, the historical-critical method encouraged "an unwholesome preoccupation" with the historicity of Scripture, "rather than a vivid sense of the elements in it which completely transcend environment and speak a 'timeless' Word of God to our souls." At the same time, it was fruitless to insist on biblical inerrancy, "since the original autographs are nonexistent." Concentrating on the sources of Scripture or the doctrines that explain the Bible misses the point: what is important is what the Bible says. This was the starting point of biblical theology. Although Miller acknowledged that "it was not likely that there would be any large-scale return to the wholly uncritical approach to the Scriptures," what Scripture said should be the focus of study.[146]

Kelly and Miller wanted Scripture taken on its own terms. Understanding the Bible from a purely critical standpoint drained it of authority; yet insisting on an uncritical literalism required either suspending belief or excising whole passages for the modern Christian. Neither approach was satisfactory because neither approach built faith. What was needed was a "biblical theology" that rested firmly on the effort to grasp what Scripture had to say to the modern world. No journal existed, however, that was specifically designed to give voice to this way of looking at Scripture. Hence, it seemed obvious to them that some kind of journal should be created to fill the vacuum.

As Kelly and Miller envisioned a new journal, they talked with Henry Brimm (the librarian), and he became an enthusiastic supporter, willing to commit the library's resources to their efforts. As they began to seriously plan for their new journal, they realized that they had a huge task before them. Financing would be a problem; just trying to keep enough student housing available and hire faculty for new courses was enough to make President Lacy skeptical of their plans to pay for the journal through subscriptions and advertising. Tradition was another issue. "When the proposal was made that *Interpretation* should replace the *Union Seminary Review*, one of the older men pointed out that Union already had a journal that had stood the test of time. Moreover, he opined that if these younger professors wanted to start a new journal, they should do it on their own and be fully responsible for it." Finally, the faculty was hesitant about the scope of the proposed journal.

> The third issue causing hesitancy on the part of the faculty was the decision by Kelly and me that the new journal be specialized in the area of biblical theology. We were convinced that if it were associated with a precise mission, the journal would have more reader appeal and a greater likelihood of economic survival. Moreover, the mission of the journal, it seemed to us, had already been defined by the broad resurgence of interest in the Bible. Our intention, therefore, was to use the subtitle: *A Journal of Biblical Theology*. The faculty, however, objected, arguing that to add this subtitle would be to restrict the subject matter of the journal. In addition, there were departmental interests at work, with some faculty concerned about their own turf. Why, it was asked, should Union Seminary's official journal be weighted toward the biblical department, as though biblical studies alone were taught in the curriculum?[147]

Brimm, Kelly, and Miller, however, believed that the title *Interpretation: A Journal of Biblical Theology* was the only way to highlight the "biblical theology" emphasis. Yet John Newton Thomas vigorously opposed the title, maintaining that the focus on theology was too narrow. A compromise was finally reached with the subtitle *A Journal of Bible and Theology*.[148]

In this era Union Seminary actually housed two schools of thought when it came to biblical studies. John Bright accepted the historical-critical method and defended the basic historical accuracy of the Old Testament on archaeological grounds. He was never associated with *Interpretation* because he thought biblical theology as a means of interpreting Scripture was so broad as to be useless. At the same time, however, Bright was convinced that there was "an evangelical and Bible-centered theology" that was not "ultra-fundamentalism and certainly not radical liberalism, which lies somewhere in between and seeks to preserve the virtues and avoid the excess of both."[149] He argued that seeing the Bible in its historical light would confront Christians with its radical message, and his book *A History of Israel* reflects this position.

Miller and Kelly, though, argued that *Interpretation* would be like no other journal. Current publications in biblical studies were "highly technical, containing conversations between and among scholars about philological, archaeological, literary, historical, and cultural aspects of biblical study. It did not, however, move on from there to the theological and religious implications of these inquiries for the faith and life of the church." Still other journals were intended for the layperson or for use in sermon preparation. They wanted *Interpretation* to help working pastors think about biblical themes and apply them to life, to give their ministry a theological framework. It would neither be an esoteric university journal, nor a sermon mill furnishing ready-made sermon outlines and illustrations. Rather, *Interpretation* would prompt ministers to focus on "the theological consequences" in living the Christian life and show that the Bible is relevant to the current times.

With the faculty divided over whether a new journal was needed and President Lacy unsure whether the seminary could afford a new venture, Brimm, Kelly, and Miller invited the president to a weekend retreat in 1946. During what became known as "the weekend," President Lacy began to accept their vision, see the need for a new journal, and resolve to find money to start it up. Funding fell into place less than a year later, when several board members took the lead in convincing the entire board to underwrite this new venture. Yet there was no money for clerical help, to track subscribers, send out bills, record payments, and correspond with advertisers. Jo Brimm, Henry's wife, stepped in and volunteered to take the job with minimal compensation. She set up her small office in what had been a cloakroom under the stairs of the old library wing, with just a chair, a table, a typewriter, and some trays of index cards.[150]

Miller would later remember agonizing over how many copies to print for the first issue. In August 1946, the *Union Seminary Review* had 440 subscribers.[151] Thinking that his publication would be more popular, he decided to print 1,300 for the initial release in January 1947. But the number of subscribers for that first issue was less than 650.[152] Yet biblical theology now had a platform, and Union Seminary was publishing a scholarly journal.[153]

Biblical Theology

There has never been a commonly agreed-upon definition of "biblical theology." Indeed, the very idea of a biblical theology grew out of Kelly's desire for his students not just to learn the text as a historical document, but also to apply it to contemporary life. In 1971 the twenty-fifth anniversary issue of *Interpretation* contained an editorial observing that World War II had changed the context of world Christianity.

There should be a journal, a voice speaking for and to a contemporary current in theology that was rising and spreading with excitement and vitality. It was a direction always marked by the adjective "biblical" or the noun "Bible." In the large, it was a spirit and mood created by the achievements of dominant theologians of the time, by the discovery of the churches in the ecumenical movement that they had the Bible in common, by the breakthrough by conservative Protestantism into historical biblical study, by consuming interest in revelation, by fascination with the overwhelming, sustaining, and transcendent reality of God. More narrowly, it was the phenomenon known as the "biblical theology movement."[154]

Kelly argues, however, that they never intended to begin a "movement," but only a new way of interpreting Scripture. It is true that most of *Interpretation*'s early articles came from Reformed denominations, with a common theological orientation influenced by Karl Barth. Biblical theology, however, was not a reaction against systematic theology. Rather, it was an attitude that interpreted and connected biblical ideas to modern life. Biblical studies at that time, Kelly complained, "gave no hint of meaning for faith, no word of commitment, no concern for Christian living, or the church's role in the world."

The goal of biblical theology, therefore, was to apply the meaning of Scripture to daily living;[155] historical-critical questions were secondary. In some ways, this new way of looking at Scripture can be seen as a reaction against the sterility of historical criticism, which, in its extreme form, destroyed the unity of Scripture by supposing that each document in the Bible "was merely the creation of its own age and the whole a purely human collection, representing the confused and often contradictory gropings of men after God, of little interest save to the historian." In that view, such a confused collection of historical documents has no authority and can make no moral demands. At the same time, biblical theology rejected fundamentalism and sought "to correct those who believe Scripture is 'purely a supernatural book,' or who see only allegorical interpretations divorced from life."[156]

Interpretation symbolized the postwar changes at Union. The new journal not only reflected the biblical theology "movement," but also validated President Lacy's efforts to seek a specialized faculty from outside the southern church. Union was extracting itself from the circular fundamentalist/historical-critical argument to apply the Bible to contemporary life. E. T. Thompson argued that *Interpretation* "was one medium through which the southern Presbyterian church was at last beginning to speak to the larger Christian world."[157]

Kelly and Miller were intentional in shaping *Interpretation*'s commitment. They formed an editorial council to suggest articles; this council was composed of scholars from mainline American denominations, the United Church of Canada, and the Evangelical Church of the Czech Brethren. About half of the council was made up of biblical scholars, and the rest included theologians, philosophers, ethicists, and working pastors. The council's goal was to make *Interpretation* interdenominational, international, and interdisciplinary.[158] In 1971, Balmer Kelly observed that while "denominational journals spread the gospel of ecumenism among the churches of America, . . . no other journal published and spread among a grassroots constituency a greater amount of biblical and theological material from the ecumenical movement than did *Interpretation*." The editorial judgment that the "labor of many men at one task is one of the most eloquent forms in which the unity of the church appears today" gave a concrete example of ecumenical cooperation that could not be ignored.[159]

Alumni

Throughout this era, Union graduates could be found at all levels of the Presbyterian Church (US). Besides serving on every General Assembly board, in positions in every synod, and in many presbyteries, eight graduates served as moderators of the General Assembly. Despite the Depression and World War II, the interest in foreign missions remained high. In the 1927–47 period, 63 students went into foreign missions in Asia (2), Brazil (11), China (9), Congo (8), Formosa/Taiwan (2), Japan (7), Korea (14), Mexico (4), Philippines (2), Puerto Rico (1), Russia with the YMCA (1), South Africa (1), and Sudan (1). Six worked as home missionaries, two among Native Americans and four in Appalachia. As might be expected, many graduates were superintendents of home missions in their presbyteries and synods. John Anderson (BD, 1944) initiated the Presbyterian Urban Ministry and became executive of the Board of National Ministries.

Union alumni also continued to have an impact on theological and southern education. During this period 17 served as seminary professors (including one at Union Seminary in New York), 35 as college or university professors, and 4 as deans (including one at Duke University). Sixteen Union alumni served as college or seminary presidents, including Albert Curry Winn (BD, 1945; ThD, 1956), president of Louisville Presbyterian Theological Seminary, 1966–73; James Iley McCord (attended 1938–39), president of Princeton Theological Seminary, 1959–83; George A. Long (attended 1942–43), president of Pittsburgh-Xenia Theological Seminary, 1943–55; Marshall Scott Woodson (ThD, 1934), president of Flora Macdonald College, 1950–60; Frank Bell Lewis (BD, 1936; ThM, 1937), president of Mary Baldwin College, 1947–53; Ansley Cunningham Moore (attended 1941–45), president of St. Andrews College, 1960–70; and Louis Cossitt Lamotte (ThD, 1947), president of Presbyterian Junior College and from 1958 of the merged St. Andrews Presbyterian College, 1939–60.

Union graduates had an impact on other denominations as well. Vernon Carey Hargroves (attended 1924–25) was president of the Baptist World Alliance in 1970–75. Several Methodist bishops were Union graduates, such as Samuel B. Chilton (attended 1932–33), suffragan bishop, Episcopal Diocese of Virginia, 1960–70; and Samuel Coleman Patterson (BD, 1941), one of the founders of the Reformed Theological Seminary of the Presbyterian Church in America, in Jackson, Mississippi. During this period, 23 alumni transferred to the northern church, four to the Congregational Church, three to the Episcopal Church, two each to the Associate Reformed Presbyterian and Methodist Churches, and one each to the Disciples of Christ and the United Church of Canada.

In the 1927–47 period, 987 students attended Union, and 96 percent went into the ministry; the dropout rate was 3 percent. The graduates who did not accept a call or who left the ministry after one or two calls showed a distinct predilection for public service. Teachers, social workers, and personnel managers were the most popular choices. One became superintendent of the blind for the Department of Welfare, state of New Hampshire. One became the dean of the law school at the University of Richmond; one became superintendent of schools in Portsmouth, Virginia; and one finished his career as a staff member of the Brookings Institution. Several worked as chaplains for state institutions, writers, editors, and nursing home administrators.

The Threads of History

Union Seminary refined the idea of an educated ministry between 1927 and 1947. By the first part of the twentieth century, the PCUS assumed that their ministers

34. Aerial view of campus, 1935. Notice streetcar tracks in the lower left.

would be educated in a seminary that would indoctrinate them into traditional southern Calvinism. President Benjamin Rice Lacy, though, had a larger vision. He wanted a first-class seminary to educate professional ministers through a graduate-level curriculum, by a specialized faculty, and a graduate program supported by an unequaled research library. Although the Depression delayed his vision, he achieved his goals by the end of World War II. In 1927 the average Union graduate learned the traditional curriculum from teachers who were generalists. The 1947 graduate was considered a professional: he had attended an accredited school, experienced facets of the pastorate in supervised fieldwork, and was aware of more than the traditional Calvinism interpreted by Dabney.

Although Union was firmly tied to the PCUS and saw itself as a southern seminary, the school also began to acquire a national and even an international reputation through its new journal, *Interpretation*. Through its pages Union began to engage the wider church in theological conversation. The emphasis on research (and the library's expansion) showed a new attitude toward academics; training ministers to recite the old answers was no longer enough. Union would not just sit on the sidelines while the issues of the day were being discussed; Union would help shape the conversation. The fact that President Lacy defended E. T. Thompson announced that an era of academic freedom was entering Union's halls.

Union began to question the status quo when it came to race. The admission of Samuel Govan Stevens was but the first indication that Union was ready to end segregation. In the refectory, students recognized the need for a community based on ἀγάπη—the selfless, sacrificial, unconditional love that Jesus showed to the world—instead of status. World War II changed the student body: these students were older, married, and more serious. Professors like E. T. Thompson prompted their students to examine the doctrine of the spirituality of the church in light of what Scripture revealed.

For the first time, Union would begin to shape American theological education. As one of the founding members of AATS, Union was in the forefront of
professionalizing seminary education. By putting fieldwork and hospital visitation in the curriculum, the seminary began to implement a modern seminary
curriculum. Energized with a new outlook and fortified by their encounter with
biblical theology, Union graduates would take their knowledge, outlook, and
skills to the parish and begin to change a way of life. And through the pages of
Interpretation, Union found a distinctive voice that would be heard.

Chapter Eight (1947–66)
Faithful Scholarship

No part of American life was untouched by World War II. Socially, economically, politically, and culturally the war transformed the United States from a provincial second-rate power to the military, economic, and technological leader of the free world. Yet this new leadership role laid bare the historical tensions within American culture. The postwar generation began to question accepted norms as they exposed the contradictions between national ideals and social reality. The campus of Union Theological Seminary was a microcosm of this ferment. The insights that Union students gained from seeing society through the eyes of biblical theology led them to denounce segregation publicly and to finally discard the doctrine of the spirituality of the church. Union continued to innovate, establishing the Reigner Recording Library and radio station WRFK. While many questioned how the curriculum could be altered to better prepare students, male and female, black and white, the traditional five courses remained at the core of what every student learned.

The war changed campus life, but in an unexpected way. Besides the drop in enrollment, the biggest change on the quad was the decreasing age of the students. Throughout the war, the faculty complained that students were "immature" and took steps to encourage emotional growth. In 1945 and 1946 the faculty regularly met together to discuss each student and his particular needs. Those who were felt to be immature received personal counseling from a faculty member. Yet the problem remained. In 1946 the faculty reported that "absences and tardiness have been unusually prevalent, indicating on the part of some students a lack of discipline or a lack of interest." For the first such in a long time, the administration officially disciplined four students that year for a lack of cooperation with other students, faculty, and administrators, and the faculty complained that the general tenor of student dress, speech, and conduct was unbecoming men who were working toward ordination.[1]

A New Kind of Student

Yet in 1946 the faculty also noticed that returning veterans were adding a note of seriousness and purpose to the campus. These students were not just older. Men who had gone through the Depression and served in combat refused to be treated as naive undergraduates. They were not prepared to take at face value something that a professor said just because he had a DD degree. Veterans questioned, challenged, and began to play a critical part in reshaping curriculum and class procedures. The seminary would never be the same.[2]

Veterans transformed the campus culture as well. Many students wore their military uniforms because that was all they had: there was no money to purchase new clothes.[3] James L. Mays, who would later teach Old Testament, entered Union in 1946 in a class that was made up almost entirely of veterans. At that time the two upper classes were entirely made up of those with ministerial deferments, so the entering class was older (and had more varied and intense life experiences) than the two classes ahead of them. With colleges rushing men through in three years or less, by 1946 the median age of a Union graduate was 22 years old, with no experience outside the classroom. After 1946, the median age was 27 to 28.[4] Before World War II, students had to obtain permission from the seminary to get married. Upon demobilization, students who had gotten married while serving in the armed forces were already older than traditional seminarians and showed up on campus with their wives. Of the 80 students in the class entering in 1946, over 60 percent were married. The traditional resistance to student marriages vanished.[5]

The presence of so many married students required some unorthodox thinking. In 1948, married students outnumbered single students, and only 22 of the 80 married students could be housed on campus.[6] President Lacy heard of excess military housing: he leased one vacated barracks and officers' housing unit from the navy when the Diesel Repair School closed, with the University of Richmond and the Medical College of Virginia leasing the other eight barracks. These buildings (still standing at the corner of 34th Street and Maury on the south side) became married-student housing until Rice Apartments opened in 1954. The faculty and trustees worried that the students living at the Diesel School would be deprived of a fulfilling community life. Reminiscences of those who lived at the Diesel School, however, are filled with fond memories of hot apartments, pressure toilets, and a close community that formed the basis of lifelong friendships. To provide more space for married students, the board also authorized the purchase of the Neill Ray House in 1949 and furnished the Reigner Apartments in 1950.[7] But it was only with the opening of Rice Apartments (built with the proceeds of the Mid-Century Campaign) that dedicated on-campus married-student housing became a reality.

The veterans were not interested in tradition for tradition's sake, and they were impatient with any part of the curriculum they believed was outmoded or a professor who was not engaging. In Mays's second year, the student government critiqued the faculty, with the idea of raising standards. Professors who were used to docile and pliable students were not amused. At the same time, postwar shortages made books, like the Hebrew Bible, almost impossible to find. Tensions between veterans and nonveterans, restlessness with a tradition-minded faculty, and the lack of resources were always present, but students during this era remember a community that worked hard to get along together.[8]

The sheer number of returning students also strained facilities. In 1947 the faculty reported that the seminary had reached its capacity: there was no place to teach or house more students. In 1950 the graduate program was in danger of collapse due to high enrollment. Postwar inflation, the need to expand facilities, and the cost of technology were expensive. Board was $6.50 a week in 1946; in 1951 it was $8 per week.[9]

An Expanded Outlook: Montpellier

The presence of men who had served in Europe and Asia gave Union a new international consciousness. In the spring of 1946, Henry Brimm heard that Dr. Lucien Rimbault, the president of the French Reformed Seminary in Montpellier, France, had written a letter describing the poor condition of the seminary (including the lack of food) in the aftermath of the war. In some cases, French seminary students had to drop out due to malnutrition, and others could not afford to heat their homes in the winter. Brimm spoke to the students about the situation, and they began a food and clothing drive. The student body raised $5,000 for the French seminary's most pressing needs, collected food and clothing, and sent them to France.[10] The interest was overwhelming, and the effort soon involved the entire PCUS. It quickly became apparent, however, that it was more efficient to collect money than to ship clothing and canned goods.[11]

Many in the faculty were surprised at the outpouring of student support, but most of the students had seen the destruction of war and wanted to be part of the rebuilding. Moreover, President Lacy visited the French seminary in 1948, when he was a delegate to the initial meeting of World Council of Churches in Amsterdam. He took a side trip to Montpellier after the meeting and was moved by the devastated conditions. When he returned, he took every opportunity to strongly support the clothing and food drives organized by the students and used every opportunity to speak about Montpellier's conditions to the larger church.

Once the French economy improved, clothing and money were not needed, but students still wanted to help. Apparently from a suggestion by President Lacy, students decided to build a dormitory. After two years of fund-raising, enough money to build a dormitory was remitted to Montpellier by 1951. The building was completed in 1954 as the Centre Universitaire Protestant (CUP), enlarged in 1965, and renovated in 2001. Ironically, Union students thought they were sending food and clothing and building a dormitory as an expression of fraternal support. Montpellier students, however, thought UTS was supporting their efforts to evangelize France. Whatever the motive, the relationship with Montpellier showed an interest in international affairs that ran against the isolationism of postwar America. Indeed, what began as a clothing drive turned into an exchange program.

Wanting a closer relationship, Montpellier suggested that the seminaries exchange students, and Jean Abel arrived in Richmond for a year of study in the fall of 1946.[12] In 1948, another exchange student, Pierre Étienne, arrived. That year UTS students raised another $5,470 and collected more than a ton of clothing and books for not only Montpellier, but also for seminaries in Göttingen, Germany, and in Debrecen, Hungary (which was 50 percent destroyed during the war). In 1949 another exchange student, Freddy Reymond, was on campus, and Dr. Rimbault was a visiting professor, the first foreign visiting professor in Union's history.

In 1949, UTS students pledged $8,000 for Montpellier and medical supplies for Korea. On November 15, 1949, Dr. Lucien Rimbault presented President Lacy with the doctor of theology degree, honoris causa, and W. T. Martin Jr. (student body president) with the bachelor of theology degree, honoris causa. Both these degrees were granted in perpetuity to all successors of Lacy and Martin in their respective offices,[13] signaled by *épitoge* (the piece of cloth with white fur stripes attached by a button on the left shoulder), which is sometimes worn today by the president.

Lamar Williamson (BD, 1951) was the first UTS graduate to study at Montpellier, attending during the 1951–52 school year. He went to prepare himself to teach in the Congo (where he served in 1956–66) and to gain another viewpoint in his study of the Bible. Williamson grew up a teetotaler in Arkansas, but at Montpellier he enjoyed drinking wine like everyone else during the midday meals.[14] The student exchange continues today.

Fifty Years in Richmond

Union celebrated fifty years in Richmond in October 1948. Walter W. Lingle, who had done so much to "remove" the seminary, gave the opening address. What struck Lingle was not how modern Union was, but how Union had tried to modernize the tradition. "Seminaries don't change very markedly. Of course, there have been some changes in the curriculum since those early days in Hampden-Sydney—first the inauguration of social teaching, then speech, then music, and finally fieldwork.... But fundamentally, I am struck most today, not by the newness of the curriculum, but rather by the expansion and enrichment of the old courses."[15] Later, in an article, he wrote:

> When I was a student, there were a limited number of courses and a limited number of subjects. Two years in Dabney's "Theology" constituted the backbone of our studies. There were no electives. We had a very good library, but there were very few fresh books in it. The library was open only a very few hours a day, and students used it very little. It was a place to keep books. Our work consisted largely in memorizing the textbooks and the professors' notes, which did not develop much original thinking. There were very few lecturers or preachers from the outside. Today the number of courses and subjects taught is bewildering to an old-timer.[16]

The anniversary was important not only for the seminary, but also for the city of Richmond. President Lacy's speech marking the end of the celebrations was broadcast over WRVA, the most powerful radio station in Richmond. Echoing Walter W. Moore in the previous generation and reflecting the postwar optimism, President Lacy proudly declared that "the objectives of the Seminary will be the same for the next fifty years as they were for the last fifty years. He called for more faculty and a modernized physical plant, to "make America Christian in order that America may help to make the world Christian."[17]

Douglas Southall Freeman, winner of two Pulitzer Prizes for his biographies of George Washington and Robert E. Lee and editor of the *Richmond News Leader*, gave the keynote speech at the closing celebration. He stated that "Confederate tradition, strong church influence, tobacco business, and liquor business were the main characteristics of Richmond" at the beginning of the century. Freeman concluded: "One of the greatest contributions to the city was the raising of Union's walls in Richmond, higher and nobler than ever before."[18]

According to the *News Leader*, "Richmond, the South, [and] the nation are debtors to the faithful scholarship of Union Theological Seminary." More important, the story boasted, "Never, to our knowledge, has there been any division at Union Theological Seminary into so-called 'modernists' and 'fundamentalists.'"[19] President Lacy echoed this sentiment. In an interview he said that what struck him most about Union's fifty years in Richmond was "not the newness of the curriculum but rather the expansion and enrichment of the old courses. Scholarship has flourished and has developed in the seminary, but it has been faithful scholarship in the richest, widest meaning of that adjective."[20]

The City: Incubator of Change

Walter W. Lingle and President Lacy recognized how the city challenged the seminary. Fifty years in Richmond incubated a new kind of understanding of faith and the role of the church. While at Hampden-Sydney, Union Seminary had been a guardian of the past. Until the move to Richmond, Union (with some notable exceptions) "believed in the Old South and held tenaciously to traditional views." The views could be summed up in "five points": Reformed scholasticism, *jure divino* Presbyterianism, the doctrine of the spirituality of the church, rigid Puritanism (meaning a strict moralistic piety based on prevailing social norms), and no reunion [with the northern church]."[21] Indeed, the 1909 seminary bulletin boasted: "Throughout her long and honorable history of ninety-six years," Union Seminary has been "remarkably spared from strife that would interrupt her progress; and no shadow of suspicion of unsound teaching has been cast upon her fair name."[22]

Removing to Richmond, however, mandated change almost as if by osmosis. The doctrine of the spirituality of the church, held so dear by Dabney and Johnson (and so entrenched in the southern Presbyterian consciousness) was first challenged in 1911 by the students who worked in the Seventeenth Street Mission. In 1914, Lingle began his course on the social teachings of the Bible. The foundations had been set. In a January 28, 1931, article in the *Presbyterian of the South*, Dr. Davis H. Scanlon (1900) of Durham issued a challenge:

> Do our theological seminaries lead in any advanced thinking of progressive movement? No, . . . they are meek and only followers. They are possessed of fear lest the spirit of Palmer, Thornwell, and Dabney depart from them, and some theological censor cry aloud, "New ways." . . . We need fewer defensive and more offensive leaders of righteousness, speakers of the truth at any cost. Let our noble seminaries enter the front lines.[23]

Biblical Theology: Catalyst for Change

The students who started the Seventeenth Street Mission and listened to Walter W. Lingle's lectures in Christian sociology made a conscious break with the

Union of Hampden-Sydney days. In its first century, Union sought to conserve the past; now in its second hundred years, students envisioned a transformed future. Donald Woods Shriver Jr. (BD, 1955) represents the generation who broke the hold of the spirituality of the church doctrine. Born in Norfolk, Virginia, he graduated from Davidson, then Union—what he called the "Apostolic Succession."[24] He had thought about going to Yale but attended Union because he wanted to be a parish minister in the PCUS. Shriver went to Yale for his master's and then spent three years in Gastonia, North Carolina, after which he went to Harvard, graduating with a PhD in 1962. After Harvard he served as campus minister at North Carolina State University and director of the University Program on Science and Society and Urban Policy from 1962 to 1972. Shriver taught ethics at Candler School of Theology from 1972 until 1975, when he accepted the presidency of Union Theological Seminary in New York, serving until 1998.

In the 1950s, as in previous times, Union stressed the pastorate; graduate study was practically discouraged, and virtually all Shriver's classmates were headed to a church. The seminary, however, saw itself as more than a conduit for the pulpits; UTS aimed to be a bridge between the intellect and the parish. "To graduate from UTS in the 1950s was to be full of the Bible." But it was not the Bible of the fundamentalists or the historical-critical method. Biblical study at Union was supported by science—archaeology, history, philology—and Shriver learned to appreciate biblical study grounded in history. The most memorable book from his student days was John Bright's *Kingdom of God* (1953); each chapter ended with a contemporary reference, which made the Bible more than a historical document. John Bright made the Bible relevant to life. The connections between history and contemporary times, between faith and action, led Shriver (while on the PCUS youth council) to help integrate Montreat Conference Center in 1954.

Donald Shriver was continuing a Union tradition. It could be argued that Montreat was the place where many PCUS ministers formed an ethical consensus. By the time the Synod of North Carolina purchased the four-thousand-acre cove (that was to become the Montreat Conference Center) in 1905, "Christian Assemblies" had been held there every summer since 1897. Indeed, it could be said that Montreat was the southern version of Chautauqua. When the auditorium and hotel were completed by 1925, the summer conferences really expanded and regularly attracted ministers from around the denomination.

Union alumni influenced denominational policies through Montreat programs. Walter Lingle, for example, served as the program chair for Montreat conferences from 1910 to 1924, and in the summer of 1933 his lectures on social issues from a biblical perspective prompted those in attendance to create the Ministers' Forum. This group allowed ministers to freely discuss the lectures and the issues they faced in the pastorate.[25] Due to the number of UTS graduates in denominational positions and in the parish, Montreat's programs were often planned by and featured Union graduates. The conferences allowed ministers to network and support one another; they attracted national speakers who would not normally be heard by the PCUS.

Shriver remembers Balmer Kelly's characterization of Union's educational goals in the nineteenth century as learning "confessional theology, with the

Bible playing the role of supporting handmaid." It was no longer enough to use Scripture to support a theological system. Biblical theology grew out of the need to distinguish what the Bible said "from what many generations of church theologians have said it says, . . . to discern what the Bible brings to us and what we interpreters bring to it."[26]

Benjamin Rice Lacy combined an unwavering loyalty to the PCUS with a desire for a more specialized faculty. Biblical theology developed at Union in response to the challenges of both fundamentalism and liberalism. Balmer Kelly, Donald Miller, and James Mays did not see either the historical-critical method or the Westminster Confession as completely authoritative in interpreting Scripture. Rather, these scholars discerned a meld of faith and event in the substance of the text. As James Mays said of Bright, "In his introductory course to the Old Testament, he led students through the biblical narrative from Genesis to the Second Temple period in a way that displayed the books as essentially an historical and theological account of Israel's life. . . . No one could read his *History of Israel* without perceiving that it was also an account of the basis of the Christian faith."[27]

A generation earlier, President Lacy understood that

> the men who come to our Seminary . . . are anxious themselves to discover the true basis for our faith in a book which reveals God and is inspired by God. They are going out to minister to congregations who are asking themselves disquieting questions. . . . Many to whom they minister can be reached and helped only by one who has frankly and fearlessly faced the questions raised by [biblical] criticism and can give an answer to his faith.[28]

The historical-critical method wanted to isolate parts of Scripture into editorial subsections, and fundamentalism was preoccupied with disconnected proof texts; in contrast, "biblical theology insisted on taking the whole Bible into consideration as one tried to interpret its parts." Although E. T. Thompson was not a biblical theologian, Shriver observes that Thompson "gave us many reasons to look critically at issues of racial justice beginning then publicly to afflict the conscience of the Presbyterian Church U.S." In the process, Thompson could call Dabney a heretic because of his insistence on the spirituality of the church doctrine.[29]

Balmer Kelly was Shriver's most formative professor. In Kelly's course "Biblical Theology," Shriver and a generation of students understood how the Bible could speak to their lives. Kelly used the historical-critical method to affirm Scripture's historicity. Yet there was more to the Bible than its origins; its teachings and its faith emerged from real history and real human life. For Kelly, the primary goal was to comprehend the Bible as one, whole authoritative book across the span of its sixty-six books. In this view, the old dispute over "inerrant inspiration" was worthless. "Comparing Scripture with Scripture" meant the qualification of one by the other. Verses of the Bible were not all equally authoritative. Scripture, like the historical experience of the faithful, could overrule itself. Indeed, the very phrase "biblical theology" required students to compare one interpretation of a passage with others.

"Such teaching," Shriver recalls, "made it possible for many of us from the fifties at UTS-VA to understand the Bible, not as a collection of maps to follow literally into our futures but as a book for alerting us to landmarks on contemporary roads."[30] God's redemptive work was continuing in the present day. The implications were incredible and wide-ranging. Shriver recognizes that although social ethics was not prominent in the curriculum, the biblical courses prompted students, via their own reflections, to construct a Bible-based social ethic. Biblical theology rejected the fragmentation of the Bible into a pile of puzzle pieces through textual and canon criticism. Rather, biblical theology treated Scripture as factual history, which had contemporary meaning because the Lord was still dynamic.[31] In 1931, Davis H. Scanlon had urged, "Let our noble seminaries enter the front lines." The reaching of E. T. Thompson, Balmer Kelly, and other biblical theologians influenced Donald Shriver and his generation to look at the relationship between Scripture and life in a new way; this attitude became the foundation and context for Union Theological Seminary in the next generation.

First Signs of Change

In 1945 the student body asked the faculty for permission to sponsor the 1947 Interseminary Conference on campus. It was understood that African American students would be attending. Since the conference would require housing and feeding black delegates, the faculty referred the issue to the trustees. The board threw the issue back to the faculty, stipulating only that no women should be entertained overnight. Echoing the 1934 student body attempt to accommodate African American students, Union did not sponsor the conference.

Although state law specifically prohibited integrated education and housing, the board had been willing to skirt the law and enroll African American graduate students as long as they lived at Virginia Union University. The issue of allowing African Americans to matriculate as undergraduates had been raised as early as 1946, but the board shied away from a decision.[32] The issue, however, was taken out of their hands. On May 17, 1954, the Supreme Court ruled 9-0, in *Brown v. Board of Education*, that "separate educational facilities are inherently unequal." This decision overturned the 1896 *Plessy v. Ferguson* decision, which allowed segregation on a state-by-state basis. The *Brown* case combined five cases (one of which was *Davis v. County School Board of Prince Edward County* and filed in Virginia) and prompted uniformly negative reactions among state governments throughout the South. Virginia's reaction was particularly antagonistic. On February 24, 1956, Senator Harry F. Byrd Sr. announced the policy that would become known as "Massive Resistance." In order to avoid integration, the state would allow counties to close their public schools. Massive Resistance was centered in Prince Edward County, and every public school in Virginia closed the doors from 1958 until 1959, with Prince Edward County schools remaining closed until 1964.

Although *Brown v. Board of Education* applied only to public education, it was clear that the church needed to take a stand. On January 28, 1955, at a special meeting of the board, the faculty reported they had "received requests from two Negro students, who have families, for admission to Union Seminary." The faculty voted to refer the matter to the Executive Committee and wait for the board's annual meeting in May.[33] The board was caught in a bind. The court's decision was unambiguous, but it was unclear if private education was bound by the court's decision. At the same time, feelings in Virginia were running high, and the church was uncertain.

The faculty acted first, voting on May 20 (prior to the board meeting) to "[favor] the admission of properly qualified Negro students to the Seminary and summer clinics—including both room and board—on the same terms as all other students."[34] Before the board could take up the matter, however, the secretary reported an item of correspondence:

> The Synod of West Virginia had raised a question as to whether the seminary should admit Negro undergraduate students. The board voted to reply that when a properly qualified Presbyterian Negro student applies for admission, his application will be considered on its merits. The board requested that the Synod of West Virginia also be informed as to what Union Theological Seminary had done in the past toward the education of Negro ministers.[35]

Understanding that admission would also require housing, the board appointed a Special Committee on the Housing of Negro Students with Families, and directed the Executive Committee to call a meeting of the board before the next regular meeting to hear their report. Seven months later, on January 10, 1956, the board held a special meeting to hear the oral report of the Special Committee. The committee reported and asked to be continued until a special meeting of the board in April. The board agreed and reconvened on April 4 to hear the committee's recommendations.

Their report was in two parts. First, the committee recommended that a "graduate of Stillman Institute who wished to bring his wife and two children and enroll as a student" had since decided to come by himself. The board decided that it would be in order to admit him to the dormitories. Then, noting that "the law of Virginia still requires segregation, but that the law is presently in flux and the situation may change considerably within the next ten months," the committee recommended "that action on the housing of qualified Negro Presbyterian candidates or ordained ministers in the facilities of the Seminary be postponed until there is a definite application from a qualified student."[36]

The committee, however, made it clear where they thought Union should stand and presented the board with a positive policy: "A Brief Statement of the Practice of the Seminary in Educating Negro Students" (April 4, 1956). The committee recommended admitting and housing all qualified students regardless of "racial origin." The time for segregation was over:

> The Christian Scriptures indicate that racial distinctions have no place within the life and fellowship of Christian believers. Nowhere in the Standards of our Church are there any teachings which justify us in drawing racial distinctions within the Church itself. . . . There is no alternative but to offer to qualified Negro students the full facilities of our Seminary as they prepare themselves for leadership within the life of the Church.[37]

The committee then recommended that all housing be open to all students and that family housing be purchased in the vicinity of "Virginia Union University's residential area" if a family feels isolated in the seminary or Ginter Park community. The committee recognized the seminary's leadership role, but also their culture. "Since the above recommendations are in line with the long-established policy of the Seminary, we believe that they should be put in effect quietly, as a matter of course and without publicity that would suggest that a new policy was being established or might unnecessarily exacerbate existing relations between the races in North Richmond." The board adopted the recommendations unanimously.[38]

The End of Spirituality of the Church

The board's actions, however tentative they may seem in hindsight, would have been unimaginable just a generation earlier. To recommend admitting all students "without regard to race" signals a transformation in theology that was unencumbered by the spirituality of the church doctrine. Before the 1950s, the average Southerner had to choose between the conservatism of Dabney or rejecting faith altogether. The result was a contradiction between faith and practice. As Ace Tubbs (1948) remembers:

> At seminary I had a rude awakening in the critical issue of race relations. As a boy I was taught to refer to blacks as colored, and that colored children preferred to go to their own schools and churches. In college and seminary I learned to refer to blacks as Negroes, and that Negroes could not enroll at Presbyterian Colleges and Seminaries because the law said they couldn't; and that I must always be a law-abiding citizen.
>
> A Negro came into the Union Seminary Library one day. One of my law-abiding preacher friends got up and told the librarian, Henry Brimm, to get that Negro out of the library. Henry told my "born-again" Christian friend, who chose to love Jesus, but not the people Jesus loved, that the man was not a Negro, but the product of our missionary work in Africa. My friend said, "Oh, that's different," and sat down with the Negro and engaged in a conversation about our missionary work in Africa.[39]

The work in local ministries that began in the early 1900s bore fruit in the 1950s. The Seventeenth Street Mission became Eastminster Presbyterian Church in 1952. Eastminster's pastor, the Rev. Irvin Elligan Jr., was the first African American minister in Hanover Presbytery, and he supervised UTS and ATS students in their fieldwork at Eastminster. In 1954, K. Sherwood McKee (BD, 1953) worked as an evangelist in Creighton Court (a housing project of 2,500 people) for two years, assisted by UTS and ATS students. Woodville Church was established as a result of this mission in 1958.[40]

Jim Smylie has argued that biblical theology provided the Scriptural foundation to demolish segregation. In 1861 the PC(CSA) General Assembly affirmed that God assigned "every man by a wise and holy decree, the precise place he is to occupy in the great moral school of humanity." This place was set forever in "a vast Providential scheme." In direct opposition, biblical theology emphasized God's continuing action in the world. Faith was a dynamic relationship with God, which required each Christian to work toward a more responsible society that reflected the kingdom. God was not static.[41]

Biblical theology was in the tradition of Union Seminary. Just as John Holt Rice and Walter W. Moore sought to challenge both revivalism and "German" scholarship in the nineteenth century, so Union defied both fundamentalism and the historical-critical method in the twentieth. Walter Lingle, E. T. Thompson, and others self-consciously fashioned and taught a theology based on Scripture, which was never intended to be confined to the halls of academia. Rather, this theology would address the issues of the day. The issue that became the catalyst for biblical theology's deepest influence was race.

In the March 21, 1949, issue of the *Presbyterian Outlook*, E. T. Thompson published a Bible study showing that racism is unbiblical. He reviewed passages from Genesis through 1 John, highlighting passages seen in the popular mind to support segregation and racial superiority. There was no use of Greek; this study was meant for laypeople.[42] There was no public reaction.

Six years later, the country's mood had changed. The March 14, 1955, issue of the *Presbyterian Outlook* carried articles concerning segregation and integration. The *Outlook* reprinted a speech given by the Rev. G. T. Gillespie (BD, 1911), president emeritus of Bellhaven College, Jackson, Mississippi, before the Synod of Mississippi on November 4, 1954. In this address he argued that segregation was not based on "race prejudice," but was "one of nature's universal laws." Segregation, according to Gillespie, promoted progress, did not necessarily involve discrimination, and was based on biblical grounds. Thus segregation could not be characterized as un-Christian.

E. T. Thompson, Donald Miller (both Union professors), and John H. Marion (Secretary of Christian Relations for the PCUS) answered Gillespie. Thompson wrote two articles: "The Curse Was Not on Ham" and "Paul Said, 'God Made of One.'" These articles reflect the maturing and power of biblical theology. Thompson was not only answering Gillespie; he also fashioned his presentation to contradict the traditional arguments first put forward by Dabney in *Defence of Virginia* a century earlier. Gillespie's address made little more than general points that were congenial to southern culture. Thompson, though, speaks past him at several points. Putting an outline of *Defence of Virginia* beside "The Curse Was Not on Ham," it is clear that Thompson was not aiming at Gillespie, but rather at Dabney and southern culture. Dabney made great use of Ham's curse. Ninety years later, Thompson replied:

> There are many people who believe that God has condemned the Negroes to a position of permanent inferiority, that in his curse upon Ham, he doomed the descendants of Ham, i.e., the Negro race, to a position of perpetual servitude. This interpretation of Genesis 9:24–27 became the common one in the South in the days preceding the Civil War and remains a popular one until the present time. A slight examination of the passage, however, along with the aid of any good commentary or Bible dictionary, will make it clear, however, that this interpretation is based on three mistaken ideas. The record shows [that] (1) the curse is pronounced by Noah, not by God—and there is a difference; (2) the curse is pronounced on Canaan, and not on Ham; and (3) the descendants of Canaan are the Canaanites (see Gen. 10:15–19), white tribes every one of them.[43]

This is pure biblical theology: using Scripture alone to address a contemporary issue, exposing false interpretation, and advocating a new way of living.

Donald Miller answered Gillespie point by point and swept away all the biblical arguments for segregation. Pointing to the reality of judgment, he declared that "there should be no distinctions between us except those between sinners and saved." For Miller, the Golden Rule did away with the old categories of master-slave or black-white relations. Instead, Jesus changed the dynamics of human relationships to that of sinner and saved because God loved us all while we were still sinners.[44]

The attitude that the church should stand silently aloof from the ethical conflicts of modern life was incomprehensible to biblical theologians. E. T. Thompson, for example, taught church history for over forty years but never produced a strictly historical work. He was not interested in studying the past for its own sake, but in using history to encourage involvement in current issues and persuade people not to repeat the mistakes of the past.[45] Ben Sparks (BD, 1965) has observed that as one can draw a line from Walter Lingle to E. T. Thompson, it is apparent why Union was so involved in civil rights. Union had a tradition that enabled its graduates to respond to the times. "We drank from cisterns we did not hew." John Leith "grounded us in Reformed Theology, not as an academic discipline alone, but as fuel for illumining the public life of the troubled and hopeful days through which we were living, as well as of the fourth century, when the Nicene Creed was formulated."[46]

Civil Rights and the Seminary

Forming a theology that repudiated segregation was one thing; taking public action was entirely something else. On February 1, 1960, four African American college students sat down at a lunch counter at Woolworths in Greensboro, North Carolina, and politely asked for service. Their request was refused. When asked to leave, they remained in their seats. The sit-in was born and became a tactic of the early civil rights movement.

Students from Virginia Union University immediately targeted Thalhimers and Miller and Rhodes, downtown Richmond's most prestigious department stores, for a sit-in and picketing. Although Union Seminary students were not initially involved, E. T. Thompson pricked the seminary's conscience with his gentle question: "If this is a struggle for what is right, why are only black students involved?" This observation led to an open meeting a few nights later in the lounge of Lingle Hall. Students from Virginia Union were invited to tell the students of Union and the Presbyterian School of Christian Education (PSCE—the Assembly's Training School [ATS] had changed its name in 1959)[47] what they were doing and why. George Conn (BD, 1962), who had entered Union in September 1959, remembers a standing-room-only audience that night:

After a long and emotional evening, which included some fine examples of preaching in the Black Church tradition, which elicited more than one "Amen" from the Presbyterian audience, "God's Frozen Chosen," I made the foolish mistake of asking what we could do to help. I was immediately presented with a "time sheet" and told to sign my name when I would show up on the picket line. Trapped! Fortunately several classmates joined in responding to this "altar call."

Word quickly spread, and President James Archibald Jones (president, 1956–66) summoned those who signed to his office. According to Conn, Jones "counseled us not to go but made it clear that it was ultimately our decision and that he would take no action to block us if we felt that we should join the line."

One evening later, the seminary community gathered in Watts Chapel for a public reflection led by faculty members. Dr. Ben Lacy Rose observed that he had been a public opponent of segregation for a number of years. He said that while he did not see his role on the picket line, his position did not mean that he was not committed to the battle or that the students' role was inappropriate. Conn remembers John Leith as especially moving.

> [He warned] the student body that neither those who marched nor those who stayed on campus should feel "right" or "superior" to those who chose otherwise. He reminded us that whatever we did was made inadequate by the distortions of sin but that when offered up in faith, God had both the capacity and will to make it good. For the first time in my life I understood the Doctrine of Justification.

Less than a month after the first sit-in, the Union Seminary students marched on February 23, 1960. Their "shift" began at 2:00 p.m., but before picketing they received "a brief orientation on how to behave and react. Speak to no one, look straight ahead, do not block traffic, dress well, if struck fall to the ground in a fetal position and protect your head and genitals. The last bit of advice was not encouraging."[48] Three students from Union participated on the first day: Aubrey N. Brown III (attended 1959–61), George Conn, and T. K. Morrison (attended 1959–60). They walked for a twenty-minute shift, and then others took over. Their pictures were prominently featured in a *Richmond Times-Dispatch* story on March 6. The story and picture were picked up by the Associated Press and printed around the country.[49] George remembers wondering what his parents would think. He also discovered the tableaux of humanity revealed by the picketing.

> As the days wore on, toughs gathered to jeer us, with looks of indescribable hatred on some faces. A little spit here and there marked most days as we took the ninety-six steps from one corner to the next, four steps to make the turn, ninety-six back, and so on. There was encouragement, comedy, and sadness.
>
> Along the way I remember too the elderly black man who dared not look directly at me as I passed him, but I was renewed by his quietly muttered "God bless you." I remember the lady with the Chihuahua, which charged the police dog, entangling both leashes as the police dog cowered. I remember the frail and elderly "lady," the seeming epitome of southern gentility, who took one look at me and my sign and who hit me across the head with her pocketbook while calling me a "God-damned son-of-a-bitch."

The public action polarized the seminary community. Some students, mostly seniors, complained that the public demonstrations were jeopardizing their calls. While some faculty members disapproved of the public demonstrating, Professors Kennedy (BD, 1954; teaching Christian Education), Leith, and

35. Union students on the picket line at Thalhimers, downtown Richmond, March 6, 1960. Courtesy of *Richmond Times-Dispatch*.

Rose were outspoken in their support and encouragement.[50] A group of Union and PSCE students formed the Committee for Information on the Race Problem in March and mimeographed news reports about civil rights demonstrations for distribution "to college students in [the Richmond] area." Besides the publicized actions, Union students demonstrated their commitment in less publicized ways. In 1959, Charles Swezey (BD, 1961), Calvin Houston (BD, 1959) (an African American student), and Jimmie Ruth Erskine (a PSCE student) decided on the spur of the moment to go to the White Tower at the corner of Brook Road and Azalea to see if they could get a cup of coffee. The waitress was so upset that she spilled coffee all over the counter. They stayed long enough to make their point and then left.[51]

Officially the administration was neutral. Frank Bell Lewis, dean, told the *Times-Dispatch* that the students "are acting on individual and private decision." "The seminary," he said, "had taken no official action in the matter."[52] In a newspaper article, Aubrey Brown III said that "the faculty and administration encouraged us not to participate but left us to do as we felt we should."[53] Another student said the seminary administration had "protested strongly" but left the decision to join the picket lines "to the individual student."[54]

The public picketing caught people's attention. There were many letters to the administration threatening to withhold donations: "Neither the citizens of

Richmond nor the Presbyterians of Virginia approve of your behavior, . . . and this is going to prove a great handicap when we again attempt to raise funds to subsidize your education."[55] George Conn and the others received death threats and insults.

> On one particular day when I had just received and read a particularly seething letter, Dr. Leith met me in the hallway of Watts, and reading my face, asked what the problem was. I gave him the letter to read, and he responded, "Only a damn fool would write a letter like that, and only a damn fool would pay attention to it. Go to your room and read some theology." So I did.[56]

Most of the letters, though, were supportive. One woman wrote: "We cannot find sufficient words of thanks for the brave stand that each of you have taken in a cause we all feel to be just."[57] Another wrote: "It satiated the depth of my soul with joy to see you marching onward as Christian soldiers in our picket lines. I wish to commend each of you for your straightforwardness and zealous display. You are truly deserving of such commendation.[58]

During the 1960s Americans were on edge because the values that citizens espoused did not reflect the way the country lived. It was an argument over national priorities in a way not seen since the Civil War. Tradition, for example, sought to maintain segregation, but American ideals held the notion of equality as the basis for our national identity. In the maelstrom of contradictory and confusing principles, students felt it was important to make their voice heard, especially in civil rights legislation. The Civil Rights Act of 1964, ending segregation in public facilities and enforcing the equal protection guarantees of the Fourteenth Amendment, came before the Senate on March 30, 1964. Before the bill could reach the floor, however, eighteen southern senators (known as the "Southern Bloc") began a fifty-four-day filibuster.

The student government called for students to vote on a resolution supporting the passage of the Civil Rights Act of 1964 on May 8.[59] Before the vote was taken, however, the student body sponsored a debate, which caught the imagination of the city. James Kilpatrick, editor of the *News Leader*, appeared before the students to argue against the resolution. Senator Hubert Humphrey (D-MN) had been invited to speak in favor, but he sent his legislative assistant, John Stuart, as his representative. After a lively debate, the resolution passed 45-24. It was at this meeting that 25 students and 4 wives signed up to stand vigil in Washington, pressing for passage of the act.[60] John Kuykendall (BD, 1964) had initially been surprised when he saw his classmates demonstrating for civil rights. He did not know if he could join in the demonstrations and face his family. Nevertheless, he decided that the Civil Rights Act was too important not to join in support. He went to stand vigil for the act, and he did not care if he was on the front page of the paper.[61] The bill was finally signed into law on July 2 by President Johnson.

Selma

Once segregation was legally outlawed, the next goal was to compel enforcement of the Fifteenth Amendment by eliminating state barriers to voting, such as literacy tests exclusively given to African Americans. In order to press

President Johnson to send the Voting Rights Act to Congress, 600 people intended to walk the 50 miles from Selma to Montgomery, Alabama, on March 7, 1965. What started as an ordinary march, however, gained national prominence when state and local police attacked the marchers without provocation at the Edmund Pettis Bridge—an action that became known as "Bloody Sunday." The local civil rights leadership attempted a second march the following Tuesday, March 9. Over 2,500 protesters began the march, but police turned them around after they crossed the bridge.

The Selma March riveted the country, and Union Seminary responded. On March 15, some 300 people in Richmond marched from Virginia Union University to the state capitol to show their support for the Voting Rights Act, offer their sympathy for the deaths of Rev. James Reeb (a white Unitarian minister who had been murdered in Selma after marching the previous week) and nine others, and "protest [the] brutality and senseless violence in Selma, Alabama."[62] Newspapers identified "one of the leaders of the service [as] Dan West, of Dallas, Tex., a white Presbyterian student at Union Theological Seminary."[63]

Union students prepared for the march. In the preceding week, the student body had issued instructions for the marchers. The stress was on dignity and nonviolence. Men were instructed to wear coats and ties. Loud talking, laughing, and joking were to be avoided. Marchers were to stay on the sidewalks, observe all stoplights, and never react to "jibes, shouts, [or] ridicule." Students were not to argue or wave their signs. "Upon reaching the Capitol steps, we must be careful to leave a pathway for persons entering and leaving the building. Immediately following the benediction, we shall begin the march back to Virginia Union."[64] Every faculty member except two and most of the student body participated.

Reactions to the demonstration and student participation were immediate and strident. "The phones rang off the hook in Watts Hall, and the secretaries were targets of considerable verbal abuse." President Jones, by all accounts, was "gracious and wise." He supported the students by telling them that they were free to march if they desired. And he tried to placate enraged donors by reminding them that the march was not sanctioned by the seminary. Ben Sparks remembers how the demonstration fractured the student body.

> When the march from Selma to Montgomery engaged the energies of the entire campus, one member of our class held a press conference on the front steps of Watts Hall. He opposed our sympathy march with students and faculty from Virginia Union and PSCE from the Northside to the front steps of Mr. Jefferson's Capitol. He suffered our scorn and contempt.
>
> Another member of our class suffered because he staunchly believed in integration and worked tirelessly for it. He could not speak to his family of origin in Mississippi for almost a year. One Christmas, I think, John Ames decided not to go home.[65]

Although President Johnson sent the Voting Rights Act to Congress on March 17, 1965, civil rights leaders decided there would be a third march to pressure Congress to pass the bill. The third march began in Selma on March 16, and James Mays, together with three students—John D. Turner (BD, 1965; ThM, 1966), Dan West (BD, 1965), and Louis Weeks (BD, 1967)—joined the march on March 21, arriving in Montgomery on March 24, protected by 2,000 soldiers, 1,900 federalized Alabama National Guard troops, as well as scores of FBI agents and federal marshals.

The Fellowship of Concern

Public participation to promote civil rights had a foundation going back at least a generation. In the summer of 1933, Walter Lingle gave a series of lectures that explored current issues from a biblical perspective. Those present at Lingle's lectures founded the Ministers' Forum that summer, and the Ministers' Forum gave rise to the more ecumenical Fellowship of Southern Churchmen (FSC), organized in 1934. The FSC was a loosely knit interdenominational and interracial association of Christians who gathered periodically for study, discussion, and prayer about significant issues of their day. They "propounded a radical critique of twentieth-century southern civilization, gave like-minded Christians an opportunity to address these problems collectively, and offered a sense of community to Christians who held radical ideas and would have been isolated without the FSC." In the 1930s and early 1940s, the FSC addressed economic concerns. In the mid-1940s they began to address racial issues. Although the FSC was not an organization of Union Seminary, many UTS graduates were members and leaders; Charles M. Jones (BD, 1932), a pastor in Chapel Hill (N.C.), served as executive secretary from 1950 to 1952.[66]

The Fellowship of Concern (FoC) was the successor to the Fellowship of Southern Churchmen, and James Mays went to Selma through his involvement with the FoC. A local member of the FoC in Alabama called Randy Taylor (BD, 1954), pastor of the Church of the Pilgrims in Washington, D.C., and informed him what had happened to the first marchers. Taylor asked the leadership of the FoC to go to Selma and march. Since President Jones had always backed the FoC, Mays and the three students were able to leave campus with no problem. They connected with other members of the FoC and traveled to Alabama.[67]

Mays had been involved in civil rights throughout his parish ministry. As a seminary professor, however, he was a more public person. Right after Mays returned from Selma, Second Presbyterian Church in Petersburg, Virginia, sent a delegation of two elders to him and lovingly told him he could not preach there anymore. He had been scheduled to preach at the church in the near future and was hurt because he had been their student minister for two years. Ten years later, however, the church initiated a healing that restored their relationship. President Jones supported Mays, but there always was pressure on Jones to "do something" about his "wayward" professor.[68]

Although not a direct descendant of the Ministers' Forum, and never an organization officially affiliated with UTS, the Fellowship of Concern reflects relationships and attitudes formed at Union. In late 1963, John Randolph (Randy) Taylor, Francis Wellford Hobbie III (BD, 1949), James Mays (BD, 1949), and Don Shriver (BD, 1955) were among the leaders who founded A Fellowship of Concern.[69] This fellowship was active in 1963–68, with about five thousand members.[70] They worked to change church policies in many areas, especially regarding race and reunion with the northern church,[71] and aided ministers who suffered as a result of their witness for integration. When President Lacy retired from UTS in 1956, he accepted concurrent calls to College Church and as chaplain at Hampden-Sydney College. He did not confine his activities to Hampden-Sydney but quickly became an outspoken opponent of Massive Resistance. Prince Edward County closed its entire school system in September 1959 rather than comply with the Supreme Court's order to integrate. The schools were not reopened until 1964, when the county supervisors were threatened with prison. During this entire period he ignored death threats and publicly denounced Massive Resistance, with encouragement from the Fellowship of Concern.

The Mid-Century Campaign

While civil rights was the dramatic issue that caught everyone's attention, the postwar enrollment increases and the changes in society required Union to think of itself less as a denominational school and more like a university. Without more money, Union did not have the resources to attract excellent teachers, support research, and provide innovative programs. Synodical support was uncertain and irregular. Union's supporting synods never funded their school as fully as other synods supported their seminaries. In 1946, for example, Austin had 42¢-per-capita support, Union only 9.6¢. In 1950, Union's support increased to 13.2¢, but that was still woefully short of the seminary's needs.[72] As he considered his legacy, President Lacy decided that he needed to give fundraising one more try. With the failure of the Walter W. Moore Campaign in his mind, he initiated the Mid-Century Campaign in 1951.

President Lacy wanted, however, to first test the waters. In January 1949 he launched a drive to raise $150,000 in ten days.[73] The Richmond papers gave the effort wide and positive publicity,[74] and the campaign exceeded its goal by $6,238. Now funds were available for tennis, basketball, and handball courts, plus the construction of one faculty house. President Lacy commented that people just kept giving.[75] He was convinced that Union could conduct a successful capital campaign.

After a year of planning, UTS hosted the Mid-Century Convocation on December 4–5, 1951. This conference was designed "to discuss and attempt to find solutions to problems of church and seminary in the world today, with the emphasis on the South." Union was the denomination's flagship seminary, and the public paid attention. Both Richmond papers covered it, and the first night's program, held in the Mosque Theatre (the present-day Landmark Theatre) and broadcast throughout the Mid-Atlantic, was a panel discussion that included the governors of Virginia and North Carolina.[76]

President Lacy used the convocation to kick off the Mid-Century Campaign. He employed paid fund-raisers; the first time Union had ever used professional consultants.[77] They designed a fund-raising organization with cochairmen in every presbytery in the four supporting synods and produced a professional-looking booklet titled *For All Southern Presbyterians: A Great Door Is Opened.* The theme of the booklet was simple: the postwar economic boom brought an increase in population, which meant that Union could not produce competent ministers unless the church improved facilities and increased faculty. Indeed, projected enrollment was estimated to reach 250 for the MDiv degree in the next decade. The need was evident; already one church in six was without a minister.

The campaign's goal was to remake the seminary. President Lacy wanted to raise $2 million to build Rice Apartments (and move married students and families out of the Diesel School), increase the size of the library, add $500,000 to the endowment, fully fund the departments of graduate studies and field-work, establish chairs in preaching and biblical theology, and increase the budget for *Interpretation* and continuing education courses. The plea for donations repeated the same argument used by John Holt Rice 130 years earlier: lack of ministers for a growing country. "The war," he wrote, "with its economic mobilization, spectacularly accelerated the steady pace of Southern progress." And with this progress, Northerners would move south, rural people would move to the suburbs, and these people would need churches.[78] This time the church was ready to listen and give; by 1953 the campaign had exceeded its goal by $600,000.[79]

The campaign's success was easy to see. In 1953 the faculty court on Rennie Road was completed, and the Rice Apartments were built in 1954. Ginter Park Presbyterian Church left Schauffler Hall in 1954 (making way for the seminary's burgeoning audio department and WRFK). By 1955 the Melrose dorm had been converted to married-student housing for fifteen couples.[80]

With the campaign behind him, President Lacy announced his retirement. During his tenure undergraduate enrollment grew from 119 to 127, the total student body from 174 to 281, the faculty from 8 to 15, and the endowment increased from a little over $1 million to a little more than $4 million.[81] Perhaps the most important development to emerge from the Mid-Century Campaign, however, was the new attitude toward raising money. After its successful conclusion, the board agreed in principle to the idea of a director of development to maintain contacts made during the campaign. Union was now beginning to look and function like a modern corporation.

James Archibald Jones

As Union was growing and participating in the wider world, James Archibald "Jas" Jones became the third president on April 5, 1956. The transition from Lacy to Jones was orderly; Jones had been elected president in 1955 to provide for a complete transition period. He was also thoroughly in the "Union Family." A native of North Carolina, he was a graduate of Davidson, a member of Union's Class of 1934, and assistant to President Lacy. Jones had studied at the University of Edinburgh.[82] After his studies he pastored Presbyterian churches in North Carolina for 16 years: First Church, Henderson; and Myers Park, Charlotte. He was 41 years old. Whereas Lacy was born in the nineteenth century, Jones was born in the twentieth; he represented the new opportunities that postwar America was ready to grab. At his inauguration there were 275 students,[83] and 116 educational institutions were represented at his ceremony.[84] Truly Union was becoming a first-rate seminary, known for faithful scholarship.

36. James Archibald Jones, president, 1956–66

President Lacy was justifiably proud of the faculty he had assembled and allowed them to take positions that Walter W. Moore never would have tolerated.[85] And President Jones wanted to secure the policy of attracting professional teachers. Specialized professors would undergird the two goals he announced in his inaugural address. First, increase postgraduate opportunities. Second, initiate programs to train lay leadership.[86] Lacy had compared seminary education to medical school; now President Jones said seminaries should more closely resemble agricultural schools, which go out to farmers and teach new methods.

President Jones also echoed John Holt Rice by intentionally placing Union squarely within the ecumenical movement:

> I rejoice in the relationship that exists between this institution and a particular denomination. Here we have ecclesiastical loyalties, and we emphasize to a proper degree techniques which are calculated to strengthen the life of the Presbyterian Church in the United States. But let it be declared without any hesitation whatsoever that Union Theological Seminary in Virginia is not sectarian. Energetically it believes in the witness of the denomination which bred it and which over the years has undergirded it. But neither the Seminary, nor the Church from whose vigor it has sprung, is so misguided and so arrogant as to consider that all, or even chief, wisdom and piety reside within the boundaries of one ecclesiastical system.

Thus UTS graduates both "enrich that fealty which they have to their own church" and "become partners in sanctifying labors that transpire beyond the frontiers of their own church."[87] He gave concrete action to his ecumenical intentions and his desire for a less parochial faculty by hiring Matthias Rissi from Switzerland, the first foreign-born professor, in 1963.[88]

The Gamble Report

President Jones would preside over the largest curricular expansion in Union's history. During his administration fieldwork, pastoral counseling, and continuing education became permanent course offerings. Connolly Gamble (BD, 1945; ThM, 1950; ThD, 1952), who would later serve as the director of continuing education in 1956–76, conducted a study of the effectiveness of Union's curriculum in 1947–50. This report prompted the board to examine the course offerings and begin plans for modernization.[89] Gamble's goal was to investigate and analyze "the total education program of Union Theological Seminary." His methodology was simple; he did not refer to the Book of Order, to AATS accreditation standards, or professional societies. Rather, he surveyed 359 UTS graduates to evaluate how they thought "the curriculum of the Seminary as it was when they were undergraduates" prepared them for their work.

The survey's results not only showed that traditional course offerings were insufficient, but also spotlighted the enormous pressures on the seminary curriculum. The top subjects "thought to be inadequately treated in seminary were evangelism, biblical theology, individual Christian ethics, Christianity and secular philosophies, and pastoral work" (counseling). Although each of these subjects, except for pastoral work, had been added to the curriculum over the previous three years, they were not offered each year. Respondents further complained that the Hospital Visitation class had foundered, and visiting opportunities once offered through the SMI were now not available. The advent of biblical theology, a renewed interest in Christian ethics, and a new emphasis on ecumenics all put new demands on the curriculum.

At the same time, faculty complained that students were not as prepared as they were in the past. Before the war 50 percent of all seminary students decided to enter the ministry before age 21 and took the appropriate religion classes in college. After the war only 26 percent decided on the ministry by age 21, so many students arrived at seminary without a background in religious studies. In the Class of 1950, for example, "out of 35 men, 10 held bachelors of science or engineering. The long-held assumption that entrants to seminary would have a liberal arts education oriented toward a seminary curriculum was no longer completely valid." As a consequence, introductory courses in European history, psychology, philosophy, and Greek were now standard. "The Faculty find it difficult, if not impossible, to teach undergraduate courses on a level consonant with graduate education. Frequent concessions must be made to inadequacies in the college training of the students."[90]

Gamble argued, however, that it was the faculty who had missed the point. Citing the 1934 study by William Adams Brown, *The Education of American Ministers*, Gamble argued that the increasing specialization predicted by Brown[91] had now made seminary education disconnected from the parish. Union's curriculum was highly structured and emphasized academic courses; required courses made up 83% of the curriculum. Of the total required courses, biblical studies (including Hebrew and Greek) made up 38.7%; practical theology, 24.7%; doctrinal theology, 18.7%; church history, 13.6%; and missions, 4.3%. In surveying 36 other seminaries, he found that only 4 did not specify 50% of the courses as required, only 18 specified 75% of their courses as required, and only 16 required both Hebrew and Greek. Union, then, was in a distinct minority by having so many required courses and both biblical languages. Gamble was afraid that Union could not decide if the aim of its undergraduate education was for the benefit of the academy or the parish.

Gamble analyzed the graduate program and found the same confusion. Officially, the graduate program was designed as "further professional training for men who are in pastorates or in other forms of service in the regular ministry of the church." Union, therefore, saw both its undergraduate and graduate programs as aimed toward the parish. Yet this vision was unrealistic. Gamble argued that the undergraduate curriculum should prepare students for the parish, while graduate work should prepare ministers for research. A parish minister and an academic researcher required different skills.

Gamble had three recommendations. First, deemphasize the graduate program. The faculty had already complained in 1947 and 1949 that they feared UTS was becoming a "degree mill," and the number of graduate students was taking time away from undergraduate education. Gamble argued that Union should be primarily an undergraduate school.[92]

Second, enlarge the extension (or continuing education) program. As far back as 1928, there were those who advocated that

> the Extension Division would make it possible for every person (pastors, Sunday-school superintendents, teachers, students, societies, etc., etc.) who cannot go (or return) to a seminary, to receive some instruction and service from the Seminary. All of the Seminary's resources—faculty, schools, departments, libraries, and research material—should be available.[93]

Gamble echoed this sentiment; the best way the seminary can serve its graduates and the church at large is not through tightening admissions standards or expanding graduate education, but through continuing education. Gamble found that 82.8 percent of the respondents to his questionnaire were in favor of a more comprehensive continuing education program.[94] As a consequence, continuing education was strengthened throughout the 1950s, and Gamble was named the director of continuing education in 1956.[95]

Finally, Union had to balance the academic and the practical to meet the needs of the parish.[96] Gamble advocated establishing the position of dean of instruction to coordinate the curriculum and ensure that undergraduate courses were aimed toward the parish. Adding another year to the curriculum, as some had advocated, or adding required courses was unrealistic. Rather, a dean could promote consensus as to what was important and implement any changes.

Fieldwork

"Practical education" was the primary reason for Union's relocation to Richmond in 1898. Although the effectiveness of fieldwork was never questioned, the idea of formalizing fieldwork was never seriously discussed. Rather, upon relocating to Richmond, students saw opportunities for ministry and just did it. Their hands-on experiences in local missions were seen as the logical extension of the practical side of seminary education.[97]

The postwar population boom caused the PCUS to see more potential in fieldwork. Throughout the denomination there were a large number of country churches, with small membership and limited finances. Unable to employ a full-time minister or offer quality educational programs, they were nonetheless poised to grow due to their location near the suburbs. President Lacy, seeing that informal, student-run local missions were no longer viable, called James Appleby (BD, 1931) as director of fieldwork in 1946. Appleby developed the idea of grouping churches into a parish and assigning students from Union and PSCE to serve them. The churches in the parish were able to have preaching every Sunday and develop an education program like larger churches. When a pilot program was tried in West Hanover, the parish quickly gained members and financial strength.[98] The General Assembly was enthusiastic over the success of the pilot program and adopted the Larger Parish Plan in 1946, modeled after Appleby's model. Between 1946 and 1950, 204 rural and suburban churches were organized and were able to call students and minister according to their resources.[99]

Appleby convinced the board to require four units of fieldwork for graduation (one class each semester and during the last two summers of residency) and insisted that all requests for fieldwork be approved by his office. In this way he ensured that students were working in worthwhile ministries, supervised by responsible persons, and receiving appropriate feedback.[100] Union quickly became known for this innovative program, one of the first in the South.[101]

Several on the board and faculty, however, saw fieldwork as taking students away from the regular curriculum. Appleby responded by pointing out that the idea of fieldwork was not new. Union had moved from Hampden-Sydney because there were not enough opportunities for practical education in southside Virginia. Moore had stressed that seminary education is "not monasticism but ministry." Indeed, the Catalogue of 1897 almost required fieldwork: "During the long summer vacations students may find an opportunity to engage in practical Christian work under the direction or with the approbation of their pastors and Presbyteries. The experience thus gained with the active duties of the ministry will supplement the training of the Seminary and furnish invaluable aid in the preparation of the sacred offices."

Appleby pointed out that, for the previous fifty years, fieldwork had been voluntary; he only systematized it.[102] Whatever the qualms of some faculty and board members, however, funding from the Mid-Century Campaign institutionalized fieldwork, pastoral counseling, and continuing education as permanent parts of the curriculum.

Pastoral Counseling

Gamble noticed that a greater emphasis on pastoral care was needed in the curriculum. Indeed, graduates prior to this time continually mention how they wished they had been more prepared in the area of pastoral care. As Ace Tubbs remembers: "It did not take me long to discover that I had five other alcoholics in the three churches [where he spent a year in ministry between his second and third year]. Later, when I returned to the seminary, I reminded the professors that they did not tell me what an alcoholic is; that I might have five of them in my church; nor how to counsel the alcoholic and his/her family."[103]

Gamble, however, did not want to be seen as an advocate for pastoral counseling because it was so controversial. Many veterans, however, were interested in counseling, and graduates were pressing for more emphasis in this area. Although the board did establish the chair of pastoral counseling in 1949,[104] its acceptance was resisted by the faculty. It could be fairly said that the biggest change to the curriculum in the last half of the twentieth century was the addition of pastoral counseling.

Formal pastoral counseling classes and clinical pastoral education (CPE) are not found in any catalogue entry before the 1950s. In the nineteenth century, pastoral classes meant an exegesis course on the Pastoral Epistles, a class in Sunday school administration taught by the professor of church history, and preaching in front of the professors. After the 1920s (when Christian Education had become its own department) a class in "pastoral duties" was taught by the English Bible professor—again an exegetical study of the Pastoral Epistles.[105] As students participated in the SMI-sponsored "hospital visitation," the value of counseling became apparent to many. Some students began to seek out the newly created CPE programs springing up around the country. One of these pioneers was Bill Oglesby, who would originate Union's pastoral care program. He was appointed professor of pastoral counseling in 1952.

William Barr Oglesby Jr. (BD, 1937) was born in Mississippi and graduated from Austin College. He saw himself as a parish pastor, and his first call was to New Iberia, Louisiana. As a home mission church, they had not had a minister for fifteen years and had only twenty-three members when they called him. Oil, however, had just been found there, people were streaming into the area, and the church grew.[106] In 1942 he accepted a call to Helena, Arkansas. Where New Iberia was optimistic, Helena was tense. The area was poor (dependent on cotton), and with the poverty came depressing violence. The church had defaulted on its payments and was foreclosed before Oglesby arrived. Locked out of their sanctuary, the congregation met in a home. The Christmas before they called Oglesby, everyone pledged not to give presents for Christmas and use the money to pay off the note and call a minister. When he left Helena after five years, the church was self-supporting and he discovered a profound dimension to his ministry.

It was in Helena that Oglesby realized that his ministry was dealing with people on an intensely personal level. It was here that he confronted alcoholism for the first time. A member of his church (a deacon) was an alcoholic and became involved with Alcoholics Anonymous. Oglesby began to learn about AA, and he worked with the deacon to start the first AA group in eastern Arkansas. After five years in Helena, he was called to Little Rock in 1947, and in 1950 accepted a call to UTS.

After the war, Oglesby thought that many people had lost their way. He came to believe that the church, to be an effective agent of transformation, had to train ministers differently, and he believed Lacy understood the need to give ministers new tools for the parish. Although he received a PhD from the University of Chicago in 1961, Oglesby did not have an earned doctorate when he was first called. He had come to President Lacy's attention when he studied under Tolley Thompson and wrote his ThM thesis on pastoral counseling.

The chair of pastoral counseling at UTS was the first one established at any seminary in America. The DeFriese family (from Bristol, Virginia) who endowed the chair put a stipulation in the endowment to provide for two years of doctoral work for the person in the chair. As a consequence, Oglesby went to the University of Chicago in 1950 and took CPE in 1951 at the Topeka (Kansas) State Hospital, which became the model for the program he instituted at Union. From its inception, Oglesby wanted to separate pastoral counseling from psychology, the hospital, and the mental hospital. Following the ideas of the development stages of spirituality put forth by Lewis Sherrill in his ground-breaking 1951 work *The Struggle of the Soul*, Oglesby saw counseling as a spiritual endeavor. Since any kind of counseling was unknown in the seminary curriculum, however, he was viewed with some suspicion.

In fact, pastoral counseling was not accepted at all when Oglesby started pushing for a required class in 1952, and it took two years for a class to be approved. His primary faculty opponent was Donald Miller.[107] Miller argued that pastoral counseling was using the social sciences to interpret Scriptures. He cited Karl Barth, who thought that pastoral care was not an appropriate area of study because it took the focus off what God was doing and focused on what humans were doing.[108] Thus he accused pastoral counseling of relying on weak theology.[109]

Nevertheless, it was increasingly apparent that the traditional curriculum alone was not sufficient to prepare ministers for the modern parish. Just as Rice navigated between revivalism and skepticism, so Union had to find a way to find a path between therapeutic Christianity on one hand and psychiatry on the other. In October 1951, the Special Committee on Theological Education affirmed that "the primary function of this seminary is to train parish ministers." At the same time, the committee recognized "the new emphasis on counseling" in the functions of a parish minister. Since "the functions of the minister would determine the work of the Seminary," the committee set out to determine how best to include a program of fieldwork and clinical pastoral education in the curriculum.

The next April the faculty refused to endorse pastoral care as a subject for undergraduates. While the faculty did affirm that "the function of this Seminary is to primarily train Parish Ministers," they thought counseling would be better taught at the graduate level. Interestingly enough, six months later the faculty voted to form a "Radio and Television" committee, offer a class in religious radio in the Spring Quarter 1953, and encourage UTS students to take the audiovisual class at ATS. The faculty was therefore open to offering nontraditional, practical classes at the time—just not pastoral counseling.

As Oglesby talked about the need for his proposed classes and Gamble's report sunk in, the faculty understood the need and in 1954 required two semester hours of "The Psychology of Religious Development," three hours of "Pastoral Counseling," and two hours of "Pastoral Care" in the curriculum.[110] It had taken three years to approve a pastoral care class, and the results were far-reaching. "Something interesting happened when Bill Oglesby came here," Jim Smylie observes. "With regard to curriculum, he introduced small-group work and broke the predominant lecture system. Oglesby introduced a greater dynamic into teaching, which persists today. Most of us alternate lectures with small-group discussion methods."[111]

When Bill Oglesby gave his inaugural lecture in 1954, he was very aware that pastoral counseling was not fully accepted on campus, but that it was wanted in the parish. He stressed that pastoral care could provide a unifying framework for ministry. In an era of specialization, pastoral care prevents the pastoral office from being fragmented into specialized areas, such as preaching, worship, evangelism, administration, youth work, or education. It is pastoral care that takes each area of ministry and molds it into a minister's one purpose, "to witness to the Gospel—the reality of the redemption of God in Jesus Christ."[112]

Continuing Education

There was never any doubt as to the desirability of continuing education. The only question was how to institutionally support it. In the 1930s, Henry Brimm had established what is believed to be the first continuing education program for pastors through summer clinics and home-study guides and books, called the Directed Study Program. His idea was simple: he would recommend the latest books in a certain field to parish ministers so that they could stay current in that discipline. The readings were not sequenced or designed to fit into an overall plan. Indeed, the program was considered to be a library operation.[113]

President Jones, however, wanted a more systematic approach to keep pastors (especially those in rural areas) up-to-date and, at the same time, reach out to laypeople. With support from the Mid-Century Campaign, he appointed Connolly C. Gamble as director of continuing education in 1956. This position was a full-time faculty appointment, the first faculty position dedicated to managing a continuing education program in the country. Gamble made "brief syllabi or study guides prepared by the members of the Seminary faculty and other qualified authorities" available to those ministers who desired the training. The minister would work through the syllabus as a course, completing it on his own schedule. Academic credit was not awarded. Gamble took an expansive view of continuing education. He started the Tower Room Scholar Program in 1957 and made the Directed Study Program available to laypeople. He also initiated the Interpreting the Faith conferences in the late 1960s. In addition, Gamble expanded the Town and Country Ministers' Institute (begun in 1937), then renamed it the Town and Country Pastors' Institute in 1957, making sure to include not just ordained clergy, but also Christian educators, evangelists, and some laypeople.[114]

The Purpose of the Church and Its Ministry

By the 1950s Union was arguably one of the most innovative seminaries in the country. The flagship seminary of the PCUS had appointed a director of fieldwork in 1946, a professor of pastoral counseling in 1952, and a director of continuing education in 1956. In 1954, however, the dean informed the board that all further curriculum decisions would be postponed until the AATS Niebuhr study was issued[115] (funding had already been allocated for Connolly Gamble's appointment as director of continuing education). At first glance, it seems that the seminary merely needed time to incorporate the changes of the last decade. There could be no doubt that fieldwork, pastoral care, and continuing education were firmly established. Yet the dean's decision mirrored an anxiety in American theological education.

The American Association of Theological Schools published *The Purpose of the Church and Its Ministry* in 1956. This four-year study, directed by H. Richard Niebuhr along with Daniel Day Williams and James M. Gustafson, surveyed thirty-six seminaries in the United States and Canada. This project was a self-conscious continuation of the study conducted by Mark Arthur May in 1934. *The Purpose of the Church and Its Ministry* explored the purposes of theological education and how that education was conducted.

Niebuhr argued that the context of ministry and theological education had changed. Before World War II, Americans were bound by customs inherited from the Old World, yet also believed they were immune from events around the world. After the war, the Americans saw themselves in a new light and relationship to the world. Victory allowed them to feel free to experiment and assume new, unprecedented roles in the world and in their imaginations. Americans now saw themselves in a new role as leading the free world against the communist empire, while paradoxically denying fellow citizens full rights at home. Niebuhr pondered how the church and its ministry—and the education of its ministers—could address the new postwar context.

Niebuhr criticized the provincialism of the American church: denominationalism seemed to deny the importance of the church universal. More profoundly, however, with education being taken over by the state, declining attendance at worship services, more marriages being performed by civil authorities, and social change transforming the world—the emphasis on the denomination turned the minister into little more than a manager. Niebuhr called ministry "the Perplexed Profession" because ministers were unsure of their role. The same uncertainty, he argued, afflicted theological schools. They had lost their sense of purpose by trying to fill too many agendas; be it "social gospel, social ethics, religious education, psychological counseling, and ecumenical relations."[116] Indeed, Don Shriver relates:

> In the early 1970s, Professor W. D. Davies of the "other" Union, in New York, had a student ask him, at the end of a class on the New Testament, "Dr. Davies, why do you take this book, the Bible, so seriously?" Davies reflected that he was dealing with a generation of students who had not been brought up in a church where the answer had already been embodied in sermons and study groups addressed to a committed body of believers.[117]

Niebuhr saw mid-twentieth-century theological education as so specialized that it had become sterile and unconnected to modern life. Increasing specialization within disciplines obscured the "controlling idea" that gave unity to theological education. The tendency toward pluralism resulted in confusion and a lack of direction that led to competition between "scholarly" and practical education. Niebuhr's answer was to recover the idea of the seminary as the intellectual center of the church's life, which combines theory and practice—not to manage people, but to lead them in greater love for God and neighbor,[118] even if it made organizational concerns secondary.

Niebuhr's assessment of theological education was dismal. Since the 1920s, he accused seminaries of either rigidly maintaining the basic theological studies (Bible, history, theology) or introducing nontheological disciplines to enhance theological studies (literary analysis in the so-called basic fields; and psychology, social studies, rhetoric, and so forth in the so-called practical fields). For Niebuhr, there was no such thing as "practical" theology as distinguished from "theoretical" theology. What was lacking in seminary education was focus.

He criticized seminaries for introducing new disciplines in practical theology and fieldwork to address perceived deficiencies identified by their graduates, denomination, or research. For Niebuhr, the trend of introducing more and more classes avoided the larger issue: "Our schools, like our churches and our ministers, have no clear conception of what they are doing." He indicted modern theological education for delivering the knowledge ministers required in a piecemeal fashion that turned students into parroting a tradition, rather than seeking to be lifelong learners. Niebuhr argued that seminary education should aim to produce ministers who are biblically literate and theologically competent, and possess basic practical knowledge.[119]

President Jones gave each trustee a copy of *The Purpose of the Church and Its Ministry* in 1957. He took the Niebuhr study seriously, believing that theological education, and Union in particular, was becoming disconnected from the church and from other seminaries. He was intentional in ending Union's isolation from other institutions. Although Union had been a founding member of AATS in 1936, he took steps to make Union more active. In 1960, UTS hosted the annual meeting of AATS, and President Jones was elected president of AATS for 1960–62, perhaps the best measure of how important UTS was becoming to theological education. In March 1963, Union hosted a preseminary education conference sponsored by AATS. This conference was funded in part by the Lilly Foundation, the first mention in the board minutes of this foundation, whose support for theological education would play a large role in seminary funding starting in the 1970s. In 1958, President Jones informed the board that the faculty had held consultations with Presbyterians teaching at the University of Virginia. He was concerned that Union did not have a relationship with a university and wanted connections with the wider academic community.[120]

Union's Answer to Niebuhr

Niebuhr feared that seminary education was becoming fragmented. Specialization had resulted in a growing disconnect between professor and student, seminary and congregation. The historical-critical method, mass communications, the Holocaust, and World War II revealed a growing gap between the creeds of the churches, their traditional theologies, and contemporary biblical interpretation.[121] Niebuhr argued that the minister's first task was to serve the theological needs of people, not to be a social worker, psychiatrist, or physician. Yet Connolly Gamble had seen how ministers in the postwar world understood that their role had changed. Being the town theologian was no longer valid; fieldwork and pastoral care gave them the professional tools for the modern parish. In Niebuhr's mind, there was apparently no way to resolve the contradiction between traditional subjects and modern needs. If seminaries instituted Christian education, ethics, fieldwork, and pastoral counseling courses, there was no way to keep a coherent conception of their purpose. In contrast, Union Theological Seminary in Virginia would continue to use the traditional curriculum to focus the subjects students took in order to address contemporary life with a specific way of interpreting the Bible.

James Luther Mays (BD, 1949) taught at Union for over thirty years and held two chairs: the Archibald McFadden Chair of Biblical Interpretation and the Cyrus McCormick Chair of Hebrew and Old Testament. Born in Louisville, Georgia, he was raised in the Associate Reformed Presbyterian Church. He graduated from Erskine College in 1942, where he was known as a scholar and debater (on the debate team with John Leith). After Erskine he served in the Air Corps until 1945,[122] when he went to Columbia University to pursue a PhD in philosophy. Columbia was a disappointment; he was disillusioned with the philosophy department and his professors. After taking a class in Thomas Aquinas, he realized that he should be in seminary.

Mays had previously applied to UTS during his senior year at Erskine and was accepted. Since the country was at war, however, he had decided to take a commission in the Air Corps. President Lacy wrote and assured him that his acceptance would be held open. Mays didn't know anything about Presbyterian seminaries; he applied to Union only because he was under the care of the Winston-Salem Presbytery. He entered after his year at Columbia in 1946 and graduated three years later. Mays was ordained by Lexington Presbytery and accepted a call to Mt. Carmel Presbyterian Church in Steele's Tavern, Virginia. He took a year away from Mt. Carmel to study in Basel (1951–52) and in 1954 accepted a call to First Church, Lincolnton, North Carolina.

Mays appreciated the fact that Union believed ministers should be as intellectually competent as doctors and nurses. The seminary had a self-conscious, heavy emphasis on Bible, while other southern seminaries emphasized systematic theology. All professors taught a Bible course. The entire seminary was oriented to the pastorate and the mission field. Indeed, everyone had served in the pastorate except Balmer Kelly. Consequently, while UTS was not academically distinguished, it had a huge influence in the church. Mays later reflected, however, that some professors operated as though they were still in the church and taught students as though they were in Sunday school.

After fourteen months in Lincolnton, Mays received a telephone call from James Jones (who was then the minister of Myers Park in Charlotte, North Carolina). Jones related that President Lacy was visiting in Charlotte. Mays did not know that Jones was about to become president of UTS, but Lacy and Jones were at that time planning their transition. President-elect Jones wanted Mays for the opening in Old Testament. This was the traditional method through which Union kept a connection with the church. Presidents since Moore believed that seminary professors should come from the church. They would identify students and ministers with potential and subsidize their graduate work with an aim toward teaching at Union. Thomas Cary Johnson, E. T. Thompson, Bill Oglesby, Pat Miller, John Trotti, and others were brought to Union in that way.

Mays left Lincolnton and studied at the University of Manchester, from which he received his PhD in 1957. He would go on to be a founding member of the Fellowship of Concern, editor of *Interpretation* (1966–83), and Fulbright Lecturer at the University of Göttingen (1966–67), and was elected president of the Society of Biblical Literature in 1985. He served Union for over thirty-nine years, retiring in 1996.

James Luther Mays delivered his inaugural lecture, "Exegesis as a Theological Discipline," at a time when, as Niebuhr put it, seminaries were in a "quandary." Niebuhr argued that seminaries were not integrating faith, education, the parish, and Christian life. Mays proposed a way out of that quandary by taking Scripture as a whole, and as the focus of each part of the seminary. Indeed, Donald Shriver and others consider Mays's 1960 inaugural lecture as a still-valid critique of modern biblical criticism and its divorce from the life of the church. Mays argues that modern scholars are preoccupied by "vexed" questions as to whether the Bible portrays "real" history and whether the doctrines of systematic theology are already to be found in the Bible or are brought to the Bible from outside its text. He finds this enterprise wanting, as a violation of the nature of the Bible itself, whose authors offered testimony to events they experienced as divine revelation.[123] Since they experienced the event as divine revelation, we should approach the text the way they intended.

Mays acknowledges that modern biblical scholarship was a revolt against Protestant scholasticism (represented by Turretin), which sought to use Scripture to support confessional positions, but "it was born schizophrenic." On one hand, historical criticism sought to place Scripture in history. On the other hand, it could never tell what that history was. Thus we get the quest for the historical Jesus, which reflected modern presuppositions rather than Scripture. The result is historical exegesis, which can scientifically analyze words but cannot relate them to faith: "The Synoptic Gospels have dissolved into sources, the sources into pericopae, the pericopae into original" languages.

For Mays, much of modern exegesis "has lingered among literary fragments and sources, archaeological ruins, etymological roots, religious phenomenology," but could not explain what the text means. Consequently, modern criticism "has disrupted the continuity of the community's use of the Bible."

> By insisting that the historical character of the Bible be apprehended exclusively with the techniques, values, and perspectives of 19th century historicism, it has precluded the methodological recognition of precisely that which is distinctive in the historical which the Bible offers. . . . The center of gravity was shifted in interpretation from what the Bible says to the Church to what the original meaning was in an ancient period. The interest of the trained interpreter was focused on the correct answer to problems of historical reconstruction rather than on the question of faith for the message of the witness. . . . The question of continuity between exegesis, systematics, and homiletics is the enigma of theological education and practice today—and the dogmatism of theoretical historicism has played its part in fashioning the enigma.

For Mays, the key word is "continuity." Since World War I, he argued, biblical scholarship has used a "scientific" approach to break down Scripture into constituent parts that do nothing to nurture faith. It remains for a "third revolt" to produce scholarship that is "obedient to the nature of the Bible." This third revolt must ask questions of both theology and history. This "third revolt" is biblical theology.

Mays does not devalue the historical-critical method but only criticizes it for becoming an end in itself. History is more than a chronological sequence of cause and effect; in Scripture, revelation becomes history because what happened and interpretation are one. Thus the exegete cannot separate the "historical" from the event because people understood that they were being drawn into divine action. Biblical events are simultaneously historical and theological. Thus the right question for the interpreter is "What shall I believe?" Exegesis is always consciously theological; even so-called scientific exegesis has presuppositions. The failure "of the old quest for 'the historical Jesus'" demonstrates the failure of separating theology from history and from word. Jesus cannot be separated from his kerygma.[124]

James Mays was arguing for a mind-set informed by biblical theology. This emphasis on Scripture was an implicit answer to those who thought seminary education had lost its core, those who wanted to discard any type of biblical ethic, or those who constructed their ethics from a few out-of-context passages. As Don Shriver observes:

> Some contemporary scholarly study can seem to undermine the authority of the book as faculty lead students through a forest of text criticism, canon history, and the like. Characteristically, many seminary students these days lack deep roots in a congregation, and one wonders how they can revere the Bible when they have seldom if ever listened to the exegesis and preaching of a minister who fulfilled the office of messenger as suggested by Mays' lecture. In Mays' view, "biblical preaching" ushers listeners into the human reality of witnesses . . . vividly enough for contemporaries to perceive that the message pertains to our current reality as well as to that old one.

The result of modern biblical scholarship, Shriver argues, is an argument over methodology, instead of clarifying the meaning of the gospel.[125]

Scott McCormick (BD, 1956; ThM, 1957; ThD, 1959) has argued that the purpose of biblical theology was to "apprehend the biblical message in its historical context" in order to create and nurture faith, and it made three assumptions. First, the Bible is the Word of God and a record of God's self-revelation. Consequently, questions of inerrancy are secondary. Second, Scripture is a unity. Whereas the historical-critical method seeks to divide Scripture into constituent parts with perhaps conflicting points of view, biblical theology seeks to find how all of Scripture points to the same source. The relationship between biblical theology and systematic theology, therefore, is vague and tenuous; biblical theology is more proclaiming; systematic theology seeks a logical pattern for propositional statements. Finally, biblical theology emphasizes the ecumenical church by pointing to commonalities. In the end, it is Jesus who stands before us demanding a response.[126]

However one may criticize McCormick's definitions or argue with his thesis that biblical theology was a "movement," there is no denying that Union was teaching the Bible in a unique way from the 1940s to the 1980s. Harking back to Moore's contention that Union was "conservative in doctrine and progressive in methods," biblical studies at Union would not reduce Scripture to a document, or read it outside the context of the church. Cognizant of Niebuhr's critique, Union sought to introduce pastoral care and continuing education, to confront the culture on issues of race, to integrate its witness with the highest standards of biblical and theological scholarship.

In the 1950s, biblical studies at Union had a strong ethical bent; the Christian life was to be involved in the world. Robert Tabscott (BD, 1962) remembers how he was surprised that "we were never indoctrinated with the Jesusolatry and the civil religion of 'God Bless America.'" Rather, his teachers "were not so much concerned about our souls as they were our minds, for mind and soul were the same to them."[127] He remembers a continuity between John Bright (who was always suspicious of biblical theology, even "locking horns" with John Newton Thomas)[128] and Jim Mays and Balmer Kelly. Although John Bright relied on archaeology and the tools of the historical-critical method,

> Bright's conviction held that social justice was the indispensable expression of true piety. The 8th-century prophets were vigorous spokesmen for YHWH's justice and righteousness. . . . From his lectern, [he] never took aim on anti-Semitism, race, politics, ecumenism, or creeds. He offered no blueprints for sit-ins and marches, and a few years later in 1970, when the Seminary erupted in protest over the killing of students at Kent and Jackson State Universities, John Bright did not sign the community manifesto. But he did not have to, for his life resonated an inclusive *mishpat* . . . justice. He was an 8th-century prophet in full gear. He validated reverence and the essence of holy ground and pronounced the impending Day of Yahweh, when all the world would be judged for their crimes against each other. There would be no exception.[129]

For Bright, history preceded theology because history constituted the arena of revelation and theology. If he was suspicious of biblical theology, he recognized that his work would, and should, provoke theological reflection. But it would be a reflection "within the field of historical inquiry." Indeed, "there is no authentic understanding of God without Israel's history, and there is no true understanding of Israel's history without God."

In the end, it matters not whether Abraham's journey took place in the Middle Bronze Age, Late Bronze Age, or Early Iron Age. What matters is that the patriarch's sojourn was an act of faith, something archaeology will never be able to verify or falsify.

Bright came to see that biblical theology provided a scaffolding to build around the findings of archaeology. In 1990 he reflected: "I never grew away from Albright [William Foxwell Albright, founder of the biblical archaeology movement and Bright's teacher at Johns Hopkins] but added other things. I added an interest in biblical theology."[130]

For Don Shriver, Robert Tabscott, and other students, it was not the creeds or facts they learned at Union that formed them, but how to apply what they learned.

Some fifty of us graduated from UTS in the spring of 1962. We were on our way, but little did we know what lay ahead for the nation and for us. I do not understand how it was that so many of us showed up in Dixie after Medgar Evers was gunned down in 1963—but we did: Mac Hart, Larry Kennon, Denton McLellan, Ed Wilson, Bill Jones, Bob Lawrence, Burt Tuggle, and me were among them. Most of us were Union men. God, we were young and green, heavy laden and afraid, hardly prepared to face what we had to face: Trent Lott, Strom Thurmond, States Rights, racism, and rage, and one of the most sorrowful battlegrounds was the church in which I had been raised.[131]

H. Richard Niebuhr and James Mays saw the same fragmentation in theological education. Niebuhr argued for creating a new focus based on the needs of the postwar world. Mays, however, proposed that seminaries stop debating the "vexed" questions of whether the Bible portrayed "real" history or whether a specific doctrine was supported by Scripture. He proposed that revelation not be the specific province of biblical studies and the traditional subjects, but be integrated with pastoral care, ethics, fieldwork, and education. His model was Union Theological Seminary in Virginia.

The Library

Every major technological innovation in the postwar period was supported and advanced in some way by the library. Henry Brimm saw the library as more than a repository of books and journals. For him, the modern library had to be concerned with all forms of media. After the war, the now-expanded library contained spaces for studying and became the nexus of seminary life; students who lived off campus came to consider it their second home. In 1952 the library hours were expanded; on Monday to Friday, it was open from 8:30 a.m. to 6:00 p.m., 7:00 to 10:00 p.m.; on Saturday, 8:30 a.m. to 5:00 p.m.[132]

Brimm noticed that library use had grown from 13,102 loans with 620 registered borrowers in 1930, to 22,635 loans with 912 borrowers in 1949. By 1965 there were over 2,400 borrowers, and the library subscribed to 603 periodicals. The library's collection was also growing. In 1954 (the library's 150th year) the collection stood at 101,701 volumes. A decade later, the library held 140,000 volumes. The major technological change of the time came in November 1966 with the installation of a Xerox 914 photocopier.[133]

Brimm opened the library to other schools, denominations, and races. There was a price, however, in maintaining a first-class library. A 1951 study revealed that ATS contributed $1,000 to the operation of the library, but used a third of the library's resources. The study concluded that ATS should pay a third of the library's costs. Although ATS did end up paying more, library support continued to be a sore spot between Union and their neighbor "across the Brook."[134]

Just as other presidents "chose" faculty, President Jones sent John Trotti (1960) to the Library School at the University of North Carolina in 1963. Since Brimm's retirement was not imminent, Trotti pastored the Altavista, Virginia, Presbyterian Church from 1964 to 1968, while he finished his PhD in Old Testament from Yale. In the summer of 1968, Trotti joined the staff as assistant librarian, a full faculty position.[135]

Reigner Recording Library

Robert White Kirkpatrick (BD, 1932; ThM, 1933; ThD, 1943) taught public speaking, oversaw radio and television production, and founded the seminary's radio station. He was a child of Union; his father was a Presbyterian minister who had worked as a fund-raising agent for the seminary. Kirkpatrick lived in Westminster Hall until he was four years old. After leaving Richmond, he grew up in various pastorates in the Carolinas and decided to become a minister while in high school. He graduated from Davidson, arrived in Richmond in 1929, and stayed on for one year after graduation to earn his ThM.[136]

His first call was to South Boston, Virginia, where he became interested in the mechanics of sermon delivery. Kirkpatrick began working on his doctorate in 1938 (while still in South Boston), driving to Richmond for classes and to use the library. His field of study was so novel that before the faculty would approve his dissertation topic, they asked him to teach a class to see if his methods would produce better speakers. He designed a course and taught it to the senior class, beginning in 1939. His course was so useful that the students petitioned the faculty to include it as part of the regular curriculum. After receiving his ThD, he continued driving to campus one day a week to teach the class. In 1946 he published *The Creative Delivery of Sermons*, based on his dissertation, and accepted a call to Westminster in Richmond, where he remained for four years.

Kirkpatrick accepted a call to UTS and began teaching homiletics in September 1950. He emphasized sermon delivery because it was assumed that everyone would enter parish ministry and needed to know how to give a good sermon. His method was simple: students would preach to their classmates in class sections (usually in Watts Chapel), and he would tape the sermon. A short time later, Kirkpatrick would then have students listen to themselves, and he would talk to them individually and evaluate their preaching style. He wanted to use two tape-recording machines to allow one group of students to use one machine while another group used the second machine. The seminary, however, would only agree to purchase one $125 tape recorder, so Kirkpatrick brought his own machine. He discovered he could also tape visiting lecturers and have the students analyze the style of the speaker with a second machine.

By 1953, Kirkpatrick realized that his informal taping was getting too big and complicated for him to handle on his own. There were too many tapes to store in his office, and someone had to perform regular maintenance on the tapes and equipment. Moreover, since some of these lectures were popular, a circulation system had to be devised and maintained. The administration saw the value in taping students and visiting lecturers, and President Lacy approved $3,000 to purchase a new tape recorder and more tapes. Henry Brimm made library space available for recorded tape storage and catalogued them by speaker and subject, but there was no funding for equipment or personnel.

In 1952, Kirkpatrick had asked Dr. Charles A. Reigner of Baltimore, who taught and wrote business textbooks and was enthusiastic about the use of technology, for $4,000 to purchase a tape-duplicating machine. Sometime later he solicited Reigner for money to get another one, and Reigner came through

37. Reigner Recording Library, 1964

again. In early 1953, Kirkpatrick approached Reigner with the idea of establishing a recoding library. As he described the concept, he asked Reigner what the name of this new library should be. Reigner suggested his name, donated the funds to establish it, and the Reigner Recording Library was in business.

Kirkpatrick continually looked for new ways to enlarge the tape collection. He asked UTS in New York for tapes of their distinguished lecturers, and he began to record regular classes, especially those taught by E. T. Thompson and Howard Kuist. Students could request tapes through the extension program, and the tapes were mailed out for free. In 1956, Kirkpatrick went to the Evanston Assembly of the World Council of Churches and returned with 525 miles of tape. He also had the New Delhi WCC assembly recorded. Every time a student would leave for study in Scotland, Kirkpatrick would make sure they would tape their classes. Recording was so new that everyone was thrilled to be recorded. He also recorded proceedings of the General Assembly.

By the mid-1950s the Reigner Recording Library was the largest tape library in the United States.[137] On campus, tapes began to be so popular that Kirkpatrick began playing recordings of unusually good sermons on Tuesday night in Watts Chapel after dinner. He called it "A Time for Listening." Students would stop by on the way to the library, and the program became very popular.

WRFK

When "A Time for Listening" began, some married students did not live on campus and commented that they did not have the same opportunity to hear the Tuesday night sermons as students living on campus. Kirkpatrick thought there should be some way for the entire seminary community to hear these sermons and wondered if a low-powered radio transmitter would reach enough people. He thought that the radio station could also play tapes of especially significant lectures and speeches.[138]

Soon after President Jones assumed office in 1955, Kirkpatrick found himself on the same train to Washington, D.C., as the new president. During the trip Kirkpatrick asked him if the seminary would accept a radio station if it was donated. The president asked how much it would cost to run it. Kirkpatrick assured him it would not cost more than powering one lightbulb, and he would use volunteer student help. President Jones agreed.

That summer the Reigner Recording Library acquired an army surplus audio control console, which could be used as the broadcast control console. In the fall, Kirkpatrick and his wife donated a 10-watt FM transmitter, transmission line, and high-gain antenna. But there could be no broadcast immediately. It took eighteen months (until December 1956) to complete the FCC paperwork (filled out by a student on work study) and obtain government approval. The FCC also required that a qualified engineer be available whenever the station was on the air. Kirkpatrick did not have the money to hire one, so he studied the guidebooks, took the test, passed, and became an FCC-certified radio engineer. "President Jones," he remembers, "suggested that Helen and I choose the call letters, and we selected the initials of my father, Robert Foster Kirkpatrick, both an alumnus and former field secretary of the seminary. On the seminary's Commencement Day 1957, WRFK-FM began regular broadcasting on a frequency of 91.1 megahertz, with an effective radiated power of 12.5 watts."

The transmitter was located in the fifth-floor tower room of Watts Hall, directly under the flagpole. The antenna was clamped to the flagpole at a height of 96 feet. The radio control room was located in a small room on the north end of the second floor of Schauffler Hall, surrounded by other rooms that were part of the Audiovisual Center. It remained in that location until 1964, when it was moved to a basement room in the north end of Schauffler Hall. Right after the station began broadcasting, Kirkpatrick took an FM receiver and rode around in his car to see how far the signal would carry. Although the initial power of the station was only 12.5 watts, it was easily heard at Randolph-Macon College in Ashland, eleven miles away.

The broadcasts were an immediate hit; people in the seminary neighborhood liked the station. Some people in low-lying areas, such as behind Bryant Park, could not get the signal and called, complaining that they could not hear the "seminary's radio programs." The *Richmond News Leader* enthusiastically urged northsiders to listen to the "FM 'good music' radio station."[139] In 1960 the *Richmond Times-Dispatch* announced in an editorial: "We bought an FM radio the other day and 'discovered' WRFK."[140]

Several of President Jones's friends teased him about their small station, and their joking annoyed him. He told Kirkpatrick: "Bob, if we're going to have a radio station, we ought to have a good one." Taking him at his word, Kirkpatrick found a 1,000-watt transmitter for sale in Oak Park, Illinois, in 1958. The president was out of town, so Kirkpatrick went to the seminary's treasurer. The treasurer was reluctant to cut a check for $1,000 without specific authorization until Kirkpatrick told him that Jones wanted "a good radio station."[141]

Later that year, D. Tennant Bryan (the majority stockholder of Media General, one of the first radio and television conglomerates, based in Richmond) told Kirkpatrick that he was moving his radio and television transmitters to Broad Street Road. He then offered Kirkpatrick his 1,500-watt radio transmitter, building, and 13 acres on Wilkinson Road. Kirkpatrick readily agreed and sold the 1,000-watt transmitter he had just purchased. One year later, Kirkpatrick was offered a surplus 3,000-watt transmitter. Kirkpatrick purchased it for $2,500, boosted the output to 16,000 watts, and moved the transmitter to Wilkinson Road in 1960. The FCC assigned WRFK the frequency of 106.5 because the transmitter given by Bryan was tuned to 106.5, a commercial band. The additional power made WRFK a regional radio station; regular listeners would call in from Chapel Hill, Fort Bragg, and the Shenandoah Valley. The rest of the station, record library, studios, and offices were moved to Wilkinson Road in 1974.

The radio station was a shoestring operation; students did almost everything. Kirkpatrick gave his wife the job of music director because she complained that he did not know anything about music. He usually played different kinds of music one after another, and she complained that more thought should be given to the playlist so the same genres of music would follow one another. She listened to the station all of the time. One night when they were out to eat—she always carried a portable radio with her—she noticed that the student disc jockey had started playing the musical number on side two. Kirkpatrick claimed that no one would notice, but she made him call the studio and have the student turn the record over and begin again.

From its opening day in 1957 until 1969, each broadcast day went from 4:00 to 11:00 p.m. Classical music played from 4:00 until 6:00 p.m. and from 7:00 to 10:00 p.m. From 6:00 to 7:00 p.m. WRFK played light music, such as Cole Porter, Rogers and Hammerstein, and Leonard Bernstein. An outstanding sermon or lecture was broadcast from 10:00 to 11:00 p.m. On Saturdays, broadcasts would begin at 1:00 p.m. with novel serializations, then an opera or Broadway musical.[142] On Sundays, broadcasts began at 10:00 a.m. and ended at 1:00 p.m. The Sunday schedule consisted of an hour of religious music, such as Bach cantatas, oratorios, or requiems, then a live broadcast of the worship service at Second Presbyterian Church, followed by a delayed broadcast of the Ginter Park service.[143]

WRFK was one of the first educational radio stations in Virginia and in 1970 was one of only 70 radio stations in the United States to be a charter member of National Public Radio (NPR).[144] Affiliation with NPR was, however, a mixed blessing. On one hand, NPR brought additional financial support and access to many new programs. On the other hand, WRFK could no longer set its own policies. For example, NPR mandated an increase in the broadcast day to 8 hours on weekdays. By 1972 it was 12 hours a day. These increases put a strain on volunteer help, and professional engineers were hired, which raised operating costs.[145] Nevertheless, by 1985, Arbitron ranked WRFK as 10th in a market of 26 stations and number one in per capita fund-raising; it was on the air 22 hours a day.[146]

Television

The effectiveness of recording student preaching and the success of the Reigner Recording Library caused Kirkpatrick to consider the possibilities of television in teaching homiletics. As video began to be available, he thought he could use it so that students could critique their hand gestures, not just their voices. He purchased a 16mm camera in 1952 and would have students read Scripture in front of the camera; that was enough to critique their style. He also noticed that the lectures and programs presented in Schauffler Hall were becoming so popular that Schauffler's sanctuary could not hold the crowds. When told that there were so many invited guests that students might not be able to witness his installation in 1955, President-elect Jones said he would not be inaugurated unless students could watch it, and Kirkpatrick was ready with the suggestion that his installation be televised.[147]

The only remote camera in the state of Virginia belonged to WTAR in Norfolk. They set up their camera and lights in Schauffler's auditorium and beamed the signal to the basement for $750. A short time later Kirkpatrick came across a TV camera for sale from Blonder Tongue Laboratories, in Old Bridge, New Jersey, for $995. He went to New Jersey and saw how they could shoot a $1 bill with resolution sharp enough that he could see the bill's detail on the monitor. Returning to Richmond, he told President Jones that he could pay $750 for a onetime TV feed, or he could pay $995 for a camera the seminary could use it whenever they desired. The president told him to purchase the camera; he did not want to spend $750 and have nothing to show for it. Infrastructure was constructed on an ad hoc basis. Every time a steam line was dug up, Kirkpatrick would convince Building and Grounds to allow students to place conduit in the trench. He would then help students wire the buildings.

Kirkpatrick put a remotely operated camera in the back of Watts Chapel to record everyone who spoke, from students in preaching class to dignitaries invited for special occasions. Although he was enthusiastic about video technology, students hated seeing themselves. It was, however, a great improvement over preaching for the faculty. In 1955 an elective in Religious Programming was offered, students were taught how to produce a short religious television program,[148] and every graduate received videotapes of their preaching.

Union's closed-circuit television network was probably the first of its kind among national seminaries and the second one on a Virginia campus, the first being the Medical College of Virginia.[149] Kirkpatrick began to broadcast all seminary events. At the first commencement broadcast by the television cameras, however, the perils of new technology were all too apparent. The student cameraman, instead of pointing the camera at the pulpit all the time, opened the window and took pictures of the girls walking across the quad to attend the program in Schauffler.[150]

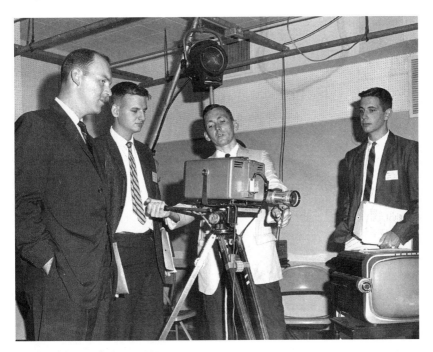

38. Closed-circuit television, 1964

While "Dr. Kirk" was on top of the latest technology, he is remembered more as an outstanding teacher and mentor. Jeff Kellam (MDiv, 1969) had some radio experience in college and had thought of somehow using radio in ministry. He had looked at Princeton and Louisville seminaries, but chose Union when he discovered that the seminary had a 16,000-watt radio station. When he applied, word got to Dr. Kirkpatrick that Kellam had previous radio experience in college. He called Kellam and offered him a job in the Audio-Visual Center as part of his "work scholarship." Kirkpatrick also promised him several hours a week on the air.

Quickly Kellam discovered that he would begin at the bottom. Much of his early work entailed cleaning 16mm film in the archives and toting A-V equipment from classroom to classroom. But as the WRFK's broadcast hours increased, Kellam got on the air, and by his last year in seminary, he was the station's primary voice. His scholarship, however, was more than a way to get through seminary. "Dr. Kirk" nurtured his call to media ministry. From 1968 to 1992 (until he was called to a part-time pastorate in a small country church in Vermont) he served Hanover Presbytery as associate for media, was WRFK's first professional staff member, and was the station director.

Kellam remembers how serious Kirkpatrick was about communicating, for more than theoretical reasons.

He stuttered. This professor of speech had overcome, with serious therapy, a severe stutter. When he preached or made formal presentations, his smooth voice was pristine in its diction and comforting timbre. When he spoke informally, however, that stutter still presented itself, if not audibly then in trembling lips. One more reason I followed him on my faith path, and with deep respect . . . and love.[151]

The Watts Hall Organ

While Union was in the forefront of acquiring the newest electronic technology, the seminary also took care to find the best in nineteenth-century music technology. The pipe organ in Watts Chapel was built in New York City in 1879 by Henry Erben, one of most prominent organ builders of the time. His organs are found in Trinity Church, New York; Second Presbyterian Church, Charleston, South Carolina; and the Washington and Lee University chapel (Lexington, Virginia). The organ found in Watts Chapel was one of Erben's last; he died in 1880. Once its manufacturing was completed in New York, it was disassembled and shipped to Liberty, Virginia (now Bedford—the words "Liberty, Va." are still visible on several of the large wooden pipes), then assembled in the Presbyterian church. The organ was originally supplied by a hand bellows. John Newton Thomas, theology professor, had pumped the bellows during his boyhood in Bedford. (The pump handle was presented to Dr. Thomas when the organ was moved to the seminary.)[152]

In 1961 the Bedford Church decided to purchase a new organ and offered the Erben to Union. In August 1961, a crew of volunteers assembled by James Sydnor (professor at PSCE) went to Bedford, took the organ completely apart, loaded it on a U-Haul trailer, brought it to Richmond, and lugged it up the stairs in Watts Hall. Lawrence Walker, a Richmond organ technician, rebuilt the organ. Over a three-month period he reconditioned hundreds of parts, replacing all the leather pieces in the valves and joints, and put it all back together. The case was designed by Mr. Allen Dryden, an architect in Kingsport, Tennessee, a seminary trustee.

When the organ was being installed, a hole had to be cut through the wall into the second-floor landing, to fit the pipe for the blower. When the hole for the air duct was cut, the workmen discovered a black pipe, which indicated gas. Everyone was afraid to touch it, so the work stopped. No one knew of any natural gas connections, so someone had to find the original blueprints, as well as meeting minutes and architect's notes, to figure out where the natural gas connections would be. The answer was finally found in the Trustees' minutes. When Watts Hall was built, it was decided to run pipes for gas lighting because there was some doubt that electricity was here to stay. It was planned that the gas pipes would be connected to the city supply when it was needed. Although faculty homes and Westminster Hall had gas connections for a short time, by the time Watts Hall could have been connected to the city connection, it was already more economical, more reliable, and safer to use electricity. This pipe, therefore, never contained gas and could be cut to make way for the air duct, with no fear of explosion.[153] The organ was dedicated on April 24, 1962.[154]

Curriculum Revision

The increasing specialization in theological education and the decreasing influence of the PCUS can be seen in the 1957 self-study and the 1964 curriculum revision. The 1957 self-study was the first time Union had ever completed a systematic examination of its curriculum. As a result of this self-study (using guidelines from AATS, not PCUS), the number of electives increased in 1958, and the graduate program underwent a complete change, limiting candidates for the ThM to eleven and for the ThD to three. Continuing Education was also detached from the Graduate Department and became its own entity. Finally, reacting to an AATS recommendation, UTS went back to the semester system in the 1960–61 academic year.[155]

The 1957 self-study did not, however, address the feeling that many students arrived on campus unprepared for the course work. Although a summer Greek course was instituted in 1943 to preserve ministerial deferments, the faculty only made "Summer Greek" a requirement in 1960.[156] The next year, the catalogue listed required undergraduate courses in Religion and Bible before admission would be granted.[157] Requiring summer Greek coincided with the first indications of declining enrollment: as attendance decreased during the early 1960s, summer Greek became the scapegoat. In 1961 the board wondered if the experiment of requiring summer Greek should be cancelled in light of declining enrollment, but the faculty supported the requirement, even if it was responsible for smaller classes.

In late 1963, the Presbytery of Appomattox overturned the Synod of Virginia to eliminate the Summer Greek requirement. They complained that requiring a summer Greek class was a burden because it robbed students of the opportunity to earn money, hopefully in a church that needed their services. Moreover, the presbytery feared an "overemphasis" on academics at Union. The Synod of Virginia brought the matter before the UTS board, but both faculty and administration held firm, and the synod did not press the matter further. No part of the church tried to bend the academic to the ecclesiastical again.[158]

The addition of summer Greek and requiring undergraduate Religion and Bible courses were just patches on a larger problem. President Jones believed that the curriculum was fragmented and did not address the needs of the church. In the fall of 1964, the faculty announced a new curriculum, reducing the number of required courses, and increasing electives and independent study opportunities. At this point, classes such as "Ethical Issues in the American South" and "Religion in the Changing South"[159] begin to appear.

Enrollment

The presidency of James (Jas.) A. Jones can be seen as encompassing two distinct eras. Prior to 1960, average attendance was 179 undergraduates per year, and most students came from church-related colleges and majored in Religion. John Kuykendall (BD, 1964) is typical of that time. He first saw the Union campus as a seventh or eighth grader. The church sponsored a trip to Virginia for the high school youth group of which his older brother was a member. Kuykendall tagged along because his mother drove one of the cars. In addition to Natural Bridge, Luray Caverns, and other sites, the group spent two days in Richmond, visiting the Board of Christian Education, PSCE, and ATS. John's grandfather went to UTS (attending in both Hampden Sydney and Richmond), and Union seemed like the natural choice after his graduation from Davidson.[160]

After 1960 the average enrollment was 169 per year, and most students did not come from church-related colleges.[161] Merwyn Johnson (BD, 1963; ThM, 1964), for example, had attended the University of Virginia and entered UTS in 1960. He had no deep ties to the PCUS and applied to Union only because his father—a navy chaplain—had advised him to go to seminary with the people where he intended to have his ministry. The change in student background meant that many students did not have experience with the PCUS culture and did not understand the demands of theological education. The dropout rate became a concern for the first time in 1962,[162] and the faculty considered the new curriculum as an effort to educate "pilgrim learners"—those who did not have experience in the church.[163]

Between 1946 and 1966, 40% of all students came from Virginia, and 30% from North Carolina. More students came from Davidson than any other college (33%) with Hampden-Sydney College and King College, in Bristol, Tennessee, each supplying 10%. In 1957 and continuing throughout the period, however, King College supplied more students to Union than Hampden-Sydney. After the war the percentage of northern students doubled (to about 6%), and students from western states (such as Illinois, Iowa, Michigan, Minnesota, Oklahoma, Washington, and Wisconsin) began to attend in greater numbers than ever before. During this time there was at least one student from the northern church in each class, with twenty in 1963. Illustrating Union's national reputation, there was at least one student from every Ivy League college enrolled from 1948 through 1966. Students from East Pakistan (now Bangladesh), India, Indonesia, Ireland, San Salvador, Switzerland, and Taiwan were in attendance for the first time.

More students required a larger corporate organization. In 1952 the board approved the position of dean of the faculty, and in 1953, the positions of registrar (who had previously also functioned as the admissions officer) and dean of instruction were created, and the assistant to the president became the de facto dean of students. Although the growth of the administration reflected the increasingly corporate nature of America and might well have been necessary, Ben Lacy was uneasy with the new bureaucracy. In his final year as president he remarked: "The growth of the seminary has resulted in an increased administrative staff and a division of work which has removed the president from much of the direct participation and contacts which characterized the early years of my administration."

The growing corporate organization and postwar inflation finally eliminated Moore's dream of a free seminary education completely supported by the church. Tuition was made permanent after the war, and by 1956 (President Jones's first year), tuition and "yearly fees" were $650; in 1957 they shot up to $805. President Jones observed that since so many students drove "first-rate" cars and maintained other luxuries, they could afford the increase. He argued: "It may very well be that we are doing theological education a disservice by cheapening it."[164] In 1950, students began to be assessed $10 per year in Student Government dues, and in 1953 a $10 application fee was charged for the first time.[165] The postwar enrollment boom also strained resources. In 1950, due to the increase in applications, the board limited the number of non-Presbyterian students to an eighth of the entering class. In 1952 the scholarship funds were exhausted for the first time.[166]

39. Refectory, Richmond Hall, 1940s

Harbingers of a New Society

Beginning in 1949, the previous class's graduation picture was included in the Catalogue. The graduates are all male and all dressed in suits. The caption says it all:

> These 153 graduates comprise the largest student body in our 138 years. They come from 21 states and foreign countries, and received their college training in 111 institutions here and abroad. Over half of them are married and over two-thirds are former servicemen.[167]

There was an order to campus life that reflected an earlier time. Ed Stock remembers that all the students wore coats and ties. Everyone, including faculty and staff, went to chapel, and everyone (except for the married students at the Diesel School) lived on campus, which facilitated a close-knit community. Attendance at Sprunts was mandatory; if someone did not attend, he had to write a paper. And a student said grace before every meal.[168]

The student body, however, was changing. In the 1954–55 Catalogue, the student body picture reflects the change in society; Allix Bledsoe James (ThD, 1957), a graduate of Virginia Union University, is pictured with the student body. He was the first African American student of the postwar era. There was no announcement of his attendance; his picture just appeared in the Catalogue.

40. Refectory, Richmond Hall, around 1964

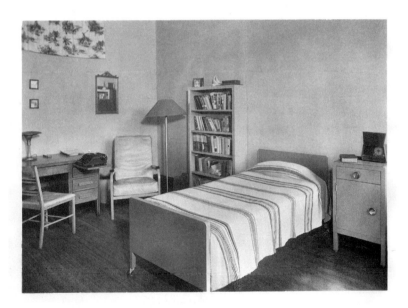

41. Dorm room, Westminster Hall, early 1950s

42. Isaac Crosby, Class of 1962

Robert Benjamin Hooper Jr. (ThM, 1957), also a graduate of Virginia Union, would follow in 1956.[169]

Isaac Crosby (BD, 1962; ThM, 1966; ThD, 1970) was the first African American admitted to the Bachelor of Divinity Program. Born in Bay Springs, Mississippi, his parents died while he was a young child, and he was raised by an uncle "who sorta encouraged me to go to school." He rode the bus thirty miles to the colored school and washed his only pair of pants every night "so they would look clean and nice for school the following day." Crosby graduated from Stillman College in 1958 and attended Union. He accepted a call to Pine Bluff, Arkansas, for three years and returned to Union to work on his graduate degrees. Crosby served on the PCUS Board of World Missions from 1969 to 1971 and was appointed professor of philosophy and religion at Stephens College, Columbia, Missouri, in 1972. He died from cancer in 1983. Like Samuel Govan Stevens a generation earlier, Crosby's recollections of campus life were positive, and he kept a correspondence going with several classmates and professors until he died. What set him apart from Samuel Govan Stevens, however, is that Isaac Crosby lived on campus.

While Union was intentionally wrestling with the issue of race, gender was not a subject for discussion. Since the PCUS did not ordain women until 1964, there was no need to admit women for the BD degree. Union took pride in

Mrs. J. E. ETCHISON

43. Elizabeth Duncan Etchison, Class of 1951

the fact that the Assembly's Training School (later PSCE) was founded largely on Moore's initiative. Administrators reminded people that Union allowed women to prepare themselves for mission work by taking classes on campus before ATS was founded, and current classes (according to the instructor's wishes) were often open to the students "across the Brook."[170]

"A middle-aged Methodist woman" would force the issue of women and theological education at Union. Elizabeth Duncan Etchison (BD, 1951) began taking classes at PSCE in 1944 and transferred to UTS (without taking a degree at ATS) in 1949. Her classmates and some faculty members were aware that she was covertly planning to qualify for a BD degree.[171] She had taken classes at ATS that would transfer to UTS, and she never took enough classes each semester to arouse suspicion that she wanted a degree.

Etchison had done too much to let anyone hold her back. A native of Norfolk, Virginia, she enlisted in the YMCA in 1918 and went to France with the American Expeditionary Forces. After the armistice she worked for the YWCA in the newly formed Czechoslovakia. Then she spent three years as headmistress of a girls' boarding school in Brussels.[172] When she returned to the United States, she attended Birmingham-Southern College (graduating in 1925) and became the first religious instruction teacher in the Birmingham, Alabama, schools. After several years of teaching, she married and settled in Richmond.

44. Mary Faith Carson, Class of 1961

Feeling restless, however, Etchison with her daughter returned to Belgium to teach in an American school. When the Germans invaded Poland in 1939, she and her thirteen-year-old daughter left Brussels on a Norwegian-flagged ship, which struck a mine on the second day out and sank in the North Sea. Half the crew and passengers (including Etchison's daughter) were lost, and she was rescued after three days in a lifeboat.[173]

Etchison's goal was to prepare herself for teaching by studying the Scriptures in the original languages. By 1951 she had accumulated enough course credits to receive her degree from UTS. The faculty agreed to award it, but the board expressly stated that this should not set a precedent. Mrs. Etchison taught at Stillman College during the remaining years of her life. She died in 1964.

Etchison's "exceptional" case, however, did become a precedent, and in 1957 the Union Seminary Board approved the admission of women candidates for the BD degree. Mary Faith Carson (BD, 1961) is the first regularly matriculated woman to graduate from UTS. Hailing from Marion, North Carolina, she graduated from Salem College in 1951 and PSCE in 1953. Carson accepted a call as director of Christian Education (DCE) to Fourth Presbyterian, Greenville, South Carolina, for three years. Then she accepted the job of DCE at Chapel Hill Presbyterian Church, where she spent three years. While at Chapel Hill, Carson decided to go to seminary. She was not interested in ordination; she just thought a BD degree would make her a more effective Christian educator. Her ultimate goal was to start a lay academy in Chapel Hill.[174]

Carson wrote, asked what she needed for admission, and was told the only thing she lacked was Greek. Not being able to afford to spend the summer in Greek school, she purchased a copy of Machen's *New Testament Greek for Beginners*, and a retired classics professor tutored her over the summer. Before arriving in Richmond in September 1959, she had finished the entire textbook, which the UTS summer Greek classes did not.

Mary Faith Carson recalls UTS as "the best years of my life," and what stands out in her recollections was the excellent teaching. She felt very accepted in class and never had a problem because she was a woman. Carson did not eat in Richmond Hall; she ate at PSCE, where she lived, since there was no housing for women at Union. Her Biblical Theology class helped her work through the issue of women in the Bible. She later used her notes from this class to debate Mary Daly—who had preached the first sermon by a woman in Harvard Chapel and then walked out to protest the patriarchal nature of the church—taking the position that the Bible was not antiwoman.

Mary Faith Carson graduated first in her class and was given a fellowship for graduate study. When she was presented with the award, President Jones remarked that the men who gave the money for the fellowship would be rolling in their graves if they knew a woman had walked off with it. She taught at Queens University in Charlotte, North Carolina, from 1961 to 1964, while working on her doctorate at Princeton. Carson graduated with her PhD in 1967 and spent her career teaching at Moravian College, in Bethlehem, Pennsylvania, from 1967 until her retirement in 2000.

Although Mary Faith Carson was ordained in 1979, she never really considered ordination while she was at UTS because the PCUS did not ordain women until 1964. Throughout the church, female ordination was an issue that divided churches and roiled the General Assembly. On campus, though, the ordination of women was discussed in the pages of *Expression* during the early years of the 1960s. Just after women's ordination had been approved by the General Assembly in 1964, Kay Speegle wrote an article that identified the dilemma of women at the beginning of the drive for gender equality and reflected the debate for years to come. Speegle (who entered Union in 1962 and ultimately graduated from Austin Seminary in 1965) compared the "door to ordination" as a "Dutch door, half open and half closed." Her classmates fell into two groups. The "for yous . . . endorse you before he asks your name. He will slap your back as a true colleague, and laud you for your courageous pioneering spirit." On the other hand, the "against yous" function as "the stern-faced judge who charges you with blasphemy for denying the God-given duty of Woman, whose place is three steps behind the man, to carry his burden. There are the ones who will sit you down to try to straighten you out of your obviously confused and misguided state." All she—and other women—wanted is "a colleague or two who see you simply as a person with a purpose and a call to a ministry."[175]

Student Community

As older, more mature students flooded onto campus at the end of the war, Union's pace quickened. An automatic bell was installed in Watts Hall in 1950 to remind professors to end their classes on time. That same year, driving on the quadrangle was prohibited due to the increase in traffic. Beginning in 1950, the original green and black trim on the seminary building was replaced by the "more attractive" chocolate and brown colors.

In 1956, in President Jones's first report to the board, he stated that he was concerned with student morale. He identified the lack of community as the primary reason for the low morale and urged the board to approve an area for a student union and additional dormitory space to promote a sense of cohesiveness. One year later, he reported to the board that the Student Center (which included a lounge and snack bar located next to the bookstore, in the basement of Richmond Hall), had been set up and was functioning well.[176]

In an effort to engender community, President Jones encouraged the establishment of a student newspaper, which was to be the student voice for both Union and PSCE. The first issue of *Expression* was published in February 1956, and it mirrored the times. President Jones was interviewed for the first article. He discussed how the Bible would be taught at Union, stressing "its meaningfulness" and assuring students that the administration was working to alleviate the strains on student housing, classroom space, and teaching personnel.[177] This interview was the last time an administrator would be prominently featured in the paper. Although faculty members later wrote short articles and letters or were quoted in the student newspaper, never again would the president or a professor be so prominently featured; this was to be a student newspaper, addressing student concerns.

The issue of race and civil rights was ever present for this generation of students. They had grown up in segregation and were struggling with how to end it. *Expression* carried many searching and emotional articles about the propriety of participating in demonstrations[178] and the failure of the church.[179] The most personal and emotional articles, however, concerned Massive Resistance. Student articles were absolutely against Massive Resistance, and it was clear that the student voice was being heard in the church. On one occasion, a couple from Prince Edward County wrote to *Expression* in reply to an earlier article, accusing the students of hypocrisy for condemning the whites of Prince Edward without living there.[180]

Although Union students had struggled over the issue of race since the 1830s, the first time a student openly expressed doubts about segregation appeared in the first issue of *Expression*. Bob Gustafson argued that "if a person takes the Christian faith with honesty," he will "toss aside conventional Christian thinking."[181] Other students argued that "the south and Negroes were not ready for integration."[182] Nevertheless, Ben Lacy Rose, who taught homiletics, observed: "When Jesus was on earth in the flesh, he did not hesitate to disregard the social customs of his day which required segregation."[183]

Most articles in *Expression* supported integration and repudiated the traditional scriptural interpretation that mandated segregation. Even those who argued for equality, however, understood the personal emotions of the issue. One student who attended the Ecumenical Student Conference in Athens, Ohio, in 1960 confessed: "It is difficult for old-line Southerners from Richmond to get used to seeing a student from Africa treating a white student of the opposite sex to a soda."[184] Articles in *Expression* reflected the struggles over the civil rights movement waged within each student. There was soul-searching over proper tactics and motivation, such as whether sit-ins were seeking publicity. Those who returned from summer internships were disappointed that the people they served had no use for civil rights, but still claimed to show God's love.

Students did not, however, just write about issues from afar. Faculty and students who participated in demonstrations and conferences reported on their experiences in *Expression*. William Kennedy, a Christian Education professor, wrote about his participation in the March on Washington on August 28, 1963.[185] In 1964 a representative from the Student Interracial Movement spoke on campus to recruit students for "summer situations in interracial situations," and the Student Council called for a fast on November 15 "in support of impoverished Negroes in Mississippi."[186] That summer Donnie Cross (MDiv, 1965) reported on his work with a voter registration project in rural Virginia.[187]

In 1965 four students went to Montgomery, Alabama, and Dan West concluded that "the Church needs the Freedom Movement, much more than the Freedom Movement needs the Church."[188] One student traveled to the First Southern Regional Conference sponsored by the Student Interracial Ministry in Atlanta at the Interdenominational Theological Center, "a Negro Seminary."[189] In November 1966 three students attended a speech by James Farmer, former national director of the Congress of Racial Equality, which caused some controversy in the national press. The students wrote articles describing their impressions of his speech; they concluded that Black Power was nothing to be feared and interracial groups must continue.[190]

As Union students protested, marched, and attended lectures and conferences, some felt the tension between their faith and their politics: "Is one a Christian first and then a 'liberal' or a 'civil rightist'?"[191] Students argued whether it was right to march, and one concluded: "This march was for me not a protest, as virtually everyone has called it, but a witness."[192] Others concluded that there was no scriptural warrant for marching: "As ministers, we can to show enough love so that marching will become unnecessary. . . . Marching can divide the community."[193]

The drive for civil rights soon expanded to include concerns about the inner city and the place of the church in society. In 1961 some students called for the student body to open up a storefront mission, but nothing ever came of that initiative.[194] Three years later one student challenged his classmates: "We are called to go forth bravely and boldly into the world. But are we giving serious consideration to going into [the city]?" He concluded: "God is calling some of us to go into the heart of crowded cities in the south."[195]

Many students began to see Union as a middle-class island, catering to other middle-class islands, and ignoring the raging sea around them. In 1965 one student reported: "Several weeks ago a few of us went to Washington to a conference on the inner city." The conference was an eye-opener for the students.

"The church cannot baptize some people and retreat from others. I first met my most recent God-child on a picket line downtown. This is New Theology."[196] Another student lamented:

> Our brother, who has been divorced, stands before the church bulletin board. The "Adult Bible Class" announcement glitters. But he cringes within at the thought of the cold shoulders from some, the barbed thoughts which he fears would festoon his seat there. Our brother, released from prison and jobless, walks past the church without a glance. The homeless, those who belong [nowhere], or feel that they belong nowhere, they are around us. These homeless ones have been given to us. We, the church, are a home to many. Who knows this better than we of PSCE and UTS?[197]

The idea that students conformed too easily and were too middle class is often seen in *Expression*. In 1961, A. Donovan Cross complained in his article "Suburban Captivity of the Seminary":

> I had a course called "Types of Ministry" last semester. We talked all about a lot of sociological studies; we even wrote papers on inner city work, migrant farm work, and other "different" types of ministries. But I do not believe that any of us really seriously considered any of this as something we might do. So I don't believe we are going to get men to do anything but the "nice," "clean" work of the suburban church.[198]

Summer interns related their experiences, and many were bitter: "My work this past 2½ months has confirmed my growing suspicion that the Church is well nigh dead or at least lost in the deep woods of confusion. . . . The Church is no longer a redemptive center in society [and] has no good news for people."[199] Another asked, "[What] does a verb being *niphal*-perfect, [or] Calvin's concept of sin and grace, have to do with living in a society where people don't even know their next-door neighbors?"[200]

The seminary made an effort to be open to the community. After they were constructed, the basketball, tennis, and handball courts were open to everyone in the Ginter Park neighborhood. Some students and faculty complained, however, that tennis playing on Sunday was a violation of the Fourth Commandment. Although a posted sign asked people to observe the Sabbath and the courts were locked on Sunday, people climbed over the fence anyway, and the issue went away.[201] In the late 1950s, PSCE professor Wade Boggs invited an African American teenager named Arthur Ashe to play on the seminary tennis courts, when the city courts were closed to him.[202] Ashe went on to play tennis at UCLA (where he won the NCAA singles title); he was the first African American selected for the United States Davis Cup team and the only African American male to win Wimbledon, the US Open, and the Australian Open. Ashe was ranked number one in the world in 1968 and 1975. He retired in 1980 and died in 1993. In 1962, Tolly Thompson organized an interracial meeting of Richmond high school students on campus. Thompson wanted the students to get to know each other, so integration would not seem so threatening. Lisa Cross, Thompson's granddaughter, remembers everyone holding hands in the middle of the campus and singing "We Shall Overcome" at the end of the day.[203]

Foreign exchange students wrote articles about their churches and their impressions of Union and the United States as their year came to a close. Many were dismayed at the assumptions Americans made about God.

> For the inauguration of President Johnson, the Presbyterian minister said, in his prayer, that the Western world would not be able to live without the United States. To this I say No! The United States is not the center of the world, and life is certainly possible without them. God is no more in America than anywhere else. He is maybe used in America more than anywhere else, that is all.
>
> My major problem in adjustment was with the church, or at least the part of the church I have seen so far. I have been in about twenty five churches, and maybe twenty times, I've felt that I was entering a club where one speaks about God, but is very careful not to live with Him.[204]

Looking at a fractured country, students wondered why Presbyterians could not unite. Every time the issue of reunion came up before the General Assembly, student articles were uniformly in favor of merging with the northern church.[205] In 1965 the student body passed a resolution to remain in the National Council of Churches and begin exploring reunion with the United Presbyterian Church.[206] Union hosted moderators of the northern church in 1957[207] and 1963.[208]

The pages of *Expression* showed that students were aware of the world around them. After the Suez Crisis in July 1956 (in which England, France, and Israel invaded Egypt after Gamal Abdel Nasser nationalized the Suez Canal), Hartley Hall argued that Israel did not have a divine right to that "narrow stretch of land between the Jordan River valley and the Mediterranean Sea."[209] Throughout this period students wrote on Christian-Muslim relations,[210] the Catholic and Protestant churches in Ireland, and the arms race. They criticized repression under Chiang Kai-shek (who ruled mainland China from 1926 to 1948 and Taiwan from 1948 to 1975), the authoritarianism of Park Chung Hee (who ruled South Korea from 1961 to 1979), and how foreign policy toward Brazil and other countries favored American industry.[211] In 1957, Will H. Terry argued that "the church is not called to formulate foreign policy, but to remind the people that Christian ethics applies to foreign policy."[212]

Politics were uniformly democratic and liberal. When the Supreme Court banned prayer in public schools in 1963, one student commented, "I believe that we need to move the religious education of our children back into the homes and the church. We really can't expect the State to take over the function of having devotions for our children."[213] Before the 1964 election "an unscientific poll" showed such overwhelming student support for Johnson and the Democratic ticket that the editor had to find someone who was pro-Goldwater and convince him to write an article favorable to the Republican nominee.

Throughout the late 1950s and into the 1960s, the curriculum was the subject of constant and lively debates. In the 1950s, students called for more electives. In the 1960s, many articles were directed to the New Curriculum Committee, calling for a mandatory intern year. In addition, students were critical of the grading system and asked UTS to do away with letter grades.

Undergraduates were concerned that graduate studies were shortchanging their education.

> I have been told that the faculty is going to get a new man or maybe two men to replace Dr. Miller in the Bible Department. This, I am further told, is to strengthen the graduate school to a large extent. Now I say, if this is true, to Hell with the graduate school! We need pretty desperately some sort of chair in ethics beyond what we have now. [And] it is pretty obvious that seniors preach poor sermons for the most part in chapel.[214]

Students also complained that the lack of ethics classes made them unable to explain their positions on civil rights to potential congregations.[215]

One of the constants in seminary life was the feeling that students did not live up to the ideal of community. In 1956 one student accused his classmates of not helping to build community. He complained that the "average" student

> abhors courses that disturb the even tenor of the mind, and that raise questions about one's lifelong prejudices, that is, of fifteen years' standing. He finds the refectory no match for his mother's cooking, and he complains to a silent heaven about it. He never walks if he can ride, never takes a bus if he can drive his car, never drives an old car if he can possibly borrow the money for a new one. The professors' organization of the classes he probably does not like, and so he reorganizes the absence requirements, dates for term papers and all, more in line with his own requirements.[216]

In 1964 another student complained, "A truly unfortunate situation exists on this small campus when one can live here three years and upon graduation count no more than one member of the faculty his friend."[217] Every year there are gripes that someone is taking reserve books from the Reserve Room so that no one else in a class can use them.[218] Students just wanted Union to be different from the impersonal world they saw.

> There is the student in the dining hall who sits with one of the cliques, who is seen but not really seen, whose presence is not even affirmed, who perhaps is grasping out for someone . . . to listen to him but who finds no one to listen while he speaks. There are also the married and single students who sit with the same people, talk the same things, who never really cross over into other groups.
>
> Consider the professors who say they are more than happy to meet the students where they are but who make you cross their determined line, or who are too busy with committees, books to write, meetings to attend that they just haven't time to talk.[219]

There was also the fear that "too many of us on this campus make Intellect the god we worship. . . . Yet we seldom recognize the worth and contribution of the deeply compassionate, loving, friendly, Christ-like individual."[220]

The issue of attendance and participation symbolized a lack of community for some. There were regular complaints that students did not attend chapel and campus-wide events. One student proposed that "there be two chapels a day, the morning one mainly conducted by the faculty and the evening one conducted by the students just before the evening meal." He also suggested "two weekend retreats could be held during each academic year, one in the spring and the other in the fall." Finally, he asked that "all students and faculty be required to eat in the refectory at the noon meal. The students and faculty would be requested not to eat with particular groups but rather that all seek to eat with different people each day and thereby become better acquainted with one another."[221]

At the same time, however, students bristled at being required to attend seminary events and questioned the need for the pledge that "I will faithfully and diligently attend on all the instructions of this Seminary." In 1961, President Jones had spoken to the student body concerning their lack of attendance at Sprunts and reminded them that the pledge compelled them to support seminary activities. Student reaction was immediate and negative. Using the pledge to force attendance, one student complained, was no more than an attempt to bind his conscience and enforce conformity to an artificial ideal. "Instead of trying so hard (and so futilely) to impose a community upon ourselves, a body composed of too many diverse elements, we should endeavor to make the most of diversity."[222] Although accepting the pledge had been required of every student since 1811, strident arguments "for" and "against" the pledge, or any sort of enforced attendance at seminary events, continued until 1965. The pledge no longer appeared in the student handbook, but all students still signed it when they matriculated.

There was universal concern that relations between Union and PSCE were not what they should be. Although there were social activities, such as drama groups, choirs, and dinners between both student bodies, Union students continually accused themselves of thinking that PSCE was "somewhat inferior in theological sophistication." One UTS student complained that his classmates did not appreciate that "those who study 'across the Brook' will be fulfilling ministries that are vital and rewarding within the life of the Church. . . . [They] are none other than our colleagues, our contemporaries, within the work of the Church."[223] Sara Little, professor of Christian education at both PSCE and UTS, pointed out that "Christian education is considered to be supplementary to the preaching ministry, not competitive with it."[224]

The administration did try to foster community. Beginning in 1947, an annual retreat was held at the beginning of the school year,[225] faculty homes were opened to students one night a week,[226] and each student was assigned a faculty adviser.[227] A wives' club is mentioned for the first time in 1948, and ushering at the Mosque Theatre was finally an approved way of making money.[228] Recognizing the stresses of seminary life, the notice that "Professor Oglesby is available for counseling" first appeared in 1952.[229]

Theological issues (besides race, capitalism, and foreign adventures) were barely mentioned in the immediate postwar period. There was only one article defending infant baptism in 1957.[230] The issue of alcohol was also settled. In 1961, students seemed to decide that a minister could go to cocktail parties, but not get drunk. The student council voted to ban alcohol on campus in 1964, and some letters criticizing the decision appeared in the paper for a short while thereafter.[231] In 1958 the Student Council saw "the need for improvement in the realm of dress, recommending that all students "wear coats and ties, in an effort to improve this area of personal witness."[232] There was no mention of dress after 1964.

Expression was not just an outlet for political opinion. Every issue had a book, television, or movie review, and usually a poem. In 1957 one student discussed the relationship between William Faulkner, John Steinbeck, Thornton Wilder, Robert Frost, and Tennessee Williams.[233] In 1958 and 1960, there was a parody of *The Screwtape Letters* (by C. S. Lewis), with Wormwood enticing Union students into a dull and ineffective faith through lack of participation in ecumenical and missionary societies and by an overemphasis on academics. Indeed, some students considered that *Expression* was too oriented toward reviews of popular culture. In January 1959 the *No-Name Gazette* was published as a protest to *Expression*. The editors of the new paper accused the editors of the "established" paper of fostering "an attitude of indifference" on campus. They wanted fewer book and movie reviews and more "columns for those who have something to say which would be of value for our whole community."[234] The editors replied that they print what they receive. The *No-Name Gazette* lasted for three issues.

Six years later, other students got together and distributed the first (and only) issue of *Depression*. The complaint was the same: too many "pernicious movie reviews." The editor of *Depression* pointed out that in the previous year *Expression* published 122 pages; of these, 31 were consumed by movie reviews.[235] Just as before, the editors replied that they print what they receive, and nothing more was heard.

While complaints about cliques in the refectory appear regularly, and students were conflicted over required attendance at seminary events, there was a real sense of ownership over what students considered "theirs": the snack bar. Students managed the bookstore until the Depression. After the war, students managed a small snack bar in the basement of Richmond Hall. In 1965 (after losing money on the snack bar for some time) the administration took action. The dining hall management was put in charge of the snack bar. The new policies were immediately noticed, and students were vociferous in their reaction. One student summed it up: "Our refreshment center was left open at night and on weekends: but now, suddenly, locks have clamped the doors shut."[236]

After the war, Union no longer fielded interscholastic sports teams. Instead, intramural football, basketball, softball, and sometimes tennis scores and stories were a staple of *Expression*. Although the UTS softball team won the 1952 Virginia State Intercollegiate Championship[237] and Union teams sometimes played other seminaries (Union defeated Westminster Seminary in football in 1961),[238] the touch or flag football of the Calvin Bowl was the highlight of the year. It was argued that this clash between intramural football teams had "relevance to our existential situation in a theological school." The sports reporter observed, "Conservatives placed their greatest emphasis on a strong and rugged defense, . . . [using] the orthodox 'single-wing' formation, with the line unbalanced to the right." At the same time, "liberals emphasized a varied offense, . . . quite flexible as the situation demanded."[239]

On April 1, 1966, *Expression* published *Prayboy*, a seminary-themed satire of *Playboy*. The *Prayboy* philosophy was simple and repeated the plea for a gym.

The bodies of the prayboys and praymates must be healthy and beautiful things. This can be so only through physical expression. Therefore, it is imperative that UTS PSCE have a gymnasium soon.[240]

And *Prayboy*'s "Party Jokes" required a passing knowledge of the Old Testament.

A young seminarian was making his calls on a bicycle to save money during his summer fieldwork. One day one of the elders in the church saw him walking and asked where his bicycle was.

"I can't find it," said the young seminarian, "and I'm afraid someone may have stolen it."

"Well," said the elder, "you are having a series of services this week. Why don't you preach on the Ten Commandments? . . . Maybe whoever has the bicycle will get the hint when you get to 'Thou Shalt Not Steal.'"

Later that week the elder saw the seminarian on his bicycle and asked, "Did the sermon do what I said it would?"

"Not exactly," admitted the seminarian. "When I got to the Seventh Commandment, I remembered where I left the bicycle."[241]

But the students could also bite, as in this satirical creed:

The Seminary Creed

I believe in Union the Seminary Almighty, maker of ministers; And in her Average Student, Our exemplar in the faith; who was conceived by the status quo, born of unwilling exposure to Hebrew and Greek, staggered under unwanted smatterings of theology, kept in anguish by practical work; he descends into despair about the church; After three years, he graduates to serve her; ascends into the inanities of Sunday mornings, and sits at the right hand of the middle class; from thence he judges the weak and the sinful.

I believe in self-accomplishment; in the Southern Presbyterian Church; in the communion of recreation, administrative know-how, the avoidance of crises, and the life everlastingly dull. Amen.[242]

A Changing World

The world was changing, but not in a way anyone could imagine. With the passage of the Civil Rights Act of 1964 and the Voting Rights Act of 1965, students confidently allowed themselves to think that society was conforming to their vision. Vietnam was barely on the horizon, but the echoes of war could be heard. In March 1966, *Expression* recorded that two students attended "the meeting of the Theological Students for Viet Nam Peace Talks, held in New York on February 9, 1966." In the same issue, the editors conducted a poll of Union and PSCE students which showed that 74% of students and 75% of faculty favored "the current involvement and policy of the U.S. in the Vietnamese conflict," and 95% of students and 88% of faculty were against "the immediate withdrawal of all U.S. troops from Vietnam." Moreover, 85% of students and 100% of faculty considered the "containment of Communism in Southeast Asia within its present limits as important to the security of the free world," and 70% of students and 57% of faculty were against "public demonstrations in behalf of an early peace in Viet Nam."[243] The next month, the UTS Social Action Committee invited the Richmond Council for Peace Education to meet in the basement of Schauffler Hall.[244]

Perhaps the biggest postwar change in the lives of students was the ordeal of senior preaching. Prior to 1956, Tuesday nights were reserved for seniors to preach in front of the entire community. Dinner included candles and table-cloths; males wore coats and ties, and women—if invited (and usually from PSCE)—wore hats and gloves. After dinner everyone would go to chapel. Three faculty members would critique the sermon in front of the entire congregation.[245] Lawton Posey (BD, 1960) remembers that on his night John Leith raked him "over the theological coals, barefooted, and in both directions," but Leith affirmed that "I had some potential."[246] In 1956, President Jones announced that senior preaching before the entire student body had been eliminated, and no one objected.[247]

Hartley Hall has observed that senior preaching was seen as a rite of passage and worked because the faculty was very involved with the students. Every faculty member was in a prayer group with seven or eight students, which met once a week. Consequently, the community was close and clearly defined.[248] Although formidable at the time, senior preaching was seen by many as a time of affirmation and shared fears, which created an empathetic and long-lasting community.

This is not to say, however, that students stopped preaching. Until the middle of the 1960s, every second- and third-year student was assigned to fill empty pulpits at churches around Richmond, and in Virginia and North Carolina. Just as before the war, these churches were the first time most students had to deal with difficult and disappointing congregations. Such experiences made some doubt their call, while others were encouraged.

Technology began to infiltrate the lives of students. Term papers in the archives were mostly handwritten prior to 1950, then typewritten papers predominate. In 1950, telephones could be installed in dorm rooms for the first time.[249] The installation fees and monthly rate, however, were considered too expensive for most students, so the pay phones were constantly in use. By 1956, six "Telephone Pay Stations" were on campus for student use: Watts Hall (third floor), Westminster Hall (second floor), Richmond Hall (first-floor lobby), Neill Ray House (second floor), Melrose Hall (second floor), and Rice Apartments (basement).

Despite the changes in culture and curriculum, the class schedule remained consistent with previous decades. Throughout this era, class periods were 55 minutes in length (except on Saturdays, when they were 50 minutes) with 10 minutes between classes. In 1947, chapel began at 8:45 a.m. and lasted for 15 minutes. Classes then ran from 9:00 a.m. to 5:00 p.m. On Saturday, there was no chapel.[250] In 1959, chapel began after first period (at 9:25 and lasted for 15 minutes).

The refectory served breakfast at 7:30 (8:15 on Sunday), lunch at 1:10 (12:25 on Saturday), and dinner at 6:00 p.m. (no dinner on Sunday). In 1964 the refectory began serving breakfast cafeteria style, but the board was assured that both lunch and dinner were still "sit-down" occasions.[251] Students were required to eat in the refectory, and complaining about the food was a consistent topic in

Expression. One student thought that the Advance Campaign should include $20,000 for "not less than ten jars of peanut butter to be present at all meals; fresh bread at every meal; meat at all breakfasts and other meals, [and] a new minimum serving of french fries: 10 fries per student."[252] Some tried to improve the situation on their own. Consequently, throughout this period the administration continually warned students: "The Southeastern Underwriters Association, which has supervision of our fire insurance, has been most emphatic in warning us against any such practices. Those who cook in their rooms will be asked to withdraw from the dormitories."

In the 1949 Student Handbook, the prohibition against pets appears for the first time.[253]

The pages of *Expression* reflect concerns with civil rights, Union's middle-class orientation, the burgeoning consumer society, and America's growing involvement in Vietnam. Yet student life still involved going to class and living in a community. In the archives, next to the student newspapers is a box stuffed with handbills and sign-up sheets, showing the variety of student life. One announces the second dose of Sabin Oral Polio Vaccine on January 22, 1964, at Neill Ray House at 4:00 p.m. Another announces choir rehearsals for *Messiah*, presented in December 1962; a handbill invites students to participate in the Civil Rights Vigil on April 15, 1964. There are fliers for numerous picnics, ice-cream socials, garden plot sign-ups, Calvin Bowl invitations, and Real Award nominations. The community held together.

Beyond a Regional Seminary

John Holt Rice's dream of Union's scholarship contributing a voice in the wider theological conversation was unrealized until the 1950s. Publishing was never a priority because professors who were generalists did not see original research as important to the preparation of educated ministers for the parish. The publication of John Bright's *Kingdom of God* in 1953 and the growing influence of *Interpretation* changed the faculty's orientation. *The Kingdom of God* was one of the first theological works by a Southerner to gain national attention and respect; it symbolized that the seminary was moving out of a distinctly southern context.[254] *Interpretation* also enhanced Union's reputation. Paul Achtemeier, editor of *Interpretation* from 1984 to 1990, reported that when he traveled to Europe, he was, quite naturally, asked where he was from. The first several times he replied, "I am from Union Theological Seminary in Richmond, Virginia," and all he received were blank looks. Then he began to tell people he was "from Union Seminary, where *Interpretation* is published," and everyone could place him and was impressed.[255]

Interpretation gave institutional voice to Rice's dream as it sought to build "bridges between the exegete and the theologian . . . that within the pages of one journal, as within the one church, biblical scholar and theologian live and work as one."[256] Balmer Kelly observed that two of the most widely read religious quarterlies of the 1940s and 1950s were published from Presbyterian seminaries: *Theology Today* (Princeton) and *Interpretation*. From less than 650 subscribers in 1947, paid circulation grew to 1,500 by 1949, and to 6,300 by 1970.[257] By 1966, *Interpretation* was sent to all 50 states and 85 countries. It was on the shelves of 661 seminary, university, and public libraries.[258] *Interpretation* fostered the faithful scholarship that helped make Union a national seminary.

Union's reputation attracted visitors. Perhaps the most renowned guest was Karl Barth, arguably the most influential theologian of the twentieth century. Princeton Seminary had invited him to deliver the B. B. Warfield Lectures in October 1962. This was his only visit to the United States, and he also lectured at the University of Chicago, San Francisco Theological Seminary, and Union in Virginia. While in Richmond, Barth (who was fascinated by the Civil War) toured battlefields and fired a musket. Ann Logan, daughter of President Jones, remembers Barth with his shock of white hair sitting in their house in the evening, listening to Mozart.[259] Others were scandalized when the great theologian asked for beer with his evening meals.

Alumni

Tom Currie, dean of the Charlotte campus, recalls that in the 1950s tall-steeple congregations in Texas wanted "Union men" (either undergraduate or graduate) to fill their pulpits, and Union graduates became known as "The Wise Men from the East." Whatever the satire, there was no denying that Union remained the flagship seminary of the PCUS. By 1950, about 50% of all PCUS ministers were UTS graduates (75% in Virginia, 70% in West Virginia, and 70% in North Carolina),[260] and these figures generally hold between 1948 and 1966. Service to the church remained a hallmark for Union graduates: three of them served as moderators of the General Assembly, and they were found on all boards and committees of the General Assembly and on most synods and presbyteries. During this time, 111 Union graduates entered the mission field, with 31 serving in Congo (now Zaire), 23 in Brazil, 12 in Korea, 10 in Japan, 9 in Taiwan, 7 in Mexico, 5 in Portugal, 3 in Indonesia, 2 in East Pakistan (now Bangladesh), and 1 each in Colombia, Ecuador, Ethiopia, India, Iran, Ivory Coast, Liberia, the Panama Canal Zone, and Spain.

In previous periods the dropout rate was no more than 4%; then in 1948–66 the total dropout rate was 7%, reaching 15–20% in 1962–66. Many students arrived at Union on a personal spiritual journey and left when faced with the academic rigor or a crisis of faith; others attended to maintain their draft deferment. Of the 1,722 graduates during this era, 23% left the ministry within 10 years—an unprecedented figure. While some apparently returned to their previous professions in business, electrical engineering, medicine, or the law, there were others who entered totally new fields as librarians, civil servants, and Peace Corps workers. Public service and education were still important to Union graduates. In the 1948–66 period, 2% of Union graduates became social workers (including an administrator for the state of Delaware) and counselors (a totally new field); 10% ended up as deans, secondary education teachers and principals, campus ministers, and professors, including Robert Hawks (BD, 1955), who served as the executive director of the Davis-Stuart Children's Home in Lewisburg, West Virginia, from 1961 to 1974.

Union had an enormous impact on theological education. Fred Stair (BD, 1947) and Hartley Hall (BD, 1957) served as presidents of Union. San Francisco Theological Seminary called Randy Taylor (BD, 1954) as its president from 1985 through 1994. Donald Shriver (BD, 1955) was president of Union Seminary in New York from 1975 to 1991. Doug Oldenburg (BD, 1960) was called as president of Columbia Theological Seminary from 1987 to 2000. Kenneth Orr (BD, 1960; ThM, 1961) was president of the Presbyterian School of Christian Education from 1974 to 1979. This influence also extended beyond the PCUS: Allix James (ThM, 1949; ThD, 1957) served in a series of positions in the administration of Virginia Union University, beginning in 1950, and ultimately serving as president from 1970 to 1979. Neely McCarter (ThM, 1958) served as president of Pacific School of Religion from 1979 to 1991. Robert Stamper (ThD, 1950) served as vice president of Columbia Theological Seminary from 1955 to 1964.

Union graduates were important to college education as well. William Kadel (ThD, 1951) was president of Eckerd College from 1958 to 1968. Robert Patterson (BD, 1952) served as vice president of Southwestern (now Rhodes) College from 1952 to 1977. James Frye (BD, 1955) served in the administration of King College, Bristol, TN, from 1960 to 1967, then St. Andrews Presbyterian College (now University) from 1967 to 1985. John Kuykendall (BD, 1964) was president of Davidson College from 1984 to 1997, then served as its interim president in 2010–11. Dan West (BD, 1965) was president of Arkansas (now Lyon) College from 1972 to 1988.

Advance Campaign

At the end of the 1950s, Union Theological Seminary in Virginia was a national seminary in optimistic times. It was known through its graduates, its professors, and the influence of *Interpretation*. Yet many supporters thought that the physical plant and curriculum did not match its reputation and influence. In 1957, President Jones reported to the board that the seminary needed $5 million to increase the endowment; construct an administration/classroom building, a dorm for single men, a dorm for graduate students, apartments for married students; and secure additional faculty. He predicted an enrollment of 400 by 1968. When there was an unexpected operating deficit in 1958, his previous year's report became the basis for the Advance Campaign.[261]

President Jones recognized that the success of the Mid-Century Campaign at the beginning of the 1950s was largely due to professional fund-raisers. Although the board had agreed in principle to hire a director of development after the success of the Mid-Century Campaign in 1953, no real follow-up action was ever taken. In early 1964, President Jones met with Balmer Kelly in New York (as Kelly was returning from Europe) and explained his plan to establish a development office. He wanted a professional to manage the Advance Campaign and stay in touch with the seminary's base of support after the campaign was completed. The president asked Kelly to chair the development committee. Kelly readily agreed and later came to believe that the establishment of the development office and committee was a more significant change to UTS than anything else in its history.[262]

The mall in the center of Union Seminary's Main Quadrangle is a useful as well as attractive part of the campus. It, and Schauffler Hall (visible in the background of this photograph), will be retained in the rebuilding program now planned for the Seminary's physical plant. As suggested in the site plan in this brochure, the beauty of the mall and its trees will be enhanced by small reflecting pools at either end, and new walks. These projects are now scheduled for Phase II.

Below, an architect's concept of how the Main Quadrangle buildings might relate to each other when all three building phases have been completed. The upper sketch shows the north side of the campus and the lower sketch shows the south side, as seen from the mall. Schauffler Hall is shown in cross-section in both sketches. These sketches are intended to show building sites and relationships only, and do not necessarily suggest the final appearances of the buildings.

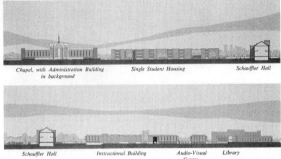

Chapel, with Administration Building in background   Single Student Housing   Schauffler Hall

Schauffler Hall   Instructional Building   Audio-Visual Center   Library

45. Site plan of the campus: Advance Campaign, 1965

The Advance Campaign was originally designed to last from 1965 to 1967 and be conducted in three phases: to expand the facilities to accommodate a student body of 300, then of 400, and eventually of 500. The phase-one goal was $6 million, to come from the congregations in the controlling synods.[263] The $6 million raised in phase one was designated to build an instructional building and an audiovisual center, add three floors to the library, build married-student housing on Westwood tract (Advance Apartments), and construct faculty housing. In addition, there was to be an unspecified endowment for fieldwork. The goal for phase two was $6.8 million and would construct a new chapel and administration building and an athletic building (with swimming pool), and provide for a $500,000 scholarship fund. Phase three would raise $5.2 million to provide the new buildings with furniture and equipment, for a total goal of $19 million.[264]

Just as the map of the proposed campus for the Walter W. Moore fund reveals a triumphal vision, so the literature for the Advance Campaign betrays a desire to obliterate the past. In the 1960s the construction of the interstate highway system and urban renewal projects resulted in neighborhoods being obliterated and stately homes being torn down for superhighways, public housing, and high-density apartments. Union almost followed that trend.

The Advance Campaign envisioned demolishing the buildings around the quad in favor of uniform, windowless, utilitarian buildings in modern square-block style. Taking a cue from the Walter W. Moore campaign, Westwood tract would

46. Proposed Quad plan: Advance Campaign, 1965

be the site of married-student housing, faculty housing, and a gymnasium. Additional buildings, however, were not the only goal; funding from the Advance Campaign would enable the seminary to establish five endowed chairs—Church and Society, American Church History, Greek New Testament, Old Testament Studies, and Biblical Studies—to offer more electives and research opportunities. Funding was also needed to obtain the latest in technology and expand the library.[265]

The Advance Campaign was unveiled at commencement on May 18, 1965. The *Richmond Times-Dispatch* called the $19 million campaign "the virtual rebuilding of Union Theological Seminary"[266] and excitedly printed a map of what the campus would look like after the buildings were completed. The assumption was that the current enrollment of 207 would grow to 500 in 20 years. When an anonymous donor gave $1 million, it seemed like the ultimate $19 million goal was within reach.[267]

In the midst of the Advance Campaign, the seminary recorded its operating budget of $1 million, along with a $40,000 deficit in 1965.[268] The promotional booklet, *Training for Excellence*, claimed that on March 31, 1965, the book value of the endowment was $7.5 million and "the seminary has no indebtedness." But *Training for Excellence* also argued that Union did not have the resources to cope with the new challenges faced by the church and the seminary: "a world

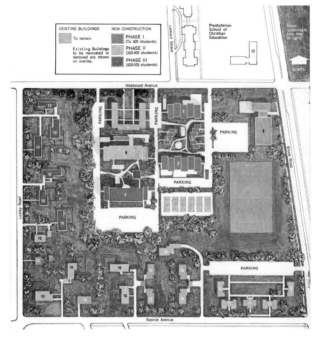

47. Proposed expansion on Westwood tract: Advance Campaign, 1965

in which God seems less and less important to many, . . . a world haunted by the specter of secularism, . . . and a world of broken homes and sagging moral values, bursting suburbs and inner-city decay."

Training for Excellence proudly trumpeted Union's impact on the church:

> In its 153 years, Union Seminary has prepared more than half of the ministers of the Presbyterian Church in the United States, in addition to preparing ministers in many other Protestant denominations. Union leads all our denomination's seminaries in the number of B.D. graduates who are missionaries. Union Seminary alumni number 1,948 in North America (including 1,939 in the United States), 39 in the Far East, 32 in South America, 30 in Europe, 20 in Africa, and two in India.

The booklet emphasized that Union's influence was ongoing. In the 1964–65 school year,

> 342 men from the four controlling Synods (131 more than in the previous year) pursued specific courses of study under faculty direction. Another 134 pastors came to the campus as Tower Room Scholars for resident study in twelve-day programs which included daily group conferences with faculty members.[269]

The churches came through, and the $6 million goal for phase one was quickly met, but it was not a portent of success. The Advance Campaign never made it beyond the first phase; the inflation of the 1960s exploded the cost estimates. In 1965 the estimated cost of phase one was $3,544,000, but total costs turned out to be $5,994,000. As new estimated costs were revised 30 percent above previous estimates and donations dried up due to the economy, it was clear that the Advance Campaign would be a failure. By 1969, after completing less than half the projects originally outlined in the program's first phase, all new construction was halted (including the gym and pool); only the married-student apartments, faculty housing, library expansion, and chapel renovation were completed. Three new professors were hired, and continuing education was endowed. At the same time, enrollment did not keep up with expectations. President Jones had predicted a total 1970 enrollment of 400, but it reached only 350.[270]

Although the Advance Campaign never reached its goal, it had a profound effect on the campus. There were now buildings on the Westwood tract, and the faculty was now able to take sabbaticals (which were unknown in previous years). At the same time, the Advance Campaign showed how American society had changed. Instead of reflexively supporting the institution, the campaign bothered many students because it offered a vision of blandness. One of the promotional tools distributed by the seminary was a movie titled *The Training of the Minister*. One student complained:

> The UTS portrayed in the film (except for occasional slices of humor) was tranquil, insipid, innocuous, and inoffensive. It was all of these, and in such extremes that its total effect was very offensive; for it projected an image of the minister which (hopefully and thankfully) is fast becoming an unreality. Perhaps the money will come in, ringing and tinkling; but if there is any credence given to the observation that these sorts of money-raising efforts have an effect on enrollment, then a progression of knitted brows on the admissions committee is imminent. Can you imagine any college student, having seen the film, considering UTS for training unless he were as tranquil, insipid, innocuous, and inoffensive as the film itself?
>
> There is so much more that is stimulating and exciting. A professor from this school actually went to Selma, and gave as his report on the trip what was one of the best and most encouraging addresses heard on campus this year. Many more faculty joined the students in their Richmond demonstration. And those on the faculty responsible for the new curriculum deserve the highest praise; it is enough to make the seniors turn on the underclassmen with envy.[271]

Students were asked to make phone calls to donors, stuff envelopes, and speak in churches. They griped that their participation cut into their study time and grumbled that the entire campaign encouraged a superficial vision by focusing on money; the administration "seems to put more vigor into the campaign than it ordinarily expends on preaching the gospel." With inflation and dwindling receipts (and second thoughts about tearing down beloved buildings), everyone was relieved when the Advance Campaign was over.

President Jones hoped that the Advance Campaign would enable Union to compete with the best seminaries in the country. In response to the AATS call for a higher level of professionalization in theological education, Union began offering the master of sacred theology (STM) degree (in addition to the BD,

ThM, and ThD) in the fall of 1966. The STM was a master's-level professional degree, primarily designed for ministers actively serving in a pastorate who could not leave for periods of residence on a seminary campus. The degree required four years, and STM classes were held once a week.[272] The STM program, however, would soon be eclipsed by the introduction of the DMin.

Just as it became apparent that Union would raise $6 million in the phase-one goal of the Advance Campaign, President Jones died of a heart attack on November 17, 1966.[273] Although President Jones's death was completely unexpected and there was no succession plan, the board quickly named Balmer Kelly as acting president because he was the dean.[274]

President Jones had built a corporate structure and established a specialized faculty, which was completely unprecedented. President Lacy had called Ken Goodpasture (BD, 1955) in the middle of his senior year and asked him to be the president's assistant. Although the selection process was informal, the duties of this assistant were important. He would assign housing, conduct public relations, enforce student discipline, recruit new students, and plan for special events (including helping with the transition to President Jones).[275] A decade later, all of these jobs, plus development, would be handled by full-time professionals. President Jones institutionalized the administrative shift from ecclesiastic to academic, from the board to the faculty.[276] By the time of his retirement in 1974, Balmer Kelly compared Union to a corporation.

President Jones had also begun to treat the faculty as professionals. In 1956 he convinced the board to allow sabbaticals and improve the faculty's retirement plan. There was one area, however, where he continued the previous informal tradition: identifying and educating promising men for the faculty, such as William Kennedy in education and James Mays in Old Testament. In 1958 President Jones reported to the board that he saw two basic methods of gaining faculty: either enlisting "new scholars" from pastors in the church, or by "sheep stealing"—hiring established scholars away from other institutions. He preferred recruiting from the church. In 1962 he suggested to the board the idea of "visiting professorships," bringing individuals to campus to be tried out before hiring them. Jim Smylie was brought to campus under this program in 1962 and was the only person hired this way.[277]

Balmer Hancock Kelly

According to most recollections, there was one person who was always present to give the campus tensions a biblical context and who tried to bridge the campus divisions: Balmer Hancock Kelly. Balmer Kelly (BD, 1939) represents a bridge between the Union of the Old South and the Union that was becoming a national and even international seminary. While Kelly was never particularly well known outside Union, he was involved in virtually every major initiative at Union in the mid-twentieth century. From *Interpretation* to biblical theology, from managing the Advance Campaign to being an advocate for the seminary during student protests—Kelly was always present and always contributing. He was appointed dean in 1965[278] and was the logical choice to serve as acting president from 1966 to 1968.

48. Balmer Hancock Kelly, interim president, 1966–68

Consistently remembered as an effective and inspiring teacher, Kelly was trusted by the board, faculty, and students. He continually advocated for more public relations and pushed for a permanent development office. Kelly was most proud of shepherding the curriculum review of the late 1950s, although it ultimately resulted in dropping his biblical theology class in favor of CPE.[279] He was able to convince the faculty and board to move away from the semester system, and when the revised curriculum was in place for two years, UTS was picked as one of the nation's top theological schools.

Kelly was known to academia as an editor of *Interpretation* and to the church as editor of the Layman's Bible Commentary (which he considered to be his most important work). In his view, the Layman's Bible Commentary was an attempt to bring biblical theology to laypeople, such as those who were teaching Sunday school. There were overtures from three presbyteries to stop publication of the Layman's Bible Commentary because, they claimed, the series deviated from traditional views of Scripture, but the General Assembly never acted on them.

Kelly had arrived at UTS in the middle of the Depression. He remembered that classes were small, 25 to 30 students, and the seminary was run like a church. Faculty were not bound by their departmental designation; any professor could basically teach in whatever subject area he desired. But seminary was an awakening for him: he began to focus on biblical studies as an outgrowth of his love of biblical languages.

Although economics certainly played a part in its failure, Kelly saw the Advance Campaign as symbolic of the times. At the beginning of the 1960s, Union had the confidence of the denomination and the church. Yet as the decade wore on, Union and American institutions in general lost credibility with their constituencies. Kelly concluded that by the time President Jones died, UTS did not have the support it once had. He observed that during the 1960s, the questioning of authority weakened the sense of call to a church. Moreover, as the church became politicized, UTS became politicized; it was becoming more and more difficult to find common ground.[280]

Nonetheless, the community remained. Doug Miller, son of Donald Miller, lived on Westwood Avenue from 1945 to 1961. He remembers the seminary as a giant playground: safe, lots of places to play, and the seminarians were like big brothers. He had a paper route around Ginter Park and remembers climbing the magnolia trees and playing with the sons of other professors and staff members.[281] When it was hot, he and his friends would run into Schauffler Hall or the library and take a drink from the "ice-cold" water fountains. When they needed a snack, they would buy candy and soda from the student store. The Missionary Closet was in Dr. Baer's house, and all the seminary kids wore clothes from it.

Doug Miller went to Ginter Park School until sixth grade. In 1959, when he was entering seventh grade, he went to a military school because of the uncertainty over integration, as he remembers it. His father, Dr. Donald Miller, became president of Pittsburgh Theological Seminary in 1962, and the family never moved back to Richmond. Doug Miller's experience was representative of the decisions seminary families had to make. Everyone supported civil rights, but the feared violence surrounding integration made personal choices difficult. According to most recollections, the campus (faculty, students, and staff) was able to accommodate divergent opinions during the civil rights movement; it would be Vietnam that would divide the school.

The Threads of History

Students admitted to Union Theological Seminary in Virginia in 1948 entered an atmosphere of "Reformed scholasticism, *jure divino* Presbyterianism, the doctrine of the spirituality of the church, rigid Puritanism, and no reunion [with the North]."[282] Students who graduated in 1966 rebelled against each of these five points. During the nineteen years from 1947 to 1966, the definition of an educated minister changed from one who knew and could defend the southern Calvinist tradition, to one who could criticize southern Calvinism from the viewpoint of other theologians. Students who graduated in the 1950s and 1960s could also apply the latest counseling techniques and brought at least some field experience to their first pastorate. What remained constant was the emphasis on the traditional curriculum.

By 1966 the interplay between a southern and national seminary was largely resolved. The spread of biblical theology and the increasing circulation of

Interpretation gave Union a national impact, albeit unapologetically serving the PCUS. During this era the primary institutional tension was not between north and south, but between church and seminary. Throughout American culture, people began to question the traditional sources of authority. With the increasing specialization of the faculty, reliance on accreditation rather than General Assembly standards, and support of the civil rights movement, connections with the local church were loosened. Perhaps this was natural. As the appearance of the seminary went from single white men to a student body that began to include all races and women, from student pranks to kids playing on the quad, Union led the church in showing how to make room for all. Veterans who had seen the worst and best of humanity could not be told they knew nothing of life. Students who rejected segregation could not abide its scriptural justification.

Union engaged the world in subtle and public ways. The use of technology—as seen in the Reigner Recording Library, the use of television, and the beginning of WRFK—was not dramatic but led to a continuing, lifelong influence. Getting used to radio and television enabled students to understand the power of mass communications and employ it in their ministry. While the interest in foreign missions declined, students engaged the world in other concrete ways. From funding a dormitory in France to registering voters and marching, UTS reflected the new dreams and divisions in American society.

The tension between reform and status quo was seen most clearly in the civil rights struggle. Students could no longer abide the slow pace in race relations. The public demonstrations of the early 1960s would have been unthinkable to the previous generation. As students began to ask questions about racial equality, concerns over the lack of women in leadership positions and the agony of urban America followed.

During this period, Union continued to be known for its innovation. The support for continuing education and the introduction of pastoral counseling and fieldwork in the curriculum were unprecedented. As H. Richard Niebuhr had hoped, UTS began to function as a "think tank" for the denomination, most notably in organizing and supporting the Larger Parish Plan. Union Seminary's most important contribution, not just to the church or theological education, however, was biblical theology. Biblical studies at Union was simply doing what seemed obvious: emphasizing the content of the biblical message instead of questions of authorship. Biblical theology, with its insistence on rigorous scholarship, allowed Union students and alumni to confront the culture with integrity. It was the approach of biblical theology that finally demolished the spirituality of the church doctrine. Despite its doubts about catering to the middle class or serving a corrupt culture, Union remained distinctive. Its graduates had influence throughout the church, the South, and the country. Although Union's traditional constituency may have felt a sense of alienation, they still trusted "the Wise Men from the East."

Chapter Nine (1967–97)
Scholarship or Praxis?

The successful passage of the Civil Rights Act (1964) and the Voting Rights Act (1965), the ambition to spread American values around the world, the conviction that the War on Poverty could end privation in American society, and the confidence of a rich society whose children had access to education and disposable income—all these combined in the early 1960s to engender an optimism that made all things seem possible. That confidence in the inevitability of a more just culture was shaken with the assassination of President Kennedy in 1963. The national mood of hopefulness finally dissolved as the Vietnam War continued, as race riots occurred with depressing regularity throughout the 1960s (beginning with "Long Hot Summer" of 1964, when 158 race riots from Watts in Los Angeles to Detroit to New York scarred virtually every large American city), and as more leaders were assassinated: Martin Luther King Jr. (in April 1968) and Robert Kennedy (in June 1968). A feeling of chaos and collapse descended on American society and caused an anxiety not felt since 1861 or 1929. Americans struggled over sexual ethics, the draft, and the place of women and minorities in society.

A generation earlier, H. Richard Niebuhr worried that ministry had become "the Perplexed Profession," and theological schools were trying to fulfill too many agendas. He argued that seminaries had lost their sense of purpose because the specialized curriculum led to a competition between "scholarly" and practical education. Union responded by preserving the traditional five subjects at the core of its curriculum while continuing the tradition of innovation. From experimenting with the newly conceived DMin degree to seeking a national faculty, from insisting upon the equal treatment of women and minorities to expanding the physical plant of the campus to the Westwood tract, Union continued to serve the church and society in a time of transformation. By confronting the seismic shifts in American culture and the challenges to theological education, Union Theological Seminary would show society and the church the possibilities of a new inclusive society.

The Poor People's Campaign

On May 18, 1968, six weeks after the assassination of Dr. Martin Luther King Jr., about 450 participants in the Poor People's March on Washington arrived in Richmond before heading on to Washington. The Poor People's Campaign had been planned by Dr. King and was carried out by the Southern Christian

Leadership Conference (SCLC). UTS, PSCE, and Virginia Union University (who would join together to become the Richmond Theological Center within a year), along with assistance from private individuals, offered to provide food and overnight accommodations for the marchers, and most of them ended up camping on the Westwood tract and the grounds of PSCE.

The marchers arrived in south Richmond on buses, met a crowd of other demonstrators, and marched through the city to Ginter Park. Hosting the marchers was a huge operation: approximately 250 volunteers cooked a meat-loaf dinner, which was served in Lingle Hall, and some marchers were given rooms in which to sleep (it was summer break, and some students had made their rooms available). A rally was held at Virginia Union's Hovey Field that night, and volunteers provided breakfast before the marchers departed the next day.

Since PSCE was the primary staging area and Union students were involved, both institutions were identified with the marchers, and public criticism was intense. On Sunday, May 28, Dr. Charles E. S. Kraemer, president of PSCE in 1954–74, wrote a letter to the *Richmond Times-Dispatch* with the heading, "Thanks Expressed for Help Given Poor." President Kraemer stressed that everything done for the marchers was accomplished by volunteers with donated items "so that there was no expense to the two schools." He lauded the "conduct and courtesy" of the police, while reminding his critics that "this movement is dedicated to nonviolence." More important, he stressed, the marchers "are children of God." Consequently, "institutions dedicated to sharing the gospel of the love of God in Jesus Christ would have to think long and hard before locking their doors against weary, hungry men and women and little children."[1] Nevertheless, individuals and churches threatened to withhold donations from both institutions because they allowed the marchers to stay on their respective grounds. The Poor People's March was the last major demonstration of the civil rights era.

Three weeks after the Poor People's Campaign passed through Richmond, the election of Fred Rogers Stair Jr. (BD, 1947; ThM, 1948) as Union's fourth president was announced at graduation in 1968, but he was not inaugurated until November 10,[2] two years after President James Jones died of a heart attack. Balmer Kelly had served as interim president during that time to provide administrative continuity, especially for the Advance Campaign. President Stair was a native of Knoxville, Tennessee, graduated from Davidson in 1939, and taught at a boys' school for a year. He entered Union in 1940 but discontinued his studies after Pearl Harbor and served as an infantry officer in World War II. After his discharge he studied at the University of Edinburgh for a year and returned to Richmond to complete his degree. Stair served as an assistant to President Lacy in 1948–53; as pastor at First Church, Hickory, North Carolina, in 1953–59; then at Central Presbyterian in Atlanta for eight years.

As with other presidents, his inauguration was front-page news in the Richmond papers.[3] At the same time, however, he faced a campus and student body that would have been unrecognizable to previous presidents. Bill Oglesby observed that when he was a student in the late 1930s and when he began teaching in 1950, students addressed their professors as "Dr." But during the 1960s students began to address professors by their first names.[4] He also

49. Frederick Rogers Stair Jr., president, 1967–81

noticed that in the 1950s it was difficult to interest students in the wider world. It was the opposite in the 1960s: students had no interest in the interior life since they were out to change the world. But by the 1970s students just wanted to analyze their inner experience and put much less emphasis on social justice issues. John Bright agreed; he thought students from the 1960s believed that the pastorate was irrelevant. By the 1970s he detected a change: students were seeking a more practical education.[5] The tone of American society was exemplified by the April 8, 1966, cover story of *Time* magazine. In the postwar period of the 1950s, *Time* had featured theologians and religious leaders on its covers: C. S. Lewis, 1947; Reinhold Niebuhr on *Time*'s 25th anniversary issue, March 8, 1948; Billy Graham, 1954, for the first time; Paul Tillich, 1959; Karl Barth, 1962; plus cover stories of American bishops or the pope about once a year. Now *Time* asked on its cover, "Is God Dead?"

Shortly before he died, President Jones wrote an article for the journal *Theological Education*, in which he gave his views on how seminaries should confront modern society. Echoing President Lacy forty years earlier, Jones observed that the minister was no longer the smartest person in town: the context had changed. Consequently, the profession of ministry had to rigorously maintain its theological competence (to understand what it believed), cultural sophistication (to credibly speak to society), and ecclesiastical orientation (to keep the church relevant). The changed context of ministry demanded that seminaries become places of exploration rather than indoctrination. Jones proposed a new way of learning, balancing "involvement" (personal participation) and academics (learning orthodox theology). Students, he argued, "come alive in homiletics only when they engage in actual preaching to actual congregations, not to make-believe pew-men sitting at pupils' benches."[6]

On Sunday, April 7, 1968, the *Richmond Times-Dispatch* featured an interview with the new president on the front page of section D. President Stair stressed his continuity with Jones; the prime purpose of UTS remained the training of "men and women for the Presbyterian ministry." But the context of ministry had changed. "Ministers of all faiths," he insisted, "must know and understand the beliefs of other faiths" and "function in an urban civilization," which was fragmented and individualistic. "Today's minister must be flexible and function in wholeness, and it is up to the seminary to make him aware of this."[7] By 1967, UTS had trained a little over half of all the ministers serving in the Presbyterian Church (US),[8] and he wanted to complete Union's shift in emphasis from a "technical school" to a first-rate graduate school.[9] He believed that a new kind of education was needed for the future.

On the morning of President Stair's inauguration, the seminary hosted a colloquy titled "Partnership in Education." Participating were Dr. John Coleman Bennett, president of Union Theological Seminary, New York; Dr. Edgar F. Shannon Jr., president of the University of Virginia; and Virginius Dabney, editor of the *Richmond Times-Dispatch*. Bennett argued that "the student at times knows better than the theologian what is relevant to life." The student, therefore, should have a part in the institution and should have a responsibility to keep the institution "on the road of its commitments."[10]

And the new president of UTS was ready to accept more student participation. He included the students in his inauguration by having the student body president, James Blackmon Graves (MDiv, 1969), address the inaugural luncheon. Graves acknowledged contradictions of the times:

> On the one hand we are students, your students, a real part of today's turned-on student generation, students who are working and concerned with the revolutionary upheaval of outmoded and dehumanizing structures, students who feel concerned to identify to some extent with the new Left and whose political nature cannot be denied. At the same time we are about to become and are, in fact, now your colleagues, brothers, fellow-ministers in the Church of Jesus Christ, a call to which we are committed. And so as ministers in this Church as we attempt to affirm our vocation in this stance, we are also caught up in the fears and ambiguities that face us as we affirm this vocation.[11]

President Stair's inaugural speech did not set goals or urge alumni to do more. Rather, it was a call for UTS to stay within its tradition of orientation toward the church. He did not want Union to join the trend "for seminaries to cluster together and for graduate departments of religion to merge in[to] universities supported by tax or foundation funds." In the spirit of John Holt Rice, he proposed that UTS "interact" between the extremes, as both "a theological seminary for ministry and a graduate school of religion." He also recognized that Union students reflected the tensions in society in a particular way:

Although they come from "our" homes and "our" congregations, they also reflect the pluralism of thought and the secularism which mark society today, the conflicts over war and peace, the criticisms of the Church from within and from without. Our students desire to do something with their lives, and they seek here a faith which can be understood with meaning, which can be applied in particular action, and which can be commended with relevance to others.

It was the seminary's job to confront America's "crisis of faith" by pointing out that "the basic questions of our time and the chief problems of our society are once again theological and demand answers which are theological." The seminary could only address society's spiritual uncertainties by clarifying the essentials of faith and ending what he saw as Union's isolationism.[12] A new curriculum, a more modern organization, and professors from outside the South would, President Stair hoped, bring Union into the national conversation.

Searching for the Right Curriculum

From Robert Kelly's groundbreaking survey of seminaries in 1924, to the Brown-Adams study published a decade later, to the 1956 Niebuhr-Williams-Gustafson report—theological schools continually questioned how they could address the context in which they lived. Although postwar seminaries no longer struggled with the stifling lack of resources that afflicted seminaries before World War II, Glen T. Miller argues that the Niebuhr-Williams-Gustafson report raised a "central issue" for theological education. How could seminaries in the postwar period serve a fragmented culture, a culture that made the "clear vision" of traditional denominationalism an anachronism? Without a central focus, "what was theological about theological education?"[13]

Union responded by maintaining the traditional core curriculum, while adding electives in an effort to fine-tune how the church encounters the modern world. Bill Oglesby has reflected that during his time at Union (1952–85), there were four major curriculum revisions, one every eight years. He mused that there were so many revisions because it was so difficult "to spell out what a seminary" should be: a graduate school or a professional school? Indeed, what was the relationship between scholarship and praxis? He was afraid that Union would be trapped by the past if the traditional curriculum was not adapted to the times. As an example, he reported that the 1892 Catalogue listed a curriculum largely unchanged from 1812: Theology (Systematic, Pastoral, and Polemical), Ecclesiastical History and Polity, Oriental Literature (Hebrew and Old Testament), Biblical Introduction, and New Testament Literature. The only training in the pastoral function was preaching in front of classmates as a junior and preaching in front of the seminary community as a senior.

Oglesby argued that Moore wanted to keep the traditional curriculum, yet steer away from the European model of lectures to give students the opportunity for the praxis of ministry; he moved the seminary to Richmond because the urban environment afforded more opportunities for "practical work." Moore thought that students could pursue the traditional seminary course of study while engaging in the practice of ministry. Consequently, Christian Sociology and Christian Education were established in the curriculum, and by 1919 the demonstration church was functioning in Schauffler Hall. Continuing to innovate, UTS created the Department of Field Work after World War II.

Clinical pastoral education (CPE), however, changed Union more than any curricular review. In 1954 UTS had one required class in pastoral counseling, the first seminary in the country to do so (yet CPE is not mentioned in the UTS *Catalogue* until 1970). Yet the legacy of CPE extends beyond the fights over theology and biblical interpretation. Oglesby argued that CPE influenced the process of theological education through the utilization of small peer groups and student participation in the process of learning. When students demanded greater say in their education and more hands-on experience in the 1960s, they were reflecting their CPE experiences. After CPE was firmly entrenched in the curriculum, lectures remained the dominant teaching format but were never again the only way to teach.[14]

During the 1960s students throughout the country came to believe they were competent to critique their education. Richard Vaught (attended 1969–70; transferred to Garrett Seminary, Evanston, Illinois) declared that seminary students of the late 1960s were "not going to be pushed, poked, and refined into what the Seminary believes is the image of the ideal minister."[15] The civil rights movement became a prism through which many people came to view American society. Frustrated by continuing injustices, they refused to see the issue of civil rights in isolation and wanted the institutions of which they were a part to participate in the positive changes the country needed to make. The editor of the irregularliy issued "underground" student newspaper (published between October 1969 and May 1970) *Perspective* argued that Union's curriculum had to change if it was going to be effective in contemporary society:

> The three major dilemmas of this country are war, race, and socio-economic system of control. Where in our curriculum do we find a course which relates to these issues? What courses are oriented to the Christian responsibility in war, the amplification of our primitive knowledge of what racism is and does, the understanding of various economic systems and their implications for Christian living?[16]

Beginning in 1968, in response to the desire for greater student involvement in seminary decision making, faculty and students began meeting every second Wednesday at 7:30 p.m. in the UTS Student-Faculty Colloquy. The stated purpose was "so that students and faculty members may bring before the body any grievances or suggestions that are of general interest to the school."[17] Since student concerns were presented in an open forum, the traditional structure of student government was replaced. Student representatives were no longer chosen by class, but by residential structure. Within a couple years, however, there were complaints that fewer and fewer people were attending these Wednesday night meetings, so the class-based student government organization was reinstituted. The administration also tried to include students in decision making by allowing them to attend faculty meetings and instituting a system of student evaluation of faculty in 1969. In 1970 the board was receptive when a student delegation presented their resolution after Kent State and voted the students the privilege of the floor at the upcoming board meeting. By 1971 six students were regularly attending faculty meetings, and twenty-three students were serving on various faculty committees.[18]

At the urging of students, Balmer Kelly and the administration began to experiment with different kinds of fieldwork. For the previous twenty years, students were assigned to work in a church for the summer. In 1968, students were placed not just in churches but also in local ministries in "urban fields and rural parishes, work in institutions such as jails and hospitals, service on evangelistic teams, and leading youth groups." The new fieldwork was designed to "give students a firsthand look at many of the social changes" in society and how the church was meeting those changes.[19]

The Interseminary Program in Church and Society is an example of the then-novel interdisciplinary, ecumenical, outside-the-church approach. This course also started in 1968 (in cooperation with Duke Divinity School and Virginia Theological Seminary) and allowed students to work as interns "within industrial complexes, political organizations, and financial institutions under the direction of faculty members from the three institutions."[20] Another curricular experiment was the "January Term," first held in 1967 and designed to give students an intensive monthlong immersion in an area of their choosing.[21] The course in Experimental Ministry, held during January 1968, "involved members of the UTS junior class in the everyday life of the city of Richmond, in conjunction with the Task Force for Renewal, Urban Strategy and Training (TRUST). David King (MDiv, 1971) wrote that the course deeply affected the students and prompted him "to try to draw some conclusions about how the Church might enter to provide an outlet for mission within the urban-technopolitan society."[22] The new vision for fieldwork did not, however, last more than a few years. The legacy of this new attitude toward fieldwork, however, continues in visits to World Council of Churches meetings, the United Nations, Washington (D.C.), the Middle East, Central America, and Ghana. The Ghana trips, started in 1986 (funded by a 1981 PCUS Women of the Church Birthday Offering of $112,000), were intended to internationalize seminary education, expose students to Reformed churches that originated in traditions other than the PCUS, and increase awareness of world missions.[23] But Union did not stop with just one-way visits; it hosted pastors and scholars from Ghana and other countries, to give them time and resources to conduct research and view the American context of the church universal.

The curriculum revision of 1971 solidified the soul-searching of the previous decade. By 1969 the number of elective subjects had increased by approximately 50 percent,[24] and this revision also stressed electives. The 1971 curriculum revision made structural changes to Union's offerings as well. It ended the Town & Country Pastors' Institute, established in 1937.[25] The reach of mass communication, easier transportation, and the development of the DMin degree made it superfluous. The 1971 curriculum revision not only changed what was taught, but for the first time also called for new teaching methods beyond the lecture.

Perhaps the most public change stemming from the 1971 curriculum review was the Competency Paper. In theory, this paper spelled out the "skill and knowledge areas which the faculty deems necessary for the performance of ministry." The aim of the competency paper was to make sure every course at Union served a purpose in preparing students for ministry. Most students, however, found the competency paper too verbose and irrelevant.

> A new literary masterpiece has just been released (or perhaps it escaped on its own) from the UTS Underground Press. This nascent classic is, of course, the Competence paper (2nd ed., 6 pp., Richmond, Va., 1974). The author, like this reviewer, has chosen for obvious reasons to remain anonymous. The current edition is destined to become a best seller among those who received free copies.
>
> The Competency Paper is an exciting new addition to that rare genre, theological fiction; not since Barth's *Church Dogmatics* has a book been so clearly intended to keep its audience roaring with laughter from beginning to end. Every page, every paragraph, brings chuckles and guffaws of laughter at the improbable situations and unbelievable characterization. The author has done for seminarians what J. R. R. Tolkien did for the Hobbits, providing a lovely fantasy world in which their little minds and bodies could feel at home. . . . The story is presented in the form of a morality play with 2 acts and a million scenes. The plot never thickens; it is that way from the beginning.
>
> As a test of the impact the Competence Paper is having on the community outside the Seminary, this reviewer conducted a public opinion poll of 10 persons. They were asked to describe the Competence Paper. They replied:
>
> a. "It's so squeezably soft." (43%)
> b. "More absorbent than Bounty." (19%)
> c. "Ideal for Christmas Wrapping." (27%)
> d. "It keeps chopped liver fresher than tinfoil." (11%)[26]

Students being students, there were constant complaints about workload. In 1969 the Student Council passed a resolution asking for "a short reading period" to "allow for more competent preparation" for finals. They argued that "UTS NY, Yale, Harvard, and Princeton Seminaries" all have reading periods of up to nineteen days, and that "beginning school earlier in September and ending later in May would be worth inclusion of the proposed reading period."[27] In 1975, representatives of the first-level students met with faculty who were teaching first-level courses and formally complained about the workload. The students let the matter drop when Dr. Leith offered to give more surprise tests as an evaluative procedure during courses.[28] Fred Moon (attended 1973–75) mirrored the complaints of many: "There seems to be such a heavy load that little else (family life, wife, husband, children, spiritual life) gets its just dues [*sic*]. The level system, originally designed to allow students to develop at a more individual pace, is deteriorating into the old 'Run 'em in and run 'em out in three years' (or 'push 'em through four and give 'em a D.Min. lollipop') system."[29]

Throughout 1977 and 1978, curriculum continued to be a popular and controversial topic. Students met among themselves and with faculty committees concerning the academic calendar, grading, and course offerings. The administration was looking for ways to balance course work with a "variety of types of learning," while students just wanted to delete some requirements and add more elective courses. The faculty, however, believed that the best way to combine classroom and practical learning was to change the academic calendar from two semesters to one of two options: the 1–3–1–3–1, or the 3–10–4–10–3.

The arcane discussions left students puzzled: "Try to explain it to a non-student friend without a pen or pencil in your hand." The faculty was seeking ways to reduce class size, decrease the workload on students, and "allow for flexibility of teaching styles and learning experiences."[30] While students appreciated the faculty's sentiment, the whole issue was too complicated and "most people didn't care."[31] Ironically, the major change was not initiated by the students. The "credit/no credit" grading system was changed to honors, credit, marginal credit, or no credit: "a way to determine if someone was in trouble and to better examine academic performance."[32] "This change," Richard Hamm (MDiv, 1979) reported, "came from the faculty review committee; students at the forum had voted overwhelmingly to keep credit, no credit."[33]

Students still pressed for different kinds of courses. February 16, 1978, saw forty-eight students (more than 60 percent of all the MDiv enrollment) attending a forum that called for more interdisciplinary courses, more coordination with RTC schools, courses in ecumenics and social ethics, smaller classes in required courses, a greater emphasis on small-group work, the inclusion of reading days before exams, and keeping the credit/no credit grading system.[34] At the end of 1978, students asked the faculty to consider "the importance of FAITH QUESTIONS and SPIRITUAL DEVELOPMENT as part of the course structure."[35] There were also concerns that Union was concentrating on training students for large churches and ignoring the rural congregations.[36] Many students were grateful that the seminary was finally recognizing and encouraging those who were working toward ministries outside the parish. J. Christopher Mullen (MDiv, 1985) declared: "Let us own our academic heritage and take some comfort in the fine preparation given to those entering the parish ministry. Let us improve that preparation, though, and broaden it to include this growing segment of ministers who will be working outside the purview of the local church."[37]

Out of these conversations of what seminary students should know, courses emerged that would have been inconceivable just a generation earlier. By the late 1980s, UTS offered courses and seminars on Feminist Theology, Women's Experience/Women's Faith, Proverbs from a Latin American Perspective, Modern Jewish History and Thought, the Spirituality and Growth of Korean Churches, Methodist Studies, and Rural and Global Missions, plus travel seminars to Appalachia, Latin and Central America, Ghana, the Middle East, and the Virginia Legislature.

Interestingly enough, throughout the discussions over what makes an "ideal minister," the UTS community never wavered from its commitment to the traditional curriculum, which would be recognizable to the student of any era. Required courses (15 out of 28 credits) for the master of divinity degree continued to emphasize the traditional areas: two courses each in Old and New Testaments (plus one course in Hebrew and one in Greek), two courses each in church history, theology, field education, and preaching, and one course in ethics and pastoral care—all required for graduation.[38] Union took pride in the way it prepared its students in the five core areas. Between 1983 (the first year of the PC(USA)) and 1997, Union students consistently scored an average of 9.5 points higher on the denominational ordination exams than students from other seminaries.

MDiv and DMin: Hallmarks of the Professional Minister

Between 1960 and 1980, church attendance in the United States declined by 20 percent.[39] Social commentators theorized that the rise of the welfare state, the pervasive mistrust of American institutions, or the political, programmatic, racial, and sociological shortcomings of the institutional church were at the root of the decline in church attendance and influence.[40] Many theological educators were also concerned that a lack of professional credentials in an increasingly specialized society put ministers at a disadvantage compared with other professions. Consequently, their influence waned, and students did not want to become ministers. Although the doctor of ministry degree had been discussed as early as the 1930s and 1940s, it was not until the 1960s that many schools felt the need to compete with other professional degrees.[41]

In a roundtable discussion, President Hartley Hall once observed that the UTS curriculum was defined by the parish, on what was called the "professional" model. Sara Little, however, pointed out that many in the American Association of Theological Schools (the AATS changed its name to the Association of Theological Schools [ATS] in 1978)[42] no longer considered the "professional model" viable.[43] What President Hall labeled the "professional" track aimed to train ministers for the parish. Sara Little understood that ATS sought to encourage seminaries to educate professionals for a wide variety of fields (such as counseling or teaching), of which parish ministry was but one facet of the profession.

ATS sought to resolve the tension between focused training for pastoral needs and the broad educational requirements of a true profession by abolishing the bachelor of divinity degree. Since the BD took three years to complete, many theological educators came to believe that by denoting the first ministerial degree as a "bachelor's," it was inferior to master's degrees in other disciplines.[44] In 1968, President Stair told the board that many theological schools were reexamining the nomenclature of their degrees and deciding to award the master of divinity degree. It was, he argued, difficult to ask undergraduates to work for three additional years for a bachelor's degree. Union, acting on ATS recommendations and following the lead of Louisville, Columbia, and Austin,[45] began awarding the MDiv in 1971, after seventy years of awarding the BD.[46]

If the first degree signaled an increased level of professionalism, there had to be another degree to encourage graduates to pursue advanced professional education. Union began offering the master of sacred theology (STM) degree in 1967. This precursor of the DMin was designed for pastors living near the seminary who were already serving a congregation. They could take classes part-time while serving a church and still have structured access to the resources of the seminary.[47] The STM represented the attempt to differentiate between continuing education, which was designed to give pastors more tools to serve a congregation, and graduate education, which granted the ThM and ThD to produce scholars in a specific field of study.

At the beginning of the 1972 school year, Union became the first seminary, in both the ATS and the denomination,[48] to introduce a new curriculum enabling a student to earn an MDiv degree in three years and a doctor of ministry (DMin) degree in four.[49] The "in-sequence DMin" required an intern year after two years of classes, then returning for a fourth year, consisting of classwork and submitting a written research project. The DMin was designed to be the terminal professional degree for ministry, and the ThD the terminal degree for research (Union replaced the ThD with the PhD in 1982).[50] Many in the ATS believed that an in-sequence doctor of ministry degree would give pastors a more professional standing in an increasingly credentialed world. The move to the in-sequence DMin, however, had unintended consequences: the MDiv was now seen by many as little more than an adjunct to the DMin, and the STM degree was phased out by 1973 after six years.

The DMin degree was a source of pride. In 1970, Union had the highest proportion of its students taking a voluntary intern year of any theological seminary in the country.[51] The 1977 report to the synods boasted: "Our Doctor of Ministry program is one of only a few in North America that is fully accredited without any notations and the only one that has both 'in sequence' and 'in ministry' options." In his 1977 report, President Stair saw the seminary dedicating itself to "improve what we are doing and adding strength to strength."[52]

President Stair was, however, too optimistic about Union's ability to make the DMin program work. As early as the fall of 1974, UTS had proposed "enhancing" the requirements for the DMin by requiring an additional year on campus, and then requiring a year's participation with a "satellite DMin group" in another city after the student was in the field. By requiring a year's worth of seminars, Union intended to answer those who criticized the DMin degree for not requiring enough parish experience.[53] The satellite concept, although never implemented, represents the first thought of putting more separation between the MDiv and the DMin degrees.

By 1976 the in-sequence DMin was under increasing attack. Union, however, continued to support the degree, and at their 1976 meeting ATS voted to make no changes. The primary criticism was that the seminary was awarding a doctorate to students who were not ordained and had no experience as an installed pastor. Criticism grew as other schools discarded the in-sequence DMin. By 1978 only two schools—UTS and Claremont—accounted for 84 percent of all in-sequence DMin degrees. UTS continued to advocate for the degree but understood that it was losing support.[54] The faculty recognized that the in-sequence DMin was not working as intended and began to phase it out in 1982 (those already in the program could continue). The MDiv would be the primary degree, and the DMin would be advanced professional training exclusively for those with at least three years in ministry.[55] In 1983 the change in emphasis was complete: the Doctor of Ministry Program was shifted to the continuing education office, and serving in a pastorate was a requirement for admission to the program.

The Corporate Seminary

Walter W. Moore did not see the need for a secretary; and just before his retirement, President Lacy lamented that he felt insulated from the students as his staff increased. The reality was, however, that new administrative demands, such as constant fund-raising, planning to meet accreditation requirements, and preparing government paperwork for GI benefits after World War II,[56] required more people with a variety of skills. These administrators had to be organized efficiently to provide what a modern seminary needed.

Since ministry now required a more professional degree to gain credibility in society, the seminary needed to adopt a more corporate nature to support these increased expectations. President Stair realized that his background did not prepare him to manage a modern corporate seminary. In 1973 he spent part of his sabbatical at the Advanced Management Program at Harvard Business School. The seminary organization was growing in complexity, and the Self-Study Reports provide an interesting glimpse into the expansion of the administration.

One cannot discern a formal administration until Walter W. Moore was appointed president in 1904; the job of the seminary was to teach, and professors could take care of everything else. Indeed, President Moore had to be forced to accept a secretary. It was not until 1928 that the catalogue contained a separate listing for administration. In 1928 there were 5 full-time professors and 5 staff positions (the seminary treasurer, the president's secretary, 1 bookkeeper, 1 matron, and 1 "special representative" to manage the Walter W. Moore campaign). By 1935 the total positions were 12, evenly split between faculty and nonfaculty. The job of "special representative" had been eliminated, and 2 positions in finance were added: assistant treasurer and his secretary. In 1941 the positions totaled 14, again evenly split, with the addition of a "stenographer" to the staff. It was not until 1945 that staff outnumbered professors (9 to 8), with a new position in the finance office and a secretary for the library.

Although President Lacy had added the position of treasurer in 1928, and assistant treasurer by 1935, it was President Jones who created the corporate scaffolding for Union's administration. He created the business office in 1950 and the president's office by 1955. In 1950, staff outnumbered professors 15 to 8, with 3 new positions in the business office. In 1955, positions totaled 26, with 16 nonfaculty (3 new positions in the president's office); 1965 saw 35 positions, with 27 nonfaculty, including 7 in the president's office, 6 in the business office (including the superintendent of buildings and grounds), 4 in the office of the dean, 3 in the audio-visual center and radio station, and the new position of registrar.

President Stair built on previous growth. There were 45 total positions in 1970, and 35 of them were nonfaculty (the bulk of the new positions coming in the library, business office, and the audio-visual center and WRFK. There were 72 total positions in 1980 (61 of them nonfaculty), and by 1985 there were 70 total permanent positions, including 62 nonfaculty in nine departments: Library and Media Services (18 positions), Administration (14 positions, including Communications and Physical Plant), Development (19 positions), Academic Affairs (8 positions, including the registrar), Business and Finance (6 positions), WRFK (6 positions), Continuing Education (3 positions), and *Interpretation* (3 positions).[57] In the last three-fourths of the twentieth century, Union's bureaucracy grew first to meet the needs of financial accountability, then also the requirements of managing the library, raising funds, and providing student services. Paradoxically, the demands on the administration did not originate within the church, but from students' increased expectations and a growing national educational establishment. As corporate standards of accountability, the standard of living, and specialized educational regulations increased throughout the twentieth century, Union's bureaucracy grew in response.

The corporate seminary needed secular credentials. Although Union was already accredited by ATS, President Stair worked for accreditation by the Southern Association of Colleges and Schools (SACS) in 1971. Traditionally, theological seminaries had been accredited only by ATS.[58] Since more graduates were entering teaching and many schools were suspicious of graduate theological degrees due to the "the current state of disrepair" in professional accreditation, the seminary decided to seek this parallel accreditation.[59] Responding to the increasing and constant demands of accreditation (and perhaps symbolizing a tilt toward the academy), the Office of Institutional Effectiveness (OFINE) was established in 1996 to maintain and monitor accreditation compliance.[60]

In 1972 the board granted tenure for the first time and gave curricular oversight to the faculty to gain SACS accreditation. Both actions diminished denominational influence and meant that the board had to work through the administration and president.[61] President Stair placed Union in the mainstream of higher education, and the educational establishment noticed. During his administration, Union was voted among the ten best theological seminaries in the United States associated with ATS, and of these, the only school not associated with a major university.[62]

The Advance Campaign

The Advance Campaign had been launched with great fanfare at graduation in 1965. The vision was breathtaking: raising $19 million to accommodate a student body of 500 by 1980, with a modern instructional building, an audio-visual center, renovated library, married-student housing on Westwood tract (Advance Apartments), more faculty housing, a new chapel and administration building, and a gym. In addition, adequate funds would be raised for chairs in Church and Society, American Church History, and Biblical Studies, as well as an endowment for fieldwork. The campaign, however, never succeeded in completing more than half of the proposed first phase construction. In addition, total enrollment never approached the optimistic estimates of the mid-1960s.

Upon his inauguration, President Stair decided that Advance Apartments would be the first priority, and they were the only buildings completely constructed as the result of the campaign (for $1.5 million). The original 1967 plans for a new instructional building had called for the demolition of four faculty residences (only one was actually razed), and in 1971 what would become Moore, Johnson, and Dabney Halls were renovated (along with Schauffler and Richmond, and the first two floors of Watts). The library was also remodeled, and the Reigner Recording Library was created by closing off the East Reading Room. Once again a gym was put on hold, but a new maintenance facility on Westwood tract was constructed in 1976.[63] President Stair canceled all fund-raising plans in the fall of 1975. Although the disappointment over the incomplete campaign was widespread, it forced the administration to stress renovation, and within a decade Union was proud of its historic campus.

A National Seminary

President Stair recognized that renovated facilities and a modern organization were not enough to keep Union in the front ranks of national seminaries. A decade earlier, H. Richard Niebuhr had identified that faculty formed the core of theological education, and Union's new president wanted different voices for a seminary serving a more diverse culture. President Stair wanted UTS to be more than just a "fine regional seminary" and felt the need to open up to a larger constituency because he thought the northern and southern churches would reunite sooner rather than later. More immediately, he wanted a professor who was interested in religious pluralism and brought Donald Dawe to UTS.[64]

Dawe taught theology at UTS from 1969 to 1996 and was the first Northerner since 1838 (when Elisha Ballantine and Hiram Goodrich resigned during the Old School–New School split) to have a career at Union. A native of Detroit, he served in the army during World War II, where he experienced a crisis of faith and came to consider God and the church as superfluous. After the war he attended Wayne State University, intending to be a research chemist. After reading Reinhold Niebuhr's *Nature and Destiny of Man*, Dawe realized that he could connect piety and intellect. He left chemistry behind, attended Union Seminary (NY), was ordained in the United Presbyterian Church (UPC), and was called to a small church in upstate New York for five years. He then served as a student pastor in Chicago and returned to Union (NY), graduating with a PhD in 1961. Dawe then taught at Macalester College (a Presbyterian school) in St. Paul (Minn.) before being called to Union. Dawe liked UTS and never regretted staying. He appreciated Union's emphasis on community and felt he was part of a changing church, which the seminary was helping to shape.

President Stair, however, had plans beyond one teacher from the North. Indeed, not since John Holt Rice would the seminary be so intentional in reaching out to the North and other theological traditions. In the 1967 Self-Study Report, UTS reported that the Advance Campaign would allow the addition of two professors in "Philosophy and Comparative Religions" and "World Christianity."[65] In 1974, Stair recommended that the board amend the UTS bylaws to encompass teachers beyond the PCUS—to allow those of the Reformed faith, and not only southern Presbyterians, to join the faculty. The board dithered, and in 1977 President Stair raised the issue more forcefully, stating that the change would strengthen the faculty, give a broader denominational view to students, and put the seminary "in good stead along with other leading national seminaries." The board finally made the change in 1980, and went one step further. The trustees decided to allow faculty from other Reformed traditions, but also outside of the Reformed faith, but only on the recommendation of the president, in consultation with the faculty, and with a two-thirds vote of the board.[66]

After President Stair recruited Donald Dawe, professors from around the country were no longer anomalous. Paul J. Achtemeier, a native of Nebraska, was called as a New Testament professor in 1973. He was a graduate of Elmhurst College, near Chicago, and received his BD and ThD from Union Seminary (NY), and was ordained in the United Presbyterian Church (UPC). He also studied at Princeton Seminary, Heidelberg University (Germany), and the University of Basel (Switzerland) under Karl Barth. He was the New Testament editor for the commentary series Interpretation: A Bible Commentary for Preaching and Teaching, general editor of *Harper's Bible Dictionary* (1985; rev., 1996), and an editor of the journal *Interpretation*. He was the first non-Catholic elected as president of the Catholic Biblical Association of America and served as president of the Society of Biblical Literature, giving the presidential address in 1989.

W. Sibley Towner, a native of Nebraska, was called as an Old Testament professor in 1975. After graduating with a BA from Yale in 1954, "Sib" served as a short-term missionary teacher in Lebanon. After three years he returned to Yale, where he earned his BD, was ordained in the UPC, and continued his studies, earning his PhD in 1965. Towner was a research fellow at Hebrew University, Jerusalem, for one year and a visitor at Mansfield College, Oxford, for two years. He taught at Yale and Princeton, and was Old Testament professor and dean at University of Dubuque Theological Seminary before being called to Union. Towner wrote articles for the *Interpreter's Dictionary of the Bible* and *Daniel* for the Interpretation Commentary series.

Jack Dean Kingsbury, a native of California, was called as a New Testament professor in 1977. He graduated from Concordia Seminary, St. Louis (BA, 1956; BD, 1959), studied at the University of Tübingen (Germany), received his Dr. theol. from the University of Basel in 1967, and was ordained in the Lutheran Church–Missouri Synod. Kingsbury served as an assistant pastor in Minneapolis and taught at Luther Seminary in St. Paul. He authored over ten books and served as editor of *Interpretation*.

Douglas F. Ottati was called as a theology professor in 1977. A native of Indianapolis, he graduated from the University of Pennsylvania (AB, 1972) and earned an MA in ministries and a PhD from the Divinity School of the University of Chicago. He served two churches in the Chicago area as an assistant to the pastor. Ottati was an Instructor in Religion at King's College, Wilkes-Barre, Pennsylvania, and Instructor in Theological Ethics at Concordia College, Moorhead, Minnesota, before being called to Union. He was called as the Craig Family Distinguished Professor of Reformed Theology at Davidson College in 2007.

S. Dean McBride, a native of California, was called to UTS as an Old Testament professor in 1985. He graduated from Pomona College (BA), Harvard Divinity School (STB), and Harvard University (PhD, in the department of Near Eastern Languages and Literatures). McBride taught at Pomona College, Yale University, Northwestern University Graduate School, and Garrett-Evangelical Theological Seminary before joining the faculty at Union. He has also held visiting appointments at Cambridge University, Brown University, the University of Chicago, and the College of William & Mary. McBride served on the Revised Standard Version Bible Committee and the editorial board of the commentary series Hermeneia. In 1980–81 he was a member of the archaeological field staff of the Meiron Excavation Project when the Roman period village of Nabratein was excavated in Upper Galilee, Israel. On five occasions in 1990–2000, he and

Sibley Towner shared leadership of Union's Middle East Travel Seminar. These six professors signified a break with the past and represented the new outlook of a truly national seminary.

While the theological and geographical traditions were expanding, the community was atomizing. Jim Mays has observed that when he arrived on campus, all faculty were scholars who had served a congregation, and students felt that they were connected to the church. President Lacy would pick out graduates to pursue a PhD, have them serve a church, and then call them to the seminary. Accreditation, however, dictated that faculty be chosen by a faculty committee, as in other graduate schools. By the 1970s professional associations determined careers, not involvement in the church.[67] President Stair was balancing the inherent tension in seminary education. The church expected UTS to adhere to a certain tradition, while the academy expected current scholarship regardless of denominational standards.[68] He wanted nationally recognized scholars, but ones that the PCUS would accept.

The Challenge to Biblical Theology

Union had been known as ground zero for the biblical theology movement throughout the postwar period. Yet the combination of social upheaval and the proliferation of the new theologies prompted many to wonder if the assumptions and methods of biblical theology were still valid. Brevard S. Childs, in *Biblical Theology in Crisis* (1970), argued that the biblical theology movement was no longer a useful way of interpreting the Bible.

Childs acknowledged that since the 1940s, biblical theology had offered an alternative to both fundamentalists, who rejected historical criticism, and liberal Christians, who "lost themselves in the minutiae of literary, philological, and historical problems." As a result, the Bible had been hopelessly fragmented, and the essential unity of the gospel was distorted and forgotten." He agreed that by the end of World War II, biblical scholarship had deteriorated into trivialities. In his view, biblical theology opened the way to accept historical criticism, while keeping the focus on the church and providing an opening to the ecumenical movement. Childs identified Donald Miller and Balmer Kelly as the leading proponents of this point of view, the journal *Interpretation* as its mouthpiece, and the Christian Faith and Life curriculum as "the first creative venture" in bringing the newer insights of biblical theology down to the grassroots level of Christian education. Biblical theology pointed out that "the church had suffered from its misunderstanding of the Bible and needed to hear its fresh notes in order to be awakened to its real task."

What was new in 1948, however, was too constricted by the last half of the twentieth century. According to Childs, the biblical theology movement had not been able to define what the unity of Scripture meant through the different forms of literature, or show a consistent theology within Scripture, among other issues. Biblical theology was bound by its "strongly Protestant" orientation and "the needs of the Christian church." Thus, by the late 1960s, pressures were building that finally ended biblical theology "as a major force"[69] in the last third of the twentieth century.

Childs maintained that a "new" biblical theology was needed. There were those who argued that biblical theology was too simplistic: all you had to do was examine the Bible, assuming that the biblical analysis would naturally apply to today's problems.[70] Childs was not so direct, but he also doubted whether biblical theology could address the period of tremendous political and social change the United States was now in. He proposed focusing on the text of the canon in its final form. For him, defining the origins, structure, and history of the text was not helpful; it was the meaning of the text in its final form that was essential for the church.

Childs proposed another way of examining Scripture: "canonical criticism" (although he rejected the term). The use of canonical criticism gave new ethical insights to the gray areas of life. Violence, abortion, minority rights, and other issues could be approached from different perspectives. In his view, biblical theology had failed because its horizon was too narrow. "The challenge of the Christian interpreter in our day is to hear the full range of notes within all of Scripture, to wrestle with the theological implication of this Biblical witness, and above all, to come to grips with the agony of our age before a living God who still speaks through the prophets and apostles."[71] Biblical theology, Childs argued, could not answer the questions that were being raised by feminists, liberation theologians, and the other emerging schools of thought in the 1970s.

John Haddon Leith

Although Union became known for biblical theology, there were advocates for other ways of understanding Scripture. John Haddon Leith called students, faculty, and the church into a conversation with history in order to faithfully address modern life. A native of Due West, South Carolina, he graduated from Erskine College in 1940 (where he was on the same debate team as Jim Mays) and Columbia Seminary in 1943. He then received an MA from Vanderbilt in 1946 and a PhD from Yale in 1949. After graduation from Columbia, he founded Spring Hill Presbyterian Church in Mobile. He was called as pastor of Second Presbyterian Church, Nashville, shortly thereafter and took the opportunity to study at Vanderbilt. After Yale, Leith served as pastor of First Presbyterian Church, Auburn, Alabama, from 1949 to 1958, when he was called to Union. In 1956 he was a member of a special committee of East Alabama Presbytery that concluded, "There is no Scriptural basis for racial segregation in the Church." When ministers were hounded out of their pulpits because they favored integration, he was instrumental in helping them receive other calls. After his death in 2002, First Presbyterian Church, Auburn, established the Leith Lecture Series to bring distinguished speakers to the church as a commemoration of his life, ministry, and scholarship.

John Leith was dedicated to the pastoral ministry, and it would not be too much to say that his writings grew out of his teaching experience as a minister. His numerous books—especially *Creeds of the Churches: A Reader in Christian Doctrine, from the Bible to the Present* (1963), *Assembly at Westminster: Reformed Theology in the Making* (1973), *An Introduction to the Reformed Tradition: A Way of Being the Christian Community* (1977), *Basic Christian Doctrine* (1993), and *Crisis in the*

Church: The Plight of Theological Education (1977)—were written for congregational use and reflection and remain influential. *The Church: A Believing Fellowship* (published in 1965, republished 1981), was written for young people in the communicants' classes at First Presbyterian, Auburn. It was published in the Covenant Life Curriculum as a Sunday school text for junior high students and continues to be used by churches today for adult education and officer training.

Leith's inaugural lecture set the outlines of his career and theological project. He argued that modern life "uprooted" a consciousness of history, which prevented a conversation with the past; people had "no inner direction and no tradition to give strength to their lives." American Protestants were especially prone to ignore history, to jump over the twenty centuries from the ministry of Jesus to the present day without understanding the forces that shaped their lives and how those forces influence their interpretation of Scripture. Without an understanding of Christian history, contemporary believers are like children who do not understand their family. The secular traditions of society may be substituted for the traditions of the Christian church, "but no [one] can sit down traditionless to interpret the Bible." The question for our time, then, is not whether to accept or reject tradition, "but the proper relation which must exist between" tradition and the modern life of the believer.

The study of historical theology, Leith maintained, balances the tradition and the time in which people live. As such, historical theology is not abstract; it is "not the history of Christianity nor the history of theological texts," but takes the life of the church seriously. Education in historical theology, therefore, is vital for the church because history corrects doctrine in a constant conversation between present and past, resulting "in the renewed lives of plain people." He observed that there is really nothing new but the history we do not know. "There are few if any theological problems or difficulties for faith which Christian people face today which Christian people have not faced in essential substance before." History of theology allows the minister to see through contemporary language that presents old heresies in new ways, while at the same time it "is a protection against the blind spots and the overemphasis of particular ages." Historical theology, therefore, both prompts the believer into faithful action while curbing useless speculation.

Since theology both influences and is a product of a specific culture, the study of historical theology "makes one aware of the cultural conditioning and the cultural idiom of all theology and of the necessity of translating every theology into the cultural idiom of one's own society." If the church is to confront the modern scientific revolution, participate in conversations with other religions, and address the fragmentation of modern life, ministers will have to understand the tradition in which they stand and explain it so the people they serve can appropriate it.

> Christian people have a right to expect from ministers and professors guidance and help in the theological understanding of the radical changes which are taking place and guidance and help in obedience to Jesus Christ in the midst of the changes. The really critical test of theological teaching will not be found in classrooms but in the embodiment of this teaching in the life of the Church.

Tradition, then, supplies the definitions that keep the church in conversation with the "Great Cloud of Witnesses" and focuses contemporaneous thought on Jesus Christ. There is a nineteen-century-long conversation between the church and the world that prepares Christians to address the intellectual and cultural crises of the present. Historical theology recovers the "Christian memory which is indispensable to an understanding of the Christian faith."[72]

When Leith arrived on campus in 1958, the theology of the PCUS was grounded in the Westminster Confession.[73] Rote memorization of Westminster and Calvin (through Turretin or Augustus Strong) could not, however, prepare the modern minister to help God's people make sense of modern life in light of the gospel. He expanded Union's theological horizons, teaching seminars on Friedrich Schleiermacher and Reinhold Niebuhr, and his class on Calvin was always popular. Leith wrote extensively, showing how the Reformed tradition could show the church how to take principled, consistent, and loving stands on civil rights, capital punishment, nuclear and conventional war, economics, homosexuality, and other topics that caused church members to often speak past one another. George Conn remembered that Leith could let students see that picketing Thalhimers Department Store was more than defying a worn-out tradition or embarrassing one's family: it was a divine act.

Throughout the majority of his career, Leith was concerned that the church listen to the full spectrum of its history, albeit through the lens of the Reformed tradition. Perhaps his best-known work, *Creeds of the Churches* (1963, with revised editions), is remarkable for its catholicity. For the previous century, theology at Union had been bound to Calvin as interpreted by Turretin, yet here was a book that included not only the expected ante-Nicene documents but also Lutheran, Anglican, Baptist, and Methodist confessions in the modern age, as well as current ecumenical pronouncements. Phillip Schaff published his magisterial three-volume *Creeds of Christendom* in 1877, as an exercise in history. Leith wanted his work to be used in the parish; he includes short introductions to each confession as a help for any minister or layperson to wrestle with its meaning. Theology was never an end in itself, merely a product of "the relative isolation of the scholar's study." Creeds were the product of their times, written to articulate the Christian faith in reflection upon "moments of historical intensity," to make faithful sense of the turmoil in which believers lived.[74]

Leith arguably had a greater impact on Union Seminary and the church after the 1970s. As theological education was experimenting with more degrees and various curriculum changes, it was Leith who reminded everyone that faculty and students lived, worked, and studied on a continuum that should be mindful of the past, current in its thinking, and focused on the parish. Near the end of his career, he presented a lecture titled "Teaching Theology at Union Theological Seminary in Virginia" as part of the observances of the 175th anniversary of Union's founding in 1987. He began his address by noticing the 1940 Catalogue's boast that students had previously been trained

> in one system of theology only, and that was old-line Calvinism. Since 1940 they have been made increasingly aware of a wider spectrum of theological thought. Calvinism has remained the accepted system of theology, but it is not the rigid unyielding Calvinism of earlier years; it is rather a Reformed theology prepared to accept insights from modern theologians, all subject to revision in the light of a growing understanding of Scripture.

He declared that the theology taught at Union had always been practical and aimed at the minister serving a parish, to communicate doctrine to ordinary people. The ideal Presbyterian minister was the model of the scholar-pastor who combined scholarship with the work of the ministry. But Leith perceived a dilemma in the modern teaching of theology: "Are theology teachers interpreters of the tradition or inventors of a new theology?" Secular universities may produce theologians "who are technically superior to those of a previous time, but are they better equipped to pastor a church?"[75] Just as the historical-critical method tended to divide and subdivide Scripture into unrelated and perhaps unintelligible parts, so Leith saw that the so-called new theologies were obscuring the past and inhibiting a conversation with the church's history. Historical theology could give unity to an increasingly fragmented field.

Leith never saw himself as an original thinker, nor was he primarily concerned with the academy. Indeed, he described himself as "critically orthodox." "I have attempted to reaffirm the classic catholic and Reformed faith in the contemporary idiom of ordinary discourse while taking seriously the spirit and methods of the Enlightenment and the nineteenth century without their dogmas."[76] He saw himself as the transmitter of a tradition and saw the field of theology becoming fragmented. Leith advocated historical theology as a way to unify disparate theological efforts and give a common vocabulary to the church. In one of this last books, *Crisis in the Church: The Plight of Theological Education* (1997), Leith lamented that by discarding its history, "the long-term wisdom of the Christian community," seminaries were leading the church away from historic theological boundaries and affirmations into theological nihilism. "No church," Leith argues, "has endured for long without the clear affirmation" of historic doctrines. For him, the greatest danger facing the modern church is a corrupted proclamation. "The task of theology is to test the proclamation of the church in light of the Word of God in Jesus Christ as attested in Scripture." Without the tradition as a guide, proclamation leads away from Jesus, and then there is no church.[77]

John Leith was a supportive, and even inspirational, mentor for many. Ted Wardlaw (DMin, 1978) remembers his first year at Union as a time of crisis; Hebrew made him question his call, and he even applied for a job in his hometown with thoughts of leaving Richmond. His classmates were no help; when he talked with them, they would just repeat the problem back to him (since they were "trained in active listening"). He went to talk to Dr. Leith, and his response was what Wardlaw needed to hear. "Reinhold Niebuhr once told Paul Lehmann, who told me, that in everyone's life there is always an SOB. And right now the SOB in your life is you. Now quit your navel-gazing, quit your bellyaching, quit whining, quit being such a baby, and get to the library, eat well, exercise well, and get to work."[78] Wardlaw went to the library and got to work.

In the 1980s, Leith came to be seen as an enigma. Disturbed by what he saw as the devaluing of the life of the church, he complained that whereas professors had previously been drawn from the church and were UTS graduates, professors were now "drawn from divinity schools, lack appreciation for the church's life and traditions, are not graduates of UTS, and have no interest in the traditions or the future of the seminary" (quote adapted). In his opinion, professors who were recruited from outside the church led to the breakdown of the old theological consensus.[79] The crisis he saw in the seminaries was interwoven with the crisis in the church; the secularization of educational institutions led seminaries to move away from their primary responsibility: preparing pastors for ministry.

Despite his critique of Union and the church, he remained an imposing presence. In one of his last public appearances, Leith carried the seminary's copy of Calvin's *Institutes* into the new library in 1996.[80] His call to a traditionless people to recapture an unknown tradition may have made him an anachronism in the minds of some. Nevertheless, without that tradition the church is an orphan.

Commitment to Richmond

There is arguably no piece of legislation that has altered the American landscape more than the Interstate Highway Act in 1956. Besides the intended effects of providing Americans with high-speed limited-access roadways, there was an obvious and permanent unintended consequence: interstates prompted the trend toward "urban renewal" and transformed the American cityscape. Historically, African American neighborhoods in Richmond were particularly dismembered. The Richmond-Petersburg Turnpike (opened in 1958) devastated the Jackson Ward neighborhood; the mid-1960s completion of I-64 and I-95 through Richmond destroyed Navy Hill, Fulton, and parts of Westwood; and the Downtown Expressway (completed in 1976) virtually wiped out Oregon Hill. At the same time, the turmoil caused by integration caused many Americans to flee from the cities. In Richmond, the city's annexation of northern Chesterfield County (roughly Bon Air in the north to US Route 1 on the south) in 1970 and court-mandated busing in 1971 caused whites to flee to the suburbs. In Ginter Park, the stately old homes were torn down for apartments.[81]

Union Seminary felt the strain of the city. East of the quad, across Chamberlayne Avenue, grand old houses of Ginter Park were demolished to make way for high-density apartments by the mid-1960s. The seminary felt the need to keep up. The prospectus for the Advance Campaign includes a site map that previews the proposed new buildings. Mirroring what was happening all over Ginter Park, every "old" building is depicted as being replaced by block-style, stucco buildings; only the facades of Schauffler and Latta Library remain. Although some count it fortunate that the Advance Campaign did not have the money to renovate the buildings on the quad, the drive to change the environment perhaps reflected deeper concerns about Union's urban location.

As the neighborhood underwent a transformation, the seminary community no longer felt the same about the area around the quad. At the called meeting following the death of President Jones in 1966, the trustees approved a new faculty housing policy, which let professors choose between seminary-provided housing and a housing allowance, thereby allowing them to move off campus.[82] The 1967 Self-Study Report revealed that many were thinking Union's time in Richmond had come to an end.

At the time of the intensive study preparing for the Advance program, serious consideration was given to the question regarding the location of the seminary. After careful investigation, it was concluded that the seminary is strategically located to accomplish its function and that the Ginter Park area within the greater Richmond community provides a unique milieu for the training of ministers.[83]

In the November 1990 board meeting, the issue of education for faculty children was a contentious topic. Many on the faculty wanted to live outside of Richmond due to the perceived poor quality of the city's schools.

Many wondered how Union would contribute to the new urban ecology. Most faculty had always sent their children to the neighborhood public schools. At the beginning of Richmond's efforts to desegregate their schools in the late 1960s, they continued to support the public schools as a positive statement about integration.[84] Yet many of their children had a tough time; they were often the only white children in class. Being a distinct minority in an atmosphere filled with tension, they could be targets of abuse and did not feel accepted. Several faculty families then enrolled their children in private schools, but their children were not accepted there either.[85] What should have been a joyful attempt to create a better society left a legacy of bitterness in some instances.

The concerns over quality of life and education were factors in recruiting and retaining students and faculty from the 1980s onward. Indeed, education became the touchstone that determined the seminary's relationship to the city. Mark Peters (MDiv, 1996) observed that some students wanted the seminary to create a private school for seminary children. He was suspicious that more malevolent motives were in play:

> We all know how bad (read "unchristian") the public school systems have become. Some parents maintain that they want their children taught in a school environment that promotes Christian values. It is only coincidental that most of these too happen to have a majority of white students in their enrollment.
>
> I say to all of you, to the childless and the parents, when we abandon the public school system, we abandon the children we leave behind. And for the Christian, whether he/she likes it or not, those are his/her children too.[86]

In early 1992, President Hall submitted a paper to the board titled "An Obstacle to Our Mission." This paper outlined the three primary issues influencing faculty recruitment and retention: salary, housing costs (to allow faculty to live near campus), and education for children. President Hall did his best to sustain Moore's vision of an urban theological community, where students lived on one side of the quad and faculty on the other side, but it was a dream of the past.

Hall reported that faculty morale was low because many professors did not want to live on or close to campus, due to the issues of crime and the reputation of the city schools.[87] Indeed, UTS was experiencing a high rate of faculty turnover because other institutions could offer more money and a better quality of life. In addition, the issue of children's education affected not only faculty but also student and staff recruitment. Yet the administration was largely hamstrung in addressing these issues: budgetary restrictions precluded any increases in salaries, housing allowances, or subsidies for private schools.

The pressures built up; by the 1990s there were comments, albeit "only half in jest," that the campus should be sold to the Baptist Theological School in Richmond (BTSR), and Union should move to Charlotte.[88] Many also saw that with increased use of technology, the viability of the residential community model of education could be outmoded in the near future.[89] For the first time in its history, many openly wondered if Union had a future as a residential school in Richmond.

Security was another consistent concern, and this only became more urgent by the 1990s. In 1969 typewriters were stolen from dorm rooms, along with the color television in the Richmond dorm common area. An "interloper" was also caught in Melrose Dorm. In 1975, students complained about vandalism, and a student was attacked (suffering a concussion) on the way home from the library. Another student chased the attacker away.[90] Students called for more lighting around campus, and the administration responded. The realities of urban life, however, continued to intrude. Students began to call for uniformed security officers in 1978,[91] and uniformed security officers were patrolling the campus within two years. In 1994 the Spouses Council conducted a survey, which called for more lighting, a campus crime-watch program, and a "regular safety newsletter informing [the] campus of safety issues." While some worried that the security initiatives would isolate the campus community,[92] the Spouses Council made their commitment to the city clear.

> Living in an urban setting, even within a seminary campus, invites unfortu-
> nate circumstances to enter our lives. We do not, however, have to allow these
> circumstances to limit our enjoyment of our time here. Working together, we
> can promote a safe and productive environment for the study of God's Word
> and become an example for the community at large.[93]

In 1996, off-duty Richmond City Police officers began patrolling the campus in two shifts.[94]

Richmond Theological Center

The Richmond Theological Center (RTC) quickly became the barometer of Union's commitment to Richmond. In 1968, President Stair noticed the trend for theological seminaries to cluster with university centers. He proposed a formal relationship between the School of Theology of Virginia Union University (STVU) and PSCE. The RTC was designed to allow students at one school to take courses at another RTC institution. Moreover, all three schools would share resources. On June 10, 1969, the presidents of all three schools announced the formation of the RTC. Under the initial agreement, UTS paid 54 percent of Lingle Hall's (the cafeteria and conference rooms) operating costs and 60 percent of the library's costs, with the other two schools sharing the remaining overhead.[95]

The UTS community had high hopes for the RTC. The 1972–73 Catalogue prominently displays a picture of the RTC sign,[96] and Union dedicated staff to distribute the "RTC Calendar" each week so everyone in the RTC community could keep up with events and news of the three institutions. The 1974 Self-Study Report was glowing:

Our experience these five years is that the RTC has strengthened each of the three schools: more course offerings at lesser costs, more realistic community integration, more learning from each other. It would be the intention of the UTS administration to recommend the RTC for another three years.[97]

Living in community can, however, be difficult. During an intramural basketball game in 1975, Virginia Union students "became angry at what seemed to be bad officiating against their team in particular" because they were black and the referee was white. After two meetings between the teams, they identified that the officiating problem was that "one referee had been trained to officiate high school basketball and the other was calling a much looser game." After the issue was settled, many thought that the "willingness with which all parties to the dispute entered into the attempt at reconciliation" was positive and would stimulate better communications with the RTC community.[98]

Perhaps in an effort to emphasize the independence of its constituent part, the Richmond Theological Center became the Richmond Theological Consortium in the early 1980s. In the UTS community, however, the name change was merely window dressing; many wondered if the RTC was really working. Students complained that the lack of calendar coordination, no common cross-registration procedures, and the absence of a common chapel prevented real community from being formed.[99] By 1980 Union's trustees were also discouraged. They observed that UTS was providing more services and taking up more of the cost for RTC's operation, even though PSCE and the STVU depended on the UTS library for their accreditation. At its founding in 1942, STVU was unaccredited and had 23 students; by 1993 it had 120 students and was accredited.[100] In 1982 one student complained: "It is obvious that there is not a great deal of interaction between the three schools on the academic level." Indeed, Union students seemed to want to stay in the family. In the 1992–93 school year, 83 percent of all cross registrations by UTS students was for courses offered at PSCE. The continual problems of cross-registration and lack of a common calendar were recurrent themes. Sara Little lamented: "There is an intercultural, interracial experience here we have not utilized."[101]

There was also the uneasy feeling that UTS was isolated from the community around it. From its inception, some saw the RTC as a way for Union and PSCE to feel smug about racism without actually having to confront the culture. Students were proud that the seminary, through its building program, was "going to stay in a changing neighborhood." They were also glad to see that the PSCE kindergarten "has long since integrated, and last year the Seminary and PSCE community participated in an effort to encourage people to keep their children in schools which were becoming integrated." They were also pleased that Union and PSCE have "provided space for controversial speakers on both the left and the right, and we have thereby declared our belief in free speech and civil liberties." Yet Kit Havice (BD, 1969) detected a glaring omission in the Union's witness:

What does the world hear us saying when we invite the Seminary Community to a banquet to greet Dr. Stair or to the Smith open house and fail to invite the Building and Grounds staff?

What do we mean to proclaim when our students receive minimum wage for doing unskilled work in the dining hall and the kitchen staff does not [even receive that]?[102]

And Paul Rader (MDiv, 1984) was disappointed; he saw Union as an isolated preserve, not engaging with the world around it.

> January 15 was the date of the thirteenth annual Martin Luther King Jr. Memorial Service here in Richmond. As far as I know, and I hope I am wrong, only two students from UTS and no faculty or administration members attended. The celebration was ecumenical in nature, well publicized, and was fortunate to have a nationally respected speaker. Common courtesy would suggest that at least one representative from the seminary be there.[103]

A New Language

The biggest change on campus between 1967 and 1996 was the presence of women.[104] Following Mary Faith Carson (BD, 1961), Nancy Miller (attended 1957–58, 1959–61), and Ellen Thomasson (attended 1959–60), fifteen women were on campus by 1968.[105] Elaine Rhodes (DMin, 1976) arrived at UTS in July 1970, with only four other women in her class (Glenda Lisk [attended 1970–71]; Margaret Peery [MDiv, 1974]; Sara Payne [MDiv, 1972], and Lucy Rose [DMin, 1975]).[106] At first she was not bothered by the use of traditional language; she was more concerned about placement for ministry.

Rhodes remembers that women students were invited to meetings of the student wives' club, and they attended because it provided some fellowship. It was at one of these meetings that some of the wives asked why the language used in chapel and on campus was not gender-neutral. Elaine did not think deeply about the issue until she heard Edna Mason Pickett (DMin, 1974) preach in chapel and had the congregation sing "O Brother Man," by John Greenleaf Whittier, with gender-neutral words. The traditional hymn begins: "O brother man, fold to thy heart thy brother," and Pickett changed the words to "O loved of God, hold to your hearts each other. . . ." This change made such an impact on Rhodes that she began to think of ways she and others could get the student body and faculty to think about how we speak of God and God's people. Although her ultimate concern remained equal placement in a church that was decidedly ambivalent (at best) on the issue of women in ministry, she soon realized that inclusive language was fundamental to changing attitudes. Hence she initiated the process that, with the help of others, became the inclusive-language policy and a vehicle for women's concerns to be heard.

Margaret Peery, Elaine Rhodes, Nancy Rowland (DMin, 1977), and Judy Sutherland (MDiv, 1974) drafted the "Inclusive Language Paper," and the faculty was receptive. A task force on language composed of both faculty (Donald Dawe and Patrick Miller) and the students presented the study paper to the faculty on May 3, 1974. While acknowledging that language is a "controversial issue, even among us seminary women," the paper argues that language is "an expression of our attitudes, our values, our culture, and of who and where we are." Consequently, "just as changing our attitudes helps to change our language, so it may be possible for alterations in our language to help to effect change in our attitudes."

The authors were blunt: "There are those of us who feel very much left out when people consistently use the masculine words as generic." The use of this language fosters "a real sense of exclusion and [a sense] that we are not being taken seriously." They asked the seminary to show leadership on this issue.

> Our concern is the role that we as a seminary can play in attending to this matter, which is one of liberation. The seminary is where the leaders of the church are being trained, and it is a place to which the church and its leadership looks for guidance. As such, the seminary is a leader, whether it wishes to claim that role or not. One of the most concrete ways the seminary can responsibly carry out this role is to help to inform its students of issues requiring prophetic leadership.

The paper also asked professors to use and encourage others to use gender-neutral language when appropriate. They also asked the administration to prepare a style manual so all seminary publications would employ gender-neutral language. Finally, they asked students to consider the language used in chapel and on campus. The issue was not merely political posturing. Inclusive language was not an end in and of itself: the goal was to change the world. "Let us make our language a means by which the gospel may be heard anew."[107]

The "Inclusive Language Paper" was well received and opened the faculty's eyes to the vulnerability and abandonment women could feel. Two weeks later, on May 15, 1974, Pat Miller, Margaret Peery, and Judy Sutherland presented "Recommendations to the Faculty from the Women Students" to the faculty. These recommendations went beyond language to placement and support.

Placement of Women

Student pulpit supply was a particular area of concern. It had been customary for churches to ask for a specific "type" of student to supply their pulpits. Instead, the paper asked that a "rotation" system for pulpit supply be implemented: churches could no longer pick who they wanted to fill their pulpits. Students, without regard to gender, would be assigned to preach in churches as each church called, seeking a pulpit supply. If a church refused a student, "the Associate to the Dean and the offended student will confront them by phone or letters and try to find out why they refused to have the student and will also encourage the church to accept this person." If the church continued to reject the student originally assigned, the official policy was that "someone else will be sent to them."[108] In reality, however, the dean of students sent no one if the church only wanted male students.[109] The paper also called on the seminary to guarantee that all students would be able to interview for summer work positions. If a church refused to interview a woman, they would interview no one. The faculty readily agreed.

The "Recommendations" also called for the seminary to assist all graduates through the call process by establishing a Personnel Advisory Committee. This committee, to be appointed annually by the president and composed of faculty members, would ensure that all students receive fair treatment in the call process, including explaining "the denominational [call] processes and provide suitable forms for them to fill out in order to place their names with the proper denominational agencies." The students also called on the administration to include in the 1974 graduate picture book "a paragraph encouraging people in the church to give careful consideration to women students as they fill vacancies in their professional leadership," and on appropriate occasions to "recommend specific women students for consideration." Further, they requested that the administration send "a communication to the Stated Clerks of the Synods of the Virginia and North Carolina, reviewing the statements on written policies about placement of women, and stating the seminary's concern about the response and the responsibility of the courts of the church for women who have a vocation for ministry." The faculty promised they would act.

The paper also called for personal support for female students. The administration, in consultation with women students, was asked to "explore opportunities for providing access to a female counselor who is sensitive to those issues which are part of the feminist perspective." The paper insisted that women should be part of the public face of Union Seminary; pictures of women should be included in seminary publications, and the viewpoints of female students, staff, and faculty should be reported whenever opinions were solicited. Finally, the paper wanted the faculty and administration to "make an express effort to identify women who are qualified for candidacy for position on the faculty." It also requested "that the community plan for a symposium next spring in continued exploration and investigation of the Women, Theology, and Language theme."[110] The faculty agreed.

Adopting a paper was not going to be sufficient; the issue of women in ministry was not unique to Union and would continue to be a source of contention. Although the PCUS and the northern church had permitted the ordination of women since 1965 and 1956, respectively, many churches refused to consider a woman for their pulpit and questioned whether women should even be in seminary. Changing language was but a first step, one that embodied "the example of respect for one another through our language" and reflected the love that our Lord commands us to show one another.[111]

Union continued to take a strong stand; the faculty passed a resolution concerning inclusive language on May 26, 1980, and reaffirmed it on March 11, 1982. This resolution called not only for gender-neutral language, but also "language that includes persons of different races and ethnic backgrounds, different ages, and different family circumstances." The faculty further committed themselves by issuing guidelines for the use of inclusive language in chapel and tasked the Christian Life and Action Committee to standardize the language in the *Worshipbook*. Perhaps most important, the faculty directed the dean of students "to devise ways of alerting incoming students to the concern of the Faculty, Administration, and Student Body of this matter,"[112] and the policy was printed in the catalogues. There would be no ambiguity as to Union's position on women in ministry and on the atmosphere of learning on campus.

A New Presence of Women

Environments do not change by resolutions, but by human action. The 1967 Self-Study Report officially acknowledged the growing numbers of women on campus and the need to support them. The Advance Campaign directed funding to create living space for women on campus so that they would not need to live across the Brook at PSCE. Union would also show its commitment publicly; the 1967–68 Catalogue's back cover shows a female student leaving the library.[113]

Although Mary Faith Carson[114] and Elaine Rhodes[115] felt encouraged and accepted, Union could be a baffling place for women. Mary Jane Winter (MDiv, 1976) arrived on campus in July 1969 for Greek school, and then went to Harvard Divinity School, where she received an MTS. She returned to Richmond in 1974 with her husband and was the first married woman on campus.[116] A native of Arkansas and a graduate of Mary Baldwin College, she was nonetheless taken aback at the "Virginian" formality of Union. Her mail was addressed to "Mrs. Theodore H. Winter." When she complained, a secretary told her that this was how they did it, and there would be no "Ms."

In her experience most of the faculty were supportive; it was her male colleagues who were the most difficult. The first day Mary Jane was on campus, a male colleague asked her why she was here and then said she was not called; she was a "Women's Libber," and it was not biblical for her to be a pastor. Yet Mary Jane felt that the seminary as an institution tried to help women. Nealy McCarter (dean) and Mac Turnage (third-level adviser) were especially helpful. They were encouraging and ensured that women had an equal opportunity for pulpit supply.

Nevertheless, the church was not always welcoming. Mary Elizabeth Goin (MDiv, 1978) explained the contradictions between what churches wanted in a candidate and what candidates wanted in a church:

> I get discouraged at those times when I hear worried church members wonder if they'll ever find the right man for their pulpit. . . . The word around here is that pulpit committees are all looking for that 25-year-old man with 30 years' experience, who is independently wealthy and looking for the challenge of a small church that can offer only minimal salary. And all of us are looking for that little church with 110% attendance and contributions from its members, where we will have plenty of time for study, visiting, and leisure.[117]

Jeff Sconyers (attended 1976–79) pointed out the differences in perceptions that made being a female seminarian frustrating:

> Why is it that no one asks male seminarians how they intend to handle marriage and a church, while the question invariably arises regarding women in seminary?
> No matter how supportive and understanding we may be here, no matter how high our consciousnesses have been raised, it is important that we be prepared for hard times in the church when we speak out for what comes down simply to the full humanity of women. We are quick to say that we will work for the full rights of women in the church. And yet women graduating from Union Seminary can expect, in the main, second-rate jobs at low pay, or no jobs at all. It will not be easy.[118]

Although Annie Wilson enrolled as an experiment in 1907, and Elizabeth Etchison covertly took enough classes to graduate in 1951, their presence was accidental and left no lasting influence. In the same way, female professors added to Union's mission before they were fully acknowledged. Miss Eugenia L. Anspaugh taught speech in the fall of 1901. Forty men enrolled, and more took individual instruction.[119] The first female professor on record at Union Theological Seminary was Mlle. Suzanne De Dietrich, ThD, resident lecturer at Ecumenical Institute of Celigny, Switzerland, who was a visiting professor during academic year 1954–55. During academic year 1970–71, Roberta Cowan Chestnut, DPhil, was appointed Visiting Instructor in Old Testament.

Elizabeth R. Achtemeier was appointed as visiting professor of homiletics in 1973 and continued as adjunct professor of Bible and homiletics until 1997; yet due to Union's nepotism policy, she was never appointed professor because her husband, Paul J. Achtemeier, taught New Testament. Sara P. Little served as adjunct professor of Christian education from 1967 to 1973. In 1974 she was appointed professor of Christian education (a joint appointment with PSCE, where she had been a professor since 1951), and in 1976 she became a member of the UTS faculty (without an official connection with PSCE).[120] She was the first female full-time professor at Union and served as professor of Christian education from 1974 until her retirement in 1990.

A native of Charlotte, Little graduated from Queens College (now Queens University), and received her master's degree from PSCE and her PhD from Yale. With her unfailing sense of humor and shrewd understanding of human nature, she understood how to effect change, but she also knew that change came slowly. Among some angry articles in the December 1985/January 1986 issue of *In Medias Res*, the "Women's Issues Issue," Sara counseled grace. She first recalled listening to a tape "of my summary at the end of a consultation on women in ministry on March 31–April 1, 1973" and ruminating on what it takes to transform any human organization.[121]

> You may be saying, "Interesting, but so what?" The "so what" is the outcome of that consultation. A task force that worked for the next year did a careful analysis and made recommendations about our life together. Then they invited the faculty for an evening in Schauffler 104 to hear the report, beginning with a clever media takeoff on "Rise Up, O men of God." I think I have never been prouder of UTS women than when they presented their recommendations about curriculum, about field placement, about policies for accepting invitations to preach when a church refused to have a woman, about appointing monitors for each class to check the language used, and a host of other items. Questions and comments (critical, sometimes) were handled with all the precision and clarity of an experienced leader. And the group monitored the follow-through of the recommendations afterwards, sometimes through tedious procedures. Indeed, those of us here now benefit from many of those actions.[122]

Rebecca Harden Weaver served as the early church historian from 1984 until her retirement in June 2012; she is the longest serving female professor. A native of Texas, she graduated from the University of Texas, received her MDiv from Austin Seminary, and her PhD from Southern Methodist University. Weaver served as associate pastor of the West Plano, Texas, Presbyterian Church. She remembers seeing the advertisement for the church history position, and Hartley Hall, in the tradition of presidential selection of professors, made the first contact.[123] She was particularly interested in the church's controversies over nature and grace and the role of women in the Middle Ages. Among her numerous publications, Weaver is perhaps best known for *Divine Grace and Human Agency: A Study of the Semi-Pelagian Controversy* (1984) and "Augustine's Use of Scriptural Admonitions against Boasting in His Final Arguments on Grace" (in *Studia Patristica* 27 [1993]). Although she is known for rigorous and exacting scholarship, Rebecca Harden Weaver is appreciated for her gracious nature, which made her a mentor for many Union women and men.

Women were found not just in the classroom, however. The first female members of the seminary's board of trustees were Mrs. Alice Gifford, who served from 1972 to 1976, and Mrs. Elinor Henderson Swaim, who served in 1972–80. Their election made front-page news.[124] In the board minutes through 1975, female members were identified by their husbands' names: Mrs. R. P. Gifford, Mrs. Wilborn S. Swaim, and Mrs. Lewis H. Evans Jr. But in the May 1976 minutes, women were identified by their own given names: Martha A. Beery, Colleen T. Evans, Betsy K. McCreight, and Elinor S. Swaim. In the next meeting, women were identified by their own name but with the title of Mrs. Subsequent meetings simply identified women in the minutes by their own name. At this May meeting the board also adopted a resolution to appoint a committee, partly comprising female seminarians, to outline a strategy to be used to assist women in locating challenging positions in the church. The first female chair of the board was Jane D. Rourk, who served as such in 2002–5.

Sara Little was right: by tedious steps, progress was made. The board minutes from November 1981 report the highest percentage of women in Union's history admitted that fall. In January 1983 the board incorporated gender-inclusive language into the seminary bylaws. And in November 1986 the board moved that the 1954 policy concerning the cemetery at Hampden-Sydney be modified: the word "wives" was changed to "spouses." The November 1988 board minutes reported that after thirty years of accepting female students, of the 186 women the seminary had graduated to that date, only 2 (who were recent graduates) had not received initial placement: "No other seminary has produced this placement record."

Beginning in 1985, the Office of Field Education and Placement (OFEP) held a special seminar for women who were engaged in the placement process (the seminars were eliminated in 1995 due to budget restrictions). The results of this seminar showed that the issue of women in ministry was a churchwide dilemma, but Union was making a difference. Reports from 1995 show that 70 percent of female graduates were appreciative of the UTS faculty, and 66.7 percent felt that fellow students were supportive, yet women were placed at a slower rate than men. Indeed, of the 65 churches in attendance at the 1995 face-to-face week-end-long intensive interview event (where churches and candidates could theoretically have up to 8 interviews), 21 did not ask to interview a woman.[125] These churches, however, were assigned female candidates to interview because all attending churches were required to interview at least one woman.

Yet, whatever progress had been made, many women still found UTS awkward at best. In 1990, Shirley Hutchins published "Some Thoughts from the 'Girl' Seminarian" in *In Medias Res*. She was frustrated that after so many years and an official policy, many people still resisted using inclusive language. Hutchins complained that language was "a BIG DEAL," and the lack of inclusive language on campus revealed deeper assumptions and attitudes. "Inclusivity is more than words. It is an attitude. It is a way of life."[126] Indeed, many felt that the church itself was not supportive. Union hosted A Convocation of Women on April 12–13, 1991. Writing about the conference, Martha Lane Moore (MDiv, 1994) sadly observed, in words that could have been written twenty years earlier: "Whatever may be our own assessment of the feminist critique of Christian patriarchy, we cannot deny that there are women in the ministry and in our future congregations who do not feel that the church has fully affirmed them as creations of God."[127]

Nora Tubbs Tisdale (DMin, 1979), who taught homiletics and worship from 1988 to 1993, left to teach at Princeton Theological Seminary while "disappointed in the lack of gender and racial-ethnic diversity," sensing little interest "to alter the old, informal, and comfortable ways of networking and doing business in order to embrace newcomers and to make room (in informal as well as formal processes) for voices and perspectives which are different."[128] At the May 1994 board meeting, Rebecca Weaver reported:

> Repeatedly, female students have told me of being either ridiculed or verbally abused by our male students. I am convinced that this situation will continue as long as the membership of the faculty and of the administration is almost exclusively male. Despite the conscientious efforts of men on the faculty and in the administration to encourage our female students, the almost total absence of women in these positions reinforces the bias of many of our male students that women's theological scholarship and women's issues in the church are not only unworthy of serious consideration but even appropriate subjects for ridicule.[129]

The board was alarmed and tasked their Campus Life Committee and the president to conduct a study "about concerns that women and others have for a more hospitable UTS campus." The committee reported on May 1, 1995, that they found a "chilly climate" on campus that made Union unwelcoming and even hostile to women and dismissive of nontraditional theological perspectives. The committee recommended that the president appoint an oversight committee to assure "that the UTS community continues to encourage diversity in gender, age, ethnic, and theological perspective on its board, faculty, invited speakers, administration, student body, etc." The board also stated "its desire for the hiring/retention of women and other under-represented groups as well as the maintenance of a hospitable campus atmosphere which recognizes differences and promotes learning." It called for the inclusive-language policy to be enforced by "giving feedback to students, worship leaders, invited speakers, administrators, and others concerning their use of inclusive language."[130]

The presence of women on campus grew dramatically throughout this period. In 1967 about 12 percent of the entering class was female; in 1997 the figure was almost 50 percent. The 1996 Self-Study Report contained the first extensive section on women's concerns. The administration had already formed a special committee to resolve difficulties in recruiting and retaining female faculty; it also pledged to poll alumnae and survey current students to improve the atmosphere and support for women in ministry.[131]

Frances Taylor Gench (MDiv, 1982; PhD, 1988) represents a traditional Union paradigm in a new way; she is a Davidson graduate, and her parents and grandparents went to Union. She is, however, a woman (and she met her husband on campus). Her first memories of Union were the hot Richmond summer and the Greek school. Bill Carl taught the class and had the students say the Lord's Prayer in Greek. He sometimes brought his son, Jeremy, who was "just out of diapers" and would amaze the class by reciting the Lord's Prayer in Greek.[132] She grew to love the combination of rigorous academics with the strong sense of community. Loving God with the mind led her to see how exegesis and context mattered in recognizing how God worked; reading the Bible in a disciplined, informed manner changed her life. The story of women in the church can seem like a series of unfulfilled promises and false hopes. Yet, when Elaine Rhodes challenged Union in 1974 with the "Inclusive Language Paper," the seminary responded with a consistent commitment to women in ministry that has changed the church.

Thomas Hartley Hall IV

In March 1981, Hartley Hall was called as the fifth and last PCUS president of Union Seminary. He was a native of Macon, Georgia, and in high school had been elected the international president of Key Club, a Kiwanis-sponsored service organization. Hall was a Phi Beta Kappa graduate of Davidson College, with a degree in business and economics. At Davidson he was designated cadet commander of its ROTC unit, and the day after his graduation in 1951, he reported for active military duty. He served as an infantry officer in Korea during 1952–53, first as platoon leader, then company commander, and (at twenty-three years old) Headquarters Commandant of the 32nd Infantry Regiment. He received the Bronze Star with Oak Leaf Cluster, and the Silver Star for gallantry in combat. In 1954 he left a family real estate business (and his real estate license, held since he was nineteen) and entered Union Seminary, where so many of his twenty-nine Davidson classmates who went on to seminary had gone.[133] He attended UTS because the Davidson seminarians he respected the most had opted for Union: he simply relied on their judgment and followed them. In spite of his having graduated cum laude and with a Phi Beta Kappa key, the UTS faculty found deficiencies in his prior academic preparation. They assigned him required readings in moral philosophy and modern European history, on which he was examined and tested upon return from his first summer's fieldwork. Union was very much a southern school, and the seminary tried to acculturate the few non-Southerners in attendance. A classmate from Ohio, John Dozier (BD, 1957), was assigned *The Mind of the South*, by J. W. Cash, and other books on the South prior to entering.

More in the mold of students in succeeding generations, President Hall did not intend to become a minister when he arrived in Richmond. He wanted to address questions that confronted him as the result of his combat experiences. He fell in love with biblical studies during his first year. In his first summer he served as a student assistant in Lumberton, North Carolina. This experience of ministering to the congregation in Lumberton was the beginning of his sense of

50. T. Hartley Hall IV, president, 1981–94

call to the pastorate. After receiving his BD in 1957 and a faculty fellowship, he attended Yale University Divinity School and received an STM in 1958.

East Hanover Presbytery ordained Hall in 1957 before he entered Yale, so he could serve as assistant pastor of the First Congregational Church in Branford, Connecticut, and he continued as their interim pastor through 1959. For 1959–61 he was called as campus minister and Presbyterian chaplain at North Carolina State University. Then Hall served First Presbyterian in Lenoir, North Carolina, during 1961–66; went to First Presbyterian in Tyler, Texas, for 1966–73; and to Westminster Presbyterian in Nashville in 1973–81. While at Westminster, he also served as an adjunct professor in homiletics at Vanderbilt University Divinity School.

The search process that resulted in President Hall's call reflected Union's corporate nature. President Lacy handpicked James Jones (who had served as Lacy's assistant in 1934) and had identified Fred Stair (who had served as Lacy's assistant from 1948 to 1953) for a potential leadership position. Hall was the first president chosen by a board committee. In his inaugural address, he recognized that reunion was just over the horizon, and Union was no longer just a regional seminary. He called for UTS to stop thinking geographically and reach beyond "our historic formal ties to the Synods of Virginia and North Carolina." Union should work with "all those parts of the church who share with us a concern for those ministers and lay persons who will in such large measure determine the quality of life—the health, if you please—of our congregations."

Yet, however well the seminary did its job, the school was ultimately dependent on the denomination:

> It is my firm conviction that if the church is healthy, then Union Seminary is going to prosper. And if the church is sick, then we will have problems of such magnitude that no amount of tinkering with curriculum or admissions and degree requirements—not even massive infusions of new endowments—will solve them.[134]

By the 1980s the Presbyterian family was growing smaller: the 1960 combined membership of both the UPC and PCUS was a little over 4 million; in 1983, the first year of reunion, there were 3.1 million members; and in 2012 the PC(USA) had 1.8 million members. In addition, denominational identity was declining; some churches were thinking of themselves as "community" churches.[135] And with the drift away from denominational loyalties, seminaries stood to lose both funding and students.

Reunion

Although "Reunion" (the organic merging of the largest northern and southern Presbyterian churches) was first broached in 1865 and proposed in 1870, history kept the northern and southern churches apart. While a large number of Cumberland Presbyterian Churches united with the northern church in 1906, and six synods of the northern church (majority African American) were located in the South,[136] the PCUS would not entertain any hint of organic union. John MacKay, the president of Princeton Seminary, again raised the call for southern and northern Presbyterian churches to reunite at the dedication of the Latta Library Extension in 1944,[137] but the idea of reunion was not taken seriously until 1962, when the Consultation on Church Union (COCU) was formed. COCU was part of the post–World War II ecumenical impulse. The four original members of COCU were the Episcopal Church, the Methodist Church, the United Presbyterian Church in the USA (the northern body), and the United Church of Christ—itself formed in 1958 as the result of a merger of the Congregational Church and the Evangelical and Reformed Church. The Presbyterian Church in the United States was a member by 1967.

In May 1966, COCU called for the union of its ten member denominations. They proposed that a Plan of Union be approved within 13 years, followed by 30 years of federation, then full organic union. Although the Plan of Union was soundly defeated, negotiations between the Evangelical United Brethren Church and the Methodist Church resulted in the creation of the United Methodist Church in 1968. Presbyterians wondered why they could not overcome their history and began to lumber their way toward reunion—to the way things were in 1860.

Professor James Smylie represented the reasoning of many of those in the PCUS who favored reunion. Forming a national church was seen as a way to renounce past actions.

> In 1861, John A. Smylie traveled from his home in Mississippi to Augusta, Georgia, where, as a Presbyterian minister, he signed the address to "all the churches

of Jesus Christ thought the Earth," justifying the organization of the Presbyterian Church of the Confederacy, the Confederacy, and even slavery itself. His uncle, the Rev. James Smylie, also a Mississippian and owner of fifty-three slaves, according to the census of 1850, wrote one of the earliest tracts defending slavery as a positive good. If my genealogy is correct, I am a direct descendant of these two Smylies since my paternal grandparents were cousins.[138]

Many also argued that Reunion was a theological imperative. The body of Christ had to be united as part of a faithful Christian witness in fulfillment of the aim of Jesus' prayer in John 17.[139]

For all the history and theology, the idea of reunion did not excite the campus. John Leith argued that the emphasis on uniting with the UPC was misplaced. The energy put into Reunion should be spent in strengthening the PCUS and building up membership through evangelizing.[140] The editor of the student newspaper, *In Medias Res*, reported that just a slim majority of students seemed "to lean toward the proposal favorably."

> Most students thought reunion would be good for both churches; the northern church had a more international outlook, and the southern church had a stronger confessional heritage. Many were concerned with the northern church's corporate style, in contrast to a "just folks" way of doing things in the southern church. [One student said,] "The PCUS has a southeastern mentality. It needs to be given a broader outlook, a national [outlook], and PCUS can give the UPCUSA a back-to-basics mentality—our evangelism, biblical and Reformed thinking, [and] our conservatism can be moderating influences on the northern church."[141]

Despite apathy and opposition, the United Presbyterian Church and the Presbyterian Church in the United States merged in 1983 to form the Presbyterian Church (USA)—a return to the pre-Civil War name.

Whatever the hopes and romantic appeals, Reunion had two immediate consequences for Union: admissions and finances. Like many others in the southern church, Roger Nicholson (MDiv, 1972) went to UTS because it was "the" seminary. After graduation he served churches in Louisiana, Alabama, and Tennessee and was a campus minister before he became director of admissions in 1986.[142] President Hall and Nicholson realized that Reunion made the traditional student pipeline unreliable. Students from Virginia and North Carolina, no longer bound by regional and denominational loyalties, now felt more free to attend other Presbyterian seminaries and nondenominational schools.

In a national environment, it was not enough to "keep" the students from Virginia and North Carolina. President Hall directed Nicholson to begin recruiting students. The idea of designing a systematic program to attract students was unprecedented. It would no longer be enough for professors to visit the synod's denominational colleges once a year or for alums to steer students to Richmond. Union now needed to sell itself and attract students with competitive financial aid offers. Moreover, Nicholson oversaw the accreditation of the DMin program to attract students who may have attended other seminaries.

Nicholson developed what became a nationally recognized marketing strategy for attracting students, especially from the western states. UTS began to produce admissions materials that could match the quality of pamphlets from colleges and universities. The new advertising and admissions pamphlets reflect a transformation in the way Union saw itself. Before 1987, Union's admissions materials usually contained a map that showed Richmond in relation to Virginia and North Carolina. After Nicholson's redesign, the catalogue's maps show Richmond in relation to Washington (D.C.), Atlanta, and the Mid-Atlantic states. Recruiting pamphlets feature students who are not from the South. Fresh water and a healthful climate are no longer enough: Richmond is portrayed as cosmopolitan, with

> something for everyone. The city's parks and museums, the Richmond Symphony and Ballet, the Virginia Museum Theater, the new Center for the Performing Arts, the Planetarium, Dogwood Dell, the opera, and the Richmond Braves are all accessible, affordable treats for the student in search of diversion.[143]

Besides admissions, it was apparent that Reunion would result in a changed financial relationship between seminary and church. The theological turmoil in the northern Presbyterian church during the preceding century had created a climate of suspicion, resulting in weak support of the church's seminaries. New ministerial students in the northern church did not necessarily go to the seminaries of the northern General Assembly, such as Princeton and Pittsburgh, but attended independent seminaries, such as UTS (NY), Auburn, and others. In the old PCUS, however, it was virtually an unspoken requirement that a minister should attend a PCUS seminary. Consequently, Reunion forced a clash of cultures and expectations. In 1983 the majority of UPC candidates were not attending Presbyterian seminaries, while in the old PCUS the precise opposite was true.

At the same time, the northern church funded their theological institutions differently than the southern church. Financial support (and also control of) UPCUSA seminaries was lodged with the General Assembly. As a result, these schools therefore had no great incentive to orient their educational programs in support of the congregations or judicatories where each happened to be located. In contrast, financial support for PCUS seminaries had always come from the synod in which it happened to be located, and from the synods that controlled them. The survival of a PCUS seminary depended on its relationship of trust and support of the congregations in whose midst it lived. Prior to Reunion, each PCUS seminary had its own defined geographical area of support. After Reunion, southern schools lost their protected economic support base, while northern schools retained their previous synodical financial support.

Union had been the flagship seminary of the PCUS: its board members came from the population centers of PCUS membership (the Synods of Virginia, North Carolina, West Virginia, and Appalachia), and over 40 percent of the General Assembly's minister-moderators were UTS graduates. As late as 1970 the theological institutions of the former PCUS on average received 74 percent of their total income from synods. By 1980 those contributions had dropped to 32 percent. The new denomination nationalized funding for theological education. In the new denomination, churches and synods were asked to send their donations for seminary education to the national church (who would theoretically support all seminaries equally). Thus the seminaries became just one of many constituents competing for funds. Seminary boards drew their members from around the country and not just from the supporting synods; southern interest in supporting the operation of "our own" schools waned. In 1985, Union Seminary received less than 6 percent of its budget from its supporting synods.[144]

On top of the new dynamics of Reunion, the inflation of the 1970s and early 1980s decimated not only the Advance Campaign but also the endowment. Between 1971 and 1981 the endowment lost almost 30 percent of its purchasing power. When President Hall was called in 1981, the endowment stood at $24.2 million, and some were concerned that the seminary would be bankrupt within four years if finances were not improved. Although a skeleton development office had been operating since the Advance Campaign, fund-raising was never more than a part-time concern. After the Advance Campaign and the renovation of Richmond Hall in 1977, those assigned to fund-raising went back to their primary duties. President Hall hired Robert Carlson as the first advancement director in 1983. During his eight years at Union, he established the infrastructure for fund-raising, such as a donor database and endowment fund accounting, and hired dedicated advancement staff for the first time. New (for Union) ways of raising money, energy conservation, and systems of financial management instituted by Bob Huntley, board chairman, and Bill Berry, the CEO of Virginia Power and chair of the board's Finance Committee—these strategies had the intended effect. When President Hall retired in 1994, the endowment stood at $72.5 million.

A New Context

The wider church recognized that the assumptions by which its seminaries had operated were transformed by Reunion. Whereas Union had been the leading PCUS seminary, supplying close to 30 percent of its ministers, overnight it was now just one of ten schools and was graduating about 8 percent of the PC(USA)'s ministers. The 1993 General Assembly formed a committee tasked with a "study of the new denomination's relationship with its inherited Presbyterian 'theological institutions,' that is, the ten Presbyterian seminaries and the Presbyterian School of Christian Education."[145] The committee concluded that Presbyterian seminaries faced a new world: a secular society that devalued religious education, diverse students without a traditional Presbyterian background, and disparate demands that encouraged an increasingly disjointed curriculum. Union, however, would continue to keep the traditional curriculum at its core.

The committee observed that it was not just Reunion affecting Presbyterian theological education; the context of the culture had changed. President Hall agreed, pointing out that in 1947 over half of all American baccalaureate degrees were awarded by private, church-related colleges. By 1989 the number was under 10 percent. Undergraduate education had changed into a secular experience.[146] The committee also saw that family life had become fragmented and Christian education deemphasized:

The lack of effective Christian education in the congregation, and the near demise of religious publications, the near extinction of the student Christian movement, and decline of the denominational college have made it far more difficult for theological schools to do their job. Vast networks of spiritual formation, leadership recruitment, and pre-seminary academic preparation have dissipated. Those responsible for the theological education of clergy are now charged with accomplishing many tasks and dimensions of preparation that were once shared within a vital configuration.

Students had also changed: "The demographic profile of the North American seminarian has changed more in the twenty years since 1970 than in the prior two hundred years." No longer were seminarians "predominantly white, male, in their early-to-mid-twenties." Although 77% of MDiv students were still white, 44% of Presbyterian students were female, and only 44% of all students were enrolled in the MDiv program. By 1991, students were older than in the past, with 62% of PC(USA) students 30 years of age or older; and 34% of those enrolled at Presbyterian seminaries were not Presbyterian. At the same time, 15% of all students were studying part-time, and more were living off campus.

The academy, not the church, now set the standards and culture in higher education. Into this mix, theological pluralism made it difficult and controversial to decide what was basic knowledge.[147] President Hall echoed the report. He saw the church losing confidence in its schools; in 1994 the presbyteries accepted almost as many candidates and ministers from non-Presbyterian seminaries and divinity schools as those graduated from PC(USA) seminaries.[148]

The traditional seminary community was, the report acknowledged, breaking down; theological schools would be "hard pressed to maintain the nineteenth-century model of a fully residential community, with all its possibilities for creating a formative ethos that is expressed in activities within and beyond the classroom." The lack of "traditioning" due to parental and church indifference to Christian education over the last two decades" meant that the seminary "would begin to function as a catechumenate, a place to discover how to orient oneself to a religious experience . . . and how to become a member of a Christian community." The lack of community tradition and consciousness would require remedial tasks unimaginable just a generation earlier.

Seminary education, the report concluded, had become badly fragmented, making it difficult if not impossible to integrate its various parts into a coherent educational experience. With so many specialized fields and disciplines, each developing in its own direction without reference to the others, what students were asked to learn seemed confused and disorganized: the parts of the theological curriculum no longer fit together into an understandable pattern.[149]

President Hall made it clear that the only way to resist these trends was to stick with the traditional curriculum taught in a residential setting:

We begin with an institutional commitment to provide and maintain a full-time, residential community of scholars, faculty, and students, with a required curriculum focusing on the "classic" theological disciplines. It is a community of learning in which persons may be shaped and formed into the kinds of persons/ministers the Presbyterian Church has found helpful and productive in the life of its congregations.

We recognize the fact that some "jobs" are also a way of life. Farming, for instance, or the military. Ministry falls into this category as well. This "ministerial" way of life is an alien experience to many of our students coming to campus. You can't learn it via extension courses. It takes an extended experience in community to convey an understanding of what it's all about.

The job of the seminary was not to be "trendy" or "relevant" for its own sake. Rather, by being healthily "old-fashioned," Union would seek to "ground a person in the basics, to tradition them in our particular brand of Christian faithfulness, and assume that this is going to be applicable and transferrable in changing circumstances during the course of time."

Union had always assumed that students did not need to learn about prayer, ministry, or the Christian life in a course because they had already been exposed to the "ordinary means of grace" (worship—preaching and sacraments, prayer, and Bible study) in the life of the congregation. They would understand the demands of ministry from growing up within the church. Connolly Gamble, however, detected that the demands on ministry had changed. He found that students wanted pastoral counseling courses, and Union introduced them into the curriculum in the 1950s. These courses, however, had put the school in a quandary: "While [students] are busy learning about ministry—they are not learning other things: like Bible and theology and church history."

What happens to a seminary curriculum when we can no longer assume a Protestant Ethos "out there," or that students will have all drunk deeply at the well of Reformed community and its theology before they come here?

What happens to a seminary curriculum when we can no longer assume that students will come here firmly grounded in the liberal arts—English, history, philosophy, literature, languages, and the values of Western Christian Civilization?[150]

President Hall's commitment to the full-time student model (with no part-time jobs to take focus away from studies) had enormous financial implications: more financial aid than ever before would be required because the cost of a seminary education was more expensive than ever before. Indeed, by the 1986–87 school year, financial aid was 25 percent of the total budget, at $1.2 million.[151] This level of aid was unprecedented. Traditionally it was accepted that it was the church's mission to provide a theological education for its future ministers "gratis," as the 1866 Catalogue put it. By 1891 the seminary charged "an annual fee of $5.00," which Walter W. Moore considered a betrayal and a signal that the church was not supporting theological education. While $5.00 in 1891 certainly had more purchasing power then than it does now, this amount was clearly assessed to cover certain overhead and administrative expenses, but not to "pay" for the education itself.

As late as 1940, income from endowment met 81 percent of the total operating budget. It was not until 1946 that Union Seminary began to charge tuition on a permanent basis; it assessed tuition only in response to the influx of post–World War II students who were able to take advantage of the GI Bill. Veterans were allowed to use their educational benefit only toward tuition, so tuition became a way to defray expenses for an exploding student population.

Prior to World War II, seminary students could be married only with faculty permission, and very few were. Students who did marry while enrolled were automatically disqualified from receiving any financial assistance. Graduates from this time remember joking that the church expected their ministers to be single at graduation and married a month later, when they moved into the manse. As late as 1957 the room/board/fee/tuition costs for a full academic year amounted to $700. Yet this expense could be offset by an automatic $200 grant from the PCUS Board of Christian Education, and the balance largely met through savings from the required summer fieldwork stipend.[152] It was not until 1967 that student costs exceeded $1,000 a year.[153] By the 1970s the concept of financial aid was redefined to cover the student's family needs while engaged in preparation for ministry. Family health insurance, to say nothing of food and clothing for children, now became legitimate expenses used in calculating financial aid.[154] Extending the range of financial aid left the seminary open to increasing costs beyond its control.

For President Hall, budgets were not just management measures: money undergirded Union's tradition of spiritual formation. UTS traditionally expected the community to prompt and guide spiritual formation. In this paradigm, the ideal of full-time students living in subsidized housing, in the atmosphere of a Reformed ethos, with faculty living on the premises in seminary-maintained residences—these features were vital to spiritual formation and traditioning. Money, then, was not just tied to facilities and faculty, but was directly related to the formative process of the students in this community.[155]

Financial aid enabled students to participate in the community, yet money was now limited. By the 1980s, Union was budgeting for more financial aid than it received in tuition income.[156] Moreover, students were now arriving on campus with considerable undergraduate indebtedness. Adding seminary debt on top of college debt put seminary graduates in a precarious financial position and caused them to look beyond small churches, who could only pay the presbytery minimum.

Although the General Assembly committee applauded experimentation with "satellite centers," more extensive DMin programs, and efforts to modernize curriculum (while warning against "program sprawl"),[157] President Hall made it clear that he wanted Union to stick with its traditional curriculum, offered in a full-time residential program. Ministry, for him, was "a calling from God employing certain 'gifts' to serve a particular people in God's name," rather than a "profession performing certain tasks and exercising particular skills." In his view, seminaries were now tempted to view the ministry as a profession. Many schools offered programs that increased their enrollment but did not lead to ordination; they designed programs for part-time students and increasingly offered off-campus programs in order to survive, but did not necessarily meet the needs of the church. In 1970, for example, 80 percent of all those enrolled in American seminaries were working toward an MDiv degree; by 1990 that figure had sunk to 53 percent.[158]

President Hall did acknowledge that the presence of non-Presbyterians on campus would increase, but he had reservations. President Lacy was proud to see "two Methodists, a Disciple, and one northern Presbyterian" in the Class of 1927,[159] and non-Presbyterians had always been a relatively small percentage of Union's enrollment. But as the number of non-Presbyterians increased, President Hall asked: "How many non-Presbyterians on campus is desirable? Or helpful? At what point do the presence of non-Presbyterians marginalize the Reformed heritage, especially in an era when Presbyterian students are, as a group, far less rooted and grounded in the tradition than previous generations?" It was a new era. At the end of his presidency, he reflected: "Whereas today we are concerned with 'traditioning' people, in the 1950s UTS encouraged students to step outside the tradition because the 'natural traditioning' was so strong." President Hall wondered aloud if the new mission of the modern seminary was "to tradition a traditionless people."[160]

Sale of WRFK

Perhaps the most public symbol of Union's change in context and concentration on funding theological education was the sale of WRFK. From the time Robert White Kirkpatrick purchased a 12-watt transmitter and began broadcasting on Commencement Day 1957, the "seminary's radio station" had become a Richmond institution. WRFK had been the first Virginia radio station, one of 73 in the country, to be an original part of the National Public Radio network formed in 1970.[161] As early as 1968 there were offers to purchase the operation, but the board refused all offers, wanting to find some way to keep WRFK's seminary identity intact. In 1969 the board investigated incorporating WRFK and running it as a separate commercial venture, but the taxation requirements could have threatened the seminary's tax-exempt status. At the same time, a group called "Save Fine Music" approached the seminary and offered to subsidize the station if it would broadcast classical music for 17 to 18 hours a day. The subsidy was to be in the form of the classical music collection owned by EZ Communications, from the music library of radio station WFMV. For the next 17 years, WRFK was able to expand its broadcasting day to 18 hours by using the donated library.

By 1980 the "seminary's radio station" was a success.[162] It was popular in Richmond and identified the seminary to the public. "It's not just a radio station," one listener insisted; "it's a way of life."[163] As the only noncommercial radio station in Richmond, WRFK represented a break from an increasingly homogenized mass media. Yet the truth was that radio broadcasting was becoming a financial drag on the seminary. By 1980 the Corporation for Public Broadcasting had issued rules prohibiting sectarian programming. Consequently, WRFK had to purchase more and more of its shows. The expense of replacing local religious-oriented programs with shows acquired from other sources was a drain on Union's budget.

By the time President Hall was inaugurated in 1981, the seminary was subsidizing WRFK's operations at a level equivalent to 10 percent of the faculty salaries—money that was lost for education.[164] Although WRFK had strong listener support (as the tenth-most-popular radio station in the Richmond market in 1987, with over 50,000 listeners),[165] there was no reason for Union to own a radio station that was prohibited from broadcasting religious programming. Hall argued that WRFK could no longer fulfill its original mission, and people who donated to the seminary gave money for theological education, not radio programming. Nevertheless, he was roundly criticized on campus, by Hanover Presbytery,[166] and in the press when plans to sell WRFK were announced in 1985.[167] Devoted listeners petitioned the Federal Communications Commission (FCC),[168] initiated lawsuits,[169] held benefit concerts,[170] and conducted letter-writing campaigns[171] to prevent its sale. At the August 1985 meeting of the board, protestors (including Annie Hall, President Hall's wife) gathered on campus and protested the proposed sale.[172] In response, the board took out a series of advertisements in the local newspapers defending the sale.[173] Robert Huntley, chair of the board of trustees, wrote an editorial outlining the seminary's position,[174] and President Hall gave numerous interviews explaining why the seminary was getting out of the radio business.

In the end, the economics of radio broadcasting and theological education just did not go together. Despite the fact that the 1985 fund drive had been successful, radio broadcasting was a distraction and a budgetary drain. The board voted to sell WRFK in August 1985 and hired a consultant to facilitate finding a buyer. UTS sold WRFK to Clear Channel Communications on December 1986 for $4.1 million.[175] There was no doubt, however, that something was lost. WRFK was, as a *Richmond Times-Dispatch* editorial mourned, "beloved." It was part of what made Richmond unique and added to its character.[176] Although public radio continues to be heard in central Virginia as WCVE, many graduates still remember the pride they felt while hearing, at the station breaks, that WRFK was broadcast by Union Theological Seminary.

Divided Country, Divided Church, Divided Campus

Reunion may have rejoined the Presbyterian divisions caused by the Civil War, but American society was becoming more fragmented. Students of the 1960s were concerned with social justice; now the Jesus movement of the 1970s—with its emphasis on an emotional commitment to a personal, inward faith—could be seen as a reaction to the 1960s. In the view of some faculty, there were students who showed up on campus with plenty of emotion but did not understand that following Jesus required intellectual rigor.[177] Yet UTS did its best to welcome those outside the "frozen chosen" who were willing to tackle the academics. Doug Beacham (DMin, 1976) reflected:

> As a non-Presbyterian, and feeling somewhat like the "token" Pentecostal on the campus in 1972, I am deeply appreciative of the Christian love and acceptance that was shown me by faculty and students alike.
>
> I remember introducing my parents to President Fred Stair on the Sunday I received my DMin. My father was an executive with the Pentecostal Holiness Church, and while introducing him, I remarked to Dr. Stair that as a Pentecostal family, we appreciated the seminary arranging graduation on Pentecost Sunday. He smiled and warmly replied, "We Presbyterians prefer to call that predestination!"[178]

Throughout the rest of the era, students increasingly divided themselves between conservative and liberal, Pentecostal and progressive, in ways not seen since the 1830s.

Students in the 1960s were not as interested in missions as previous generations: they did not want to impose their faith on others.[179] In the early 1970s, students also seemed to ignore missions, but for a different reason: missions did not seem to have much to do with a personal faith. By the end of the decade, a concern for missions was growing again. In 1978, Jay Click (DMin, 1981) complained, "Chaplaincy gets an airing à la Oglesby and Arnold, and even teaching is encouraged in subtle yet very real ways. However, what of missions and the minister as missionary?"[180]

Throughout the 1980s, inclusive language came to be the screen upon which the theological divisions of the church were cast. Kathy Sykes (spouse of a student) voiced the concern that "the flagrant usage of inclusive language may soon become a threat to historic Christianity"[181] and replace Trinitarian vocabulary.[182] Another woman, H. Pride Carson (MDiv, 1989), saw the "Women's Issue" in the context of the larger human struggle:

> Would someone mind telling me what a woman's issue is? With all the inclusiveness that is discussed around these two campuses, it seems to be a very exclusive term. Are there really any issues besides menstruation and pregnancy that are exclusively female issues? Don't basic human and societal rights belong to each of us, both female and male? . . . I, personally, have grown very tired of women who are defensive about what they perceive to be their own private minority battle, but what seems in actuality to be a battle with their own femaleness in light of their unacceptance of men and their intrinsic maleness. Perhaps the real "women's issues" lie not in trying to fit ourselves into another realm of being (male), or in trying to force those completely different from ourselves to change into something more closely resembling what we are. . . . Then, perhaps, we can move on to "people's issues," and fight an equitable fight against what is exclusive and unjust for all of us.[183]

Some men began to feel defensive, perceiving that the emphasis on inclusive language made them "the enemy." Garet Aldridge (MDiv, 1987) remarked: "Don't attack us. I think we need each other."[184] Almost a decade later, in 1994, Jonathan Van Deventer (MDiv, 1995) complained that students tried so hard not to offend that they were afraid to talk about anything.[185]

Students also wrestled with the issue of abortion. *In Medias Res* had articles and opinion pieces about it every year from the 1970s to the 1990s. John Doubles (MDiv, 1994) urged fellow students to remember that abortion was a painful pastoral concern:

> There are no winners in this debate. The opponents are no longer champions of their cause but vultures haggling over the carrion of a permissive society. But debate and decide we will, and our church will adopt a position on the matter, and thousands of people will continue to live their decision daily. What is our response and responsibility to them as good practicing Christians striving to emulate our Savior?[186]

The campus reflected the nation. Some saw abortion as ending a life, while others saw the issue as one of individual rights. Keith Reeves (PhD, 1998), like many others, struggled to make sense of what role the church should take in the ongoing debate.

> You will have to make your own decision regarding abortion. But it seems to me that the unborn child is a member of a silent minority of underdeveloped and according to society inferior humans. Should we not be concerned that everyday little humans are destroyed by others simply because they are a burden to the ones who are responsible for them? Think about it.[187]

The other consistent challenge to the church's pastoral ministry was the advent of AIDS. While many in popular culture and media were discussing "how" people contracted AIDS or "whether" AIDS was a specific judgment against homosexuals, Union students recognized that AIDS represented "A New Challenge to Ministry." In 1993, Phil Oehler typified the thoughts of many on campus:

> I do not believe that this will be the only case of AIDS in this small town or in any other small town. I believe that the Church must be prepared to deal with this issue. The Church must be prepared to deal with people who have AIDS, and not treat them like lepers. The Church must instead treat these people with Christian love and compassion.[188]

James McTyre (MDiv, 1991) argued that the UTS community had to wake up or else the pastoral response would be controlled by someone else.

> As persons who are going to spend a good portion of our lives in and around churches, we are going to be given the rank of "expert." Sooner or later, if not already, we are going to be asked in so many words what God thinks about AIDS and how it should be addressed by the church. We, as ministers, need to realize that television evangelists, fundamentalist denominations, and news media have beaten us to the punch, . . . [and] our silence speaks to affirm a prevailing [ignorance]. This silence, as say AIDS activists, equals death.[189]

As the church considered various study papers on human sexuality, homosexuality, and the ordination of lesbians and gays, campus debates reflected the arguments within the denomination and grew heated. McTyre recognized the explosiveness of this issue in 1991: "Show me someone on this campus who hasn't been asked about the Human Sexuality Report, and I'll show you someone who isn't looking for a call." Nevertheless, he recognized that most people's minds were already made up. "My uneducated guess is that having read the Report, I will fall into a group comprising, very graciously estimating, about 10 percent of the denomination's members: People Who Have Read the Sexuality Report and Are Willing to Discuss It."[190]

Two students attended the 1991 General Assembly that debated the human sexuality report, and the students were grateful for the process that allowed everyone to speak. Though it would be another two decades before the assembly would give definitive guidance allowing it, Union students remained generally in favor of the ordination of lesbians and gays.

Although there were always varieties of opinion on campus, by the late 1970s students detected a growing campus rift between conservatives and liberals. A decade apart, Jim Singleton (MDiv, 1983) and Jon Burnham (MDiv, 1994) called for recognition and an appreciation of a more diverse theological spectrum.

> For all the talk of inclusivity here, one could feel excluded if she happened to come from the wrong side of the theological tracks. Scarcely a week goes by without my hearing some rightist group or individual dragged through the mud in class. Charismatics are weird; conservatives are blind to proper scholarship; evangelicals are suspicious, pietists are otherworldly, fundamentalists are all of the above, and those poor fellows from Congaree Presbytery are worse yet! Oral Roberts, Billy Graham, Fanny Crosby, and Pat Robertson are some of those for whom seldom is heard an encouraging word at this bastion of inclusiveness. . . . It just does my heart good to know that we have a paper on inclusive language.[191]
>
> We don't want to put all the Muslim fundamentalists into the bad-apple category. But we seem to put all Christian fundamentalists into the bad-apple category. My idea is this: If we really want to be inclusive, let's include theological conservatives as well as liberals.[192]

When copies of the *Presbyterian Layman* were stolen shortly after arriving on campus, Dave Duquette (MDiv, 1994) complained: "Isn't this the kind of oppressive behavior that *The Layman* and other staunch conservatives are so often condemned for? Aren't they the ones who are exclusive?"[193] By the mid-1990s, students who wanted to reclaim the term "evangelical" from the labels and stereotypes of "fundamentalist" formed the Theological Student Fellowship, and there was a chapter of Presbyterians Pro-Life. The increasing diversity of the student body was reflected in the establishment of the Black Caucus and the Women in Ministry groups.

Louis Bonzano Weeks

Louis B. Weeks was called as the sixth president of Union Seminary in May 1994. A native of Memphis, he received his AB degree from Princeton University in 1963 and immediately enrolled at Union. He took a year off from seminary in 1965–66 and served as a missionary of the PCUS, an instructor at the Centre de Jeunesse et École Publique Secondaire in the Republic of Zaire (now the Democratic Republic of the Congo). Upon returning from Africa, he graduated with his BD in 1967. Weeks was then ordained and entered the doctoral program at Duke University, graduating with his PhD in 1970. While at Duke he served as stated supply at Little River Presbyterian Church in Hurdle Mills, North Carolina.

After graduating from Duke, he was called as assistant professor of Church History at Louisville Presbyterian Theological Seminary. Weeks was promoted to associate professor in 1974 and professor in 1978. From 1979 through 1993, he was dean of the seminary. During his time in Louisville, he served four churches as interim and parish associate, and as chair of the General Assembly Task Force on the Use and Authority of the Bible from 1979 to 1982. From 1989

51. Louis Bonzano Weeks, president, 1994–2007

to 1994 he, along with John Mulder and Joe Coalter, directed research on the seven-volume series The PC(USA) as a Case Study in Mainline American Protestantism. He was also the founding chair of the Academic Committee for the Appalachian Ministries Educational Resource Center.

Weeks was the first Union president who did not graduate from Davidson, the first president from the west (Tennessee), and the first with extensive experience in the administration of theological education. Seeing the divisions within the church, he continually sought to make Union into a place that welcomed both conservatives and liberals.[194] He was intentional in encouraging Union to be hospitable to women and minorities and to recruit women, African Americans, Asians, and native Spanish speakers to the faculty and board of trustees.[195]

Recognizing the national environment in which Union found itself, President Weeks worked to strengthen the endowment throughout his tenure. On assuming the presidency, he invigorated the Enduring Commitment Campaign to raise funds for building the new William Morton Smith Library and increasing resources to recruit students and increase faculty pay. Under the leadership of Hal Todd, Enduring Commitment raised $3.5 million more than its $31 million goal by the time it concluded in 1999.[196] The most successful fund-raising effort in Union's history, the One In Mission campaign, was conducted from

2001 to 2007 and raised $50 million. When Weeks was inaugurated in 1994, Union's endowment stood at $72.5 million; when he retired in 2007, it was worth nearly $123 million.

Just as President Stair took over amid protest over civil rights and Vietnam, President Weeks landed in the middle of a fractious time. The disputes over biblical interpretation, women in ministry, and gay ordination came boiling to the surface in the decade after Reunion, and the controversies were mirrored on campus. He faced three issues that, arguably, defined the changing nature of the church and modern theological education: the federation of Union and PSCE, the establishment of a campus in Charlotte, and the controversy personified by Jack Dean Kingsbury and Douglas F. Ottati over how to interpret the Reformed tradition.

The Consensus Breaks Down

Ken Goodpasture once remarked that Union Seminary had always been characterized by consensus and balance. Students, faculty, and staff traditionally strove for common ground upon which to agree in order to carry out the work of the church and train ministers for the pastorate.[197] Collegiality held throughout 1960s and 1970s. In the 1980s, however, American Protestantism splintered into several camps. The so-called mainline denominations (of which Presbyterians were prominent) lost influence, and fundamentalist and evangelical churches gained members. Traditionally, more conservative Christians had stayed out of politics, but as evangelicals followed the mainline into political involvement in the 1980s, religion and politics became partisan, divisions hardened, and verbal combat became aggressive and expected.[198] The vocabulary of theological debate was transformed throughout the American church from friendly persuasion to the vocabulary of attack. The Union faculty from the 1980s were keenly aware of a sense of fragmentation, a "lack of ethos" that promoted disagreement and critical exchange of ideas.[199]

In 1989, Professor Douglas Ottati published *Jesus Christ and Christian Vision*, in which he argued that "contemporary Christology was in crisis." That is, the modern world interprets Jesus Christ in many ways: liberator, revolutionary, wise teacher, friend, crucified God, and risen Lord. "The result is that Christian theology today often appears to be a historical inquiry that has lost its coherence as well as its traditional bearings."

Ottati proposed "a contemporary statement of the Christian community's center of meaning." He further criticized "a narrowly traditional Christology, which merely repeats the past tradition" as incapable of addressing the needs of this present crisis. Ottati questioned traditional Christologies as "representing the thought form of a particular time and place, which is finally inadequate for reflection about the historic reality of Jesus Christ." While affirming "the centrality and particularity of Jesus Christ," he also argued that the Chalcedonian definition "long since has lost is significance" and tried to reinterpret what Jesus Christ means for modern life. Ottati was careful, however, to frame his argument in the context of historical Christianity.

If what I now interpret the definition to mean to the ongoing community of the church is not identical with what it likely meant to those who produced it, then at least there is a historical chain of connection between my present interpretation and what the definition originally meant.

In his paradigm the Chalcedonian tradition just informs "one's contemporary reflections about what Jesus Christ says, does, and endures without being confined to a specific formulation or set of images."[200] What contemporary Christians say about the person of Jesus Christ is not necessarily bound to historical affirmations.

The use of new, nontraditional language to describe the person and work of Jesus Christ was challenged on campus, but the dispute quickly became public. David Green (MDiv, 1997), student body president, saw in this dispute a seminary with deeply conflicted ideas about how to educate ministerial students. "Two sides are vying with each other for control. The faculty is deeply divided; so is the student body." He saw in this division an uncertainty over "the use and teaching of Scripture. Whereas some faculty seem to regard Scripture as authoritative for faith and practice, others give the impression that contemporary experience is really what counts. The difference is fundamental and not merely cosmetic."[201] At the same time Professor Jack Dean Kingsbury, professor of New Testament, publicly questioned Ottati's orthodoxy and fitness to teach in a Presbyterian seminary.

Alums chose sides, presbyteries weighed in (Coastal Carolina even questioning the fitness of Union graduates), and denominational papers gave the story wide coverage. Even the *Richmond Times-Dispatch* featured the unfolding events on campus. In November 1996, the controversy made front-page news. Kingsbury accused the administration of "trying to force him out over philosophical and theological differences." He identified this particular dispute as part of a continuum "that has been simmering on the campus for almost twenty years: a conflict between those who want to update the Christian message for the twenty-first century and those who believe traditional teachings should remain untouched by modern influence."[202]

The students chose sides. While some agreed with David Green that the seminary was a transmitter of a specific tradition, Kerra Becker (MDiv, 1996) and others saw theological education in a different light:

> The diversity of opinion here on campus is an asset. I do not want that taken away from the seminary environment. We are here to learn and be challenged by our critics as well as be nurtured and upheld by those who are like-minded in faith. Our theology will be tested enough by the Committees of Preparation for Ministry. Here, we have the unique opportunity to grow and experiment with "trying on" new perspectives.[203]

Frank Wyche (MDiv, 1998) pleaded for a middle ground of understanding:

> It seems to me that a common point of view of the extreme left and of the extreme right is that each believes itself to be the sole possessor of ultimate truth, and that anyone disagreeing certainly must belong to the other extreme.[204]
>
> Most people I know at UTS, students, faculty and staff alike, do not belong on either extreme, but are sensible people who see more than one point of

view and who, even when they are sure of things for themselves, do not insist that others think as they do. There is no great mystical insight to all of this, but I somehow think this point is worth saying from time to time.[205]

Amid claims for academic freedom, orthodox theology, and the church in the modern world lay the wider question of the place of the seminary and theological education in the late twentieth century. Following in the footsteps of Robert Kelly in 1924, Mark Arthur May in 1934, and H. Richard Niebuhr in 1956, Paul Wilkes surveyed theological education in the December 1990 issue of the *Atlantic Monthly*. He concluded that American seminaries "have squandered a legacy, and in their hearts they nurse the fear that perhaps it has been lost forever. Each of them knows well that no group, denomination, or faith is exempt." He asked whether American seminaries would be places of instruction in a specific tradition, or places to "experiment with new perspectives."

Just as Niebuhr found American seminaries to be "perplexed," Wilkes also detected confusion in theological education. "Seminaries have failed," he wrote, "because seminaries have not decided what theological education is. . . . Seminaries can't decide whether they are passing on a tradition or exposing students to a wide range of theologies. Without a tradition in which to place themselves, personal stories take the place of theology and critical analysis." He argued that the increasing professionalization of the ministry pulled the seminary away from the church, making it resemble a university more than a church-related institution dedicated to preserving and transmitting a specific theology and worldview.[206] Just as Union had kept the traditional curriculum in the 1950s, now Union resolved the pressures of specialization and the tensions between the academy and seminary by continually reaffirming the traditional curriculum.

Enrollment

Union Theological Seminary's enrollment between 1967 and 1996 reflected the loss of membership throughout the Presbyterian Church (USA), the transition to a national seminary, and the questioning over what a seminary should be. Throughout this period the average enrollment was 203 (including MDiv, in-sequence DMin students, and dual-degree students), with a high of 283 in 1974, and a low of 127 in 1995 (ten years after in-sequence DMin had been discontinued). The effects of Reunion in 1983 had a dramatic impact on enrollment. The average enrollment before Reunion was 34 more students than after Reunion. Davidson continued to provide the majority of students, with 12%, but the University of North Carolina at Chapel Hill was second at 6%. Hampden-Sydney and King College were the alma mater of 5% of the student body, and Presbyterian College supplied 4%. Public institutions provided over 65% of all students. Virginia continued to be the home of most students (46%), with North Carolina at 23% and (surprisingly) Pennsylvania and Florida each at 5%. During this time 40 of the 50 states were represented in the student body. Union also became more international in this period. Besides the usual European countries, students came from Brazil, Congo, Ghana, Iceland, India, Indonesia, New Guinea, New Zealand, Nigeria, and Uruguay.

The 1967 Self-Study Report seemed to fulfill the ecumenical vision of President Lacy. The report bragged that out of 350 students, 66 came from outside the PCUS. Among the students were 17 United Presbyterians, 14 Methodists, 8 Baptists, 6 from the Reformed Church in America, 4 Lutherans, 3 from the Associate Reformed Presbyterian Church, and 2 Cumberland Presbyterians; 1 each as Mennonite, Seventh-day Adventist, Church of God, Disciples of Christ, and Church of the Brethren; plus students from 7 overseas churches. In the STM course, 10 denominations were represented. Prior to Reunion at least 80% of all students (at all levels) were from the PCUS. In the early 1990s, 49% of the students were from the PC(USA).

The 1967 Report declared that "opportunity has been given to various students whose transcripts do not fit the traditional pattern of the ministerial candidate." Students could be admitted without an undergraduate degree, when approved by their presbytery, but "when students are admitted without out a bachelor's degree, the deficiency must be made up before the BD can be awarded."[207] The 1974 Self-Study Report, however, reflected the growing professionalization of the ministry: UTS was "strongly" discouraging presbyteries from recommending students who had not graduated from college.[208]

With the ordination of women and integration of American society, the composition of Union's student body changed more between 1967 and 1996 than in the previous two centuries. In the 1967–68 school year, 14 female students were enrolled. A decade later Union had 47 female students, over one-third of the student body. By 1985, women comprised 42% of all students. Yet attendance by students from minority groups remained low. Before the 1990s, some years found no African Americans, Asians, or Hispanics in the incoming MDiv class, despite efforts to recruit such.[209] By 1995, however, more than 20% of students at all levels were Asian and African American.[210] The number of married students held steady throughout this period, at 50 to 60%, while the number of second-career students fluctuated between 20% and 65% of the student body.[211] Indeed, the average age rose from 27 in 1980 to almost 32 in 1985.

The most dramatic statistic from this era is the dropout rate. Between 1948 and 1966, the total dropout rate was 4 to 7%. Although the records can be difficult to interpret for this period, between 1967 and 1973 (the year the draft ended) the dropout rate soared to around 20%. At the same time, up to 30% of the students who identified themselves as affiliated with the PCUS were not under the care of a presbytery. Apparently some students enrolled without a clear call to ministry. Once the draft ended, the average dropout rate fell back to between 6% and 8%. The vast majority of those who disenrolled did not pursue a vocation in the church. Yet others transferred to other Presbyterian seminaries. Some went to Louisville, Columbia, Austin, or Pittsburgh. But most went to schools with a more conservative reputation, such as Gordon-Conwell, Fuller, Reformed Theological Seminary, Erskine, and Westminster.

In addition to the traditional five-course curriculum, the graduate program was a consistent emphasis through this era. Although enrollment figures can be confusing due to changing degrees (usually accepting a ThM instead of finishing the PhD program), it is clear that the graduate program was important. Attendance in the STM program beginning in 1967 was responsible for making the 1968–69 school year the highest enrollment in seminary history, although the number of first degrees awarded dropped. Indeed, MDiv enrollment continued to decline in the 1970s, while graduate enrollment increased, so that for the first time since the Depression graduate students approached the number of undergrads. With the decline of the STM and the advent of the in-sequence DMin, it is difficult to compare numbers for the professional graduate programs. After the in-sequence DMin degree was phased out, the average enrollment in the DMin program was around 30. In 1982, the trustees authorized replacing the ThD with a PhD (which symbolized a graduate degree on par with a university degree),[212] and enrollment for research graduate degrees was robust. Between 1967 and 1997, the average enrollment for the ThM degree was 9, and 60 for the PhD, though some of the latter had virtually ceased working on their dissertation.

Vietnam

The Vietnam War dominated student concerns until the mid-1970s. An October 1968 poll in the student paper *Expression* found 60% of the student body favoring Hubert Humphrey for president, 36% for Nixon, and 2% for Wallace. Despite the overwhelming antiwar sentiment on campus, a dramatic change from surveys done just two years earlier (in 1966), Isabel Rogers (who taught Applied Christianity at PSCE) urged the Union-PSCE community in 1969 to be an example of Christian love and forbearance and not let the divisions over Vietnam tear the community apart:

> Vietnam is a case in point. All too easy is it to want to force everybody to fit one pattern, to conform to one viewpoint and to call that the Christian answer. But Christians must be free to differ with each other and to respect each other in their differences; there is no place for a party line in the Christian community.[213]

The tensions, however, were close to the surface. Sara Little remembers walking across campus in 1970 and feeling dismayed that the students seemed so angry.[214] She was not the only perplexed faculty member; James Mays recalls that the faculty was somewhat unprepared for students arriving on campus with other commitments than to the church.[215] It was obvious that the expectations of students had changed in a generation. In the Class of 1949, veterans composed 80% of entering students, and the vast majority had graduated from Presbyterian colleges with majors in religion. In 1962, under the care of a presbytery were 67% of the students; in 1966 only 48% were, and in 1969 that number had sunk to 44%. The 1967 Self-Study Report recognized that a new kind of student was now on campus: application forms no longer requested "motives for entering the ministry," but "motives for seeking theological education."[216]

Yet the student community remained cohesive and dedicated to the church. A few students published an "alternative" student newspaper, *Perspective*, to vent their frustrations. But there were so many angry responses to their negative views that *Perspective* lasted only seven issues, between October 1969 and May 1970.[217] Many students from that time remember painful divisions on campus. Some students saw the church exclusively as an agent of social change, while others saw the church in more traditional ways. Several students remember the "draft dodgers" (who never intended to serve a church). At their 1967 meeting the board was informed that some students had been involved in protests and marches against the war, but "a far larger group of students on the Campus have been rigorously supporting the government policy."[218]

The administration, however (like most of America), misjudged the extent of antiwar feeling as the war dragged on. Although Union students and faculty had participated in civil rights marches, the level of their public protest against the war in Vietnam was unprecedented. The first formal report of students involved in an antiwar protest came when two women students (one from UTS and one from PSCE) attended the Conference of Clergy and Laymen Concerned about Vietnam in Washington, February 5–6, 1968. Marybeth Hermanson (MDiv, 1969) wrote in the student newspaper *Expression*:

> We protested against war in the name of peace; dictatorship in the name of democracy; censorship in the name of freedom; lies in the name of truth. We protested a scorched-earth policy in the name of life; strafing and bombing of homes in the name of protection; the use of riot-control gas in the name of humaneness.

Betsy Gessler, as a junior at PSCE, wrote that she found "a warmth and a unity of purpose" at the conference, but also "wondered why the conference did not condemn Viet Cong atrocities."[219] The entire April 1968 issue of *Expression* was devoted to Vietnam. The editors asked several students, from both PSCE and UTS, to comment on the war, and all were against it.[220] Throughout the rest of the American involvement in Vietnam, antiwar letters to the editor appeared regularly in *Expression*, and antiwar sentiment was a consistent feature of the alternative paper *Interrobang* (named after the nonstandard punctuation mark combining the question mark and the exclamation point: ?).

The first organized student antiwar protest came in October 1969, when the student body petitioned the faculty to observe the national Moratorium against the Vietnam War on October 15.[221] Students around the country had called for a "National Moratorium on Business as Usual in response to President Nixon's call for a Moratorium on Criticism." The student body passed a resolution calling for a moratorium at Union.[222] The faculty agreed and canceled classes on October 15, 1969; Union students became part of the nationwide protest.[223] The moratorium took place in two parts: a morning rally at Monroe Park and a teach-in at Union to begin at 2:30. John Mack Walker (BD, 1970; ThM, 1972) expressed the frustration of many students:

> The church is us—each one of us who stand by and watch Vietnam and Laos and South America and New York and Richmond and Union Theological Seminary and says nothing. And Jesus Christ says, IF YOU ARE NOT FOR ME, YOU ARE AGAINST ME, and all us other niggers [*sic*] say, IF YOU'RE NOT A PART OF THE SOLUTION, YOU'RE PART OF THE PROBLEM.[224]

From May 1 to June 30, 1970, American forces engaged in a series of operations that crossed the border between South Vietnam and Cambodia in what became known as the "Cambodian Incursion." The military aim of these operations was to deny the Vietcong bases in ostensibly neutral Cambodia. This perceived widening of the war caused American campuses to explode. During an antiwar protest at Kent State University on May 4, 1970, Ohio National Guardsmen killed four students. American campuses erupted; strikes by four million students around the country closed hundreds of universities, colleges, and high schools.

The day after the shootings at Kent State, on May 5, an informal group of students and faculty gathered in Watts Chapel after dinner to pray and share their concerns over the crisis in the country and the world. The group drafted a statement that deplored "the extension of the Vietnam War into Cambodia as the pursuit of a concept of nationalistic glory and honor which we find incompatible with our Christian faith in the Lordship of Jesus Christ over all earthly powers." They further opposed "the policy of political repression at home fostered by the philosophy of the present administration." After a day of canvassing, 240 members of the RTC signed the statement; of that number 109 were students and faculty at Union Seminary. The statement was then sent to President Richard M. Nixon, Vice President Spiro T. Agnew, Virginia Senators Harry F. Byrd Jr. and William B. Spong Jr., Representative David E. Satterfield III (of Virginia's Third Congressional District), and Virginia Governor A. Linwood Holton Jr. and Ohio Governor James A. Rhodes.

The students, however, wanted to do more than issue a statement. They declared "A Week of Concern" and elected a steering committee of Richmond Theological Center students and faculty to plan additional ways of expressing to the church the dimensions of "the crisis of these days and its meaning for the Christian faith." The next night, Wednesday, the committee presented a plan of action that was adopted. They urged students and faculty to boycott classes the next Friday. In lieu of classes, students were urged to demonstrate by handing out antiwar leaflets along Brook Road and Chamberlayne Avenue. Since Interstate 95 was not yet completed, every commuter entering Richmond from the north saw the demonstration.

A "Teach-In" for the entire RTC community (conducted in part by history professor James Smylie, theology professor Donald Dawe, and ethics professor Terrance Anderson), in which approximately seventy-five students and faculty participated, was held in the afternoon. A team of six RTC students had previously requested to meet with Governor Linwood Holton on Friday afternoon. At this meeting they asked that if National Guard troops had to be used on campuses in Virginia, they would not be given live ammunition. On Saturday twenty students joined the national demonstration in Washington, while others produced a one-hour radio show on WRFK "dealing with both sides" of the Vietnam War and the Kent State shootings.

Perhaps the most interesting aspect of the "Week of Concern" was the effort to address local congregations the next Sunday morning. The committee contacted seven Richmond Presbyterian churches (Bon Air, First, Second, Westminster, Grace Covenant, Ginter Park, St. Giles) and asked that a team of students be allowed to "read the statement on Cambodia and the Kent killings to their congregation" and remain after church to have an exchange of views."

The response was tepid. Only one congregation allowed the students time during worship to express their concerns. However, two ministers did mention the statement from the pulpit and invited discussion following the service. Of the remaining five churches, four permitted students to visit Sunday school classes. The fifth church invited representatives to meet with the session at another time. The committee was pleased with the responses they received; in one way or another all seven churches were visited; twenty-eight faculty and students made their views known. On Sunday evening the committee organized a memorial service for "Kent State students and victims of war, led by Professor Bill Russell, [Instructor in] the pastoral department, and assisted by students from the RTC." Approximately seventy-five students and faculty members joined in this service.

At a debriefing on Monday, the students and faculty members who participated in the Week of Concern gathered in Lingle to discuss their feelings about the events of the previous five days. Robert Tabscott (BD, 1962; ThM, 1970) recorded the thoughts of most students that much had been accomplished: "The overwhelming consensus was that we had engaged in a meaningful enterprise in which we had not only worked through some of our frustrations as students and faculty but had also engaged the church at large in dialogue." One student, however, told him that he had become disillusioned with the church: "This week has sharpened my perspective and demonstrated to me what a pitiful situation many of our churches are in."[225]

It seemed as though the violence would not stop. On May 10, 1970, a riot broke out in Augusta, Georgia, and the governor called out state police and the National Guard to restore order. Six African American students were shot by police for looting following the civil rights demonstrations. Shortly after midnight on May 15, a group of African American students at Jackson State College (now Jackson State University) in Jackson, Mississippi, were demonstrating against the Cambodian incursion. After the students were confronted by city and state police, the police opened fire, killing two students and injuring twelve—only eleven days after Kent State and five after Augusta. At the end of commencement on May 26, faculty, staff, 162 graduates, and family members signed a letter "to give public expression to their grief over the death of those Black persons who were tragically and unjustly killed in Jackson and Augusta." The letter also called upon "the constituency of the Presbyterian Church in the United States and all men of good will to redouble their efforts to work for justice, mercy, peace, and reconciliation in our troubled land."[226]

The student body sent this letter to the Synod of Mississippi, which prompted Arthur Michael Warren (BD, 1965), who was serving a church in Mississippi, to pen a personal reply. He argued that the people of Mississippi were being unfairly condemned for what was a national problem:

> I can remember the entire Seminary community hustling around for special prayer and meetings when something would happen in Mississippi, such as the march in Selma, Ala., and the murders in Philadelphia, and yet carrying on business as usual when something of a similar nature would happen in Richmond. I can remember especially the frantic prayers on the day President Kennedy was shot, and there being no mention of the Negro woman who was raped and shot the same day within a half mile of our "hallowed walls." I am not trying to escape our guilt down here by drawing attention to the guilt of others, but I would remind you that it is often easy and very much safer to "involve" yourself in something that is far removed.

As students and faculty began to wrestle with the issue of integration in Richmond schools, Warren's observation would give pause to many. "The problems here are deeper than surface idealism, and they cannot be solved in one summer's fieldwork."[227]

The students on the steering committee continued to make sure the seminary and the church knew where they stood. Members of the committee presented the letter signed at commencement to the board's annual meeting and asked for its prayerful consideration. A member of the senior class requested and was granted permission by the board to speak at the commencement exercises on student opposition to the war in Southeast Asia and to the Kent State, Jackson State, and Augusta killings. The students had instructed the student body president "to communicate our resolution to the Synods of Appalachia, North Carolina, Virginia, and West Virginia, and that we request their prayerful consideration of this resolution." At the June 30, 1970, meeting of the Synod of West Virginia, Dean K. Thompson (BD, 1969; ThM, 1970; ThD, 1974) spoke to the synod about the antiwar efforts of UTS students. The result was that the synod passed an antiwar resolution and printed it.[228]

Student Life

It would be easy to characterize the period between 1967 and 1997 as one of strife. While there is no question that American society and the church (specifically the Presbyterian Church) wrestled with unprecedented challenges, it is also true that as students went from class to class, there was a grace and humor in their daily lives together. While former students could all identify the issues upon which there was disagreement, everyone remembered a cohesive, accepting, and even loving community. Many students retreated to Tom-Tom's after the library closed, just to talk. Dinners in the student-friendly neighborhood of the Fan (adjacent to Virginia Commonwealth University) and cheap movies at the Byrd Theatre also gave students a break from the anxiety of studying.

Students wanted the seminary community to embody Christian ideals not just in politics but also in their corporate investments. In 1978 a group of students wrote the board, asking them to disclose Union's stock portfolio.[229] They were concerned that Union owned stock in companies that did business in South Africa (which many companies boycotted due to its apartheid policies) and J. P. Stevens (which was accused of unfair labor practices). What was an issue of human rights for the students was a matter of fiduciary responsibility for the board, and they were reluctant to publicize the seminary's stock holdings. Some students pointed out that other educational institutions, including Davidson, and many other seminaries had "policies of social responsibility which guide their investments practices."[230] Students held public meetings throughout 1978, arguing for a policy of socially responsible investing, which would mean making the seminary's investments public. While some students objected to telling the board how to invest the UTS money,[231] by 1979 the board was moving toward a more open policy on seminary investments.[232]

In addition to the Vietnam War and socially responsible investing, some of the issues that attracted intense but transitory attention were the status of the Panama Canal, nuclear disarmament, opposition to an antimissile defense (Star Wars) program, American policy in Central America (especially Nicaragua), and the call for a snack bar in the basement of Lingle Hall.[233] Several other topics garnered consistent attention throughout the era: the quality of the campus community, relations with the city, security, minority student recruitment, abortion, AIDS, human sexuality, the seemingly insurmountable divide between theological conservatives and liberals, and computers.

As men and women called into ministry, many students expected the community on the quad to demonstrate Christian ideals in interpersonal relations. Philip Oehler (MDiv, 1994) was concerned that by stressing academics over *agapē*, the Union community was not living up to its ideals.

> In this community, I see personal attacks, fierce competition in class, and community destruction instead of community building. I am as guilty as the next member in this community of these types of attacks.
> Why can't the "School House" meet the "Beloved Community"? Could not an institution of higher learning become a place where people are accepted for their heart and not for their theological views, political stance, or lack of Biblical language skill?[234]

There was also a certain friction between Union and PSCE. Many at PSCE accused Union students and faculty of feeling superior to PSCE. Although PSCE and Union students regularly produced plays together—such as *No Exit* on March 5 and 7, 1982—letters to the editor continually bemoaned how "the Brook" separated them. Isabel Rogers sadly reported in October 1968: "Saturday night I heard a group of PSCE-UTS students talking about the old communications problems between students of the two schools—wanting desperately to be able to do something about them."[235] Sara Little was seen by many as a bridge between both campuses; she often lamented that since pastors and Christian educators would inevitably work closely in the field, they should begin to learn to appreciate one another's gifts in school.[236] The fact that she continued to remind students of their mutual ministry during these years is an indication of how wide the Brook was.

Hal Breitenberg (MDiv, 1991; PhD, 2004), however, identified that the increasing numbers of commuter students were challenging Union's traditional self-understanding. He argued that while UTS continued to describe itself as residential, it was in fact becoming nonresidential.

> But the bonds that contribute to a sense of community must not be reduced to the location of one's domicile. Rather than emphasizing proximity of students' domiciles to campus, which may contribute to a sense of community, but in no way guarantee it, it may be best to speak of the UTS community in terms of participation. Our seminary community is characterized by a high level of participation in the life, joys, and concerns of those closely associated with the ongoing task of theological education at Union; this includes students, their spouses and children, faculty and staff. Such participation, I think, contributes more significantly to a sense of community than does the location of our residences.
> Union is indeed blessed with a strong sense of community. Fortunately, many of us who commute would maintain that this sense of community is

not restricted to those who reside on campus, although we know that living on campus often contributes to and enhances the community spirit. If community is thought of in terms of participation rather than in terms of the proximity of domiciles, and efforts are directed toward this end, positive steps can be made toward an increased sense of community for all.[237]

Union, however, would cling to the residential model. The 1996 Mission Statement declared that "Union Theological Seminary in Virginia . . . sustains a residential community of full-time students" and declared that "75 percent of degree students live in campus housing."[238]

If there were doubts about the RTC and tensions with PSCE, there were no uncertainties over the value of the campus community. By the 1990s, the wives' club became the Union-PSCE spouses' group and included men. While the spouses banded together to serve "as a support group for the spouses of the RTC Community by providing opportunities for spiritual growth, study, fellowship, and service to others," Becky Teague was afraid that spouses were treated as "anonymous."

> Approximately half of the student body of Union Seminary is married. However, we spouses are not mentioned as being a part of the residential community referred to in the Seminary's Mission Statement, even though our number is greater than that of the faculty, and many of us are providing the primary means of financial support that enables our own particular student to be here.
>
> In a community that prides itself on its emphasis on concern and caring for the marginalized, where is the awareness and appreciation for the depersonalized, not-quite-part-of-it-all, *spouse*?[239]

For everyone, though, the campus community was family. Becky Falter, a spouse, wrote about her first and second trimesters in *In Medias Res*.[240] Carson Brisson, Hebrew professor, wrote about his son, who was then nearly three years old at the time. And students wrote about school issues and how members of the community had helped their families during illnesses, death, and the birth of triplets.

Some feared that the perceived isolation hampered efforts to recruit minority students. In 1988, Karen Brown noticed a "Black Phenomenon" on campus: an entering class that brought the number of African American students to four—herself, Ernest Hood (MDiv, 1991), Kecia McMillian (attended 1988–89), and Michael Simpson (attended 1988–91)—and hoped this class of African Americans would be just the beginning.

> This constituency would like to affirm Union for its efforts in being inclusive. However, we hope this number does not remain a phenomenon, for its own sake as well as for the sake of the church. The seminary is moving in the right direction, as it prepares for the second annual Racial Ethnic Conference in the spring. The church is one, and this is an ideal atmosphere for all to grow in our diversity. As of this writing, the seminary has broken this phenomenon as Cheryl Watts will be joining our community in January.[241]

Karen Brown and Shirley Hutchins (MDiv, 1992) reported they had to rub their eyes when they saw Luther Ivory (DMin, 1987) on his first day as the first

African American professor at Union.[242] A graduate of the University of Tennessee, he served as a naval officer for five years, received his PhD from Candler School of Theology, and taught Theology and Ethics.

Despite Union's history and self-criticism, African American students valued their experience at Union. Hoffman Brown (DMin, 1981) arrived on campus in July 1977.[243] He had just graduated from William and Mary and was recruited by Chuck Mendenhall. Brown was wondering where he should attend seminary, and Mendenhall took the time to write to him. Brown was impressed by the personal attention and decided to enroll. He was the only African American student on campus and felt accepted, yet recognized some southern provincialism. The only adverse reaction he received came from other Baptist ministers and STVU students who felt that he was abandoning his tradition.

UTS had a real sense of community, which Brown loved. At the same time, it was the RTC that kept him invested with UTS. He took preaching at STVU, and most of his friends were at PSCE. He enjoyed the plays that he and other RTC students gave for the community, but eating in Lingle "was the best part." He never sensed a division between married and single students, or between students from the other schools.

Brown took the in-sequence DMin degree. He thought the program was valuable because it gave him a taste of the pastorate. Looking back over a thirty-year career in which he served three churches, Brown felt that UTS did a good job of preparing him for the professional side of ministry, but that it was weak on the practical side (such as dealing with people, etc.). Only a congregation can teach some things.

Union began to address the issue of diversity in a systematic way in the 1990s. In the 1996 Self-Study Report, for the first time, there appears a section titled "Commitment to Student Diversity and Support" (which was also a formal accreditation standard). The administration pledged to "seek greater representation among African American and Korean-American students." Moreover, ten-year targets were set to achieve a goal of 20 percent of the student body as persons of color.[244]

Technology crept onto the campus. In 1978, students could look up books available through the Ohio College Library Center (OCLC) and order them though the interlibrary loan system. The Ibycus system (designed to search the Greek text of the New Testament) was available in the mid-1980s on a closed CD-ROM system. By the mid-1980s, students were comparing notes about the popular word-processing programs, debating the comparative values of dot-matrix and the new laser-jet printers, complaining about incomprehensible technical support, and all the other irritations that are now an accepted part of the digital age. Virtually every issue of *In Medias Res* from the late 1980s shows a growing, if wary, familiarity with technology. Students were generally complimentary about the library's increasing use of technology, and they enthusiastically supported the new Technology Committee (formed in September 1995), but a March 1999 *In Medias Res* editorial complained that the UTS-PSCE Web page was a "failure."[245]

While students went to class, studied, and discussed the issues of the day, children of seminary families and many students remember roller-skating in the basement of Lingle Hall. When Lingle Hall first opened, PSCE initiated a program to build community throughout Ginter Park and within the RTC by providing recreational opportunities. In 1969, neighborhood children could choose roller-skating, drama, folk dancing, arts and crafts, or puppetry in the afternoon. On Thursday and Friday nights, adults could skate and learn folk dancing.[246] These programs were run by students (with the programs varying year by year). During the late 1980s, PSCE's summer camp was attracting 180 children. Roller-skating was the most consistent offering; when the program finally ended in the early 1990s, everyone felt that something valuable had been lost.

Families in Advance Apartments still remember impromptu dinners together, and single students would have their own group meals. For several Thanksgivings, students (single and married) gathered for a "Potluck Thanksgiving Feast" in the Schauffler basement. The Westminster Christmas Party, Pig & Profligacy barbeque, preaching in different presbyteries during the fall and spring Caravan, Current Events Lunch, the summer ice-cream socials between memorizing Greek vocabulary cards, the T-Pool, Sprunt Lectures, and the Real Awards (lovingly satirizing the eccentricities and foibles of professors and students alike)—all built memories and lifelong friendships outside of the classroom.

Each class continued the tradition of forming its own flag football team in the fall and playing a small schedule against each other. The top two teams then played in the Calvin Bowl, followed by the "homecoming dance," called the "Calvin Ball." The halftime show, however, was the highlight of the sports year.

> Excitement ran down the spine of the crowd as they witnessed the musical instruments being dispensed to the chosen few. "Ah yes," a tower scholar stuttered in awe, "this is the pride of the South, the heartthrob of the upright, the grandeur of western man's achievement, yes—the Kazoo Marching Band."[247]

Every time Union played another seminary in a sport, it was a featured story. UTS defeated Columbia in flag football 39–33 in November 1988, and a sporadic tradition called the "Bible Bowl" was born. While some were disappointed that winning seemed to take precedence over fellowship,[248] there was a real sense of ownership of the Calvin Bowl. In 1990 the RTC Athletic Committee, "in an attempt to 'foster' inclusivity, sent a motion to the RTC Executive Committee asking for the Calvin Bowl and Ball to be turned over to the RTC and to change the name to (pardon me while I yawn) the RTC Bowl (does the Blockbuster Bowl come to mind?)."[249] The response by Union students was overwhelmingly negative, and the Calvin Bowl remained. And after the Calvin Bowl, students repaired to the Neill Ray House for the Calvin Ball.

Although Frisbee playing could always be found on campus, it had always been informal. Ultimate Frisbee was first mentioned in 1993, with regular games held on Mondays and Wednesdays at 5:00 p.m.[250] Games are now held (weather and tests permitting) on the quad every afternoon. After Lingle Hall was closed in 2009 (and was leased, along with the Newbury Building and DuBose Hall, to J. Sargeant Reynolds Community College in July 2010), Ultimate Frisbee became an integral part of campus social life.

Humor was the usual way of keeping perspective, and no subject was off-limits. In 1974 the following notice appeared in *In a Mirror*:

> The Academic Credentials Committee of Theological Colleges and Schools in the U.S. has ruled that anyone receiving the D.Min. degree must write the "Dr." in front of his or her name with lower case letters, only. If anyone has any questions about this matter please see dr. Chuck Mendenhall.

New students were advised "not to forget the cardinal rule of seminary: request a first-floor apartment." And graffiti from other seminaries was reprinted with glee.

> Jesus said unto them: "Who do you say that I am?"
> And they replied: "You are the eschatological manifestation of the ground of our being, the kerygma in which we find the ultimate meaning of our interpersonal relationships."
> And Jesus said: "What?"

"Quotable Quotes" was an important part of *In Medias Res* and showed that student sermons were as painful as ever.

> "That sermon took us to hell." Nora Tubbs Tisdale offers some constructive criticism on a student sermon.

Amy (MDiv, 1994) and Steve (MDiv, 1994) Willis went to Union for different reasons, but both appreciated Union because of the community feeling. Amy went to Erskine College as a Roman Catholic and joined the Associate Reformed Presbyterian Church while attending there. Although she had visited Yale, she went to UTS because of the Erskine-Presbyterian connection and because Union was devoted to the small church.[251] Steve went to the University of North Carolina at Chapel Hill. Although he grew up in the Presbyterian Church, he had never heard of Union until an adviser at UNC recommended UTS. Although he visited Princeton, it was Union's community that attracted him. Amy never felt alienated as a woman, perhaps because "those battles had already been fought." Moreover, they never detected a hostile atmosphere on campus. Only later did they realize that there was a lot of controversy during their time; the faculty kept their disagreements among themselves, so there was a peaceful atmosphere on campus. They met on campus and were married right after graduation.

The world was changing, and Union had to address it. By 1978, Professors Oglesby and Arnold gave psychological evaluations to entering students and went over the results with each student when requested. Counseling was also offered to students and their families.[252] In 1980, students had to be reminded that they could be dismissed if their manner of life (their spiritual, moral, and social character) was inconsistent with seminary expectations.[253] The grievance procedure first appeared in 1992,[254] the Sexual Misconduct Policy was introduced in 1994,[255] and the Alcoholic Beverage Policy in 1995.[256]

Despite everything that happened during these thirty years, the Union community remained a witness to God's grace. Beat Abegglen (accompanied by his wife, Susanna) was a Swiss exchange student from the University of Bern in the 1988–89 school year. He has always thought that being in Richmond gave both of them "an awareness of the Body of Christ in its larger meaning."[257] In 1991, Cla Famos looked out of his dorm window and saw Union from a "Swiss" perspective.

> First of all, there is this nice lawn in front of me, surrounded by trees. Right now some people have started playing Frisbee on it. I think that's a great sport; but not only that, for me it became like a symbol of the welcoming community we have on this campus. I still remember my first day at Union, when I hardly knew anybody. But as soon as I joined this game, I got to know people and was accepted. I hope Union can become as a whole what the "Frisbee people" are: a welcoming community where everybody can join the game.
>
> On the right of the lawn lies the Chapel building. The services held in there were very meaningful for me and gave me many impulses on my faith journey. I did not only enjoy the good American preaching, but [also] the atmosphere of tolerance where there was room for different theology under one roof.[258]

Alumni and Alumnae

While the substance and aim of theological education was being challenged by many during this era, Union graduates continued to focus on the parish. Between 1967 and 1997, some 85 to 90% of all graduates served a church after graduation in congregations that were almost entirely east of the Mississippi, with 5 to 15% attending graduate school. The 10% who graduated with an MDiv and did not seek ordination usually entered teaching, counseling, medicine, or law. During this time 13 graduates entered the mission field in Brazil (3) and Zaire (now Democratic Republic of the Congo, 3), Japan (2), and 1 in each of Iran, Italy (Sicily), Taiwan, Thailand, and Zambia.

These MDiv, DMin, and PhD graduates had an impact on undergraduate education. Over thirty alumni taught in colleges and universities at some point in their career, with Craven Edward Williams (DMin, 1973) serving as the president of Gardner-Webb College in North Carolina from 1976 to 1986. Union graduates of this era influenced theological education. Numerous graduates taught as adjunct professors, and at least twelve taught in seminaries. Serving as president of Louisville Presbyterian Theological Seminary were Albert Curry Winn (BD, 1945; ThD, 1956) in 1966–73 and Dean K. Thompson (BD, 1969; ThM, 1970; ThD, 1974) in 2004–10. Ted Wardlaw (DMin, 1978) was called as the president of Austin Presbyterian Theological Seminary in 2002, and Louis Weeks (BD, 1967) was Union's president from 1994 to 2007.

As they had throughout its history, Union graduates served at all levels of the church, from presbytery committees to General Assembly boards and staff. Between 1967 and 1996, eight graduates served as moderators of the General Assembly: Marshall Coleman Dendy (attended 1945–46), in 1967; Patrick Dwight Miller Sr. (BD, 1926; ThM, 1927), in 1968; Robert Matthew Lynn (BD, 1927), in 1969; Benjamin Lacy Rose (BD, 1938; ThM, 1950; ThD, 1955; professor, 1956–73), in 1971; Jule Christian Spach (attended 1949–51), in 1976; Albert Curry Winn (BD, 1945; ThD, 1956), in 1979; John Franklin Anderson Jr. (BD, 1944), in 1982; and John Randolph Taylor (BD, 1954), in 1983.

Library

Throughout Union's history, the library symbolized Union's aspirations. Brown Library at Hampden-Sydney signaled the school's intention to achieve a high level of scholarship. Spence Library was ready on the first day of class in Richmond because Walter W. Moore insisted that Union would be in the forefront of American seminaries. The 1944 Latta Addition confirmed Union's status as a national institution. Through the turmoil of the 1960s and the debates of the 1980s, the library stood as an emblem of consistency and stability, serving everyone who walked into the circulation room.

Throughout this era the librarian's reports to the board of trustees show the library's explosive growth and how technology was now influencing higher education. In 1965 the library report claimed 140,000 volumes in its holdings. In 1970 the library inventory counted 151,717 holdings, including 315 microforms and 356 disc recordings for the first time (tape recordings having been held in the Reigner Recording Library for over 20 years). There were 777 periodical subscriptions, 2,904 registered borrowers, and a circulation of 56,492.[259] In 1976 the collection surpassed 200,000 volumes. In 1987 there were 248,534 volumes (with a circulation of 61,605), 1,502 periodical subscriptions, 41,176 microforms, and 58,387 audiovisual pieces. In 1996 the library held 285,000 volumes, subscribed to 1,447 periodicals, and was open 81 hours each week. Between 1990 and 1995 the average circulation was 41,586, and it was declining due to increasing use of the photocopier and the beginning of online resources.[260]

The collection was crowding the library by 1970, and John Trotti (who had just taken up the position of librarian) added the fifth and sixth floors to the library that year. He also raised fines for late books from 3¢ to 5¢ per day and produced the seminary form manual, *Jots and Tittles*, based on the *Chicago Manual of Style* and the shorter *Guide to Form and Style* by Kate L. Turabian. In 1972, Trotti established the Media Services Department. In 1973 the library's first floor was completely renovated to provide a more spacious area for the circulation desk and more lighting in the Reference Room.

As with other places on campus, security became a concern for the library. In 1976, losses due to theft cost some $11,000. That summer the magnetic tape security system was installed. Special teenage workers were hired as "pushers" (who brought the books shelf by shelf to workstations) and "strippers" (who put the security strips in place). The acquisition and installation cost over $30,000, but losses were reduced to near zero.

In 1978, David Vines Miller (BD, 1954) was on furlough from mission work in Africa. Seeing the sale table on which duplicate and withdrawn items were put out for sale to students and other patrons, Miller asked if there would be some way of sharing these volumes with the seminary in Lesotho. John Trotti offered the volumes for free and volunteered to pack the books for shipping. He also secured $1,200 to cover shipping costs, and the International Theological Library Book Project began to supply theological libraries all around the world with books.

When technology arrived on campus, it came to the library first. In November 1978 the library joined the digital future: it became a member of the Southeastern Online Network (Solinet) and through that body gained access to the

Ohio College Library Center (OCLC). Through the database maintained by OCLC, any Union student could locate a book, paper, or periodical anywhere throughout the country and obtain it (if it was available) though the interlibrary loan system. As John Trotti stated: "It was only a small beginning, but everyone knew the camel's nose was in the tent." From one OCLC terminal there began a steady progression of word processors, terminals for database searching, and eventually Wi-Fi.

After dealing with mold on the upper two floors of the library in the summer of 1984 and recognizing that the miles of wiring in the ceilings were impeding maintenance, everyone realized that the library was inadequate for the school's growing needs. In 1986 John Trotti presented a paper detailing nineteen factors pointing to the need for a new library facility. The board of trustees authorized a search for architects and consultants to study facility options. After nine months of working with consultants, it was obvious that a fifth expansion of the present library building would not move the library into the twenty-first century. After considering several options (building on the Westwood tract, leveling houses and building a long building on the south side of the campus, etc.), it was finally decided to renovate Schauffler Hall (which was underutilized) and extend it into the quad.[261]

From initial planning to checking out the first book, the William Smith Morton Library (named for a prominent early-twentieth-century Richmond Presbyterian and insurance executive) cost $13.8 million and took a decade to complete. The 68,000-square-foot Morton Library is more than twice as large as the "old" Spence Library (at 31,000 sq. ft.). It holds more than 420,000 volumes, compared to 290,000 books (in a space designed for 250,000) in the old facility.[262]

Before the Morton Library would open, there was an electrical fire in the Spence Library in the spring of 1996. Trevor Waters and Larry DeSoso of the physical plant were injured and hospitalized (but recovered after extensive treatment), and the old library was closed for several days. Although there was minimal damage to the building and no damage to the book collection, the building inspector deemed the building unsafe and closed it to the public. After extensive negotiations with city officials, the library reopened with a plan to close it once Morton Library was ready.

Before moving into the new library, the Smithsonian Institution contacted Union, seeking a card catalogue. Students who had used computers all their lives did not know what a card catalogue looked like. The Smithsonian wanted a card catalogue with the old handwritten cards, typed cards (with red-ribbon subject headings), multilith cards, and computer-produced cards. The Union catalogue held all these formats. On October 3, 1996, Union donated and shipped a sixty-drawer Library Bureau oak catalogue (40 drawers from the author-title catalog, and 20 from the subject catalog) to Washington, where it now represents the end of an era in library technology.

As the Morton Library neared completion, various schemes for the transfer of books were considered. Some advocated having the community form a human chain and move the 300,000 volumes and all the media pieces hand to hand across the campus. This was ruled out as impractical. Others suggested that in honor of the removal of the library from Hampden Sydney in 1898, the books should be loaded in tobacco hogsheads and rolled across the campus.

This idea was also rejected. It was decided to employ professional library movers. Yet some kind of symbolic move was needed to show the change from old to new.

On November 21, 1996, all faculty and executive staff members of the RTC schools carried two volumes each they had selected as having special significance. In addition, President Weeks loaded a wheelbarrow with faculty writings. Dr. John Leith led the procession as faculty emeritus and carried the rare second edition of John Calvin's *Institutio Christianae religionis*, dated 1559, the most expensive single volume the library ever purchased (in 1995). It was also determined that this book was the library's 300,000th catalogued item.

There was a worship service in the circulation area of the old library: the community gave thanks for the old facility and all those persons who had established it, worked in it, or studied there. With banners and full academic regalia, the procession moved out of the old library and paraded through a sizeable crowd of students, staff, and community onlookers to the new William Smith Morton Library. Although the library was not in use, the entourage made its way into the rare-book room, where the books were deposited and another brief service of thanksgiving and dedication was held.[263]

The progress of library construction and the transfer of books on opening day were given prominent coverage by the *Richmond Times-Dispatch*. A new library was not only positive news in the middle of controversy; Morton Library also meant something more. Roger Nicholson, at a staff meeting before approving the library, remembers suggesting liquidating both PSCE and UTS and rebuilding in Charlotte. There was also discussion about moving to the Research Triangle near Raleigh.[264] Thus the vote to build the new library symbolized the seminary's commitment to Richmond.[265]

Federation of UTS and PSCE

One of the unintended consequences of Reunion in 1983 was the loss of PSCE. Until 1959 the PCUS did not allow the Assembly's Training School (ATS) to have its own endowment because it was considered an agency of the General Assembly. Once the PCUS General Assembly made the Training School a free-standing institution in 1959, the school changed its name to the Presbyterian School of Christian Education, and it was able to raise money on its own. Although the General Assembly did not provide funding to its seminaries, it promised to provide funding to PSCE.[266] Since the United Presbyterian Church (UPC) did not have a comparable institution and did not understand its unique place within the southern church, this funding arrangement ended with Reunion. Consequently, PSCE automatically became the weakest theological institution in a new denomination with eleven theological schools and less than three million members.[267]

In addition to the change in funding, Reunion also transformed the position of Christian educator. The old southern church adopted the ordained offices of the northern church, and congregations began to employ associate pastors as Christian educators, rather than hiring PSCE graduates. Since the MA degree granted by PSCE did not lead to ordination, potential PSCE students now opted to attend seminary instead. Consequently, PSCE, with no funding and a diminishing mission, became an anomaly in the new denomination; even the 1993 General Assembly Report was not sure what to do with such a single-mission institution.[268] Seeing that PSCE would be devalued in the new denomination, UTS President Hartley Hall and PSCE President Wayne Bolton began exploring ways in which Union and PSCE could cooperate. In the fall of 1993 the boards of UTS and PSCE resolved that "program, personnel and faculty, effort and resources, may be shared to the fullest extent,"[269] which resulted in the dual-degree program. In August 1994 the idea was floated that Union and PSCE could combine in a state college–type system in which both schools would retain their boards and presidents, but the presidents would report to a chancellor.

The Union board, however, rejected this option, and President Weeks was asked to assemble a plan for merger. He enlisted three well-known consultants, worked with the Union Development office to secure two foundation grants, and worked with the two administrations and faculties to offer a plan to afford a merger in February 1995.[270] A lack of time, however, began to drive developments. By 1994, PSCE was spending more than 13 percent per year of its $3 million endowment (compared with Union's $75.5 million endowment) on expenses. More ominously, there were fewer than a hundred students in the Master of Christian Education Program, many of them part-time.[271] By mid-1995 some estimated that PSCE was eighteen months from bankruptcy.[272] Although PSCE had one of the highest percentages of giving by alumni and alumnae of all Presbyterian theological institutions, the average gift was small, and the total realized through annual giving did not support the annual operating costs. The school did everything it could to save money. In 1992, PSCE dismissed 26 percent of its support staff. In 1996, Watts Hall (a PSCE dorm) and a half-interest in Lingle were sold to the newly established Baptist Theological Seminary at Richmond. In addition, PSCE-owned faculty homes were sold as they were vacated to buy more time.[273] But PSCE continued to lose money.

In 1995 both boards authorized a joint committee to conduct "a study which will engage both UTS/PSCE in exploring mutual collaboration and partnerships for the enhancement of the mission of the Church." The study recognized PSCE's financial problems resulting from excess space and cost of deferred maintenance. This study argued that PSCE's finances would not allow it to operate into the future, and it recommended a federation of the schools.[274]

Pamela Mitchell-Legg represented both the promise and the dilemma of PSCE. A graduate of the University of Virginia, she went to PSCE to learn to write curriculum, graduating with an MA in 1979. She then became PSCE's first EdD graduate in 1986 and accepted a job at United Seminary in Dayton, Ohio.[275] Mitchell-Legg enjoyed her time at PSCE but always felt that Union looked down on PSCE because of Union's emphasis on biblical languages. In contrast, PSCE was proud that they were not "bound" by one academic model. She returned to teach at PSCE in 1994 and, although no one told her about the financial situation, soon realized that the school was in serious trouble. There was no money to fix faculty housing, and the deferred maintenance around the campus was obvious.

Some in the UTS community questioned why the seminary would take on the debt and physical plant of an institution with a declining enrollment and diminishing mission. The official reason was that if PSCE disappeared, the Christian education resources PSCE had already developed would no longer be just across the Brook, and Union would need to develop those resources on its own.[276] Yet behind the official, logical reason lay the feeling that PSCE represented a casualty of the modern church, a unique identity from the PCUS that must be preserved.[277] There was virtual unanimity on the UTS board in favor of taking over PSCE.[278]

President Weeks presented the strategic plan for federation with PSCE to the board at their May 1997 meeting.[279] PSCE did not want to use the word "merger" because it implied an inferior position in relationship to UTS, so the word "federation" was used. There was immediate opposition to federation among some on the Union faculty, although most professors saw the necessity for the action. Students seemed to be in favor of federation, and the PSCE faculty was mostly all for it.[280] Union's faculty was initially opposed because they felt that PSCE was academically inferior, and adding a Christian education degree would detract from Union's main mission. Opposition intensified when it was announced that, over a three-year period, PSCE professors' salaries were to be equalized with those of Union's professors.[281] The salary equalization, plus the property UTS was now responsible for, caused a financial drain on the seminary and divided the faculty community.[282]

Many in the UTS community believed that the advantages of federation far outweighed the disadvantages. Union would now have more practical theologians, more women on the faculty, and different pedagogies, and could offer an MA in Christian Education. Perhaps just as important, the new name (perhaps a bit awkward) reflected the hope that the identities of both institutions would be preserved and a little bit of the PCUS uniqueness could be salvaged.[283] Thus, on July 1, 1997, Union Theological Seminary in Virginia changed its name after 171 years and federated with the Presbyterian School of Christian Education to become Union Theological Seminary and Presbyterian School of Christian Education.

It quickly became apparent that it was not only the name that was unwieldy. The boards merged into one, with forty-two members. Both campuses would have a dean, serving under the president. The new institution would own all the property on both sides of the Brook (along with the massive deferred maintenance needs), and PSCE degree programs would continue.[284] Thus the new Union-PSCE offered ten degree programs, with a total student enrollment of 330 (48% female) and twenty-two denominations represented on campus (52% Presbyterian).

The Threads of History

Denominational seminaries are inexorably tied to the church. Throughout its history, Union exerted an important and even defining role in the PCUS. In civil rights, the ordination of women, and discussions about the Vietnam War, Union often led the church in the stances it ultimately took. With the changes in

American culture in the last third of the twentieth century and in the national church created by Reunion, Union Seminary found itself facing a church with declining membership and stymied by doubt. The definition of an educated ministry had changed within a generation. Union's commitment to the traditional curriculum, however, never wavered.

The secularization of culture meant that most students had lost the nurturing framework found in the life of the local southern Presbyterian church. Prior to this era, it was expected that students would grow up in a local congregation and arrive in Richmond with a liberal arts education and a specific understanding of ministry. They came onto campus knowing the tradition they felt called to serve. The calls for classes in spirituality and ministry during these years are evidence that many students had not known lengthy involvement and responsibility in the life of a local congregation.[285] The challenge for Union was to address this new culture. Biblical theology no longer clarified the theological meaning of contemporary life. Professors faced students who did not necessarily accept the church's traditions or agree with the residential model, students who questioned many of the assumptions of what defined an educated ministry.

Although Union had always attracted students from outside the South, Reunion changed its context. In the newly formed PC(USA), Union was no longer the flagship seminary. How to distinguish itself and retain its identity remained a challenge; federation with PSCE was an attempt to save part of the PCUS heritage while marketing itself to a new denomination. If Union had always struggled with the interplay between a "southern" and a "national" institution, its challenges were now more than geographical. Professor Bill Arnold noticed that a new pluralism (diverse communities and ways of thinking) challenged Union to balance its tradition with unexpected trends.[286]

In past eras, Union had always engaged the world by graduating pastors and missionaries. With the rise of the corporate seminary, specialized professors, and the professional minister, UTS was expected to produce not only excellent candidates, but also present itself with stellar credentials to a secular world. Many alumni and professors feared that during this period Union put more emphasis on academics than on the parish.[287] Jim Mays taught under four presidents (Jones, Stair, Hall, and Weeks). When he began teaching, almost all faculty had some experience in serving a church as pastor. Time in the pastorate gave a shared sense of purpose to the teaching enterprise. After thirty years of teaching, Mays felt as though Union lost some of its cohesion because faculty were now pursuing individual careers without reference to the church.

Mays also reflected that before the 1980s, Union had a great deal of credibility with the church at large because it navigated between advocating for reform and holding fast to the status quo. This unique ethos was reflected in biblical theology.[288] As process theology, liberation theology, feminist theology, and other such new developments came upon the scene in the 1960s and 1970s, faculty and students struggled with how to embrace new theological insights while holding on to what was valuable in the tradition. Nevertheless, the curriculum remained centered on the traditional five areas, and most students still aimed to serve a congregation.

During this period Union continued to influence the denomination and theological education. Although the seminary was seen as one of the leading theological institutions in the country and continued to graduate professors and presidents, the context was changing. Students lacking a tradition in the church (and the tradition itself was questioned), denominational fractiousness, campus divisions, the pace of technology, the commitment to the residential model, the decline of biblical theology, and the energy taken up by Reunion and federation caused some to wonder if Union even had a viable place in the modern world. Yet students—both male and female, no longer exclusively just out of college, coming from African American, Spanish-speaking, and Asian churches—still arrived on campus because Union's unwavering commitment to the traditional curriculum remained the bedrock of the seminary's life. The challenge was how to convey the value of this curriculum in a new way to a new church.

Chapter Ten (1998–2012)
Union Presbyterian Seminary

As the twentieth century opened, Union Theological Seminary was just settling into its new campus in Richmond. Walter W. Moore, the faculty, and students joined the rest of the dominant culture in looking forward to the new century with a comfortable triumphalism. In 1900 there were 70 million Americans in 45 states, and the country was recovering from the financial panic of 1896. The Spanish-American War had come to a victorious conclusion a year earlier, and the Philippines, Puerto Rico, Cuba, Guam, and American Samoa had become possessions of the United States. The country was predominantly rural, 60 percent of the population lived outside cities, and less than 12 percent of all Americans had a high school diploma. There were only ten miles of paved roads and 8,000 registered automobiles.

Americans at the turn of the twentieth century were religiously uniform: 97% identified themselves as Christian. Of the almost 68 million American Christians, 85% identified themselves as Protestant (in over 180 denominations) and 13% identified themselves as Roman Catholic.[1] Americans were also sure of their faith. As part of their classic study of American culture, *Middletown* (1924), Robert and Helen Lynd interviewed high school students from Muncie, Indiana (renamed "Middletown") and asked for a response to the statement "Christianity is the one true religion, and all peoples should be converted to it": 91% agreed.[2]

In the early twentieth century many Americans were concerned that unchecked immigration from Ireland and southern Europe would overwhelm the United States (due to the Roman Catholicism of the immigrants). Besides limiting immigration, many white Southerners believed that Reconstruction should be reversed in order to keep society stable. Consequently, southern states began to revise their constitutions in 1890, codifying Jim Crow segregation and disenfranchising African Americans. Virginia ratified its new, segregationist constitution in 1902, and elected African American office holders (at the state and federal level) disappeared within two elections. Throughout the country, there were 115 lynchings in 1900.

Walter W. Moore shared the predominant culture's optimism. As a result of the Removal (from Hampden Sydney), he saw enrollment increase from 68 in 1897 to 72 in 1900, and the number of students would rise above 100 for the first time in 1911. The move to Richmond anticipated the new urban America. Although Union's students were white (and integration was culturally unthinkable and legally prohibited), they initiated ministries, especially the Seventeenth Street Mission, which would have been unthinkable just 5 years earlier.

447

The campus and library were among the most modern buildings in Richmond and the equal to seminary facilities anywhere in the country. Moore's expansive vision emphasized "practical" work and Christian education to serve the Presbyterian Church (US); Union's student body was 93 percent southern and 97 percent Presbyterian.

Union Theological Seminary and Presbyterian School of Christian Education approached the year 2000 in a context that would have been unrecognizable to Americans in 1900. At the turn of the new millennium, there were 281 million Americans in 50 states. The country was predominantly urban, with only 21% living outside cities. More than 80% of all adult Americans had graduated from high school. There was almost one registered vehicle per driver, and 70% of all Americans drove to work.

Americans became more religiously diverse as the twentieth century progressed. In 1963, some 90% of Americans claimed to be Christians; 2% professed no religious identity. By 2000, about 78% self-identified as Christian, and of these roughly 75% were Protestant and 20% Roman Catholic. Muslims made up just over 2% of the population, and 13% of Americans claimed no religious identity. A 1999 follow-up study revisited Middletown (Muncie, Ind.) and asked the high school students if "Christianity is the one true religion and all peoples should be converted to it": only 42% agreed.

Although church attendance was not reliably measured until 1943, Gallup polls found that between 1943 and 2000 roughly 40% of the American population claimed to attend church (or synagogue) in the previous week. What changed, however, was that the so-called mainline denominations lost members: the United Methodist Church, the Evangelical Lutheran Church in America, the PC(USA), the Episcopal Church, the American Baptist Church, the United Church of Christ, the Disciples of Christ, and the Reformed Church in America. Meanwhile, more conservative churches, such as the Southern Baptist Convention, grew from 2.2% of the population in 1900 to 5.3% in 1998.[3] At the same time, the number of Presbyterians (northern, southern, and Cumberland branches) declined from 2.5% of the population in 1900[4] to roughly 1% of the population in 2000. Faced with a more secular society and a shrinking denomination, President Weeks sought to position Union-PSCE to meet the demands of the new millennium. The new school offered ten degree programs to attract more students and seemed to realize the ecumenical vision President Lacy had at the 1927 senior class graduation banquet, when he saw "an Asian, a Persian, two Methodists, a Disciple, and one northern Presbyterian" and remarked that he would have never seen such diversity in his student days. By 2000, Union's MDiv student body was even more diverse: 51% female, 12% African American, and 10% Korean American. In 1995, Weeks succeeded in making the Reformed educational tradition available to others when the United Methodist Church approved UTS for the education of Methodist students, renewing an accreditation that had lapsed in the 1980s.[5]

Union remained proudly Presbyterian in a time when being a denominational school was difficult. In 1960, mainline theological schools educated 50% of all Protestant seminarians. By the year 2000, that figure had dropped to 40%.[6] President Weeks searched for new ways the seminary could thrive in this changing context. His research on the Presbyterian Church, with John Mulder and Milton Coalter, convinced him that it was vital for the seminary to provide new resources for congregations and pastors and lay leaders. In response, he worked with faculty and development officers to secure grants and other funding for several institutes, to serve the rapidly growing Korean churches and help the church address questions dealing with faith and science. New platforms, such as the campus in Charlotte and the Extended Campus Program, were initiated to meet the needs of a new culture.

Nevertheless, questions persisted as to what it meant to be a Presbyterian seminary. In the year 2000, Presbyterians comprised just 52% of the student body. While the endowment had risen from $86.6 million in 1997 to $120.3 million in 2000, the equalization of pay between UTS and PSCE professors and the increased demands in maintaining the physical plant were still straining resources. America was entering a post-Christian culture, and Union-PSCE prepared pastors to serve a country that looked more like the skeptical post-Revolutionary country of 1812 than the triumphal Christian nation of 1900.

New Name, Consistent Mission

Union approached the twenty-first century with a solid foundation. The administration conducted a survey of UTS and PSCE graduates in January and February 1998. Approximately 6,000 surveys were sent out to all living graduates, as far back as the 1940s. The results were encouraging: 94% believed their education at UTS or PSCE prepared them for their work, 87% felt that their education helped them grow spiritually, and 81% thought the housing facilities were satisfactory.[7] This survey showed that the new federated institution would need to work hard to live up to the reputation of its predecessors.

However necessary Federation may have been, combining Union and PSCE was more than just changing a name, ordering new stationery, and walking across the Brook. Uniting what had been Union and PSCE into Union-PSCE was as much an emotional transformation as it was an organizational restructuring. In 1997 the Office of Institutional Effectiveness (OFINE) polled current students, faculty, and support and administrative staff on Federation's effects, in the Federation Climate Survey. The 181 responses showed that combining UTS and PSCE, despite optimistic intentions, was like grinding gears. Respondents complained that they were unsure of the goals or shape of the new school; PSCE "people" were afraid that the old UTS was burying the legacy of PSCE because Union had always looked down upon PSCE as an inferior school. At the same time, UTS "people" were offended because they felt like they had to work to protect the feelings of former PSCE people. On both sides of the Brook, there were feelings of anxiety that everyone was spending too much time building a new institution instead of educating for the future of the church.[8]

Jane Vann, professor of Christian Education at UTS, began researching the learning cultures of Union Theological Seminary and Presbyterian School of Christian Education in the summer of 1998 by interviewing faculty and students of both institutions. She hoped to show that ways could be found to preserve the distinctive styles of PSCE and UTS in the federated institution. Vann described PSCE as a place of "praxis." Collegial and holistic, PSCE believed that teaching and learning included virtually all aspects of the life of the school, both in the classroom and outside it, seeking "to teach habits of mind (intellect), heart (affections), and body (practices)." PSCE emphasized nonhierarchical relationships among students, staff, and faculty. Students felt that previous experience mattered, and the educational processes were designed for each individual with the goal of academic engagement and spiritual formation.

Union's culture was different, shaped by a concern for orthodoxy and transmission of the Reformed tradition. Professors did not encourage innovation; instead, they wanted students to understand themselves as a part of a historical continuum. The curriculum was designed for students to encounter the Bible and classic theological texts within the framework of the Reformed tradition, with the aim of handing on the tradition to future generations. Students at Union were asked to develop critical judgment, understanding that all theological positions cannot be correct. Vann noticed that while Union professors were adamant, they were careful not to indoctrinate students. There was always a recognition that Union students would need to take ordination exams and face their presbyteries in order to be ordained. The denomination and presbyteries expected ministerial candidates to know, teach, and defend a standard of orthodoxy. Although pastoral care classes, the biggest curricular change in the twentieth century, had been in the curriculum for over forty-five years, Union professors and students agreed that their education was largely concerned with matters of the mind.

In trying to find a way to preserve the distinctive learning styles of both Union and PSCE, Vann confirmed OFINE's Federation Climate Survey. She saw confusion and frustration in the merging of both schools. Indeed, their respective cultures were almost incompatible. Many students in the new Union-PSCE questioned the mission of the federated institution. Students in the MDiv program understood the mission of the school to be the preparation of ministers. Students outside of the MDiv program saw Union-PSCE's mission as more of a divinity school, stressing academics. After arriving on campus, one student in the survey declared: "If you want to study to be a pastor, go someplace else. This is where you go to become a theologian." Another student commented:

> I think this school does like to have this kind of facade that it is training people to go on and get the PhD, not to be pastors. But I don't think it's the faculty and professors that are giving that facade; I think it's the students. . . . It's what the students think this mighty ivory [tower] institution is, versus what the faculty thinks. And the faculty I know feel they are training pastors. It's a difference in the facade that the students want to portray versus the faculty.

Vann argues that the frustration with the "intellectual" side of ministry manifested itself by student calls for more practical classes. Throughout her study, students continually asked for a reorientation of the curriculum toward a stronger emphasis on preaching and on classes that would help them gain practical hands-on skills for leadership in congregations.

Vann saw a disturbing "culture of competition" emanating from the students and permeating the school. This competition manifested itself in the struggle for grades and the perceived demand for uniformity in certain theological views. In her view, teachers tried hard to create an environment for students to explore topics in an open way. Students, however, resisted and seemed less willing to grant this openness to their peers. Many complained that they focused on academic achievement and dismissed gifts for ministry in favor of scholastic success.[9] Moreover, Federation led to resentment on the UTS campus over PSCE having resources given to it, with a resulting competition for those resources.[10]

Federation not only challenged Union-PSCE to meld two campus cultures, but also speak to the "traditionless" students who began attending Union-PSCE in greater numbers. Without a strong background in a congregation, many students found themselves adrift in an unfamiliar community, using a strange language. If professors complained that students were not adequately prepared for theological study in the previous century, by 2000 many students were also feeling that same deficiency. One student felt the lack of traditioning acutely.

> I think that this school assumes several things, which are not true. One is that you have a liberal arts background and that you took a humanities course at a liberal arts college, that you've read Plato and Aristotle. I was in class . . . where a [student asked], "What is an Enlightenment paradigm?" which if you went to a university and majored in business is not an unreasonable question. You wouldn't know. I think [the school] also assumes that you will get skills for ministry in your supervised field education, which I don't think is true. . . . I think the school also assumes that you grew up in the church . . . and are schooled in the practices of the community of faith, and that is also not true. That is what has been difficult for me. First of all, all of those things are true about me: I did go to a liberal arts college, and I did grow up in the church. And I know that if I were to leave here and enter a church, I would feel really unprepared. That's disconcerting for me because I know that a majority of students probably don't fit that exact profile, and I wish that the school did more to meet the needs of all students instead of assuming that everyone fits the paradigm of fifty years ago.

Besides academics, some students arrived on campus expecting the seminary to nurture their spiritual growth. The traditional notion that the seminary is not the church did not resonate with many students. For them, the campus community was their community of faith because the demands of academics and family kept them away from local congregations. Vann lamented the lack of involvement in local congregations and the decline in chapel participation as troublesome trends.[11]

Worship Rebuilds the Consensus

If students expected the seminary to help them cultivate their spiritual lives, Jane Vann was concerned that Union was not ready to meet those expectations. Yet Edna Banes, dean of students from 2001 to 2012, identified the transformation in chapel as symbolic of the new institution trying to find its identity. Throughout the 1960s, students had complained that compulsory attendance policies for chapel, Sprunt Lectures, graduation, and other campus-wide events were childish. Moreover, since more faculty were living off campus and the number of commuter students was increasing, mandatory attendance policies were placing an undue burden on these two groups.[12] The board responded in

1974 by agreeing to end compulsory student attendance at commencement,[13] and attendance at other events soon became optional.

The price for making attendance discretionary was a decline in participation, which weakened campus programs and the sense of community. Edna Banes argues that the evolution of chapel is a barometer of how the campus community has changed. In the early 1970s, chapel was straightforward:

> Thirty years ago worship at Union Theological Seminary was undergoing transition. For many years chapel had been led by faculty (three days a week) and senior students (two days a week). The majority of students and faculty were resident. Attendance at chapel was expected, though not required, and most did attend. Although the services focused on preaching, chapel was not an academic activity. Student sermons and worship leadership were not graded or evaluated in chapel. Rather, community services were held on Thursday evenings. At those services, seniors would preach and be evaluated by faculty and peers.

Chapel was seen as providing a balance to the classroom. Since most of the faculty had previously served churches, they saw chapel as an opportunity to model worship for the students and share their faith. As professors began to live away from campus (and many of the new professors had not served in churches), however, chapel and many other formal community activities were not seen as a priority. In line with the laid-back ethos of the 1960s, the faculty decided not to process or wear robes at convocation for several years.

Many students and faculty came to see the purpose of seminary education as imparting academic knowledge, with spiritual formation playing an increasingly minor role. Consequently, corporate worship suffered and the meaning of chapel changed. Watts Chapel, with its fixed pews and pulpit as the focus of the room, resembled the church many of the students could expect to serve. At the same time, the liturgical movement encouraged experimentation and challenged how worship was conducted. Indeed, for several years in the 1980s and 1990s, students could write a liturgy instead of a sermon on the denominational ordination exams. The sermon was deemphasized; dialogues, narrative, poetry, dance, and drama became accepted in chapel. If there was an expected order of service (i.e., Scripture/sermon/prayer/hymn) for most of Union's history, by the late 1980s there were no restrictions placed on what would take place in chapel. Indeed, Banes argues that the committee carrying responsibility for chapel could not decide what controls or parameters, if any, should be imposed on worship.[14] Chapel as a mode of traditioning was largely lost. The long-held assumption that "the seminary is not the church," that students would be nurtured by their church, and the seminary existed to provide academic preparation—that was, according to Lee Zehmer (MDiv, 1991), no longer helpful. The idea that the seminary is not the church

> has excused the powers that be from any responsibility of meeting the spiritual needs of the students. "We expect them to get involved with a local congregation," it is said. Let me tell you: with 50 verses of Greek to translate, 150–200 pages of Barth to read, ordination exams to study for, PIFs [personal information forms] to write, it is a wonder that anybody has time to go to the church on Sunday, let alone get involved.

> Whether we would like to admit it or not, we are a gathered fellowship of believers who are preparing for the service of God. More attention needs to be paid both to our spiritual and pastoral needs.[15]

By the early 2000s, Banes found that students were not always sure how to approach chapel. Indeed, Federation highlighted differences in the cultures of the old schools. Worship at UTS traditionally emphasized preaching and an identifiable order of worship; liturgical innovations were viewed with suspicion. In contrast, PSCE encouraged creativity: many chapel services included liturgical dance, drama, poetry, clowning, or mime.[16] At the same time, Korean, African American, Methodist, evangelical, and international students all wanted to bring their contributions to the chapel experience through different preaching and music styles. Commuter students wanted a more flexible chapel schedule, while other students wanted set times of worship. Younger students, who were more familiar with contemporary music as part of their worship, found the traditional chapel music "very dry and uninspiring."[17] Other students missed the traditional hymns and worried that poor chapel participation by faculty abdicated the opportunity to model good preaching.

Chapel became a source of friction. In response to the varied schedules, tastes, and traditions of the students, the administrations tried various strategies: chapel was conducted at various times and intentionally included different styles of worship. At the time of Federation in 1997, Union-PSCE alternated chapel worship between Sydnor Chapel (the former PSCE chapel) and Watts Chapel (on the Union campus). In the year 2000, however, the building that housed Sydnor Chapel was sold, and all chapel worship became centered in Watts Chapel. The change in worship space amplified the conflicting legacies of both schools. The architecture of Watts Chapel, with its fixed pews, limited the experimentation invited by the flexible seating of Sydnor Chapel.[18]

By 2001 more than 50 percent of faculty and students commuted to campus, making early morning and late afternoon services difficult, and some were afraid that chapel now offered little opportunity for the community to cohere. Yet it was the changing composition of the community that showed how chapel could become a vehicle of consensus. In the fall of 2001 the traditional pattern of five services each week was replaced by a block of two and a half hours on Wednesdays. This new schedule allowed for an hour-long chapel service followed by a community lunch for all faculty, staff, and students. Chapel and lunch now became a contact point for many students and the foundation for a renewed sense of community.

What Kind of School?

Chapel attendance was a concern at other schools as seminaries felt their way into the new century. Chapel symbolized Union-PSCE's dilemma: was chapel (and by extension seminary education) a vehicle to nurture student spirituality, or a component in teaching students a tradition they would transmit to their congregations? Edna Banes contended that Union-PSCE's purpose was reflected in its worship and that the new school was at a crossroads. Was it a place of academic education in a specific tradition, or a place to find spiritual nurture? Traditionally, the spiritual nurture of students had been the responsibility of the congregation. The seminary's job was to reinforce the conventions of worship and the customary habits of southern Presbyterian spiritual life. Yet that tradition was gone, and students "often complain that their education is far more head than heart." This tension, however, was an old one. During her research, Banes discovered

> a survey conducted by two students at UTS in 1934–35 to measure the devotional life of the student body. After decrying the hypocrisy of students who claim to lead very spiritual lives but do not attend chapel, they state; "One suggestion which occurs again and again is to have classes more devotional and inspiring in character; less rattling of dry bones; less about the Bible and more of the Bible."

Although students in the 1930s and at the beginning of the twenty-first century may have voiced the same longings for "heart" in their seminary education, the student in the 1930s was more likely to have a connection with a local church. The student in the early 2000s was, in contrast, more of a seeker. The question facing the new school was stark: How can Union-PSCE prepare students to serve Presbyterian congregations, while appealing to those who are much less likely to have a connection with a local congregation?[19]

Union-PSCE tried to meld the missions and legacies of both schools while appealing to a student who did not see the local church as the focus of ministry. At Federation, Union-PSCE offered ten degree programs. The master of divinity (MDiv) and the master of arts in Christian education (MACE) were the basic professional degrees, with the master of arts in theological studies (MATS) offered beginning in 2002. In addition, there were four dual degrees: the master of arts in Christian education / master of divinity (MACE/MDiv) offered at the seminary; and three offered in conjunction with Virginia Commonwealth University: the master of arts in Christian education / master of social work (MACE/MSW); the master of divinity / master of science in criminal justice (MDiv/MS), and the master of divinity / master of social work (MDiv/MSW), offered in cooperation with Virginia Commonwealth University. The doctor of education (EdD) was folded into a PhD in Christian education, so the three advanced degrees—the master of theology (ThM), the doctor of ministry (DMin), and the PhD—remained the same.[20]

While President Weeks was trying to make Union-PSCE more attractive to students through wider degree offerings, he was simultaneously trying to give the school more impact in the church and community. He integrated two PSCE programs into Union-PSCE. The Center on Aging, directed by Henry Simmons, was the only program in any Presbyterian seminary specializing in gerontology. The Josephine Newbury Center for Childhood Education taught students and church leaders the most effective techniques for teaching children. Union-PSCE also continued *Interpretation*, and the Office of Professional Development became the Center for Ministry and Leadership Development, charged with administering the DMin program and other continuing education events.

Six new centers, institutes, and programs were established during this time to enable Union to address contemporary issues. The Carl Howie Center for Science, Art, and Theology began in 1996. Carl Gordon Howie (BD, 1944; ThM,

1947) was an Old Testament scholar who earned a PhD from Johns Hopkins University in 1949. After serving as a navy chaplain in the Pacific and China during World War II, he pastored congregations in Lynchburg (Virginia), Washington (D.C.), San Francisco, Detroit, and Dearborn (Michigan) for thirty-six years. While studying at Johns Hopkins in 1947 with W. F. Albright, Howie was involved with the original verification of the Dead Sea Scrolls and spent the rest of his life studying them. He wrote five books on the Dead Sea Scrolls and several commentaries.

Howie wanted his center to "recognize and engage the insights and implications of the interplay of science, art, and theology" to inform the modern practice of ministry. He helped raise $800,000 to begin the Center,[21] and more than $1 million in endowment and gifts had been received by 1999.[22] The Center continues to sponsor yearly conferences, with speakers from around the world. Lecture topics have included "The Inner Garden" (1996), "Science and Religion: Imagining the Mystery / Christian Hope in the Age of Science" (2001); "Taking Care and Dying Well" (2006); "Evolution, God, and Becoming Human" (2009); and "The Environment and Human Agency" (2012).

The Asian American Ministry Center was established in 1998, with Syngman Rhee as director. The center supports one of the fastest-growing parts of the Presbyterian Church by studying Asian American congregations and recruiting gifted Asian American students to careers in ministry. The Center also sponsors yearly continuing education opportunities for Asian American pastors, educators, and laity.

The Institute for Reformed Theology was also initiated in 1998 and, until it closed in 2013, sponsored annual colloquies. The institute both published an e-journal and invited internationally known theologians to address colloquies on issues facing the church. In 2006, for example, the topic was "John Calvin as Teacher, Pastor, and Theologian."

Project Burning Bush and the Rehoboth Project were designed for personal renewal and aimed at two different groups of people. Project Burning Bush was launched in 2000 to help high school students explore their call to ministry. Over three hundred high school youths have completed a two-week summer program, during which they engaged in Christian vocational discernment through theological reflection, intentional community building, workshops, outreach, and worship. Having sought to clarify God's call in their lives, they returned to their home congregations to accomplish a project based on what they learned. The Rehoboth Project, started in 2002 and ending in 2009, allowed pastors to design peer learning groups to nourish and sustain their calls. In the seven years of its operation, 566 pastors and 69 laypeople participated, representing 527 congregations.

Besides the Sprunt Lecture Series, Union inaugurated the Dawe Lecture series in 2007 to honor Donald Dawe's commitment to multireligious and multicultural understanding and interfaith dialogue. The Dawe Lecture Series has addressed such topics as "A Cross-Cultural Dialogue between Christian Faith and East Asian Worldview" (2007); "Living Islam: Translating Faith into Action" (2009); "Without Buddha I Could Not Be a Christian" (2011); and "Godly Self-Care" (2012). As in the past, Union continued to invite guest speakers to provide unique insights and faithful challenges to the student body. In

2012, Timothy Tyson presented a lecture based on his book exploring lynching and the church's silence, "Blood Done Sign My Name." Other topics have included "The Vocation of a Christian Intellectual" (2008), given by Cornel West, "Faith and Freedom: The Common Root of King's Nonviolence" (2010), and "The State of Our Religious Union" (2012).

Perhaps the most important signpost of the professionalization of seminary education and the critical importance of accreditation was the establishment of the Office of Institutional Effectiveness (OFINE) in April 1996. This was initiated in response to a self-study that "revealed serious weaknesses in the planning and evaluation processes" of Union. ATS and SACS "imposed notations and recommendations regarding institutional effectiveness," which would have to be addressed if Union was going to keep its accreditation.[23] In response, President Weeks created OFINE with its own director, administrative assistant, and budget. OFINE was charged with creating a strategic plan for the board, the administration, and the students, and later assessing how the goals were being met.[24]

The varied degrees, centers, programs, and projects, however, never interfered with Union's foundation: the Bible and the traditional curriculum. From 2002 to 2004, Bible classes accounted for 8 out of 21 required credits; in 2012, biblical languages, Bible courses, theology, and church history took 39 of the 51 required credit hours. Costs, however, continued to rise. A normal course load taken in the 2002 academic year cost $7,000;[25] in 2009 the cost rose to $11,520.[26] UTS, however, remained committed to making education affordable. Almost all students were eligible for considerable subsidy, and fewer than 10 percent increased their educational debt while at Union-PSCE.

The Vision of a New Campus

After fusing together two campuses, two traditions, and two cultures into one institution, Union-PSCE broadened its reach by establishing a satellite campus in Charlotte, North Carolina. A campus with dormitories and support facilities had been Union's model of theological education since 1812. Yet even in 1974 there was a recognition that the seminary's reach had to be expanded, if only including "satellite DMin groups" in other cities.[27] It was obvious to some that with the rise of two-income families, the inroads made by nondenominational seminaries, and new possibilities created by Internet technology, the idea of a residential campus was becoming only one of several options of "delivering" theological education. Indeed, the 1993 General Assembly Special Committee to Study Theological Institutions worried that those seminaries who did not increase their geographical influence would be "stranded."[28] Moreover, by the late 1990s, many seminaries were experimenting with satellite campuses.

Although Walter W. Moore probably hoped to move the Hampden Sydney campus to Greensboro or Charlotte, once George Watts and Lewis Ginter got together, there was no question that Union Theological Seminary would move to Richmond. Bill White (Chairman of the Board, 1980s) remembers that James Jones, when pastor of Myers Park Presbyterian Church (in Charlotte) in the late 1940s, first broached the idea of either moving Union Seminary to Charlotte, or establishing some kind of campus in the city.[29] His idea went nowhere, but it continued to simmer for years, especially among members of the board from North Carolina. When creating a satellite campus in Charlotte was raised in the early 1980s, President Hall was opposed.[30] Besides believing that Union's strength lay in its residential model, he was sorting out Union's place in a reunited denomination and building up the inflation-ravaged endowment.

When Louis Weeks was inaugurated as Union's president in 1994, he was immediately aware of the calls for a Charlotte campus.[31] The board and the new president, however, first wanted to address the challenges presented by Federation. Yet, in the spring of 1996, Alan Elmore, Charlotte Presbytery Executive (in conversation with Charlotte-based members of the board and President Weeks), made it plain that establishing a PC(USA) seminary in Charlotte had become a priority for the presbytery. A student at Gordon-Conwell Theological Seminary had petitioned unsuccessfully for ordination. The presbytery was "in turmoil concerning the equity and advisability" of requiring students to attend a Presbyterian seminary or a residential seminary with Presbyterian presence for at least one year in preparation for ordination. The board of trustees decided to explore some type of extension campus in Charlotte.[32]

As part of this exploratory process, President Weeks asked the Research Services Department of the PC(USA) to provide demographic data and arguments for a Charlotte campus in the fall of 1996. He also commissioned a study by seminary faculty and staff to address the feasibility of a satellite campus in Charlotte. While the Research Services report provided data to support a degree-granting, satellite campus in Charlotte, the faculty report concluded that a branch campus in Charlotte would not work. The faculty's reasoning was simple: a branch campus had been unsuccessfully tried by others before and would undercut Union's traditional commitment to the residential model. The report proposed, instead, that Union increase its presence in Charlotte by offering frequent continuing education events for pastors, public lectures aimed at congregations, leadership events for Charlotte-area business and civic leaders, and a continuing commitment by the faculty to preach in Charlotte-area churches.[33]

The idea of a satellite campus would be a hard sell. In the mid-1990s, Columbia Theological Seminary (CTS) and San Francisco Theological Seminary (SFTS) had tried to establish satellites in Orlando (Florida) and Pasadena (California), respectively. The CTS efforts in Orlando ended quickly, and SFTS was struggling with that southern California campus (which opened in 1991 and closed in 2011): no one wanted to repeat those experiences.[34] Some also argued that with Gordon-Conwell and Reformed Theological Seminary (RTS) already in Charlotte, there was no need for another Reformed seminary. Perhaps the most emotional argument was that Union had always prided itself on the residential model.[35] Yet the facts were plain: in 1995, of the twenty-five MDiv candidates from Charlotte Presbytery alone, only five were enrolled in Union-PSCE, and that number was decreasing.[36]

Calls for a Charlotte campus, however, continued. In the spring of 1997, President Weeks began to meet informally with ministers from the Charlotte area, and out of those conversations momentum began to grow. Charlotte Presbytery polled other PC(USA) seminaries to determine whether they were interested in establishing a Charlotte campus. Only Columbia and Union-PSCE responded affirmatively. In September 1997, President Douglas Oldenburg of Columbia Seminary and President Louis Weeks of Union attended a meeting with Charlotte Presbytery representatives to discuss what could be done. With Columbia's recent negative experience fresh in his mind, President Oldenburg indicated that Columbia was not interested in establishing a presence in Charlotte. If there was going to be a PC(USA) seminary presence in Charlotte, the field was open to Union-PSCE.[37]

It was easy to see why a Presbyterian seminary in Charlotte would be a good fit. Almost two-thirds of all Presbyterians live within 250 miles of a line between Pittsburgh (Pennsylvania) and Charlotte (North Carolina).[38] In the year 2000, there were 130,000 PC(USA) members in 518 congregations living within 100 miles of Charlotte; more Presbyterians lived within 100 miles of Charlotte than lived within 100 miles of Chicago and Richmond combined. More Presbyterians lived within 100 miles of Charlotte than lived within 100 miles of Atlanta and San Francisco combined. Yet all four of those cities had PC(USA) seminaries.[39] Growth potential was also important. The seven-county Charlotte area added 268,000 people between 1990 and 1997, including growth in the Asian American and Hispanic communities.[40]

Gordon-Conwell opened its Charlotte campus in 1992, and one year later five students under the care of Charlotte Presbytery were attending.[41] A survey of sixty potential seminarians conducted in the Charlotte Presbytery indicated that the presence of a PC(USA) seminary would influence their decision to pursue theological education in Charlotte.[42] On top of that, it seemed to most church leaders in Charlotte that the number of UTS graduates filling pulpits in Charlotte was declining.[43] More ominously, none of Charlotte's seven existing seminaries had the PC(USA) as their primary focus.[44]

Determined to show the need for a seminary in Charlotte, former PC(USA) moderator Price Gwynn responded to Union-PSCE's fall 1996 study (which concluded that Union-PSCE should not establish a satellite campus) at a Charlotte Presbytery committee meeting on September 30, 1997. Drawing on his background as chairman of the Presbyterian Publishing Corporation Board of Directors, he critiqued the seminary report as being based on inadequate market research. The primary argument against a Charlotte presence was that since the satellite campuses established by Columbia and San Francisco were unsuccessful, Union's effort would be reinventing a failed wheel. Gwynn answered by observing that the Orlando satellite of CTS collapsed due to lack of funding, and the SFTS campus in Pasadena was failing due to the presence of Fuller Theological Seminary. In 1997, Fuller "graduated more students who are ordained as Presbyterian ministers than does any other seminary with the single exception of Princeton . . . and granted more MDiv degrees than Columbia and Union combined." SFTS was, therefore, unwisely trying to challenge Fuller in its own backyard.[45] No single seminary had a secure presence in Charlotte; establishing a satellite campus of Union-PSCE would not be in direct competition with RTS (in Charlotte since 1990) or Gordon-Conwell (in Charlotte since 1992) because those seminaries competed for the same conservative students; Union-PSCE offered a distinct alternative.[46]

While some argued that the residential ethos of Richmond formed leaders of the church, Gwynn argued that it was time to realize that the platforms for the delivery of theological education were expanding. With two-income families unable to pick up and move for three years, second-career people looking for a transition, and advances in computer technology, there were growing pressures for alternatives to the residential experience. Just as army officers who graduate from West Point and those who complete Officer Candidate School are considered officers, so graduates from Richmond and Charlotte would have the same education and meet the same high standards, but reach that goal in different ways. "The pool of candidates who can relocate and also pay the tariff for a three-year residency is shrinking. If all our eggs are in that basket, we could wake up some September and be in serious trouble. Alternative education is not a cancer—it simply reaches a different market."[47] His presentation was persuasive. The Charlotte Presbytery and the Union Board of Trustees voted to finalize their plans for a Charlotte campus.

Charlotte Presbytery then created the Task Force on a Theological Seminary Presence in Charlotte. This task force, with Malcolm Brownlee as moderator, had a twenty-one-member coordinating council, with fifteen additional members in three subcommittees. In concert with Union-PSCE supporters in the area and with the seminary administration, the task force asked four other North and South Carolina presbyteries (Coastal Carolina, Providence, Salem, and Western North Carolina) to join them. The task force would advise the presbyteries how to coordinate their efforts to support the establishment of a seminary in Charlotte. They also met with representatives from Columbia (CTS), Reformed Theological Seminary, and Gordon-Conwell, as well as Barbara Wheeler, president of Auburn Seminary, and Max Muhleman, a marketing consultant with the professional sports teams in Charlotte, who would focus on the "market" for students and some financial issues. They also met with Jack Rogers, vice president for the Southern California Program of San Francisco Theological Seminary,[48] to study how San Francisco did the planning and budgeting for the extension.

In January 1998, Katherine M. Dunlop, of the University of North Carolina, presented a study to the task force titled "Potential Models for Seminary Education." She reviewed the advantages and disadvantages of five models of education: the "university" model and four "nontraditional" models (night school, intensive semesters, cohort, and electronic).[49] In addition, Barbara Wheeler recommended a "feeder" model.[50] That is, students would spend one or two years in Charlotte and then go to Richmond.[51] Students, however, wanted to attend Charlotte precisely because they did not want to move. Requiring them to move to Richmond would undermine the entire concept of a satellite campus.

The Task Force selected the cohort model (in which students admitted at the same time would remain together throughout their education, by moving through the curriculum collectively instead of individually selecting classes) leading to the MDiv and MACE degrees as the best option for the Charlotte campus. The cohort model would allow Charlotte's calendar to be designed for and organized around part-time students. The MDiv coursework would be the same as Richmond, yet since classes would be held at nights and on weekends, it would take almost six years to complete (while the MACE coursework would take about four). Whereas some wanted technology (such as interactive television and electronic self-study courses) to be Charlotte's centerpiece,[52] President Weeks insisted that tenure-track faculty in Charlotte was vital because it would give Charlotte students the same education as found on the Richmond campus and make Charlotte eligible for accreditation.[53]

For the next two years the Charlotte Task Force worked to finalize details. The proposal to establish an accredited institution granting the master of divinity (MDiv) and the master of arts in Christian education (MACE) was presented to Charlotte Presbytery at its February meeting in 2000. The Presbytery Council voted 14-1 to support the proposal and to take it to the floor of the presbytery. On February 22, Charlotte Presbytery heard a forty-minute presentation from nine members of the Charlotte Task Force. The presentation was based on four primary issues: the requirement for a new method of delivering theological education, the need to serve African American churches, a recommitment to serve small churches, and the assurance of financial viability.[54]

Price Gwynn and Basil Irwin led the presentations on the floor of the presbytery by arguing that the denomination and its seminaries had to move into the future and explore new methods of making theological education available. Echoing Walter W. Moore in his arguments for building Schauffler Hall, Gwynn pointed out that an extension campus in Charlotte would teach the denomination how to deliver theological education in a new way and broaden Union's "brand."[55] By establishing a part-time school in Charlotte, students would not be dislocated from their homes and would remain active in their local congregations. "A new model of seminary education is not the wave of the future. It's the mode of the present. We mainline Presbyterians need to get with the program, and Charlotte is the place to be."[56]

Local support was the missing ingredient in the previous attempts to establish satellite campuses. A Union-PSCE presence in Charlotte would allow people in Charlotte and surrounding communities "the opportunity to think of Union as our seminary," and students would migrate to that campus.[57] The program would be streamlined and simple; MDiv and MA students only. The targets were for 20 new students each year, with 60 at the end of 3 years, and as many as 120 at the end of 6 years.[58]

Katherine Dunlap then spoke about how a Union-PSCE campus in Charlotte would provide education for African American Presbyterian pastors, educators, and other leaders. Charlotte is the center of African American Presbyterianism, with 20 percent of all African American Presbyterians in the country.[59] More African American communicants and churches were in Charlotte Presbytery than any other presbytery in all the PC(USA), including Los Angeles, New York, and the District of Columbia. In 2000 there were 73 African American students enrolled in all PC(USA) seminaries combined. Of those, 30 were at Johnson C. Smith Theological School in Atlanta. The other 43 were scattered among nine seminaries. Of the 73 current students, only 50 were interested in parish ministry. Thus the church could expect roughly 15 new African Americans entering the ministry each year. Those 15 would be expected to fill the anticipated 147 vacant pulpits in African American churches across the denomination. By graduating just four African American students each year, the

Charlotte campus could increase the available pool by 33 percent[60] and perhaps make more candidates available to Charlotte churches.[61]

Besides exploring a new model of theological education and serving African American congregations, Nellie Evans spoke about the need to recommit to small churches and how a Union-PSCE presence would lead this effort. In 2000, more than half of all Presbyterian seminarians were from congregations with more than 500 members. Only 12 percent of those students said they would consider a call from a church of 200 members or less. The thought was that in a denomination of small churches (8,000 out of 11,000 congregations in 2000), making it easy for students to attend seminary near where they live might make them more likely to serve a small church.[62]

Dreams cost money, and the training of ministers would require extensive financial support; the projected budget was $700,000 a year. In his presentation, Bill White pointed out that this figure was far less than a residential campus; the Charlotte campus was designed so its fixed cost would be lower than that of a residential campus. He reported that the two largest fixed costs of a conventional seminary are maintenance (upkeep and replacement of the physical plant) and library expenses. The president of Queens College, Billy Wireman (who was also a Presbyterian elder), offered office and classroom space in Trexler Hall (above the cafeteria) as long as classes were held on the weekends.[63] "We won't have a dime in bricks and mortar, and only a few books in a corner of somebody else's library."[64] More important, Charlotte Presbytery had pledged $100,000 toward the new campus, and the four other presbyteries (Coastal Carolina, Providence, Salem, and Western North Carolina) would be asked to pledge a total of $200,000. White proposed a fund-raising campaign to generate $300,000 from individuals and $100,000 from churches. He estimated that the first twenty students would generate $50,000 in fees and tuition and proposed asking Queens College for a $50,000 subvention. Finally, he proposed raising an endowment from institutions and foundations to generate $100,000.

John Kuykendall, UTS-PSCE board president, then told the presbytery that Charlotte was the ideal place for the satellite campus and the time was now. Charlotte was already a center for theological education. As he spoke, a thousand seminary students in the Charlotte area were enrolled in seven institutions, four of them started in the decade of the 1990s, and all theologically conservative. "We need a Presbyterian voice, a moderate option, a PC(USA) presence."

Malcolm Brownlee, moderator of the Task Force, placed a two-part motion before the presbytery. First, "that the Presbytery endorse the concept of a PC(USA) Charlotte seminary provided adequate funding be secured." Second, "that the Task Force be instructed to pursue the matter vigorously with Union/ PSCE and the four neighboring presbyteries in anticipation of a September opening in the year 2001 or 2002."[65] After the report was given, Leighton Ford (on the board of Gordon Conwell, which had about 200 students) stood on the floor of the presbytery and endorsed the plan for a satellite campus by saying Gordon-Conwell would work with Union-PSCE as colleagues.[66] Charlotte Presbytery voted overwhelmingly in favor of supporting a Union campus in Charlotte, and the other presbyteries followed suit by the end of June.[67]

The Task Force and President Weeks were determined not to repeat the experience of Columbia and San Francisco. Union-PSCE, in partnership with all five supporting presbyteries (Charlotte, Coastal Carolina, Providence, Salem, and Western North Carolina) pledged to raise $2.4 million for three years' operating funds.[68] By August 2001 already, $6 million[69] had been raised for the endowment for professors and student aid, with an additional $3 million by 2003.[70] This initial funding would give the impetus to hire four resident professors and allow Charlotte to be accredited.[71] Morton Library had been setting aside books since 1995 and would send 6,000 volumes to the new library in Charlotte, and Dr. Randolph Taylor, former pastor of Myers Park Presbyterian Church in Charlotte and the first moderator of the PC(USA), donated his extensive library to the Charlotte campus.[72] The enthusiasm was evident; in the end the money raised would provide operating funds for four years.[73]

Union-PSCE at Charlotte

Once agreement on the need for a new kind of educational platform was reached and funding was guaranteed, personnel had to be found to staff the new campus. Thomas W. Currie was called as professor of theology and the first dean of Union-PSCE Charlotte. A native of Texas and the son of a Presbyterian minister, Currie graduated from Austin Seminary and won a fellowship to the University of Edinburgh, where he received his PhD in theology.[74] He then served a church in Brenham, Texas, where he stayed for twelve years, and also served as adjunct faculty in theology in Austin's extension program; Currie began serving in Kernville, Texas, in 1989. President Weeks called him in the summer of 2000, asking if he would be interested in the job of dean of the Charlotte campus. Currie was offered the position in April 2001 and moved to Charlotte that June.

During the fall of 2001, the Charlotte campus held three open houses for prospective students. About 20 twenty students attended each open house, and the first cohort of 20 students began on February 2, 2002. Currie taught a course titled "The Christian Life." Richard N. Boyce taught Hebrew and would later teach practical theology and preaching. Pamela Mitchell-Legg moved from Richmond to Charlotte to teach Christian education, and Rodney Sadler started teaching Hebrew, Greek, and all the Bible classes in the fall of 2002. Another cohort of 16 was admitted that fall, bringing the total enrollment to 38, exceeding the original goal for first-year admissions. Thereafter, students were only admitted in the fall so as to keep the cohorts together as much as possible.

Charlotte attracted mostly older students. The traditional seminarian was right out of college, with an average age of 22 to 24. The average age of the Charlotte student was 30 to 35. Moreover, the Charlotte campus attracted students not just from the metropolitan area but also from all over the state and beyond. Students drove from Anderson, South Carolina; and Raleigh, Greensboro, and Black Mountain in North Carolina. One student rode the Megabus on an 8-hour round-trip from Atlanta.[75] On Friday night some would stay with members of area churches who had volunteered to put them up. The hosts became known as "Friday-night friends."

This nontraditional model has had to contend with issues that a residential campus usually never has to face. The rising price of gas made transportation an important cost factor. One student estimated that he drove the circumference of the earth in the five years he drove to and from the seminary. In addition, students are only on campus for one or two days a week, so losing a day due to weather is a big handicap. The time factor could also be off-putting; completing the MDiv degree in six years required an enormous commitment on the part of both student and family. Nevertheless, Charlotte has been a success. Beginning with 20 students in February 2002, by 2012 there were 81 enrolled, and 67 MDiv and 18 MACE students had graduated and were serving over 50 congregations, from Pennsylvania to Florida and South Korea.[76]

After eleven years at Queens University, the Charlotte campus moved to a new building on the grounds of Sharon Presbyterian Church in September 2012. The building was 22,000 square feet and cost $5.2 million. Just like Watts Hall in 1898, classes had to begin a week late because the building was behind schedule. And like the new campus in Richmond, when Charlotte's building was completed, it was already paid for.[77]

Its ability to attract highly motivated, competent students dedicated to parish ministry says a lot about Union's vitality.[78] And while the Charlotte campus is about three hundred miles from Brook Road, Walter W. Moore's commitment to tradition and progress remains symbolically intact; a stained-glass window removed from Schauffler Hall during the library renovation is prominently located in Charlotte's building.

The Extended Campus Program (ECP)

In addition to a satellite campus, Union established a digital presence with the Extended Campus Program (ECP). This innovative program was conceived by PSCE in the early 1990s to expand the school's reach. The PSCE administration understood that churches often hired a director of Christian education (DCE) with no formal training. Moreover, these DCEs were most often adults who needed flexible schedules. By putting a PSCE degree within reach from a long distance, these educators would be more effective in their jobs, show the value of a trained educator to their congregations, and increase their professional value to the church. At its inception, the ECP was envisioned as a summer program.

After Federation, ECP's popularity grew. From three graduates in 2004, ECP had 25 graduates by 2012. Yet the program's graduates are only part of the picture. From a January term program at Federation, it grew into an online program combined with yearly periods on campus. A student following the recommended calendar could graduate with an MACE degree in five years. Yet like other Internet courses, most students take only the courses they want without working for a degree. The number of students fluctuated from 43 in 2001–2 to 37 in 2006–7, and 16 at the beginning of the 2012 school year.

Utilizing the Internet has given Christian education students the ability to stay at home and draw on Union's expertise. The ECP also allowed churches flexibility; they were now able to encourage individuals to consider working as a DCE without the barrier of cost and travel.[79] At the same time, ECP gave Union an Internet presence, upon which it can build in the future.

Enrollment

The effects of Federation, the advent of the Charlotte campus, and the Extended Campus Program were seen in a more diverse and more national student body. In the 1998–99 school year (one year after Union and PSCE became one institution), total enrollment in Richmond was 330 (with 134 in the MDiv program, plus 82 in the MA track). Women comprised 46% of the MDiv students and 69% of those pursuing the MA degree; African Americans made up 5% of the MDiv students and 9% of the MA contingent, with one Hispanic person seeking the MDiv. Students came from 31 states and 12 foreign countries; they had graduated from over 130 colleges and universities. Presbyterians comprised 50% of the student body, and 26 other denominations were represented on campus.[80] The median age was 27 (5 years younger than 1993), and 50% were second-career students.[81] The average student age was 33.8, and slightly more than half were married.[82] Faculty-student ratio was about 1:13.[83]

The Charlotte campus opened in 2002, and by 2006 total enrollment in Richmond and Charlotte increased to 365 (with 178 seeking the MDiv, and 91 the MACE; the MA was phased out in 2006). Women comprised almost 60% of all students (48% of MDiv'ers, 58% of MACE seekers); African Americans made up 7% of MDiv students and 6% of MACE ones; Asian Americans composed 3% of MDiv'ers and 2% of MACE students; Hispanics and American Indians / Native Alaskans together were about 1% of each track. The geographical distribution of the student body on both campuses remained steady. Presbyterians increased their presence to 62% of the student body, and 20 other denominations were represented on campus. The average age of a basic degree student in Richmond declined to 31.2 years; students in the Extended Campus Program averaged 45.4 years; those in Charlotte averaged 42.9 years. The faculty-student ratio was 1:9.[84]

In 2012, at the end of 200 years, total enrollment in Richmond and Charlotte dropped to 221 (138 studying for the MDiv, plus 10 for the MACE). Women comprised 55% of the MDiv'ers and 70% of the MACE students; African Americans made up 12% of the MDiv'ers and 60% of the MACE students; Asian Americans composed 4% of the MDiv'ers and 1% of the MACE students; Hispanics and American Indian / Native Alaskans together were less than 1% of each track. Represented were 26 states and 8 foreign countries. The number of Presbyterians remained consistent at around 60%, as did the number of other denominations on campus, and students in Charlotte were generally older. The enrollment decline throughout this era mirrored national trends (nationally, seminaries were seeing a 7.5% decrease);[85] between 2002 and 2012, MDiv enrollment dropped from 176 (148 in Richmond, 28 in Charlotte) to 138 (79 in Richmond, 59 in Charlotte).

Graduate enrollment was also diverse. In 1998 there were 6 working for the ThM, 65 for the PhD (29% female, 6% African Americans), 16 for the EdD (56% female, 12% African Americans, 1 Hispanic) and 24 for the DMin (8%

female, 12% African Americans). In 2006 there were 6 working for the ThM (33% female, 16% African Americans), 53 for the PhD (45% female, 5% African Americans, and 6% Asian Americans), and 32 for the DMin (40% female, 9% African Americans). By 2012 there were two ThM and 32 PhD candidates (34% female, 5% African Americans, and 12% Asian Americans); the DMin degree had been suspended in 2008, and the final four students in the program graduated in 2012.

Student Life

Students in the first decade of the twenty-first century stood on a continuum with the Union students at the beginning of the twentieth century. Both took the same core classes, both wanted the seminary to reach out to the world, and both wanted courses that would prepare them for the contemporary church. Yet the average student (usually from a more uniform background) in 1900 understood the traditions and expectations of the church, but the average twenty-first-century student (who was not just male and not just white) felt freer to define what "the Tradition" meant for them as individuals. With specific issues being debated in the church, some observers were afraid that students were beginning to think of themselves as advocates for specific causes,[86] rather than preparing to serve the church.[87] Students and administrators detected confusion in the seminary community over issues of identity: "Why are we here?"[88]

Helen Byrd (MDiv, 2007) was a second-career student (formerly a teacher) and a Presbyterian from Norfolk.[89] She wanted to attend Union because it was close to her home, but she was initially reluctant because of the seminary's roots in southern history. Byrd did, however, feel welcomed as an African American and second-career student, and she enjoyed her time in Richmond. She remembers being surprised at the generational divide. Byrd had attended a Presbyterian boarding school and was active in her congregation, but many of her younger classmates did not have a background in the church. She was dismayed that there was drinking in the dorms (by both those with a church background and those lacking such). Byrd was also uncomfortable with the informality of the younger students, such as calling the president by his first name. She felt as though the professors did not see themselves as church leaders, and this attitude was reflected in the lack of interest in worship.

Many conversations have produced evidence that the perceived campus divisions of that time were manifested in three ways. First, there was a divide between students and faculty over the curriculum. Many students, both those who had grown up in the church and those for whom the church was relatively new, wanted more "practical" courses, such as the "Church in the World," which gave hands-on ministry experiences in the city. The faculty was initially resistant because they feared that practical courses were not "academic" enough.[90] The "Church in the World," however, was immensely popular and developed into the whole campus taking on daylong service projects in Richmond.

The second divide was over the use of technology. Students had now grown up with technology and were comfortable with the digital world. Consequently, they clamored for more technology in the classroom. The use of Blackboard software, online discussion groups, some distance learning, and dedicated Web sites became a reality. Like teachers at other institutions making the transition to using the Internet, many of the faculty were resistant because they did not see how learning could take place outside of the classroom.[91] Yet the popularity of the Extended Campus Program (ECP) showed that a digital presence was necessary. The resources devoted to wiring classrooms and securing the latest equipment meant that Union would use the latest technology to teach what Presbyterian ministers must know.

Third, while "practical" classes and technology can be seen as generational divides, church controversies were also felt on campus. The multiplicity of student organizations was unlike that of any other period. In 2001, for example, there were fifteen student organizations on campus: ARTS, Asian Women Alliance, Black Caucus, Commuter Students, Theophilus Fellowship (for conservative students), the Graduate Students Association, International Student Organization, Korean Students, Student Government Assembly, Union-PSCE Spouses, Whosoever/Safe Place, Handbell Choir, Koinonia, Liturgical Dancers, and Peace Fellowship.[92]

Despite the tendency to divide up, students found common ground. Veronica Thomas (MDiv, 2007) was a second-career student and found Union to be very welcoming. For her, however, the seminary's biggest challenge was not that she was African American or a woman, but that she was Pentecostal. Other students were uncomfortable with her style of worship and praying; one student even asked her not to "praise" in chapel. Like Helen Byrd, she was also surprised at the informality of the younger students. While she also did not like some of the behavior she saw, she decided to minister to the younger students. Thomas always kept extra food in her room and encouraged classmates and others to use her fax machine. When they were hungry or wanted to send a fax, they would talk with her, and many came to see her as a mother.[93]

Perhaps the biggest change from past years was that by 2006 students were officially allowed to store food in their rooms. "One compact refrigerator, which clearly conforms to proper electrical standards, operates on no more than 2.5 amps, has a capacity not exceeding 5 cubic feet, and whose maximum outside dimension does not exceed 48 inches, is permitted in each room." Auxiliary heaters, halogen lamps, and window air-conditioning units, however, were not.[94]

Reflecting the litigious tendencies in American society and the growing influence of the accreditation process, the 2000 Catalogue contains warnings never thought necessary in previous generations. It issues guidance about submitting work on time; cautions against plagiarism and cheating (outlining the way to report it); exhortations for students to treat one another with "civility, collegiality, and respect", admonishments against "gossip, rumor, secret accusations, and disregard for the needs and rights of others to pursue study, family life, recreation, and friendships" (along with grievance and mediation procedures); and admonitions against sexual misconduct and any form of "discrimination against others on the basis of race, national origin, ethnicity, sex, religion, color, creed, disability, sexual orientation, marital status, or age" (including harassment, intimidation, threats, and "disrupting the peaceful or orderly conduct of lectures, meetings, and worship services led or sponsored by those with whom one may disagree").[95]

But the routine of student life, despite the surface divisions, remained recognizable to the student of any era. The Calvin Ball and Bowl, impromptu dinners, the Current Events Lunch, picnics, Sprunts, and Pig & Profligacy barbeque remained highlights of the year, registering fond memories of those events. The daily schedule would also have been familiar to any student of the previous two centuries. Classes commenced at 8:30 a.m. Monday through Friday and lasted until 8:30 p.m., but 5:00 p.m. on Fridays.[96]

The *Richmond Times-Dispatch* still turned to Union to give perspective on current events. In March 2006, ethics professor Katie Cannon (who was the first African American woman ordained in the United Presbyterian Church and was initially reluctant to consider teaching at Union due to Robert Lewis Dabney's long shadow) and two other female ministers were interviewed by the *Times-Dispatch* for Women's History Month, on the hurdles still faced by women in ministry.[97] That November, John Carroll, New Testament professor, was interviewed in a front-page story on the Saturday before the vote to allow same-sex marriage in Virginia. Carroll argued that the fundamental issue was not marriage, but "the broader biblical concern with compassionate care for the marginalized" and "the way we approach the specific and contested matter of the treatment of sexual minorities in the church."[98] In January 2007, the *Washington Post* did a feature story on Alpheaus Zobule, a doctoral student from Ranonga, in the Solomon Islands, who translated the New Testament from Greek into the Lungga language. Lungga was not written until Zobule wrote two grammars that allowed it to become written. He was at Union for his PhD in biblical studies, and his dissertation compared parts of the Septuagint with the Hebrew Bible in preparation for his project to translate the Old Testament from Hebrew into Lungga.[99]

The 2001 Catalogue announced that Union-PSCE was part of the Washington Theological Consortium (WTC).[100] This meant that Union-PSCE students could take classes for credit at theological schools in Washington (D.C.), such as Howard, Wesley, and the Virginia Theological Seminary. At one point about twenty students from all member seminaries took classes at one another's school. By 2010, however, there is no mention of the WTC; driving to Washington was not a popular option. Each year's Catalogue also mentioned the Richmond Theological Consortium (RTC). The RTC still officially existed, but calendars were not coordinated, there was virtually no cross registration between schools, and the library agreement collapsed in 2008.

Alumni and Alumnae

For the first time in Union's history, a sizeable minority of graduates did not serve a congregation. The ten degrees offered by Union-PSCE after Federation represented an attempt to appeal to a wide variety of students and exert an influence through educated laypeople. Just as other Christian educational institutions, such as Liberty University in Lynchburg and Regent University in Virginia Beach, attracted students by their ethos, so Union sought students who would bring their faith to the fields of social work and criminal justice. Nevertheless, roughly 50% of the graduates of each class during this period went into the pastorate, 10% became directors of Christian education, 10% went to graduate school, 10% entered CPE programs, and 10% entered secular work (with the remaining entering the chaplaincy, teaching, and the administration of higher education). Union's impact on the denomination remained strong. Douglas Wayne Oldenburg (BD, 1960) was elected moderator of the General Assembly in 1998, and Syngman Rhee (director of the Asian-American Ministry Center, 1998–2011) was elected moderator in 2000.

Library

The Morton Library had been John Trotti's dream, and once it was built, he retired. (He passed away in 2014.) His successor, Milton J. Coalter, was called as librarian in 2004. A graduate of Davidson, he received his MDiv and ThM from Princeton Seminary. He was ordained by Palisades Presbytery and served for twenty years at Louisville Presbyterian Theological Seminary, first as library director, and later as vice president for library and information technology. Coalter served as acting president of Louisville Seminary in 2003 while an interim president was being sought. Along with President Weeks and John Mulder, he was a codirector and coeditor of *The Presbyterian Predicament* (1990), a major study of the Presbyterian Church and other mainline Christian denominations. By the year 2000 the library held 315,636 volumes and 98,803 nonprint items, and it received 1,358 periodicals and scholarly journals.[101] The William Smith Morton Library was the center of campus; 81,500 people had entered Spence Library during its last year, while 96,000 entered the new library during the 1999–2000 school year.[102] By 2006 there were 342,253 volumes, along with 85,426 nonprint items held in Richmond, and 14,666 volumes in Charlotte.

The widespread availability of digital resources (such as Google Books and Christian Classics Ethereal Library: CCEL) affected the library by the turn of the century. In the year 2000, circulation stood at 44,621, but declined steadily every year thereafter. In 2005, circulation was 33,336; in 2012 it was down to 21,002. Students are now able to access reserve reading for their classes online through Blackboard and other Internet resources, rather than going to the Reserve Book Reading Room. Also, classes require fewer research papers than in the past. The library, however, kept pace with the technological changes, as it always has. More periodicals and books are now available electronically. Beginning in 2011 the library began keeping statistics on student "borrowing" from proprietary databases. By 2012 there were 15,659 inquiries, 35,802 searches, and 15,607 full text downloads from the 36 online research databases and 519 journals. The William Smith Morton Library was the 29th largest theological library in the country in 2012.

Morton Library carried forward the seminary's aspirations: Brown Library at Hampden-Sydney signaled that Union intended to be a research institution. Spence Library on the new campus in Richmond declared that Union would be modern. And Latta Library asserted that Union would be the equal of any research seminary in the country. Now Morton Library anchored Union to Richmond and became the de facto center of the RTC. Although students may not have been able to take classes on one another's campuses, the library allowed

STVU and BTSR to be accredited. Indeed, the library was originally designed to serve UTS, PSCE, STVU, and BTSR.

Because of scheduling issues and calendars, the RTC remained an unrealized ideal. It finally unraveled in 2008. An ATS accreditation team visiting STVU thought that the support agreement with the library was not advantageous to STVU, so STVU canceled the agreement in April 2008. The library lost $500,000 in income per year,[103] and the loss of STVU students caused a huge decline in circulation. In addition, as BTSR saw its enrollment decline, they reduced their library support, and the library was forced to cut staff, book acquisitions, and journal subscriptions. Just as the library symbolized the hopes for the RTC, it also symbolized the end of the ideal.

Facing the Future

President Weeks presided over more changes to the Union campus than any other president other than Walter W. Moore. He combined Union Theological Seminary and the Presbyterian School of Christian Education into one institution. During his term UTS established a new campus in Charlotte, thereby adding an alternative to the residential campus model. In addition, the ECP began to establish itself. Schauffler Hall was remade into Morton Library, and the old Latta Library was renovated and became the Allen and Janette Early Center for Christian Education and Worship. He established the Carl Howie Center for Science, Art, and Theology; the Asian-American Ministry Center; and the Institute for Reformed Theology. He supported Project Burning Bush and the Rehoboth Project, as well as initiating the Dawe Lecture series.

Just as John Holt Rice needed money to establish his "school of the prophets," President Weeks knew that the vision of Union Seminary in the twenty-first century would not be cheap. The One In Mission Campaign was launched on June 1, 2001, and ended on June 30, 2007, with his retirement. Over 6,100 donors gave more than $56 million (exceeding the original goal by $6 million), and Union added more than 2,000 new donors to its rolls. The One In Mission Campaign was unique in that it combined individual, congregational, and corporate donations. Eleven donors gave more than $1 million each, including Mr. and Mrs. J. Roy Davis Jr., the Dickson Foundation, Mrs. Janette B. Early, Mr. and Mrs. F. O'Neil Griffin, the Lilly Endowment, Dalton L. McMichael, Dr. and Mrs. Samuel W. Newell, Mr. and Mrs. Josiah P. Rowe III, and the family of Alice Jones Thompson and Will McIlwaine Thompson.[104] Despite the national apprehension from the attacks on 9/11 and turmoil in the church, Union remained dear to the hearts of Presbyterians. This campaign was the largest in Union's history.[105]

Right before his retirement, Louis Weeks made his last report to the board. He stated that the endowment had grown from $70.3 million in 1994 to $122.8 million in 2007 (despite the economic downturn), making Union eighth among American theological seminaries in financial resources.[106] He had also brought about the federation of Union and PSCE, established the campus in Charlotte, and initiated Union's digital presence by expanding the ECP. By 2005 the campus was wireless, and the software for the library and business offices had the latest versions available.[107] Besides the graduates, President Weeks was most proud of what he saw as a change in ethos. In his view, seminary was no longer a "boot camp," but a school with a "winsome learning environment for folk in every degree program."[108] He related what others had told him: "Union had a sense of being Reformed that is more distinct than any other Presbyterian seminary."[109]

Brian Keith Blount

In previous years, even with the advent of search committees, Union traditionally looked to its own graduates for a president. To find a successor to Louis Weeks, however, the search committee looked at other candidates, and Brian K. Blount quickly stood out. Born in Smithfield, Virginia, he was raised a Baptist. He received his BA from the College of William & Mary in 1978 and his MDiv from Princeton Theological Seminary in 1981. In January 1982 he was taken under the care of Southern Virginia Presbytery and was installed as pastor of Carver Memorial Presbyterian Church at Newport News on June 2, 1982. He served Carver Memorial in 1982–88. Between 1988 and 1992 he studied for his PhD at Emory University and served as an instructor at Candler School of Theology and Columbia Theological Seminary. Upon graduating from Emory in 1992, he was called as an assistant professor at Princeton Theological Seminary, and in 1998 he was promoted to associate professor. In 2003 he was named professor of New Testament interpretation.

President Blount originally did not want to be president of Union, but John Kuykendall visited him in Princeton, and he decided to go ahead with the process because he sensed that the presidency of Union was a true call. He had always been interested in growing things, and being president was an opportunity to grow something important. Brian Blount was inaugurated as Union's seventh president on July 1, 2007, appointed to the Walter W. Moore and Charles E. S. Kraemer Presidential Chairs, and also appointed as professor of New Testament.

Although not a Union graduate, Blount was more like Walter W. Moore than any other president. He had served a church, was a noted biblical scholar, and was concerned that Union "should be the place where people (students, church members) [could] satisfy their intellectual curiosity in a way that serves the church." He saw himself as a guide, to help the seminary understand that it was now in a national context, and as a healer, to mend the divisions in the seminary community.

President Blount was also unlike Union's previous leaders in that he was African American. In an address contemplating the meaning of the inauguration of Union's first African American president, and the first African American president of any Presbyterian seminary, Professor Samuel K. Roberts emphasized the historical improbability of Blount's inauguration. Using E. T. Thompson's *Days of Our Years* (1962), Roberts noticed the irony that John Holt Rice "served for eight years as pastor of the Cub Creek Church in Charlotte County, Virginia. The salary was altogether inadequate for his support, so Dr. Rice had

52. Brian Keith Blount, president, 2007–

run a small farm with the help of a few slaves brought to him by his wife."[110] The cultural context of Union Seminary was slavery and sectionalism; the legacy of Robert Lewis Dabney could still be felt.[111] But it was also Union students who initiated the Seventeenth Street Mission and marched for civil rights. If President Blount symbolized the contradictions and tensions of the past, he also embodied the hopes for the future.

Although separated by two centuries, President Blount's inaugural speech was in the tradition of John Holt Rice. The new president did not have to explain the need for an educated ministry, argue for a Presbyterian contribution to the wider theological conversation, or place Union in the scheme of a national denomination; these issues had been settled. Yet Rice and Blount both saw that their institutions faced a changing culture and context. Rice wanted his school of the prophets to address deism and revivalism, but within a confident and even triumphal context. Using the image of Lazarus from John 11, President Blount urged the seminary to see that times had changed. Just as Lazarus had been healthy, so Union had a beautiful campus, an impressive faculty, supportive alumni, eager students, and a transformative history.

Yet the new president saw that Lazarus was ill. He recognized that the Presbyterian Church (USA) was hemorrhaging members, that the seminaries "of all denominational and religious stripes" were threatened by shrinking finances, and graduates were burdened by crushing debt at graduation. Closer to home he noted: "After 10 years, we're still fighting the ghosts of federating Presbyterian School of Christian Education and Union Theological Seminary. After 5 years, we're still trying to work out the complexities of having two campuses more than 300 miles apart," along with mounting financial and identity problems.

Yet in the middle of this bleak picture, President Blount was confident in the hope of a loving Lord. Just as Jesus let Lazarus die in order to resurrect him, so the Lord was ready to renew Union. There was no doubt that this renewal process would be difficult and painful.

> This is how God's love works in John's Gospel and in this Lazarus story. It is how God's love is at work in our stories today. In our seminary story. Are we ready for this kind of renewing love?
>
> As we gather this day to inaugurate not just my time in a new office, but to imagine the renewal of this venerable institution, we gather together in love for this community, for what it has been and for what we believe God intends it can be. If this Lazarus love story has anything to say to us at this moment in time, it says that if we love Union Theological Seminary and Presbyterian School of Christian Education to the degree that Jesus loved Lazarus, then, even as we so deeply treasure and cherish all that it has been to and for us, we must be willing to let the Union Theological Seminary of the last two centuries, the Presbyterian School of Christian Education of the last nine decades, and the Union-PSCE of the last ten years go so that God can renew us, despite how difficult, how painful, how glorious that renewal process might be. Like Jesus, we look at the difficulties that face us and do what it takes to provoke the confrontation necessary to bring about God's glorification, knowing that the path to such glory may well travel the road of a cross. For Jesus, that meant staying put. For us, it means moving out.

Just as Walter W. Moore challenged Union Seminary to be a transformative leader at the beginning of the twentieth century, President Blount challenged the seminary community to commit to renewal at the beginning of the twenty-first; to be ready to sell old buildings, transform the curriculum to meet the needs of a new church and student body, coordinate two geographically separated campuses, transition to a digital environment, and solve the seminary's financial issues. Just as Jesus called to Lazarus to come out of the tomb, President Blount was certain that the Lord was calling Union to leave its comfortable past and begin to serve in a new way.[112] The "copious fountain" that John Holt Rice saw so clearly would continue to water the church and the world with faithful, educated, and sensitive ministers to preach, teach, and heal in a new context.

President Blount spent his first year talking to students, staff, administrators, alums, and consultants to determine where the seminary stood and how it should proceed. He prompted the Union community to begin rethinking what Union could be by issuing the "Catalyst for Conversation" in 2008. This paper was an analysis of Union's position in four areas: financial, programmatic, physical plant, and identity. Perhaps the most immediate concern was funding. As a result of the 2007 financial meltdown, Union's endowment plummeted from $122.8 million to $114 million in 2008 (and it would decline to $90 million in 2009 before increasing again). While most institutions tried to withdraw less than 4.5% from their endowment for current operating expenses, in 2004 Union withdrew 6.8%, in 2005 7.2% was withdrawn, in 2006 7.4%, and in 2007 and 2008 7.8%. If the 2009 budget was to be sustained, 8.25% of the endowment would have to be withdrawn. To reduce the rate of withdrawal under 5% by 2014 would take difficult choices, requiring Union-PSCE to clarify its purpose.[113]

Finances required that Union's programs be focused. President Blount argued that "Union-PSCE, instead of doing a few things well, attempts to do many things sufficiently." The feeling persisted that "many programs have been added because they represented opportunities that appeared for one reason or another to enhance the profile of the institution." A comparison of the 1991 and 2007 Catalogues demonstrates a veritable "program explosion" that stretched the seminary's resources too thin and resulted in a "curricular maze." In short, Union-PSCE offered too many degrees for the size of its faculty and student body.

Programmatic concerns extended to the PhD program and the seminary's outmoded "delivery platforms." President Blount argued that the PhD program funding be increased or the program disbanded. "Union-PSCE too often loses applicants because it cannot offer competitive scholarships." The decision was made to suspend the PhD and DMin programs for a year to restructure them. He observed that Union had three platforms: the traditional residential model in Richmond, the commuter model in Charlotte, and the online model with the Extended Campus Program (ECP). Some in Richmond were suspicious of ECP because it was online and apprehensive of the Charlotte campus because it was not a full-time residential program. Nevertheless, both programs were working; the ECP was attracting students; by 2008 the count showed 14 of the 19 MDiv Charlotte graduates as serving congregations in Virginia, North Carolina, South Carolina, and Alabama. Of the 4 MACE graduates, 2 were serving churches: 1 in Pennsylvania and 1 in South Korea.

As a result of Federation, Union-PSCE acquired the property and buildings once owned by the Presbyterian School of Christian Education. Although the former PSCE campus represented a significant emotional bond with the past, these buildings also caused Union-PSCE to expend twice as much on property and related costs as any other PC(USA) seminary. In 2006–7, Union-PSCE allocated 16.9% of total expenditures on physical plant maintenance; the peer median amount was 7.7%. Moreover, a 2002 engineering study estimated it would cost almost $2 million to renovate Rice alone; meanwhile all student housing needed renovation.[114]

Behind these figures was the reality of American Presbyterianism and contemporary theological education. Nationally, MDiv enrollment was declining.[115] While enrollment in the Richmond MDiv program fell, enrollment at the Charlotte campus was on the upswing. The fall of 2003 saw 109 students enrolled in the Richmond MDiv program and 42 in Charlotte. In 2007, Richmond MDiv enrollment dropped to 83, while Charlotte rose to 73. The trend was the same for the MACE program: the fall of 2003 had 42 students enrolled in Richmond and 9 in Charlotte; in the fall of 2007, that number dropped to 18 in Richmond and 14 in Charlotte.

The DMin program also reflected the changing realities of theological education. The in-sequence DMin degree had been abolished in 1982 in favor of a generalist DMin degree designed for pastors who had served a church for at least three years. The program was put under continuing education in 1983, but enrollment remained fairly small throughout the 1990s. In March 2000, the Practical Theology Department voted to suspend admissions to the PhD program in practical theology, replacing it with the DMin. Many felt that placing the DMin program in the Practical Theology Department would boost the importance of the degree and attract more serving pastors.

The DMin degree, as in most other seminaries, became more specialized in 2004 when a small-church ministry track was added and ministers from small churches were not charged tuition (although there were no gifts or grants to underwrite the program). Response was positive, and the DMin program grew to a maximum of 42 students by 2005, but enrollment then declined. As questions began to be asked about the proliferation of programs, the DMin degree was seen as redundant. Admission to the program was suspended for two academic years from 2008 to assess its viability. The DMin degree was eliminated—along with the MATS, and the MDiv/MSW and MACE/MSW (offered in conjunction with Virginia Commonwealth University).

With a declining enrollment and shrinking finances, President Blount focused Union's resources. By 2009, nine degree programs had been pared to four: the MDiv, the MACE, the ThM, and (after a one-year hiatus) the PhD.[116] Moreover, he insisted on using technology to integrate the Charlotte campus and the ECP, envisioning a "digital campus."

> I would argue that a more creative approach to the three different delivery platforms in the seminary system would allow for the kind of flexibility that would be attractive to students in every degree program that we offer. Students could also begin commuter-type studies at the Charlotte campus and finish up in the residential Richmond campus. Students could also begin in Richmond and finish up in either the Charlotte or the ECP platform. An even more creative approach would enable a connection between the ECP platforms and the Richmond and Charlotte platforms. This would, of course, presuppose that even some MDiv courses would be offered via the ECP platform.[117]

The physical plant was reduced to a more manageable size to reduce costs: Lingle Hall, DuBose Hall, and the Newbury building were leased to J. Sargeant Reynolds Community College. In addition, Mission Court was razed in May 2010. As the demand for missionary housing lessened, the board of trustees for Mission Court had transferred the buildings to the seminary in 1992. They had been vacant for almost a decade and had fallen into disrepair. It was too expensive to renovate the structures, even with tax credits available for the restoration of historic buildings.[118]

Federation had not only resulted in stretched finances, confusion in programs, and deferred building maintenance. Combining the two schools had also blurred Union's identity and reflected contradictory visions between the seminary as an academic institution or a church-oriented school. President Blount declared:

Union-PSCE is more a treaty than a name. It is certainly not a descriptive name. Union Theological Seminary and Presbyterian School of Christian Education does not describe the primary identity of the institution. It is no longer a school of Christian Education; it is a theological seminary. The name should reflect this identity.

President Blount wanted to grow something new, and a new beginning would be reflected in a new name. He hired a branding consultant who would "help us reach some consensus, no matter how agonizingly achieved, on a new name."[119] On May 15, 2009, the board of trustees voted to change the name of Union Theological Seminary–Presbyterian School of Christian Education to Union Presbyterian Seminary.

The Threads of History

Theological education, like the Christian faith, must resolve several tensions. On one hand, faith is intensely personal. Every follower of Jesus Christ has to personally claim what they believe. On the other hand, Christian faith has a corporate expression. What we believe was formulated almost two millennia ago; a seminary both transmits what has been handed down by the "great cloud of witnesses" and gives each student the tools to reinterpret the faith tradition for their own time and place. A seminary that serves a specific faith tradition faces additional tensions. The school must decide how, and by what proportion, it will appropriate the scholarship of the church universal and apply that learning to its own specific tradition. Then the institution must decide how to appropriate and teach that tradition to its students, while reinterpreting it to meet the demands of the modern world.

To teach its ministerial candidates, American Presbyterianism adopted the theological curriculum from the Church of Scotland. The Book of Discipline (1560) did not require indoctrination in specific details of the Bible or theology. Rather, the traditional curriculum ensured that each student would be firmly grounded in the Reformed tradition by mastering five subjects: Hebrew, Greek, theology, church history, and polity. Presbyterians accepted the scaffolding of John Knox's curriculum, confronting the emotionalism of revivals and the skepticism of the Enlightenment with critical inquiry, competent exposition, and faithful engagement with the world. Moses Hoge and John Holt Rice used these five subjects as the foundation for Union Theological Seminary.

No one seriously questioned the traditional curriculum until Robert Lewis Dabney submitted his "Memorial on Theological Education" to the Committee on Seminaries at the 1869 General Assembly. He recommended reorganizing the seminary curriculum and adding more classes in theology, specifically apologetics. The fact that the General Assembly rejected Dabney's Memorial, based on Benjamin Mosby Smith's arguments that Dabney's proposals would diminish the prominence of biblical languages, shows how important the traditional curriculum was to the Presbyterian Church. Although some questioned the emphasis on learning Greek and Hebrew from the late 1880s up to 1963, the biblical language requirement was never in serious danger of elimination.

Additions to the curriculum were built around the five traditional subject areas. English Bible was added to the curriculum in the 1890s, Christian sociology was a required course by the second decade of the twentieth century, Christian education was fully integrated into course offerings by the 1920s, fieldwork was required by the end of the 1940s, and pastoral care was part of the curriculum by the end of the 1950s. None of these additions ever threatened the primacy of biblical languages and exegesis, theology, church history, and polity.

During the twentieth century, however, many outside Union questioned the need for the first-degree seminarian to know Hebrew and Greek. The studies on theological education in 1920, 1924, 1934, and H. Richard Niebuhr's 1956 survey all questioned whether the resources dedicated to teaching biblical languages might be better employed for subjects more obviously connected with contemporary church life. Union Theological Seminary in Virginia, however, never altered the commitment to the traditional curriculum. Instead, it struggled against becoming "a Moody Institute on the one hand or a theological university on the other."[120] While the definition of an educated minister has changed in the last two hundred years, Union's dedication to the traditional curriculum has remained firm.

From its inception Union has tried to be open to the church universal. In his report to the Synod of Virginia in 1816, Moses Hoge made it clear that "our theological seminary is not intended exclusively for the advantage of any denomination." He wanted his students "to distinguish between the essentials of the Christian religion, respecting which the Protestant churches are so generally agreed, and the circumstantials, about which there have been so many worse than fruitless debates." John Holt Rice institutionalized Union's expansive outlook by raising money and attracting students from the North and other faith traditions. While George Baxter and Robert L. Dabney tried to turn Union into an exclusively southern institution, Benjamin Mosby Smith kept Rice's vision alive. Although Walter W. Moore had no use for a reunited church, it was his devotion to scholarship and innovative teaching methods that caused him to move the campus from rural Hampden Sydney to Richmond.

Union Presbyterian Seminary has, for most of its history, thought of itself as a "southern" institution. Yet it has always drawn students and support from the North and, beginning with Walter W. Moore, Union has participated in the national and international theological conversation. Benjamin Rice Lacy and James A. Jones made Union a force in theological education through their activities with the American Association of Theological Schools (AATS). At the beginning of the post–World War II era, Union was leading the PC(US) out of its theological shell and engaging the wider world through biblical theology. Professors so inspired their students that many renounced the culture of their birth and demonstrated for civil rights. Union was early in recognizing the ministry and gifts of women. With Reunion and Federation, Union seeks to take the best of the PC(US) tradition into a new church in a new century.

Union has always engaged the world. From graduating a majority of PC(US) missionaries to students debating topical subjects, UTS has always prompted its graduates to confront their context. Walter W. Moore understood that the Hampden-Sydney campus was too isolated to challenge students to grow, and the relocation to Richmond released a hitherto unknown desire for local missions. Faced with unprecedented urban challenges in a new century, students organized new types of ministries and began to dismantle Dabney's legacy of the spirituality of the church.

At the same time, Union embodied the tension between reform and the status quo in our national life. The students at Hampden-Sydney campus left their books and fought for the Confederacy. About a century later, many of them led the drive for civil rights. Throughout its history, Union's students have been acutely aware of the contradictions between the society they served and the ideals espoused by that society. While everyone did not always agree on methods, timing, and the fundamental issues of the day, Union students were aware of the world around them and were involved in the turmoil of their times.

Union's influence on the denomination and theological education has been more subtle. While UTS, throughout its history, graduated over 40 percent of PCUS moderators and its share of PC(USA) moderators, Union's hallmark has been its willingness to combine innovation and tradition. The campus moved to Richmond as America was urbanizing. Union led the PCUS and most of the American Protestant church in practical education by putting Christian sociology, Christian education, pastoral care, and fieldwork in the curriculum. The Reigner Recording Library and WRFK showed how technology could impact American theological education in the 1950s. By adding a campus in Charlotte and offering the Extended Campus Program, UPS is following Walter W. Moore's progressive ideas for theological education. The creative tension between innovation and tradition has sometimes been uncomfortable, but it has also given the graduates a distinctive heritage while moving the church forward.

On January 25, 2000, John Trotti (BD, 1960) gave a speech at the alumni/ae luncheon. Everyone had heard about the discord on campus: the Kingsbury/ Ottati controversy was still raw, Federation was an emotional issue, and Charlotte was on the horizon. What would become of Union? Trotti acknowledged that the "giants in the land of our day are gone." But he reminded his listeners that "giants are still here, praying over classes." The best days were not behind beloved Union. "Some may look back and say in this day or that, 'There were such bright and wonderful students, the best and the brightest.' Well, friends, there were, and I am here to say, 'There [still] are.'"[121]

John Trotti was right. The dynamism of Union Presbyterian Seminary is still there for all to see. Earlier generations may not recognize the names of the new buildings (and there is a new building in Charlotte), but they would recognize the academic rigor, the devotion to the church, and the camaraderie of classmates.

Along with other seminaries, Union faces real challenges in the future. The increasing specialization of seminary education, the decline in denominational membership, and the rise in student debt—these have led to a fraying of connections with local congregations. Indeed, with a shrinking denomination and a decline in MDiv enrollment (a nationwide trend),[122] there are some who wonder if Union Presbyterian Seminary has anything to offer contemporary life. And the reply is simple: Union's definition of an educated minister has not changed in two centuries. Armed with biblical languages, theology, church history, and polity, Union graduates have confronted deism, skepticism, romanticism, transcendentalism, Marxism, Darwinism, existentialism, postmodernism, and the psychobabble of the twentieth century. They have proclaimed the gospel with integrity, stood up for faith, and challenged both heart and mind because they did "not turn to the right or to the left" (Deut. 5:32).

Afterword

One of my most enjoyable experiences in writing this book has been to take a break, leave the rare-book room, walk down the quad, and sit on a bench near the "old" library on a warm summer night. Walter W. Moore and generations of students, professors, and staff would still recognize the campus. There are no cars on the quad now, and the paths are paved, but the bookstore is back in Richmond Hall. Spence Library is largely quiet; most of the foot traffic comes from Morton Library, and students still live in Westminster. The lights may be brighter, but the campus buildings would be recognizable.

The one constant in Union's history has been the drive to educate ministers to confront the culture. John Holt Rice employed the traditional curriculum to challenge both the simplistic answers of the revival tent and the skeptical culture that declared "Reason" would make faith irrelevant. The challenges have shifted with each generation, but a learned ministry continues to meet the world head-on. Rice's vision remains Union's purpose: to educate students to confront an antagonistic world with a ministry intellectually equipped not just to defend faith and critique the poverty of human knowledge, but also to be with people as they die and assure them of life in Jesus Christ.

I have been asked many times whether Union has something to say to our church and culture. While it would be tempting to support one camp or another, Union's history shows how the seminary can be a healing agent. In 1857, Matthew Lyle Lacy from Douglas Church, a New School church in Prince Edward County and under the care of the New School Second Presbytery of Philadelphia, was admitted to Union, the bastion of Old School Presbyterianism.[1] Lacy should have attended Princeton, but he chose Union instead. Undoubtedly he wanted to stay close to home, but his presbytery also had the confidence to approve his presence at the Hampden-Sydney seminary. Faculty minutes record nothing special about this student, yet it is clear that despite Union's Old School position, the church had confidence in the education it offered.

As long as Union maintains its devotion to biblical learning in service of the entire church, it will retain the confidence of all parts of the church; there is still a lot of history to be written. At the seventieth-anniversary exercises in 1894, Robert Burwell (1826; he knew Rice personally) was certain of Union's future and rejoiced that in 1964 "another will stand here to tell the story, and what a glorious history will it be of the mercy and truth and faithfulness of our Covenant God and Father through Jesus Christ."[2] He could not have imagined World Wars I and II, the civil rights movement, the ordination of women, and the Internet. Yet he was certain that whatever challenges the future held, Union would faithfully confront them and remain vital to the proclamation of Jesus Christ. Although Union Presbyterian Seminary will continue to face many divisive issues and trials, I share his certainty.

Endnotes

CHAPTER 1: Congregations Are Perishing for Lack of Ministers

1. *Minutes of the Presbyterian Church in America, 1706–1788*, ed. Guy Klett (Philadelphia: Presbyterian Historical Society, 1976), viii.

2. Charles Augustus Briggs, *American Presbyterianism* (New York: Charles Scribner's Sons, 1885), 1.

3. *Minutes of the Presbyterian Church in America, 1706–1788*, 1.

4. William B. Sprague, *Annals of the American Pulpit*, vol. 3, *Presbyterian* (New York: Robert Carrier and Brothers, 1860), 1.

5. Robert P. Davis and James H. Smylie, *Virginia Presbyterians in American Life: Hanover Presbytery (1755–1980)*, ed. Patricia Aldridge (Richmond, VA: Hanover Presbytery, 1982), 8.

6. *Minutes of the Presbyterian Church in America, 1706–1788*, 3.

7. Sprague, *Annals of the American Pulpit*, 3:6.

8. R. P. Davis and Smylie, *Virginia Presbyterians in American Life*, 9.

9. Ibid., 7; *Minutes of the Presbyterian Church in America, 1706–1788*, 10.

10. Wilbur E. Garrett, ed., *Historical Atlas of the United States* (Washington, DC: National Geographic Society, 1988), 82, 142.

11. John Knox and William Croft Dickinson, *John Knox's History of the Reformation in Scotland*, vol. 2 (New York: Philosophical Library, 1950), 298.

12. Ibid.

13. John H. S. Burleigh, *A Church History of Scotland* (London: Oxford University Press, 1960), 167.

14. Ibid., 169.

15. R. P. Davis and Smylie, *Virginia Presbyterians in American Life*, 9.

16. *Minutes of the Presbyterian Church in America, 1706–1788*, 4, 9.

17. Ernest Trice Thompson, "The First Years," in *The Days of Our Years: The Historical Convocations Held April 24–27, 1962, as a Feature of the Celebration of the Sesquicentennial of Union Theological Seminary in Virginia* (Richmond, VA: Union Theological Seminary, 1962), 7.

18. Herbert C. Bradshaw, *History of Hampden-Sydney College*, vol. 1, *From the Beginnings to the Year 1856* (Durham, NC: Fisher-Harrison, 1976), 6.

19. *Minutes of the Presbyterian Church in America, 1706–1788*, 104, 122, 153–54, 157, 174, 177–79, 182, 186, 212.

20. G. MacLaren Brydon, "The Anti-Ecclesiastical Laws of Virginia," *Virginia Magazine of History and Biography* 64, no. 3 (July 1956): 264.

21. Bradshaw, *History of Hampden-Sydney College*, 1:5.

22. *Minutes of the Presbyterian Church in America, 1706–1788*, 157.

23. *Report of a Committee of the General Assembly of the Presbyterian Church, Exhibiting the Plan of a Theological Seminary* (New York: J. Seymour, 1810), 9.

24. *Minutes of the Presbyterian Church in America, 1706–1788*, 212.

25. Bradshaw, *History of Hampden-Sydney College,* 1:7.

26. *Minutes of the Presbyterian Church in America, 1706–1788,* 211–13.

27. Bradshaw, *History of Hampden-Sydney College,* 1:6.

28. Leonard J. Trinterud, *The Forming of an American Tradition: A Re-Examination of Colonial Presbyterianism* (Philadelphia: Westminster Press, 1949), 64.

29. Ibid., 65.

30. *Minutes of the Presbyterian Church in America, 1706–1788,* 213, 341, 368.

31. William Henry Foote, *Sketches of Virginia, Historical and Biographical, Second Series* (Philadelphia: J. B. Lippincott, 1855), 158; Sprague, *Annals of the American Pulpit,* 3:140.

32. Foote, *Sketches of Virginia,* 490–91.

33. William E. Thompson, *Her Walls before Thee Stand: The 235-Year History of the Presbyterian Congregation at Hampden-Sydney, Virginia* (Hampden Sydney, VA: William E. Thompson, 2010), 161. Hampden Sydney is the place name and may be hyphenated as a compound adjective, such as Hampden-Sydney College. However, the sources often hyphenate the place name too.

34. Sprague, *Annals of the American Pulpit,* 3:426.

35. Henry Richard Mahler Jr., "A History of Union Theological Seminary in Virginia, 1807–1865" (ThD diss., Union Theological Seminary in Virginia, 1951), 18–19.

36. Bradshaw, *History of Hampden-Sydney College,* 1:122.

37. James H. Smylie, "Clerical Perspectives on Deism: Paine's *The Age of Reason* in Virginia," *Eighteenth Century Studies* 6, no. 2 (Winter 1972–73): 217.

38. Mahler, "A History of Union Theological Seminary in Virginia, 1807–1865," 20, 29.

39. Edwin Scott Gaustad, *Historical Atlas of Religion in America* (New York: Harper & Row, 1962), 3.

40. *Minutes of the Presbyterian Church in America, 1706–1788,* 2.

41. Gaustad, *Historical Atlas of Religion in America,* 3, 19.

42. *Minutes of the General Assembly, 1789,* ed. William M. Engles (Philadelphia: Presbyterian Board of Publication, 1847), 21.

43. Ibid., 23–24.

44. *Minutes of the General Assembly of the Presbyterian Church in the United States of America, from Its Organization A.D. 1789 to A.D. 1820 Inclusive* (Philadelphia: Presbyterian Board of Publication, 1847), 92.

45. Ibid., 93.

46. E. T. Thompson, "The First Years," 8–9.

47. Trinterud, *The Forming of an American Tradition,* 6, 266–67.

48. E. T. Thompson, "The First Years," 9.

49. W. E. Thompson, *Her Walls,* 120.

50. Garrett, *Historical Atlas of the United States,* 88.

51. W. E. Thompson, *Her Walls,* 120.

52. George M. Marsden, *The Evangelical Mind and the New School Experience* (Eugene, OR: Wipf & Stock, 1970), 9.

53. W. E. Thompson, *Her Walls,* 120, 132.

54. John Luster Brinkley, *On This Hill: A Narrative History of Hampden-Sydney College, 1774–1994* (Hampden Sydney, VA: Hampden-Sydney College, 1994), 10n.

55. Joseph Dupuy Eggleston, "Extracts from the Minutes of the Virginia Synod and Hanover Presbytery, on Liberty Hall Academy, Hampden-Sydney College, and Union Theological Seminary, 1771–1824, with Explanatory Notes" (unpublished manuscript in the Union Theological Seminary Library, 1947), 18, Synod of Virginia.

56. Foote, *Sketches of Virginia,* 456.

57. *Minutes of the General Assembly, 1789–1820,* 368.

58. Ibid., 44.

59. R. P. Davis and Smylie, *Virginia Presbyterians in American Life*, 11.

60. Stephen L. Longenecker, *Shenandoah Religion: Outsiders and the Mainstream, 1716–1865* (Waco: Baylor University Press, 2002), 22.

61. R. P. Davis and Smylie, *Virginia Presbyterians in American Life*, 18.

62. Eggleston, "Extracts from the Minutes," 5, Synod of Virginia.

63. Wesley M. Gehwer, *The Great Awakening in Virginia, 1740–1790* (Durham, NC: Duke University Press, 1930), 74.

64. *Minutes of the Presbyterian Church in America, 1706–1788*, 158, 163.

65. R. P. Davis and Smylie, *Virginia Presbyterians in American Life*, 18–19.

66. Bradshaw, *History of Hampden-Sydney College*, 1:3.

67. *Minutes of the Presbyterian Church in America, 1706–1788*, 278–79, 298.

68. Bradshaw, *History of Hampden-Sydney College*, 1:8.

69. *Minutes of the Presbyterian Church in America, 1706–1788*, 380, 389, 530, 535.

70. Gaustad, *Historical Atlas of Religion in America*, 21.

71. Eggleston, "Extracts from the Minutes," 18, Synod of Virginia.

72. Ibid., 1, Synod of Virginia.

73. Ibid., 1, Hanover Presbytery.

74. Foote, *Sketches of Virginia*, 441.

75. Eggleston, "Extracts from the Minutes," 2, Hanover Presbytery.

76. Ibid., 73, Synod of Virginia.

77. Ibid., 77, Hanover Presbytery.

78. Ibid., 14, Hanover Presbytery.

79. Foote, *Sketches of Virginia*, 474–77.

80. Ibid., 23, Hanover Presbytery.

81. Ibid., 79–81, Synod of Virginia.

82. Ibid., 69, Hanover Presbytery.

83. Ibid., 13, Synod of Virginia.

84. Ibid., 24, Synod of Virginia.

85. Ibid., 26, Hanover Presbytery.

86. Ibid., 3, Synod of Virginia.

87. Ibid., 5, Synod of Virginia.

88. Mahler, "A History of Union Theological Seminary in Virginia, 1807–1865," 9.

89. Eggleston, "Extracts from the Minutes," 2, 4–6, Hanover Presbytery.

90. *Minutes of the Presbyterian Church in America, 1706–1788*, 1.

91. Foote, *Sketches of Virginia*, 410.

92. R. P. Davis and Smylie, *Virginia Presbyterians in American Life*, 56.

93. Sprague, *Annals of the American Pulpit*, 3:336.

94. Mahler, "A History of Union Theological Seminary in Virginia, 1807–1865," 29.

95. Samuel Stanhope Smith, "Academy in Prince Edward," *Virginia Gazette* (Williamsburg, VA), September 1775, 3.

96. Eggleston, "Extracts from the Minutes," 6, Synod of Virginia.

97. Stephen L. Longenecker, *Shenandoah Religion: Outsiders and the Mainstream, 1716–1865* (Waco: Baylor University Press, 2002), 27–29.

98. Joseph T. Rainer, "Commercial Scythians in the Great Valley of Virginia: Yankee Peddlers' Trade Connection to Antebellum Virginia," in *After the Backcountry: Rural Life in the Great Valley of Virginia, 1800–1900*, ed. Kenneth E. Koons and Warren R. Hofstra (Knoxville: University of Tennessee Press, 2000), 72.

99. Donald Robert Come, "The Influence of Princeton on Higher Education in the South before 1826," *William and Mary Quarterly* 2, no. 3 (1945): 366.

100. Ibid., 367, 371.

101. Brinkley, *On This Hill*, 32.

102. Arthur Dicken Thomas Jr., "Moses Hoge: Reformed Pietism and Spiritual Guidance," *American Presbyterians* 71, no. 2 (Summer 1993): 5.

103. Bradshaw, *History of Hampden-Sydney College*, 1:19.

104. Ibid., 1:20.

105. S. S. Smith, "Academy in Prince Edward," 3.

106. Bradshaw, *History of Hampden-Sydney College*, 1:27–28.

107. Smylie, "Clerical Perspectives on Deism," 211.

108. Bradshaw, *History of Hampden-Sydney College*, 1:28.

109. William Hill, *Autobiographical Sketches of Dr. William Hill, Together with His Account of the Revival of Religion in Prince Edward County and Biographical Sketches of the Life and Character of the Reverend Dr. Moses Hoge of Virginia*, vol. 4, *Historical Transcripts* (Richmond, VA: Union Theological Seminary in Virginia, 1968), 5–7, 9–11.

110. Ernest Trice Thompson, *Presbyterians in the South*, vol. 1, *1607–1861* (Richmond, VA: John Knox Press, 1963), 126.

111. Ibid., 1:127.

112. Bradshaw, *History of Hampden-Sydney College*, 1:134.

113. Ibid., 1:82.

114. Come, "The Influence of Princeton," 373.

115. Brinkley, *On This Hill*, 34, 61.

116. John Holt Rice, "The Influence of Christianity on the Political and Social Interests of Man," *Virginia Evangelical and Literary Magazine* 6 (1823): 7.

117. Eggleston, "Extracts from the Minutes," 20, Synod of Virginia.

118. Ibid., 21, Hanover Presbytery.

119. Bradshaw, *History of Hampden-Sydney College*, 1:62.

120. Ibid., 1:77.

121. Eggleston, "Extracts from the Minutes," 23, Hanover Presbytery.

122. Ibid., 1, Synod of Virginia.

CHAPTER 2: Poor and Pious Youth

1. John Adams, "The Political Writings of John Adams," in *The Political Writings of John Adams*, ed. George W. Carey (Washington, DC: Regnery Publishing, 2000), 701–2.

2. Nathan O. Hatch, "The Christian Movement and the Demand for a Theology of the People," *Journal of American History* 67, no. 3 (December 1980): 567.

3. Wilbur E. Garrett, ed., *Historical Atlas of the United States* (Washington, DC: National Geographic Society, 1988), 114–15.

4. *Minutes of the Presbyterian Church in America, 1706–1788*, ed. Guy Klett (Philadelphia: Presbyterian Historical Society, 1976), 248.

5. Joseph Dupuy Eggleston, "Extracts from the Minutes of the Virginia Synod and Hanover Presbytery, on Liberty Hall Academy, Hampden-Sydney College, and Union Theological Seminary, 1771–1824, with Explanatory Notes" (unpublished manuscript in the Union Seminary Library, 1947), 18, Hanover Presbytery.

6. *Addresses Delivered at the Celebration of the Centennial of the General Assembly of the Presbyterian Church* (Philadelphia: MacCalla & Co., 1888), 17.

7. Ibid.

8. Eggleston, "Extracts from the Minutes," 39, Hanover Presbytery, April 4, 1806.

9. Ibid.; Henry Richard Mahler Jr., "A History of Union Theological Seminary in Virginia, 1807–1865" (ThD diss., Union Theological Seminary in Virginia, 1951), 11.

10. Mahler, "History of Union Theological Seminary," 11; Eggleston, "Extracts from the Minutes," 39, Hanover Presbytery, April 4, 1806.

11. Eggleston, "Extracts from the Minutes," 39, Hanover Presbytery, April 4, 1806.

12. William Henry Foote, *Sketches of Virginia, Historical and Biographical, Second Series* (Philadelphia: J. B. Lippincott & Co., 1855), 372.

13. Herbert C. Bradshaw, *History of Hampden-Sydney College*, vol. 1, *From the Beginnings to the Year 1856* (Durham, NC: Fisher-Harrison, 1976), 144.

14. *Minutes of the Presbyterian Church in America, 1706–1788*, ed. Guy Klett (Philadelphia: Presbyterian Historical Society, 1976), 248.

15. Phillip B. Price, "The Life of Reverend John Holt Rice, D.D.," in *The Life of Reverend John Holt Rice, D.D.*, reprinted from the *Central Presbyterian*, 1886–1887 (Richmond, VA: Library of Union Seminary in Virginia, 1963), 197–99.

16. Henry M. Brimm, "The Library of Union Theological Seminary, 1806–1944," *Union Seminary Review* 55, no. 4 (August 1944): 286, as found in the Presbytery of Hanover Minutes, 3:225.

17. John B. Trotti, "The History of the Union Theological Seminary Library" (unpublished manuscript in the author's files, 2008), 6. The original books had been on display in a special replica bookcase since the 1940s. When the move was made from the old Spence/Latta Library to the new William Smith Morton Library in 1994, it was discovered that none of these original volumes had been catalogued and were only then officially included in the library's holdings. Surviving more than 190 years in insecure public display, these books are now in the rare books collection of the Morton Library.

18. Ibid., 15.

19. Bradshaw, *History of Hampden-Sydney College*, 1:146–47.

20. John Luster Brinkley, *On This Hill: A Narrative History of Hampden-Sydney College, 1774–1994* (Hampden Sydney, VA: Hampden-Sydney College, 1994), 137.

21. Brinkley, *On This Hill*, 137.

22. Trotti, "Union Theological Seminary Library," 7, 16.

23. William B. Sprague, *Annals of the American Pulpit*, vol. 3, *Presbyterian* (New York: Robert Carrier & Brothers, 1860), 428.

24. Sprague, *Annals of the American Pulpit*, 3:429.

25. Brinkley, *On This Hill*, 49.

26. Leonard Wesley Topping, "A History of Hampden-Sydney College in Virginia, 1771–1883" (Union Theological Seminary, 1950), 166.

27. G. MacLaren Brydon, "The Anti-Ecclesiastical Laws of Virginia," *Virginia Magazine of History and Biography* 64, no. 3 (July 1956): 262.

28. William E. Thompson, *Her Walls before Thee Stand: The 235-Year History of the Presbyterian Congregation at Hampden-Sydney, Virginia* ([Hampden Sydney, VA]: William E. Thompson, 2010), 63.

29. Bradshaw, *History of Hampden-Sydney College*, 1:123.

30. Mahler, "History of Union Theological Seminary," 20.

31. *Minutes of the General Assembly of the Presbyterian Church in the United States of America, from Its Organization A.D. 1789 to A.D. 1820 Inclusive* (Philadelphia: Presbyterian Board of Publication, 1847), 2.

32. Arthur Dicken Thomas Jr., "Moses Hoge: Reformed Pietism and Spiritual Guidance," *American Presbyterians* 71, no. 2 (Summer 1993): 2.

33. Sprague, *Annals of the American Pulpit*, 3:427.

34. John Blair Hoge, *Sketch of the Life and Character of the Rev. Moses Hoge, D.D.*, Historical Transcripts 2 (Richmond, VA: Union Theological Seminary, 1964), 150.

35. Ernest Trice Thompson, "Union Theological Seminary," *Commonwealth*, February 1952, 1.

36. A. D. Thomas, "Moses Hoge," 5, 11–12.

37. J. Hoge, *Rev. Moses Hoge*, 13.

38. A. D. Thomas, "Moses Hoge," 8.

39. *Extracts from the Minutes of the General Assembly of the Presbyterian Church in the United States of America, A.D. 1808* (Philadelphia, 1808), 185–87.

40. Mark A. Noll, *The Princeton Theology, 1812–1921: Scripture, Science, and Theological Method from Archibald Alexander to Benjamin Breckinridge Warfield* (Phillipsburg, NJ: Presbyterian & Reformed Publishing Co., 1983), 51.

41. Ibid.

42. *Celebration of the Centennial*, 17.

43. Noll, *The Princeton Theology*, 53.

44. Foote, *Sketches of Virginia*, 368.

45. J. B. Hoge, *Rev. Moses Hoge*, 150.

46. W. E. Thompson, *Her Walls*, 101.

47. Eggleston, "Extracts from the Minutes," 55, Hanover Presbytery.

48. Noll, *The Princeton Theology*, 55.

49. *A Letter from the General Assembly of the Presbyterian Church in the United States of America to the Churches under Their Care* (Philadelphia: Jane Aitken, 1810), 7.

50. *Report of a Committee of the General Assembly of the Presbyterian Church, Exhibiting the Plan of a Theological Seminary* (New York: J. Seymour, 1810), 4.

51. *A Letter from the General Assembly* (1810), 3–4.

52. *Exhibiting the Plan of a Theological Seminary*, 7, 9–11, 17–18.

53. *The Plan of a Theological Seminary Adopted by the General Assembly of the Presbyterian Church in the United States of America in Their Sessions of May Last, A.D. 1811: Together with the Measures Taken by Them to Carry the Plan into Effect* (Philadelphia: Jane Aitken, 1811), 15, 19.

54. *Exhibiting the Plan of a Theological Seminary*, 13–14, 18–19.

55. T. Hartley Hall IV, "The Lower Gifts" (paper presented at the opening convocation in Watts Chapel, Union Theological Seminary in Virginia, September 9, 1987), 3.

56. *The Plan of a Theological Seminary, . . . 1811*, 23–26.

57. Eggleston, "Extracts from the Minutes," 53, 57, 59, Hanover Presbytery.

58. Ibid., 25–27, Synod of Virginia.

59. Mahler, "History of Union Theological Seminary," 36.

60. W. E. Thompson, *Her Walls*, 61.

61. Trotti, "Union Theological Seminary Library," 1.

62. Brinkley, *On This Hill*, 137. Moses Hoge played the central part in the development of theological education, but the term "president" was not used by the seminary until 1904 (the same year the University of Virginia created the post and adopted the term), and the seminary did not award academic degrees until 1899.

63. Eggleston, "Extracts from the Minutes," 69, Hanover Presbytery.

64. Brinkley, *On This Hill*, 61.

65. Moses Hoge, Drury Lacy, and Matthew Lyle, "The Presbytery of Hanover," *Virginia Argus* (Richmond, VA), October 26, 1810, 3.

66. Foote, *Sketches of Virginia*, 231, 366, 563.

67. Brinkley, *On This Hill*, 80–81.

68. A. D. Thomas, "Moses Hoge," 12.

69. W. E. Thompson, *Her Walls*, 59.

70. William Maxwell, *A Memoir of the Rev. John H. Rice, D.D.* (Richmond, VA: R. I. Smith, 1835), 49.

71. J. B. Hoge, *Rev. Moses Hoge*, 145–46.

72. Eggleston, "Extracts from the Minutes," 49; Hanover Presbytery, October 24, 1807; Sprague, *Annals of the American Pulpit*, 3:428.

73. Eggleston, "Extracts from the Minutes," 24, Synod of Virginia.

74. Ernest Trice Thompson, "The First Years," in *The Days of Our Years: The Historical Convocations Held April 24–27, 1962, as a Feature of the Celebration of the Sesquicentennial of Union Theological Seminary in Virginia* (Richmond: Union Theological Seminary, 1962), 10.

75. Mahler, "History of Union Theological Seminary," 39.

76. M. Hoge, D. Lacy, and Lyle, "Presbytery of Hanover," 1.

77. Mahler, "History of Union Theological Seminary," 40; Synod of Virginia Minutes, 3:18.

78. Eggleston, "Extracts from the Minutes," 30, Synod of Virginia, October 23, 1813.

79. Ibid., 31, Synod of Virginia, October 29, 1814.

80. Bradshaw, *History of Hampden-Sydney College*, 1:139.

81. Foote, *Sketches of Virginia*, 369–74.

82. Topping, "History of Hampden-Sydney College," 59.

83. Bradshaw, *History of Hampden-Sydney College*, 1:139.

84. Eggleston, "Extracts from the Minutes," 32, Synod of Virginia, October 29, 1814.

85. Ibid., 32, Synod of Virginia, October 15, 1815.

86. Mahler, "History of Union Theological Seminary," 42.

87. Eggleston, "Extracts from the Minutes," 33–35, Synod of Virginia, October 25, 1816.

88. Mahler, "History of Union Theological Seminary," 44.

89. Eggleston, "Extracts from the Minutes," 32, Synod of Virginia, October 12, 1815.

90. Foote, *Sketches of Virginia*, 370.

91. Mahler, "History of Union Theological Seminary," 49.

92. Eggleston, "Extracts from the Minutes," 50, Synod of Virginia, October 19, 1818.

93. Ibid., 59, Synod of Virginia, October 24, 1819.

94. Ibid., 6, Synod of Virginia, October 19, 1820.

95. J. B. Hoge, *Rev. Moses Hoge*, 145; Mahler, "History of Union Theological Seminary," 13.

96. Bradshaw, *History of Hampden-Sydney College*, 1:28.

97. Mahler, "History of Union Theological Seminary," 45.

98. Eggleston, "Extracts from the Minutes," 36–37, 39–41, Synod of Virginia, October 25, 1816.

99. Brinkley, *On This Hill*, 57–60.

100. Bradshaw, *History of Hampden-Sydney College*, 1:148.

101. Brinkley, *On This Hill*, 49.

102. Eggleston, "Extracts from the Minutes," 43, Synod of Virginia, October 17, 1817.

103. Brinkley, *On This Hill*, 66–68, 81.

104. W. E. Thompson, *Her Walls*, 59–60.

105. Foote, *Sketches of Virginia*, 372.

106. Eggleston, "Extracts from the Minutes," 43, 45, 47, Synod of Virginia, October 20, 1817.

107. Mahler, "History of Union Theological Seminary," 46.

108. J. B. Hoge, *Rev. Moses Hoge*, 236.

109. Mahler, "History of Union Theological Seminary," 48.

110. Eggleston, "Extracts from the Minutes," 55–56, 58, Synod of Virginia, October 24, 1819.

111. Mahler, "History of Union Theological Seminary," 51; Synod of Virginia Minutes, 4:226.

112. Eggleston, "Extracts from the Minutes," 35, Synod of Virginia, October 25, 1816.

113. Ibid., 57, Synod of Virginia, October 24, 1819.

114. Mahler, "History of Union Theological Seminary," 51, 54.

115. J. B. Hoge, *Rev. Moses Hoge*, 236.

116. Mahler, "History of Union Theological Seminary," 57.

117. J. B. Hoge, *Rev. Moses Hoge*, 151.

118. Brinkley, *On This Hill*, 79–80.

119. Robert R. Howison, *A History of Virginia from Its Discovery and Settlement by Europeans to the Present Time* (Philadelphia: Carey & Hart, 1846), 397.

120. Eggleston, "Extracts from the Minutes," 32, Synod of Virginia, October 15, 1815.

121. House of Delegates, Commonwealth of Virginia, *Journal of the House of Delegates of the Commonwealth of Virginia* (1815–16), 35.

122. Foote, *Sketches of Virginia*, 271, 332.

123. House of Delegates, *Journal of the House of Delegates*, 88.

124. David E. Swift, "Thomas Jefferson, John Holt Rice, and Education in Virginia, 1815–1825," *Journal of Presbyterian History* 49, no. 1 (Spring 1971): 317.

125. P. A. Bruce, *History of the University of Virginia*, vol. 1 (New York: MacMillan, 1919), 19.

126. House of Delegates, *Journal of the House of Delegates*, 153.

127. John Holt Rice, *An Illustration of the Character & Conduct of the Presbyterian Church in Virginia* (Richmond: Du-Val and Burke, 1816), 4.

128. Ibid., 4, 18, 20, 38.

129. Swift, "Thomas Jefferson, John Holt Rice, and Education," 55.

130. J. H. Rice, *Presbyterian Church in Virginia*, 44–45.

131. Eggleston, "Extracts from the Minutes," 35, Synod of Virginia, October 25, 1816.

132. John Holt Rice, "Memorials to the General Assembly of Virginia," *Virginia Literary and Evangelical Magazine* (Richmond, VA), January 1826, 30–49.

133. Theological Society Minutes, 1812–1823 (1823), preamble.

134. Ibid., January 16, 1813, and November 26, 1813.

135. Ibid., December 9, 1814; February 20, 1815; July 27, 1815; November 24, 1815; January 19, 1816; July 10, 1818; December 10, 1818; July 10, 1818.

136. Ibid., June 14, 1816; March 7, 1817; November 27, 1818; January 8, 1819; March 5, 1819; June 25, 1819; March 3, 1820.

137. Ibid., January 7, 1814; February 20, 1818.

138. Ibid., September 30, 1818.

139. Ibid., January 21, 1814.

140. Ibid., August 6, 1819.

141. Ibid., August 20, 1819.

142. Ibid., March 31, 1820.

143. Ibid., June 12, 1813.

144. Society of Missionary Inquiry, Minute Book 1: 1818–1830, January 18, 1818.

145. H. McKennie Goodpasture, "Our Field Is the World: Mission Studies at Union Theological Seminary in Virginia, 1812–1897," an address given on the 175th anniversary of the founding of Union Seminary, October 12, 1987, 1.

146. Society of Missionary Inquiry, Minute Book 1: 1818–1830, April 6, 1818.

147. Goodpasture, "Our Field Is the World," 1, 3.

148. Society of Missionary Inquiry, Minute Book 1: 1818–1830, July 6, 1818; December 7, 1818; January 18, 1819.

149. Ibid., August 21, 1820.

150. Ibid., December 18, 1820.

151. Society of Missionary Inquiry, Correspondence Book 1, 1818–1836, February 24, 1818.

152. Sprague, *Annals of the American Pulpit*, 3:429; Mahler, "History of Union Theological Seminary," 54.

153. A. D. Thomas, "Moses Hoge," 3.

154. Mahler, "History of Union Theological Seminary," 55–56.

155. Eggleston, "Extracts from the Minutes," 64, Synod of Virginia, October 25, 1821.

156. Society of Missionary Inquiry, Correspondence Book 1, 1818–1836, letters 5–6.

157. Bradshaw, *History of Hampden-Sydney College*, 1:150–51.

158. Herbert C. Bradshaw, *History of Prince Edward County, Virginia, from Its Earliest Settlements through Its Establishment in 1754 to Its Bicentennial Year* (Richmond, VA: Dietz Press, 1954), 159.

159. Robert P. Davis and James H. Smylie, *Virginia Presbyterians in American Life: Hanover Presbytery (1755–1980)*, ed. Patricia Aldridge (Richmond, VA: Hanover Presbytery, 1982), 67.

160. Stephen L. Longenecker, *Shenandoah Religion: Outsiders and the Mainstream, 1716–1865* (Waco: Baylor University Press, 2002), 27–29.

161. Joseph T. Rainer, "Commercial Scythians in the Great Valley of Virginia: Yankee Peddlers' Trade Connection to Antebellum Virginia," in *After the Backcountry: Rural Life in the Great Valley of Virginia, 1800–1900*, ed. Kenneth E. Koons and Warren R. Hofstra (Knoxville: University of Tennessee Press, 2000), 72.

162. Maxwell, *Memoir of the Rev. John H. Rice*, 186.

163. Lucas [John Holt Rice], Letter to the editor, *Virginia Evangelical and Literary Magazine and Missionary Chronicle* 4, no. 6 (June 1821): 302, 305–6, 309.

164. Swift, "Thomas Jefferson, John Holt Rice, and Education," 54.

165. E. T. Thompson, "The First Years," 11.

166. Native Virginian, "Sketch of Lower Virginia," *Virginia Evangelical and Literary Magazine* 6, no. 6 (June 1823): 306–8.

167. Ezra Hall Gillette, *History of the Presbyterian Church in the United States of America*, vol. 2 (Philadelphia: Presbyterian Board of Publication and Sabbath-School Work, 1864), rev. ed. (1873), Michigan Historical Reprint Series (Ann Arbor: University of Michigan Library, 2005), 226.

168. Mahler, "History of Union Theological Seminary," 4.

CHAPTER 3: No Ism but Bibleism

1. Henry Richard Mahler Jr., "A History of Union Theological Seminary in Virginia, 1807–1865" (ThD diss., Union Theological Seminary in Virginia, 1951), 62; Synod of Virginia Minutes, 4:317.

2. John Luster Brinkley, *On This Hill: A Narrative History of Hampden-Sydney College, 1774–1994* (Hampden Sydney, VA: Hampden-Sydney College, 1994), 87, 91.

3. George W. Dame, "Sketch of the Life and Character of Jonathan P. Cushing, M.A.," *American Quarterly Register* 11, no. 2 (November 1838): 118.

4. Brinkley, *On This Hill*, 90.

5. Walter Rüegg, ed., *A History of the University in Europe*, vol. 3, *Universities in the Nineteenth and Early Twentieth Centuries (1800–1945)* (Cambridge: Cambridge University Press, 2005), 5–6.

6. Ralph P. Rosenberg, "Eugene Schuyler's Doctor of Philosophy Degree: A Theory concerning the Dissertation," *Journal of Higher Education* 33, no. 7 (1962): 383.

7. Brinkley, *On This Hill*, 92.

8. Society of Missionary Inquiry, Correspondence Book 2 (Hampden Sydney, VA, 1818–1832), letter 6.

9. William Maxwell, *A Memoir of the Rev. John H. Rice, D.D.* (Richmond, VA: R. I. Smith, 1835), 183.

10. Daniel W. Crofts, "Late Antebellum Virginia Reconsidered," *Virginia Magazine of History and Biography* 107, no. 3 (Summer 1999): 260.

11. Robert D. Mitchell, *Commercialism and Frontier: Perspectives on the Early Shenandoah Valley* (Charlottesville: University Press of Virginia, 1977), 148.

12. Mahler, "History of Union Theological Seminary," 92.

13. Maxwell, *Memoir of the Rev. John H. Rice*, 183; William Henry Foote, *Sketches of Virginia, Historical and Biographical, Second Series* (Philadelphia: J.B. Lippincott & Co., 1855), 183, 374.

14. Foote, *Sketches of Virginia*, 375.

15. Ibid.

16. J. D. Eggleston, "Extracts from the Minutes of the Virginia Synod and Hanover Presbytery, on Liberty Hall Academy, Hampden-Sydney College, and Union Theological Seminary, 1771–1824, with Explanatory Notes" (unpublished manuscript in the Union Seminary Library, 1947), 74, Synod of Virginia.

17. Ibid., 73, 75, Synod of Virginia.

18. Maxwell, *Memoir of the Rev. John H. Rice*, 186.

19. Foote, *Sketches of Virginia*, 241–42, 375–76.

20. Mahler, "History of Union Theological Seminary," 75, 77.

21. Benjamin Mosby Smith, address, in *Addresses at the Unveiling and Dedication of the Memorial Tablet in Honor of the Rev. John H. Rice, D.D., Delivered in the Chapel of Union Theological Seminary, Va., May 5, 1885* (Richmond, VA: Whittet & Shepperson, 1885), 9.

22. Foote, *Sketches of Virginia*, 242, 244–45.

23. Mahler, "History of Union Theological Seminary," 78.

24. Walter W. Moore, "Dr. John H. Rice," *Union Seminary Magazine* 9 (1898): 266.

25. Mahler, "History of Union Theological Seminary," 78–79.

26. Maxwell, *Memoir of the Rev. John H. Rice*, 37.

27. Mahler, "History of Union Theological Seminary," 79.

28. W. Moore, "Dr. John H. Rice," 267.

29. Ernest Trice Thompson, *Presbyterians in the South*, vol. 1, *1607–1861* (Richmond, VA: John Knox Press, 1963), 277.

30. Ernest Trice Thompson, "John Holt Rice," *Union Seminary Review* 43, no. 1 (October–November 1932): 177.

31. W. Moore, "Dr. John H. Rice," 267.

32. David E. Swift, "Thomas Jefferson, John Holt Rice, and Education in Virginia, 1815–1825," *Journal of Presbyterian History* 49, no. 1 (Spring 1971): 33.

33. Herbert C. Bradshaw, *History of Hampden-Sydney College*, vol. 1, *From the Beginnings to the Year 1856* (Durham, NC: Fisher-Harrison, 1976), 152.

34. E. T. Thompson, *Presbyterians in the South*, 1:277.

35. Mahler, "History of Union Theological Seminary," 84.

36. E. T. Thompson, *Presbyterians in the South*, 1:277.

37. Mahler, "History of Union Theological Seminary," 81, 83, 85.

38. David E. Swift, "Yankee in Virginia: James Marsh at Hampden-Sydney, 1823–1826," *Virginia Magazine of History and Biography* 80, no. 3 (July 1972): 312.

39. Swift, "Thomas Jefferson, John Holt Rice, and Education," 33.

40. Maxwell, *Memoir of the Rev. John H. Rice*, 174.

41. Swift, "Yankee in Virginia," 321.

42. Alfred J. Morrison, *"The Virginia Literary and Evangelical Magazine, 1818–1828," William and Mary Quarterly* 19, no. 4 (April 1911): 268, 270.

43. Swift, "Thomas Jefferson, John Holt Rice, and Education," 33.

44. Morrison, *"Virginia Literary and Evangelical Magazine,"* 268.

45. Benjamin Mosby Smith, "The Brown Memorial Library: Address at the Laying of the Corner-Stone of the Library Building of Union Theological Seminary, Hampden-Sydney, Va., September 1, 1879," *Central Presbyterian* (Richmond, VA), September 17, 1879, reprinted in *Union Seminary Review*, August 1944, 296.

46. John Holt Rice, *A Sermon on the Duties of a Minister of the Gospel: Preached at the Opening of the Presbytery of Hanover at Dee Ess Church, October 11, 1809* (Philadelphia: William W. Woodward, 1809), 7.

47. Ibid., 12.

48. Swift, "Thomas Jefferson, John Holt Rice, and Education," 32–34.

49. Robert Burwell, "The Early Days of Union Seminary," in *Septuagesimal Celebration of Union Theological Seminary in Virginia, 1824–1894* (Richmond, VA: Whittet & Shepperson, 1894), 51.

50. Benjamin Rice Lacy, "A Look Backward and Forward," *Union Seminary Review* 38, no. 1 (October 1926): 30.

51. Maxwell, *Memoir of the Rev. John H. Rice*, 186, 274.

52. Holem [John Holt Rice], "Observations on the Manner of Educating Young Men for the Ministry of the Gospel," *Virginia Evangelical and Literary Magazine* 5, no. 8 (August 1822): 412.

53. Ibid., 412, 414–17.

54. John Holt Rice, *New England Memorials* (1823), 424.

55. Maxwell, *Memoir of the Rev. John H. Rice*, 232.

56. James H. Smylie, "Theological Education, Academia, and the Ministry" (a paper given at the 1976 Faculty Workshop), 4.

57. Maxwell, *Memoir of the Rev. John H. Rice*, 240.

58. E. T. Thompson, *Presbyterians in the South*, 1:277.

59. Maxwell, *Memoir of the Rev. John H. Rice*, 232–33.

60. Foote, *Sketches of Virginia*, 383–85.

61. Burwell, "Early Days of Union Seminary," 50.

62. Maxwell, *Memoir of the Rev. John H. Rice*, 159.

63. John Holt Rice, "Theological Seminary, Andover, Mass.," *Virginia Evangelical and Literary Magazine* 5, no. 5 (May 1822): 225–27.

64. Mahler, "History of Union Theological Seminary," 71.

65. Swift, "Thomas Jefferson, John Holt Rice, and Education," 37–38.

66. Theological Society Minutes, 1812–1823, September 25, 1822.

67. Mahler, "History of Union Theological Seminary," 65.

68. T. Hartley Hall IV, "The Lower Gifts" (1987), 2.

69. Theological Society Minutes, November 30, 1822.

70. Mahler, "History of Union Theological Seminary," 86–87.

71. William B. Sprague, *Annals of the American Pulpit* (New York: Robert Carter & Brothers, 1859), 3:329.

72. Eggleston, "Extracts from the Minutes," 76, Hanover Presbytery.

73. William E. Thompson, *Her Walls before Thee Stand: The 235-Year History of the Presbyterian Congregation at Hampden-Sydney, Virginia* ([Hampden Sydney, VA]: William E. Thompson, 2010), 121.

74. Maxwell, *Memoir of the Rev. John H. Rice*, 250–51.

75. J. H. Rice, *New England Memorials*, 1–2, dated September 27, 1823.

76. Union Theological Seminary Board of Trustees Minutes (1823–1840), loose pages.

77. Benjamin Rice Lacy Jr., "Historical Address Delivered at the Opening of the Seminary on Wednesday, September 15th, 1937," *Union Seminary Review* 49, no. 1 (October 1937): 5.

78. Ernest Trice Thompson, "The Ideals of John Holt Rice," *Union Seminary Review* 43 (1932): 295–96.

79. Phillip B. Price, "The Life of Reverend John Holt Rice, D.D," in *The Life of Reverend John Holt Rice, D.D.*, reprinted from the *Central Presbyterian*, 1886–1887 (Richmond: Library of Union Seminary in Virginia, 1963), 102.

80. H. McKennie Goodpasture, "Our Field Is the World: Mission Studies at Union Theological Seminary in Virginia, 1812–1897," an address given on the 175th anniversary of the founding of Union Theological Seminary (October 12, 1987), 3.

81. E. T. Thompson, *Presbyterians in the South*, 1:457.

82. Goodpasture, "Our Field Is the World," 3.

83. E. T. Thompson, *Presbyterians in the South*, 1:283.

84. Walter W. Moore, "Historical Sketch of Union Theological Seminary," *Union Seminary Magazine* 9, no. 4 (March–April 1898): 232.

85. John Holt Rice, *An Inaugural Discourse, Delivered on the First of January, 1824* (Richmond, VA: Nathan Pollard, 1824), 5, 9, 42–43.

86. Maxwell, *Memoir of the Rev. John H. Rice*, 330.

87. Rice, *Sermon on the Duties of a Minister*, 12.

88. Walter W. Moore, "Historical Sketch," in *Septuagesimal Celebration*, 12.

89. Ernest Trice Thompson, "The First Years," in *The Days of Our Years: The Historical Convocations Held April 24–27, 1962, as a Feature of the Celebration of the Sesquicentennial of Union Theological Seminary in Virginia* (Richmond, VA: Union Theological Seminary, 1962), 15.

90. Rice, *Inaugural Discourse*, 12–13, 16–18, 20, 28.

91. E. T. Thompson, "The First Years," 14.

92. John Holt Rice, "The Power of Truth and Love: A Sermon Preached before the American Board of Foreign Missions," *National Preacher* 3, no. 5 (October 1, 1828): 76.

93. Ibid., 74.

94. Rice, *Inaugural Discourse*, 17, 26.

95. E. T. Thompson, "The First Years," 15.

96. E. T. Thompson, "Ideals of John Holt Rice," 290–91.

97. Rice, *Inaugural Discourse*, 29–33, 35–36, 44–45.

98. Eggleston, "Extracts from the Minutes," 77.

99. Bradshaw, *History of Hampden-Sydney College*, 1:153.

100. W. Moore, "Historical Sketch," *Union Seminary Magazine* 9:232; W. E. Thompson, *Her Walls*, 101.

101. Burwell, "Early Days of Union Seminary," 54; and in *Union Seminary Magazine* 5, no. 3 (January–February 1894): 151–52.

102. Theodorick Pryor, address, in *Addresses at the Unveiling and Dedication*, 15.

103. Burwell, "Early Days of Union Seminary," *Union Seminary Magazine*, 152.

104. Ibid., 150; and in *Septuagesimal Celebration*, 54, 56.

105. T. H. Hall, "The Lower Gifts," 3.

106. Rice, *Inaugural Discourse*, 42; Presbytery of Hanover Minutes, 3:356.

107. Rice, *Inaugural Discourse*, 41.

108. T. H. Hall, "The Lower Gifts," 14.

109. Rice, *Inaugural Discourse*, 40, 41, 44.

110. Board of Trustees Minutes, loose pages.

111. T. H. Hall, "The Lower Gifts," 2, 12.

112. Rice, *Inaugural Discourse*, 44.

113. T. H. Hall, "The Lower Gifts," 14.

114. Maxwell, *Memoir of the Rev. John H. Rice*, 295.

115. G. MacLaren Brydon, "The Anti-Ecclesiastical Laws of Virginia," *Virginia Magazine of History and Biography* 64, no. 3 (July 1956): 260.

116. Maxwell, *Memoir of the Rev. John H. Rice*, 266, 295.

117. John Holt Rice, "Theological Seminary in Prince Edward," *Virginia Literary and Evangelical Magazine* 9, no. 1 (January 1826): 612.

118. Herbert Clarence Bradshaw, *History of Prince Edward County, Virginia, from Its Earliest Settlements through Its Establishment in 1754 to Its Bicentennial Year* (Richmond, VA: Dietz Press, 1954), 160.

119. Mahler, "History of Union Theological Seminary," 103.

120. Maxwell, *Memoir of the Rev. John H. Rice, D.D.*, 274, 276–77.

121. Foote, *Sketches of Virginia*, 399.

122. William Henry Foote, *Sketches of North Carolina* (New York: Robert Carter, 1846), 535.

123. Ibid., 550.

124. Maxwell, *Memoir of the Rev. John H. Rice*, 288.

125. W. E. Thompson, *Her Walls*, 113–14.

126. Maxwell, *Memoir of the Rev. John H. Rice*, 300–301.

127. Foote, *Sketches of North Carolina*, 552.

128. Maxwell, *Memoir of the Rev. John H. Rice*, 302.

129. Foote, *Sketches of Virginia*, 374–476. See also Mahler, "History of Union Theological Seminary," 111, 113–14; Presbytery of Hanover Minutes 4:123, September 29, 1824; 194, May 5, 1826; 237–47, October 3, 1826.

130. Ezra Hall Gillette, *History of the Presbyterian Church in the United States of America*, vol. 2 (Philadelphia: Presbyterian Board of Publication and Sabbath-School Work, 1864), rev. ed. (1873), Michigan Historical Reprint Series (Ann Arbor: University of Michigan Library, 2005), 92.

131. Maxwell, *Memoir of the Rev. John H. Rice*, 301–2.

132. Mahler, "History of Union Theological Seminary," 109; Hanover Presbytery Minutes, 4:196.

133. T. H. Hall, "The Lower Gifts," 3, 7, 14.

134. Foote, *Sketches of Virginia*, 40; *General Assembly Minutes, 1821–35*, 212–13.

135. Maxwell, *Memoir of the Rev. John H. Rice*, 278, 284–85.

136. Burwell, "Early Days of Union Seminary," *Union Seminary Magazine*, 147. *Rob Roy* is the title of an 1817 novel by Walter Scott, and the character is based on Robert Roy MacGregor (ca. 1671–1734). MacGregor, known as "Rob Roy," was a famous Scottish folk hero because he was thought to steal from the rich and give to the poor.

137. Maxwell, *Memoir of the Rev. John H. Rice*, 288.

138. W. Moore, "Historical Sketch," in *Septuagesimal Celebration*, 9.

139. Maxwell, *Memoir of the Rev. John H. Rice*, 258.

140. Mahler, "A History of Union Theological Seminary," 142; Board of Trustees Minutes, 1:27, 31, 41, 42, 56, 70, 72.

141. Bradshaw, *History of Hampden-Sydney College*, 1:156.

142. Brinkley, *On This Hill*, 139.

143. T. Hartley Hall IV, "The Lower Gifts" (a paper presented at the opening convocation, Watts Chapel, Union Theological Seminary in Virginia, September 9, 1987), 12; Board of Trustees Minutes, 1:66.

144. Brinkley, *On This Hill*, 141.

145. Maxwell, *Memoir of the Rev. John H. Rice*, 258.

146. Brinkley, *On This Hill*, 139.

147. Mahler, "History of Union Theological Seminary," 96.

148. W. Moore, "Historical Sketch," *Union Seminary Magazine* 9:233.

149. T. Hartley Hall IV, "Administrative History of Union Theological Seminary" (notes in the author's papers, 1986), 14–15.

150. Maxwell, *Memoir of the Rev. John H. Rice*, 352.

151. Francis R. Flournoy, "The Early Life of Benjamin Mosby Smith," *Union Seminary Review* 55, no. 1 (November 1943): 16.

152. John B. Trotti, "The History of the Union Theological Seminary Library" (unpublished manuscript in the author's files, 2008), 15.

153. Francis R. Flournoy, *Benjamin Mosby Smith, 1811–1893* (Richmond, VA: Richmond Press, 1947), 17.

154. Pryor, address, in *Addresses at the Unveiling and Dedication*, 16–17.

155. W. E. Thompson, *Her Walls*, 106.

156. Mahler, "History of Union Theological Seminary," 144.

157. T. H. Hall, "Administrative History of Union," 15.

158. Henry M. Brimm, "The Library of Union Theological Seminary, 1806–1944," *Union Seminary Review* 55, no. 4 (August 1944): 287; Trotti, "Union Theological Seminary Library," 175.

159. Maxwell, *Memoir of the Rev. John H. Rice*, 316, 329–30, 332, 357.

160. Iota, "Theological Seminaries," *Virginia Literary and Evangelical Magazine* 9, no. 8 (August 1826): 408.

161. John Holt Rice, "Education for the Gospel Ministry," *Virginia Literary and Evangelical Magazine* 10, no. 4 (April 1827): 175.

162. Ibid., 179.

163. Rice, "Theological Seminary in Prince Edward," 611–12.

164. Maxwell, *Memoir of the Rev. John H. Rice*, 295–96; E. T. Thompson, "Ideals of John Holt Rice," 182.

165. Board of Trustees Minutes, loose pages.

166. Mahler, "History of Union Theological Seminary," 105; Board of Trustees Minutes, October 14, 1825, 10.

167. Mahler, "History of Union Theological Seminary," 102, 105.

168. Ibid., 139; Board of Trustees Minutes, 1:50.

169. Mahler, "History of Union Theological Seminary," 140.

170. Board of Directors, "Report on the Course of Study to Be Pursued in the Union Theological Seminary," *Virginia Literary and Evangelical Magazine*, October 1828, 513–21.

171. Mahler, "History of Union Theological Seminary," 137.

172. Ibid.; Board of Trustees Minutes, 1:63.

173. Board of Directors, "Report on the Course of Study," 522, 524–25.

174. Maxwell, *Memoir of the Rev. John H. Rice*, 328.

175. Mahler, "History of Union Theological Seminary," 129; Synod of Virginia Minutes, 5:177.

176. Gillette, *History of the Presbyterian*, rev. ed., 2:353.

177. Maxwell, *Memoir of the Rev. John H. Rice*, 313, 317, 319, 320 21, 323 26.

178. *Minutes of the General Assembly of the Presbyterian Church in the United States of America* (1828), 253.

179. Mahler, "History of Union Theological Seminary," 123.

180. Foote, *Sketches of Virginia*, 418.

181. Maxwell, *Memoir of the Rev. John H. Rice*, 330.

182. Mahler, "History of Union Theological Seminary," 88, 134.

183. Maxwell, *Memoir of the Rev. John H. Rice*, 348, 352.

184. Board of Directors, "Report on the Course of Study," 526; Board of Trustees Minutes, 1:19.

185. Trotti, "Union Theological Seminary Library," 3, 5, in the chapter for the 1824–97 time period.

186. Balmer H. Kelly, "No Ism but Bibleism: Biblical Studies at Union Theological Seminary in Virginia, 1812–1987" (paper presented on the 175th anniversary of the founding of Union Theological Seminary, October 12, 1987), 4.

187. Balmer H. Kelly, in the 1976 General Catalog, 44–48.

188. Balmer H. Kelly, ed., *A General Catalog of Trustees, Professors, and Students of Union Theological Seminary in Virginia* (Richmond, VA: Union Theological Seminary, 1976), 42–44.

189. William Spottswood White, *The African Preacher* (Philadelphia: Presbyterian Board of Publication, 1849), 1.

190. W. E. Thompson, *Her Walls*, 66.

191. Board of Trustees Minutes, loose pages.

192. Mahler, "History of Union Theological Seminary," 138; Board of Trustees Minutes, 1:63.

193. W. Moore, "Historical Sketch," in *Septuagesimal Celebration*, 15.

194. Mahler, "History of Union Theological Seminary," 137.

195. T. H. Hall, "The Lower Gifts," 13.

196. Faculty Minutes, 1828–59 (Hampden Sydney, VA), cover page and December 23, 1828.

197. Ibid., November 18, 1830.

198. Society of Missionary Inquiry, Minute Book 1: 1818–1830, September 1826.

199. Ibid., April 19, 1830.

200. Ibid., November 19, 1821.

201. Ibid., December 15, 1821.

202. Ibid., February 4, 1828.

203. Ibid., March 1, 1830.

204. Ibid., February 20, 1821.

205. Ibid., August 21, 1821.

206. Ibid., February 5, 1829.

207. J. B. Hoge, *Rev. Moses Hoge*, 230; Mahler, "History of Union Theological Seminary," 27.

208. W. E. Thompson, *Her Walls*, 64.

209. Arthur Dicken Thomas Jr., "Moses Hoge: Reformed Pietism and Spiritual Guidance," *American Presbyterians* 71, no. 2 (Summer 1993): 8.

210. Stephen L. Longenecker, *Shenandoah Religion: Outsiders and the Mainstream, 1716–1865* (Waco: Baylor University Press, 2002), 125.

211. Jewel L. Spangler, "Proslavery Presbyterians: Virginia's Conservative Dissenters in the Age of Revolution," *Journal of Presbyterian History* 78, no. 2 (2000): 116.

212. Louis Weeks III, "John Holt Rice and the American Colonization Society," *Journal of Presbyterian History* 46 (1968): 35–41.

213. E. T. Thompson, *Presbyterians in the South*, 1:334.

214. Bradshaw, *History of Hampden-Sydney College*, 1:365.

215. A. D. Thomas, "Moses Hoge," 8.

216. Society of Missionary Inquiry, Minute Book 1: 1818–1830, July 10, 1819.

217. Ibid., July 10, 1819; July 17, 1820; January 14, 1821; August 21, 1821.

218. Ibid., July 10, 1819.

219. John Haddon Leith, "Teaching Theology at Union Seminary in Virginia" (paper presented on the 175th anniversary of the founding of Union Theological Seminary, October 13, 1987), 2.

220. Wilbur E. Garrett, ed., *Historical Atlas of the United States* (Washington, DC: National Geographic Society, 1988), 40.

221. Bradshaw, *History of Hampden-Sydney College*, 1:359.

222. Spangler, "Proslavery Presbyterians," 117.

223. Ibid.

224. Bradshaw, *History of Hampden-Sydney College*, 1:359–61.

225. *Minutes of the Presbyterian Church in America, 1706–1788*, ed. Guy Klett (Philadelphia: Presbyterian Historical Society, 1976), 567.

226. Ibid., 627.

227. Robert Livingston Stanton, *The Church and the Rebellion: A Consideration of the Rebellion against the Government of the United States; and the Agency of the Church, North and South, in Relation Thereto* (New York: Derby & Miller, 1864), 372.

228. Spangler, "Proslavery Presbyterians," 113.

229. Longenecker, *Shenandoah Religion*, 135–37.

230. *Extracts from the Minutes of the General Assembly of the Presbyterian Church in the United States of America A.D. 1818* (1818), 692.

231. David E. Swift, "Progress and Impasse in Virginia: A Study in American Humanism and Calvinism, 1770–1830" (PhD diss., Wesleyan University, Middletown, CT, 1969), 238.

232. F. R. Flournoy, "Early Life of Benjamin Mosby Smith," 13.

233. E. T. Thompson, "John Holt Rice," 177.

234. Swift, "Progress and Impasse in Virginia," 241–42.

235. John Holt Rice, "Thoughts on Slavery," *Virginia Evangelical and Literary Magazine* 2, no. 7 (July 1819): 293.

236. Rice, *New England Memorials*, 474.

237. Rice, "Thoughts on Slavery," 295.

238. Ibid., 301.

239. Ibid., 295, 301.

240. Rice, *New England Memorials*, 474.

241. Rice, "Thoughts on Slavery," 293.

242. E. T. Thompson, *Presbyterians in the South*, 1:328.

243. Rice, "Thoughts on Slavery," 299.

244. Maxwell, *Memoir of the Rev. John H. Rice*, 306–7.

245. Morrison, "*The Virginia Literary and Evangelical Magazine*, 1818–1828," 270.

246. Maxwell, *Memoir of the Rev. John H. Rice*, 307.

247. Rice, "Thoughts on Slavery," 298.

248. E. T. Thompson, *Presbyterians in the South*, 1:333–34.

249. *Minutes of the General Assembly of the Presbyterian Church* (1818), 693.

250. *Minutes of the Presbyterian Church in America, 1706–1788*, 627.

251. *Minutes of the General Assembly of the Presbyterian Church* (1818), 692.

252. Price, "Life of Reverend John Holt Rice," 131–32.

253. Philological Society Minutes (Hampden Sydney, VA, 1828–1830), 1, March 1, 1828.

254. Ibid., March 13, 1828.

255. Ibid., March 28, 1828.

256. Ibid., July 26, 1828.

257. Ibid., December 5, 1828.

258. Ibid.: "Joseph Brown read an essay, written in answer to the question: Does בָּרַךְ ever mean to blaspheme or curse?"

259. Ibid., February 6, 1829: "Robert L. Caldwell read an essay on the meaning of נָחַשׁ (to practice divination) with a view particularly, to examine the interpretations given to that word by Dr. Adams Clark."

260. Ibid., March 6, 1829.

261. Ibid., March 5, 1830.

262. Ibid., January 23, 1829.

263. Ibid., February 6, 1829.

264. Ibid., February 20, 1829.

265. Ibid., March 19, 1830.

266. Price, "Life of Reverend John Holt Rice," 140–42.

267. Society of Missionary Inquiry, Correspondence, Book 2, January 13, 1832.

268. Ernest Trice Thompson, "Union Theological Seminary," *Commonwealth*, February 1952, 1.

269. E. T. Thompson, "The First Years," 14, 18.

270. Mahler, "History of Union Theological Seminary," 163.

271. E. T. Thompson, *Presbyterians in the South*, 1:278–79.

CHAPTER 4: Our Southern Zion

1. Faculty Minutes, vol. 1, *1828–1859* (Hampden Sydney, VA), December 10, 1831.

2. Union Theological Seminary Board of Trustees Minutes, 1:75.

3. Henry Richard Mahler Jr., "A History of Union Theological Seminary in Virginia, 1807–1865" (ThD diss., Union Theological Seminary in Virginia, 1951), 215.

4. Jon Meacham, *American Lion: Andrew Jackson in the White House* (New York: Random House Trade Paperbacks, 2009), 46, 132.

5. Society of Missionary Inquiry, Correspondence, Book 2 (Hampden Sydney, VA, 1818–1832), letter 10, April 9, 1828.

6. Ibid., letter 21, March 19, 1833.

7. William E. Thompson, *Her Walls before Thee Stand:. The 235-Year History of the Presbyterian Congregation at Hampden-Sydney, Virginia* ([Hampden Sydney, VA]: William E. Thompson, 2010), 146.

8. Society of Missionary Inquiry, Correspondence, Book 2, letter 27, December 11, 1835.

9. William E. Thompson, "The Seminary Moves to Richmond, Part 4," *Museum: Newsletter of the Associates of the Esther Thomas Atkinson Museum of Hampden-Sydney*, Spring 2001, 38.

10. William B. Sprague, *Annals of the American Pulpit*, 4 (New York: Robert Carter & Brothers, 1859), 193.

11. Henry A. White, "George Addison Baxter," *Union Seminary Magazine* 9, no. 4 (March–April 1898): 274–77; William Henry Foote, *Sketches of Virginia, Historical and Biographical, Second Series* (Philadelphia: J. B. Lippincott & Co., 1855), 260–69, 280–94.

12. Faculty Minutes, vol. 1, 1828–1859, December 10, 1831.

13. Sprague, *Annals of the American Pulpit*, 4, 194.

14. H. A. White, "George Addison Baxter," 275.

15. Ernest Trice Thompson, *Presbyterians in the South*, vol. 1, *1607–1861* (Richmond, VA: John Knox Press, 1963), 331.

16. Harold M. Parker, *United Synod of the South: The Southern New School Presbyterian Church*, Presbyterian Historical Society Publications 26 (New York: Greenwood Press, 1988), 2; cf. unpublished manuscript notes in the files of James H. Smylie.

17. T. Hartley Hall IV, "The Lower Gifts" (1987), 5.

18. George A. Baxter, *Inaugural Address of the Rev. G. A. Baxter, D.D., on His Induction into the Professorship of Christian Theology, in Union Theological Seminary: Delivered at the College Church, Prince Edward County, Virginia, April 11, 1832* (Richmond, VA: J. Macfarlan, 1832), 4–6.

19. Ernest Trice Thompson, "The First Years," in *The Days of Our Years: The Historical Convocations Held April 24–27, 1962, as a Feature of the Celebration of the Sesquicentennial of Union Theological Seminary in Virginia* (Richmond, VA: Union Theological Seminary, 1962), 14.

20. Baxter, *Inaugural Address*, 7–9, 15–16.

21. Foote, *Sketches of Virginia*, 456–59.

22. Baxter, *Inaugural Address*, 22.

23. T. H. Hall, "The Lower Gifts," 4.

24. Sprague, *Annals of the American Pulpit*, 4, 196.

25. Moses D. Hoge, "An Address," *Union Seminary Magazine* 5, no. 3 (January–February 1894): 161.

26. H. A. White, "George Addison Baxter," 277.

27. M. Hoge, "An Address," 160.

28. Jacob Harris Patton, *A Popular History of the Presbyterian Church in the United States of America* (New York: R. S. Mighill & Co., 1900), 301, 313.

29. Society of Missionary Inquiry, Correspondence, Book 2, letter 16, January 13, 1832.

30. T. Hartley Hall IV, "Administrative History of Union Theological Seminary" (notes in the author's papers, 1986), 16. Also Board of Trustees Minutes, 1:120. It is not clear which contractor had to be paid.

31. Mahler, "History of Union Theological Seminary in Virginia, 1807–1865," 174; Board of Trustees Minutes, 1:112.

32. Foote, *Sketches of Virginia*, 418.

33. Robert Livingston Stanton, *The Church and the Rebellion: A Consideration of the Rebellion against the Government of the United States; and the Agency of the Church, North and South, in Relation Thereto* (New York: Derby & Miller, 1864), 369–70.

34. *Extracts from the Minutes of the General Assembly of the Presbyterian Church in the United States of America A.D. 1818* (1818), 692.

35. Parker, *United Synod of the South*, 1.

36. Mahler, "History of Union Theological Seminary," 191; Board of Trustees Minutes, 1:113–14.

37. Sprague, *Annals of the American Pulpit*, 176–79.

38. E. T. Thompson, *Presbyterians in the South*, 1:377–79.

39. George Junkin, *The Vindication, Containing a History of the Trial of the Rev. Albert Barnes by the Second Presbytery and by the Synod of Philadelphia* (Philadelphia: Wm. S. Martien, 1836), xxiii.

40. Board of Trustees Minutes (1823–1840), 1:128, April 12, 1836.

41. Ibid., 1:161.

42. Ibid., 1:132–34, April 13, 1836.

43. Ibid., 1:137, September 27, 1836.

44. Foote, *Sketches of Virginia*, 511, 514–18.

45. E. T. Thompson, *Presbyterians in the South*, 1:392.

46. Foote, *Sketches of Virginia*, 525, 530–33.

47. W. E. Thompson, *Her Walls*, 131.

48. *Minutes of the General Assembly of the Presbyterian Church of United States of America* (1837), 507–8.

49. W. E. Thompson, *Her Walls*, 133.

50. Parker, *United Synod of the South*, 4.

51. George M. Marsden, *The Evangelical Mind and the New School Experience* (Eugene, OR: Wipf & Stock, 1970), 9.

52. Parker, *United Synod of the South*, 2.

53. Harold M. Parker, "The Urban Failure of the Southern New School Presbyterian Church," *Social Science Journal* 14, no. 1 (January 1977): 139.

54. Marsden, *Evangelical Mind and the New School*, 3.

55. Anne C. Loveland, "Presbyterians and Revivalism in the Old South," *Journal of Presbyterian History* 57 (1979): 39.

56. Charles Washington Baird, *Eutaxia, or, the Presbyterian Liturgies* (New York: M. W. Dodd, 1855), 245–46.

57. Henry Woods, *The History of the Presbyterian Controversy, with Early Sketches of Presbyterianism* (Louisville, KY: N. H. White, 1843), 41.

58. Parker, *United Synod of the South*, 13–14.

59. E. T. Thompson, *Presbyterians in the South*, 1:384, 386.

60. Stanton, *Church and the Rebellion*, 376.

61. Foote, *Sketches of Virginia*, 511–12.

62. E. T. Thompson, *Presbyterians in the South*, 1:396–97, 404.

63. Herbert C. Bradshaw, *History of Hampden-Sydney College*, vol. 1, *From the Beginnings to the Year 1856* (Durham, NC: Fisher-Harrison, 1976), 228.

64. Parker, *United Synod of the South*, 26.

65. Richard McIlwaine, *Memories of Three Score Years and Ten* (New York: Neale Publishing Co., 1908), 42.

66. William Hill, *History of the Rise, Progress, Genius, and Character of American Presbyterianism: Together with a Review of "The Constitutional History of the Presbyterian Church in the United States of America," by Chas. Hodge* (Washington City: J. Gideon Jr., 1839), 2.

67. Bradshaw, *History of Hampden-Sydney College*, 1:227–28.

68. Synod of North Carolina Minutes, 2:37–38, September 1837.

69. Board of Trustees Minutes, 1:145.

70. Foote, *Sketches of Virginia*, 541; Minutes of the Synod of Virginia, 6:200.

71. Board of Trustees Minutes, 1:149–50, April 10, 1838.

72. Walter W. Moore, "Historical Sketch," in *Septuagesimal Celebration of Union Theological Seminary in Virginia, 1824–1894* (Richmond, VA: Whittet & Shepperson, 1894), 14.

73. Foote, *Sketches of Virginia*, 541.

74. Board of Trustees Minutes, 1:150–51, April 10, 1838.

75. Society of Missionary Inquiry, Correspondence, Book 2, letter 14, August 11, 1839.

76. James H. Smylie, "The Burden of Southern Church Historians: World Mission, Regional Captivity, Reconciliation" (inaugural address as professor of American church history at Union Theological Seminary in Richmond, VA, March 7, 1968); see *Affirmation*, November 4, 1968: 31.

77. E. T. Thompson, *Presbyterians in the South*, 1:404.

78. W. E. Thompson, *Her Walls*, 126.

79. Board of Trustees Minutes, 1:159.

80. Mahler, "History of Union Theological Seminary," 203.

81. Board of Trustees Minutes, 1:149-151, April 10, 1838.

82. T. H. Hall, "Administrative History of Union," 19.

83. Board of Trustees Minutes, 1:162–63, April 10, 1838.

84. Ibid., 1:154, 162, 183.

85. Synod of North Carolina Minutes, 2:10, 22–23, November 1836.

86. Board of Trustees Minutes, 1:142.

87. John Luster Brinkley, *On This Hill: A Narrative History of Hampden-Sydney College, 1774–1994* (Hampden Sydney, VA: Hampden-Sydney College, 1994), 164.

88. Mahler, "History of Union Theological Seminary," 183.

89. Parker, *United Synod of the South*, 26.

90. Faculty Minutes, vol. 1, 1828–1859, December 8, 1838.

91. Board of Trustees Minutes, 1:170, September 24, 1839.

92. Mahler, "History of Union Theological Seminary," 209.

93. Minutes of the Synod of Virginia, 7:56.

94. Synod of North Carolina Minutes, 2:22.

95. Minutes of the Synod of Virginia, 7:85, 106–7, 125.

96. Society of Missionary Inquiry, Minute Book 2, 1830–1861 (Hampden Sydney, VA), April 4, 1831.

97. Society of Missionary Inquiry, Correspondence, Book 2, letter 24, June 11, 1834.

98. Society of Missionary Inquiry, Missionary Correspondence, letter 13.

99. Henry McKennie Goodpasture, "Our Field Is the World: Mission Studies at Union Theological Seminary in Virginia, 1812–1897," an address given on the 175th anniversary of the founding of Union Theological Seminary (October 12, 1987), 4.

100. Society of Missionary Inquiry, Minute Book 2, 1830–1861, February 1, 1844; February 28, 1857.

101. Ibid., September 1, 1845.

102. Ibid., December 1, 1853.

103. Ibid., February 1, 1850.

104. Faculty Minutes, vol. 1, 1828–1859, January 19, 1844.

105. Ibid., January 23, 1844.

106. Ibid., January 25, 1844.

107. W. E. Thompson, "Seminary Moves, Part 4," 39.

108. Board of Trustees Minutes, 1:121.

109. William E. Thompson, "Gone but Not Forgotten," an address given for the dedication of the Presbyterian Seminary historic marker sign (April 27, 1991), 4. Boston House was finished in 1829. Its first inhabitants were the Rice family, then the Baxter family. The Coleman Guest Cottage may have been the slave quarters for Boston House. North Carolina House was completed in 1830. Today, from the College Road side, one can see the words "North Carolina" and "May 1830" painted on the tall brick chimneys. This house served as the residence of the president of Hampden-Sydney College from 1904 until 1939; since its restoration in 1990, it is the permanent home of the college's dean of the faculty. William E. Thompson also argues that there was another slave cabin behind North Carolina House. Westminster Hall was also finished in 1830. It served as the seminary's dining room (although seminary and college students alike ate at a half-dozen boarding houses in the village). There were privies behind all the buildings. Eastcourt was built for Anne Rice after John Holt Rice died in 1831.

110. W. Moore, "Historical Sketch," in *Septuagesimal Celebration*, 15.

111. T. H. Hall, "Administrative History of Union," 20.

112. Board of Trustees Minutes, loose pages, April 10, 1832.

113. Society of Missionary Inquiry, Minute Book 2, 1830–1861, January 1, 1848.

114. Faculty Minutes, vol. 1, 1828–1859, December 8, 1848.

115. Ibid., February 21, 1850.

116. Society of Missionary Inquiry, Correspondence, Book 2, letter 20, March 7, 1833.

117. Faculty Minutes, vol. 1, August 24, 1847.

118. Ibid., February 10, 1848.

119. Frank Bell Lewis, "Times of Crisis," in *Days of Our Years*, 27.

120. Society of Missionary Inquiry, Minute Book 2, 1830–1861, November 3, 1832.

121. Ibid., February 2, 1835.

122. Ibid., January 1, 1838.

123. Ibid., June 30, 1838.

124. Ibid., December 31, 1842.

125. Ibid., June 1, 1848.

126. Ibid., June 7, 1849.

127. Ibid., various dates.

128. Ibid., November 3, 1832.

129. Faculty Minutes, vol. 1, 1828–1859, November 11, 1836.

130. Society of Missionary Inquiry, Minute Book 2, 1830–1861, November 15, 1836.

131. Faculty Minutes, vol. 1, 1828–1859, November 23, 1836.

132. Society of Missionary Inquiry, Minute Book 2, 1830–1861, November 25, 1836.

133. Ibid., December 21, 1836.

134. Faculty Minutes, vol. 1, 1828–1859, December 26, 1836.

135. Society of Missionary Inquiry, Minute Book 2, 1830–1861, June 1, 1840.

136. Ibid., December 1, 1849.

137. Ibid., various dates.

138. Ibid., December 31, 1842, and May 31, 1845.

139. Ibid., letter 24, June 11, 1834.

140. Francis R. Flournoy, *Benjamin Mosby Smith, 1811–1893* (Richmond, VA: Richmond Press, 1947), 22–38.

141. Faculty Minutes, vol. 1, 1828–1859, November 6, 1832.

142. F. Lewis, "Times of Crisis," 28; Board Minutes, 1:193, 196.

143. Board of Trustees Minutes, 1:215.

144. UTS Catalogue, 1833–1834, 8.

145. John Blair Hoge, *Sketch of the Life and Character of the Rev. Moses Hoge, D.D.*, Historical Transcripts 2 (Richmond, VA: Union Theological Seminary, 1964), 64.

146. Board of Trustees Minutes, loose pages, September 28, 1836.

147. Faculty Minutes, vol. 1, 1828–1859, March 31, 1835.

148. Ibid., June 15, 1835.

149. Ibid., November 2, 1835.

150. W. Moore, "Historical Sketch," in *Septuagesimal Celebration*, 17.

151. Faculty Minutes, vol. 1, 1828–1859, July 5, 1836.

152. W. Moore, "Historical Sketch," in *Septuagesimal Celebration*, 16.

153. Board of Trustees Minutes, 1:174, April 7, 1840.

154. Ibid., 1:231–32, 234.

155. James H. Smylie, "UTS Opens the Family Photo Album," *Focus* 2, no. 4 (Winter 1987): 10.

156. W. Moore, "Historical Sketch," in *Septuagesimal Celebration*, 15.

157. T. H. Hall, "Administrative History of Union," 17, 22.

158. Mahler, "History of Union Theological Seminary," 221.

159. Robert Lewis Dabney, "Francis S. Sampson, D.D.," *Union Seminary Magazine* 9 (March–April 1898): 282, 284.

160. T. H. Hall, "Administrative History of Union," 22.

161. Mahler, "History of Union Theological Seminary," 215; Board of Trustees Minutes, 1:197.

162. Board of Trustees Minutes, 1:181.

163. Faculty Minutes, vol. 1, 1828–1859, June 28, 1841.

164. F. Lewis, "Times of Crisis," 29.

165. T. H. Hall, "The Lower Gifts," 4.

166. Walter W. Moore, "Historical Sketch of Union Theological Seminary," *Union Seminary Magazine* 9, no. 4 (March–April 1898): 236–37.

167. Minutes of the Synod of Virginia, 8:39–45.

168. Ibid., 1:6 as printed; Board of Trustees Minutes, 1:210.

169. T. H. Hall, "Administrative History of Union," 20; Board of Trustees Minutes, 1:191.

170. Mahler, "History of Union Theological Seminary," 221; Board of Trustees Minutes, 1:197, 208.

171. T. H. Hall, "Administrative History of Union," 21.

172. Smylie, "Family Photo Album," 10.

173. T. H. Hall, "Administrative History of Union," 21–22.

174. Board of Trustees Minutes, 1:159–60.

175. Faculty Minutes, vol. 1, 1828–1859, September 14, 1843.

176. Board of Trustees Minutes, 1:141.

177. Synod of North Carolina Minutes, vol. 2, October 1837, 8.

178. Minutes of the Synod of Virginia, 6:123.

179. Ibid., 7:193.

180. Bruce S. Greenwalt, "The Lord Watch between Us: White and Black Southern Presbyterians, 1864–1874" (unpublished manuscript in the author's files, 1982), 2.

181. Faculty Minutes, vol. 1, 1828–1859, September 26, 1842.

182. Board of Trustees Minutes, 1:220.

183. Minutes of the Synod of Virginia, 1:57.

184. Board of Trustees Minutes, 1:334.

185. T. H. Hall, "The Lower Gifts," 8.

186. Goodpasture, "Our Field Is the World," 4.

187. Society of Missionary Inquiry, Missionary Correspondence, letter 1.

188. F. Lewis, "Times of Crisis," 30.

189. F. R. Flournoy, *Benjamin Mosby Smith*, 1, 3.

190. Francis R. Flournoy, "The Early Life of Benjamin Mosby Smith," *Union Seminary Review* 55, no. 1 (November 1943): 3–4.

191. Flournoy, *Benjamin Mosby Smith*, 6–11, 13, 22–38.

192. F. R. Flournoy, "Early Life of Benjamin Mosby Smith," 1.

193. W. E. Thompson, *Her Walls*, 126.

194. Bradshaw, *History of Hampden-Sydney College*, 1:370.

195. W. Lacy, "Benjamin Mosby Smith," 286.

196. F. R. Flournoy, *Benjamin Mosby Smith*, 49.

197. Benjamin Mosby Smith, "The Brown Memorial Library: Address at the Laying of the Corner-Stone of the Library Building of Union Theological Seminary, Hampden-Sydney, Va., September 1, 1879," *Central Presbyterian* (Richmond, VA), September 17, 1879; reprinted, *Union Seminary Review*, August 1944, 298.

198. Board of Trustees Minutes, 1:166.

199. Mahler, "History of Union Theological Seminary," 241.

200. Board of Trustees Minutes, 1:215.

201. Thomas Cary Johnson, *The Life and Letters of Robert Lewis Dabney* (Carlisle, PA: Banner of Truth, 1977), 34.

202. Ibid., 35.

203. Topping, "History of Hampden-Sydney College," 75.

204. Robert Lewis Dabney, *A Discourse on the Uses and Results of Church History Delivered by Robert L. Dabney, May 8, 1854, at His Induction into the Professorship of Ecclesiastical History and Polity in Union Theological Seminary, Virginia* (Richmond, VA: Ritchies & Dunnavant, 1854), 3.

205. Ibid., 4, 6–13.

206. Lorie Mastemaker, "Hampden-Sydney in the 1850s: Part 1, The Quiet before the Storm," *Museum: Newsletter of the Associates of the Esther Thomas Atkinson Museum of Hampden-Sydney*, Spring 2004, 21.

207. McIlwaine, *Three Score Years and Ten*, 45.

208. Brinkley, *On This Hill*, 203–4.

209. W. Moore, "Historical Sketch," in *Septuagesimal Celebration*, 15.

210. Mastemaker, "Hampden-Sydney in the 1850s," 22.

211. H. Clarence Bradshaw, *History of Farmville, Virginia, 1798–1948: Reprint of the Sesquicentennial Edition of the Farmville Herald, Dated October 22, 1948* (Farmville, VA: Farmville Herald, 1994), 17.

212. Mastemaker, "Hampden-Sydney in the 1850s," 24–25, 28.

213. W. E. Thompson, *Her Walls*, 179.

214. McIlwaine, *Three Score Years and Ten*, 57.

215. Brinkley, *On This Hill*, 211.

216. McIlwaine, *Three Score Years and Ten*, 105.

217. Brinkley, *On This Hill*, 211.

218. T. H. Hall, "Administrative History of Union," 23.

219. Mastemaker, "Hampden-Sydney in the 1850s," 16.

220. W. Moore, "Historical Sketch," in *Septuagesimal Celebration*, 15.

221. T. H. Hall, "Administrative History of Union," 24.

222. Robert Fishburne Campbell, "Rev. Thomas E. Peck, D.D., L.L.D.," *Union Seminary Magazine* 9 (1898): 299.

223. E. T. Thompson, *Presbyterians in the South*, 1:459.

224. W. E. Thompson, "Gone but Not Forgotten," 10.

225. Faculty Minutes, vol. 1, 1828–1859, September 7, 1855.

226. Ibid., November 30, 1854.

227. Board of Trustees Minutes, 1:326–28.

228. Minutes of the Synod of Virginia, 1:146.

229. Board of Trustees Minutes, 1:388.

230. Ibid., 2:54.

231. T. H. Hall, "Administrative History of Union," 27.

232. Mahler, "History of Union Theological Seminary," 270, 273.

233. Board of Trustees Minutes, 2:8.

234. Catalogue, 1854–1855, 12–13.

235. Board of Trustees Minutes, 1:246.

236. McIlwaine, *Three Score Years and Ten*, 52–53.

237. Catalogue, 1854–1855, 12–13.

238. McIlwaine, *Three Score Years and Ten*, 108–9.

239. Minutes of the Synod of Virginia, 1:220.

240. Board of Trustees Minutes, 1:356, 368.

241. T. H. Hall, "Administrative History of Union," 27.

242. Board of Trustees Minutes, 1:399.

243. Minutes of the Synod of Virginia, 1:164.

244. Board of Trustees Minutes, 1:393.

245. Minutes of the Synod of Virginia, 1:184, 202–3.

246. T. H. Hall, "Administrative History of Union," 24.

247. Catalogue, 1856, 5.

248. Ibid., 1854–1855, 14–15.

249. Ibid., 1856, 14.

250. Faculty Minutes, vol. 1, 1828–1859, September 14, 1857.

251. Board of Trustees Minutes, 1:214, 234, 344.

252. Robert Lewis Dabney, "The Course of Studies in Union Seminary, Part 1," *Central Presbyterian* 1, no. 33 (August 16, 1856): 130; "The Course of Studies in Union Seminary, Part 2," *Central Presbyterian* 1, no. 33 (August 29, 1856): 134.

253. Ibid., 130.

254. Ibid., 134.

255. Ibid., 130.

256. Board of Trustees Minutes, 1:358, 437.

257. E. T. Thompson, *Presbyterians in the South*, 1:533–34.

258. W. E. Thompson, *Her Walls*, 184.

259. Patricia P. Hickin, "Antislavery in Virginia, 1831–1861" (PhD diss., University of Virginia, June 1968; in James H. Smylie's Papers), 338.

260. E. T. Thompson, *Presbyterians in the South*, 1:535.

261. F. Lewis, "Times of Crisis," 35.

262. E. T. Thompson, *Presbyterians in the South*, 1:535, 555, 559.

263. F. Lewis, "Times of Crisis," 35–36.

264. J. Treadwell Davis, "The Presbyterians and the Sectional Conflict," *Southern Quarterly* 8 (January 1970): 120.

265. Ibid., 121–22.

266. Maurice W. Armstrong, Lefferts A. Loetscher, and Charles A. Anderson, eds., *The Presbyterian Enterprise: Sources of American Presbyterian History*, Presbyterian Historical Society Publication Series 1 (Philadelphia: Westminster Press, 1956), 211–12.

267. Ernest Trice Thompson, *Presbyterians in the South*, vol. 2, *1861–1890* (Richmond, VA: John Knox Press, 1973), 63.

268. W. E. Thompson, *Her Walls*, 208.

269. J. T. Davis, "Presbyterians and the Sectional Conflict," 121–22.

270. E. T. Thompson, *Presbyterians in the South*, 1:561.

271. F. R. Flournoy, *Benjamin Mosby Smith*, 75.

272. E. T. Thompson, *Presbyterians in the South*, 1:559.

273. F. Lewis, "Times of Crisis," 35–36.

274. Brinkley, *On This Hill*, 276.

275. W. E. Thompson, *Her Walls*, 200, 204.

276. Board of Trustees Minutes, 2:85.

277. Mahler, "History of Union Theological Seminary," 283.

278. Minutes of the Synod of Virginia, 1:287.

279. F. R. Flournoy, *Benjamin Mosby Smith*, 75–76.

280. Brinkley, *On This Hill*, 280: "Turretin" refers to Francis Turretin (1623–87), author of the primary Latin textbook Robert Lewis Dabney used to teach his brand of Calvinism: *Institutio theologiae elencticae*, translated as *Institutes of Elenctic Theology*, 3 vols. (Phillipsburg, NJ: Presbyterian & Reformed Publishing Co., 1992–97).

281. Brinkley, *On This Hill*, 279. The paroling of prisoners ended on April 17, 1864, with the massacre at Fort Pillow, Tenn. (north of Memphis). Confederate forces, commanded by Nathan Bedford Forrest, murdered Union soldiers, mostly U.S. Colored Troops, who were in the act of surrendering. Ulysses S. Grant ordered General Benjamin F. Butler, who was negotiating prisoner exchanges with the Confederacy, to demand that in the exchange and treatment of prisoners, black prisoners had to be treated identically to whites: a failure to do so would "be regarded as a refusal on their part to agree to the further exchange of prisoners, and [would] be so treated by us." The Confederacy refused, and there were no further prisoner exchanges in the war.

282. Faculty Minutes, vol. 2, 1859–1892 (Hampden Sydney, VA), September 9, 1861.

283. W. E. Thompson, *Her Walls*, 211.

284. Johnson, *Life and Letters of Robert Lewis Dabney*, 262–63.

285. Smylie, "Family Photo Album," 11.

286. Board of Trustees Minutes, 2:91–92.

287. W. E. Thompson, *Her Walls*, 211.

288. E. T. Thompson, *Presbyterians in the South*, 2:77.

289. Board of Trustees Minutes, 2:93.

290. Mahler, "History of Union Theological Seminary," 285.

291. Board of Trustees Minutes, 2:95, May 12, 1862.

292. E. T. Thompson, *Presbyterians in the South*, 2:79.

293. Mastemaker, "Hampden-Sydney in the 1850s," 16.

294. F. R. Flournoy, *Benjamin Mosby Smith*, 77.

295. Faculty Minutes, vol. 2, 1859–1892, September 8, 1862.

296. Ibid., August 23, 1862.

297. Ibid., September 8, 1862.

298. Ibid., January 20, 1864.

299. F. R. Flournoy, *Benjamin Mosby Smith*, 97, 112.

300. Herbert C. Bradshaw, *History of Prince Edward County, Virginia, from Its Earliest Settlements through Its Establishment in 1754 to Its Bicentennial Year* (Richmond, VA: Dietz Press, 1954), 391.

301. Board of Trustees Minutes, 2:115–18, 120.

302. T. H. Hall, "Administrative History of Union," 28.

303. F. Lewis, "Times of Crisis," 39.

304. Minutes of the Synod of Virginia, 1:353.

305. Board of Trustees Minutes, 2:128–29, 131.

306. F. R. Flournoy, *Benjamin Mosby Smith*, 79.

307. W. E. Thompson, *Her Walls*, 215–16.

308. Bradshaw, *History of Farmville, Virginia*, 32.

309. Board of Trustees Minutes, 2:131.

310. W. Moore, "Historical Sketch," *Union Seminary Magazine* 9:239.

311. F. R. Flournoy, *Benjamin Mosby Smith*, 75.

312. Minutes of the Synod of Virginia, 1:373.

313. John B. Trotti, "The Seminary during the Civil War, 1861–1865," *Focus*, Summer 1994, 3. These surviving books possibly include Enoch Pond, *Swedenborgianism Reviewed* (Portland, ME: Hyde, Lord & Duren, 1846); Johann F. I. Tafel, *Vergleichende Darstellung und Beurtheilung der Lehrgegensätze der Katholiken und Protestanten* (Tübingen: Zu-Guttenberg, 1835).

314. F. R. Flournoy, *Benjamin Mosby Smith*, 240.

315. W. E. Thompson, *Her Walls*, 207.

316. J. T. Davis, "Presbyterians and the Sectional Conflict," 125–26.

317. John T. Ames Jr., "The Relationship between Northern and Southern Presbyterian Churches, 1861–1882" (a term paper written for a directed study supervised by Dr. James H. Smiley, Union Theological Seminary in Virginia, Richmond, May 1965), 4.

318. John H. Leith, "Teaching Theology at Union Seminary in Virginia" (paper presented on the 175th anniversary of the founding of Union Theological Seminary, October 13, 1987), 4.

CHAPTER 5: Fighting Yankees and Moving to Richmond

1. Francis R. Flournoy, *Benjamin Mosby Smith, 1811–1893* (Richmond, VA: Richmond Press, 1947), 79.

2. James Appleby, "Rebuilding," in *The Days of Our Years: The Historical Convocations Held April 24–27, 1962, as a Feature of the Celebration of the Sesquicentennial of Union Theological Seminary in Virginia* (Richmond: Union Theological Seminary in Virginia, 1962), 47.

3. Walter W. Moore, "Historical Sketch," in *Septuagesimal Celebration of Union Theological Seminary in Virginia, 1824–1894* (Richmond, VA: Whittet & Shepperson, 1894), 21.

4. T. Hartley Hall IV, "Administrative History of Union Theological Seminary" (notes in the author's papers, 1986), 28.

5. Ernest Trice Thompson, *Presbyterians in the South*, vol. 2, *1861–1890* (Richmond, VA: John Knox Press, 1973), 371.

6. W. Moore, "Historical Sketch," in *Septuagesimal Celebration*, 21.

7. UTS Catalogue, 1866, 2–4.

8. F. R. Flournoy, *Benjamin Mosby Smith*, 79–80; Walter W. Moore, "Historical Sketch of Union Theological Seminary," *Union Seminary Magazine* 9, no. 4 (March–April 1898): 240.

9. Henry Richard Mahler Jr., "A History of Union Theological Seminary in Virginia, 1807–1865" (ThD diss., Union Theological Seminary in Virginia, 1951), 87–89.

10. Herbert C. Bradshaw, *History of Prince Edward County, Virginia, from Its Earliest Settlements through Its Establishment in 1754 to Its Bicentennial Year* (Richmond, VA: Dietz Press, 1954), 476.

11. W. Moore, "Historical Sketch," in *Septuagesimal Celebration*, 22–23.

12. T. H. Hall, "Administrative History of Union," 29.

13. Robert Lewis Dabney, *A Defence of Virginia and through Her, of the South in Recent and Pending Contests against the Sectional Party* (New York: E. J. Hale & Son, 1867), 25, 43, 356.

14. F. R. Flournoy, *Benjamin Mosby Smith*, 82, 103–4.

15. E. T. Thompson, *Presbyterians in the South*, 2:373.

16. F. R. Flournoy, *Benjamin Mosby Smith*, 97.

17. Samuel B. Wilson, "History of Union Theological Seminary" (a report for the board of directors, given at their meeting on May 14, 1867), 16.

18. E. T. Thompson, *Presbyterians in the South*, 2:138–39.

19. William E. Thompson, *Her Walls before Thee Stand: The 235-Year History of the Presbyterian Congregation at Hampden-Sydney, Virginia* ([Hampden Sydney, VA]: William E. Thompson, 2010), 236.

20. F. R. Flournoy, *Benjamin Mosby Smith*, 104.

21. W. E. Thompson, *Her Walls*, 238.

22. J. Treadwell Davis, "The Presbyterians and the Sectional Conflict," *Southern Quarterly* 8 (January 1970): 130.

23. Ibid., 130.

24. Thomas Cary Johnson, *The Life and Letters of Robert Lewis Dabney* (Richmond, VA: Presbyterian Board of Publication, 1903; reprint, Carlisle, PA: Banner of Truth, 1977), 335.

25. F. R. Flournoy, *Benjamin Mosby Smith*, 108.

26. T. Hartley Hall IV, "The Lower Gifts" (paper presented at opening convocation, Watts Chapel, Union Theological Seminary in Virginia, September 9, 1987), 11.

27. F. R. Flournoy, *Benjamin Mosby Smith*, 70.

28. Benjamin Mosby Smith, *A Sermon, Occasioned by the Death of Charles T. Edie, Who Was Killed by Edward A. Langhorne* (Petersburg, VA: Express Book and Job Office, 1857), 10–12.

29. F. R. Flournoy, *Benjamin Mosby Smith*, 72, 122–23.

30. Ernest Trice Thompson, *Presbyterians in the South*, vol. 1, *1607–1861* (Richmond, VA: John Knox Press, 1963), 470.

31. F. R. Flournoy, *Benjamin Mosby Smith*, 125.

32. Peck, *Miscellanies of Rev. Thomas E. Peck, D.D., LL.D.* 3 vols., ed. Thomas Cary Johnson (Richmond, VA: Presbyterian Committee of Publication, 1895–97), 3:26.

33. John H. Leith, "Teaching Theology at Union Seminary in Virginia" (paper presented on the 175th anniversary of the founding of Union Theological Seminary, October 13, 1987), 8; referring to Robert Lewis Dabney, *Syllabus and Notes of the Course of Systematic and Polemic Theology Taught in Union Theological Seminary, Virginia* (Richmond, VA: Shepperson & Graves, 1871).

34. Richard McIlwaine, *Memories of Three Score Years and Ten* (New York: Neale Publishing Co., 1908), 103.

35. Faculty Minutes, vol. 3, 1892–1911 (Hampden Sydney and Richmond, VA, 1892–1911), March 31, 1893.

36. *1869 Constitution and Plan of Union Theological Seminary in Virginia, Amended 1892* (Richmond, VA: Whittet & Shepperson, 1893), 13–15.

37. *Report of a Committee of the General Assembly of the Presbyterian Church, Exhibiting the Plan of a Theological Seminary* (New York: J. Seymour, 1810), 18.

38. William B. Oglesby Jr., "Faith in Action: Preparing Students for the Work of Ministry" (paper presented on the 175th anniversary of the founding of Union Theological Seminary, October 12, 1987), 5.

39. Robert Lewis Dabney, *Discussions by Robert L. Dabney*, vol. 2, ed. C. R. Vaughan (Richmond, VA: Presbyterian Committee of Publication, 1891), 47, 57, 72.

40. F. R. Flournoy, *Benjamin Mosby Smith*, 63.

41. Glenn T. Miller, *Piety and Professionalism: American Protestant Theological Education, 1870–1970* (Grand Rapids: William B. Eerdmans Publishing Co., 2007), 86–87.

42. Francis B. Simkins, "Robert Lewis Dabney, Southern Conservative," *Georgia Review* 18 (1964): 406.

43. Ibid., 407.

44. E. T. Thompson, *Presbyterians in the South*, 2:489–90.

45. Charles Reagan Wilson, "Robert Lewis Dabney: Religion and the Southern Holocaust," *Virginia Magazine of History and Biography* (Richmond) 89, no. 1 (January 1981): 82–83.

46. E. T. Thompson, *Presbyterians in the South*, 2:112–13.

47. William E. Thompson, "From the Hill to the Brook: The Story of the Removal of the Seminary to Richmond" (an address given on October 5, 1998), 9.

48. William E. Thompson, "Railroads, Racism, and Religion: A Re-Examination of the Reasons for the Removal of Union Theological Seminary from Hampden-Sydney to Richmond, with a View to a Modern Day Ministry amidst the Continuing Reasons for the Departure" (DMin diss., Union Theological Seminary, 1992), 90.

49. Faculty Minutes, vol. 2, 1859–1892 (Hampden Sydney, VA), September 9, 1874.

50. W. E. Thompson, "Railroads, Racism, and Religion," 90.

51. John Luster Brinkley, *On This Hill: A Narrative History of Hampden-Sydney College, 1774–1994* (Hampden Sydney, VA: Hampden-Sydney College, 1994), 334.

52. J. Gray McAllister, *The Life and Letters of Walter W. Moore: Second Founder and First President of Union Theological Seminary in Virginia* (Richmond, VA: Union Theological Seminary, 1939), 368.

53. E. T. Thompson, *Presbyterians in the South*, 2:216–17.

54. Brinkley, *On This Hill*, 350–51.

55. W. E. Thompson, *Her Walls*, 256.

56. E. T. Thompson, *Presbyterians in the South*, 2:375–76.

57. C. R. Wilson, "Dabney: Religion and the Southern Holocaust," 84.

58. Editorial, "Dedication Exercises," *Union Seminary Magazine* 10, no. 1 (October–November 1898): 194.

59. W. E. Thompson, *Her Walls*, 287.

60. Editorial, "Dedication Exercises," 195.

61. Robert Lewis Dabney, *Syllabus and Notes of the Course of Systematic and Polemic Theology Taught in Union Theological Seminary, Virginia* (Richmond, VA: Published by the Students, Shepperson & Graves, printers, 1871), 2, 4, 26–38, 139, 172.

62. Balmer H. Kelly, "No Ism but Bibleism: Biblical Studies at Union Theological Seminary in Virginia, 1812–1987" (paper presented on the 175th anniversary of the founding of Union Theological Seminary, October 12, 1987), 7–8.

63. Ibid., 8.

64. E. T. Thompson, *Presbyterians in the South*, 2:414.

65. Catalogue, 1873, 9–10.

66. James H. Smylie, "The Burden of Southern Church Historians: World Mission, Regional Captivity, Reconciliation" (inaugural address as professor of American church history at Union Theological Seminary in Richmond, VA, March 7, 1968), 6; cf. *Affirmation*, November 4, 1968, 25–50.

67. John B. Trotti, "The History of the Union Theological Seminary Library" (unpublished manuscript in the author's files, 2008), 23.

68. W. Moore, "Historical Sketch," in *Septuagesimal Celebration*, 26.

69. Walter W. Moore, "The First Fifty Years," *Union Seminary Magazine* 24, no. 1 (1912–13): 298.

70. Henry M. Brimm, "The Library of Union Theological Seminary, 1806–1944," *Union Seminary Review* 55, no. 4 (August 1944): 289.

71. Catalogue, 1896, 13, 15, 22, 25.

72. Benjamin Mosby Smith, "The Brown Memorial Library: Address at the Laying of the Corner-Stone of the Library Building of Union Theological Seminary, Hampden-Sydney, Va., September 1, 1879," *Central Presbyterian* (Richmond, VA), September 17, 1879; reprinted, *Union Seminary Review*, August 1944, 298.

73. W. E. Thompson, "From the Hill to the Brook," 8.

74. William E. Thompson, "The Seminary Moves to Richmond, Part 2, The Guiding Force: Walter W. Moore," *Museum: Newsletter of the Associates of the Esther Thomas Atkinson Museum of Hampden-Sydney*, Spring 2000, 18.

75. Johnson, *Life and Letters of Robert Lewis Dabney*, 439.

76. W. E. Thompson, "Railroads, Racism, and Religion," 30–31.

77. Miller, *Piety and Professionalism*, 272–78.

78. William E. Thompson, "The Hidden Reasons for Union Seminary's 1898 Move to Richmond" (a paper given to the St. James Fellowship, 1996), 5.

79. W. E. Thompson, "Railroads, Racism, and Religion," 31.

80. Miller, *Piety and Professionalism*, 272.

81. W. E. Thompson, "Railroads, Racism, and Religion," 32.

82. Miller, *Piety and Professionalism*, 232–33.

83. W. E. Thompson, "Railroads, Racism, and Religion," 27, 33–34.

84. T. H. Hall, "Administrative History of Union," 32.

85. Catalogue, 1881, 16.

86. T. H. Hall, "Administrative History of Union," 36.

87. W. Moore, "Historical Sketch," in *Septuagesimal Celebration*, 31.

88. Miller, *Piety and Professionalism*, xi.

89. Appleby, "Rebuilding," 42.

90. T. H. Hall, "Administrative History of Union," 39.

91. Appleby, "Rebuilding," 49. *Union Seminary Magazine* became *Union Seminary Review* with the October–November 1913 issue.

92. Walter W. Moore, "The Passing of Ussher's Chronology," *Union Seminary Magazine* 13, no. 2 (December 1901–January 1902): 73–81.

93. Russell Cecil, "The Psychological Aspects of the Conversion of the Apostle Paul," *Union Seminary Magazine* 9, no. 3 (January–February 1898): 168–76.

94. Franklin Pierce Ramsay, "Textual Emendation and Higher Criticism," *Union Seminary Magazine* 13, no. 1 (October–November 1901): 13–18.

95. Egbert Watson Smith, "Some Impressions of Radical Old Testament Criticism," *Union Seminary Magazine* 19, no. 2 (December 1907–January 1908): 163–72.

96. Samuel G. Wilson, "Bahaism," *Union Seminary Review* 25, no. 3 (February–March 1914): 214–24.

97. Parke P. Flournoy, "The Bugle from Berlin: The Retrocession of Harnack," *Union Seminary Magazine* 11, no. 1 (October–November 1899): 10–15.

98. Givens B. Strickler, "The New Theology, Part 1," *Union Seminary Magazine* 12, no. 1 (October–November 1900): 1–6; G. B. Strickler, "The New Theology, Part 2," *Union Seminary Magazine* 12, no. 2 (December 1900–January 1901): 89–99; G. B. Strickler, "The New Theology, Part 3," *Union Seminary Magazine* 12, no. 3 (February–March 1901): 175–84; G. B. Strickler, "The New Theology, Part 4," *Union Seminary Magazine* 12, no. 4 (April–May 1901): 268–75.

99. Givens B. Strickler, "The Bible and Science," *Union Seminary Magazine* 8, no. 4 (March–April 1897): 253–55.

100. William Caven, "Biblical Theology and Systematic Theology," *Union Seminary Magazine* 11, no. 4 (April–May 1900): 245–50.

101. Booker T. Washington, "The Relation of the Races in the South," *Union Seminary Magazine* 11, no. 4 (April–May 1900): 274–79.

102. D. Clay Lilly, "Colored Labor in Relation to the Prosperity of the Southern Farmer," *Union Seminary Magazine* 13, no. 4 (April–May 1902): 274–76.

103. J. B. Warren, "Evolution as It Stands Related to Christian Faith," *Union Seminary Magazine* 22, no. 4 (April–May 1911): 253–81.

104. Neal L. Anderson, "Evolution as a Science and a Philosophy," *Union Seminary Review* 33, no. 4 (July 1922): 288–98.

105. William T. Riviere, "Some Impressions of Philosophy in a French University," *Union Seminary Review* 31, no. 1 (October 1919): 34–38.

106. W. H. Woods, "Is the Church Meeting the Changed Conditions in the Social and Business World?," *Union Seminary Magazine* 15, no. 3 (February–March 1904): 225–32.

107. J. M. Wells, "The Christian and the Theatre," *Union Seminary Magazine* 13, no. 2 (December 1901–January 1902): 102–11.

108. Thomas Cary Johnson, "The Seminary Course of Study—Its Range, Standard, Examinations, and Tests," *Union Seminary Magazine* 9, no. 2 (November–December 1897): 14–31.

109. Walter W. Lingle, "The Latin Thesis," *Union Seminary Magazine* 13, no. 2 (December 1901–January 1902): 98–101.

110. Editorial, "Lack of Preparation among Ministerial Students," *Union Seminary Magazine* 10, no. 2 (December 1898–January 1899): 138–40.

111. Mary E. Richmond, "First Principles in the Relief of Distress," *Union Seminary Magazine* 17, no. 3 (February–March 1906): 185–92.

112. L. B. Turnbull, "The Lord's Supper—a Plea for Its More Frequent Observance," *Union Seminary Magazine* 9, no. 1 (September–October 1897): 32–37.

113. Hugh W. White, "Romish Obstacles to Mission Work in China," *Union Seminary Magazine* 11, no. 1 (October–November 1899): 47–50.

114. "Odd Moments," *Union Seminary Magazine* 1 (October–November 1889): 61.

115. "Among the Periodicals," *Union Seminary Magazine* 1 (October–November 1889): 77.

116. W. M. Junkin, "Inter-Seminary Missionary Alliance," *Union Seminary Magazine* 3, no. 4 (March–April 1892): 311.

117. Edward R. Leyburn, "The Student Volunteer Movement and the Detroit Convention," *Union Seminary Magazine* 5, no. 4 (March–April 1894): 272, 276.

118. Miller, *Piety and Professionalism*, 272–78.

119. W. E. Thompson, "Seminary Moves, Part 2," 11.

120. Catalogue, 1882, 13–14; 1886, 20–21.

121. Faculty Minutes, December 9, 1885.

122. T. H. Hall, "Administrative History of Union," 33.

123. Faculty Minutes, September 25, 1894.

124. T. H. Hall, "Administrative History of Union," 33.

125. Johnson, *Life and Letters of Robert Lewis Dabney*, 196.

126. Catalogue, 1892, 14.

127. Brinkley, *On This Hill*, 334.

128. Turner Ashby Wharton, *Then and Now: A Sketch of the Major Changes which Three Score Years Have Wrought in Man's Attitude Toward "the Faith of Our Fathers"* (Sherman, TX: The author's children, 1935), 53.

129. John Leighton Stuart, *Fifty Years in China: The Memoirs of John Leighton Stuart, Missionary and Ambassador* (New York: Random House, 1954), 23.

130. Ibid., 27.

131. Brinkley, *On This Hill*, 353.

132. W. E. Thompson, *Her Walls*, 281.

133. Faculty Minutes, September 19, 1876.

134. Ibid., September 13, 1876.

135. Ibid., December 22, 1879.

136. Ibid., October 27, 1880.

137. R. L. Wharton, "Student Life at Union Seminary," *Union Seminary Magazine* 9 (1898): 314.

138. Ibid.

139. T. H. Hall, "Administrative History of Union," 40.

140. R. Wharton, "Student Life at Union Seminary," 316.

141. "The Hampden-Sydney B. B. Nine," *Hampden-Sydney Magazine*, November 1884, 14.

142. R. Wharton, "Student Life at Union Seminary," 317.

143. W. E. Thompson, *Her Walls*, 249–50.

144. E. T. Thompson, *Presbyterians in the South*, 2:374–75.

145. T. H. Hall, "Administrative History of Union," 30–31.

146. Faculty Minutes, May 4, 1885.

147. Ibid., November 2, 1892.

148. T. H. Hall, "Administrative History of Union," 38.

149. T. H. Hall, "The Lower Gifts," 9.

150. Faculty Minutes, November 18, 1874.

151. Ibid., March 22, 1893.

152. T. H. Hall, "Administrative History of Union," 31–32.

153. T. H. Hall, "The Lower Gifts," 4.

154. Society of Missionary Inquiry, Minute Book 3, 1866–1877 (Hampden Sydney, VA), various dates.

155. Ibid., Minute Book 4, 1886–1898, various dates.

156. Henry McKennie Goodpasture, "Ecumenical Mission: A Visit with Robert E. Speer as Historian and Interpreter; An Inaugural Address," *Affirmation* 1, no. 5 (September 1973): 25.

157. Missionary Inquiry, Minute Book 4, 1886–1898, October 30, 1890; October 30, 1897.

158. W. M. Junkin, "Inter-Seminary Missionary Alliance," 311.

159. Society of Missionary Inquiry, Minute Book 4, 1886–1898, March 12, 1892.

160. Ibid., Minute Book 3, 1866–1877, February 3, 1866; January 2, 1869; March 2, 1872; January 2, 1874; November 5, 1875.

161. Ibid., Minute Book 4, 1886–1898, various dates.

162. Rhetorical Society Minutes, 1872–1894, March 6, 1885.

163. Ibid., October 21, 1887.

164. H. McKennie Goodpasture, "Our Field Is the World: Mission Studies at Union Theological Seminary in Virginia, 1812–1897," an address given on the 175th anniversary of the founding of Union Theological Seminary (October 12, 1987), 5.

165. Rhetorical Society Minutes, 1872–1894, March 21, 1879; December 23, 1881. The Presbyterian Assurance Company was started in Philadelphia in the early 1800s as what we would call a life insurance company. It tried to expand into the South in the 1870s but was never able to sustain much business in the PCUS.

166. Rhetorical Society Minutes, 1872–1894, various dates; Society of Missionary Inquiry, Minute Book 3, 1866–1877; Minute Book 4, 1886–1898, various dates.

167. Rhetorical Society Minutes, 1872–1894, September 12, 1884.

168. Ibid., various dates.

169. Goodpasture, "Our Field Is the World," 6.

170. Society of Missionary Inquiry, Minute Book 3, 1866–1877, January 2, 1869; Minute Book 4, 1886–1898, February 4, 1887.

171. Ibid., Minute Book 4, 1886–1898, October 3, 1890.

172. Rhetorical Society Minutes, 1872–1894, January 9, 1874.

173. T. Wharton, *Then and Now*, 46, 50, 54.

174. Faculty Minutes, October 18, 1893.

175. Appleby, "Rebuilding," 58.

176. W. E. Thompson, *Her Walls*, 150, 228.

177. Thomas R. English, "Our China Mission Work," *Union Seminary Magazine* 9, no. 4 (March–April 1898): 344.

178. W. E. Thompson, "From the Hill to the Brook," 7.

179. Catalogue, 1885, 21.

180. Brinkley, *On This Hill*, 373.

181. W. E. Thompson, "Seminary Moves, Part 2," 25–30.

182. Ernest Trice Thompson, *Presbyterians in the South*, vol. 3, *1890–1972* (Richmond, VA: John Knox Press, 1973), 201–2.

183. Walter L. Lingle, "The Last Fifty Years," *Union Seminary Magazine* 24, no. 1 (1912–13): 49–50.

184. W. E. Thompson, "The Hidden Reasons," 7.

185. E. T. Thompson, *Presbyterians in the South*, 3:202.

186. W. E. Thompson, "From the Hill to the Brook," 8.

187. Benjamin Rice Lacy Jr., "Historical Address Delivered at the Opening of the Seminary on Wednesday, September 15th, 1937," *Union Seminary Review* 49, no. 1 (October 1937): 8.

188. W. Moore, "Historical Sketch," in *Septuagesimal Celebration*, 27, 31, 33.

189. W. E. Thompson, "Railroads, Racism, and Religion," 34.

190. Miller, *Piety and Professionalism*, 30, 39–41.

191. Appleby, "Rebuilding," 62.

192. W. E. Thompson, "The Hidden Reasons," 4.

193. W. E. Thompson, "Railroads, Racism, and Religion," 73–76.

194. William E. Thompson, "Seminary Moves to Richmond, Part 4," *Museum: Newsletter of the Associates of the Esther Thomas Atkinson Museum of Hampden-Sydney*, Spring 2001, 26.

195. Arthur Y. Beatie, *Walter W. Moore and Union Seminary* (Richmond: Union Theological Seminary in Virginia, 1927), 19.

196. W. E. Thompson, "Seminary Moves, Part 2," 23.

197. Appleby, "Rebuilding," 62.

198. Mahler, "History of Union Theological Seminary," 40; Synod of Virginia Minutes, 3:18.

199. Robert Fishburne Campbell, "Address at the Twenty-Fifth Anniversary of the Removal of Union Theological Seminary to Richmond, Va., May 8, 1923," *Union Seminary Review* 34, no. 4 (July 1923): 293.

200. B. Lacy, "Historical Address," 9–10.

201. Editorial, "Modern Missions as a Part of the Seminary Curriculum," *Union Seminary Magazine* 7, no. 1 (September–October 1895), 124.

202. Howard Campbell, "Rev. Thomas E. Peck, D.D., LL.D.," *Union Seminary Magazine* 9 (1898): 296.

203. W. E. Thompson, "Railroads, Racism, and Religion," 35.

204. William E. Thompson, "The Seminary Moves to Richmond, Part 3, The Parish Responds," *Museum: Newsletter of the Esther Thomas Atkinson Museum of Hampden-Sydney*, Fall 2000, 14.

205. Ibid., "Part 2," 33–34.

206. Ibid., "Part 3," 14–15.

207. Brinkley, *On This Hill*, 381.

208. W. E. Thompson, "Railroads, Racism, and Religion," 9.

209. Brinkley, *On This Hill*, 382.

210. W. E. Thompson, "From the Hill to the Brook," 13.

211. W. E. Thompson, "Railroads, Racism, and Religion," 11.

212. W. E. Thompson, "From the Hill to the Brook," 13.

213. W. E. Thompson, "Railroads, Racism, and Religion," 46–47, 51–53, 55.

214. W. E. Thompson, "Seminary Moves, Part 3," 15.

215. W. E. Thompson, "Railroads, Racism, and Religion," 15, 58–59.

216. Brinkley, *On This Hill*, 382.

217. Ibid., 384 n. 180.

218. W. E. Thompson, "Railroads, Racism, and Religion," 14.

219. McAllister, *Life and Letters of Walter W. Moore*, 253.

220. W. E. Thompson, "Railroads, Racism, and Religion," 17.

221. W. E. Thompson, "From the Hill to the Brook," 14.

222. W. E. Thompson, "Railroads, Racism, and Religion," 47, 50, 59.

223. W. E. Thompson, "Seminary Moves, Part 3," 24.

224. W. E. Thompson, "Railroads, Racism, and Religion," 51.

225. W. E. Thompson, "Seminary Moves, Part 4," 49.

226. W. E. Thompson, "The Hidden Reasons," 14.

227. E. T. Thompson, *Presbyterians in the South*, 3:202–3.

228. W. E. Thompson, "Railroads, Racism, and Religion," 50, 57.

229. W. E. Thompson, "Seminary Moves, Part 3," 26.

230. W. E. Thompson, *Her Walls*, 279.

231. W. E. Thompson, "Seminary Moves, Part 3," 29–30.

232. W. E. Thompson, "Railroads, Racism, and Religion," 60.

233. W. E. Thompson, "Seminary Moves, Part 3," 30.

234. Ibid., "Part 2," 30–31.

235. Editorial, "Modern Missions," 126–27.

236. W. E. Thompson, "The Hidden Reasons," 14–15.

237. W. E. Thompson, "Railroads, Racism, and Religion," 97–100.

238. W. E. Thompson, "From the Hill to the Brook," 12.

239. W. E. Thompson, "Railroads, Racism, and Religion," 101–3.

240. W. E. Thompson, "From the Hill to the Brook," 12.

241. W. E. Thompson, "Railroads, Racism, and Religion," 105–7, 109.

242. David D. Ryan and Wayland W. Rennie, *Lewis Ginter's Richmond* (Richmond, VA: Whittet & Shepperson, 1991), 15.

243. W. E. Thompson, "Railroads, Racism, and Religion," 111, 113, 115.

244. W. E. Thompson, "The Hidden Reasons," 1–2, 16.

245. W. E. Thompson, "Seminary Moves, Part 3," 30, 33.

246. E. T. Thompson, *Presbyterians in the South*, 3:202–3.

247. Appleby, "Rebuilding," 63.

248. W. E. Thompson, "Railroads, Racism, and Religion," 19.

249. Brinkley, *On This Hill*, 385.

250. W. E. Thompson, "Railroads, Racism, and Religion," 68.

251. W. E. Thompson, "Seminary Moves, Part 3," 35–36.

252. Brinkley, *On This Hill*, 385.

253. W. E. Thompson, "Railroads, Racism, and Religion," 21.

254. Editorial, "Modern Missions," 129.

255. Ibid., 128.

256. W. E. Thompson, "Seminary Moves, Part 3," 21, 36–37.

257. McIlwaine, *Three Score Years and Ten*, 351–52.

258. W. E. Thompson, "From the Hill to the Brook," 16.

259. Walter W. Moore, "Union Seminary Men in Korea," *Union Seminary Magazine* 9 (March–April 1898): 247.

260. W. Moore, "Historical Sketch," *Union Seminary Magazine* 9:248.

261. W. Moore, "Union Seminary Men in Korea," 249.

262. T. H. Hall, "Administrative History of Union," 41.

263. William E. Thompson, "Gone but Not Forgotten" (an address given for the dedication of the Presbyterian Seminary historic marker sign, April 27, 1991), 11.

264. T. H. Hall, "Administrative History of Union," 41.

265. Lingle, "The Last Fifty Years," 50–51.

266. Trotti, "Union Theological Seminary Library," 44–45.

267. W. E. Thompson, "From the Hill to the Brook," 17.

268. Trotti, "Union Theological Seminary Library," 45.

269. W. E. Thompson, "From the Hill to the Brook," 16–17.

270. E. T. Thompson, *Presbyterians in the South*, 2:265, 268–69, 287–88.

271. W. Moore, "Historical Sketch," *Union Seminary Magazine* 9:246.

272. R. L. Wharton, "Valedictory," *Union Seminary Magazine* 9 (March–April 1898): 320.

273. Robert Burwell, "The Early Days of Union Seminary," *Union Seminary Magazine* 5, no. 3 (January–February 1894): 155.

CHAPTER 6: Conservative in Doctrine, Progressive in Methods

1. "Coming of Union Theological Seminary," *Richmond Dispatch*, January 1, 1898, 6; January 1, 1899, 8; these are good examples of how the paper thought UTS would improve Richmond.

2. Editorial, "Dedication Exercises," *Union Seminary Magazine* 10, no. 1 (October–November 1898): 45–46, 53.

3. Thomas Cary Johnson, "An Aim of the Ministerial Student: A Faculty Address Delivered by Prof. T. C. Johnson in the Seminary Chapel, Richmond, VA, October 6th, 1898," *Union Seminary Magazine* 10, no. 1 (October–November 1898): 11, 19.

4. Editorial, "Dedication Exercises," 54.

5. Ernest Trice Thompson, "The Twentieth Century," in *The Days of Our Years: The Historical Convocations Held April 24–27, 1962, as a Feature of the Celebration of the Sesquicentennial of Union Theological Seminary in Virginia*, ed. Ernest Trice Thompson (Richmond, VA: Union Theological Seminary, 1962), 65.

6. Robert Winthrop, "Campus Tour of Union Theological Seminary" (Library archives, 1980), 1–2.

7. David D. Ryan and Wayland W. Rennie, *Lewis Ginter's Richmond* (Richmond, VA: Whittet & Shepperson, 1991), 3.

8. Winthrop, "Campus Tour," 5.

9. Henry M. Brimm, "The Library of Union Theological Seminary, 1806–1944," *Union Seminary Review* 55, no. 4 (August 1944): 289.

10. Winthrop, "Campus Tour," 1a, 2a, 4, 7.

11. "In Their New Home," *Richmond Times-Dispatch*, October 6, 1898, 1.

12. Edward E. Lane, "The Buildings," *Union Seminary Magazine* 10 (1898): 61.

13. J. Edmunds Brown Jr., "In Salutation," *Union Seminary Magazine* 11, no. 1 (October–November 1899): 59.

14. Robert Foster Kirkpatrick, "The Chapel," *Union Seminary Magazine* 11, no. 2 (December 1899–January 1900): 142.

15. Lane, "The Buildings," 61–62.

16. Edward E. Lane, "The New Chapel," *Union Seminary Magazine* 10, no. 4 (April–May 1899): 301.

17. Brimm, "Library of Union," 289.

18. UTS Catalogue, 1898, 36.

19. Lane, "The Buildings," 63.

20. John B. Trotti, "The History of the Union Theological Seminary Library" (unpublished manuscript in the author's files, 2008), 43, 46–48.

21. Lane, "The Buildings," 63.

22. Catalogue, 1907, 40.

23. Trotti, "Union Theological Seminary Library," 9, 49–52 (re 1898–1930).

24. William E. Thompson, *Her Walls before Thee Stand: The 235-Year History of the Presbyterian Congregation at Hampden-Sydney, Virginia* ([Hampden Sydney, VA]: William E. Thompson, 2010), 281.

25. John Luster Brinkley, *On This Hill: A Narrative History of Hampden-Sydney College, 1774–1994* (Hampden Sydney, VA: Hampden-Sydney College, 1994), 389.

26. Editorial, "Hampden-Sydney's Opportunity," *Hampden-Sydney Magazine* (1895): 50.

27. Robert Fishburne Campbell, "Address at the Twenty-Fifth Anniversary of the Removal of Union Theological Seminary to Richmond, Va., May 8, 1923," *Union Seminary Review* 34, no. 4 (July 1923): 300.

28. Student Handbook, 1905–1906 (Richmond, VA: Union Theological Seminary), 13–15.

29. R. F. Campbell, "Twenty-Fifth Anniversary of the Removal," 300.

30. "The Seminary," *Union Seminary Magazine* 12, no. 2 (December 1900–January 1901): 163.

31. Catalogue, 1898, 35–36.

32. Editorial, "Union Theological Seminary," *Union Seminary Magazine* 10, no. 1 (October–November 1898): 34–35.

33. J. E. Brown, "In Salutation," 42–43.

34. William E. Thompson, "Railroads, Racism, and Religion. A Re-Examination of the Reasons for the Removal of Union Theological Seminary from Hampden-Sydney to Richmond, with a View to a Modern Day Ministry amidst the Continuing Reasons for the Departure" (DMin diss., Union Theological Seminary, 1992), 126.

35. Ryan and Rennie, *Lewis Ginter's Richmond*, 23.

36. Samuel C. Shepherd Jr., *Avenues of Faith: Shaping the Urban Religious Culture of Richmond, Virginia, 1900–1929* (Tuscaloosa: University of Alabama Press, 2001), 17.

37. Ibid., 35.

38. "In Their New Home," 1–2.

39. Editorial, "Dividends on the Seminary," *Richmond News Leader*, October 12, 1922; editorial, "An Outsider on Richmond's Assets," *Richmond News Leader*, July 13, 1925.

40. Shepherd, *Avenues of Faith*, 60–63.

41. Glenn T. Miller, *Piety and Professionalism: American Protestant Theological Education, 1870–1970* (Grand Rapids: William B. Eerdmans Publishing Co., 2007), xi.

42. Catalogue, 1898, 40.

43. "The Progress of Union Seminary," *Central Presbyterian* (Richmond, VA), April 6, 1904, 1–2.

44. Catalogue, 1915–1916, 22–24.

45. T. Hartley Hall IV, "Administrative History of Union Theological Seminary" (notes in the author's papers, 1986), 45.

46. Catalogue, 1924–1925, 48.

47. James H. Smylie, "Theological Education, Academia, and the Ministry" (a paper given at the 1976 Faculty Workshop, 1976), 6.

48. Connolly Currie Gamble Jr., "The Education of Southern Presbyterian Ministers: A Survey of the Program and Possibilities of Union Theological Seminary, Richmond, Virginia" (Union Theological Seminary, May 1950), 22.

49. Catalogue, 1898, 16–20.

50. Ibid., 1902, 37.

51. Gamble, "Education of Southern Presbyterian Ministers," 22.

52. T. H. Hall, "Administrative History of Union," 45.

53. Catalogue, 1915–1916, 25.

54. Gamble, "Education of Southern Presbyterian Ministers," 23.

55. T. H. Hall, "Administrative History of Union," 51.

56. Gamble, "Education of Southern Presbyterian Ministers," 23.

57. Catalogue, 1920–1921, 23.

58. Gamble, "Education of Southern Presbyterian Ministers," 23.

59. Catalogue, 1925–1926, 13.

60. Gamble, "Education of Southern Presbyterian Ministers," 23.

61. Trotti, "Union Theological Seminary Library," 50.

62. Ernest Trice Thompson, *Presbyterians in the South*, vol. 3, *1890–1972* (Richmond, VA: John Knox Press, 1973), 470.

63. E. T. Thompson, "The Twentieth Century," 67.

64. Walter W. Moore, *Inaugural Address: Exercises in Connection with the Inauguration of the Rev. Walter W. Moore, D.D., LL.D. as President of Union Theological Seminary* (Richmond, VA: L. D. Sullivan & Co., 1905), 13.

65. Ibid., 13.

66. T. H. Hall, "Administrative History of Union," 48–49.

67. E. T. Thompson, "The Twentieth Century," 74.

68. T. H. Hall, "Administrative History of Union," 50–51.

69. Trotti, "Union Theological Seminary Library," 82, re 1930–70.

70. Miller, *Piety and Professionalism*, 291–92.

71. Parke P. Flournoy, "When Were the Gospels Written?," *Union Seminary Magazine* 11, no. 3 (February–March 1900): 214.

72. Walter W. Moore, "The Passing of Ussher's Chronology," *Union Seminary Magazine* 13, no. 2 (December 1901–January 1902): 73–81. Based upon a literal reading of Scripture, Bishop James Ussher calculated the date of creation and determined that the universe was brought into being the night prior to Sunday, October 23, 4004 BC.

73. Editor, "Criticisms and Reviews," *Union Seminary Magazine* 5, no. 3 (January–February 1894): 223.

74. Walter W. Moore, "The Great Fish of Jonah," *Union Seminary Magazine* 7, no. 1 (September–October 1895): 24–35.

75. Walter W. Moore, "The Period of the Israelites' Sojourn in Egypt, in the Light of Archaeological Research," *Presbyterian Quarterly* 13, no. 47 (January 1899): 24–43.

76. Walter W. Moore, "The Oppression in Egypt," *Union Seminary Magazine* 3, no. 1 (September–October 1891): 241–50.

77. E. T. Thompson, *Presbyterians in the South*, 3:212, 216–17.

78. Givens Brown Strickler, "The New Theology, Part 1," *Union Seminary Magazine* 12, no. 1 (October–November 1900): 1.

79. Ibid., "Part 3," *Union Seminary Magazine* 12, no. 3 (February–March 1901): 268.

80. Ibid., 274.

81. Shepherd, *Avenues of Faith*, 256.

82. John H. Leith, "Teaching Theology at Union Seminary in Virginia" (paper presented on the 175th anniversary of the founding of Union Theological Seminary, October 13, 1987), 8.

83. Shepherd, *Avenues of Faith*, 257–58.

84. E. T. Thompson, *Presbyterians in the South*, 3:224.

85. Balmer H. Kelly, "No Ism but Bibleism: Biblical Studies at Union Theological Seminary in Virginia, 1812–1987" (paper presented on the 175th anniversary of the founding of Union Theological Seminary, October 12, 1987), 9–10.

86. E. T. Thompson, *Presbyterians in the South*, 3:358–59.

87. Robert Lewis Dabney, "Thomas Cary Johnson," *Union Seminary Magazine* 3, no. 4 (March–April 1892): 271–73.

88. Thornton Whaling, "The Church and Social Reforms," *Union Seminary Review* 25, no. 1 (October–November 1913): 32.

89. William E. Thompson, "Would You Believe? A Social Liberal at Hampden-Sydney!," in *The Opening of the Lewis Wicks Hine Photography Exhibit* (Atkinson Museum of Hampden-Sydney College, March 26, 2000), 6.

90. Ibid., 10.

91. E. T. Thompson, *Presbyterians in the South*, 3:264.

92. J. Wayne Flynt, "Feeding the Hungry and Ministering to the Broken Hearted: The Presbyterian Church in the United States and the Social Gospel, 1900–1920," in *Religion in the South*, ed. Charles Reagan Wilson (Jackson: University Press of Mississippi, 1985), 92.

93. Walter L. Lingle, *The Bible and Social Problems: The James Sprunt Lectures, 1929* (New York: Fleming H. Revell Co., 1929), 7.

94. Flynt, "Feeding the Hungry and Ministering to the Broken Hearted," 106–7.

95. Shepherd, *Avenues of Faith*, 65.

96. E. T. Thompson, *Presbyterians in the South*, 3:265.

97. Catalogue, 1914, 40.

98. Flynt, "Feeding the Hungry," 84–85, 109.

99. Lingle, *The Bible and Social Problems*, 11–13.

100. Flynt, "Feeding the Hungry," 104.

101. Robert Benedetto, *Index to the Union Seminary Magazine and Union Seminary Review, 1889–1946* (Richmond, VA: Union Theological Seminary, 1995), xi.

102. Walter W. Lingle, editorials, *Union Seminary Review* 25, no. 1 (October–November 1913): 51–52.

103. Flynt, "Feeding the Hungry," 110.

104. Peter H. Hobbie, "Walter L. Lingle, Presbyterians, and the Enigma of the Social Gospel in the South," *American Presbyterians* 69, no. 3 (Fall 1991): 194.

105. Andrew W. Blackwood, "The Social Message of Micah," *Union Seminary Review* 26, no. 1 (October 1914): 22–33.

106. Walter L. Lingle, "The Unrevised and Revised Confessions of Faith Compared," *Union Seminary Review* 29, no. 2 (January 1918): 89–90.

107. Peter Hairston Hobbie, "Ernest Trice Thompson: Prophet for a Changing South" (PhD diss., Union Seminary in Virginia, May 1987), 140.

108. Thomas Cary Johnson, *A History of the Southern Presbyterian Church* (New York: Christian Literature Co., 1894), 423.

109. James H. Smylie, "The Burden of Southern Church Historians: World Mission, Regional Captivity, Reconciliation" (inaugural address as professor of American church history at Union Theological Seminary in Richmond, VA; March 7, 1968), 40.

110. Johnson, *A History of the Southern Presbyterian Church*, 476–77.

111. Walter Lee Lingle, *Presbyterians, Their History and Belief* (Richmond, VA: Presbyterian Committee of Publication, 1928), 178–79.

112. Ibid., 181–98.

113. Lingle, *The Bible and Social Problems*, 7, 9.

114. "The Centennial Celebration," *Union Seminary Magazine* 24 (1912): 9.

115. Egbert W. Smith, "Union Seminary in Home Missions," *Union Seminary Magazine* 24, no. 1 (1912–13): 110.

116. James I. Vance, "Union Seminary in Foreign Missions," *Union Seminary Magazine* 24, no. 1 (1912–13): 118–19.

117. E. W. Smith, "Union Seminary in Home Missions," 115.

118. Robert Fishburne Campbell, "Union Seminary in the Pastorate," *Union Seminary Magazine* 24, no. 1 (1912–13): 78.

119. Ibid., 81–82.

120. "Letters of Congratulations," *Union Seminary Magazine* 24 (1912): 128–54.

121. Theron H. Rice, "Union Seminary in Theological Education and Religious Thought," *Union Seminary Magazine* 24, no. 1 (1912–13): 101, 103, 104–6.

122. Robert Haydon Bullock, "The Past Fifty Years of Presbyterianism in Richmond, Virginia" (ThD diss., Union Theological Seminary in Virginia, 1943), 105.

123. Walter L. Lingle, "The Last Fifty Years," *Union Seminary Magazine* 24, no. 1 (1912–13): 68.

124. E. T. Thompson, "The Twentieth Century," 69.

125. Ernest Trice Thompson, *Presbyterians in the South*, vol. 2, *1861–1890* (Richmond, VA: John Knox Press, 1973), 288–89.

126. Ibid., 2:290.

127. *1869 Constitution and Plan of Union Theological Seminary in Virginia, Amended 1892* (Richmond, VA: Whittet & Shepperson, 1893), 14–15.

128. Thomas Cary Johnson, "The Study of the English Bible Is Demanded by the Needs of Our Day," *Presbyterian Quarterly*, no. 21, July 1892, 374.

129. E. T. Thompson, *Presbyterians in the South*, 3:206–7, 473.

130. T. H. Hall, "Administrative History of Union," 44.

131. Walter W. Moore, *The Preparation of the Modern Minister*, pamphlet 4 of *The Claims and Opportunities of the Christian Ministry*, ed. John R. Mott (New York: International Committee of Young Men's Christian Associations, 1909), 19.

132. Catalogue, 1910, 42.

133. R. L. McKinnon, Richmond, Society of Missionary Inquiry, End of Year Report, May 6, 1917.

134. Society of Missionary Inquiry, Minute Book 6, March 1912–March 1932 (UTS), December 7, 1913.

135. Ibid., September 22, 1913.

136. Student Handbook 1916–1917 (UTS), 37.

137. Catalogue, 1925–1926, 75.

138. R. F. Campbell, "Twenty-Fifth Anniversary of the Removal," 303–4.

139. William B. Oglesby Jr., "Faith in Action: Preparing Students for the Work of Ministry" (paper presented on the 175th anniversary of the founding of Union Theological Seminary, October 12, 1987), 7.

140. E. T. Thompson, "The Twentieth Century," 68.

141. Cothran G. Smith, "The Seventeenth Street Mission," *Union Seminary Review* 33, no. 4 (July 1922): 317.

142. Ibid., 319.

143. Bullock, "The Past Fifty Years of Presbyterianism in Richmond, Virginia," 99, East Hanover Presbytery Minutes, April 26–28, 1915, 23–26; April 21–23, 1919, 38; April 21–23, 1924, 34; April 13–15, 1925, 36.

144. C. G. Smith, "The Seventeenth Street Mission," 320–24.

145. Bullock, "Presbyterianism in Richmond," 96.

146. C. G. Smith, "The Seventeenth Street Mission," 321.

147. H. McKennie Goodpasture, "Our Field Is the World: Mission Studies at Union Theological Seminary in Virginia, 1812–1897" (an address given on the 175th anniversary of the founding of Union Theological Seminary, October 12, 1987), 7.

148. Ibid.

149. E. T. Thompson, "The Twentieth Century," 72; James H. Smylie, "UTS Opens the Family Photo Album," *Focus* 2, no. 4 (Winter 1987): 13.

150. E. T. Thompson, *Presbyterians in the South*, 3:389, 397.

151. Flynt, "Feeding the Hungry," 99, 101.

152. Catalogue, 1909, 42.

153. Ibid., 1910, supplement.

154. Walter W. Moore, "The Training School for Lay Workers and the A. L. Phillips Memorial Fund," in *1915 PC (US) General Assembly* (1915); PSCE Notebook in the Library archives, in the papers of Dr. James W. Smylie, 1; T. H. Hall, "Administrative History of Union," 45.

155. T. H. Hall, "Administrative History of Union," 38.

156. Editorial, "James Sprunt, LL.D.," *Union Seminary Review* 31, no. 2 (January 1920): 89, 91–95.

157. Ibid., 95.

158. Walter W. Moore, "Mr. Bryan at Union Seminary," *Presbyterian of the South* 23 (November 1921): 1.

159. Ibid.

160. William Jennings Bryan, *In His Image* (New York: Fleming H. Revell, 1922), 8.

161. Ibid., 86–135.

162. E. T. Thompson, *Presbyterians in the South*, 3:308.

163. H. McKennie Goodpasture, "Ecumenical Mission: A Visit with Robert E. Speer as Historian and Interpreter; An Inaugural Address," *Affirmation* 1, no. 5 (September 1973): 27.

164. B. H. Kelly, "No Ism but Bibleism," 8.

165. Oglesby, "Faith in Action," 8, 9.

166. Winthrop, "Campus Tour of Union," 8.

167. W. M. Junkin, "Inter-Seminary Missionary Alliance," *Union Seminary Magazine* 3, no. 4 (March–April 1892): 311.

168. Catalogue, 1903, 4, back cover.

169. Ibid., 1904, back cover.

170. T. H. Hall, "Administrative History of Union," 45.

171. T. Hartley Hall IV, "The Lower Gifts" (paper presented at opening convocation, Watts Chapel, Union Theological Seminary in Virginia, September 9, 1987), 7.

172. Walter W. Moore, "Address at the Dedication of Schauffler Hall," *Union Seminary Review* 33, no. 1 (October 1921): 29.

173. Shepherd, *Avenues of Faith*, 66.

174. W. Moore, "Dedication of Schauffler Hall," 1.

175. Catalogue, 1912, 35.

176. Ibid., 1922–1923, 38.

177. *Glimpses of 75 Years* (Richmond, VA: Ginter Park Presbyterian Church, 1982), 2–3.

178. Archibald Rutledge, "Things We Can't Explain," *Reader's Digest* (New York), November 1942, 30–32.

179. E. T. Thompson, "The Twentieth Century," 73.

180. Minutes of East Hanover Presbytery, May 8, 1919, 52.

181. Robert P. Davis and James H. Smylie, *Virginia Presbyterians in American Life: Hanover Presbytery (1755–1980)*, ed. Patricia Aldridge (Richmond, VA: Hanover Presbytery, 1982), 170.

182. Goodpasture, "Our Field Is the World," 8.

183. Willard B. Gatewood, "Embattled Scholar: Howard W. Odun and the Fundamentalists, 1925–1927," *Journal of Southern History* 31, no. 4 (November 1965): 377.

184. William E. Leuchtenburg, *The Perils of Prosperity, 1914–1932* (Chicago: University of Chicago Press, 1973), 204–24.

185. Shepherd, *Avenues of Faith*, 258, 279.

186. Editor, "Around the Seminary," *Union Seminary Magazine* 13, no. 2 (December 1901–January 1902): 137.

187. Catalogue, 1911, 35.

188. Ibid., 1923–1924, 40.

189. Ibid., 1898, 42.

190. Ibid., 1914–1915, 27.

191. Goodpasture, "Our Field Is the World," 9.

192. Catalogue, 1922–1923, 39.

193. Ibid., 1907, 38–39.

194. Union Theological Seminary in Virginia Alumni Association, Organization, Places of Meeting, Schedules of Reunions, Officers of the Association (1970).

195. Ibid.

196. Catalogue, 1898, 36.

197. Ibid., 1925–1926, 22.

198. Student Handbook, 1919–1920, 44.

199. Ibid., 1900–1901, 5, 21.

200. Ibid., 1915–1916, 24–25, 27.

201. Ibid., 1914–1915, 21, 23.

202. Ibid., 1900–1901, 24–25.

203. Catalogue, 1898, 40.

204. Ibid., 1916–1917, 51.

205. Student Handbook, 1905–1906, 7, 10, 13, 15–18, 23–25, 29, 32.

206. Augustus C. Summers, letter from DeBary, FL, to President T. Hartley Hall, March 23, 1990.

207. Student Handbook, 1907–1908, 33.

208. Ibid., 1921–1922, 26.

209. T. H. Hall, "Administrative History of Union," 46.

210. Summers, letter to T. H. Hall, March 23, 1990.

211. Givens B. Strickler Society Minutes, 1914–1917 (Richmond, VA), March 9, 1914.

212. Catalogue, 1914, 47.

213. Givens B. Strickler Society Minutes, 1914–1917, January 10, 1916.

214. Shepherd, *Avenues of Faith*, 249.

215. T. H. Hall, "Administrative History of Union," 47.

216. Student Handbook, 1926–1927, 30.

217. Walter W. Moore, "The Seminary and the War," *Union Seminary Review* 30, no. 1 (October 1918): 1–6.

218. Student Handbook, 1921–1922, 50.

219. Edward Mack, "Our Church in the Reconstruction after War," *Union Seminary Review* 30, no. 2 (January 1919): 99–110; Edward R. Leyburn, "The Church and Reconstruction," *Union Seminary Review* 30, no. 2 (January 1919): 137–46.

220. Student Handbook, 1921–1922, 26, 41–42.

221. E. T. Thompson, *Presbyterians in the South*, 3:226.

222. Student Handbook, 1905–1906, 21.

223. Ibid., 1923–1924, 57.

224. Louise McComb, *The First Seventy Years: A History of the Presbyterian School of Christian Education* (Richmond, VA: Presbyterian School of Christian Education, 1985), 16.

225. Student Handbook, 1926–1927, 31–32.

226. E. T. Thompson, "The Twentieth Century," 69.

227. Oglesby, "Faith in Action," 8.

228. Catalogue, 1925–1926, 25, 31, 40–42.

229. Summers, letter to T. H. Hall, March 23, 1990.

230. Bullock, "Presbyterianism in Richmond," 106.

231. J. Gray McAllister, *The Life and Letters of Walter W. Moore: Second Founder and First President of Union Theological Seminary in Virginia* (Richmond, VA: Union Theological Seminary, 1939), title.

232. R. F. Campbell, "Twenty-Fifth Anniversary of the Removal," 300.

233. Smylie, "Family Photo Album," 14.

234. R. F. Campbell, "Twenty-Fifth Anniversary of the Removal," 302.

235. Benjamin Rice Lacy Jr., "Historical Address Delivered at the Opening of the Seminary on Wednesday, September 15th, 1937," *Union Seminary Review* 49, no. 1 (October 1937): 12.

236. Miller, *Piety and Professionalism*, 106.

237. Walter W. Moore, *Appreciations* (Richmond, VA: Presbyterian Committee of Publication, [1914?]), 100–101.

238. R. F. Campbell, "Twenty-Fifth Anniversary of the Removal," 302.

CHAPTER 7: A First-Class Seminary

1. "Union Seminary Elects New Head," *Richmond Times-Dispatch*, May 12, 1926, 1.

2. *World Survey by the Interchurch World Movement of North America*, vol. 1, *American Volume* (New York: Interchurch Press, 1920), 200.

3. Robert L. Kelly, *Theological Education in America: A Study of One Hundred Sixty-One Theological Schools in the United States and Canada* (New York: George H. Doran Co., 1924), vii.

4. Glenn T. Miller, *Piety and Professionalism: American Protestant Theological Education, 1870–1970* (Grand Rapids: William B. Eerdmans Publishing Co., 2007), 268, 314, 316–17, 322–27, 329, 334–35.

5. Benjamin Rice Lacy, "Union Theological Seminary in This Present Age: On the Occasion of His Inauguration as President of Union Theological Seminary in Virginia, May 11, 1927," *Union Seminary Review* 38, no. 4 (July 1927): 356–65.

6. Arthur Y. Beatie, *Walter W. Moore and Union Seminary* (Richmond: Union Theological Seminary in Virginia, 1927), 26–27, 45.

7. B. Lacy, "Seminary in This Present Age," 365–66.

8. Ernest Trice Thompson, *Presbyterians in the South*, vol. 3, *1890–1972* (Richmond, VA: John Knox Press, 1973), 465.

9. T. Hartley Hall IV, "Administrative History of Union Theological Seminary" (notes in the author's papers, 1986), 59.

10. "Campbell Talks on Freedom and Restraint," *Richmond Times-Dispatch*, January 16, 1930, church page.

11. "Not Heim Alone," *Richmond News Leader*, February 1, 1935, 3.

12. UTS Catalogue, 1937–1938, 12.

13. Ibid., 1940–1941, 12.

14. Glenn T. Miller, *A Community of Conversation: A Retrospective of the Association of Theological Schools and Ninety Years of North American Theological Education* (Pittsburgh: Association of Theological Schools, 2008), 2, 4.

15. Jesse H. Ziegler, *ATS through Two Decades: Reflections on Theological Education, 1960–1980* (Worcester, MA: Heffernan Press, 1884), 44.

16. Catalogue, 1936–1937, 20.

17. T. Hartley Hall IV, "The Lower Gifts" (paper presented at opening convocation, Watts Chapel, Union Theological Seminary in Virginia, September 9, 1987), 10.

18. Mark Arthur May et al., *The Education of American Ministers*, vol. 1, *Ministerial Education in America* (New York: Institute of Social and Religious Research, 1934), 143.

19. T. H. Hall, "Administrative History of Union," 54, 78.

20. May et al., *Education of American Ministers*, 1:107–8, 123.

21. Maurice W. Armstrong, Lefferts A. Loetscher, and Charles A. Anderson, eds., *The Presbyterian Enterprise*, Presbyterian Historical Society Publication Series 1 (Philadelphia: Westminster Press, 1956), 251–54.

22. Herbert S. Turner, "Old Testament Criticism," *Union Seminary Review* 41, no. 1 (October 1929): 15.

23. E. T. Thompson, *Presbyterians in the South*, 3:326–27.

24. T. H. Hall, "Administrative History of Union," 56.

25. Connolly Currie Gamble Jr., "The Education of Southern Presbyterian Ministers: A Survey of the Program and Possibilities of Union Theological Seminary, Richmond, Virginia," Union Theological Seminary (May 1950), 24.

26. T. H. Hall, "Administrative History of Union," 56.

27. Peter Hairston Hobbie, "Ernest Trice Thompson: Prophet for a Changing South" (PhD diss., Union Theological Seminary in Virginia, May 1987), 408.

28. Balmer H. Kelly, "No Ism but Bibleism: Biblical Studies at Union Theological Seminary in Virginia, 1812–1987" (paper presented on the 175th anniversary of the founding of Union Theological Seminary, October 12, 1987), 8.

29. James L. Mays, e-mail from Richmond, Va., to the author, "Some Notes on Biblical Studies at Union: [19]30s–50s," August 13, 2011.

30. Interview with Balmer H. Kelly, UTS Video History Project (1989).

31. J. L. Mays, "Biblical Studies at Union."

32. Interview with Balmer H. Kelly, UTS Video History.

33. J. L. Mays, "Biblical Studies at Union."

34. T. H. Hall, "Administrative History of Union," 72–73.

35. Catalogue, 1940–1941, 13.

36. Hobbie, "Ernest Trice Thompson: Prophet," 158.

37. Interview with E. T. Thompson, UTS Video History (1964).

38. Catalogue, 1927–1928, 61.

39. J. L. Mays, "Biblical Studies at Union," 1.

40. B. H. Kelly, "No Ism but Bibleism," 9.

41. Interview with E. T. Thompson, UTS Video History.

42. Hobbie, "Ernest Trice Thompson: Prophet," 106–9.

43. Interview with E. T. Thompson, UTS Video History.

44. Hobbie, "Ernest Trice Thompson: Prophet," 124.

45. Robert McNeill, *God Wills Us Free: The Ordeal of a Southern Minister* (New York: Hill & Wang, 1965), 60.

46. E. T. Thompson, *Presbyterians in the South*, 3:207–8.

47. John H. Leith, "Teaching Theology at Union Seminary in Virginia" (paper presented on the 175th anniversary of the founding of Union Theological Seminary, October 13, 1987), 1.

48. E. T. Thompson, *Presbyterians in the South*, 3:493–94.

49. Leith, "Teaching Theology at Union Seminary," 11.

50. Interview with E. T. Thompson, UTS Video History.

51. Hobbie, "Ernest Trice Thompson: Prophet," 139.

52. Ernest Trice Thompson, "Is the Northern Church Theologically Sound?," *Union Seminary Review* 42, no. 2 (January 1931): 134.

53. Hobbie, "Ernest Trice Thompson: Prophet," 202–10.

54. E. T. Thompson, *Presbyterians in the South*, 3:328.

55. Hobbie, "Ernest Trice Thompson: Prophet," 212–13, 218–19.

56. Tom Glasgow, *Shall the Southern Presbyterian Church Abandon Its Historic Position?* (Charlotte, NC: Privately published, 1940), 2, 19.

57. E. T. Thompson, *Presbyterians in the South*, 3:335–37.

58. Hobbie, "Ernest Trice Thompson: Prophet," 316, 322; East Hanover Presbytery Minutes, October 15–16, 1940, 18; November 25, 1940, 43–51.

59. E. T. Thompson, *Presbyterians in the South*, 3:338.

60. Hobbie, "Ernest Trice Thompson: Prophet," 349.

61. E. T. Thompson, *Presbyterians in the South*, 3:338–39.

62. John Haddon Leith, "Ernest Trice Thompson: Churchman," in *Ernest Trice Thompson: An Appreciation* (Richmond: Union Theological Seminary in Virginia, 1964), 44.

63. Robert P. Davis and James H. Smylie, *Virginia Presbyterians in American Life: Hanover Presbytery (1755–1980)*, ed. Patricia Aldridge (Richmond, VA: Hanover Presbytery, 1982), 194.

64. B. H. Kelly, "No Ism but Bibleism," 10.

65. Ernest Trice Thompson, "The Twentieth Century," in *the Days of Our Years. The Historical Convocations Held April 24–27, 1962, as a Feature of the Celebration of the Sesquicentennial of Union Theological Seminary in Virginia*, ed. Ernest Trice Thompson (Richmond: Union Theological Seminary in Virginia, 1962), 74.

66. John B. Trotti, "The History of the Union Theological Seminary Library" (unpublished manuscript in the author's files, 2008), 1, 16–17, on 1898–1930; 18, 48, 54, 56–61, 65–66, 69, 72, on 1930–70.

67. T. H. Hall, "Administrative History of Union," 57.

68. Trotti, "Seminary Library," 30, on 1930–70.

69. T. H. Hall, "Administrative History of Union," 57.

70. Henry M. Brimm, "The Library of Union Theological Seminary, 1806–1944," *Union Seminary Review* 55, no. 4 (August 1944): 291.

71. "Union Theological to Start Construction on New Library," *Richmond News Leader*, August 21, 1941, 2.

72. Trotti, "Seminary Library," 21, 23, 77, on 1930–70.

73. John F. Anderson, "Expanded Theological Library Awaits Presbyterian Students," *Richmond Times-Dispatch*, April 3, 1944, IV–1.

74. John Alexander Mackay, "The Heritage of Yesterday," *Union Seminary Review* 60, no. 4 (August 1944): 277, 283, 285.

75. Hobbie, "Ernest Trice Thompson: Prophet," 195.

76. Robert Benedetto, *Index to the* Union Seminary Magazine *and* Union Seminary Review, *1889–1946* (Richmond, VA: Union Theological Seminary, 1995), xii.

77. Lewis J. Sherrill, "The Barrenness of the Southern Presbyterian Pen," *Union Seminary Review* 42, no. 4 (May 1931): 278–89.

78. Benedetto, *Index*, xii.

79. John H. Grey, "The Rediscovery of the Southern Presbyterian Pen," *Union Seminary Review* 48, no. 1 (October 1936): 54–60.

80. Ernest Trice Thompson, "Southern Presbyterians: What We Can Learn from the Past," *Union Seminary Review* 48, no. 1 (October 1936): 15–31.

81. Allen Cabaniss, "Liturgy in the Southern Presbyterian Church," *Union Seminary Review* 54, no. 1 (October 1942): 11–27.

82. Rachel Henderlite, "The Need for Theology in Religious Education," *Union Seminary Review* 57, no. 1 (October 1945): 1–14; Benedetto, *Index*, xiii.

83. Karl Barth, "Miserable Lazarus," *Union Seminary Review* 46, no. 4 (May 1935): 259–68.

84. Emil Brunner, "The Absoluteness of Jesus," *Union Seminary Review* 46, no. 4 (May 1935): 269–82.

85. Alexander Christie, "The Doctrine of Holy Scripture in Calvin and Brunner, Part I," *Union Seminary Review* 52, no. 1 (October 1940): 19–33; "Part II," *USR* 52, no. 2 (January 1941): 116–27; "Part III," *USR* 52, no. 4 (May 1941): 325–51.

86. Adolf Keller, "A Battle of Life or Death in European Protestantism," *Union Seminary Review* 49, no. 4 (May 1938): 334–42.

87. Adolf Keller, "Totalitarian Faith on the European Continent," *Union Seminary Review* 50, no. 4 (May 1939): 327–36.

88. Wolfgang Schweitzer, "The Confessional Church in Germany," *Union Seminary Review* 56, no. 2 (November 1945): 166–81.

89. B. Lacy, "Seminary in This Present Age," 367.

90. Catalogue, 1941–1942, 8, 89.

91. Benjamin Rice Lacy Jr., "Historical Address Delivered at the Opening of the Seminary on Wednesday, September 15th, 1937," *Union Seminary Review* 49, no. 1 (October 1937): 13.

92. Society of Missionary Inquiry, Minute Book 6, April 1932–March 1939, November 19, 1934.

93. June Percell Guild, *Black Laws of Virginia* (Richmond, VA: Whittet & Shepperson, 1936), 181, 184; see the 1902 Constitution of Virginia, art. IX, §140: this 1902 article, renewed in 1928 yet overruled by *Brown v. Board of Education* in 1954, was not formally superseded until the 1971 Constitution of Virginia.

94. Samuel Govan Stevens, letter from Richmond, Va., to Dr. Ben R. Lacy Jr., December 20, 1934 (in the Union Seminary Library archives).

95. Benjamin Rice Lacy, memorandum from Richmond, Va., to Dr. Edward Mack, December 21, 1934 (in the Union Seminary Library archives).

96. Edward Mack, letter from Richmond, Va., to Rev. Samuel Govan Stevens, January 3, 1935 (in the Union Seminary Library archives).

97. Donald W. Richardson, letter from Richmond, Va., to Rev. E. D. McCreary Jr., August 3, 1944 (in the Union Seminary Library archives).

98. Society of Missionary Inquiry, Minute Book 5, March 1912–March 1932 (Richmond, VA), March 8, 1927; April 20, 1938; April 27, 1938.

99. Student Handbook, 1927–1928, 55–56.

100. Society of Missionary Inquiry, Minute Book 6, April 1932–March 1939, April 29, 1933; October 2, 1935; T. H. Hall, "Administrative History of Union," 58. Ralph Buchanan cut grass and pulled weeds.

101. T. H. Hall, "Administrative History of Union," 58.

102. E. T. Thompson, "The Twentieth Century," 87.

103. Society of Missionary Inquiry, Minute Book 6, April 1932–March 1939, October 2, 1935; February 9, 1937.

104. Student Handbook, 1938–1939, 4.

105. Society of Missionary Inquiry, Minute Book 5, March 1912–March 1932, March 30, 1930.

106. Ibid., Minute Book 6, April 1932–March 1939, May 1, 1935.

107. McNeill, *God Wills Us Free*, 55–57.

108. Society of Missionary Inquiry, Minute Book 6, April 1932–March 1939, April 13, 1932; September 21 and 27, 1937; April 27, 1938.

109. Louise McComb, *The First Seventy Years: A History of the Presbyterian School of Christian Education* (Richmond, VA: Presbyterian School of Christian Education, 1985), 29.

110. McComb, *The First Seventy Years*, 34–35.

111. Society of Missionary Inquiry, Minute Book 6, April 1932–March 1939, October 24, 1937.

112. McComb, *The First Seventy Years*, 42.

113. Society of Missionary Inquiry, Minute Book 6, April 1932–March 1939, March 17, 1936.

114. "Calvin Bowl Game Planned Again for Thanksgiving Day," *Richmond News Leader*, November 23, 1956, 21.

115. Society of Missionary Inquiry, Minute Book 6, April 1932–March 1939, November 17, 1932; November 22, 1932; March 13, 1935; March 14, 1933.

116. Catalogue, 1928–1929, 92.

117. Society of Missionary Inquiry, Minute Book 6, April 1932–March 1939.

118. McNeill, *God Wills Us Free*, 60.

119. Society of Missionary Inquiry, Minute Book 6, April 1932–March 1939, March 17, 1933; October 7, 1936; November 3, 1936; March 19, 1937.

120. Student Handbook, 1927–1928, 21.

121. Balmer H. Kelly, "What Union Seminary Has Taught Me" (speech given to the alumni board during Sprunt Lecture week, no date given), Union Seminary Oral History Project.

122. T. H. Hall, "Administrative History of Union," 55.

123. Society of Missionary Inquiry, Minute Book 6, April 1932–March 1939, April 21, 1933; April 27, 1938; November 21, 1934.

124. T. H. Hall, "Administrative History of Union," 51, 69.

125. "Presbyterian Seminaries' Merger Set," *Richmond News Leader*, July 21, 1943, 1.

126. "Seminary Merger Story 'Premature,'" *Richmond News Leader*, July 22, 1943, 29.

127. T. H. Hall, "Administrative History of Union," 75–76.

128. Catalogue, 1946–1947, 38–39.

129. "Union Seminary and Our Armed Forces," *Union Seminary Bulletin* 2/20, no. 4 (April–June 1943): 2–3.

130. E T. Thompson, "The Twentieth Century," 76.

131. Student Handbook 1947–1948, 1.

132. Catalogue, 1945–1946, 3, 18–20.

133. Ibid., 1947–1948, 41, 69.

134. Ibid., 1946–1947, 8, 17–18, 24.

135. Ibid., 1947–1948, 32.

136. Ibid., 1946–1947, 17–18.

137. Student Handbook, 1947–1948, 2, 8.

138. Catalogue, 1946–1947, 53.

139. Student Handbook, 1947–1948, 1.

140. T. H. Hall, "Administrative History of Union," 61, 72–74.

141. "Are the Well-Springs Drying Up?," *Richmond News Leader*, February 2, 1945, 10.

142. T. H. Hall, "Administrative History of Union," 66.

143. "Rev. Fred R. Stair, Jr., Named Assistant to Dr. B. R. Lacy, Jr.," *Richmond Times-Dispatch*, May 19, 1948, 16.

144. Balmer H. Kelly, "In Retrospect," *Interpretation* 25, no. 1 (January 1971): 11–12.

145. Donald G. Miller, "The Birth of a Journal," *Interpretation* 50, no. 2 (April 1996): 117, 119.

146. E. T. Thompson, *Presbyterians in the South*, 3:497.

147. D. G. Miller, "Birth of a Journal," 118, 120.

148. Hobbie, "Ernest Trice Thompson: Prophet," 412.

149. E. T. Thompson, *Presbyterians in the South*, 3:497.

150. D. G. Miller, "Birth of a Journal," 121–24, 126.

151. Hobbie, "Ernest Trice Thompson: Prophet," 411.

152. D. G. Miller, "Birth of a Journal," 127.

153. Benedetto, *Index*, xiii.

154. Editorial, "The Twenty-Fifth Anniversary," *Interpretation* 25, no. 1 (January 1971): 3.

155. B. H. Kelly, "In Retrospect," 15–17, 22.

156. H. H. Rowley, "The Relevance of Biblical Interpretation," *Interpretation* 1, no. 1 (January 1947): 3–4.

157. E. T. Thompson, *Presbyterians in the South*, 3:498.

158. D. G. Miller, "Birth of a Journal," 124.

159. B. H. Kelly, "In Retrospect," 21–22.

CHAPTER EIGHT: Faithful Scholarship

1. T. Hartley Hall IV, "Administrative History of Union Theological Seminary" (notes in the author's papers, 1986), 79.

2. William B. Oglesby Jr., "Faith in Action: Preparing Students for the Work of Ministry" (paper presented on the 175th anniversary of the founding of Union Theological Seminary, October 12, 1987), 11.

3. Interview with James Luther Mays (June 5, 1999), UTS Video History.

4. T. H. Hall, "Administrative History of Union," 79.

5. Interview with Balmer Kelly (1989), UTS Video History.

6. *For All Southern Presbyterians: A Great Door Is Opened*, promotional booklet for the Mid-Century Campaign (Richmond, VA: Whittet & Shepperson, 1952), 10.

7. Ernest Trice Thompson, "The Twentieth Century," in *the Days of Our Years: The Historical Convocations Held April 24–27, 1962, as a Feature of the Celebration of the Sesquicentennial of Union Theological Seminary in Virginia*, ed. Ernest Trice Thompson (Richmond, VA: Union Theological Seminary, 1962), 87.

8. Interview with James L. Mays, UTS Video History.

9. T. H. Hall, "Administrative History of Union," 68–69, 76.

10. "Honorary Membership in French School Body to Be Conferred on Two Seminary Officers," *Richmond Times-Dispatch*, November 11, 1949, B-3.

11. Interview with Fred Stair, Martha Aycock, and John Trotti (March 27, 1990), UTS Video History, Montpelier Exchange Program; Parts 1–3.

12. Ibid.

13. "Honorary Membership," B-3.

14. Interview with Stair, Aycock, and Trotti.

15. "Anniversary Rites Opened at Seminary," *Richmond Times-Dispatch*, October 6, 1948, 10.

16. Ernest Trice Thompson, *Presbyterians in the South*, vol. 3, *1890–1972* (Richmond, VA: John Knox Press, 1973), 469–70.

17. Benjamin Rice Lacy, "Through Our Next Fifty Years" (an address given on the fiftieth anniversary of the move from Hampden-Sydney to Richmond, October 5, 1948), 1–2.

18. "Objectives of UTS Outlined by Dr. Lacy at Anniversary," *Richmond News Leader*, October 6, 1948, 23.

19. Editor, "Faithful Scholarship at Union," *Richmond News Leader*, October 6, 1948, 10.

20. "Objectives of UTS," 23.

21. E. T. Thompson, "The Twentieth Century," 84.

22. UTS Catalogue, 1909, 44.

23. E. T. Thompson, "The Twentieth Century," 85.

24. Interview with Donald G. Shriver (in person, April 27, 2011).

25. E. T. Thompson, *Presbyterians in the South*, 3:507–8.

26. Donald W. Shriver, "Biblical Theology: A Personal History" (unpublished manuscript in the author's possession, 2011).

27. Ibid., 2.

28. Ibid.

29. Ibid., 3.

30. Ibid., 6.

31. Ibid., 7.

32. T. H. Hall, "Administrative History of Union," 80–81.

33. Board of Trustees Minutes, 1950–1959, 800.

34. Faculty Minutes, 1955, 711.

35. Board of Trustees Minutes, 1950–1959, 800.

36. Ibid., 802.

37. Ibid., 803.

38. Ibid., 800–806.

39. Ace Tubbs, *The Story of My Life: Memoirs of the Rev. Ace Leonard Tubbs, Ed.D.* (Montreat, NC: Self-published, 2000), 15–16.

40. William Newton Todd, "The Atomic Era," in *Virginia Presbyterians in American Life: Hanover Presbytery (1755–1980)*, by Robert P. Davis and James H. Smylie, ed. Patricia Aldridge (Richmond, VA: Hanover Presbytery, 1982), 237.

41. James H. Smylie, "The Bible, Race and the Changing South," *Journal of Presbyterian History* 59, no. 2 (Summer 1981): 204–5.

42. Ernest Trice Thompson, "Jesus among People of Other Races," *Presbyterian Outlook* 126 (March 21, 1949): 13.

43. Ernest Trice Thompson, "The Curse Was Not on Ham," *Presbyterian Outlook* 14 (March 14, 1955): 1–3, 7.

44. Smylie, "Race and the Changing South," 208.

45. Peter Hairston Hobbie, "Ernest Trice Thompson: Prophet for a Changing South" (PhD diss., Union Seminary in Virginia, May 1987), 541.

46. "A Century in the City" (the program for celebrating the centennial of the move of Union Theological Seminary from Hampden Sydney to Richmond, October 5, 1998), 12, 15.

47. Louise McComb, *The First Seventy Years: A History of the Presbyterian School of Christian Education* (Richmond, VA: Presbyterian School of Christian Education, 1985), 58.

48. George M. Conn Jr., "96 Steps and Turn" (personal memoirs of George M. Conn Jr., 1989, in the author's possession).

49. "Some Students from UTS Join Picket Line at Downtown Store," *Richmond Times-Dispatch*, March 6, 1960, D-1.

50. Conn, "96 Steps and Turn," 2.

51. Interview with Charles Swezey (in person, January 22, 2010), 2.

52. "Students from UTS Join Picket Line," D-1.

53. "Seminary Students Tell Reason for Picketing," *Richmond Times-Dispatch*, March 8, 1960, D-1.

54. "Students from UTS Join Picket Line," D-1.

55. Copy of letter in the author's files.

56. Conn, "96 Steps and Turn," 3.

57. Letter from Maude Robeson to Union students (copy of letter in the author's possession).

58. Letter from Lois Betty White to Union students (copy of letter in the author's possession).

59. A Resolution on Civil Rights Adopted by the Student Body of Union Theological Seminary (May 8, 1964), 1.

60. Dan West, "UTS and Civil Rights," *Expression* (Richmond, VA) 9, no. 2 (Summer 1964): 5.

61. Interview with John Kuykendall (in person, September 2, 2011), 2.

62. The Student Body of Union Theological Seminary, "A Christian Witness of Conviction and Sympathy" (March 15, 1964), 1.

63. Allan Jones, "700 March in Four Cities," *Richmond Times-Dispatch*, March 16, 1965, 1.

64. The Student Body of Union Theological Seminary, "March Procedure" (March 15, 1965), 1.

65. "A Century in the City," 5, 7–8.

66. Robert F. Martin, "Critique of Southern Society and Vision of a New Order: The Fellowship of Southern Churchmen, 1934–1957," *Church History* 52, no. 1 (March 1983): 66–68.

67. Interview with James Luther Mays (in person, April 7, 2011), 3.

68. Interview with James L. Mays, UTS Video History.

69. F. Lindsay Moffett, "'A Fellowship of Concern' Remembered," *Presbyterian Outlook*, April 8, 2002, 8.

70. "Presbyterians: Concern v. Concerned," *Time*, October 13, 1967, 1.

71. Moffett, "'A Fellowship of Concern' Remembered," 8.

72. T. H. Hall, "Administrative History of Union," 71.

73. "UTS Drive for $150,000 Opens Today," *Richmond Times-Dispatch*, January 24, 1949, 4.

74. "Contribution to an Ideal," *Richmond News Leader*, January 31, 1949, 10.

75. "UTS Succeeds in Campaign for $150,000," *Richmond News Leader*, January 5, 1950, 3.

76. "Presbyterian Men and Women of South Are Invited to Attend Mid-Century Convocation Here," *Richmond Times-Dispatch*, December 2, 1951, B-14.

77. T. H. Hall, "Administrative History of Union," 68.

78. *For All Southern Presbyterians*, 1, 3, 7, 17.

79. "Mid-Century Victory," *Union Seminary Bulletin*, January–March 1954, 1.

80. T. H. Hall, "Administrative History of Union," 82.

81. E. T. Thompson, "The Twentieth Century," 88.

82. T. H. Hall, "Administrative History of Union," 61, 73.

83. "Union Theological Installs President," *Richmond Times-Dispatch*, April 5, 1956, 3.

84. "116 Schools Represented at UTS Inauguration," *Richmond News Leader*, April 4, 1956, 25.

85. T. H. Hall, "Administrative History of Union," 67.

86. "Union Theological Installs President," 3.

87. James Archibald Jones, "The Church and Its Ministry" (inaugural address delivered April 4, 1956, in Schauffler Hall, Union Theological Seminary, April 4, 1956), 12, 14–16.

88. James H. Smylie, "UTS Opens the Family Photo Album," *Focus* 2, no. 4 (Winter 1987): 20.

89. T. H. Hall, "Administrative History of Union," 77.

90. Connolly Currie Gamble Jr., "The Education of Southern Presbyterian Ministers: A Survey of the Program and Possibilities of Union Theological Seminary, Richmond, Virginia" (Union Theological Seminary, May 1950), 1–2, 5–6, 8–9.

91. William Adams Brown, *The Education of American Ministers*, vol. 1, *Ministerial Education in America* (New York: Institute of Social and Religious Research, 1934), 208.

92. Gamble, "Education of Southern Presbyterian Ministers," 11, 13, 14, 26, 28, 30.

93. Marshall B. Waytt, "The Seminary and Extension," *Union Seminary Review* 39 (April 1928): 272.

94. Gamble, "Education of Southern Presbyterian Ministers," 36, 56.

95. T. H. Hall, "Administrative History of Union," 61.

96. Gamble, "Education of Southern Presbyterian Ministers," 6–7.

97. Interview with Shriver, 2.

98. E. T. Thompson, *Presbyterians in the South*, 3:413.

99. *For All Southern Presbyterians*, 2.

100. Oglesby, "Faith in Action," 12.

101. James Appleby, "Field Work and Evangelism" (inaugural address delivered September 10, 1947, in Schauffler Hall, Union Theological Seminary, Richmond, VA), 3.

102. Ibid., 6, 8.

103. Tubbs, *The Story of My Life*, 23.

104. T. H. Hall, "Administrative History of Union," 56.

105. E. T. Thompson, *Presbyterians in the South*, 3:471.

106. Interview with William B. Oglesby (August 1, 1985), UTS Video History.

107. Interview with Shriver, 1.

108. Interview with Oglesby, UTS Video History.

109. Interview with Shriver, 2.

110. Faculty Minutes, 1951–1954, 557, 575–76, 593, 685.

111. Smylie, "Family Photo Album," 17.

112. William B. Oglesby Jr., "Implications of Anthropology for Pastoral Care Counseling" (lecture delivered March 2, 1954, in Schauffler Hall, Union Theological Seminary, Richmond, VA), 8.

113. T. H. Hall, "Administrative History of Union," 77.

114. Catalogue, 1957–1958, 10, 43.

115. T. H. Hall, "Administrative History of Union," 78.

116. H. Richard Niebuhr, *The Purpose of the Church and Its Ministry* (New York: Harper & Brothers, 1956), 40, 48, 55–56, 95–96.

117. Shriver, "Biblical Theology: A Personal History," 9.

118. Niebuhr, *The Purpose of the Church and Its Ministry*, 97, 99–101, 107, 131–32.

119. Charles Swezey, "Remarks to UTS Faculty on 'The Niebuhr Reports'" (delivered in Faculty Workshop, Richmond, VA, September 1981), 4–10. I thank Dr.

Swezey for his insights into the Niebuhr report and for sharing his remarks on it in the 1981 faculty workshop.

120. T. H. Hall, "Administrative History of Union," 86–87.

121. Shriver, "Biblical Theology: A Personal History," 7.

122. Interview with James L. Mays, UTS Video History.

123. Shriver, "Biblical Theology: A Personal History," 8.

124. James Luther Mays, "Exegesis as a Theological Discipline" (inaugural address delivered April 20, 1960, in Schauffler Hall, Union Theological Seminary, Richmond, VA, April 20, 1960), 8–12, 14–16, 22–23.

125. Shriver, "Biblical Theology: A Personal History," 9.

126. Scott McCormick, *Biblical Theology in the Years 1947–1956 as Reflected through Interpretation* (ThM thesis, Union Theological Seminary in Virginia, May 1957), 9–10, 14, 19, 37, 48, 54.

127. Robert Tabscott, "A Moral Reckoning" (tribute to John Bright, in the papers of James Smylie), 2.

128. John B. Trotti, "There's a Sweet, Sweet Spirit in This Place," *Focus*, Spring 2000, 12.

129. Tabscott, "A Moral Reckoning," 3–4.

130. William P. Brown, Introduction, *A History of Israel*, John Bright, 4th ed. (Louisville, KY: Westminster John Knox Press, 2000), 3, 21–22.

131. Tabscott, "A Moral Reckoning," 4.

132. Student Handbook, 1952–1953, 17.

133. Trotti, "Seminary Library," 77, 91, 99, 101, on 1930–70.

134. T. H. Hall, "Administrative History of Union," 1930–70, 69.

135. Trotti, "Seminary Library," 1, on 1968–96.

136. Interview with Robert White Kirkpatrick (September 5, 1985), UTS Video History.

137. "Sound of Learning Is a UTS Hit," *Richmond Times-Dispatch*, April 19, 1965, 8.

138. Robert White Kirkpatrick, "The Early Years of WRFK-FM" (a reminiscence by Robert W. Kirkpatrick on the early years of WRFK, Richmond, VA, July 5, 1979), 1.

139. "UTS Gets Anonymous Grant to Build Radio Station Here," *Richmond News Leader*, December 6, 1956, 21.

140. "Those FM Sounds in the Air," *Richmond Times-Dispatch*, October 12, 1960, 12.

141. Interview with Robert W. Kirkpatrick, UTS Video History.

142. "Those FM Sounds in the Air," 12.

143. R. W. Kirkpatrick, "The Early Years of WRFK-FM," 2.

144. Dallas R. Long, "Local Radio Station Will Join Network," *Richmond Times-Dispatch*, July 22, 1970, B-19.

145. R. W. Kirkpatrick, "The Early Years of WRFK-FM," 3–4.

146. Interview with R. W. Kirkpatrick, UTS Video History.

147. Ibid.

148. "Sound of Learning Is a UTS Hit," 8.

149. "UTS Has Closed-Circuit TV Network on Campus," *Richmond Times-Dispatch*, April 6, 1956, 6.

150. Interview with R. W. Kirkpatrick, UTS Video History.

151. Jeff Kellam, "Forty I Followed: Robert White Kirkpatrick," in *Peace, Grace, and Jazz!* (Internet blog, March 12, 2011, https://jeffkellam.wordpress.com/2011/03/12/forty-i-followed-robert-white-kirkpatrick/).

152. "UTS to Dedicate Rebuilt Pipe Organ Tuesday," *Richmond News Leader*, April 21, 1962, D-2.

153. Ted Hale, Reminiscence about the installation of the organ (July 5, 2011), 1.

154. "UTS to Dedicate Rebuilt Pipe Organ," D-2.

155. T. H. Hall, "Administrative History of Union," 92–93.

156. Catalogue, 1959–1960, insert.

157. Ibid., 1961–1962, 17–20.

158. T. Hartley Hall IV, "The Lower Gifts" (paper presented at opening convocation, Watts Chapel, Union Theological Seminary in Virginia, September 9, 1987), 10.

159. Catalogue, 1965–1966, 29, 31.

160. Interview with Kuykendall, 1.

161. Interview with Merwyn Johnson (in person, September 29, 2012); Dr. Johnson alerted me to this trend.

162. T. H. Hall, "Administrative History of Union," 94.

163. Interview with Merwyn Johnson, 1.

164. T. H. Hall, "Administrative History of Union," 72–73, 95.

165. Catalogue, 1953–1954, 74.

166. T. H. Hall, "Administrative History of Union," 68, 78.

167. Catalogue, 1949–1950, 25.

168. Interview with Ed Stock (interviewed by Rob Collins, Richmond, VA).

169. Catalogue, 1956–1957, 40, 58.

170. E. T. Thompson, *Presbyterians in the South*, 3:468.

171. Interview with James L. Mays, 2.

172. "139-Year Tradition to Be Broken Tomorrow When Mrs. Etchison Receives Degree at UTS," *Richmond Times-Dispatch*, May 21, 1951, 3.

173. Ibid.

174. Interview with Mary Faith Carson (in person, January 20, 2012).

175. Kay Speegle, "Reflections on the New Open Door Policy," *Expression* 2, no. 2 (Summer 1964): 1.

176. T. H. Hall, "Administrative History of Union," 82, 94.

177. "Dr. Jones and the Future," *Expression* 1, no. 1 (February 1956): 1.

178. Bill Holshouser, "A Private Case for Demonstrating," *Expression* 9, no. 1 (October 1, 1963): 6–8.

179. Tom Mainor, "Some Thoughts on Civil Rights and the Church," *Expression* 9, no. 1 (October 1, 1963): 4–5.

180. Letter to the editor, *Expression* 6, no. 10 (March 22, 1961): 2.

181. Bob Gustafson, "Seeking to Be Christian in Race Relations," *Expression* 1, no. 1 (February 1956): 2.

182. Richard Harbison, "The Minister in the Present Crisis," *Expression* 3, no. 2 (December 1957): 9.

183. Ben L. Rose, "Racial Segregation in the Church," *Expression*, April 1957, 2.

184. "Reports on the Inter-Seminary Movement and the 18th Ecumenical Student Conference in Athens, Ohio," *Expression* 5, no. 2 (Winter 1960): 6.

185. William B. Kennedy, "Reflections on the March to Washington," *Expression* 9, no. 2 (November 1, 1963): 1.

186. "Representative from the Student Inter-Racial Movement Will Speak on Campus November 11," *Expression* 9, no. 6 (November 13, 1964): 11.

187. Donnie Cross, "Voter Registration," *Expression* 9, no. 3 (September 18, 1964): 8.

188. Dan C. West, "Impressions at Montgomery," *Expression* 9, no. 14 (April 12, 1965): 10.

189. Gerald Niece, "Niece Attends Conference on Student Interracial Ministry," *Expression* 10, no. 8 (April–May 1966): 11.

190. Editor, "Reaction to Speech by Dr. James Farmer," *Expression* 11, no. 2 (November 1966): 6.

191. H. Alton Loo Jr., "In Search of the Will of God," *Expression* 9, no. 13 (March 22, 1965): 1.

192. Ibid., 2, 4.

193. G. Aiken Taylor, Letters to the Editor, *Expression* 9, no. 10 (April 12, 1965): 11.

194. Anonymous, "Proposed: A Store-Front Mission," *Expression* 6, no. 10 (March 22, 1961): 3.

195. Donnie Cross, "Letter to Seminarians," *Expression* 9, no. 7 (April 17, 1964): 1, 3.

196. A. Donovan Cross, "Reflections on the Inner-City," *Expression* 9, no. 13 (March 22, 1965): 8.

197. Allen Reynolds, "The Beloved Country," *Expression* 7, no. 10 (November 21, 1962): 3.

198. A. Donovan Cross, "The Suburban Captivity of the Seminary," *Expression* 7, no. 8 (March 31, 1962): 4.

199. Maurice Allen, "Judgments from the Parish," *Expression* 9, no. 8 (November 25, 1964): 1.

200. Editor, "Interning Students Report," *Expression* 10, no. 5 (January 1966): 7.

201. Interview with Ben Lacy Rose, UTS Video History (December 13 and 19, 1991).

202. Interview with Heath Rada (interviewed by Rob Collins, Richmond, VA).

203. Interview with Lisa Cross (interviewed by Rob Collins, Richmond, VA).

204. F. M. Dhombres, "Crazy America—I Love You," *Expression* 9, no. 13 (March 22, 1965): 6.

205. Editorial, *Expression* 4, no. 4 (Spring 1959): 10–11; John Ames, "The One Hundred and Fifth Year—for What?," *Expression* 9, no. 14 (April 12, 1965): 1.

206. Ames, "One Hundred and Fifth Year," 20.

207. Catalogue, 1956–1957, 9.

208. Ibid., 1963–1964, 25.

209. T. Hartley Hall IV, "The Middle East Situation—from a Christian Perspective," *Expression* 2, no. 1 (October 1956): 1.

210. William W. Bloom, "The Middle East Situation—from a Christian Perspective," *Expression* 2, no. 1 (October 1956): 4.

211. Harold Wallof Jr., "'News' for Yankees," *Expression* 7, no. 8 (March 31, 1962): 1.

212. Will H. Terry, "The Christian Church in International Life," *Expression*, February 1957, 3.

213. David J. Causey, "The Supreme Court on Prayer," *Expression* 9, no. 2 (November 1, 1963): 4.

214. Cross, "Suburban Captivity of the Seminary," 4.

215. James M. Davis, "*Rerum Novarum*—UTS," *Expression* 11, no. 4 (October 2, 1964): 1.

216. "What Is Wrong with Seminary Students?," *Expression*, February 1956, 6.

217. O. Ben Sparks, "Community—or Chaos," *Expression* 9, no. 8 (May 14, 1964): 1.

218. Richard S. Watt, "Bookshelf Christianity," *Expression* 6, no. 5 (November 23, 1960): 4.

219. Dave Mullen, "The Courage to Care," *Expression* 6, no. 10 (March 22, 1961): 1, 4.

220. Pamela Cameron, "UTS: Stored Heads and Unmoved Hearts?," *Expression* 9, no. 5 (October 16, 1964): 1.

221. John M. Watkins, "To Be or Not to Be a Community," *Expression* 6, no. 11 (April 12, 1961): 1–2.

222. George Ramsey, "Re: The Pledge and 'Community,'" *Expression* 6, no. 11 (April 12, 1961): 6.

223. Bob Martin, "Towards an Adequate Perspective between UTS and PSCE," *Expression* 5, no. 1 (Fall 1959): 6–7.

224. Sara Little, "About PSCE . . . ," *Expression* 6, no. 9 (March 8, 1961): 3.

225. Student Handbook, 1947–1948, 1.

226. Ibid., 1948–1949, 10.

227. Ibid., 1947–1948, 1.

228. Ibid., 1948–1949, 10, 14.

229. Ibid., 1952–1953, 10.

230. Sam Rochester, "Defending Infant Baptism," *Expression* 2, no. 3 (January 1957): 2.

231. Bob Maclin, Letter to the editor, *Expression* 9, no. 7 (April 17, 1964): 2, 4.

232. Student Handbook, 1958–1959, 71.

233. Richard L. Meath, "The Influence of Contemporary Fiction Writers on American Christianity," *Expression* 2, no. 3 (January 1957): 4.

234. "No Name Gazette," *No Name Gazette* (Richmond, VA), no. 1 (January 26, 1959): 1.

235. "Quid—Me Vexari?," *Depression* (Richmond, VA) 1, no. 1 (March 4, 1965): 3.

236. Editor, "For Those Who Hunger and Thirst . . . ," *Expression* 9, no. 12 (March 5, 1965): 4.

237. Catalogue, 1952–1953, 33.

238. "Fighting UTES" (a play on the name of the Native American tribe and the abbreviation of Union Theological Seminary), *Expression* 7, no. 3 (November 1, 1961): 2.

239. "Theology on the Gridiron," *Expression* 6, no. 5 (November 23, 1960): 1.

240. "The Prayboy Philosophy," *Prayboy* (Richmond, VA), April 1, 1966, 1.

241. "Prayboy's Party Jokes," *Prayboy*, April 1, 1966, 3.

242. Bill Melton, "The New Curriculum," *Expression* 11, no. 4 (October 2, 1964): 6–8.

243. "Vietnam Poll," *Expression* 10, no. 6 (March 1966): 1, 10.

244. Tom Byrd, "UTS Is Site of Peace Seminar," *Expression* 10, no. 8 (April–May 1966): 10–11.

245. Interview with T. Hartley Hall IV, UTS Video History.

246. Lawton Posey, e-mail to the author, May 27, 2010 (Lawton Posey Letter).

247. T. H. Hall, "Administrative History of Union," 94.

248. Interview with T. Hartley Hall, UTS Video History.

249. Student Handbook, 1949–1950, 6.

250. Ibid., 1947–1948, 4.

251. T. H. Hall, "Administrative History of Union," 95.

252. "Life That Lives On," *Expression* 9, no. 8 (May 14, 1964): 3.

253. Student Handbook, 1949–1950, 6.

254. Interview with T. Hartley Hall, UTS Video History.

255. Interview with Paul Achtemeier (in person, January 13, 2012).

256. Balmer H. Kelly, "In Retrospect," *Interpretation* 25, no. 1 (January 1971): 23.

257. Ibid., 14–15.

258. James H. Mays, editorial, *Interpretation* 20, no. 1 (January 1966): 78.

259. "Interview with Ann Logan (interviewed by Rob Collins, Richmond, VA).

260. E. T. Thompson, "The Twentieth Century," 4.

261. T. H. Hall, "Administrative History of Union," 84.

262. Interview with Balmer H. Kelly, UTS Video History.

263. T. H. Hall, "Administrative History of Union," 84–85.

264. "$19,000,000 Rebuilding Plan Detailed by Union Seminary," *Richmond Times-Dispatch*, May 18, 1965, 1.

265. *Training for Excellence* (fund-raising booklet for the Advance capital campaign, Richmond, VA: Trevvett, Christian & Co., 1965), 7, 10.

266. "$19,000,000 Rebuilding Plan," 1.

267. Editorial, "The Union Seminary Drive," *Richmond Times-Dispatch*, February 13, 1966.

268. T. H. Hall, "Administrative History of Union," 85.

269. *Training for Excellence,* inside front cover, 2–3.

270. Mary Lacy, "Inflation Is Choking UTS $19-Million Building Plan," *Richmond News Leader,* June 1, 1970, 15.

271. Editor, "Documented Inconsistency," *Expression* 9, no. 14 (April 12, 1965): 2.

272. "Master of Sacred Theology Courses to Begin at UTS in Fall," *Richmond News Leader,* May 28, 1966, 22.

273. "Dr. James A. Jones, UTS President, Dies," *Richmond Times-Dispatch,* November 18, 1966, 1.

274. "UTS Names Acting President," *Richmond Times-Dispatch,* November 30, 1966, 2.

275. Interview with Ken Goodpasture (interviewed by Stan Skreslet, July 7, 1999, Richmond, VA), UTS Video History.

276. T. H. Hall, "The Lower Gifts," 8.

277. T. H. Hall, "Administrative History of Union," 89.

278. "Dr. Kelly to Become Dean of Seminary," *Richmond News Leader,* May 18, 1965, 15.

279. Interview with Balmer H. Kelly, UTS Video History.

280. Interview with Ben Lacy Rose, UTS Video History.

281. Interview with Doug Miller (by telephone, March 24, 2011).

282. E. T. Thompson, "The Twentieth Century," 84.

CHAPTER 9: Scholarship or Praxis?

1. Louise McComb, *The First Seventy Years: A History of the Presbyterian School of Christian Education* (Richmond, VA: Presbyterian School of Christian Education, 1985), 8, 85–86.

2. Alberta Lindsey, "President for UTS Named," *Richmond News Leader,* May 16, 1967, A-1.

3. "UTS President Inaugurated," *Richmond Times-Dispatch,* November 10, 1968, 1.

4. Interview with William B. Oglesby, UTS Video History Project (August 1, 1985).

5. John Bright, "John Bright Observes a 'Good Spirit' at UTS," *Union Theological Seminary Bulletin,* 1975, 2.

6. James A. Jones, "And Some, Pastors," in *Horizons of Theological Education: Essays in Honor of Charles L. Taylor, John B. Coburn, Walter D. Wagoner, and Jesse H. Ziegler* (Dayton, OH: AATS, 1966); also in *Theological Education* 2, no. 4 (Summer 1966): 59–63.

7. James K. Sanford, "The Training of Ministers 1968 Style: Changing Times Dictate Changes in Education," *Richmond Times-Dispatch,* April 7, 1968, D-1.

8. "President for UTS Named," *Richmond News Leader,* May 16, 1967, 1.

9. Sanford, "Training of Ministers 1968 Style," D-1.

10. "UTS President Inaugurated," 1, 17.

11. Fred Rogers Stair Jr., "At the Seminary and in the World: An Inaugural Address," *Affirmation* 1, no. 4 (May 1969): 31.

12. Ibid., 31, 34–36.

13. Glenn T. Miller, *A Community of Conversation: A Retrospective of the Association of Theological Schools and Ninety Years of North American Theological Education* (Pittsburgh: Association of Theological Schools, 2008), 10.

14. William B. Oglesby Jr., "Faith in Action: Preparing Students for the Work of Ministry" (paper presented at the 175th anniversary of the founding of Union Theological Seminary, October 12, 1987), 2–6, 10, 12–13.

15. Vaught, "The Student and U.T.S." *Perspective* (Richmond, VA), issue 6, 4.

16. Editor, "Perspective: Community and Curriculum," *Perspective* (Richmond, VA), issue 3, 2.

17. President Nowlin, "UTS Colloquy Holds First Meeting," *Interrobang* (Richmond, VA), issue 4 (1969): 1.

18. T. Hartley Hall IV, "Administrative History of Union Theological Seminary" (notes in the papers of the author, 1986), 123.

19. Sanford, "Changing Times Dictate Changes," D-1.

20. UTS Catalogue, 1968–1969, 40.

21. T. H. Hall, "Administrative History of Union," 120.

22. David King, "An Experimental Course in Experimental Ministry," *Expression* (Richmond, VA), February 1968, 1.

23. Interview with Ken Goodpasture, UTS Video History (interviewed by Stan Skreslet, July 7, 1999, Richmond, VA).

24. Sanford, "Changing Times Dictate Changes," D-1.

25. Catalogue, 1971–1972, 22.

26. Perfidious Twit, "Rogue's Review of the Competence Paper," *In a Mirror* (Richmond, VA), December 1974, 7–8.

27. Dick Short, Letter to the editor, *Expression*, December 1968–January 1969, 3.

28. Barbara Horney, "UTS Students and Faculty Meet to Discuss Academic Load," *In a Mirror*, February 1975, 10.

29. Fred Moon, "Comments," *In a Mirror*, April 1975, 7.

30. Rick Dietrich, "A Disorganized Look at the Academic Calendar, Part 1, The Party Line," *In Medias Res* (Richmond, VA), November 29, 1978, 1.

31. Ibid., "Part 2, The Anti-Party Line," December 1978, 1.

32. William V. Arnold, "In Case You Wondered: Faculty Review Committee," *In Medias Res*, January 25, 1978, 3.

33. Richard Hamm and Marsha Wilfong, "Curriculum, or, What I Did Last Year," *In Medias Res*, November 8, 1978, 6.

34. Michael T. Condrey, "Regarding Curriculum at UTS," *In Medias Res*, March 15, 1978, 3.

35. Hamm and Wilfong, "Curriculum," 6.

36. Bob Knox, "The Rural Church," *In Medias Res*, March 15, 1978, 5.

37. J. Christopher Mullen, "Of Competencies and Koinonia," *In Medias Res*, November 1982, 4.

38. Catalogue, 1988–1990, 15.

39. Raphaël Franck and Laurence R. Iannaccone, "The Decrease in Religiosity in the Twentieth Century" (Bar-Ilan University Discussion Paper, 2009, http://www .thearda.com/asrec/archive/papers/Franck%20&%20Iannaccone%20ASREC%202009 .pdf.2009), 42.

40. Ibid., 22–23.

41. G. T. Miller, *Community of Conversation*, 19.

42. Jesse H. Ziegler, *ATS through Two Decades: Reflections on Theological Education, 1960–1980* (Worcester, MA: Heffernan Press, 1984), 44.

43. "A New Spirit Soars on the Wings of Tradition: A Candid Interview about the Future of UTS," *Focus* 2, no. 4 (Winter 1987): 2.

44. G. T. Miller, *Community of Conversation*, 19.

45. T. H. Hall, "Administrative History of Union," 107, 118.

46. "UTS Announces Shift to Master's [Degree]," *Richmond News Leader*, February 22, 1971, 22.

47. Union Theological Seminary in Virginia, 1967 Self-Study Report, 54.

48. T. H. Hall, "Administrative History of Union," 121.

49. UTS, 1974 Self-Study Report for the ATS and the SACS, 30.

50. "UTS Announces Shift to Master's," 22.

51. James H. Smylie, "UTS Opens the Family Photo Album," *Focus* 2, no. 4 (Winter 1987): 22.

52. T. H. Hall, "Administrative History of Union," 120.

53. UTS, 1974 Self-Study Report, 41.

54. T. H. Hall, "Administrative History of Union," 108, 120.

55. Patrick D. Miller, "Report from the Dean of Faculty," *In Medias Res*, November 1982, 1.

56. G. T. Miller, *Community of Conversation*, 8.

57. T. H. Hall, "Administrative History of Union," 112, 130–31.

58. G. T. Miller, *Community of Conversation*, 4–8.

59. T. H. Hall, "Administrative History of Union," 109.

60. UTS, 1996 Self-Study Report Prepared for the ATS and the SACS, 97.

61. T. Hartley Hall IV, "The Lower Gifts" (paper presented at opening convocation, Watts Chapel, Union Theological Seminary in Virginia, September 9, 1987), 10.

62. Smylie, "UTS Opens the Family Photo Album," 21–22.

63. T. H. Hall, "Administrative History of Union," 126–28.

64. Interview with Donald Dawe, UTS Video History Project (interviewed by Stan Skreslet, December 13, 2002, Richmond, VA).

65. UTS, 1967 Self-Study Report, 12.

66. T. H. Hall, "Administrative History of Union," 117–18.

67. Interview with James Luther Mays, UTS History Project (June 5, 1999).

68. Interview with Donald Dawe (interviewed by William B. Sweetser Jr., January 21, 2010, Richmond, VA).

69. Brevard S. Childs, *Biblical Theology in Crisis* (Philadelphia: Westminster Press, 1970), 13, 15, 19, 21, 27–28, 61–87.

70. Interview with Donald Dawe, 2.

71. Childs, *Biblical Theology in Crisis*, 91–93, 163, 183.

72. John Leith, "The Significance of Historical Theology in the Education of Ministers" (inaugural address, Union Theological Seminary, Richmond, VA, April 20, 1960; in the author's files), 1–3, 5–13.

73. John H. Leith, "Teaching Theology at Union Seminary in Virginia" (paper presented on the 175th anniversary of the founding of Union Theological Seminary, October 13, 1987), 4.

74. John H. Leith, ed., *Creeds of the Churches: A Reader in Christian Doctrine from the Bible to the Present* (New York: Anchor Books, 1963), 2.

75. Leith, "Teaching Theology at Union," 1, 10–12.

76. John H. Leith, *Pilgrimage of a Presbyterian*, ed. Charles E. Raynal (Louisville, KY: Geneva Press, 2000), xix.

77. John H. Leith, *Crisis in the Church: The Plight of Theological Education* (Louisville, KY: Westminster John Knox Press, 1997), 30, 35.

78. Theodore J. Wardlaw, "Laughter in the Church—for God's Sake" (a sermon delivered at the 2005 Sprunt Lectures, January 25, 2005, Richmond, VA; unpublished manuscript in the author's files), 4.

79. Interview with John Leith, UTS Video History (date unknown).

80. Alberta Lindsey, "Procession of Favorite Books Will Hail Seminary's New Library," *Richmond Times-Dispatch*, November 20, 1996, B-6.

81. Selden Richardson, *Built by Blacks: African-American Architecture in Neighborhoods in Richmond, VA* (Charleston, SC: History Press, 2008), 109–31.

82. T. H. Hall, "Administrative History of Union," 114.

83. UTS, 1967 Self-Study Report, 7.

84. Interview with Ken Goodpasture, UTS Video History.

85. Interview with Dean McBride and Sib Towner (Kilmarnock, VA, October 14, 2011), 1.

86. Mark Peters, "Christian Witness in Our Community and the Debate over Public Schools," *In Medias Res*, Spring 1993, 9–10.

87. Board of Trustees Minutes, 1992, 2.

88. Faculty Lunch Meeting, May 28, 1993, 1, 2, 4.

89. Faculty Workshop, September 1993, 4.

90. Sandy Durham, "The Great Ivy Rip-Off," *In a Mirror*, April 1975, 1.

91. John Oldman, "Campus Security (or, Rather, Lack Thereof)," *In Medias Res*, January 25, 1978, 6.

92. Ron Buckalew, "One Person's Perspective," *In Medias Res*, April 2, 1978, 1.

93. Jeff Falter, "UTS Safety Survey Results," *In Medias Res*, April 1994, 4.

94. Board Reports (November 1996), 5.

95. T. H. Hall, "Administrative History of Union," 108.

96. Catalogue, 1972–1973, 8.

97. UTS, 1974 Self-Study Report, 19.

98. Randy Jackson, "The Way It Was," *In a Mirror*, February 1975, 9.

99. Mark Holmes, "Reflections," *In a Mirror*, February 1975, 3.

100. Interview with T. Hartley Hall, UTS Video History (interviewed by Rebecca H. Weaver, Richmond, VA, May 5–6, 1999).

101. Editor, "Ask Not Only What the RTC Can Do for You," *In Medias Res*, December 1982, 2.

102. Kit Havice, "Social Action," *Expression*, October 1967, 3.

103. Paul Rader, "Letter to the UTS Community," *In Medias Res*, January 1983, 7.

104. Interview with Dean McBride and Sib Towner.

105. T. H. Hall, "Administrative History of Union," 122.

106. Interview with Elaine Rhodes (Davidson, NC, January 3, 2012).

107. Nancy Duff et al., "Information from the Steering Committee on Women's Concerns and Their Task Forces for the Members of the Faculty" (Richmond, VA, May 15, 1974; in the author's files), 2, 8–10.

108. Ibid., 8.

109. Interview with Mary Jane Winter (Richmond, VA, January 20, 2012).

110. Duff et al., "Steering Committee on Women's Concerns," 2–6.

111. Sally Nurnberger, "Being Included," *In Medias Res*, November 1979, 2.

112. Faculty Resolution on Inclusive Language (Union Theological Seminary, Richmond, VA, March 11, 1982), 1–3.

113. Catalogue, 1967–1968, back cover.

114. Interview with Mary Faith Carson (Black Mountain, NC, June 27, 2012), 2.

115. Interview with Elaine Rhodes.

116. Interview with Mary Jane Winter.

117. Mary Elizabeth Goin, "Of Jobs and Calls," *In Medias Res*, March 15, 1978, 1.

118. Jeff Sconyers, "One Person's Opinion," *In Medias Res*, January 25, 1978, 2.

119. Editor, "Around the Seminary," *Union Seminary Magazine* 13, no. 2 (December 1901–January 1902): 137.

120. T. H. Hall, "Administrative History of Union," 117.

121. Sara Little, "Women at Union," *In Medias Res*, January 1986, 4.

122. Ibid., 5.

123. Interview with Rebecca Weaver (Richmond, VA, January 20, 2010), 1.

124. "First Women Are Elected to UTS Board," *Richmond Times-Dispatch*, November 21, 1972, A-1.

125. Susan Elizabeth Fox, "Perceptions of the Placement Process: Presbyterian Women Candidates at Union Theological Seminary in Virginia" (PhD diss., Union Theological Seminary in Virginia, 1995), 1, 42, 95.

126. Shirley Hutchins, "Thoughts from the 'Girl' Seminarian," *In Media Res*, Spring 1990, 3.

127. Martha Lane Moore, "Faith, Feminism, and the Church," *In Medias Res*, May 1991, 15.

128. Board Minutes, April 30–May 1, 1993, 69.

129. Board Minutes, May 6–7, 1994, 72.

130. Campus Life Committee of the Board of Trustees, Report to the President on Women's Concerns, May 1, 1995, 1–3.

131. UTS, 1996 Self-Study Report, 104–5.

132. Interview with Frances Taylor Gench (Richmond, VA, October 11, 2011), 1.

133. Interview with T. Hartley Hall, UTS Video History.

134. "New Seminary President Seeks to Raise Quality of Students," *Richmond Times-Dispatch*, April 30, 1982, B-4.

135. T. Hartley Hall IV, "Curriculum Consultation" (Richmond, VA, October 30, 1989; in the author's files), 1.

136. National Black Presbyterian Caucus, *Blacks in the United Presbyterian Church in the U.S.A., 1807–1982* (New York: United Presbyterian Church, 1982), 33–35.

137. John Alexander Mackay, "The Heritage of Yesterday," *Union Seminary Review* 60, no. 4 (August 1944): 285.

138. James H. Smylie, "Imperative: Presbyterian Reunion," *In Medias Res*, January 1983, 2.

139. Ibid.

140. John H. Leith, "Church Union: A Practical Necessity but Not the Critical Issue Confronting Presbyterians," *Presbyterian Outlook*, December 20–27, 1982: 5.

141. Editor, "Students Speak on Reunion," *In Medias Res*, January 1983, 3.

142. Interview with Roger Nicholson (by telephone, March 8, 2012).

143. Catalogue, 1984–1985, 65.

144. Union Theological Seminary in Virginia, 1985 Self-Study Report Prepared for the ATS and the SACS, 67.

145. Thomas K. Tewell et al., *The General Assembly Special Committee to Study Theological Institutions: Draft Report to the 1993 General Assembly* ([Louisville, KY]: Presbyterian Church (U.S.A.), 1993), 9.

146. T. H. Hall, "Curriculum Consultation," 2.

147. Tewell, *Committee to Study Theological Institutions*, 9–10, 13, 29–31.

148. T. Hartley Hall IV, president, Union Theological Seminary in Virginia, "Trends in Theological Education and How UTS Fits In," in Board of Trustees Meeting (Richmond, VA, February 18, 1994; copy of address in the author's files), 7.

149. Tewell, *Committee to Study Theological Institutions*, 11, 29–31.

150. T. H. Hall, "Curriculum Consultation," 8, 10, 11.

151. "A New Spirit Soars on the Wings of Tradition," 4.

152. T. Hartley Hall IV, "Reflections on Admissions, Enrollment, and Financial Aid" (address given to the Board of Trustees, ca. 1989; in the author's files), 1–2.

153. Catalogue, 1967–1968, 58.

154. T. H. Hall, "Admissions, Enrollment, and Financial Aid," 2.

155. "A New Spirit Soars," 5.

156. T. H. Hall, "Admissions, Enrollment, and Financial Aid," 2.

157. Tewell, *Committee to Study Theological Institutions*, 20.

158. T. H. Hall, "Trends in Theological Education," 3, 6.

159. Benjamin Rice Lacy, "Union Theological Seminary in This Present Age: On the Occasion of His Inauguration as President of Union Theological Seminary in Virginia, May 11, 1927," *Union Seminary Review* 38, no. 4 (July 1927): 367.

160. Interview with T. Hartley Hall, UTS Video History.

161. "Local Radio Station Will Join Network," *Richmond Times-Dispatch*, July 22, 1970, B-19.

162. T. H. Hall, "Administrative History of Union," 111–13.

163. Douglas Durden, "Saga of WRFK Nears End," *Richmond Times-Dispatch*, February 28, 1988, B-1.

164. Interview with T. Hartley Hall, UTS Video History.

165. "WRFK Ranks 10th in Ratings," *Richmond Times-Dispatch*, October 20, 1987, B-7.

166. "Save WRFK, Presbytery Says," *Richmond Times-Dispatch*, October 27, 1985, B-9.

167. Sam Forrest, "Criticizes Seminary on WRFK Issue," letter to the editor, *Richmond Times-Dispatch*, March 22, 1988, A-12.

168. "WRFK Backers Seek Ruling Review," *Richmond Times-Dispatch*, February 6, 1987, 44.

169. Durden, "Saga of WRFK Nears End," B-1.

170. "WRFK Benefit Set for Nov. 2," *Richmond Times-Dispatch*, October 27, 1985, K-2.

171. Katherine Phillips, "Letter-Writing Urged to Keep WRFK on the Air," *Richmond Times-Dispatch*, February 6, 1988, A-8.

172. Douglas Durden, "Listeners to Protest WRFK Sale Effort," *Richmond Times-Dispatch*, August 30, 1985, B-1.

173. Douglas Durden, "Seminary Ads Defend Action on WRFK," *Richmond Times-Dispatch*, June 27, 1986, B-11.

174. Robert E. R. Hunley, "Transfer Will Ensure WRFK's Future," *Richmond Times-Dispatch*, June 23, 1986, 10.

175. Katherine Phillips, "Sale of WRFK Radio Is Approved by FCC," *Richmond Times-Dispatch*, December 16, 1986, 1.

176. "WRFK," *Richmond Times-Dispatch*, August 29, 1985, 14.

177. Interview with Ken Goodpasture, UTS Video History.

178. Doug Beacham, letter from Oklahoma City to Dr. James Smylie, January 23, 2003.

179. Interview with Ken Goodpasture, UTS Video History.

180. Jay Click, "Missions and Missionaries," *In Medias Res*, December 1978, 5.

181. Kathy Sykes, "Examining Inclusive Language," *In Medias Res*, January 1986, 1.

182. Ibid., 6.

183. H. Pride Carson, "One Woman's Opinion on 'Women's Issues,'" *In Medias Res*, January 1986, 9.

184. Garet Aldridge, "Free Advice," *In Medias Res*, January 1986, 12.

185. Jonathan Van Deventer, "A Cautionary Tale," *In Medias Res*, February 1994, 6.

186. John Doubles, "Abortion: The Problem of Christian Concern," *In Medias Res*, Summer 1992, 5.

187. Keith Reeves, "A Short Treatise on Abortion," *In Medias Res*, January 1986, 10.

188. Philip Oehler, "AIDS and the Rural Church: A New Challenge to Ministry," *In Medias Res*, Spring 1993, 3.

189. James McTyre, "The Worst Haircut I've Ever Had: The Church's Response to AIDS Begins at the Barber's Chair and Ends at the Bedside," *In Medias Res*, Fall 1990, 12.

190. James McTyre, "The Sexuality Report-Event," *In Medias Res*, May 1991, 3.

191. Jim Singleton, "Is Our Language Really Inclusive?," *In Medias Res*, January 1983, 5.

192. Jon Burnham, "On Theological Security," *In Medias Res*, Spring 1993, 15.

193. Dave Duquette, "Help, Monarchists!," *In Medias Res*, April 1994, 1.

194. Interview with Louis Weeks, "A Visual History of Louis B. Weeks," UTS Video History (interviewed by Joe Coalter, Richmond, VA, April 2008).

195. Ibid., disc 1.

196. Louis Weeks, President's Report to the Board (Richmond, VA, Spring 1999), 1.

197. Interview with Ken Goodpasture, UTS Video History.

198. George M. Marsden, *Fundamentalism and American Culture*, 2nd ed. (New York: Oxford University Press, 2006), 243–47, 251–57.

199. Union Theological Seminary, Faculty Workshop, September 1993, 5.

200. Douglas F. Ottati, *Jesus Christ and Christian Vision* (Minneapolis: Augsburg Fortress, 1989), 1–2, 47–48.

201. David Green, "Will the Seminary Be True to Its Traditional Mission?," opinion, *Richmond Times-Dispatch*, December 30, 1995, A-8.

202. Alberta Lindsey, "Dispute at Seminary Has Deep, Wide Roots," *Richmond Times-Dispatch*, November 1, 1996, A-1.

203. Kerra Becker, "In Response to *The Presbyterian Layman*," *In Medias Res*, Fall 1995, 2.

204. Frank Wyche, "The Majority in the Middle," *In Medias Res*, Fall 1995, 7.

205. Ibid.

206. Paul Wilkes, "The Hands That Would Shape Our Souls," *Atlantic Monthly*, December 1990, 59, 65, 68.

207. UTS, 1967 Self-Study Report, 6, 82.

208. UTS, 1974 Self-Study Report, 24.

209. UTS, 1985 Self-Study Report, 41.

210. Reports to the Board of Trustees, Union Theological Seminary in Virginia (November 1–2, 1996), 3.

211. Catalogue, 1996–1997, 2–8.

212. T. H. Hall, "Administrative History of Union," 122.

213. Isabel Rogers, "Community: Gift and Demand," *Interrobang*, November 21, 1969, 1.

214. "A New Spirit Soars," 2.

215. Interview with James L. Mays (Richmond, VA, April 7, 2011).

216. UTS, 1967 Self-Study Report for the AATS, 83.

217. Editorial, *Perspective*, issue 7, 4.

218. T. H. Hall, "Administrative History of Union," 126.

219. Marybeth Hermanson and Betsey Gessler, "Reactions to the Washington Conference," *Expression*, February 1968, 2.

220. "An International Outlook on Vietnam," *Expression*, April 1968, 1–6.

221. T. H. Hall, "Administrative History of Union," 123.

222. Mike Bye, "Vietnam?," *Interrobang*, October 10, 1969, 1.

223. "UTS to Cancel Classes Wednesday," *Richmond News Leader*, October 10, 1969, 3.

224. John Mack Walker, "Our Justice," *Perspective*, May 1970 (?), issue 7, 4.

225. Robert W. Tabscott, "Report on the Week of Concern at U.T.S." (Richmond, VA, 1970), 1–4.

226. James P. Martin et al., "Commencement Petition of May 26, 1970" (Richmond, VA), 1–2.

227. Michael Warren, letter from Liberty, MS, to Fred R. Stair ("Warren Letter concerning Jackson State," September 2, 1970), esp. 2.

228. Synod of West Virginia, "A Report Outlining the Anti-War Efforts of UTS Students" (Elkins: Synod of West Virginia, 1970), 54, 58, 59.

229. Mary Marshall Clark, "A Letter to Faculty and Students," *In Medias Res*, April 2, 1978, 1.

230. Ty Sugg, "Toward a Policy of Social Responsibility," *In Medias Res*, April 2, 1978, 4.

231. Steve Hodges and Ty Sugg, "On Investments," *In Medias Res*, January 9, 1979, 1.

232. Ty Sugg, "A Report to Union Seminary Board of Trustees from Student Government Committee on Investments," *In Medias Res*, May 14, 1979, 6.

233. "Little Things That Add Up," *Expression*, October 1967, 2.

234. Philip W. Oehler, "The Beloved Community," *In Medias Res*, Summer 1992, 3.

235. Isabel Rogers, "Community: Gift and Demand," 1.

236. Editor, "Ask Not Only What the RTC Can Do for You," *In Medias Res*, December 1982, 2.

237. Hal Breitenberg, "Communion of the Commuters: Dorms and Demographics," *In Medias Res*, Spring 1992, 11–12.

238. UTS, 1996 Self-Study Report, 1, 37.

239. Becky Teague, "A View from across the Street," *In Medias Res*, Spring 1993, 7.

240. Becky Falter, "The Perils of Pregnancy, Part 1, The First Trimester or . . . the Journey to Hell and Back," *In Medias Res*, February 1994, 9.

241. Karen Brown, "The Black Phenomenon," *In Medias Res*, September 1988, 7.

242. Karen Brown and Shirley Hutchins, "The Welcome We Received," *In Medias Res*, Fall 1991, 5.

243. Interview with Hoffman Brown (by telephone, May 25, 2012).

244. UTS, 1996 Self-Study Report, 19–20.

245. Argen Tunge, editorial, *In Medias Res*, March 1999, 1.

246. Gail Sneddon, "Letter to the Editor," *Interrobang*, November 7, 1969, 2.

247. Laura Cole, "Up the Great Goal Post," *In a Mirror*, December 1974, 1.

248. Dick Davis, "On Winning," *Perspective*, issue 3, 6.

249. Stewart Rawson, "The State of RTC Football," *In Medias Res*, Fall 1991, 3.

250. Stewart Rawson and Pete Swanson, "The Ultimate Reality," *In Medias Res*, November 1993, 13.

251. Interview with Amy and Steve Willis (Spruce Pine, NC, August 12, 2011).

252. Student Handbook, 1978–1979, 10, 34.

253. Catalogue, 1980–1981, 47.

254. Ibid., 1992–1993, 133.

255. Ibid., 1994–1995, 139.

256. Ibid., 1995–1996, 149.

257. Beat Abegglen, e-mail to the author, January 29, 2014.

258. Cla Famos, "Union from a Swiss Perspective," *In Medias Res*, May 1991, 5.

259. John B. Trotti, "The History of the Union Theological Seminary Library" (unpublished manuscript in the author's files, 2008), 4, on 1968–96.

260. UTS, 1996 Self-Study Report, 80–83.

261. Trotti, "Seminary Library," 2, 4, 6, 8, 9, 11, 14, 21, on 1968–96.

262. Lindsey, "Procession of Favorite Books," B-6.

263. Trotti, "Seminary Library," 30–35, on 1968–96.

264. Interview with Roger Nicholson, 2.

265. Interview with Dean McBride and Sib Towner, 1.

266. McComb, *The First Seventy Years*, 58.

267. "The Proposal for Federation: The Presbyterian School of Christian Education and Union Theological Seminary in Virginia" (February 24, 1997), 3.

268. Tewell, *Committee to Study Theological Institutions*, §2.

269. Laura Lewis, Tony Ruger, and Ellis Nelson, "Report to the Boards of Trustees, Presbyterian School of Christian Education (PSCE) and Union Theological Seminary (UTS)" (September 12, 1995), 1.

270. Interview with Louis Weeks, UTS Video History, disc 3.

271. Louis B. Weeks, "How to Merge Two Seminaries," *Faith and Leadership* (Duke Divinity School, August 31, 2010; an online offering of leadership education at Duke Divinity School, https://www.faithandleadership.com/how-merge-two-seminaries.

272. Interview with Louis Weeks, UTS Video History, disc 3.

273. "Proposal for Federation" (February 24, 1997), 3.

274. L. Lewis, Ruger, and Nelson, Report to the Boards of Trustees (September 12, 1995), 2, 20, 32.

275. Interview with Pamela Mitchell-Legg (Charlotte, NC, November 13, 2009), 1.

276. Interview with Louis Weeks (Williamsburg, VA, October 11, 2011).

277. Interview with Art Ross (Little Switzerland, NC, May 8, 2011), 1.

278. Interview with Bill White (Charlotte, NC, September 23, 2011), 1.

279. Louis Weeks, President's Report to the Board of Trustees (Richmond, VA, May 1997), 1.

280. Interview with Louis Weeks, UTS Video History, disc 1.

281. Interview with Stan and Paula Skreslet (Richmond, VA, October 17, 2011), 1.

282. Interview with Art Ross, 1.

283. Interview with Louis Weeks, UTS Video History, disc 3.

284. "Proposal for Federation" (February 24, 1997), 6–8.

285. William V. Arnold, "A Message from the Dean," *Focus* 2, no. 4 (Winter 1987): 1.

286. Ibid.

287. Interview with Ben Lacy Rose, UTS Video History (December 13 and 19, 1991).

288. Interview with James Luther Mays, UTS History Project.

CHAPTER 10: Union Presbyterian Seminary

1. Edwin Scott Gaustad, *Historical Atlas of Religion in America* (New York: Harper & Row, 1962), 44.

2. Robert S. Lynd and Helen Merrell Lynd, *Middletown: A Study in American Culture* (New York: Harcourt, Brace & World, 1929), 316–21.

3. Theodore Caplow, Louis Hicks, and Ben J. Wattenberg, *The First Measured Century: An Illustrated Guide to Trends in America, 1900–2000* (Washington, DC: AEI Press, 2000), 109–15.

4. Gaustad, *Historical Atlas of Religion*, 91.

5. Edna Jacobs Banes, "Worshipping as One" (DMin diss., Columbia Theological Seminary, 2003), 1.

6. Glenn T. Miller, *A Community of Conversation: A Retrospective of the Association of Theological Schools and Ninety Years of North American Theological Education* (Pittsburgh: Association of Theological Schools, 2008), 18.

7. Kurtis Hess, "Alumni/ae Survey" (1998), 1.

8. Kurtis Hess, "Federation Climate Survey" (February 16, 1998), 9–12.

9. Jane Rogers Vann, "The Teaching and Learning Cultures of Presbyterian School of Christian Education and Union Theological Seminary: Two Portraits 1999 (draft report in the author's files, 2000), 1–3, 7, 11, 14, 18, 21–22, Postscript.

10. Interview with Jane Vann (Asheville, NC, July 11, 2011).

11. Vann, "Teaching and Learning Cultures," 19–21.

12. Edna Banes, "Qualifying Examination I" (DMin diss., Columbia Theological Seminary, 2003), 6.

13. T. Hartley Hall IV, "Administrative History of Union Theological Seminary" (notes in the author's files, 1986), 124.

14. Banes, "Qualifying Examination I," 5–8.

15. Lee Zehmer, "This Is Not a Church," *In Medias Res*, Fall 1990, 5.

16. Edna Banes, "Qualifying Examination II" (DMin diss., Columbia Theological Seminary, 2003), 11.

17. Banes, "Worshipping as One," 7.

18. Banes, "Qualifying Examination I," 9.

19. Banes, "Worshipping as One," 3–4, 11, 15, 21.

20. UTS Catalogue, 2002–2004, sect. 1, p. 1.

21. Reports to the Board of Trustees, Union Theological Seminary in Virginia (November 1–2, 1996), 5.

22. Louis Weeks, President's Report to the Board (Richmond, VA, Spring 1999), 7.

23. Union Theological Seminary and Presbyterian School of Christian Education, Self-Study Report (February 2002), 16.

24. Ibid., 21.

25. Catalogue, 2002–2004, sect. 3, p. 12.

26. Catalogue, 2009–2010, sect. 5, p. 1.

27. Union Theological Seminary in Virginia, 1974 Self-Study Report for the ATS and the SACS, 41.

28. Thomas K. Tewell et al., *The General Assembly Special Committee to Study Theological Institutions: Draft Report to the 1993 General Assembly* (Louisville, KY: Presbyterian Church (U.S.A.), 1993), 19.

29. Interview with Bill White (Charlotte, NC, September 23, 2011).

30. Interview with Price Gwynn (Charlotte, NC, September 30, 2011).

31. Union-PSCE, "A Prospectus to the Southern Association of Colleges and Schools to Initiate Extension Education Master of Divinity and Master of Arts in Christian Education Degree Programs in Charlotte, North Carolina," C-1.

32. Ibid., C-1.

33. Ibid., Exhibit C-2–4.

34. Interview with Louis Weeks (Williamsburg, VA, October 11, 2011).

35. Interview with Richard Boyce, 2.

36. Union-PSCE, "Prospectus," C-1.

37. Interview with Price Gwynn, 1.

38. Gaustad, *Historical Atlas of Religion*, 90.

39. Price H. Gwynn III, "Presentation on the Floor of Charlotte Presbytery" (February 22, 2000), 6–7.

40. Union-PSCE, "Prospectus," Exhibit Z-7.

41. Interview with Bill White, 1.

42. Union-PSCE, "Prospectus," Exhibit Z-7.

43. Interview with Richard Boyce (Charlotte, NC, September 23, 2011).

44. Union-PSCE, "Prospectus," Exhibit Z-7.

45. Price H. Gwynn III, "Remarks by Price H. Gwynn to a Charlotte Presbytery Ad Hoc Committee Convened by Alan Elmore to Discuss Theological Education in the Greater Charlotte Area" (September 30, 1997), 1–2.

46. Interview with Price Gwynn, 1.

47. Gwynn, "Remarks by Price H. Gwynn to a Charlotte Presbytery Ad Hoc Committee," 3–4.

48. Union-PSCE, "Prospectus," C-1–3.

49. Ibid., Exhibit M.
50. Interview with Richard Boyce, 2.
51. Interview with Pamela Mitchell-Legg (Charlotte, NC, November 13, 2009).
52. Union-PSCE, "Prospectus," Exhibit M-2-7.
53. Interview with Pamela Mitchell-Legg, 2.
54. Union-PSCE, "Prospectus," Exhibit AA, 1.
55. Ibid., Exhibit F-2.
56. Gwynn, "Presentation on the Floor of Charlotte Presbytery," 7.
57. Gwynn, "Remarks by Price H. Gwynn to a Charlotte Presbytery Ad Hoc Committee," 4.
58. Gwynn, "Presentation on the Floor of Charlotte Presbytery," 2.
59. Thomas W. Currie and Louis B. Weeks, "Union-PSCE at Charlotte: A Presbyterian Partnership and Its Promise," *Presbyterian Outlook* 183, no. 31 (September 17, 2001): 6.
60. Gwynn, "Presentation on the Floor of Charlotte Presbytery," 4–5.
61. Union-PSCE, "Prospectus," Exhibit AA, 4–5.
62. Ibid., Exhibit AA, 5.
63. Interview with Tom Currie (Charlotte, NC, June 24, 2009).
64. Gwynn, "Presentation on the Floor of Charlotte Presbytery," 10–11.
65. Union-PSCE, "Prospectus," Exhibit AA, 6–10.
66. Interview with Price Gwynn, 2.
67. Union-PSCE, "Prospectus," Exhibit Z-8.
68. Gwynn, "Presentation on the Floor of Charlotte Presbytery," 2.
69. Currie and Weeks, "Union-PSCE at Charlotte," 7.
70. Louis Weeks, President's Report to the Board (Richmond, VA, Spring 2003), 5.
71. Union-PSCE, "Prospectus," Exhibit Z-8.
72. Currie and Weeks, "Union-PSCE at Charlotte," 7.
73. Interview with Tom Currie, 2.
74. Ibid., 1–2.
75. Michael Gordon, "A Bright Light for Us: Union Presbyterian Seminary Opens the Doors at Its New Campus in South Charlotte," *Charlotte Observer*, October 6, 2012, E-1.
76. Interview with Tom Currie, 2.
77. Gordon, "A Bright Light for Us," E-1, 3.
78. Interview with Tom Currie, 2.
79. Interview with Louis Weeks, 2.
80. Catalogue, 1998–1999, 2-11.
81. Weeks, President's Report to the Board (Spring 2003), 9.
82. Union-PSCE, "Fact Book 1999," 12.
83. Catalogue, 1998–1999, 2-11.
84. Catalogue, 2001–2002, 2-13.
85. Barbara G. Wheeler and Anthony T. Ruger, "Sobering Figures Point to Enrollment Decline," *In Trust*, Spring 2013, 6.
86. Interview with Susan Fox (Richmond, VA, October 17, 2011).
87. Interview with Bill Arnold (Richmond, VA, January 20, 2012).
88. Interview with Susan Fox, 1.
89. Interview with Helen Byrd (Richmond, VA, January 24, 2012).
90. Interview with Susan Fox, 1.
91. Ibid.
92. Student Handbook, 2001–2002, 45–47.
93. Interview with Veronica Thomas (Richmond, VA, January 24, 2012), esp. 1.
94. Student Handbook, 2007–2008, 72.

95. Catalogue, 2000–2001, AA-11–12.

96. Student Handbook, 2004–2005, 57.

97. Alberta Lindsey, "Answering the Call," *Richmond Times-Dispatch*, March 28, 2006, B-1.

98. Alberta Lindsey, "What Does Scripture Say?," *Richmond Times-Dispatch*, November 4, 2006, A-1.

99. Michelle Boorstein, "Found through Translation," *Washington Post*, January 27, 2007, B-1.

100. Catalogue, 2001–2002, 1-5.

101. Union-PSCE, "Factbook 2000," 34.

102. UTS and PSCE, 2002 Self-Study Report, 199.

103. Interview with Frances Taylor Gench (Richmond, VA, October 12, 2011).

104. *One in Mission: Campaign Report, July 1, 2001–June 30, 2007* (Richmond, VA: UTS and PSCE, 2007), 3.

105. Weeks, President's Report to the Board (Spring 2003), 3.

106. Louis Weeks, President's Report to the Board (Richmond, VA, Spring 2007), 1.

107. Louis Weeks, President's Report to the Board (Richmond, VA, Spring 2005), 2.

108. Weeks, President's Report to the Board (Spring 2005), 1.

109. Interview with Louis Weeks, "A Visual History of Louis B. Weeks," UTS Video History (interviewed by Joe Coalter, Richmond, VA, April 2008).

110. Samuel K. Roberts, "For a Time Such as This: Reflections on the Historical Significance of the Inauguration of Brian Blount as President of Union Theological Seminary-Presbyterian School of Christian Education" (May 5, 2008), 5.

111. Ibid., 6.

112. Brian K. Blount, "Are You Ready?" (inaugural sermon as president of Union-PSCE, Richmond, VA, July 1, 2007; in the author's files), 3–5, 12.

113. Brian K. Blount, "A Catalyst for Conversation for Union Theological Seminary and Presbyterian School of Christian Education" (2008), 2–5.

114. Ibid., 2–6, 8, 13, 15, 18.

115. Wheeler, "Sobering Figures Point to Enrollment Decline," 6.

116. Blount, "Catalyst for Conversation," 34.

117. Ibid., 16, 34, 40.

118. Will Jones, "Union-PSCE to Raze 5 Old Buildings in Richmond," *Richmond Times-Dispatch*, April 29, 2010, B-1.

119. Blount, "Catalyst for Conversation," 6, 9, 25.

120. Thomas C. Johnson, "The Seminary Course of Study—Its Range, Standard, Examinations, and Tests," *Union Seminary Magazine* 9, no. 2 (November–December 1897): 20.

121. John B. Trotti, "There's a Sweet, Sweet Spirit in This Place," *Focus*, Spring 2000, 14.

122. Wheeler, "Sobering Figures Point to Enrollment Decline," 6–7.

Afterword

1. Faculty Minutes, vol. 1, 1828–1859, September 14, 1857.

2. Robert Burwell, "The Early Days of Union Seminary," *Union Seminary Magazine* 5, no. 3 (January–February 1894): 155.

Bibliography

Library archives: at Union Presbyterian Seminary, Richmond, Virginia.

Minutes

General Assembly

Extracts from the Minutes of the General Assembly of the Presbyterian Church in the United States of America: A.D. 1808–1818, and 1821–1839. Philadelphia: General Assembly, published in the year the General Assembly was held.

Minutes of the General Assembly, 1789. Edited by William M. Engles. Philadelphia: Presbyterian Board of Publication, 1847.

Minutes of the General Assembly of the Presbyterian Church in the United States of America, from Its Organization A.D. 1789 to A.D. 1820 Inclusive. Philadelphia: Presbyterian Board of Publication, 1847.

Minutes of the Presbyterian Church in America, 1706–1788. Edited by Guy Klett. Philadelphia: Presbyterian Historical Society, 1976.

Supporting Synods

Synod of North Carolina Minutes. Vols. I–IV. Library archives.

Synod of Virginia Minutes. Vols. I–VIII. Library archives. Note: The first printed minutes begin with 1848 and are numbered beginning with I (1848–1865).

Synod of West Virginia Minutes. "A Report Outlining the Anti-War Efforts of UTS Students," 54–59. Elkins, WV: Synod of West Virginia, 1970.

Presbytery

Presbytery of East Hanover Minutes. Vols. 1–3. Library archives.

Presbytery of Hanover Minutes. Vols. 1–5. Library archives.

Seminary Administration

Board of Trustees Minutes, Union Theological Seminary (including reports of the president and committees). Library archives.

Faculty Minutes, 1828–2012. Library archives.

Self-Study Reports, 1967, 1974, 1985, 1996, 2002. Library archives.

Seminary Strategic Plan, 1997

"The Proposal for Federation: The Presbyterian School of Christian Education and Union Theological Seminary in Virginia." February 24, 1997. Library archives.

"A Prospectus to the Southern Association of Colleges and Schools to Initiate Extension Education [with the] Master of Divinity and Master of Arts in Christian Education Degree Programs in Charlotte, North Carolina." Library archives.

"Union Theological Seminary and Presbyterian School of Christian Education Institutional Peer Profile Report, 2006–2007." 2007. Library archives.

Student Societies

Givens B. Strickler Society Minutes, 1914–1917. Library archives.

Philological Society Minutes. Hampden Sydney, VA, 1828–1830. Librray archives.

Rhetorical Society Minutes, 1872–1894. Library archives.

Society of Missionary Inquiry. *See also* McKinnon

———. Correspondence, Book 1, 1818–1836 (mainly with other seminaries). Correspondence, Book 2, 1818–1832 (primarily with missionaries). Correspondence, Book 3, 1834–1839 (almost exclusively letters from missionaries). After 1839 all correspondence appears in the minutes. Library archives.

———. Minute Book 1, 1818–1830. Minute Book 2, 1830–1861. Minute Book 3, 1866–1877. Minute Book 4, 1886–1898. Minute Book 5, March 1912–March 1932. Minute Book 6, April 1932–March 1939. Library archives.

Theological Society Minutes, 1812–1823. Library archives.

Union Seminary Magazine Association

Magazine Association Minutes, 1890–1896. Hampden Sydney, VA, 1890–1896. Library archives.

General Catalogues, Catalogues, and Other Official Publications

Factbooks, 1999–2007. Library archives.

Catalogues, 1830, 1833–1834, 1854–1859, 1861–1862, 1866, 1870, 1873–2012. Library archives.

General Catalogues, 1884, 1907, 1976. Library archives.

Student Handbooks, 1900–1901, 1905–1928, 1938–1939, 1947–1988, 1995–2012. Library archives.

Interviews

Union Seminary Video History Project

Dawe, Donald, December 2002.

Goodpasture, Ken, July 1999.

Hall, T. Hartley, May 1999.

Hale, Ted, July 2011

Kelly, Balmer, 1989.

Kirkpatrick, Robert White, September 1985.
Leith, John, date unknown.
Mays, James Luther, June 1999.
Oglesby, William B., August 1985.
Rose, Ben Lacy, December 1991.
Stair, Fred, Martha Aycock, and John Trotti. Montpelier Exchange Program; Parts 1, 2, 3, March 1990.
Thompson, Ernest Trice, 1964.
Weeks, Louis, April 2008.

Bicentennial History Video, by Rob Collins

Cross, Lisa.
Logan, Ann.
Rada, Heath.
Stock, Ed.

Personal Interviews

Achtemeier, Paul.
Arnold, Bill.
Banes, Edna.
Blount, Brian K.
Boyce, Richard.
Brown, Hoffman.
Bryant, Bob.
Byrd, Helen.
Cannon, Katie.
Carson, Mary Faith.
Currie, Tom.
Dawe, Donald.
Fox, Susan.
Gench, Frances Taylor.
Gwynn, Price.
Hall, T. Hartley.
Hobbie, Peter.
Johnson, Merwyn.
Kingsbury, Jack Dean.
Kuykendall, John.
Mays, James L.
McBride, Dean.
Miller, Doug.
Mitchell-Legg, Pamela.
Nicholson, Roger.
Ottati, Douglas F.
Shriver, Donald G.
Rhodes, Elaine.
Ross, Art.
Skreslet, Paula.
Skreslet, Stan.
Swezey, Charles.
Towner, Sib.

Thomas, Veronica.
Vann, Jane.
Weaver, Rebecca.
Weeks, Louis.
White, Bill.
Willis, Amy.
Willis, Steve.
Winter, Mary Jane.

Books, Reference Works, Journals, Periodicals, and Correspondence

"5 Fellowships Given Divinity Students Here." *Richmond Times-Dispatch*, January 19, 1933.
"5 Gain Coveted Fellowships in Annual Award at Seminary." *Richmond Times-Dispatch*, March 6, 1935.
"116 Schools Represented at UTS Inauguration." *Richmond News Leader*, April 4, 1956.
"139-Year Tradition to Be Broken Tomorrow When Mrs. Etchison Receives Degree at UTS." *Richmond Times-Dispatch*, May 21, 1951.
1869 Constitution and Plan of Union Theological Seminary in Virginia, Amended 1892. Richmond, VA: Whittet & Shepperson, 1893.
"$19,000,000 Rebuilding Plan Detailed by Union Seminary." *Richmond Times-Dispatch*, May 18, 1965, 1–2.
Abegglen, Beat. E-mail to the author. January 29, 2014.
Adams, John. "The Political Writings of John Adams." In *The Political Writings of John Adams*, edited by George W. Carey. Washington, DC: Regnery Publishing, 2000.
Adams, Mindy Douglas. "Binding Up the Broken Hearted: Love and Justice in Central America." *In Medias Res* (Richmond, VA), Summer 1993.
Addresses Delivered at the Celebration of the Centennial of the General Assembly of the Presbyterian Church. Philadelphia: MacCalla & Co., 1888.
Adelphos. "Hints to the Presbytery of Hanover." *Virginia Evangelical and Literary Magazine* 5, no. 4 (April 1822): 208–10.
Aldridge, Garet. "Free Advice." *In Medias Res* (Richmond, VA), January 1986.
Allen, Julie. "General Assembly." *In Medias Res* (Richmond, VA), October 10, 1979.
———. "Simple Living." *In Medias Res* (Richmond, VA), November 19, 1978.
Allen, Maurice. "Judgments from the Parish." *Expression* (Richmond, VA) 9, no. 8 (November 25, 1964): 1, 3–4.
Ames, John T., Jr.. "The One Hundred and Fifth Year—for What?" *Expression* (Richmond, VA) 9, no. 14 (April 12, 1965): 1, 6.
———. "Oxford—Impressions." *Expression* (Richmond, VA) 7, no. 10 (November 21, 1962): 1, 3, 5.
———. *A Defence of Virginia*, by Robert Lewis Dabney. Unpublished term paper written for a course supervised by Dr James H. Smiley. Union Theological Seminary in Virginia, Richmond, VA, November 1964. In the author's files.
———. "The Relationship between Northern and Southern Presbyterian Churches, 1861–1882." Unpublished term paper written for a directed study supervised by Dr. James H. Smiley. Union Theological Seminary in Virginia, Richmond, VA, May 1965. In the author's files.
"Among the Periodicals." *Union Seminary Magazine* 1 (October–November 1889): 77–80.
Anderson, John F. "Expanded Theological Library Awaits Presbyterian Students." *Richmond Times-Dispatch*, April 3, 1944, IV-1.

Anderson, Neal L. "Evolution as a Science and a Philosophy." *Union Seminary Review* 33, no. 4 (July 1922): 288–98.

"Anniversary Rites Opened at Seminary." *Richmond Times-Dispatch*, October 6, 1948, 10.

Anonymous. "Proposed: A Store-Front Mission." *Expression* (Richmond, VA) 6, no. 10 (March 22, 1961): 3.

Anonymous. "Rev. Thomas E. Peck, D.D., LL.D." *Union Seminary Magazine* 4 (March–April 1898): 224–42.

Appleby, James. "Field Work and Evangelism: Inaugural Address Delivered September 10, 1947, in Schauffler Hall." Richmond, VA: Union Theological Seminary, 1947.

———. "Rebuilding." In *The Days of Our Years: The Historical Convocations Held April 24–27, 1962, as a Feature of the Celebration of the Sesquicentennial of Union Theological Seminary in Virginia*, 41–64. Richmond: Union Theological Seminary in Virginia, 1962.

"Are the Well-Springs Drying Up?" *Richmond News Leader*, February 2, 1945.

Armstrong, Maurice W., Lefferts A. Loetscher, and Charles A. Anderson, eds. *The Presbyterian Enterprise: Sources of American Presbyterian History*. Presbyterian Historical Society Publication Series 1. Philadelphia: Westminster Press, 1956.

Arnold, William V. "In Case You Wondered: Faculty Review Committee." *In Medias Res* (Richmond, VA), January 25, 1978.

———. "A Message from the Dean." *Focus*, no. 4 (Winter 1987): 1.

Auburn Center for the Study of Theological Education and the Association of Theological Schools. *Union Theological Seminary and Presbyterian School of Christian Education, Strategic Information Report, 2006–2007*. 2007.

Baird, Charles Washington. *Eutaxia, or, the Presbyterian Liturgies*. New York: M. W. Dodd, 1855.

Banbury, Rosalind. "Report on the 1979 Clergywomen's Conference." *In Medias Res* (Richmond, VA), May 14, 1979.

Banes, Edna Jacobs. "Qualifying Examination I." DMin diss., Columbia Theological Seminary, 2003.

———. "Qualifying Examination II." DMin diss., Columbia Theological Seminary, 2003.

———. "Worshipping as One: Chapel Services on a Seminary Campus." DMin diss., Columbia Theological Seminary, 2003.

Barnett, John M., John C. Meloy, and Ebenezer Finley. *History of the Presbytery of Redstone*. Washington, PA: Observer Book & Job Print, 1889.

Barth, Karl. "Miserable Lazarus." *Union Seminary Review* 46, no. 4 (May 1935): 259–68.

Basham, R. Robert, Jr. "Perspective for the Pledge." *Expression* (Richmond, VA) 6, no. 11 (April 12, 1961).

Baxter, George A. *Inaugural Address of the Rev. G. A. Baxter, D.D., on His Induction into the Professorship of Christian Theology, in Union Theological Seminary: Delivered at the College Church, Prince Edward County, Virginia, April 11, 1832*. Richmond: J. Macfarlan, 1832.

———. "Responsibilities of the Ministry and Church: A Sermon Preached before the Synod of Virginia, at Staunton, October 22, 1828." *National Preacher* 3, no. 5 (October 1828): 105–12.

Beacham, Doug. Letter from Oklahoma City to Dr. James Smylie, January 23, 2003.

Beard, Delemo L. "Origin and Early History of Presbyterianism in Virginia." ThM thesis, Union Theological Seminary, Richmond, Virginia, 1932. Printed at Bridgewater, VA, 1932.

Beatie, Arthur Y. *Walter W. Moore and Union Seminary*. Richmond: Union Theological Seminary in Virginia, 1927.

Beattie, Francis R. "A Message to the Young Minister." *Union Seminary Magazine* 11, no. 1 (October–November 1899): 16–22.

Becker, Kerra. "In Response to *The Presbyterian Layman*." *In Medias Res* (Richmond, VA), Fall 1995.

Benedetto, Robert. *Index to the Union Seminary Magazine and Union Seminary Review, 1889–1946*. Richmond, VA: Union Theological Seminary, 1995.

Benedetto, Robert, and Kathryn Washington Addo. *The Virginia Evangelical and Literary Magazine [and Missionary Chronicle]: An Index to the Monthly Magazine of John Holt Rice*. Richmond, VA: Union Theological Seminary and Presbyterian School of Education, 1998.

Blackwood, Andrew W. "A Clinic in Homiletics." *Union Seminary Review* 31, no. 1 (October 1919): 7–20.

———. "A Clinic in Homiletics." *Union Seminary Review* 31, no. 3 (April 1920): 235–52.

———. "The Social Message of Micah." *Union Seminary Review* 26, no. 1 (October 1914): 22–33.

Bledsoe, Lewis W. "One Man's Opinion." *Expression* (Richmond, VA) 6, no. 5 (November 23, 1960).

Bloom, William W. "The Middle East Situation—from a Christian Perspective." *Expression* (Richmond, VA) 2, no. 1 (October 1956): 1, 4.

Blount, Brian K. "Are You Ready?" Inaugural sermon as president of Union-PSCE. Richmond, VA, July 1, 2007. In the author's files.

———. "A Catalyst for Conversation for Union Theological Seminary and Presbyterian School of Christian Education." 2008. In the author's files.

Board of Directors. "Report on the Course of Study to Be Pursued in the Union Theological Seminary." *Literary and Evangelical Magazine* (Richmond, VA), October 1828, 513–26.

Boorstein, Michelle. "Found through Translation." *Washington Post*, January 27, 2007, B-1, 8.

Booth, Edward Munson. "Pulpit Bearing." *Union Seminary Magazine* 10, no. 3 (February–March 1899): 174–85.

Bradshaw, Herbert Clarence. *History of Farmville, Virginia, 1798–1948: Reprint of the Sesquicentennial Edition of the* Farmville Herald, *Dated October 22, 1948*. Farmville, VA: Farmville Herald, 1994.

———. *History of Hampden-Sydney College*. Vol. 1, *From the Beginnings to the Year 1856*. Durham, NC: Fisher-Harrison, 1976.

———. *History of Prince Edward County, Virginia, from Its Earliest Settlements through Its Establishment in 1754 to Its Bicentennial Year*. Richmond, VA: Dietz Press, 1954.

Breitenberg, Hal. "Communion of the Commuters: Dorms and Demographics." *In Medias Res* (Richmond, VA), Spring 1992.

"Brian K. Blount: President-Elect of Union-PSCE." *Focus* (Richmond, VA), Spring 2007, 16–21.

Briggs, Charles Augustus. *American Presbyterianism*. New York: Charles Scribner's Sons, 1885.

Briggs, Ed. "New Seminary President Seeks to Raise Quality of Students." *Richmond Times-Dispatch*, April 30, 1982, B-4.

Bright, John. *The Authority of the Old Testament*. Nashville: Abingdon Press, 1967.

———. "John Bright Observes a 'Good Spirit' at UTS." *Union Theological Seminary Bulletin* (1975): 2.

———. *The Kingdom of God. The Biblical Concept and Its Meaning for the Church*. Nashville: Abingdon Press, 1953.

————. *The Kingdom of God. The Biblical Concept and Its Meaning for the Church.* New York: Abingdon-Cokesbury Press, 1953.

Brimm, Henry M. "The Library of Union Theological Seminary, 1806–1944." *Union Seminary Review* 55, no. 4 (August 1944): 286–94.

Brinkley, John Luster. *On This Hill: A Narrative History of Hampden-Sydney College, 1774–1994.* Hampden Sydney, VA: Hampden-Sydney College, 1994.

Brown, Aubrey N., Jr. "Credible Discipleship in a World of Affluence and Poverty." An address given during the 1979 Sprunt Lectures at Union Theological Seminary. Richmond, VA.

————. "The Outlook—150 Years at Home in Richmond." *Presbyterian Outlook* 169, no. 43 (December 20–28, 1987): 9–12.

————. "Presbyterians, U.S.: Enroute to Broader Concerns." *Christian Century* 80 (December 18, 1963): 1577–80.

Brown, J. Edmunds, Jr. "In Salutation." *Union Seminary Magazine* 11, no. 1 (October–November 1899): 41.

————. "One Year at Richmond." *Union Seminary Magazine* 11, no. 1 (October–November 1899): 42–43.

————. "Opening Exercises." *Union Seminary Magazine* 11, no. 1 (October–November 1899): 59.

Brown, Karen. "The Black Phenomenon." *In Medias Res* (Richmond, VA), September 1988.

Brown, Karen, and Shirley Hutchins. "The Welcome We Received." *In Medias Res* (Richmond, VA), Fall 1991.

Brown, William Adams. *The Education of American Ministers.* Vol. 1, *Ministerial Education in America.* New York: Institute of Social and Religious Research, 1934.

Brown, William P. Introduction to *A History of Israel,* by John Bright. 4th ed. Louisville, KY: Westminster John Knox Press, 2000.

Bruce, Philip A. *History of the University of Virginia, 1819–1919.* Vol. 1. New York: Macmillan, 1920.

Brunner, Emil. "The Absoluteness of Jesus." Translated by Vernon S. Broyles Jr. *Union Seminary Review* 46, no. 4 (July 1935): 269–82.

Bryan, William Jennings. *In His Image.* New York: Fleming H. Revell, 1922.

Brydon, G. MacLaren. "The Anti-Ecclesiastical Laws of Virginia." *Virginia Magazine of History and Biography* 64, no. 3 (July 1956): 259–85.

Buckalew, Ron. "One Person's Perspective." *In Medias Res* (Richmond, VA), April 2, 1978.

Bullock, Robert Haydon. "The Past Fifty Years of Presbyterianism in Richmond, Virginia." ThD diss., Union Theological Seminary in Virginia, 1943.

Burleigh, John H. S. *A Church History of Scotland.* London: Oxford University Press, 1960.

Burnham, Jon. "On Theological Security." *In Medias Res* (Richmond, VA), Spring 1993.

Burrell, Charles Edward. *A History of Prince Edward County, Virginia.* Richmond, VA: Williams Printing Co., 1922.

Burwell, Robert. "The Early Days of Union Seminary." *Union Seminary Magazine* 5, no. 3 (January–February 1894): 143–55.

————. "The Early Days of Union Seminary." In *Septuagesimal Celebration of Union Theological Seminary in Virginia, 1824–1894,* 48–64. Richmond, VA: Whittet & Shepperson, 1894.

Butterworth, John, III. "Here Am I—Send Me Not!" *Expression* (Richmond, VA) 2, no. 2 (December 1956).

Button, Bob. "Middler Editorial." *Expression* (Richmond, VA) 9, no. 8 (November 25, 1964).

Buzard, Laura. "Interrobang." *Interrobang* (Richmond, VA), October 10, 1969.

Bye, Mike. "Vietnam?" *Interrobang* (Richmond, VA), October 10, 1969.

Byrd, Tom. "UTS Is Site of Peace Seminar." *Expression* (Richmond, VA) 10, no. 8 (April–May 1966), 10–11.

Cabaniss, Allen. "Liturgy in the Southern Presbyterian Church." *Union Seminary Review* 54, no. 1 (October 1942): 11–27.

Caccamo, Rita. *Back to Middletown: Three Generations of Sociological Reflections.* Stanford, CA: Stanford University Press, 2000.

Caldwell, Dan T., and Benjamin L. Bowman. *They Answered the Call.* Richmond, VA: John Knox Press, 1952.

"Calvin Bowl Game Planned Again for Thanksgiving Day." *Richmond News Leader,* November 23, 1956, 21.

Cameron, Pamela. "UTS: Stored Heads and Unmoved Hearts?" *Expression* (Richmond, VA) 9, no. 5 (October 16, 1964), 1, 5–6.

"Campaign to Raise $2,510,000 for UTS Due Early in 1952; Campus Will Double Facilities." *Richmond News Leader,* December 5, 1951.

Campbell, Robert Fishburne. "Rev. Thomas E. Peck, D.D., LL.D." *Union Seminary Magazine* 9 (1898): 298–301.

———. "Address at the Twenty-Fifth Anniversary of the Removal of Union Theological Seminary to Richmond, Va., May 8, 1923." *Union Seminary Review* 34, no. 4 (July 1923): 291–305.

———. "Dangers Threatening the Purity of the Church." *Union Seminary Magazine* 12, no. 1 (October–November 1900): 7–15.

———. "Union Seminary in the Pastorate." *Union Seminary Magazine* 24, no. 1 (1912–13): 78–85.

"Campbell Talks on Freedom and Restraint." *Richmond Times-Dispatch,* January 16, 1930.

Campus Life Committee of the Board of Trustees. "Report to the President on Women's Concerns." 1995.

Cannon, John F. "The Deacon's Office and Work." *Union Seminary Magazine* 6, no. 4 (March–April 1895): 235–46.

Caplow, Theodore, Louis Hicks, and Ben J. Wattenberg. *The First Measured Century: An Illustrated Guide to Trends in America, 1900–2000.* Washington, DC: AEI Press, 2000.

Carkuff, Casey. "When Our Humor Becomes Tragic: A Student Speaks Out." *In Medias Res* (Richmond, VA), Summer 1993.

Carson, H. Pride. "One Woman's Opinion on 'Women's Issues.'" *In Medias Res* (Richmond, VA), January 1986.

Causey, David J. "The Supreme Court on Prayer." *Expression* (Richmond, VA) 9, no. 2 (November 1, 1963): 1, 4.

Caven, William. "Biblical Theology and Systematic Theology." *Union Seminary Magazine* 11, no. 4 (April–May 1900): 245–50.

Cecil, Russell. "The Psychological Aspects of the Conversion of the Apostle Paul." *Union Seminary Magazine* 9, no. 3 (January–February 1898): 168–76.

"The Centennial Celebration." *Union Seminary Magazine* 24 (1912): 9–13.

"A Century in the City." The program for celebrating the centennial of the move of Union Theological Seminary from Hampden Sydney to Richmond. Union Theological Seminary, Richmond, VA, October 5, 1998.

"Challenge of Tradition to the Present Stressed by Speaker at Library Dedication." *Richmond Times-Dispatch,* May 9, 1944.

Chester, S. H. "The War and Missions." *Union Seminary Review* 30, no. 2 (January 1919): 147–53.

Childs, Brevard S. *Biblical Theology in Crisis*. Philadelphia: Westminster Press, 1970.

Christie, Alexander. "The Doctrine of Holy Scripture in Calvin and Brunner, Part I." *Union Seminary Review* 52, no. 1 (October 1940): 19–33.

———. "The Doctrine of Holy Scripture in Calvin and Brunner, Part II." *Union Seminary Review* 52, no. 2 (January 1941): 116–27.

———. "The Doctrine of Scripture in Calvin and Brunner, Part III." *Union Seminary Review* 52, no. 4 (May 1941): 325–51.

Chumbley, C. M. "The Proper Sphere of Woman's Activity." *Union Seminary Magazine* 8, no. 3 (January–February 1897): 166–75.

Clark, Gray. "Are You Willing to Be Crucified?" *Perspective* (Richmond, VA), ca. 1970, issue 6.

Clark, Mary Marshall. "A Letter to Faculty and Students." *In Medias Res* (Richmond, VA), April 2, 1978.

Clements, Richard. "Inner City Faith." *In Medias Res* (Richmond, VA), Summer 1993.

Click, Jay. "Missions and Missionaries." *In Medias Res* (Richmond, VA), December 1978.

Coffman, Julie. "Meeting the World." *In Medias Res* (Richmond, VA), May 1991.

Cole, Laura. "Up the Great Goal Post." *In a Mirror* (Richmond, VA), December 1974.

Come, Donald Robert. "The Influence of Princeton on Higher Education in the South before 1826." *William and Mary Quarterly* 2, no. 3 (1945): 359–96.

"Coming of Union Theological Seminary." *Richmond Times-Dispatch*, January 1, 1898, 6.

"A Communication Having Been Lately Brought to Our Attention." *Expression* 3, no. 3 (February 1958).

Condrey, Michael T. "Regarding Curriculum at UTS." *In Medias Res* (Richmond, VA), March 15, 1978.

Conn, George M., Jr. "96 Steps and Turn." 1989. Personal memoirs of George M. Conn Jr., in the author's files.

Constitution and Plan of Union Theological Seminary in Virginia. Richmond, VA: Whittet & Shepperson, 1893.

"Contribution to an Ideal." *Richmond News Leader*, January 31, 1949, 10.

Crofts, Daniel W. "Late Antebellum Virginia Reconsidered." *Virginia Magazine of History and Biography* 107, no. 3 (Summer 1999): 253–86.

Cross, A. Donovan. "Letter to Seminarians." *Expression* (Richmond, VA) 9, no. 7 (April 17, 1964): 1, 3.

———. "Reflections on the Inner-City." *Expression* (Richmond, VA) 9, no. 13 (March 22, 1965): 8–10.

———. "The Suburban Captivity of the Seminary." *Expression* (Richmond, VA) 7, no. 8 (March 31, 1962).

———. "Voter Registration." *Expression* (Richmond, VA): 9, no. 3 (September 18, 1964): 8.

Currie, Thomas W., and Louis B. Weeks. "Union-PSCE at Charlotte: A Presbyterian Partnership and Its Promise." *Presbyterian Outlook* 183, no. 31 (September 17, 2001): 6–7, 24.

Dabney, Charles William. *Universal Education in the South*. Vol. 1, *From the Beginning to 1900*. Chapel Hill: University of North Carolina Press, 1936.

Dabney, Robert Lewis. "The Course of Studies in Union Seminary, Part 1." *Central Presbyterian* 1, no. 33 (August 16, 1856): 130.

———. "The Course of Studies in Union Seminary, Part 2." *Central Presbyterian* 1, no. 34 (August 23, 1856): 134.

———. *A Defence of Virginia and through Her, of the South in Recent and Pending Contests against the Sectional Party.* New York: E. J. Hale & Son, 1867.

———. *A Discourse on the Uses and Results of Church History Delivered by Robert L. Dabney, May 8, 1854, at His Induction into the Professorship of Ecclesiastical History and Polity in Union Theological Seminary, Virginia.* Richmond, VA: Ritchies & Dunnavant, 1854.

———. *Discussions by Robert L. Dabney.* Edited by C. R. Vaughan. Vols. 1–2. Richmond, VA: Presbyterian Committee of Publication, 1891.

———. "The Examination Rule." *Central Presbyterian* 2, no. 45 (November 7, 1857): 178.

———. "Francis S. Sampson, D.D." *Union Seminary Magazine* 9 (March–April 1898): 282–84.

———. *Life and Campaigns of Lieut.-Gen. Thomas J. Jackson.* New York: Blelock & Co., 1866.

———. *Syllabus and Notes of the Course of Systematic and Polemic Theology Taught in Union Theological Seminary, Virginia.* Richmond, VA: Published by the Students, Shepperson & Graves, printers, 1871.

———. "Thomas Cary Johnson." *Union Seminary Magazine* 3, no. 4 (March–April 1892): 271–73.

Dame, George W. "Sketch of the Life and Character of Jonathan P. Cushing, M.A." *American Quarterly Register* 11, no. 2 (November 1838): 113–28.

Dart, John. "The Value of a Theological Education: Is It Worth It?" *Christian Century* 120, no. 4 (February 22, 2003): 32–35.

Davidson, Charles N., Jr. "Reflections upon the Week of May 3, 1970, at R.T.C." Richmond, VA, May 7, 1970.

Davies, Samuel. "A Demand for the Gospel in Some Parts of North Carolina." *Virginia Evangelical and Literary Magazine* 4, no. 11 (November 1821): 572.

———. "Origin of Presbyterianism in Virginia." *Virginia Evangelical and Literary Magazine* 2, no. 8 (May 1819): 345–53.

Davis, Dick. "On Winning." *Perspective* (Richmond, VA), issue 3, 1969.

Davis, E. Mac. "Inter-Seminary Missionary Alliance." *Union Seminary Magazine* 7, no. 1 (October–November 1894): 144–49.

Davis, J. Treadwell. "The Presbyterians and the Sectional Conflict." *Southern Quarterly* 8 (January 1970): 117–33.

Davis, James M. "*Rerum Novarum*—UTS." *Expression* (Richmond, VA) 11, no. 4 (October 2, 1964): 1.

Davis, Joseph L. "J. Calvin and J. Sprunt." *Expression* (Richmond, VA) 6, no. 11 (April 12, 1961).

Davis, Robert P., and James H. Smylie. *Virginia Presbyterians in American Life: Hanover Presbytery (1755–1980).* Edited by Patricia Aldridge. Richmond, VA: Hanover Presbytery, 1982.

Dawe, Donald G. "The Humanity of Christ and the Future of Man: An Inaugural Address." *Affirmation* 1, no. 5 (September 1973): 5–22.

———. *Jesus: The Death and Resurrection of God.* Atlanta: John Knox Press, 1985.

Dhombres, F. M. "Crazy America I Love You." *Expression* (Richmond, VA) 9, no. 13 (March 22, 1965): 5–6.

Dietrich, Rick. "A Disorganized Look at the Academic Calendar: Part 1, The Party Line." *In Medias Res* (Richmond, VA), November 29, 1978.

———. "A Disorganized Look at the Academic Calendar: Part 2, The Anti-Party Line." *In Medias Res* (Richmond, VA), December 1978.

Doubles, John. "Abortion: The Problem of Christian Concern." *In Medias Res* (Richmond, VA), Summer 1992.

"Dr. J. A. Jones Is Named Seminary President-Elect." *Richmond Times-Dispatch*, January 31, 1955.

"Dr. James A. Jones, UTS President, Dies." *Richmond Times-Dispatch*, November 18, 1966.

"Dr. Jones and the Future." *Expression* (Richmond, VA) 1, no. 1 (February 1956): 1.

"Dr. Kelly to Become Dean of Seminary." *Richmond News Leader*, May 18, 1965, 15.

"Dr. Richards to Be Sprunt Lecturer." *Richmond News Leader*, November 26, 1937.

"Dr. W. F. Albright to Give Sprunt Lectures at Seminary." *Richmond News Leader*, January 14, 1949.

Duff, Nancy, et al. "Information from the Steering Committee on Women's Concerns and Their Task Forces for the Members of the Faculty." Richmond, VA, May 15, 1974. In the author's files.

Duffield, George, Jr. *American Presbyterianism: A Sermon Delivered on the Lord's Day, November 11, 1853*. Philadelphia: Isaac Ashmead, 1854.

Dunaway, Wayland F. *The Scotch-Irish of Colonial Pennsylvania*. Chapel Hill: University of North Carolina Press, 1944.

Duquette, Dave. "Help, Monarchists!" *In Medias Res* (Richmond, VA), April 1994.

———. "Is It Safe?" *In Medias Res* (Richmond, VA), February 1994.

Durden, Douglas. "Listeners to Protest WRFK Sale Effort." *Richmond Times-Dispatch*, August 30, 1985, B-1.

———. "Saga of WRFK Nears End." *Richmond Times-Dispatch*, February 28, 1988, B-1.

———. "Seminary Ads Defend Action on WRFK." *Richmond Times-Dispatch*, June 27, 1986, B-11.

Durham, Sandy. "The Great Ivy Rip-Off." *In a Mirror* (Richmond, VA), April 1975.

Eagan, J. J. "Church Officers and Their Relation to the Sabbath-School." *Union Seminary Magazine* 16, no. 2 (December 1904–January 1905): 139–41.

East, Arlan. "The March on Washington." *Expression* (Richmond, VA) 9, no. 1 (October 1, 1963): 1, 5–6.

Editor. *See also* Editorial; Editors; *individual names of known editors*

———. "Advance: A Fond Farewell." *Expression* (Richmond, VA) 10, no. 6 (March 1966): 1, 4.

———. "Around the Seminary." *Union Seminary Magazine* 13, no. 2 (December 1901–January 1902): 137.

———. "Ask Not Only What the RTC Can Do for You." *In Medias Res* (Richmond, VA), December 1982.

———. "Criticisms and Reviews." *Union Seminary Magazine* 5, no. 3 (January–February 1894): 223.

———. "Documented Inconsistency." *Expression* (Richmond, VA) 9, no. 14 (April 12, 1965): 2.

———. "The Double Standard." *Expression* (Richmond, VA) 9, no. 11 (February 19, 1965).

———. "Dr. Jas. A. Jones." *Richmond News Leader*, November 18, 1966, 6.

———. "Expression Poll." *Expression* (Richmond, VA), October 1968.

———. "Faithful Scholarship at Union." *Richmond News Leader*, October 6, 1948, 10.

———. "For Those Who Hunger and Thirst . . ." *Expression* (Richmond, VA) 9, no. 12 (March 5, 1965).

———. "Interning Students Report." *Expression* (Richmond, VA) 10, no. 5 (January 1966): 6–10.

———. "It Matters Not Who Won or Lost. . . ." *Expression* (Richmond, VA) 10, no. 2 (September 1965): 2.

———. "New Horizons for the New Curriculum Committee." *Expression* (Richmond, VA) 9, no. 10 (January 21, 1965): 1, 5.

———. "Operation Overbrew." *Perspective* (Richmond, VA), issue 5, 1970.

———. "Perspective: Beyond the War." *Perspective* (Richmond, VA), issue 2, 1969.

———. "Perspective: Community and Curriculum." *Perspective* (Richmond, VA), issue 3, 1969.

———. "Perspective: Statement of Purpose." *Perspective* (Richmond, VA), October 1969.

———. "Reaction to Speech by Dr. James Farmer." *Expression* (Richmond, VA) 11, no. 2 (November 1966): 1, 6.

———. "The Rev. James S. Jones, D.D." *Richmond Times-Dispatch*, November 19, 1966, A-8.

———. "Shall the Seminary Be Moved?" *Hampden-Sydney Magazine* (1895), 50–51.

———. "Students Speak on Reunion." *In Medias Res* (Richmond, VA), January 1983.

———. "To Students Attending the Weekend of Theological Inquiry." *Perspective* (Richmond, VA), issue 6, 1970.

Editorial. *See also* Editor; Editors; *individual names of known editors*

———. "Dedication Exercises." *Union Seminary Magazine* 10, no. 1 (October–November 1898): 45–60.

———. "Dividends on the Seminary."*Richmond News Leader*, October 12, 1922.

———. *Expression* 4, no. 4 (Spring 1959): 10–11.

———. *Interrobang* 1, no. 1 (September 26, 1969): 1.

———. "The Funeral of Dr. Dabney." *Union Seminary Magazine* 9, no. 3 (January–February 1898): 194–96.

———. "Hampden-Sydney's Opportunity." *Hampden-Sydney Magazine* (1895): 50–54.

———. "James Sprunt, LL.D." *Union Seminary Review* 31, no. 2 (January 1920): 89–95.

———. "Lack of Preparation among Ministerial Students." *Union Seminary Magazine* 10, no. 2 (December 1898–January 1899): 138–40.

———. "The Latin Thesis." *Union Seminary Magazine* 13, no. 2 (December 1901–January 1902): 134.

———. "Modern Missions as a Part of the Seminary Curriculum." *Union Seminary Magazine* 7, no. 1 (September–October 1895): 48–49.

———. *No Name Gazette*, February 3, 1959, 1.

———. "One Year at Richmond." *Union Seminary Magazine* 11, no. 1 (October–November 1899): 42–43.

———. "An Outsider on Richmond's Assets." *Richmond News Leader*, July 13, 1925.

———. *Perspective* (Richmond, VA), issue 7, 1970.

———. "The Removal of the Seminary." *Union Seminary Magazine* 6, no. 1 (October–November 1894): 279–80.

———. "The Removal of the Seminary to Richmond." *Union Seminary Magazine* 7, no. 2 (November–December 1895): 124–28.

———. "Salutatory." *Union Seminary Magazine* 1, no. 1 (October–November 1889): 35–37.

———. "Some Observations on the Removal of the Seminary." *Union Seminary Magazine* 7, no. 2 (November–December 1895): 129–31.

———. "Student Life at Union Seminary." *Union Seminary Magazine* 9, no. 3 (January–February 1898): 314–17.

———. "The Twenty-Fifth Anniversary." *Interpretation* 25, no. 1 (January 1971): 3–10.

———. "The Union Seminary Drive." *Richmond Times Dispatch*, February 13, 1966.

———. "Union Theological Seminary." *Union Seminary Magazine* 10, no. 1 (October–November 1898): 34–37.

———. "Why So Few Candidates?" *Union Seminary Magazine* 7, no. 3 (January–February 1896): 198–99.

Editors. *See also* Editor; Editorial; *individual names of known editors*

———. "New Editorial Policy for *In Medias Res.*" *In Medias Res* (Richmond, VA), February 1994.

Edlich, Janet S. "Qualified Minister Wanted." *Expression* (Richmond, VA) 6, no. 8 (February 22, 1961).

Eggleston, Joseph Dupuy. "Extracts from the Minutes of the Virginia Synod and Hanover Presbytery, on Liberty Hall Academy, Hampden-Sydney College, and Union Theological Seminary, 1771–1824, with Explanatory Notes." Manuscript in the Union Theological Seminary Library, 1947.

English, Thomas R. "A Call to the Ministry." *Union Seminary Magazine* 7, no. 2 (November–December 1895): 103–14.

———. "The Decline of the Pulpit." *Union Seminary Magazine* 12, nos. 304–316 (April–May 1901).

———. "How an Elder May Help His Pastor." *Union Seminary Magazine* 15, no. 4 (April–May 1904): 335–40.

———. "Our China Mission Work." *Union Seminary Magazine* 9, no. 4 (March–April 1898): 344–47.

———. "A Plea for the Inductive Study of the Bible." *Union Seminary Magazine* 11, no. 3 (February–March 1900): 165–71.

———. "The Text: Its Use and Abuse." *Union Seminary Magazine* 8, no. 4 (March–April 1897): 256–62.

"Evolution or Revolution?" *Richmond Times-Dispatch*, April 13, 1964.

Faculty Resolution on Inclusive Language. Union Theological Seminary, Richmond, VA, March 11, 1982.

Falter, Becky. "Here's My Point of View." *In Medias Res* (Richmond, VA), February 1994.

———. "The Perils of Pregnancy: Part 1, The First Trimester or . . . the Journey to Hell and Back." *In Medias Res* (Richmond, VA), February 1994.

Falter, Jeff. "UTS Safety Survey Results." *In Medias Res* (Richmond, VA), April 1994.

Famos, Cla. "Union from a Swiss Perspective." *In Medias Res* (Richmond, VA), May 1991.

"Fighting UTES." *Expression* (Richmond, VA) 7, no. 3 (November 1, 1961): 2. ("Fighting UTES" is apparently a play on the name of the Native American tribe and the abbreviation of Union Theological Seminary.)

Finley, G. W. "A Sketch of Religious Life in Some Northern Prisons during the War between the States." *Union Seminary Magazine* 13, no. 4 (April–May 1902): 268–73.

"First Women Are Elected to UTS Board." *Richmond Times-Dispatch*, November 21, 1972, A-1.

Flournoy, Francis R. *Benjamin Mosby Smith, 1811–1893*. Richmond, VA: Richmond Press, 1947.

———. "The Early Life of Benjamin Mosby Smith." *Union Seminary Review* 55, no. 1 (November 1943): 1–20.

Flournoy, Parke P. "The Bugle from Berlin: The Retrocession of Harnack." *Union Seminary Magazine* 11, no. 1 (October–November 1899): 10–15.

———. "When Were the Gospels Written?" *Union Seminary Magazine* 11, no. 3 (February–March 1900): 214–16.

Flow, J. E. "The Character of Jesus Christ Is a Proof of His Historicity." *Union Seminary Review* 31, no. 4 (July 1920): 317–35.

Flynt, J. Wayne. "Feeding the Hungry and Ministering to the Broken Hearted: The Presbyterian Church in the United States and the Social Gospel, 1900–1920." In

Religion in the South, edited by Charles Reagan Wilson, 83–137. Jackson: University Press of Mississippi, 1985.

Foote, William Henry. *Sketches of North Carolina*. New York: Robert Carter, 1846.

———. *Sketches of Virginia, Historical and Biographical, Second Series*. Philadelphia: J. B. Lippincott & Co., 1855.

For All Southern Presbyterians: A Great Door Is Opened. Promotional booklet for the Mid-Century Campaign, 17. Richmond, VA: Whittet & Shepperson, 1952.

Foreman, Amanda. *A World on Fire: Britain's Crucial Role in the American Civil War*. New York: Random House, 2010.

Forrest, Sam. "Criticizes Seminary on WRFK Issue." Letter to the editor. *Richmond Times-Dispatch*, March 22, 1988, A-12.

"Four-Year Seminary School Is Urged at Alumni Dinner." *Richmond Times-Dispatch*, February 5, 1937.

Fox, Susan Elizabeth. "Perceptions of the Placement Process: Presbyterian Women Candidates at Union Theological Seminary in Virginia." DMin diss., Union Theological Seminary in Virginia, 1995.

Fox-Genovese, Elizabeth, and Eugene D. Genovese. "The Divine Sanction of Social Order: Religious Foundations of the Southern Slaveholders' World View." *Journal of the American Academy of Religion* 55, no. 2 (Summer 1987): 211–33.

Franck, Raphaël, and Laurence R. Iannaccone. "The Decrease in Religiosity in the Twentieth Century." Bar-Ilan University Discussion Paper. 2009. http://www.thearda.com/asrec/archive/papers/Franck%20&%20Iannaccone%20ASREC%202009.pdf.

Freidenberg, Walt. "Union Seminary Obtains William Blake Collection." *Richmond Times-Dispatch*, April 25, 1954.

Gamble, Connolly Currie, Jr. "*The Education of Southern Presbyterian Ministers: A Survey of the Program and Possibilities of Union Theological Seminary Richmond, Virginia*." Union Theological Seminary, Richmond, VA: Union Theological Seminary: 1950.

Gammon, Samuel R. "Union Seminary Men in Brazil." *Union Seminary Magazine* 9 (1898): 324–29.

Garrett, Wilbur E., ed. *Historical Atlas of the United States*. Washington, DC: National Geographic Society, 1988.

Gatewood, Willard B. "Embattled Scholar: Howard W. Odun and the Fundamentalists, 1925–1927." *Journal of Southern History* 31, no. 4 (November 1965): 375–90.

Gaustad, Edwin Scott. *Historical Atlas of Religion in America*. New York: Harper & Row, 1962.

Gehwer, Wesley M. *The Great Awakening in Virginia, 1740–1790*. Durham, NC: Duke University Press, 1930.

Gillette, Ezra Hall. *History of the Presbyterian Church in the United States of America*. Vol. 2. Philadelphia: Presbyterian Board of Publication and Sabbath-School Work, 1864. Rev. ed., 1873. Michigan Historical Reprint Series. Ann Arbor: University of Michigan Library, 2005. http://quod.lib.umich.edu/cgi/t/text/text-idx?c=moa;idno=AGV9128.0002.001.

Glasgow, Tom. *Shall the Southern Presbyterian Church Abandon Its Historic Position?* Charlotte, NC: Privately published, 1940.

Glimpses of 75 Years. Richmond, VA: Ginter Park Presbyterian Church, 1982.

Goen, C. C. *Broken Churches, Broken Nation: Denominational Schisms and the Coming of the American Civil War*. Macon, GA: Mercer University Press, 1985.

Goin, Mary Elisabeth. "Of Jobs and Calls." *In Medias Res* (Richmond, VA), March 15, 1978.

Goodpasture, Henry McKennie. "Ecumenical Mission: A Visit with Robert E. Speer as Historian and Interpreter; An Inaugural Address." *Affirmation* 1, no. 5 (September 1973): 23–35.

———. "Our Field Is the World: Mission Studies at Union Theological Seminary in Virginia, 1812–1987." An address given on the 175th Anniversary Celebration of the Founding of Union Theological Seminary. October 12, 1987.

Goodykoontz, Harry G. *The Minister in the Reformed Tradition.* Richmond, VA: John Knox Press, 1963.

Gordon, Michael. "A Bright Light for Us: Union Presbyterian Seminary Opens the Doors at Its New Campus in South Charlotte." *Charlotte Observer*, October 6, 2012, E-1.

Graybill, A. T. "A Sketch of Our Work in Mexico." *Union Seminary Magazine* 9 (March–April 1898): 329–31.

Green, Bill. "My Dear Wormwood." *In Medias Res* (Richmond, VA), Summer 1993.

Green, David. "Will the Seminary Be True to Its Traditional Mission?" Opinion. *Richmond Times-Dispatch*, December 30, 1995, A-8.

Green, E. M. "Pastoral Visiting." *Union Seminary Magazine* 11, no. 2 (December 1899–January 1900): 75–79.

Greenwalt, Bruce S. "The Lord Watch between Us: White and Black Southern Presbyterians, 1864–1874." 1981. Unpublished manuscript, in the author's files.

Grey, John H. "The Rediscovery of the Southern Presbyterian Pen." *Union Seminary Review* 48, no. 1 (October 1936): 54–60.

Grissett, Priscilla. "Racial Demonstrations—Why?" *Expression* (Richmond, VA) 6, no. 7 (February 8, 1961): 7.

Guerrant, Edward O. "How to Preach." *Union Seminary Magazine* 4, no. 2 (November–December 1892): 91–96.

Guild, June Percell. *Black Laws of Virginia.* Richmond, VA: Whittet & Shepperson, 1936.

Gustafson, Bob. "Seeking to Be Christian in Race Relations." *Expression* (Richmond, VA) 1, no. 1 (February 1956): 2–3.

Gwynn, Price H., III. "Presentation on the Floor of Charlotte Presbytery." February 22, 2000.

———. "Remarks by Price H. Gwynn to a Charlotte Presbytery Ad Hoc Committee Convened by Alan Elmore to Discuss Theological Education in the Greater Charlotte Area." September 30, 1997.

Hall, J. K. "The Decline in the Sense of Sin." *Union Seminary Magazine* 20, no. 4 (April–May 1909): 300–309.

Hall, T. Hartley, IV. "Administrative History of Union Theological Seminary." Unpublished notes in the author's files, 1986.

———. "Curriculum Consultation." Richmond, VA, October 30, 1989. In the author's files.

———. "The Lower Gifts." A paper presented at the opening convocation in Watts Chapel, Union Theological Seminary in Virginia, September 9, 1987. Notes for this paper in the author's files.

———. "The Middle East Situation—from a Christian Perspective." *Expression* (Richmond, VA) 2, no. 1 (October 1956): 1.

———. "Reflections on Admissions, Enrollment, and Financial Aid." Address given to the Board of Trustees ca. 1989. In the author's files.

———. "Trends in Theological Education and How UTS Fits In." In Board of Trustees Meeting. Richmond, VA, February 18, 1994.

Hamm, Richard, and Marsha Wilfong. "Curriculum, or, 'What I Did Last Year.'" *In Medias Res* (Richmond, VA), November 8, 1978.

"The Hampden-Sydney B. B. Nine." *Hampden-Sydney Magazine*, November 1884, 14.

Harbison, Richard. "The Minister in the Present Crisis." *Expression* (Richmond, VA) 3, no. 2 (December 1957): 9.

Hatch, Nathan O. "The Christian Movement and the Demand for a Theology of the People." *Journal of American History* 67, no. 3 (December 1980): 545–67.

Havice, Kit. "Social Action." *Expression* (Richmond, VA), October 1967, 3.

Hellmuth, Bart. "A Christian View of the 'New' Counseling." *Expression* (Richmond, VA) 1, no. 1 (February 1956): 5, 7.

Hemphill, W. Edwin. "Not out of This World: A Brief Interpretation of the History of Union Theological Seminary at Hampden-Sydney and in Richmond." *Record of the Hampden-Sydney Alumni Association*, April 1952, 16–17.

Henderlite, Rachel. "The Need for Theology in Religious Education." *Union Seminary Review* 57, no. 1 (October 1945): 1–14.

Henry, Stuart C. "The Lane Rebels: A Twentieth-Century Look." *Journal of Presbyterian History* 49, no. 1 (Spring 1971): 1–14.

Henry, William Wirt. "Moses Drury Hodge." *Union Seminary Magazine* 10, no. 1 (October 1899): 209–16.

———. "The Presbyterian Church and Religious Liberty in Virginia." *Union Seminary Magazine* 12, no. 1 (October–November 1900): 16–31.

Hermanson, Marybeth, and Betsey Gessler. "Reactions to the Washington Conference." *Expression* (Richmond, VA), February 1968.

Herndon, John P. "The Nature and Design of Church Discipline." *Union Seminary Magazine* 17, no. 1 (October–November 1905): 46–52.

Hess, Kurtis. Alumni/ae Survey. 1998. Library archives.

———. Federation Climate Survey. February 16, 1998. Library archives.

Hickin, Patricia P. "Antislavery in Virginia, 1831–1861." PhD diss., University of Virginia, June 1968. In the author's files.

Hill, William. *Autobiographical Sketches of Dr. William Hill, Together with His Account of the Revival of Religion in Prince Edward County and Biographical Sketches of the Life and Character of the Reverend Dr. Moses Hoge of Virginia*. Vol. 4, *Historical Transcripts*. Richmond: Union Theological Seminary in Virginia, 1968.

———. *History of the Rise, Progress, Genius, and Character of American Presbyterianism: Together with a Review of "The Constitutional History of the Presbyterian Church in the United States of America," by Chas. Hodge*. Washington City: J. Gideon Jr., 1839.

Hobbie, Peter Hairston. "Ernest Trice Thompson: Prophet for a Changing South." PhD diss., Union Theological Seminary in Virginia, May 1987.

———. "Walter L. Lingle, Presbyterians, and the Enigma of the Social Gospel in the South." *American Presbyterians* 69, no. 3 (Fall 1991): 191–202.

Hodges, Steve, and Tig Sugg. "On Investments." *In Medias Res* (Richmond, VA), January 9, 1979.

Hoge, John Blair. *Sketch of the Life and Character of the Rev. Moses Hoge, D.D.* Historical Transcripts 2. Richmond: Union Theological Seminary in Virginia, 1964.

Hoge, Moses D. "Address." In *Septuagesimal Celebration of Union Theological Seminary in Virginia, 1824–1894*, 65–76. Richmond, VA: Whittet & Shepperson, 1894.

———. "An Address." *Union Seminary Magazine* 5, no. 3 (January–February 1894): 156–65.

Hoge, Moses, Drury Lacy, and Matthew Lyle. "The Presbytery of Hanover." *Virginia Argus* (Richmond), October 26, 1810, 3.

Hoge, Peyton H. "A Gift to the Library." *Union Seminary Magazine* 11, no. 1 (October–November 1899): 55–57.

Holem [John Holt Rice]. "Observations on the Manner of Educating Young Men for the Ministry of the Gospel." *Virginia Evangelical and Literary Magazine* 5, no. 8 (August 1822): 412–18.

Holmes, Mark. "Reflections." *In a Mirror* (Richmond, VA), February 1975.

Holshouser, Bill. "A Private Case for Demonstrating." *Expression* (Richmond, VA) 9, no. 1 (October 1, 1963): 6–8.

"Honorary Membership in French School Body to Be Conferred on Two Seminary Officers." *Richmond Times-Dispatch*, November 11, 1949.

Hooper, T. W. "Relation of the Church to the Y.M.C.A." *Union Seminary Magazine* 2, no. 2 (November–December 1890): 124–28.

———. "William J. Hoge." *Union Seminary Magazine* 9, no. 3 (1898): 294–97.

Horney, Barbara. "Personal Pilgrimage toward Freedom." *In a Mirror* (Richmond, VA), October 1974.

———. "UTS Students and Faculty Meet to Discuss Academic Load." *In a Mirror* (Richmond, VA), February 1975.

House of Delegates, Commonwealth of Virginia. *Journal of the House of Delegates of the Commonwealth of Virginia*, 1815–1816.

Howison, Robert R. *A History of Virginia from Its Discovery and Settlement by Europeans to the Present Time*. Philadelphia: Carey & Hart, 1846.

Hudson, Banks. Editorial. *Interrobang* (Richmond, VA), November 7, 1969.

Hudson, David S. "$19,000,000 Rebuilding Plan Detailed by Union Seminary." *Richmond Times-Dispatch*, May 18, 1965.

Humphreys, C. W. "The Sinnott Case and the Assemblies." *Union Seminary Magazine* 23, no. 3 (February–March 1912): 241–50.

Hunley, Robert E. R. "Transfer Will Ensure WRFK's Future." *Richmond Times-Dispatch*, June 23, 1986, 10.

Hutchins, Shirley. "Thoughts from the 'Girl' Seminarian." *In Medias Res* (Richmond, VA), Spring 1990.

"Ideal of a Seminary." *Richmond News Leader*, January 2, 1945.

Ingle, Joe. "Perspective: Weekend for Theological Inquiry." *Perspective* (Richmond, VA), issue 6, 1970.

"An International Outlook on Vietnam." *Expression* (Richmond, VA), April 1968.

"In Their New Home." *Richmond Times-Dispatch*, October 6, 1898, 1–2.

Iota. "Theological Seminaries." *Literary and Evangelical Magazine* 9, no. 8 (August 1826): 408–11.

Jackson, Randy. "The Way It Was." *In a Mirror* (Richmond, VA), February 1975.

Johnson, Thomas Cary. *See also under* Peck

———. "An Aim of the Ministerial Student: A Faculty Address Delivered by Prof. T. C. Johnson in the Seminary Chapel, Richmond, Va. October 6th, 1898." *Union Seminary Magazine* 10, no. 1 (October–November 1898).

———. "A Brief Sketch of the Missions of the Southern Presbyterian Church." *Union Seminary Magazine* 7, no. 2 (November–December 1895): 79–94.

———. "Has the Assembly a Right to Veto a Change in Our Book of Church Order, Even after a Majority of the Presbyteries Have Voted for the Change?" *Union Seminary Magazine* 11, no. 1 (October–November 1899): 29–35.

———. *A History of the Southern Presbyterian Church*. New York: Christian Literature Co., 1894.

———. "Lectures on Repentance, Sanctification, and Good Works (A Revision of the Lectures LV–LVIII of Dabney's Theology)." Undated.

———. *The Life and Letters of Robert Lewis Dabney*. Richmond, VA: Presbyterian Board of Publication, 1903; Carlisle, PA: Banner of Truth, 1977.

———. "The Mental and Moral Bearing Proper to Ministerial Students." *Union Seminary Magazine* 15, no. 1 (October–November 1903): 24–38.

———. "Our Session Remiss: Hence, in Part, Our Need for More and Stronger Ministers." *Union Seminary Magazine* 4, no. 1 (September–October 1892): 33–37.

———. "The Presbyterian Church in the United States." *Union Seminary Magazine* 11, no. 4 (April–May 1900): 280–93.

———. "The Presbyteries' Practical Treatment of the Standard of Ministerial Education." *Union Seminary Magazine* 8, no. 2 (November–December 1896): 78–89.

———. "The Seminary Course of Study—Its Range, Standard, Examinations, and Tests." *Union Seminary Magazine* 9, no. 1 (September–October 1897): 14–31.

———. "The Seminary Course of Study—Its Range, Standard, Examinations, and Tests." *Union Seminary Magazine* 9, no. 2 (November–December 1897): 83–96.

———. "Should We Assert in Our Creed That All Infants Dying in Infancy Are Elect?" *Union Seminary Magazine* 13, no. 4 (April–May 1902): 243–59.

———. "A Sketch of the Missions of the Southern Presbyterian Church." *Union Seminary Magazine* 7, no. 3 (January–February 1896): 155–69.

———. "The Study of the English Bible Is Demanded by the Needs of Our Day." *Presbyterian Quarterly*, 1892, 360–84.

———. "The Veto Power of the General Assembly, Once More." *Union Seminary Magazine* 11, no. 2 (December 1899–January 1900): 99–106.

———. *Virginia Presbyterianism and Political Liberty in The Colonial and Revolutionary Times.* Richmond, VA: Presbyterian Committee of Publication, 1907.

———. "Walter W. Moore: A Sketch of His Life and Achievements." *Union Seminary Review* 38, no. 1 (October 1926): 1–29.

Jones, Allan. "700 March in Four Cities." *Richmond Times-Dispatch*, March 16, 1965, 1.

Jones, James Archibald. "And Some, Pastors." In *Horizons of Theological Education: Essays in Honor of Charles L. Taylor, John B. Coburn, Walter D. Wagoner, and Jesse H. Ziegler.* Dayton, OH: AATS, 1966. Published also in *Theological Education* 2, no. 4 (Summer 1966): 58–66.

———. "The Church and Its Ministry." Inaugural address delivered April 4, 1956, in Schauffler Hall, Union Theological Seminary, Richmond, VA.

———. *Devotional Living.* Richmond, VA: Union Theological Seminary, 1958.

Jones, Jeffrey M. "Tracking Religious Affiliation, State by State." In *Gallup: Religion and Social Trends.* June 22, 2004. http://www.gallup.com/poll/12091/tracking -religious-affiliation-state-state.aspx.

Jones, Will. "Union-PSCE to Raze 5 Old Buildings in Richmond." *Richmond Times-Dispatch*, April 29, 2010, B-1.

Juersivich, Heidi. "Dr. B. H. Kelly, 85, UTS Retiree, Dies." *Richmond Times-Dispatch*, January 10, 2000.

Junkin, George. *The Vindication, Containing a History of the Trial of the Rev. Albert Barnes by the Second Presbytery and by the Synod of Philadelphia.* Philadelphia: Wm. S. Martien, 1836.

Junkin, W. M. "Inter-Seminary Missionary Alliance." *Union Seminary Magazine* 3, no. 4 (March–April 1892): 311–18.

Kellam, Jeff. "Forty I Followed: Robert White Kirkpatrick." In *Peace, Grace, and Jazz!* Internet blog. March 12, 2011. https://jeffkellam.wordpress.com/2011/03/12 /forty-i-followed-robert-white-kirkpatrick/.

Keller, Adolf. "A Battle of Life or Death in European Protestantism." *Union Seminary Review* 49, no. 4 (May 1938): 334–42.

———. "Totalitarian Faith on the European Continent." *Union Seminary Review* 50, no. 4 (May 1939): 327–36.

Kelly, Balmer H. "In Retrospect." *Interpretation* 25, no. 1 (January 1971): 11–23.

———. "No Ism but Bibleism: Biblical Studies at Union Theological Seminary in Virginia, 1812–1987." A paper presented at the 175th anniversary celebration of the founding of Union Theological Seminary, October 12, 1987.

———. "What Union Seminary Has Taught Me." Speech given to the alumni board during Sprunt Lecture week, April 22, 1977.

Kelly, Robert L. *Theological Education in America: A Study of One Hundred Sixty-One Theological Schools in the United States and Canada*. New York: George H. Doran Co., 1924.

Kennedy, William B. "Reflections on the March to Washington." *Expression* (Richmond, VA) 9, no. 2 (November 1, 1963): 1–4.

Kerr, Robert P. *The People's History of Presbyterianism in All Ages*. 5th ed. Richmond, VA: Presbyterian Committee of Publication, 1888.

———. "A Plea for Preparation for Public Prayer." *Union Seminary Magazine* 12, no. 1 (December 1900–January 1901): 123–26.

King, Corky. "Christ, Culture and Conformity—a Memorandum to Seminary Students." *Expression* (Richmond, VA) 4, no. 3 (Winter 1959): 10–13.

King, David. "An Experimental Course in Experimental Ministry." *Expression* (Richmond, VA), February 1968.

Kirk, Harris E. "The Oriental Mystery Religions and the Christianity of Paul." *Union Seminary Review* 25, no. 4 (April–May 1914): 253–70.

Kirkpatrick, Robert Foster. "The Chapel." *Union Seminary Magazine* 11, no. 2 (December 1899–January 1900): 142.

Kirkpatrick, Robert White. "The Early Years of WRFK-FM." A Reminiscence by Robert W. Kirkpatrick on the Early Years of WRFK. Richmond, VA, July 5, 1979.

Knox, Bob. "The Rural Church." *In Medias Res* (Richmond, VA), March 15, 1978.

Knox, John, and William Croft Dickenson. *John Knox's History of the Reformation in Scotland*. Vol. 2. New York: Philosophical Library, 1950.

Lacy, Benjamin Rice. "A Dynamic Tradition." In *Our Protestant Heritage*, 185–208. Richmond, VA: John Knox Press, 1948.

———. "Historical Address Delivered at the Opening of the Seminary on Wednesday, September 15th, 1937." *Union Seminary Review* 49, no. 1 (October 1937): 1–15.

———. "A Look Backward and Forward." *Union Seminary Review* 38, no. 1 (October 1926): 29–34.

———. Memorandum by Benjamin Rice Lacy, Richmond, VA, to Dr. Edward Mack, December 21, 1934. In the library archives of Union Presbyterian Seminary.

———. *Revivals in the Midst of the Years*. Richmond, VA: John Knox Press, 1943.

———. "Through Our Next Fifty Years." An address given on the fiftieth anniversary of the move from Hampden Sydney to Richmond, October 5, 1948.

———. "Union Theological Seminary in This Present Age: On the Occasion of His Inauguration as President of Union Theological Seminary in Virginia, May 11, 1927." *Union Seminary Review* 38, no. 4 (July 1927): 353–68.

———. *Union Theological Seminary in Virginia*. Richmond: Union Theological Seminary in Virginia, 1925.

Lacy, Mary. "Inflation Is Choking UTS $19-Million Building Plan." *Richmond News Leader*, June 1, 1970.

Lacy, William Sterling. "Benjamin Mosby Smith." *Union Seminary Magazine* 9 (March–April 1898): 284–90.

———. *William Sterling Lacy: Memorial, Addresses, Sermons*. Richmond, VA: Presbyterian Committee of Publication, 1900.

Lane, Edward E. "The Buildings." *Union Seminary Magazine* 10, no. 1 (October–November 1898): 61–63.

———. "The New Chapel." *Union Seminary Magazine* 10, no. 4 (April–May 1899): 301.

————. "The Presbyterian Congo Mission." *Union Seminary Magazine* 9, no. 4 (March–April 1898): 348–49.

Lantz, Bob. "Intolerance." *In Medias Res* (Richmond, VA), Fall 1995.

Lapsley, R. A. "Books Which Every Preacher Ought to Have." *Union Seminary Magazine* 15, no. 1 (October–November 1903): 46–49.

Latimer, James Fair. *Inaugural Address*. Richmond, VA: Whittet & Shepperson, 1885.

Lawhorn, Jack W. "Through Jesus Christ Our Lord? Worship at Union Seminary." *Expression* (Richmond, VA), Winter 1959, 5–8.

Lawson, Eric. "One Person's Opinion." *In Medias Res* (Richmond, VA), April 5, 1978.

Lee, Tommy. "Presbyterians and Revivalism: The New Side / Old Side Division Which Lasted from 1741 until 1758." Unpublished paper in the author's files.

Leith, John Haddon. "The Bible and Theology." *Interpretation* 30, no. 3 (July 1976): 227–41.

————. "Church Union: A Practical Necessity but Not the Critical Issue Confronting Presbyterians." *Presbyterian Outlook*, December 20–27, 1982, 5–6.

————. *Creeds of the Churches: A Reader in Christian Doctrine from the Bible to the Present*. New York: Anchor Books, 1963.

————. *Crisis in the Church: The Plight of Theological Education*. Louisville, KY: Westminster John Knox Press, 1997.

————. "Ernest Trice Thompson: Churchman." In *Ernest Trice Thompson: An Appreciation*, 30–48. Richmond: Union Theological Seminary in Virginia, 1964.

————. "James Luther Mays." In *The Hermeneutical Quest: Essays in Honor of James Luther Mays on His Sixty-Fifty Birthday*, edited by Donald G. Miller. Allison Park, PA: Pickwick Publications, 1986.

————. *Pilgrimage of a Presbyterian*. Edited by Charles E. Raynal. Louisville, KY: Geneva Press, 2000.

————. "The Significance of Historical Theology in the Education of Ministers." In *Service of Inauguration*. Richmond: Union Theological Seminary in Virginia, April 20, 1960. In the author's files.

————. "Teaching Theology at Union Seminary in Virginia." A paper presented at the 175th Anniversary Celebration of the Founding of Union Theological Seminary. October 13, 1987.

A Letter from the General Assembly of the Presbyterian Church in the United States of America to the Churches under Their Care. Philadelphia: Jane Aitken, 1810.

Letter to the editor. *Expression* (Richmond, VA) 6, no. 10 (March 22, 1961): 2.

————. *Expression* (Richmond, VA) 9, no. 6 (March 1, 1964).

"Letters of Congratulations." *Union Seminary Magazine* 24 (1912): 128–54.

Leuchtenburg, William E. *The Perils of Prosperity, 1914–1932*. Chicago: University of Chicago Press, 1973.

Lewis, Agnes Smith. "On the Antiquity of the Syro-Antiochene Palimpsest." *Union Seminary Magazine* 15, no. 4 (April–May 1904): 359–63.

Lewis, Frank Bell. "Reformed Faith and Today's Ethical Tensions." Inaugural address, in Schauffler Hall, Union Theological Seminary, Richmond, VA, March 1, 1955.

————. "Times of Crisis." In *The Days of Our Years: The Historical Convocations Held April 24–27, 1962, as a Feature of the Celebration of the Sesquicentennial of Union Theological Seminary in Virginia*, 21–40. Richmond, VA: Union Theological Seminary, 1962.

Lewis, Laura, Tony Ruger, and Ellis Nelson. "Report to the Boards of Trustees, Presbyterian School of Christian Education (PSCE) and Union Theological Seminary (UTS)." September 12, 1995.

Leyburn, Edward R. "The Church and Reconstruction." *Union Seminary Review* 30, no. 2 (January 1919): 137–46.

————. "The Student Volunteer Movement and the Detroit Convention." *Union Seminary Magazine* 5, no. 4 (March–April 1894): 269–76.

Leyburn, George L. "The Greek Mission and Alumni of UTS." *Union Seminary Magazine* 9 (March–April 1898): 322–24.

Liedtke, M. Anne. "The Town Meetings." *In a Mirror* (Richmond, VA), January 1976.

"Life That Lives On." *Expression* (Richmond, VA) 9, no. 8 (May 14, 1964): 3.

Lilly, D. Clay. "Colored Labor in Relation to the Prosperity of the Southern Farmer." *Union Seminary Magazine* 13, no. 4 (April–May 1902): 274–76.

Lindsey, Alberta. "Answering the Call." *Richmond Times-Dispatch*, March 28, 2006, B-1, 3.

————. "Dispute at Seminary Has Deep, Wide Roots." *Richmond Times-Dispatch*, November 1, 1996, A-1.

————. "New Plan for Old Library Building." *Richmond Times-Dispatch*, November 13, 2004, B-1, 4.

————. "President for UTS Named." *Richmond News Leader*, May 16, 1967, A-1.

————. "Procession of Favorite Books Will Hail Seminary's New Library." *Richmond Times-Dispatch*, November 20, 1996, B-6.

————. "What Does Scripture Say?" *Richmond Times-Dispatch*, November 4, 2006, A-1, 8.

Lingle, Walter Lee. "About Books: Editorial." *Union Seminary Magazine* 8, no. 4 (March–April 1897): 269–71.

————. *The Bible and Social Problems: The James Sprunt Lectures, 1929*. New York: Fleming H. Revell Co., 1929.

————. Editorials. *Union Seminary Review* 25, no. 1 (October–November 1913): 51–52.

————. "The Last Fifty Years." *Union Seminary Magazine* 24, no. 1 (1912–13): 48–75.

————. "The Latin Thesis." *Union Seminary Magazine* 13, no. 2 (December 1901–January 1902): 98–101.

————. *Presbyterians, Their History and Belief*. Richmond, VA: Presbyterian Committee of Publication, 1928.

————. "The Unrevised and Revised Confessions of Faith Compared." *Union Seminary Review* 29, no. 2 (January 1918): 132–48.

Little, A. A. "The Sabbath-School: Is It a Failure?" *Union Seminary Magazine* 11, no. 3 (February–March 1900): 172–76.

Little, Sara. "About PSCE . . ." *Expression* (Richmond, VA) 6, no. 9 (March 8, 1961): 3.

————. "Women at Union." *In Medias Res* (Richmond, VA), January 1986.

"A Little Primer for Racists." *Expression* (Richmond, VA) 9, no. 1 (October 1, 1963): 2–4.

"Little Things That Add Up." *Expression* (Richmond, VA), October 1967, 2, 9.

Long, Dallas R. "Local Radio Station Will Join Network." *Richmond Times-Dispatch*, July 22, 1970, B-19.

————. "Mrs. Reynolds Gives Big Estate to UTS." *Richmond Times Dispatch*, January 4, 1972, A-1.

Longenecker, Stephen L. *Shenandoah Religion: Outsiders and the Mainstream, 1716–1865*. Waco: Baylor University Press, 2002.

Loo, H. Alton, Jr. "In Search of the Will of God." *Expression* (Richmond, VA) 9, no. 13 (March 22, 1965).

Loveland, Anne C. "Presbyterians and Revivalism in the Old South." *Journal of Presbyterian History* 57 (1979): 36–49.

Lucas [John Holt Rice]. Letter to the editor. *Virginia Evangelical and Literary Magazine* 4, no. 6 (June 1821): 302–9.

Lynd, Robert S., and Helen Merrell Lynd. *Middletown: A Study in American Culture*. New York: Harcourt, Brace & Co., 1929.

MacBryde, Duncan. "German Theologian to Give Sprunt Lecture Series Here." *Richmond News Leader*, January 31, 1935.

———. "World's Outward Progress not Matched Inwardly, Asserts Scherer at Seminary." *Richmond News Leader*, February 6, 1935.

Mack, Edward. Letter from Richmond, VA, to Rev. Samuel Govan Stevens, January 3, 1935. Copy of letter is in author's files.

———. "Our Church in the Reconstruction after War." *Union Seminary Review* 30, no. 2 (January 1919): 99–110.

MacKay, John Alexander. "The Heritage of Yesterday." *Union Seminary Review* 60, no. 4 (August 1944): 273–85.

Maclin, Bob. Letter to the editor. *Expression* (Richmond, VA) 9, no. 7 (April 17, 1964): 2, 4.

Mahler, Henry Richard, Jr. "A History of Union Theological Seminary in Virginia, 1807–1865." ThD diss., Union Theological Seminary in Virginia, 1951.

Mainor, Tom. "Some Thoughts on Civil Rights and the Church." *Expression* (Richmond, VA) 9, no. 1 (October 1, 1963): 4–5.

Marion, Forrest L. "All That Is Pure in Religion and Valuable in Society: Presbyterians, the Virginia Society, and the Sabbath, 1830–1836." *Virginia Magazine of History and Biography* 109, no. 2 (2001): 187–218.

Marsden, George M. *The Evangelical Mind and the New School Experience.* Eugene, OR: Wipf & Stock, 1970.

———. *Fundamentalism and American Culture.* 2nd ed. New York: Oxford University Press, 2006.

Martin, Bob. "Towards an Adequate Perspective between UTS and PSCE." *Expression* (Richmond, VA) 5, no. 1 (Fall 1959): 6–7.

Martin, James P., et al. "Commencement Petition of May 26, 1970." Richmond, VA. Library archives.

Martin, Robert F. "Critique of Southern Society and Vision of a New Order: The Fellowship of Southern Churchmen, 1934–1957." *Church History* 52, no. 1 (March 1983): 66–80.

Mastemaker, Lorie. "Hampden-Sydney in the 1850s: Part 1, The Quiet before the Storm." *Newsletter of the Associates of the Esther Thomas Atkinson Museum of Hampden-Sydney*, Spring 2004, 16–37.

"Master of Sacred Theology Courses to Begin at UTS in Fall." *Richmond News Leader*, May 28, 1966.

Maxwell, William. *A Memoir of the Rev. John H. Rice, D.D.* Philadelphia: J. Whetham; Richmond: R. I. Smith, 1835.

May, Mark Arthur, et al. *The Education of American Ministers.* Vol. 1, *Ministerial Education in America.* New York: Institute of Social and Religious Research, 1934.

Mays, James H. Editorial. *Interpretation* 20, no. 1 (January 1966): 78–80.

Mays, James Luther. E-mail from Richmond, Va., to the author. "Some Notes on Biblical Studies at Union: [19]30s–50s," August 13, 2011.

———. "Exegesis as a Theological Discipline." Inaugural address delivered April 20, 1960, in Schauffler Hall, Union Theological Seminary, Richmond, Virginia.

McAllister, J. Gray. "First Contributors to Union Theological Seminary." *Union Seminary Review* 23, no. 1 (October 1912): 16–20.

———. *The Life and Letters of Walter W. Moore: Second Founder and First President of Union Theological Seminary in Virginia.* Richmond, VA: Union Theological Seminary, 1939.

———. "Seminary Here since 1898." *Richmond Times-Dispatch*, October 3, 1948, IV-1.

McComb, Louise. *The First Seventy Years: A History of the Presbyterian School of Christian Education.* Richmond, VA: Presbyterian School of Christian Education, 1985.

McCormick, Scott. *Biblical Theology in the Years 1947–1956 as Reflected through "Interpretation."* ThM thesis, Union Theological Seminary in Virginia. Richmond, May 1957.

McCutcheon, Joe. "The Ubiquitous Advance." *Expression* (Richmond, VA) 10, no. 5 (January 1966), " 1.

McGirt, Bob. "Strangers at Home." *Expression* (Richmond, VA) 7, no. 10 (November 21, 1962): 4–5.

McIlwaine, Richard. *Memories of Three Score Years and Ten.* New York: Neale Publishing Co., 1908.

McKinnon, R. L. *Richmond, Society of Missionary Inquiry: End of Year Report.* May 6, 1917.

McNeill, Robert. *God Wills Us Free: The Ordeal of a Southern Minister.* New York: Hill & Wang, 1965.

McTyre, James. "The Sexuality Report-Event." *In Medias Res* (Richmond, VA), May 1991.

———. "The Worst Haircut I've Ever Had: The Church's Response to AIDS Begins at the Barber's Chair and Ends at the Bedside." *In Medias Res* (Richmond, VA), Fall 1990.

Meacham, Jon. *American Lion: Andrew Jackson in the White House.* New York: Random House Trade Paperbacks, 2009.

Meath, Richard L. "The Influence of Contemporary Fiction Writers on American Christianity." *Expression* (Richmond, VA) 2, no. 3 (January 1957): 4.

Melton, Bill. "The New Curriculum." *Expression* (Richmond, VA) 11, no. 4 (October 2, 1964): 6–8.

Mesle, C. Robert. *Process Theology: A Basic Introduction.* Danvers, MA: Chalice Press, 1993.

"Mid-Century Victory." *Union Seminary Bulletin,* January–March 1954, 1.

Miller, Donald G. "The Birth of a Journal." *Interpretation* 50, no. 2 (April 1996): 117–29.

Miller, Glenn T. *A Community of Conversation: A Retrospective of the Association of Theological Schools and Ninety Years of North American Theological Education.* Pittsburgh: Association of Theological Schools, 2008.

———. *Piety and Professionalism: American Protestant Theological Education, 1870–1970.* Grand Rapids: William B. Eerdmans Publishing Co., 2007.

Miller, Patrick D. "God and the Gods. An Inaugural Address." *Affirmation* 1, no. 5 (September 1973): 37–62.

———. "Report from the Dean of Faculty." *In Medias Res* (Richmond, VA), November 1982.

Miller-Gutsell, Marnie. "Down with Super-Mom!!" *In Medias Res* (Richmond, VA), January 1986.

Mills, W. H. "The Church's Duty to the Country Church." *Union Seminary Review* 31, no. 1 (October 1919): 39–45.

Mitchell, Robert D. *Commercialism and Frontier: Perspectives on the Early Shenandoah Valley.* Charlottesville: University Press of Virginia, 1977.

Moffett, F. Lindsay. "'A Fellowship of Concern' Remembered." *Presbyterian Outlook* 8 (April 2002): 8.

Moon, Fred. "Comments." *In a Mirror* (Richmond, VA), April 1975.

Moore, Martha Lane. "Faith, Feminism, and the Church." *In Medias Res* (Richmond, VA), May 1991.

Moore, Walter W. "Address at the Dedication of Schauffler Hall." *Union Seminary Review* 33, no. 1 (October 1921): 1–29.

————. *Appreciations and Historical Addresses*. Richmond, VA: Presbyterian Committee of Publication, 1914?

————. "The Chaldean Story of the Flood." *Union Seminary Magazine* 5, no. 4 (March–April 1894): 249–61.

————. "Dr. John H. Rice." *Union Seminary Magazine* 9 (March–April 1898): 264–73.

————. Editorial. *Union Seminary Magazine* 5, no. 3 (January–February 1894): 196–98.

————. "Fact versus Fancies." *Union Seminary Magazine* 2, no. 4 (March–April 1891): 241–50.

————. "The First Fifty Years." *Union Seminary Magazine* 24, no. 1 (1912–13): 14–47.

————. "The Great Fish of Jonah." *Union Seminary Magazine* 7, no. 1 (September–October 1895): 24–35.

————. "Historical Sketch." In *Septuagesimal Celebration of Union Theological Seminary in Virginia, 1824–1894*, 5–38. Richmond, VA: Whittet & Shepperson, 1894.

————. "Historical Sketch of Union Theological Seminary." *Union Seminary Magazine* 9, no. 4 (March–April 1898): 230–49.

————. *Inaugural Address: Exercises in Connection with the Inauguration of the Rev. Walter W. Moore, D.D., LL.D., as President of Union Theological Seminary*. Richmond, VA: L. D. Sullivan & Co., 1905.

————. "The Latest Light from Egypt." *Union Seminary Magazine* 8, no. 1 (September–October 1896): 30–38.

————. "Mr. Bryan at Union Seminary." *Presbyterian of the South*, November 23, 1921.

————. *A New Era for an Old School*. Richmond, VA: Whittet & Shepperson, 1897.

————. "Oannes and Dagon." *Union Seminary Magazine* 7, no. 3 (January–February 1896): 191–97.

————. "The Oppression in Egypt." *Union Seminary Magazine* 3, no. 1 (September–October 1891): 46–52.

————. "The Passing of Ussher's Chronology." *Union Seminary Magazine* 13, no. 2 (December 1901–January 1902): 73–81.

————. "The Period of the Israelites' Sojourn in Egypt, in the Light of Archaeological Research." *Presbyterian Quarterly* 13, no. 47 (January 1899): 24–43.

————. *The Preparation of the Modern Minister*. Pamphlet 4 of *The Claims and Opportunities of the Christian Ministry*, edited by John R. Mott. New York: International Committee of Young Men's Christian Associations, 1909. Reprinted as pages 60–83 in *The Claims and Opportunities of the Christian Ministry*, 1911. https://archive.org/details/preparationofmod00moor.

————. "Recent Discoveries in Palestine." *Union Seminary Magazine* 4, no. 3 (January–February 1893): 177–92.

————. Review of *Introduction to the Old Testament*, by S. R. Driver. *Union Seminary Magazine* 22, no. 3 (March 1911): 244.

————. Review of *The Origin and Content of the Psalter*, by Thomas Kelly Cheyne. *Presbyterian Quarterly* 6, no. 21 (July 1892): 454.

————. "The Seminary and the War." *Union Seminary Review* 30, no. 1 (October 1918)1 1 6.

————. "Some Recent Explorations in Egypt." *Union Seminary Magazine* 3, no. 3 (January–February 1892): 184–95.

————. "The Training School for Lay Workers and the A. L. Phillips Memorial Fund." In *1915 PC (US) General Assembly*, 1915.

————. "Union Seminary Men in Korea." *Union Seminary Magazine* 9 (March–April 1898): 339–43.

Morrison, Alfred J. *The College of Hampden-Sydney, Calendar of Board Minutes, 1776–1876*. Richmond, VA: Hermitage Press, 1912.

————. "*The Virginia Literary and Evangelical Magazine*, 1818–1828." *William and Mary Quarterly* 19, no. 4 (April 1911): 266–72.

"Mosque Program Discussion Debates Success of Churches." *Richmond Times-Dispatch*, December 5, 1951.

Mottley, Chuck. "In the Tension?" *Expression* (Richmond, VA) 4, no. 3 (Winter 1959).

"Mrs. Reynolds Gives Big Estate to UTS." *Richmond Times-Dispatch*, January 4, 1972.

Mullen, Dave. "The Courage to Care." *Expression* (Richmond, VA) 6, no. 10 (March 22, 1961): 1, 4.

Mullen, J. Christopher. "Of Competencies and Koinonia." *In Medias Res* (Richmond, VA), November 1982.

National Black Presbyterian Caucus. *Blacks in the United Presbyterian Church in the U.S.A., 1807–1982*. New York: United Presbyterian Church, 1982.

Native Virginian. "Sketch of Lower Virginia." *Virginia Evangelical and Literary Magazine* 6, no. 6 (June 1823): 306–11.

Nevin, Alfred, ed. *Encyclopedia of the Presbyterian Church in the United States of America, including Northern and Southern Assemblies*. Philadelphia: Presbyterian Encyclopedia Publishing Co., 1884.

"New Seminary President Seeks to Raise Quality of Students." *Richmond Times-Dispatch*, April 30, 1982.

"A New Spirit Soars on the Wings of Tradition: A Candid Interview about the Future of UTS." *Focus* 2, no. 4 (Winter 1987): 2–7.

Niebuhr, H. Richard. *The Purpose of the Church and Its Ministry*. New York: Harper & Brothers, 1956.

Niece, Gerald. "Niece Attends Conference on Student Interracial Ministry." *Expression* (Richmond, VA) 10, no. 8 (April–May 1966): 11.

Noll, Mark A. *The Princeton Theology, 1812–1921: Scripture, Science, and Theological Method from Archibald Alexander to Benjamin Breckinridge Warfield*. Phillipsburg, NJ: Presbyterian & Reformed Publishing Co., 1983.

"No Name Gazette." *No Name Gazette* (Richmond, VA), no. 1, January 26, 1959.

"Not Heim Alone." *Richmond News Leader*, February 1, 1935.

Nowlin, George. "UTS Colloquy Holds First Meeting." *Interrobang* (Richmond, VA), issue 4 (1969).

Nurnberger, Sally. "Being Included." *In Medias Res* (Richmond, VA), November 1979.

"Objectives of UTS Outlined by Dr. Lacy at Anniversary." *Richmond News Leader*, October 6, 1948, 23.

"Odd Moments." *Union Seminary Magazine* 1 (October–November 1889): 61–62.

Oehler, Philip W. "AIDS and the Rural Church: A New Challenge to Ministry." *In Medias Res* (Richmond, VA), Spring 1993.

————. "The Beloved Community." *In Medias Res* (Richmond, VA), Summer 1992.

Oglesby, William B., Jr. "Faith in Action: Preparing Students for the Work of Ministry." A paper presented at the 175th Anniversary Celebration of the Founding of Union Theological Seminary. October 12, 1987.

————. "Implications of Anthropology for Pastoral Care Counseling." Delivered March 2, 1954, in Schauffler Hall, Union Theological Seminary, Richmond, VA.

————. "Implications of Anthropology for Pastoral Care Counseling." *Interpretation* 33, no. 2 (April 1979): 157–71.

Oldman, John. "Campus Security (or, Rather, Lack Thereof)." *In Medias Res* (Richmond, VA), January 25, 1978.

O'Leary, Tommy. "The Problem of Abortion Revisited." *In Medias Res* (Richmond, VA), Summer 1993.

One In Mission: Campaign Report, July 1, 2001–June 30, 2007. Richmond, VA: Union Theological Seminary and Presbyterian School of Christian Education, 2007.

Ottati, Douglas F. *Jesus Christ and Christian Vision.* Minneapolis, MN: Augsburg Fortress, 1989.

"Our City Schools." *Richmond Times-Dispatch,* January 1, 1899.

Parker, Harold M. *United Synod of the South: The Southern New School Presbyterian Church.* Presbyterian Historical Society Publications 26. New York: Greenwood Press, 1988.

———. "The Urban Failure of the Southern New School Presbyterian Church." *Social Science Journal* 14, no. 1 (January 1977): 139–48.

Paschal, Jeff. "Why I Support a Woman's Right to Choose an Abortion." *In Medias Res* (Richmond, VA), Spring 1990.

Patterson, Curtis. "Of Ships and Shoes and Sealing Wax . . ." *Expression* (Richmond, VA) 6, no. 8 (February 22, 1961).

Patton, Jacob Harris. *A Popular History of the Presbyterian Church in the United States of America.* New York: R. S. Mighill & Co., 1900.

Paxton, John D. *Letters from Palestine.* London: Charles Tilt, 1839.

———. *Letters on Slavery: Addressed to the Cumberland Congregation, Virginia.* Lexington, KY: Abraham T. Skillman, 1833.

Peck, Thomas E. *Miscellanies of Rev. Thomas E. Peck, D.D., LL.D.* Edited by Thomas Cary Johnson. 3 vols. Richmond, VA: Presbyterian Committee of Publication, 1895–97.

Penick, Daniel A. "The Church's Opportunity among Students at State Institutions." *Union Seminary Magazine* 22, no. 3 (February–March 1911): 171–80.

Peters, Mark. "Christian Witness in Our Community and the Debate over Public Schools." *In Medias Res* (Richmond, VA), Spring 1993.

———. "An Open Letter." *In Medias Res* (Richmond, VA), February 1994.

Phillips, Alexander Lacy. "The Work of Our Church for the Negroes in the South." *Union Seminary Magazine* 4, no. 3 (January–February 1893): 206–9.

Phillips, Katherine. "Letter-Writing Urged to Keep WRFK on the Air." *Richmond Times-Dispatch,* February 6, 1988, A-8.

———. "Sale of WRFK Radio Is Approved by FCC." *Richmond Times-Dispatch,* December 16, 1986, 1.

The Plan of a Theological Seminary Adopted by the General Assembly of the Presbyterian Church in the United States of America in Their Sessions of May Last, A.D. 1811: Together with the Measures Taken by Them to Carry the Plan into Effect. Philadelphia: Jane Aitken, 1811.

"Portraits of Two Presbyterian Leaders to Be Unveiled at Union Theological Seminary during Finals Next Week." *Richmond News Leader,* May 11, 1940.

Posey, Lawton. E-mail to the author, May 27, 2010.

"Prayboy." *Prayboy* (Richmond, VA), April 1, 1966.

The Presbyterian Enterprise. See Armstrong, Maurice W.

"Presbyterian Men and Women of South Are Invited to Attend Mid-Century Convocation Here." *Richmond Times Dispatch,* December 2, 1951.

"Presbyterians: Concern v. Concerned." *Time,* October 13, 1967.

"Presbyterian Seminaries' Merger Set." *Richmond News Leader,* July 21, 1943.

"President for UTS Named." *Richmond News Leader,* May 16, 1967, 1, 6.

Price, Phillip B. "The Life of Reverend John Holt Rice, D.D." In *The Life of Reverend John Holt Rice, D.D.* Reprinted from the *Central Presbyterian,* 1886–1887. Richmond: Library of Union Seminary in Virginia, 1963.

"The Progress of Union Seminary." *Central Presbyterian,* April 6, 1904, 1–2.

Pryor, Theodorick. *Address at the Unveiling and Dedication of the Memorial Tablet in Honor of the Rev. John H. Rice, D.D., Delivered in the Chapel of Union Theological Seminary, VA., May 5, 1885*, 14–18. Richmond, VA: Whittet & Shepperson, 1885.

Purves, George T. "The Unity of Second Corinthians." *Union Seminary Magazine* 11, no. 4 (April–May 1900): 233–44.

"Quid—Me Vexari?" *Depression* (Richmond, VA) 1, no. 1 (March 4, 1965).

Rader, Paul. "Letter to the UTS Community." *In Medias Res* (Richmond, VA), January 1983.

Rainer, Joseph T. "Commercial Scythians in the Great Valley of Virginia: Yankee Peddlers' Trade Connection to Antebellum Virginia." In *After the Backcountry: Rural Life in the Great Valley of Virginia, 1800–1900*, edited by Kenneth E. Koons and Warren R. Hofstra, 62–76. Knoxville: University of Tennessee Press, 2000.

Ramsay, Franklin Pierce. "Concerning the Origin of the Pentateuch." *Union Seminary Magazine* 16, no. 2 (December 1904–January 1905): 129–33.

———. "Textual Emendation and Higher Criticism." *Union Seminary Magazine* 13, no. 1 (October–November 1901): 13–18.

Ramsey, George. "Re: The Pledge and 'Community.'" *Expression* (Richmond, VA) 6, no. 11 (April 12, 1961).

Rankin, D. C. "Union Seminary Missionaries in Japan." *Union Seminary Magazine* 9 (March–April 1898): 331–39.

Ransford, Paul. Letters to the editor. *Expression* (Richmond, VA), October 1968.

Rawson, Stewart. "The State of RTC Football." *In Medias Res* (Richmond, VA), Fall 1991.

Rawson, Stewart, and Pete Swanson. "The Ultimate Reality." *In Medias Res* (Richmond, VA), November 1993.

Reed, Richard C. "Why Two Classes of Elders?" *Union Seminary Review* 31, no. 3 (April 1920): 262–71.

Reeves, Keith. "A Short Treatise on Abortion." *In Medias Res* (Richmond, VA), January 1986.

"Religion in Eastern Va. Almost Extinct after War, Unpublished Letters at Presbyterian Seminary State." *Richmond News Leader*, October 26, 1937.

Report of a Committee of the General Assembly of the Presbyterian Church, Exhibiting the Plan of a Theological Seminary. New York: J. Seymour, 1810.

Reports to the Board of Trustees, Union Theological Seminary in Virginia, November 1–2, 1996.

"Reports on the Inter-Seminary Movement and the 18th Ecumenical Student Conference in Athens, Ohio." *Expression* (Richmond, VA) 5, no. 2 (Winter 1960).

"Representative from the Student Inter-racial Movement Will Speak on Campus November 11." *Expression* (Richmond, VA) 9, no. 6 (November 13, 1964): 11.

"A Resolution on Civil Rights Adopted by the Student Body of Union Theological Seminary." May 8, 1964.

"Rev. Fred R. Stair, Jr., Named Assistant to Dr. B. R. Lacy, Jr." *Richmond Times-Dispatch*, May 19, 1948.

Reynolds, Allen. "The Beloved Country." *Expression* (Richmond, VA) 7, no. 10 (November 21, 1962): 3.

Rice, John Holt. *See also* Holem; Lucas

———. "Education for the Gospel Ministry." *Literary and Evangelical Magazine* 10, no. 4 (April 1827): 174–79.

———. "Hints on Revivals of Religion." *Virginia Evangelical and Literary Magazine* 6 (January 6, 1823): 1–7.

———. *An Illustration of the Character & Conduct of the Presbyterian Church in Virginia*. Richmond: Du-Val & Burke, 1816.

———. "Importance of Learning to Ministers of the Gospel." *Literary and Evangelical Magazine* 11 (May 1828): 225–35.

———. *An Inaugural Discourse, Delivered on the First of January, 1824*. Richmond, VA: Nathan Pollard, 1824.

———. "The Influence of Christianity on the Political and Social Interests of Man." *Virginia Evangelical and Literary Magazine* 6 (1823): 335–474.

———. "Memorials to the General Assembly of Virginia." *Literary and Evangelical Magazine* 9, no. 1 (January 1826): 30–49.

———. *"New England Memorials,"* 1823. In the Union Presbyterian Seminary archives.

———. "The Power of Truth and Love: A Sermon Preached before the American Board of Foreign Missions." *National Preacher* 3, no. 5 (October 1, 1828): 65–80.

———. *Remarks on the Attempts Now Making to Christianize the World*. Richmond, VA: Franklin Press, 1819.

———. *A Sermon on the Duties of a Minister of the Gospel: Preached at the Opening of the Presbytery of Hanover at Dee Ess Church, October 11, 1809*. Philadelphia: William W. Woodward, 1809.

———. "Theological Seminary in Andover, Mass." *Virginia Evangelical and Literary Magazine* 5, no. 5 (May 1822): 225–28.

———. "Theological Seminary at Princeton." *Virginia Evangelical and Literary Magazine* 5, no. 6 (June 1822): 281–88.

———. "Theological Seminary in Prince Edward." *Literary and Evangelical Magazine* 9, no. 1 (January 1826): 611–13.

———. "Thoughts on Slavery." *Virginia Evangelical and Literary Magazine* 2, no. 7 (July 1819): 293–302.

Rice, Theron H. "An Ideal Course in the English Bible." *Union Seminary Magazine* 21, no. 1 (October–November 1909): 11–18.

———. "Union Seminary in Theological Education and Religious Thought." *Union Seminary Magazine* 24, no. 1 (1912–13): 100–106.

Richardson, Donald W. Letter from Richmond, VA, to Rev. E. D. McCreary Jr., August 3, 1944. Copy in the author's files.

Richardson, Selden. *Built by Blacks: African-American Architecture in Neighborhoods in Richmond, VA*. Charleston, SC: History Press, 2008.

Richmond, Mary E. "First Principles in the Relief of Distress." *Union Seminary Magazine* 17, no. 3 (February–March 1906): 185–92.

Riviere, William T. "Some Impressions of Philosophy in a French University." *Union Seminary Review* 31, no. 1 (October 1919): 34–38.

Roberts, Samuel K. "For a Time Such as This: Reflections on the Historical Significance of the Inauguration of Brian Blount as President of Union Theological Seminary–Presbyterian School of Christian Education." May 5, 2008. Library archives.

Rochester, Sam. "Defending Infant Baptism." *Expression* (Richmond, VA) 2, no. 3 (January 1957).

Rogers, Isabel. "Community: Gift and Demand." *Interrobang* (Richmond, VA), November 21, 1969.

Rolston, Holmes, III. "A Criticism of Non-Directive Counseling." *Expression* (Richmond, VA) 1, no. 1 (February 1956): 4, 7.

Rose, Benjamin Lacy. "God's Love for the World: The Message and Motive of Missions." In *World Mission Conference. A Sermon Presented at the World Mission Conference*, Montreat, NC, August 2, 1953. Nashville: Board of World Missions.

———. "Racial Segregation in the Church." *Expression* (Richmond, VA), April 1957, 2, 6.

Rosebro, John William. "The Effect of One Sermon." *Union Seminary Magazine* 9, no. 3 (January–February 1898): 185–87.

Rosenberg, Ralph P. "Eugene Schuyler's Doctor of Philosophy Degree: A Theory Concerning the Dissertation." *Journal of Higher Education* 33, no. 7 (1962): 381–86.

Rowley, Harold Henry. "The Relevance of Biblical Interpretation." *Interpretation* 1, no. 1 (January 1947): 3–19.

"Royster Completes $100,000 Gift to Seminary." *Richmond News Leader*, December 28, 1946.

Rüegg, Walter, ed. *A History of the University in Europe.* Vol. 4, *Universities in the Nineteenth and Early Twentieth Centuries (1800–1945).* Cambridge: Cambridge University Press, 2005.

Rutledge, Archibald. "Things We Can't Explain." *Reader's Digest* (New York), November 1942, 30–32.

Ryan, David D., and Wayland W. Rennie. *Lewis Ginter's Richmond.* Richmond, VA: Whittet & Shepperson, 1991.

Sanford, James K. "The Training of Ministers 1968 Style: Changing Times Dictate Changes in Education." *Richmond Times-Dispatch*, April 7, 1968, D-1.

"Save WRFK, Presbytery Says." *Richmond Times-Dispatch*, October 27, 1985, B-9.

Schweitzer, Wolfgang. "The Confessional Church in Germany." *Union Seminary Review* 56, no. 2 (November 1945): 166–81.

Sconyers, Jeff. "One Person's Opinion." *In Medias Res* (Richmond, VA), January 25, 1978.

"The Seminary." *Union Seminary Magazine* 12, no. 2 (December 1900–January 1901): 163.

"Seminary Buys Property from Presbyterian School." *Richmond Times-Dispatch*, November 3, 1996, B-4.

"Seminary Drive Here Is Launched." *Richmond Times-Dispatch*, January 6, 1954.

"Seminary Fund Drive Is Extended." *Richmond Times-Dispatch*, February 1, 1949, 4.

"Seminary Has Largest per Student Endowment." *Richmond News Leader*, August 31, 1983.

"Seminary Here Given $100,000." *Richmond Times-Dispatch*, May 16, 1977.

"Seminary Here Is $100,000 Richer." *Richmond News Leader*, February 16, 1928.

"Seminary Merger Story 'Premature.'" *Richmond News Leader*, July 22, 1943.

"The Seminary's 150 Years." *Richmond Times-Dispatch*, May 22, 1952.

"Seminary Students Tell Reason for Picketing." *Richmond Times-Dispatch*, March 8, 1960.

Shepherd, Samuel C., Jr. *Avenues of Faith: Shaping the Urban Religious Culture of Richmond, Virginia, 1900–1929.* Tuscaloosa: University of Alabama Press, 2001.

Sherrill, Lewis J. "The Barrenness of the Southern Presbyterian Pen." *Union Seminary Review* 42, no. 4 (May 1931): 278–89.

Short, Dick. Letter to the editor. *Expression* (Richmond, VA), December 1968–January 1969.

Shriver, Donald W. "Biblical Theology: A Personal History." 2011. Manuscript in the author's files.

Sieg, James McClung. "Some Features of Our Mission Work in Congo Free State." *Union Seminary Magazine* 20, no. 3 (February–March 1909): 235–46.

Siff, Mimi. "Preparing Students for Parish Ministry." A directed study, 2011.

Simkins, Francis B. "Robert Lewis Dabney, Southern Conservative." *Georgia Review* 18 (1964): 383–407.

Singleton, Jim. "Is Our Language Really Inclusive?" *In Medias Res* (Richmond, VA), January 1983.

Skreslet, Stan, and Paula Skreslet. "A Letter to Ken Goodpasture from Stan and Paula Skreslet." *In Medias Res* (Richmond, VA), April 9, 1979.

Smith, Benjamin Mosby. "Address at the Unveiling and Dedication of the Memorial Tablet in Honor of the Rev. John H. Rice, D.D." In *Addresses at the Unveiling and Dedication, Delivered in the Chapel of Union Theological Seminary, Va., May 5, 1885.* Richmond, VA: Whittet & Shepperson, 1885, 7–18.

———. "The Brown Memorial Library: Address at the Laying of the Corner-Stone of the Library Building of Union Theological Seminary, Hampden-Sydney, Va., September 1, 1879." *Central Presbyterian*, Richmond, VA, September 17, 1879. Reprinted, *Union Seminary Review*, August 1944, 294–301.

———. *A Sermon, Occasioned by the Death of Charles T. Edie, Who Was Killed by Edward A. Langhorne.* Petersburg, VA: Express Book and Job Office, 1857.

Smith, Cothran G. "The Seventeenth Street Mission." *Union Seminary Review* 33, no. 4 (July 1922): 317–26.

Smith, Egbert Watson. "Some Impressions of Radical Old Testament Criticism." *Union Seminary Magazine* 19, no. 2 (December 1907–January 1908): 163–72.

———. "Union Seminary in Home Missions." *Union Seminary Magazine* 24, no. 1 (1912–13): 109–16.

Smith, Samuel Stanhope. "Academy in Prince Edward." *Virginia Gazette* (Williamsburg, VA), September 1775.

Smith, Willard H. "William Jennings Bryan and the Social Gospel." *Journal of American History* 3, no. 1 (June 1966): 41–59.

"Smith to Hold Theology Chair at Seminary." *Richmond Times-Dispatch*, May 13, 1931.

Smylie, James H. "The Bible, Race and the Changing South." *Journal of Presbyterian History* 59, no. 2 (Summer 1981): 197–216.

———. "The Burden of Southern Church Historians: World Mission, Regional Captivity, Reconciliation." Inaugural address as professor of American church history at Union Theological Seminary in Richmond, VA, March 7, 1968. *Affirmation*, November 4, 1968, 25–50.

———. "Catch Up on Vietnam." *Expression* (Richmond, VA), October 1969, 5.

———. "Clerical Perspectives on Deism: Paine's *The Age of Reason* in Virginia." *Eighteenth Century Studies* 6, no. 2 (Winter 1972–73): 204–17.

———. "Imperative: Presbyterian Reunion." *In Medias Res* (Richmond, VA), January 1983.

———. "Theological Education, Academia, and the Ministry." Unpublished paper given at the 1976 Faculty Workshop.

———. "UTS Opens the Family Photo Album." *Focus* 2, no. 4 (Winter 1987): 8–27.

Sneddon, Gail. Letter to the editor. *Interrobang* (Richmond, VA), November 7, 1969.

"Some Students from UTS Join Picket Line at Downtown Store." *Richmond Times-Dispatch*, March 6, 1960, D-1.

"Sound of Learning Is a UTS Hit." *Richmond Times-Dispatch*, April 19, 1965, 8.

"Southern Seminary Soup." *Expression* (Richmond, VA) 9, no. 6 (October 30, 1964): 5.

Spangler, Jewel L. "Proslavery Presbyterians: Virginia's Conservative Dissenters in the Age of Revolution." *Journal of Presbyterian History* 78, no. 2 (Summer 2000): 111–23.

Sparks, O. Ben. "Community—or Chaos." *Expression* (Richmond, VA) 9, no. 8 (May 14, 1964): 1.

"Special Areas of Ministerial Service." *Expression* (Richmond, VA) 3, no. 1 (October 1957: 1–6.

Speegle, Kay. "Reflections on the New Open Door Policy." *Expression* (Richmond, VA) 2, no. 2 (Summer 1964): 1.

Sprague, William B. *Annals of the American Pulpit.* Vols. 3–4, *Presbyterian.* New York: Robert Carter & Brothers, 1859. Reprinted, New York: Arno Press, 1969.

Stair, Fred Rogers, Jr. "At the Seminary and in the World: An Inaugural Address." *Affirmation* 1, no. 4 (May 1969): 31–39.

Stanton, Robert Livingston. *The Church and the Rebellion: A Consideration of the Rebellion against the Government of the United States; and the Agency of the Church, North and South, in Relation Thereto.* New York: Derby & Miller, 1864.

Stevens, Samuel Govan. Letter from Richmond, Va., to Dr. Ben R. Lacy Jr., December 20, 1934. Copy in the author's files.

Stoessel, Horace. "Two Implications of Biblical Authority." *Expression* (Richmond, VA) 2, no. 4 (April 1957): 1, 5–6.

Strickler, Givens Brown. "The Bible and Science." *Union Seminary Magazine* 8, no. 4 (March–April 1897): 253–55.

———. "The Divine Origin of the Sacred Scriptures." *Union Seminary Magazine* 16, no. 4 (April–May 1905): 331–42.

———. "The New Theology, Part 1." *Union Seminary Magazine* 12, no. 1 (October–November 1900): 1–6.

———. "The New Theology, Part 2." *Union Seminary Magazine* 12, no. 2 (December 1900–January 1901): 89–99.

———. "The New Theology, Part 3." *Union Seminary Magazine* 12, no. 3 (February–March 1901): 175–84.

———. "The New Theology, Part 4." *Union Seminary Magazine* 12, no. 4 (April–May 1901): 268–75.

———. "The Sabbath and Modern Civilization." *Union Seminary Magazine* 15, no. 4 (April–May 1904): 299–309.

Stuart, John Leighton. *Fifty Years in China: The Memoirs of John Leighton Stuart, Missionary and Ambassador.* New York: Random House, 1954.

Student Body, Union Theological Seminary in Virginia. "A Christian Witness of Conviction and Sympathy." March 15, 1964.

———. "March Procedure." March 15, 1965.

———. "Resolution of the Student Body concerning the Cambodian Crisis." May 7, 1970.

———. "Student Planning for Cambodia Demonstrations." 1970.

Sugg, Ty. "A Report to Union Seminary Board of Trustees from Student Government Committee on Investments." *In Medias Res* (Richmond, VA), May 14, 1979.

———. "Toward a Policy of Social Responsibility." *In Medias Res* (Richmond, VA), April 2, 1978.

Summers, Augustus C. Letter from DeBary, Fla., to Hartley Hall, March 23, 1990. Copy in the author's files.

Sutton, David. "The Dangers of Professionalism." *In Medias Res* (Richmond, VA), November 29, 1978.

Sweets, David M. "Union Seminary in Religious Journalism." *Union Seminary Magazine* 24, no. 1 (1912–13): 86–95.

Swezey, Charles. "Remarks to UTS Faculty on 'The Niebuhr Reports.'" Faculty Workshop, Richmond, VA, September 1981. Copy in the author's files.

Swift, David E. "Progress and Impasse in Virginia: A Study in American Humanism and Calvinism, 1770–1830." PhD diss., Wesleyan University, Middletown, CT, 1969.

———. "Thomas Jefferson, John Holt Rice, and Education in Virginia, 1815–1825." *Journal of Presbyterian History* 49, no. 1 (Spring 1971): 32–58.

———. "Yankee in Virginia: James Marsh at Hampden-Sydney, 1823–1826." *Virginia Magazine of History and Biography* 80, no. 3 (July 1972): 312–32.

"Swiss Lecturer to Open UTS Sesquicentennial." *Richmond News Leader*, March 31, 1962.

Sykes, Kathy. "Examining Inclusive Language." *In Medias Res* (Richmond, VA), January 1986.

Tabscott, Robert W. "A Moral Reckoning." Unpublished tribute to John Bright, in the author's files.

———. "Report on the Week of Concern at U.T.S." Richmond, VA, 1970.

Taylor, G. Aiken. Letters to the editor. *Expression* (Richmond, VA) 9, no. 12 (April 12, 1965): 10–11.

Teague, Becky. "A View from across the Street." *In Medias Res* (Richmond, VA), Spring 1993.

Terry, Will H. "The Christian Church in International Life." *Expression* (Richmond, VA), February 1957, 3, 4, 6.

Tewell, Thomas K., et al. *The General Assembly Special Committee to Study Theological Institutions: Draft Report to the 1993 General Assembly.* [Louisville, KY]: Presbyterian Church (U.S.A.), 1993.

"Theology on the Gridiron." *Expression* (Richmond, VA) 6, no. 5 (November 23, 1960).

Thomas, Arthur Dicken, Jr. "Manuscript Notes on Virginia Revivalism in the 19th Century." 1980. Manuscript in the author's files.

———. "Moses Hoge: Reformed Pietism and Spiritual Guidance." *American Presbyterians* 71, no. 2 (Summer 1993): 1–15.

———. "The Panama Canal Treaty and Union Seminary's Prophetic Voice." *In Medias Res* (Richmond, VA), January 25, 1978.

Thomas, John Newton. "The Biblical and Theological Understanding of the Ecumenical Movement." An unpublished paper for a seminar at Union Theological Seminary in Virginia on the ecumenical movment (ca. 1955). In the author's files.

———. "Ernest Trice Thompson, Teacher." In *Ernest Trice Thompson: An Appreciation*, 7–19. Richmond: Union Theological Seminary in Virginia, 1964.

Thomas, Nancy White. *Five Years in Jail.* Richmond, VA: Whittet & Shepperson, 1973.

Thompson, Ernest Trice. "The Curse Was Not on Ham." *Presbyterian Outlook*, March 14, 1955, 7–9.

———. "The First Years." In *The Days of Our Years: The Historical Convocations Held April 24–27, 1962, as a Feature of the Celebration of the Sesquicentennial of Union Theological Seminary in Virginia*, edited by Ernest Trice Thompson, 7–20. Richmond, VA: Union Theological Seminary, 1962.

———. "The Ideals of John Holt Rice." *Union Seminary Review* 43 (1932): 287–99.

———. "Is the Northern Church Theologically Sound?" *Union Seminary Review* 42, no. 2 (January 1931): 109–34.

———. "Jesus among People of Other Races." *Presbyterian Outlook* 126 (March 21, 1949): 13–14.

———. "John Holt Rice." *Union Seminary Review* 43, no. 1 (October–November 1932): 175–86.

———. "Moses Hoge: First Professor of Theology in Union Theological Seminary." *Union Seminary Review* 49, no. 1 (October–November 1937): 21–34.

———. *Presbyterians in the South.* Vol. 1, *1607–1861*. Richmond, VA: John Knox Press, 1963.

———. *Presbyterians in the South.* Vol. 2, *1861–1890*. Richmond, VA: John Knox Press, 1973.

———. *Presbyterians in the South.* Vol. 3, *1890–1972*. Richmond, VA: John Knox Press, 1973.

———. "Southern Presbyterians: What Can We Learn from Their Past?" *Union Seminary Review* 48, no. 1 (October 1936): 15–31.

————. *The Spirituality of the Church: A Distinctive Doctrine of the Presbyterian Church in the United States*. Richmond, VA: John Knox Press, 1961.

————. "The Twentieth Century." In *The Days of Our Years. The Historical Convocations Held April 24–27, 1962, as a Feature of the Celebration of the Sesquicentennial of Union Theological Seminary in Virginia*, edited by Ernest Trice Thompson, 65–89. Richmond, VA: Union Theological Seminary, 1962.

————. "Union Theological Seminary." *Commonwealth*, February 1952, 1–4.

Thompson, Ernest Trice, et al. "A Statement to Southern Christians: A Report from the Council of Christian Relations." In *The Minutes of the General Assembly and Report of Assembly Agencies*, 193–98. Richmond VA: Committee of Publication, 1954.

Thompson, Graves H. "Should the Seminary and College Have Stayed Together?" In *The Record of the Hampden-Sydney Alumni Association*, Hampden Sydney, VA: Hampden-Sydney College, January 1955, 5.

Thompson, William Earl. "From the Hill to the Brook: The Story of the Removal of the Seminary to Richmond." An address given on October 5, 1998. In the author's files.

————. "Gone but Not Forgotten." An address given for the dedication of the Presbyterian Seminary historic marker sign. April 27, 1991. Copy of the manuscript in the author's files.

————. *Her Walls before Thee Stand: The 235-Year History of the Presbyterian Congregation at Hampden-Sydney, Virginia*. [Hampden Sydney, VA]: William E. Thompson, 2010.

————. "The Hidden Reasons for Union Seminary's 1898 Move to Richmond." A paper given to the St. James Fellowship, 1996.

————. "Historical Marker Commemorates Seminary." *Museum: The Newsletter of the Associates of the Esther Thomas Atkinson Museum of Hampden-Sydney*, Fall 1991, 3–9.

————. "Railroads, Racism, and Religion: A Re-Examination of the Reasons for the Removal of Union Theological Seminary from Hampden-Sydney to Richmond, with a View to a Modern Day Ministry amidst the Continuing Reasons for the Departure." DMin diss., Union Theological Seminary, 1992.

————. "The Seminary Moves to Richmond: Part 1: The Seminary Perspective." *Museum: The Newsletter of the Associates of the Esther Thomas Atkinson Museum of Hampden-Sydney*, Fall 1999, 7–34.

————. "The Seminary Moves to Richmond: Part 2, The Guiding Force, Walter W. Moore." *Museum: The Newsletter of the Associates of the Esther Thomas Atkinson Museum of Hampden-Sydney*, Spring 2000, 8–37.

————. "The Seminary Moves to Richmond: Part 3, The Parish Responds." *Museum: The Newsletter of the Associates of the Esther Thomas Atkinson Museum of Hampden-Sydney*, Fall 2000, 12–38.

————. "The Seminary Moves to Richmond: Part 4." *Museum: The Newsletter of the Associates of the Esther Thomas Atkinson Museum of Hampden-Sydney*, Spring 2001, 22–53.

————. "Would You Believe? A Social Liberal at Hampden-Sydney!" In *The Opening of the Lewis Wicks Hine Photography Exhibit*. Atkinson Museum of Hampden-Sydney College, March 26, 2000.

"Those FM Sounds in the Air." *Richmond Times-Dispatch*, October 12, 1960.

Todd, William Newton. "The Atomic Era." In *Virginia Presbyterians in American Life: Hanover Presbytery (1755–1980)*, by Robert P. Davis and James H. Smylie, edited by Patricia Aldridge, 217–67. Richmond, VA: Hanover Presbytery, 1982.

Topping, Leonard Wesley. "A History of Hampden-Sydney College in Virginia, 1771–1883." Union Theological Seminary, 1950.

Towner, W. Sibley. "Four Good Shakes and Three Desiderata." *In a Mirror* (Richmond, VA), January 1976.

Training for Excellence. Fund-raising booklet for the Advance capital campaign. Richmond, VA: Trevvett, Christian & Co., 1965.

Trinterud, Leonard J. *The Forming of an American Tradition: A Re-Examination of Colonial Presbyterianism*. Philadelphia: Westminster Press, 1949.

A Trip around the Seminary. Richmond, VA: Union Theological Seminary, May 1923.

Trotti, John B. "The History of the Union Theological Seminary Library." An unpublished manuscript in the author's files, 2008.

———. "The Seminary during the Civil War, 1861–1865." *Focus*, Summer 1994.

———. "There's a Sweet, Sweet Spirit in This Place." *Focus*, Spring 2000.

———. "Unpublished Notes for the Library's 175th Anniversary," 1987.

Tubbs, Ace. *The Story of My Life: Memoirs of the Rev. Ace Leonard Tubbs, Ed.D.* Montreat, NC: Ace Tubbs, 2000.

Tunge, Argen. Editorial. *In Medias Res* (Richmond, VA), March 1999.

Turnbull, L. B. "The Lord's Supper—a Plea for Its More Frequent Observance." *Union Seminary Magazine* 9, no. 1 (September–October 1897): 32–37.

Turner, Frederick Jackson. *The Frontier in American History*. New York: Holt, Rinehart & Winston, 1920. Reprinted, Tucson: University of Arizona Press, 1986.

Turner, Herbert S. "Old Testament Criticism." *Union Seminary Review* 41, no. 1 (October 1929): 1–15.

Turretin, Francis. *Institutes of Elenctic Theology*. 3 vols. Trans. George Musgrave Giger. Ed. James T. Dennison Jr. Translation of *Institutio theologiae elencticae*, 1679–86; new ed., 1688–89. Phillipsburg, NJ: Presbyterian & Reformed Publishing Co., 1992–97.

Twit, Perfidious. "Rogue's Review of the Competence Paper." *In a Mirror* (Richmond, VA), December 1974, 7–8.

"Union Seminary Elects New Head." *Richmond Times-Dispatch*, May 12, 1926.

"Union Seminary Gifts Total $12,000." *Richmond Times-Dispatch*, December 31, 1930.

"Union Seminary Left Large Sum." *Richmond News Leader*, August 11, 1932.

"Union Seminary and Our Armed Forces." *Union Seminary Bulletin* 2/20, no. 4 (April–June 1943).

"Union Theological Installs President." *Richmond Times-Dispatch*, April 5, 1956, 3–4.

Union Theological Seminary. Faculty Issues: Lunch Meeting of July 1, 1993.

———. Faculty Lunch Meeting of May 28, 1993.

———. Faculty Morale Ad Hoc Meeting, August 3, 1993.

———. Faculty Workshop, September 1993.

———. *A Great Door Is Opened: For All Southern Presbyterians*. Richmond: Union Theological Seminary in Virginia, 1952.

Union Theological Seminary in Virginia Alumni Association. Organization, Places of Meeting, Schedules of Reunions, Officers of the Association. 1970.

"Union Theological to Start Construction on New Library." *Richmond News Leader*, August 21, 1941, 2.

"UTS Announces Shift to Master's." *Richmond News Leader*, February 22, 1971, 12.

"UTS Campaign Ends; Workers Get $141,417." *Richmond News Leader*, February 4, 1949, 14.

"UTS Drive for $150,000 Opens Today." *Richmond Times-Dispatch*, January 24, 1949, 14.

"UTS Drive Will Seek $150,000." *Richmond News Leader*, November 9, 1948, 23.

"U.T.S. Faculty Is Picked for Term." *Richmond News Leader*, July 12, 1933.

"UTS Gets $200,000 as Anonymous Gift." *Richmond News Leader*, November 7, 1958, 21.

"UTS Gets Anonymous Grant to Build Radio Station Here." *Richmond News Leader*, December 6, 1956, 21.

"UTS Has Closed-Circuit TV Network on Campus." *Richmond Times-Dispatch*, April 6, 1956, 6.

"UTS Names Acting President." *Richmond Times-Dispatch*, November 30, 1966, A-3.

"UTS Nearing End of Project." *Richmond Times-Dispatch*, October 22, 1978, C-1

"UTS President Inaugurated." *Richmond Times-Dispatch*, November 10, 1968, A-1.

"UTS Receives $100,000 Gift." *Richmond News Leader*, November 24, 1979, 24.

"UTS Succeeds in Campaign for $150,000." *Richmond News Leader*, January 5, 1950, 3.

"UTS to Cancel Classes Wednesday." *Richmond News Leader*, October 10, 1969, D-4.

"UTS to Dedicate Rebuilt Pipe Organ Tuesday." *Richmond News Leader*, April 21, 1962, 2.

"UTS Video Circuit First in VA." *Richmond News Leader*, April 5, 1956, 21.

Vance, James I. "Union Seminary in Foreign Missions." *Union Seminary Magazine* 24, no. 1 (1912–13): 117–27.

Van Deventer, Jonathan. "A Cautionary Tale." *In Medias Res* (Richmond, VA), February 1994.

Vann, Jane Rogers. "The Teaching and Learning Cultures of Presbyterian School of Christian Education and Union Theological Seminary: Two Portraits 1999." 2000. Unpublished draft report in the author's files.

Vaughan, Clement Read. "The Millennium and the Second Advent." *Union Seminary Magazine* 20, no. 3 (February–March 1909): 212–34.

———. "The Premillennial Theory." *Union Seminary Magazine* 20, no. 4 (April–May 1909): 277–99.

Vaughan, Doug. "More on Prince Edward County." *Expression* (Richmond, VA) 6, no. 11 (April 12, 1961).

Vaught, Richard. "The Student and U.T.S." *Perspective* (Richmond, VA), 1970, issue 6.

"Vietnam Poll." *Expression* (Richmond, VA) 10, no. 6 (March 1966): 10.

Walker, John Mack. "Our Justice." *Perspective* (Richmond, VA), 1970, issue 7.

———. "A Weekend for Theological Inquiry." *Perspective* (Richmond, VA), 1970, issue 6.

Wallof, Harold, Jr. "'News' for Yankees." *Expression* (Richmond, VA) 7, no. 8 (March 31, 1962): 1.

Wardlaw, Theodore J. "Laughter in the Church—for God's Sake." A sermon delivered at the 2005 Sprunt Lectures, Richmond, VA, January 25, 2005. In the author's files.

Warren, J. B. "Evolution as It Stands Related to Christian Faith." *Union Seminary Magazine* 22, no. 4 (April–May 1911): 253–81.

Warren, K. Lewis. "Extension Work Urged for Seminary." *Richmond News Leader*, April 4, 1956, 1.

———. "U.S. Policy against Russia 'Too Weak,' Says Former German Soldier Studying Here." *Richmond News Leader*, November 11, 1948, 1.

Warren, Michael. Letter from Liberty, Miss., to Fred R. Stair: "Warren Letter concerning Jackson State." September 2, 1970. In the author's files.

Washburn, E. D. "Notes of Charge to a Pastor." *Union Seminary Magazine* 4, no. 1 (September–October 1892): 27–32.

Washington, Booker T. "The Relation of the Races in the South." *Union Seminary Magazine* 11, no. 4 (April–May 1900): 274–79.

Washington and Lee Historical Papers, No. 1. Baltimore: John Murphy & Co., 1890.

Watkins, John M. "To Be or Not to Be a Community." *Expression* (Richmond, VA) 6, no. 11 (April 12, 1961): 1–2.

Watt, Richard S. "Bookshelf Christianity." *Expression* (Richmond, VA) 6, no. 5 (November 23, 1960): 4.

Waytt, Marshall B. "The Seminary and Extension." *Union Seminary Review* 39 (April 1928): 271–75.

Webb, R. A. "Decadence in Present Day Preaching." *Union Seminary Magazine* 12, no. 3 (February–March 1901): 198–204.

Webster, Richard. *A History of the Presbyterian Church in America: From Its Origin until the Year 1760.* Philadelphia: Joseph M. Wilson, 1857.

Weeks, Louis B. "How to Merge Two Seminaries." *Faith and Leadership,* Duke Divinity School, August 30, 2010. An online offering of leadership education at Duke Divinity School. https://www.faithandleadership.com/how-merge-two-seminaries.

———. "John Holt Rice and the American Colonization Society." *Journal of Presbyterian History* 46 (1968): 26–41.

"The Welcome." *Union Seminary Magazine* 9, no. 3 (January–February 1898): 78–80.

Wellford, E. T. "The Importance of Grading Our Sabbath-Schools." *Union Seminary Magazine* 13, no. 3 (February–March 1902): 170–81.

Wells, J. M. "The Christian and the Theatre." *Union Seminary Magazine* 13, no. 2 (December 1901–January 1902): 102–11.

West, Dan C. "Impressions at Montgomery." *Expression* (Richmond, VA) 9, no. 14 (April 12, 1965): 9–10.

———. "UTS and Civil Rights." *Expression* (Richmond, VA) 9, no. 2 (Summer 1964): 5.

Whaling, Thornton. "The Church and Social Reforms." *Union Seminary Review* 25, no. 1 (October–November 1913): 30–34.

Wharton, R. L. "Student Life at Union Seminary." *Union Seminary Magazine* 9 (March–April 1898): 314–17.

———. "Valedictory." *Union Seminary Magazine* 9 (March–April 1898): 319–21.

Wharton, Turner Ashby. *Then and Now: A Sketch of the Major Changes Which Three Score Years Have Wrought in Man's Attitude toward "the Faith of Our Fathers."* Sherman, TX: The author's children, 1935.

"What Is Wrong with Seminary Students?" *Expression* (Richmond, VA), February 1956, 6–7.

Wheeler, Barbara G., and Anthony T. Ruger. "Sobering Figures Point to Enrollment Decline." *In Trust,* Spring 2013, 5–11.

White, Henry A. "George Addison Baxter." *Union Seminary Magazine* 9, no. 4 (March–April 1898): 274–77.

White, Hugh W. "The Inter-Seminary Missionary Alliance." *Union Seminary Magazine* 4, no. 1 (September–October 1892): 136–40.

———. "Romish Obstacles to Mission Work in China." *Union Seminary Magazine* 11, no. 1 (October–November 1899): 47–50.

White, William Spottswood. *The African Preacher.* Philadelphia: Presbyterian Board of Publication, 1849.

Wilkes, Paul. "The Hands That Would Shape Our Souls." *Atlantic Monthly,* December 1990, 59.

Wilson, Charles Reagan. "The Religion of the Lost Cause: Ritual and Organization of the Southern Civil Religion, 1865–1920." *Journal of Southern History* 46, no. 2 (May 1980): 219–38.

———. "Robert Lewis Dabney: Religion and the Southern Holocaust." *Virginia Magazine of History and Biography* (Richmond) 89, no. 1 (January 1981): 79–89.

Wilson, Richard. "Union Theological Installs President." *Richmond Times-Dispatch,* April 5, 1956.

Wilson, Samuel B. "History of Union Theological Seminary." An report for the board of directors, given at their meeting on May 14, 1867. Library archives.

Wilson, Samuel G. "Bahaism." *Union Seminary Review* 25, no. 3 (February–March 1914): 214–24.

Winthrop, Robert. "Campus Tour of Union Theological Seminary." Library archives, Union Theological Seminary, Richmond, VA, 1980.

"Woman's Post a First at UTS." *Richmond News Leader*, May 25, 1973.

Woods, Henry. *The History of the Presbyterian Controversy, with Early Sketches of Presbyterianism*. Louisville, KY: N. H. White, 1843.

Woods, W. H. "Is the Church Meeting the Changed Conditions in the Social and Business World?" *Union Seminary Magazine* 15, no. 3 (February–March 1904): 225–32.

World Survey by the Interchurch World Movement of North America. Vol. 1, American Volume. New York: Interchurch Press, 1920.

"WRFK." *Richmond Times-Dispatch*, August 29, 1985, 14.

"WRFK Backers Seek Ruling Review." *Richmond Times-Dispatch*, February 6, 1987, 44.

"WRFK Benefit Set for Nov. 2." *Richmond Times-Dispatch*, October 27 1985, K-2.

"WRFK Ranks 10th in Ratings." *Richmond Times-Dispatch*, October 20, 1987, B-7.

Wyche, Frank. "The Majority in the Middle." *In Medias Res* (Richmond, VA), Fall 1995.

Yonan, Isaac Malek. "The Armenian Church." *Union Seminary Magazine* 10, no. 2 (December 1898–January 1899): 143–49.

Young, Bennett H. "Division of the Presbyterian Church in Kentucky." *Union Seminary Magazine* 3, no. 1 (September–October 1891): 196–223.

Zehmer, Lee. "This Is Not a Church." *In Medias Res* (Richmond, VA), Fall 1990.

Ziegler, Jesse H. *ATS through Two Decades: Reflections on Theological Education 1960–1980*. Worcester, MA: Heffernan Press, 1984.

Index of Names

Index of Subjects